Sharing the Stage:
Biography and Gender in
Western Civilization

Sharing the Stage: Biography and Gender in Western Civilization

Jane Slaughter

Melissa K. Bokovoy

University of New Mexico

HOUGHTON MIFFLIN COMPANY　　Boston　　New York

Senior Sponsoring Editor: Nancy Blaine
Development Editor: Julie Dunn
Associate Project Editor: Martha Rogers
Editorial Assistant: Reba Frederics
Associate Production/Design Coordinator: Christine Gervais
Manufacturing Manager: Florence Cadran
Senior Marketing Manager: Sandra McGuire

Library of Congress Catalog Card Number: 2001133349

ISBN: 0-618-01178-1

1 2 3 4 5 6 7 8 9-VHG-06 05 04 03 02

CONTENTS

PREFACE

The intellectual seeds that produced this volume were gathered in many Western Civilization classes spanning almost four decades. As historians, we, the authors, represent quite distinct generations and different training, but we share ideas and goals that we believe will resonate with other teachers of introductory history courses. The power of historical insight and the thrill of historical discovery have shaped and driven our lives; our purpose is to share the quest and the excitement with students. We have experimented with different approaches and material and what we found to be most effective has shaped this volume. While many of the current generation of students are, at best, skeptical of politics, we believe that political events are among the most exciting and significant subjects in the history of western societies, and our challenge is to give these life and color. One way to do that is to bring men and women who were key players in those events onto the historical stage. We contend that to fully understand an individual's actions in regard to historical events, we must consider the gender of that individual. Gender discussed in abstract terms often falls on deaf ears; our experience has taught us that individual actions, opportunities, and expectations are far more illustrative. A tested mix of politics, biography, and gender brought from our classrooms is displayed in the chapters that follow.

Each chapter focuses on one woman and one man who grappled with fundamental problems in their societies and thought that they could change things for the better. Their lives are set within the historical context of the time and connected to historical themes, but the details of particular choices and experiences give these life. Some of the figures will be familiar and might fall into the category of great men or women, like Maria Theresa and Joseph of Austria; Maximilien Robespierre and Olympe de Gouges; and Jean-Paul Sartre and Simone de Beauvoir. In some cases, one partner will be well-known, the other not known at all (for example, Giuseppe Mazzini and Giuditta Sidoli or Galileo Galilei and Sister Maria Celeste). In other cases, neither partner in a pair will be familiar to most audiences (for example, Annie Besant and Charles Bradlaugh or Petra Kelly and Gert Bastian).

We have paired wives and husbands, brothers and sisters, parents and children, lovers, and individuals of the same circles. By pairing individuals who have intimate familial or social connections, we introduce students to the idea that they must always consider gender as an important criterion of analysis when they assess historical significance. Moving together through time, the lives of each pair illustrate how political, social, economic, or religious change affects men and women differently; a man's experience is not the universal experience, and a woman's experience is not the exception.

We have organized each of the chapters in *Sharing the Stage* into six sections: Setting the Stage; the Actors; the Acts; the Finale; Questions; and Documents. The Setting the Stage section provides historical background on the time period and society in which the individuals lived. The Actors section discusses the lives of the paired individuals, as well as some other figures who influenced their lives or society. The drama of these individuals' lives is portrayed in the Acts sections of the chapter. Here we witness how the individuals contributed to their societies and how their societies responded. The Finale section outlines the last years of the individuals' lives and attempts to provide some closure to that period of history. At the conclusion of each chapter, suggested discussion questions ask students to consider conflicting relationships, behaviors, and events and their historical meaning, thus allowing many possibilities for analysis and classroom discussion. Finally, we have included a collection of documents at the end of each chapter. Each document opens with a brief introduction and several focus questions, and all of the documents are referenced in the narrative.

We believe that students can learn to appreciate primary documents and benefit from reading and analysis of such materials. We have selected our documents carefully to include both well-known and less famous pieces. In the chapter on the French Revolution we include the *Declaration of the Rights of Man*, and the *Declaration of the Rights of Woman*, but also Robespierre's essay justifying terror, and Olympe de Gouges's essay arguing for a national referendum on the government. In addition to familiar political essays like those of Giuseppe Mazzini and V.I. Lenin, we include personal letters exchanged between partners or parents and children, some of them only now translated into English. Photographs of the sculpture of Käthe Kollwitz and an article from a U.S. newspaper in the 1930s on Fascist women illustrate the diversity of sources assembled. The materials include not only public and private statements of the central figures in each chapter, but also the accounts and ideas of other men and women of the time who express different opinions and recount different experiences. This diverse documentary evidence allows the reader to discuss in detail the possible differences between men's and women's experiences and responses in each of the movements being studied. Several questions address each document; the document is placed in context and referred to in the narrative, making it both relevant and intelligible to the reader. It is our intent that this process will acquaint students with what historians do and to encourage them to grapple with historical problems. Ideally, after reading the text and interpreting the documents, students will learn how to construct one of the most accessible of all historical stories, the biography.

Biographies give human form to textbook narratives that often seem remote and lifeless to many students. *Sharing the Stage: Biography and Gender in Western*

Civilization is conceived to accompany the Western Civilization course. Each chapter represents a discrete historical movement or event and is easy to assign for individual reading, classroom discussion, papers, and exams. This reader complements the multifaceted ways that today's instructors teach Western Civilization. It builds on historical events and personalities familiar to instructors of the course, while simultaneously offering themes suitable to teachers of history with widely ranging perspectives and interests.

Acknowledgments

Teaching introductory Western Civilization history survey courses is always challenging. The rewards are also manifold when students connect with events and people in the past and share our enthusiasms. Our thanks and acknowledgments in this volume must, therefore, begin with all the wonderful students who began to think historically and have contributed unknowingly. Oddly perhaps, we must thank each other as well. From quite different generations of historians, we found common ground in our passions for history, and our commitment to constant revision and experimentation in our teaching. We also owe a debt to friends and colleagues who validated and encouraged our plan for the volume. Most gratefully, the volume would not exist without the enthusiasm of Jean Woy and Nancy Blaine, the editors at Houghton Mifflin who understood what we were trying to do, and supported an idea others might have found risky.

From the beginning, our colleagues at UNM, Larry D. Ball, Beth Bailey, David Farber, and Virginia Scharff were our cheerleaders, intellectual advisors, and editors. The first sketches and the development of bibliography were the work of an amazing undergraduate research assistant, Bernadette Miera, who was assigned to us one summer through the university's "Research Opportunity Program." There is probably no way that we can adequately acknowledge the work that Ellen Cain did on this project. Her remarkable assistance for us in research and preparation of the manuscript was done while she wrote her dissertation in U.S. Western History at UNM. Other colleagues, students, and former students at UNM, Patricia Risso, Richard Robbins, and Lynn Schibeci provided valuable critiques and suggestions for the chapters. Robbins, as department chair, also gave us financial support. Teri Balkenende and Ute Sanchez ably translated documents and wrote summaries from Czech and German materials. We also want to acknowledge the important secondary and primary materials available at the Library of Congress, which we relied on, and even more important the work that Carol Armbruster, the French and Italian research librarian at LoC, did. She came to our rescue on many occasions, finding materials and sending them to us. Finally, the number of books, articles, and primary source materials necessary for this project meant ordering almost daily from our interlibrary loan department. The ILL staff worked rapidly and carefully on our requests and without their help our project would not have been possible.

Julie Dunn's capable hands and creative suggestions shaped the development and design of the volume. Martha Rogers carefully oversaw the copyediting and proofing. We wish to thank the following teachers and instructors for their excellent insights, critical analyses, and meticulous reading of the chapters in this volume: Jeffrey A. Auerbach, California State University–Northridge; Mary Beth Emmerichs, University of Wisconsin–Sheboygan; Amy Thompson McCandless, College of Charleston; and Richard D. Sonn, University of Arkansas.

Cohesion and Conflict in Early Modern Europe

The Scientific Revolution: Galileo Galilei (1564–1642) and Sister Maria Celeste (née Virginia Galilei, 1600–1634)

■ SETTING THE STAGE

Knowledge and learning in the centuries leading up to the seventeenth had been dominated by respect for and reliance upon philosophers and religious authorities of earlier centuries. Prevailing attitudes about the creation and acquisition of knowledge argued that instead of going directly to nature for investigation of its laws and processes, it was best to go to earlier authorities, either ancient or Christian, who were supposed to have spoken the last word on the natural world and its many phenomena. During medieval times, the most highly respected philosophers and scientists were men of the cloth. These individuals, often called "natural philosophers," did make advancements in mathematical and physical thinking, not by systematic observations of the natural world but by refined logical analysis.

Chapter 1
The Scientific
Revolution:
Galileo Galilei
(1564–1642) and
Sister Maria
Celeste (née
Virginia Galilei,
1600–1634)

Nonetheless, their conceptualizations and theories about the workings of the universe still depended upon the works and ideas of the ancient Greeks and Romans. The blending of these distinctive ways of understanding the world led to many erroneous conclusions and theoretical contradictions concerning nature and its laws.

Questioning the medieval world view and its reliance on a few ancient authorities gained momentum as Europeans abandoned religious education and training for education in secular subjects such as astronomy, mechanics, and medicine. This inquiry did not happen in a vacuum. In the sixteenth century, Europeans were challenging the authority of the Catholic Church in religious and political matters, as demonstrated by the Protestant Reformation and the religious wars that followed. It is not surprising then that as Christian unity broke down, European men and women challenged the church's authority in the intellectual realm and questioned many of the earlier interpretations of the universe and humanity's place in it. This challenge to previous knowledge and accepted truths drew the learned world into two centuries of intellectual revolt known as the Scientific Revolution.

The transformation to a new world view was not an easy one. It did not occur immediately or rapidly, nor did it displace religion from the everyday lives of Europeans. In fact, the scientists of the sixteenth and seventeenth centuries often justified their pursuit of knowledge and science in religious terms and remained faithful to the Christian church while they pursued

secular interpretations and explanations of the natural world. Such pursuits often brought scientists into conflict with religious authorities who sought to protect their monopoly on knowledge, learning, and the interpretation of the universe. Yet it is not the scientist alone who dueled with the established ecclesiastical and academic institutions of the Catholic Church for control of the minds and imaginations of Europeans. To take on the established order, think new ideas, and pursue new forms of knowledge, scientists needed allies to support their endeavors financially, to foster communication with other scientists, and to obtain social status and respectability. Humanists, protestant reformers, new merchant elites, more confident and self-assured aristocrats, princes and monarchs, and artisans helped create new institutions, social and scientific networks, and creative spaces for the growth of European culture beyond the walls of the Vatican, cathedral schools, monasteries, and convents. Relinquishing the power to control knowledge and learning would not be easy for the Catholic Church nor would it be easy for learned men and women to defy the works of the ancients and their Christian disciples.

Central to the historical understanding of the professional and personal conflicts between science and religion is the story of Galileo Galilei, which includes his scientific activity and his relationship, conflicts, and encounters with the Roman Catholic Church. Galileo's story does not have a simple plot line, with science, light, and reason standing on one side and religion, darkness, and lack of reason standing on the other. Nor did Galileo reject everything that the Catholic Church, its institutions, and its doctrines had to offer. Galileo lived in a world where he encountered the church constantly, whether it was in his personal or professional life. While rejecting the church's authority in his search for scientific truth, he remained a devout Catholic and depended on the Catholic Church for patronage and spiritual leadership and as the authority in his daughters' lives. To understand the religious, intellectual, and social milieu of the Scientific Revolution is to understand the lives of Galileo Galilei and his daughter, Sister Maria Celeste.

▩ THE ACTORS:
GALILEO GALILEI AND
SISTER MARIA CELESTE

Galileo Galilei was born in Pisa, Tuscany, on February 15, 1564, to Julia Ammanati of Pescia and Vincenzio Galilei, a cloth merchant and musician. Galileo was the first of seven children born to Vincenzio and Julia, but only three of his siblings, Virginia (b. 1573), Michelangelo (b. 1575), and Livia (b. 1587) lived to adulthood. Their mother, Julia, was a woman of education and intelligence and their father, Vincenzio, belonged to a distinguished merchant family from Florence whose wealth unfortunately was greatly diminished by the time of Galileo's birth. Vincenzio had been broadly educated in the humanist tradition. He had trained as a musician and became an accomplished lutenist and composer, but he studied and mastered mathematics and classical languages as well.

Several of Vincenzio's works on musical theory survive. In these works, he argued stridently against blind acceptance of previous musical ideas and theory. In *A Dialogue on Ancient and Modern Music*, he stated, "It appears to me that they who in proof of any as-sertion rely simply on the weight of authority without adducing any argument in support of it, act very absurdly. I, on the contrary, wish to be allowed freely to question and freely to answer you without any sort of adulation, as well becomes those who are truly in search of the truth."[1] Vincenzio would bequeath his fervent passion for music and mathematics and his distrust of and contempt for arguments based on blind obedience to intellectual authority to his eldest son.

Vincenzio had great ambitions for Galileo and began educating him, as he had been educated, in the humanist tradition. At one point as a boy, Galileo was enrolled at the monastery of Santa Maria di Vallombrosa where he learned the elements of logic. But his father was not about to allow his eldest son to enter the monastic ranks. In 1581, at great sacrifice to his impoverished family, Galileo entered the University of Pisa as a student of medicine. The choice of medicine appeared a logical one for the Galilei

---

1. *The Private Life of Galileo: Compiled Principally from His Correspondence and That of His Eldest Daughter, Sister Maria Celeste* (London: MacMillan and Co., 1870), p. 2.

Chapter 1
The Scientific
Revolution:
Galileo Galilei
(1564–1642) and
Sister Maria
Celeste (née
Virginia Galilei,
1600–1634)

family because medicine was becoming a most lucrative profession.

At the University of Pisa, Galileo encountered the works of two of the great ancient authorities in medicine and philosophy, Claudius Galen and Aristotle. Galileo read these works voraciously and attempted to engage his professors in discussion concerning the contradictions and inconsistencies in these texts. This effort to understand the ancients and then ask questions about them won Galileo the reputation of a rebel. It was soon clear that medicine and its training were not for this inquisitive young man, and he began to seek other intellectual pursuits, especially the study of mathematics.

Renaissance men and women had rediscovered the mathematics of the ancients, and they soon believed that mathematics could help explain the workings of the universe and the nature of things. In the fifteenth century, Leonardo da Vinci argued that God eternally geometrizes, and therefore nature, as God's creation, is inherently mathematical. Da Vinci and Renaissance natural philosophers grew increasingly convinced that mathematical reasoning promoted a degree of certainty about the nature of things that was impossible to deduce using only logic and observation.

Despite the embrace of mathematics during the Renaissance, it still was not a widely taught or accepted field of study in the late sixteenth century. The University of Pisa was not known for the study of mathematics and small universities throughout Europe did not teach it at all. In 1583, while on vacation, Galileo asked a friend of the family, Ostillo Ricci, who was a tutor

to the Tuscan ducal court, to instruct him in this discipline. Ricci assessed Galileo's abilities quickly and convinced Vincenzio that his eldest son's future lay in mathematical studies.

Galileo did not immediately forsake his other studies at Pisa. He continued to study both mathematics and natural philosophy and prepared himself for a future university post. In 1584, he dedicated much of his energy to the preparation of lectures on natural philosophy because it was more likely that he would find a teaching post in this discipline than in mathematics. As he prepared, he noted that this discipline rested on the foundations that Aristotle had laid eighteen centuries earlier. On all questions concerning the study of nature, Aristotle was the authority, either having the final say from his grave or having his ideas modified or altered by later authorities. Most natural philosophers, even if they observed something different from Aristotle, accepted only those results that could be reconciled with Aristotle's writings on logic, motion, and the structure of the universe. While initially bowing to the Aristotelian view, Galileo dedicated his scholarly life to criticizing, testing, and refuting Aristotle's doctrines and the commentaries of the Aristotelians, past and present.

Galileo left the University of Pisa in 1584 without obtaining his medical degree and spent the next four years in Florence with his family trying to find a university position in mathematics. During this time, Galileo began to explore bodies in motion. According to one of the romantic and mythical tales about Galileo, he had become interested in why objects move when in the cathedral of Pisa he observed a lamp swinging gently to rest after being filled with oil. Eventually this observation led him to the discovery of the isochronism of the pendulum, which he used fifty years later in the design of an astronomical clock. Whatever the truthfulness of this story, historians do know that by the late 1580s, Galileo was wrestling with several commonly held theories about the principles of motion.

The Aristotelians held that the acceleration of falling bodies depended on their weight; a heavier object fell faster than a lighter one. They also believed that an object remained at rest unless a force was applied against it, or it remained in motion only if some force propelled it. Observable fact disputed the latter theorem. Medieval philosophers had noted that a cannonball continued in the air without a force propelling it, and mathematicians and natural philosophers of the sixteenth century continued wrestling with the problem.

By the time Galileo took his first teaching post at the University of Pisa in 1589, several other scholars had worked on inertia and Galileo possibly used their work in his unpublished treatise, *On Motion.* At the University of Pisa, Galileo puzzled over the problems of falling bodies and bodies in motion, and the ideas germinated here eventually blossomed into new theories on motion. Later in life, Galileo embellished his accomplishments at Pisa by telling his biographer, Vincenzio Vivianni, how he climbed to the top of the Tower of Pisa and dropped two objects of the

same material, but of different weights, at the same time to disprove Aristotle's theory that objects fall at a rate proportional to their weight. The objects reached the ground together, disproving Aristotle. The story is not true; Galileo had reached this conclusion without actually performing the experiment. Instead of presenting his case through complicated mathematical formulas, he had invented a simple and dramatic story to illustrate his point.

In 1592, Galileo accepted the chair of mathematics at the University of Padua in the Republic of Venice. The reasons for Galileo's departure are numerous: his Pisan colleagues' discomfort with Galileo's opposition to Aristotelian principles, a higher salary at Padua, the University of Padua's better reputation, and the Republic of Venice's tradition of being an enlightened and well-ruled state. The University of Padua benefitted greatly from the patronage of Venetian nobles, many of whom appreciated all branches of learning and the arts. Some of them fancied themselves scholars and learned men. In an era when there were no formal scientific meetings, these nobles sponsored gatherings at their estates, financed experiments and equipment for the scientists they supported, and even had laboratories or workshops built in their homes. They also hired the professors at the university to teach their sons. Many professors, including Galileo, used this money to supplement their income. One of Galileo's students, Cosimo II de Medici (1590–1621), would later become his biggest patron. In 1610, Cosimo would become grand duke of Tuscany and

Chapter 1
The Scientific
Revolution:
Galileo Galilei
(1564–1642) and
Sister Maria
Celeste (née
Virginia Galilei,
1600–1634)

would lure Galileo away from Padua to Florence with the guarantee of a lifetime appointment and a generous salary.

Venice offered other opportunities as well. At this time, Venice was a great maritime empire, and its extensive trade and diplomatic networks made it easier for scientific ideas, inventions, and books from other parts of Europe to reach Galileo. Galileo also observed and benefitted from artisan innovation that emerged from the Venetian maritime industry. The intellectual and political climate created by the ruling families of Venice was reflected in the policies of the university, where the Venetians guaranteed to all scholars broad freedom of thought. The University of Padua had been founded in 1222 and by the late sixteenth century had become a European center for the study of medicine and philosophy. While many of its faculty still adhered to the works of the ancient and medieval authorities, the school of medicine and its faculty abandoned these teachings and experimented widely. This new bent toward experimentation and an openness to challenging the ancients suited Galileo's temperament.

Galileo spent eighteen years at the University of Padua, where he continued his work in mechanics, that is, the study of the action of forces on matter. He formally established the laws of falling bodies and the laws of projectiles and pondered the laws of motion, which were finally articulated by Sir Isaac Newton a century later. He also studied stationary bodies (statics) and gave the first satisfactory demonstration of the laws of equilibrium and the

principle of virtual velocities. Finally, he applied his ideas to the study of objects in water (hydrostatics) and developed the principle of flotation. Galileo virtually created the systematic study of the relationship between motion and the forces affecting motion, or what we now call the field of dynamics. Yet it is not his work in this field that is the most well known; rather, it is his invention of the telescope and his championing of Copernican astronomy.

During one of his regular visits to Venice in 1609, Galileo heard about the creation of a Dutch optician, Hans Lippershey, an invention that magnified remote objects. Recalling the events years later, he wrote, "News arrived that a Fleming had presented to Count Maurice [of Nassau] a glass by means of which distant objects could be seen as distinctly as if they were nearby. That was all. . . . [I] set myself to thinking about the problem. The first night after my return [to Padua] I solved it, and on the following day I constructed the instrument."[2] He then turned this instrument and his thoughts toward the heavens and found, using the telescope's magnification, that the Ptolemaic system could not explain what he saw. Ptolemy's geocentric cosmology, building on Aristotle's, placed the earth at the center of the universe and had the planets and sun revolving around it. Looking through his telescope, Galileo confirmed the ideas of Nicholas Copernicus (1473–1543), the Polish astronomer, who argued that the sun was at the

2. Stillman Drake, *Galileo at Work* (Chicago, Ill.: University of Chicago, 1978), p. 137.

center of universe, and the planets, including the earth, revolved around it. Galileo had privately confessed his belief in the Copernican heliocentric system in a letter to the young astronomer, Johannes Kepler (1571–1630), in 1597 but had kept his belief private lest he suffer the ridicule and humiliation experienced by Copernicus.

While not being the first to create the telescope, Galileo was the first to turn it toward the heavens and he began to see objects in the heavens that no one had even seen before. He reported his observations and discoveries in the study, *The Starry Messenger,* in 1610. Galileo's study of the heavens revealed that the seemingly perfect sphere of the moon had craters and mountains, the planet Jupiter had four small bodies or satellites revolving around it, the sun had "blemishes" on its surface, and the planet Venus moved in and out of light and dark phases. The publication of *The Starry Messenger* stunned the educated world and positioned Galileo as the foremost astronomer and scientist of his age (Document One).

The Venetian Republic rewarded its prized scholar with a lifetime appointment at the University of Padua. Despite this generous gesture, Galileo was still drawn to his home city of Florence and the Duchy of Tuscany. One of Galileo's students, Cosimo II de Medici, would later become his biggest patron. Evidence of this allegiance to Tuscany and its ruling family, the Medicis, is found in the dedication of *The Starry Messenger* to the young grand duke, Cosimo II, and in the glorification of the Medici family by naming Jupiter's moons the

"Medicean stars." In September 1610, Galileo triumphantly returned to the Medicean court at Florence as the first mathematician at the University of Pisa, with no obligation ever to work or live in Pisa. He never did. Galileo now had a powerful patron at his side, Cosimo II, but as he would soon find out, the freedom of intellectual pursuit and thought that he enjoyed in the Venetian Republic was not a freedom enjoyed by scholars in the Duchy of Tuscany (Document Two).

While at the University of Padua, Galileo's familial responsibilities increased because of the death of his father, Vincenzio, in 1591. Almost all of the family's financial burdens fell on his shoulders. His beloved sister, Virginia, married shortly after his father's death and he had to provide her dowry, a particularly onerous burden. Italy at this time was experiencing dowry inflation because of the surplus of women on the marriage market. In the late fifteenth and early sixteenth century, in Florence there were five men for every six women. To make an appropriate match for his sister, Galileo would have to pay an exorbitant price. Ten years later, his other sister, Livia, married and again the burden of the dowry fell on him. In the latter case, he asked the Venetian Republic for a two-year advance on his salary to make half of the payment. His brother, Michelangelo, assumed the other half but defaulted on the obligation. Galileo, while happy at Padua, began to seek a better patron than the Venetian Republic and in 1604 seriously entertained an offer from the duke of Mantua, but the financial terms were not to Galileo's liking and he turned

Chapter 1
The Scientific
Revolution:
Galileo Galilei
(1564–1642) and
Sister Maria
Celeste (née
Virginia Galilei,
1600–1634)

down the offer. During his years at Padua, he supplemented his income by taking students into his home, tutoring, and selling mechanical instruments from his workshop.

In the late 1590s, Galileo met and took as his mistress, Marina Gamba, a Venetian of the lower class. Why they never married has been a point of some speculation. Most likely, Marina's class position and the fact that she was from Venice discouraged any formal union; after all, Galileo came from a distinguished Tuscan family, and being linked in marriage to the Gamba family did nothing to further the family's fortune or prestige. Coming from a lower class family, Marina could not improve Galileo's financial woes by bringing a dowry to the marriage. Her family probably could offer only clothing, household items, and maybe a little cash. Until the birth of their first child, Virginia, in 1600, Marina lived in Venice and Galileo in Padua. From 1600 until Galileo's departure for Florence in 1610, Marina lived in a small house close to Galileo's residence in Padua.

Galileo and Marina had three children together, Virginia (b. 1600), Livia (b. 1601), and Vincenzio (b. 1606). Galileo's name did not appear on any of the parish documents as the father, and therefore the children were illegitimate in the eyes of the church and the Italian city-states. Galileo did recognize the children as his; took financial responsibility for them; and, in the case of his son, arranged for the grand duke of Tuscany to legitimize Vincenzio in 1619. When he left for Florence in 1610, he took his daughter, Livia, with him. Virginia had returned with

her paternal grandmother, Julia, to Florence a year earlier. Bringing his lower-class mistress to his home city would not have helped his status, and he left Marina in Padua to care for their young son. Vincenzio remained with his mother until 1612, when his father brought him to Florence on the eve of his mother's marriage to a man of Marina's own social class.

The fact that Galileo accepted responsibility for his children was not at all unusual. Men of the elite often kept mistresses. Their offspring, while not enjoying the same inheritance privileges of children born within the union of marriage, were often supported by their fathers and the boys especially could aspire to positions of privilege. This attitude toward children of such liaisons was changing, however. The Catholic Reformation of the sixteenth century sought to condemn such relationships and put an end to them. The Council of Trent (1545–1563) drew a sharp distinction between lawful childbearing, a birth following a wedding presided over by a priest, and its sinful counterpart, bastard bearing. The result of this distinction was to portray illegitimate children as products of sinful behavior and threats to the sanctity of the true family. Those accused of cohabiting without the benefit of the sacrament of marriage lived under the threat of excommunication and denunciation.[3] Both Galileo and Marina escaped such a fate but their daughters' illegitimacy, Marina's lower class

3. David I. Kertzer, *Sacrificed for Honor: Italian Infant Abandonment and the Politics of Reproductive Control* (Boston, Mass.: Beacon Press, 1993), p. 18.

status, and their parent's sinful behavior would make it difficult for Virginia and Livia to marry well.

As the mathematician and philosopher to the grand duke's court and as a scholar, Galileo had little time to devote to the care and education of his daughters. He obviously hoped that his mother or his sisters would bear the brunt of responsibility for his daughters, but his mother's ill health and quarrelsome temperament prevented such an arrangement. In 1611, he sought advice from several Catholic cardinals concerning the placement of his daughters in a convent. He was told that several obstacles stood in his way. First, Florence did not allow for two sisters to take the veil in the same Florentine convent. Second, Galileo wanted to place his daughters in the Convent of San Matteo in Arcetri. If there was no space for them and room had to be made, then the dowry for each would double. Finally, the girls were too young to enter holy life. Galileo tried to get around this last obstacle but the age requirement at first was not waived. In response to his request, Cardinal Del Monte wrote in December 1611,

> In answer to your letter concerning your daughters' claustration, I had fully understood that you did not wish them to take the veil immediately, but that you wished them to be received on the understanding that they were to assume the religious habit as soon as they had reached the canonical age [16]. But, as I have written to you before, even this is not allowed, for many reasons: in particular, that it might give rise to the exercise of undue influence by those who wished the young persons to take the veil for reasons of their own. This rule is never broken, . . . [4]

Contrary to the cardinal's assertion, the rule was broken often if the family had the right connections. Galileo used his connections at the ducal court to gain the admittance of his daughters to the Convent of San Matteo in October 1613. Virginia was thirteen and Livia twelve. One year later, they both took the veil. Virginia took the name Sister Maria Celeste and Livia, Sister Arcangela.

Why did Galileo have his daughters take their vows? In the seventeenth century, it was not unusual for young girls to be boarded and educated by nuns. Galileo's sisters had had this experience, but because of their family name and Galileo's willingness to pay the dowries of both, they left the convent and married. Galileo's daughters were illegitimate, and the dowries necessary to make a marriage arrangement with an appropriate family were probably not within Galileo's means or desires, nor were the statistical odds in his favor of finding suitable matches. Like many parents, he resorted to an acceptable life choice for his daughters and placed them in a convent, paying a modest dowry. The climate in Florence also favored such a choice. In late sixteenth-century Florence, there were 441 male friars and 2,786 nuns, out of a population of 59,000.[5]

4. Ibid., p. 69.

5. Merry Wiesner, *Women and Gender in Early Modern Europe* (London: Cambridge University Press, 1993), p. 61.

Chapter 1
The Scientific
Revolution:
Galileo Galilei
(1564–1642) and
Sister Maria
Celeste (née
Virginia Galilei,
1600–1634)

Galileo had another motive as well. In 1613, he had reached a standing within the scientific community that was unrivaled in seventeenth-century Italy. He wanted to place his daughters in a situation where "they would not burden him with new responsibilities and relieve him of all worry on the subject forever."[6] They would see their father only on the rare occasions when he visited the convent. Their mother died in 1619 with no evidence surviving that she had seen her daughters after their departure from Padua in 1613. Galileo had chosen religious lives for his daughters because it was convenient for him and socially acceptable. He chose differently for his son, Vincenzio, whom Galileo legitimized, educated, married off, and supported. His daughters would not enjoy or thrive in the life that Galileo had chosen for them. Livia would suffer numerous breakdowns and Virginia would be dead at the age of 34.

ACT I:

GALILEO, THE COPERNICAN SYSTEM, AND THE INQUISITION

The duchy of Tuscany and its ruling house, the Medicis, were intimately tied to Rome and the Catholic ecclesiastical hierarchy. Members of the Medici family served as cardinals, bishops, and popes, and these connections brought the Roman Catholic Church into the political, intellectual, and religious affairs of the duchy. This relationship between the two provided Galileo the opportunity to go to Rome in 1611 and try to convince the theologians there of the truth of the Copernican thesis. He went to Rome not as a heretic but as a man deeply committed and loyal to the Roman Catholic Church.

Galileo was a man of his time. During his lifetime, Roman Catholicism, in which he had been reared and educated, was under siege from the Reformation and threatened by the spread of Protestantism. To counter the Reformation, the church in Rome embarked upon its own reforms. In the mid-sixteenth century, the Council of Trent initiated policies to revive the clergy and papacy and instituted a new order, the Jesuits, to fight the Reformation. In addition, the church once again convened the Holy Office (Inquisition), a tribunal of church officials authorized to uncover, investigate, and prosecute heretics. Galileo understood the threat that the Reformation posed to his religion, but he did not want his church to support a view of the heavens from which it would have to retreat. His discoveries, coupled with Copernicus's and Kepler's, convinced him that a revolution in the conception of the universe was at hand and that if the church denied these scientific advances, it risked further challenge to and erosion of its

6. Ludovico Geymonat, *Galileo Galilei* (New York: McGraw-Hill, 1965), p. 55. Quoted in David F. Noble, *A World Without Women: The Christian Clerical Culture of Western Science* (New York: Oxford University Press, 1992), p. 217.

credibility.[7] Dogmatic and doctrinal principles and attitudes had brought about the Protestant Reformation, and Galileo did not want the church to lose further ground. From the favorable reception that he and his telescope received in Rome in 1611, it appeared that the church was willing to entertain discussion about the Copernican system and its implication.

In a letter to a Tuscan official, Galileo described how the learned Jesuits of the Roman College confirmed his discovery of the Medicean planets. He wrote, "The Fathers, being finally convinced that the Medicean planets are realities, have devoted the past two months to continuous observations of them, and these observations are still in progress. We have compared notes and have found that our experiences tally in every respect."[8] Pope Paul V (1605–1621) received Galileo for a private audience and Galileo met with Cardinal Bellarmine, one of the *consultors* of the Inquisition, who went so far as to look through Galileo's telescope. Galileo's final triumph was his election to the Academy of the Lincei. Founded in 1603, the academy, an exclusive association of scholars, was devoted to the study of natural phenomena and shunned the traditional natural philosophy of the universities, which at this point were bastions of conservativism and rhetorical superficiality.

The first of Galileo's confrontations with the church began when he wrote three letters in response to the ideas of Christopher Scheiner (1573–1650), a Jesuit scholar, about sunspots. Scheiner's theories on sunspots rested on Aristotelian belief in the sun's immutability and purity. Scheiner argued that the sunspots were bodies revolving around the sun and were not found on the sun's surface. In three letters to a mutual acquaintance, Mark Welser (1558–1614), Galileo proved that the sunspots could not be stars circling the sun as Scheiner hypothesized, but that they were close to the sun's surface. He also disproved Scheiner's idea that the sun stood still while these bodies revolved around it. Instead, Galileo argued that the sun turned on its axis just like the earth. These letters were published by the Lincean Academy in 1613 and it was the first time that Galileo, in print, used his own observations and discoveries as proof of the Copernican system. While carefully wording his response to avoid insulting Scheiner, Galileo could not resist a jab at the Aristotelians in general. He wrote, "They never wish to raise their eyes from those pages [Aristotle's]—as if this great book of the universe had been written to be read by nobody but Aristotle, and his eyes destined to see for all posterity."[9] Galileo had been sparring with the Aristotelians his entire academic career and he thought little of this exchange. But antagonizing a member of the most powerful priestly order in Rome, which was

7. Laura Fermi and Gilberto Bernardini, *Galileo and the Scientific Revolution* (New York: Basic Books, 1961), p. 73.

8. James Brodrick, *Galileo: The Man, His Work, His Misfortunes* (New York: Harper and Row, 1964), p. 56.

9. Ibid., p. 68.

*Chapter 1
The Scientific
Revolution:
Galileo Galilei
(1564–1642) and
Sister Maria
Celeste (née
Virginia Galilei,
1600–1634)*

charged with education matters, would not win him many friends.

Discussions and debates concerning Galileo's heavenly discoveries were not limited only to academic and religious circles, but learned men and women, mingling with scholars and priests, also contemplated the significance and meaning of Galileo's theories. During a dinner party in December 1613 at Cosimo II's residence, the grand duke's mother, Cristina of Lorraine (157?–1637), queried one of Galileo's detractors, Cosimo Boscaglia (1550?–1621), a professor at the University of Pisa and a staunch Aristotelian and Platonist, about whether or not Galileo's theories about the earth moving contradicted the Scriptures. Benedetto Castelli (1578–1643), a close ally of Galileo and a Benedictine monk, who was at the dinner, reported the incident in a letter to Galileo. Castelli wrote, "Dr. Boscaglia had had the ear of Madame for a while; and, conceding as true all of the things you have discovered in the sky, he said that only the motion of the earth had something incredible in it and could not take place, in particular because the holy scripture was obviously contrary to this view."[10] Upon receiving Castelli's letter detailing the discussion, Galileo wrote a response with the intention of setting forth clearly his views on the impropriety of mixing religion and science. In a letter addressed to Castelli and later in a revised version addressed to the Grand Duchess Cristina, Galileo argued that nature and its laws went side by side with his faith in God (Document

Three). He simply distinguished between knowledge that aimed to understand the universe and how it worked and knowledge that aimed to attain salvation. Or more simply put, according to Galileo, the Bible and religious writing teaches "humans how to go to heaven, not how the heavens go." Galileo's letters, eloquently composed and argued, circulated in both the scholarly and religious communities of Florence. Given the informalities associated with such letters, it was simply a matter of time before two church officials read or heard about the letters and denounced Galileo to the Inquisition in Rome.

In December 1615, the Inquisition launched an investigation examining the two main tenets of Copernican theory: 1) the sun is immobile and at the center of the universe, and 2) the earth rotates around the sun in daily revolutions and is not the center of the universe. Believing that he had done no wrong and wishing to defend scientific inquiry, Galileo set off to Rome "with the heroic blindness of an apostle [of science] and the enthusiastic faith of a boy."[11] In Rome, Galileo was warmly and courteously received by scholars and ecclesiastics, who listened patiently to his arguments in favor of Copernicus. As Galileo's detractors and enemies busied themselves denouncing him to the Inquisition, several influential cardinals advised him to mute his public enthusiasm for the heliocentric system. Galileo did not heed their advice and he continued his campaign. On February 23, 1616, the Inquisition completed its investi-

10. Ibid., p. 75.

11. Ibid., p. 98.

gation and declared the first of the main tenets of the Copernican system to be "false and absurd, formally heretical and contrary to Scripture" and the second to be "equally censured, philosophically false and was at least erroneous in faith."[12] It also condemned and banned any books that dealt with the Copernican theory. Prior to Galileo's championing of Copernicus's theories, they were brushed aside as indulgent intellectual musings and mathematical exercises, and only one hypothesis among many. Galileo had made these theories the subject of dinner conversations, however, and Catholic authorities could not ignore this threat to their authority. According to the church, the heliocentric system contradicted Scripture and altered a centuries old conception of the universe with a Christian god as its center. To the church, which had held a monopoly on interpreting the heavens, Galileo's advocacy meant that God's creation had become an object of direct human observation, which could be interpreted without the help of the Scriptures, a priest, or religion.[13]

The Inquisition chose not to condemn Galileo for heresy but warned him that he should abandon the idea that the heliocentric system was fact. Curious, of course, is the nuance of the Inquisition's decisions. They did not outright forbid Galileo from holding his beliefs or from teaching or defending them. Galileo could present Copernicanism as a mathematical supposition that was not supported by "real proof." Rumors flew around the learned world that Galileo had been forced to renounce his beliefs and repent. The Republic of Venice even offered him refuge.

Upon his return to Florence in June 1616, Galileo appeared content to pursue his other scientific pursuits. However, the appearance of three comets in the sky during the fall of 1618 brought his restraint to an end. Father Horatio Grassis (1590–1654), a Jesuit astronomer, used the comets' appearance to denounce the Copernican doctrine. This was too much for Galileo, who had no intention of retreating from his belief in the heliocentric system, and he searched for indirect ways to disprove the church's continuing endorsement of earth-centered heavens. Using a student as a proxy, he delivered a series of lectures and published *Discourse on Comets*, which again articulated his views. The stage was now set for Grassis to reply, which he did in *The Astronomical and Philosophical Balance*. Galileo could not bear the ignorance of the Aristotelians and the posturing of the churchmen any longer, and he crafted a brilliant and biting polemic, *The Assayer*. Published in 1623, it reiterated Galileo's belief in science, nature and its laws, and rigorous intellectual inquiry, and his contempt for those who when "philosophizing must support oneself upon the opinion of some celebrated author."[14]

The Linceans published *The Assayer* and dedicated it to the new pope, Urban VIII (1623–1644), who as the

---

12. Fermi and Bernardini, p. 83.
13. Ibid., p. 84.

14. Ibid., p. 86.

Chapter 1
The Scientific
Revolution:
Galileo Galilei
(1564–1642) and
Sister Maria
Celeste (née
Virginia Galilei,
1600–1634)

Cardinal Barberini, had befriended Galileo upon his arrival in Florence in 1611. In 1616, the cardinal had opposed the church's warning to the scientist. Galileo was quite excited about Barberini's election to the papacy, and in 1624 he visited Rome, where he was warmly and generously received by the new pope. During their cordial meetings together, Urban VIII spoke of his favorite passages in *The Assayer*, promised his old friend a pension, and listened to Galileo's ideas about the heavens. When Galileo returned to Rome, it appears that he took his old friend's generosity, warmth, and curiosity as an opportunity to write a work that openly disputed the Ptolemaic system. His continuing ill health slowed his thinking and writing and this polemic, *Dialogue on the Two Chief World Systems; Ptolemaic and Copernican,* was not published until 1632.

During the years that he was working on *Dialogue* and struggling with his health, his daughters, Sister Maria Celeste and Sister Arcangela, reappear in the historical record. They were now young women of twenty-three and twenty-two years old and had spent the last ten years of their lives coping with the austere, impoverished, and cloistered world of the Convent of San Matteo.

▓ ACT II:

GALILEO'S DAUGHTER

Sister Maria Celeste and her sister lived cloistered lives, but this circumstance did not mean that they were disinterested in the world beyond the convent's walls. Scholars have 124 of Sister Maria Celeste's letters to her father, beginning with the year 1623 and ending with her death in 1634. His letters to her have disappeared. Her letters reveal a women who was intensely interested in the affairs of her family, yearned to provide comfort and support to her father, gave advice to her brother, offered domestic help to both of them, and acted as a secretary and confidant to her father. These are not the letters of a woman who was content or satisfied with her enclosed world. As the letters reveal, Sister Maria Celeste wished to perform all of the expected duties of a dutiful daughter, albeit behind the convent's wall. Her letters also allow us to enter into the cloistered world of the Convent of San Matteo and learn of its routines, habits, rules, quality of life, and politics.

The Convent of San Matteo in Arcetri was part of the Order of the Poor Sisters, which was founded by Saint Clare of Assisi in the thirteenth century. The Poor Clares, as they were called, vowed to live a life of poverty, charity, and humility, and to devote themselves to prayer, nursing the sick, and works of mercy for the poor and neglected. The rules of the order called upon each sister and the collective group to live a life of extreme austerity and of absolute poverty. These rules symbolized the sisters' willingness to share the life of the poor through manual labor and their imitation of the poor's total dependence on others by only accepting alms for their support.

This was the most austere and severe of all the female orders.

Life as a Poor Clare had improved over the centuries. Originally the sisters slept on twigs with patched hemp for blankets. They ate little, and no meat at all. Whatever food they had was obtained by begging. By the seventeenth century, the spiritual standards of the order had changed and the abject poverty associated with the Poor Clares had lessened. The sisters now slept in beds in a large dormitory. There were a few private cells available to those sisters whose families paid an additional price beyond the dowry. The adornment of the room depended again on familial support. Some rooms sported heavy bedcurtains and door hangings, important for shutting out the cold air and draft. Early in their residence at the convent, Sister Maria Celeste and Sister Arcangela shared a small cell with another sister. When this sister relinquished the cell, Sister Maria Celeste gave it to her sister, who was suffering from ill health. Sister Maria Celeste would not have a room of her own until the last four years of her life. At times, she sought comfort and peace away from the common sleeping quarters by sleeping on the floor of another sister who kindly shared her frigid cell (Document Four).

The sisters ate together, but if they could afford extra provisions, these were allowed and shared by all members of the order. On numerous occasions over the years, Sister Maria Celeste wrote to her father asking for a supply of wine or fresh meat to make broth for herself and others when they fell ill. In keeping with the rules of the order, she distributed these provisions to the other sisters. The sisters spent long hours struggling to support themselves, growing fruits and vegetables in the convent's walled garden. Here they not only grew their own food but much of the garden was dedicated to growing medicinal herbs and plants, which they then sold for extra income. Sister Maria Celeste became the convent's apothecary, creating pills and tonics from the garden's bounty and caring for the convent's sick.[15] The convent also supplemented its meager income by baking, sewing, and embroidery. Sister Maria Celeste used these skills to attend to the needs of her father and brother, often sewing shirts, collars, and bed and table linens for them and sending them confections. She also worked as a scribe for her father as he aged. Galileo's numerous illnesses caused his handwriting to deteriorate, and Sister Maria Celeste began to copy his letters and manuscripts.

Ill health resulting from malnourishment and the cold was common among the sisters of San Matteo. Both of Galileo's daughters are often described in Sister Maria Celeste's letters as being ill or recovering from a recent bout of sickness. Sister Arcangela eventually succumbed to the privation and suffered some type of permanent breakdown. Beginning with the first of the surviving letters, dated October 1623, Sister Maria Celeste wrote letters that often detailed her sister's physical and mental health, her and the convent's need for basic foodstuffs

15. Dava Sobel, *Galileo's Daughter* (New York: Penguin Books, 2000), pp. 112–113 and 151–152.

*Chapter 1
The Scientific
Revolution:
Galileo Galilei
(1564–1642) and
Sister Maria
Celeste (née
Virginia Galilei,
1600–1634)*

and supplies, and her melancholy at being physically separated from her father and brother. Absent from the letters are sentiments expressing joy over or satisfaction with life in the convent. She confided in one letter that her fondest dream was not so much to fathom the heavens but to step foot just once inside her father's house. As her father aged, her longing to help him through his sicknesses, infirmities, bouts of loneliness, and intellectual struggles with the church increased. In his last encounter with the Inquisition, which resulted in his confinement at home in Florence, Galileo found great comfort in the attention and love bestowed upon him by his daughter.

In 1632, the most famous and controversial of Galileo's works, *Dialogue on the Two Chief World Systems; Ptolemaic and Copernican,* was published in Florence. Written in Italian, not Latin, to reach as many learned people as possible, the *Dialogue* challenged the authority of the Inquisition, which in 1616 had openly endorsed the Ptolemaic system and condemned the Copernican. In this treatise, Galileo cleverly composed a dialogue between a Ptolemist and two Copernicans. The Ptolemist was utterly confounded and defeated by the superior reasoning and proofs of the Copernicans. Church authorities perceived this work to be a defense of a theory that they had prohibited from scholarly discourse. The church reacted immediately, ordered the publisher of the book to stop selling it, and summoned Galileo to Rome.

Why Galileo was summoned before the Inquisition is a question that scholars have pondered for many years.

Some argue that Galileo's enemies, especially the Jesuits, were taking their revenge. Others argue that it was Galileo's arrogance, ambition, and naïveté. He was not content to leave his ideas in the scholarly realm but sought the church's approval for the Copernican theory. In effect, he wanted the church to reinforce his ideas and overthrow centuries of knowledge; the church was not prepared to yield to the authority of this one scientist and to the new discipline of science.

Galileo did not go to Rome immediately. He was quite ill and asked several times if he could be questioned in Florence or postpone the investigation into his suspected heresy until he was well. The church, flexing its muscle, refused and pressured him to make the trip to Rome and appear in person before the Inquisition. Galileo could have refused and fled to another state where the church's authority was not so influential. Hearing of the Inquistion's summons, the Venetians invited him to return. Galileo politely turned down the invitation and traveled to Rome in February 1633, believing he could defend his ideas before the inquisitors. He left his daughter to monitor his personal and household affairs while he was in Rome.

After spending several weeks at the residence of the Tuscan ambassador to Rome, Galileo was summoned to the Inquisition's building where he was comfortably accommodated until the beginning of the trial. On April 12, 1633, Galileo argued before the Inquisition that he did not hold nor did he teach and defend the Copernican system as fact but had merely presented the Copernican view as one supposition among many. The Inquisition was not interested in the nuance of whether Galileo accepted this view as fact or hypothesis; they wanted to put an end to Galileo's challenges and accused him of not following the Inquisition's instruction, which prohibited the discussion of the Copernican theory. He denied that he had ever received such an instruction. He argued that in 1616 he had only been warned not to teach Copernican theory as fact. The Inquisition probably manufactured the instructions. After his interrogation, Galileo fell ill. Sister Maria Celeste, knowing of her father's frail condition, the fatigue of travel, and the grueling interrogation, wrote to her father detailing the banalities of everyday life at the convent and on his estate to distract him from his trial (Document Five).

The Inquisition, after three interrogations spread over two months, found Galileo guilty of holding heretical opinions that he must denounce to be absolved (Document Six). On June 22, 1633, Galileo stood before the ten cardinals of the Holy Office and abjured (Document Seven). Galileo was then sentenced to life imprisonment in Rome. His sympathizers had the sentence softened, and he was eventually allowed to return to his home in Florence to serve his sentence. Not only would Galileo be prevented from ever again appearing publically, but the Inquistion banned all of Galileo's works, published and unpublished.

His daughter was surprised when she learned of the outcome of the trial. She wrote on July 2, 1633, ". . . what I hear from him [Signor Geri] of the resolution they have taken concerning you and your book gives me extreme pain, not having expected such a result. Dearest lord and father, now is the time for the exercise of that wisdom with which God has endowed you. Thus you will bear these blows with that fortitude of soul which religion, your age, and your profession alike demand."[16] His daughter understood the workings of the Holy Office and when two of her father's loyal supporters appeared at the convent asking her for keys to his villa so that they could get to Galileo's papers before the Inquisition did, she did not hesitate.

By December 1633, Galileo was now living on a farm and in a house next door to his daughters' convent at Arcetri. His imprisonment had begun briefly in Siena, but the pope feared that his presence in Siena would sow heretical ideas and thought it was best to send him home where he was a known quantity. During his confinement in Siena, Sister Maria Celeste encouraged her father to continue his scientific work in mechanics. She wrote, ". . . tell me what subject you are writing about at present: Provided it is something that I could understand, and you have no fear that I might gossip."[17] Galileo was composing the last of his scientific treatises, *Two New Sciences*, which was published in 1638 by a distinguished Dutch publishing firm. The Inquisition had prohibited the printing or reprinting of any of Galileo's works, and the manuscript had to be smuggled out of Tuscany. When the Holy Office heard that the book was published, however, they turned a blind

16. *The Private Life of Galileo Galilei*, p. 263.
17. Sobel, p. 333.

Chapter 1
The Scientific
Revolution:
Galileo Galilei
(1564–1642) and
Sister Maria
Celeste (née
Virginia Galilei,
1600–1634)

eye to this violation of the terms of his confinement.

Sister Maria Celeste rejoiced at her father's return to Arcetri and for several months, until her death in April 1634, they shared the same neighborhood. Galileo could not receive visitors who might engage him in scientific discussions and he could leave his property only to visit the convent. She could receive visitors only in a parlor where guests were received. However, Galileo was more than a guest. He kept the convent's clock in repair, gave advice on pruning and grafting fruit trees, and provided small carpentry services. The companionship of his daughter, her intelligence and interest in his physi-

cal and intellectual well-being, and his continued thinking and writing appear at first to have lessened the impact of Galileo's imprisonment, but to him it was still a prison. He began each letter with the phrase, "From my prison in Arcetri." His imprisonment was made all the worse when his eldest daughter died a few months after his return. In a letter to a friend shortly after Sister Maria Celeste's death, he wrote, "Here I lived on very quietly, frequently paying visits to the neighboring convent, where I had two daughters, both nuns, whom I loved dearly: but the eldest in particular, who was a woman of exquisite mind, singular goodness and most tenderly attached to me."[18]

▪ FINALE

Sister Maria Celeste's death came at the age of thirty-three after years of malnourishment, inadequate living conditions, hard work as a Poor Clare, and numerous illnesses. Her father would die eight years later at the age of seventy-seven after years of plenty; comfortable and pleasurable domestic arrangements; lively, exhilarating, and challenging scientific work and study; and occasional skirmishes with religious and scholarly authorities. Historically, Galileo and not his daughter has been portrayed as the one hindered and restrained by the religious practices and prescriptions of the day. The Inquisition did in fact condemn Galileo and his work, stifling not only the last work of his life, *Two New Sciences*, but in effect intimi-

dating others in Italy and elsewhere and preventing them from challenging sacred intellectual and philosophical traditions. In the seventeenth century, the Catholic Church wished to regain control over access to knowledge, and it was willing to vanquish one of the great scientific minds of its day in this pursuit.

Galileo's hubris did not include forsaking Catholicism. He often described his own ideas as "divinely inspired" and discredited his opponents as "contrary to Scripture." He had close collaborative scientific relations as well as close friendships with leading clerics and benefitted on occasion from papal patronage. Until his sentence, Galileo believed that an enlightened papacy could be an effective instrument of

18. *The Private Life of Galileo*, p. 271.

scientific progress. Galileo benefitted from this religious world and its world view. The Catholic Church and its clerical culture, ascetic and male-centered, created a learned world where intellectual activity and scholarly pursuit were separate from the mundane and burdensome responsibilities of everyday life. Secular institutions such as the Academy of the Lincei and universities embraced this tradition of separatism and encouraged celibacy among its members. Women were something to shed as men became scholars, essentially creating an intellectual and scholarly space that excluded women.[19]

"This world without women" meant that Galileo could justify the claustration of his daughters, not only because of the circumstance of their birth or because of the burden of the dowry, but because his chosen profession excluded the presence of women. There were a few notable women who did venture into the learned professions, like Elena Lucrezia Cornaro Piscopia (1646–1684), who was the first European woman to receive a doctorate at the University of Padua in 1678, but their success depended on familial support and scholarly climate. It is not at all surprising that Piscopia's doctorate in philosophy was obtained at

the most liberal of all Italian universities, the University of Padua.

Despite the opportunities that the University of Padua and his family had given him, Galileo did not extend to his daughters the same opportunities that he and Piscopia enjoyed. Using his prerogative as a father, he gave his daughters one choice. They entered the convent on his order, and in Sister Maria Celeste's letters, we see a woman who was not content with her life circumstances. The convent for her was not a safe haven, a place where women thrived as intellectuals and freethinking persons. The Convent of San Matteo was a place of deprivation of food, family, and friends; of petty indignities; and of countless hours spent contemplating the world outside. Both Galileo and his daughter lived lives that were bound by their class position, religion, intellectual abilities, and gender. If all these positions were equal, they would have lived similar lives. The "woman of exquisite mind," as Sister Maria Celeste's father described her, was prevented from participating in the world, not because of the illegitimacy of her birth or because of her class position or intellectual abilities, but because she was a woman.

▨ QUESTIONS

1. What type of education did Galileo receive? Why were the ancient Greeks and their medieval interpreters touted as the intellectual authorities of the day?

2. What were the necessary preconditions for questioning the church's monopoly over learning? Why did Galileo question ancient and medieval learned authorities?

19. Noble, p. 215.

Chapter 1
The Scientific
Revolution:
Galileo Galilei
(1564–1642) and
Sister Maria
Celeste (née
Virginia Galilei,
1600–1634)

3. Describe Galileo's relationship with his children. What choices did his son and his daughters have for their own lives? Why did they differ?

4. Why was Galileo's exploration of the stars and heavens threatening to the Roman Catholic Church? Was Galileo anti-Catholic? Why or why not?

5. Were education, scientific inquiry, and learned communities open to all based on merit? Why or why not?

6. Why did the Inquisition put Galileo on trial? What were his sins?

7. What role did women play during the centuries of the Scientific Revolution? What were some of the obstacles to their participation?

■ DOCUMENTS

DOCUMENT ONE

GALILEO GALILEI

The Starry Messenger
(1610)

Galileo turned the telescope to the heavens and revealed to Europeans for the first time hundreds of stars and natural phenomena. In the following excerpts, Galileo described his observation of the moon and his discovery of the four moons orbiting Jupiter. What does Galileo use for his scientific inquiries of the heavens?

But forsaking terrestrial observations, I turned to celestial ones, and first I saw the moon from as near at hand as if it were scarcely two terrestrial radii [a measure of distance, obscure today] away. After that I observed often with wondering delight both the planets and the fixed stars, and since I saw these latter to be very crowded, I began to seek (and eventually found) a method by which I might measure their distances apart. . . .

Now let us review the observations made during the past two months, once more inviting the attention of all who are eager for true philosophy to the first steps of such important contemplations. Let us speak first of that surface of the moon which faces us. For greater clarity I distinguish two parts of this surface, a lighter and a darker; the lighter part seems to surround and to pervade the whole hemisphere, while the darker part discolors the moon's surface like a kind of cloud, and makes it appear covered with spots. Now those spots which are fairly dark and rather large are plain to everyone and have been seen throughout the ages; these I shall call the "large" or "ancient" spots, distinguishing them from others that are smaller in size but so numerous as to occur all over the lunar surface, and especially the lighter part. The latter spots had never been seen by anyone before me. From observations of these spots repeated many times I have been led to the opinion and conviction that the surface of the moon is not smooth, uniform, and precisely spherical as a great number of philosophers believe it (and the other heavenly bodies) to be, but is uneven, rough, and full of cavities and prominences, being not unlike the face of the earth, relieved by chains of mountains and deep valleys. . . .

[MOONS ORBITING JUPITER]

On the seventh day of January in this present year 1610, at the first hour of night, when I was viewing the heavenly bodies with a telescope, Jupiter presented itself to me; and because I had prepared a very excellent instrument for myself, I perceived (as I had not before, on account of the weakness of my previous instrument) that beside the planet there were three starlets, small indeed, but very bright. Though I believed them to be among the host of fixed stars, they aroused my curiosity somewhat by appearing to lie in an exact straight line parallel to the ecliptic, and by their being more splendid than others of their size. Their arrangement with respect to Jupiter and each other was the following:

East　　　*****　　　*****　　　O　　　*****　　　*West*

that is, there were two stars on the eastern side and one to the west. The most easterly star and the western one appeared larger than the other. I paid no attention to the distances between them and Jupiter, for at the outset I thought them to be fixed stars, as I have said. But returning to the same investigation on January eighth — led by what, I do not know — I found a very different arrangement. The three starlets were now all to the west of Jupiter, closer together, and at equal intervals from one another as shown in the following sketch:

East　　　O　　　*****　　　*****　　　*****　　　*West*

On the tenth of January, however, the stars appeared in this position with respect to Jupiter:

East　　　*****　　　*****　　　O　　　*West*

that is, there were but two of them, both easterly, the third (as I supposed) being hidden behind Jupiter. . . . There was no way in which such alterations could be attributed to Jupiter's motion, yet being certain that these were still the same stars I had observed . . . my perplexity was now transformed into amazement. I was sure that the apparent changes belonged not to Jupiter but to the observed stars, and I resolved to pursue this investigation with greater care and attention. . . .

Chapter 1
The Scientific
Revolution:
Galileo Galilei
(1564–1642) and
Sister Maria
Celeste (née
Virginia Galilei,
1600–1634)

I had now decided beyond all question that there existed in the heavens three stars wandering about Jupiter as do Venus and Mercury about the sun, and this became plainer than daylight from observations on similar occasions which followed. Nor were there just three such stars; four wanderers complete their revolutions about Jupiter. . . .

Here we have a fine and elegant argument for quieting the doubts of those who, while accepting with tranquil mind the revolutions of the planets about the sun in the Copernican system, are mightily disturbed to have the moon alone revolve about the earth and accompany it in an annual rotation about the sun. Some have believed that this structure of the universe should be rejected as impossible. But now we have not just one planet rotating about another while both run through a great orbit around the sun; our own eyes show us four stars which wander around Jupiter as does the moon around the earth, while all together trace out a grand revolution about the sun in the space of twelve years.

DOCUMENT TWO

Giovanni Francesco Sagredo

Letter to Galileo on Intellectual Freedom
(1610)

Sagredo, a young Venetian nobleman and friend of Galileo, tried to convince Galileo to remain in the Venetian Republic where his intellectual pursuits would be protected by the republic's tradition of freedom and its ability to keep the Inquisition at bay. He warns Galileo to be careful at Cosimo II's court. What are the potential trouble spots for Galileo in Florence? Of whom must Galileo be wary?

. . . Where will you find freedom and sovereignty of yourself as in Venice? Especially since you had here support and protection, which became more weighty every day as the age and authority of your friends grew. . . . At present you serve your natural Prince, a great, virtuous man of singular promise; but here you had command over those who command and govern others, and you had to serve only yourself. You were as the ruler of the universe. . . . In the tempestuous sea of a court who can be sure not to be . . . belabored and upset by the furious winds of envy? . . . Who knows what the infinite and incomprehensible events of the world may cause if aided by the impostures of evil and envious men . . . who may even turn the justice and goodness of a prince into the ruin of an honest man? I am very much worried by your being in a place where the authority of the friends of the Jesuits counts heavily.

DOCUMENT THREE

GALILEO GALILEI

Letter to the Grand Duchess Christina
(1615)

Galileo wrote a lengthy letter to Cosimo II's mother, Christina, arguing that one needed to avoid using Scripture to understand natural phenomena. Why does Galileo object to Scripture as a source for explaining the heavens? How did Copernicus acquire his knowledge of the heavens?

To the Most Serene Ladyship the Grand Duchess Dowager:

As Your Most Serene Highness knows very well, a few years ago I discovered in the heavens many particulars which had been invisible until our time. Because of their novelty, and because of some consequences deriving from them which contradict certain physical propositions commonly accepted in philosophical schools, they roused against me no small number of such professors, as if I had placed these things in heaven with my hands in order to confound nature and the sciences. These people seemed to forget that a multitude of truths contribute to inquiry and to the growth and strength of disciplines rather than to their diminution or destruction, and at the same time they showed greater affection for their own opinions than for the true ones; thus they proceeded to deny and to try to nullify those novelties, about which the senses themselves could have rendered them certain, if they had wanted to look at those novelties carefully. To this end they produced various matters, and they published some writings full of useless discussions and sprinkled with quotations from the Holy Scripture, taken from passages which they do not properly understand and which they inappropriately adduce. . . .

Then it developed that the passage of time disclosed to everyone the truths I had first pointed out, and, along with the truth of the matter, the difference in attitude between those who sincerely and without envy did not accept these discoveries as true and those who added emotional agitation to disbelief. Thus, just as those who were most competent in astronomical and physical science were convinced by my first announcement, so gradually there has been a calming down of all the others whose denials and doubts were not sustained by anything other than the unexpected novelty and the lack of opportunity to see them and to experience them with the senses. However, there are those who are rendered ill-disposed, not so much toward the things as much as toward the author, by the love of their first error and by some interest which they imagine having but which escapes me. Unable to deny them any longer, these people became silent about them; but, embittered more than before by what has mellowed and quieted the others, they divert their thinking to other fictions and try to harm me in other ways.

Chapter 1
The Scientific
Revolution:
Galileo Galilei
(1564–1642) and
Sister Maria
Celeste (née
Virginia Galilei,
1600–1634)

. . . These people are aware that in my astronomical and philosophical studies, on the question of the constitution of the world's parts, I hold that the sun is
located at the center of the revolutions of the heavenly orbs and does not change
place, and that the earth rotates on itself and moves around it. Moreover, they
hear how I confirm this view not only by refuting Ptolemy's and Aristotle's arguments, but also by producing many for the other side, especially some pertaining to physical effects whose causes perhaps cannot be determined in any
other way, and other astronomical ones dependent on many features of the new
celestial discoveries; these discoveries clearly confute the Ptolemaic system,
and they agree admirably with this other position and confirm it. Now, these
people are perhaps confounded by the known truth of the other propositions
different from the ordinary which I hold, and so they may lack confidence to defend themselves as long as they remain in the philosophical field. Therefore,
since they persist in their original self-appointed task of beating down me and
my findings by every imaginable means, they have decided to try to shield the
fallacies of their arguments with the cloak of simulated religiousness and with
the authority of Holy Scripture, unintelligently using the latter for the confuta-
tion of arguments they neither understand nor have heard.

At first, they tried on their own to spread among common people the idea
that such propositions are against Holy Scripture, and consequently damnable
and heretical. Then they realized how by and large human nature is more inclined to join those ventures which result in the oppression of other people
(even if unjustly) than those which result in their just improvement, and so it
was not difficult for them to find someone who with unusual confidence did
preach even from the pulpit that it is damnable and heretical; and this was done
with little compassion and with little consideration of the injury not only to this
doctrine and its followers, but also to mathematics and all mathematicians.
Thus, having acquired more confidence, and with the vain hope that the seed
which first took root in their insincere mind would grow into a tree and rise
toward the sky, they are spreading among the people the rumor that it will
shortly be declared heretical by the supreme authority. . . .

[ADDRESSING THE CRITICS OF COPERNICUS'S *THE REVOLUTION OF HEAVENLY BODIES* (1543)]

. . . They always shield themselves with a simulated religious zeal, and they
also try to involve Holy Scripture and to make it somehow subservient to their
insincere objectives; against the intention of Scripture and the Holy Fathers (if
I am not mistaken), they want to extend, not to say abuse, its authority, so
that even for purely physical conclusions which are not matters of faith one
must totally abandon the senses and demonstrative arguments in favor of any
scriptural passage whose apparent words may contain a different indication.
Here I hope to demonstrate that I proceed with much more pious and religious

zeal than they when I propose not that this book should not be condemned, but that it should not be condemned without understanding, examining, or even seeing it, as they would like. This is especially true since the author never treats of matters pertaining to religion and faith, nor uses arguments dependent in any way on the authority of Holy Scripture, in which case he might have interpreted it incorrectly; instead, he always limits himself to physical conclusions pertaining to celestial motions, and he treats of them with astronomical and geometrical demonstrations based above all on sensory experience and very accurate observations. He proceeded in this manner not because he did not pay any attention to the passages of Holy Scripture, but because he understood very well that if his doctrine was demonstrated it could not contradict the properly interpreted Scripture. . . .

[THE BASIS ON WHICH NATURAL PHENOMENA MUST BE ELEVATED]

Therefore, I think that in disputes about natural phenomena one must begin not with the authority of scriptural passages but with sensory experience and necessary demonstrations. For the Holy Scripture and nature derive equally from the Godhead, the former as the dictation of the Holy Spirit and the latter as the most obedient executrix of God's orders; moreover, to accommodate the understanding of the common people it is appropriate for Scripture to say many things that are different (in appearance and in regard to the literal meaning of the words) from the absolute truth; on the other hand, nature is inexorable and immutable, never violates the terms of the laws imposed upon her, and does not care whether or not her recondite reasons and ways of operating are disclosed to human understanding; but not every scriptural assertion is bound to obligations as severe as every natural phenomenon; finally, God reveals Himself to us no less excellently in the effects of nature than in the sacred words of Scripture, as Tertullian perhaps meant when he said, "We postulate that God ought first to be known by nature, and afterward further known by doctrine—by nature through His works, by doctrine through official teaching" (*Against Marcion*, I.18); and so it seems that a natural phenomenon which is placed before our eyes by sensory experience or proved by necessary demonstrations should not be called into question, let alone condemned, on account of scriptural passages whose words appear to have a different meaning.

Chapter 1
The Scientific
Revolution:
Galileo Galilei
(1564–1642) and
Sister Maria
Celeste (née
Virginia Galilei,
1600–1634)

====== DOCUMENT FOUR ======

SISTER MARIA CELESTE

On Life in the Convent
(1623)

In the following excerpts, Sister Maria Celeste describes the cloistered life and her desire to be of assistance to her father and brother. What types of services did Sister Maria Celeste perform for her family beyond the convent's walls?

[ON DOMESTIC MATTERS, OCTOBER 20, 1623]

Most Illustrious and Beloved Lord Father

I send back the rest of your shirts which we have been working at, also the apron, which I have mended as well as I possibly could. I likewise return the letters you sent me to read; they are so beautiful that my desire to see more of them is greatly increased. I cannot begin working at the dinner napkins till you send the pieces to add on. Please bear in mind that the said pieces must be long, owing to the dinner napkins being a trifle short.

I have just placed Sister Arcangela under the doctor's care, to see whether, with the Lord's help, she may be relieved of her troublesome complaint, which gives me great anxiety.

I hear from Salvadore (the servant) that you are coming to see us before very long. We wish to have you very much indeed; but please remember that when you come you must keep your promise of spending the evening with us. You will be able to sup in the parlour, since the excommunication is for the table-cloth, and not for the meats thereon.

I enclose herewith a little composition, which, aside from expressing to you the extent of our need, will also give you the excuse to have a hearty laugh at the expense of my foolish writing; but because I have seen how good-naturedly you always encourage my meager intelligence, Sire, you have lent me the courage to attempt this essay. Indulge me then, Lord Father, and with your usual loving tenderness please help us. I thank you for the fish, and send you loving greetings along with Suor Arcangela. May our Lord grant you complete happiness.

From San Matteo, the 20th day of October 1623.

Most affectionate daughter,

S. M. C.

[ON A PACKAGE SENT TO HER BY GALILEO, OCTOBER 23, 1623]

Most Illustrious and Beloved Lord Father

If I should begin thanking you in words for the present you have sent us, besides not knowing how to quench our debt with words, I believe that you would not care for them, preferring, as you do, our gratitude, to demonstrative phrases and ceremonies. It will be better, therefore, that in the best way we know of, that is, by praying for you, we endeavour to show our sense of gratitude, and to repay this and all other great benefits which we for such a length of time have received from you.

When I asked for ten *braccia* of stuff, I meant you to get me a narrow width, not this cloth, so wide and fine, and so expensive. This quantity will be more than sufficient for us.

I leave you to imagine how pleased I am to read the letters you constantly send me. Only to see how your love for me prompts you to let me know fully what favours you receive from this gentlemen is enough to fill me with joy. Nevertheless I feel it a little hard to hear that you intend leaving home so soon, because I shall have to do without you, and for a long time too, if I am not mistaken. And your lordship may believe that I am speaking the truth when I say that except you there is not a creature who gives me any comfort. But I will not grieve at your departure because of this, for that would be to complain when you had cause for rejoicing. Therefore I too will rejoice, and continue to pray God to give you grace and health to make a prosperous journey, so that you may return satisfied, and live long and happily; all which I trust will come to pass by God's help.

Though I know it is not necessary for me to do so, yet I recommend our poor brother to your kindness; and I entreat you to forgive him his fault in consideration of his youth, and which, seeing it is the first, merits pardon. I do beg and entreat you to take him to Rome with you, where opportunities will not be wanting to give him that assistance which paternal duty and your natural kindness will prompt you to seek out.

But fearing that you will find me tiresome, I forebear to write more, though I can never cease to recommend him to your favour. And please to remember that you have been owing us a visit for a very long time.

From San Matteo, the 23rd day of October 1623.

Most affectionate daughter,

S. M. C.

Chapter 1
The Scientific
Revolution:
Galileo Galilei
(1564–1642) and
Sister Maria
Celeste (née
Virginia Galilei,
1600–1634)

[SISTER MARIE CELESTE REPORTS TO HER FATHER ABOUT A NEW SET OF DINNER NAPKINS SHE IS MAKING AND ABOUT THE HEALTH OF HER SISTER, SISTER ARCANGELA, NOVEMBER 21, 1623]

Most Illustrious and Beloved Lord Father

I cannot rest any longer without news, . . . both for the infinite love I bear you, and also for fear lest this sudden cold, which in general disagrees so much with you, should have caused a return of your usual pains and other complaints. I therefore send the man who takes this letter purposely to hear how you are, and also when you expect to set out on your journey. I have been extremely busy at the dinner-napkins. They are nearly finished, but now I come to putting on the fringe, I find that of the sort I send as a pattern, a piece is wanting for two dinner-napkins: that will be four *braccia.* I should be glad if you could let me have it immediately, so that I may send you the napkins before you go; as it was for this that I have been making such haste to get them finished.

As I have no sleeping-room of my own, Sister Diamanta kindly allows me to share hers, depriving herself of the company of her own sister for my sake. But the room is so bitterly cold, that with my head in the state in which it is at present, I do not know how I shall remain, unless you can help me by lending me a set of those white bed-hangings which you will not want now. I should be glad to know if you could do me this service. Moreover, I beg you to be so kind as to send me that book of yours which has just been published, *Il Saggiatore,* so that I may read it, for I have a great desire to see it.

These few cakes I send are some I made a few days ago, intending to give them to you when you came to bid us adieu. As your departure is not so near as we feared, I send them lest they should get dry. Sister Arcangela is still under medical treatment, and is much tried by the remedies. I am not well myself, but being so accustomed to ill health, I do not make much of it, seeing, too, that it is the Lord's will to send me continually some such little trial as this. I thank Him for everything, and pray that He will give you the highest and best felicity.

P.S. You can send us any collars that want getting up.

From San Matteo, the 21st of November 1623.

Most affectionate daughter,

S. M. C.

DOCUMENT FIVE

SISTER MARIA CELESTE

Taking Care of Business
(1633)

During Galileo's trial, Sister Maria Celeste wrote to her father often. He claimed that her letters were a great comfort to him while the trial dragged on and his health deteriorated. What duties did this most dutiful daughter perform for her father while he was in Rome?

Most Illustrious and Beloved Lord Father

Your letter written on the 10th of February was delivered to me on the 22nd of the same month, and by now I assume you must have received another letter of mine, Sire, along with one from our Father Confessor, and through these you will have learned some of the details you wanted to know; and seeing that still no letters have come giving us definite news of your arrival in Rome (and you can imagine, Sire, with what eagerness I in particular anticipate those letters), I return to write to you again, so that you may know how anxiously I live, while awaiting word from you, and also to send you the enclosed legal notice, which was delivered to your house, 4 or 5 days ago, by a young man, and accepted by Signor Francesco Rondinelli, who, in giving it to me, advised me that it must be paid, without waiting for some more offensive insult from the creditor, telling me that one could not disobey such an order in any manner, and offering to handle the matter himself. This morning I gave him the 6 scudi, which he did not want to pay to Vincenzio but chose to deposit the money with the magistrate until you have told him, Sire, what you want him to do. Signor Francesco is indeed a most pleasant and discreet person, and he never stops declaiming his gratefulness to you, Sire, for allowing him the use of your house. I heard from La Piera that he treats her and Giuseppe with great kindness, even in regard to their food; and I provide for the rest of their needs, Sire, according to your directions. The boy tells me that this Easter he will need shoes and stockings, which I plan to knit for him out of thick, coarse cotton or else from fine wool. La Piera maintains that you have often spoken to her about ordering a bale of linen, on which account I refrained from buying the small amount I would need to begin weaving the thick cloth for your kitchen, as I had meant to do, Sire, and I will not make the purchase unless I hear otherwise from you.

The vines in the garden will take nicely now that the Moon is right, at the hands of Giuseppe's father, who they say is capable enough, and also Signor Rondinelli will lend his help. The lettuce I hear is quite lovely, and I have entrusted Giuseppe to take it to be sold at market before it spoils.

Chapter 1
The Scientific
Revolution:
Galileo Galilei
(1564–1642) and
Sister Maria
Celeste (née
Virginia Galilei,
1600–1634)

From the sale of 70 bitter oranges came 4 lire, a very respectable price, from what I understand, as that fruit has few uses: Portuguese oranges are selling for 14 crazie per 100 and you had 200 that were sold. As for that barrel of newly-tapped wine you left, Sire, Signor Rondinelli takes a little for himself every evening, and meanwhile he makes improvements to the wine, which he says is coming along extremely well. What little of the old wine that was left I had decanted into flasks, and told LaPiera that she and Giuseppe could drink it when they had finished their small cask, since we of late have had reasonably good wine from the convent, and, being in good health, have hardly taken a drop. I continue to give one giulio every Saturday to La Brigida, and I truly consider this an act of charity well deserved, as she is so exceedingly needy and such a very good girl.

Suor Luisa, God bless her, fares somewhat better, and is still purging, and having understood from your last letter, Sire, how concerned you were over her illness out of your regard for her, she thanks you with all her heart; and while you declare yourself united with me in loving her, Sire, she on the other hand claims to be the paragon of this emotion, nor do I mind granting her that honor, since her affection stems from the same source as yours, and it is myself; wherefore I take pride in and prize this most delicious contest of love, and the more clearly I perceive the greatness of that love you both bear me, the more bountiful it grows for being mutually exchanged between the very two persons I love and revere above everyone and everything in this life.

Tomorrow will be 13 days since the death of our Suor Virginia Canigiani, who was already gravely ill when I last wrote to you, Sire, and since then a malevolent fever has stricken Suor Maria Grazia del Pace, the eldest of the three nuns who play the organ, and teacher of the Squarcialupi codex, a truly tranquil and good nun; and since the doctor has already given her up for dead, we are all beside ourselves, grieving over our loss. This is everything I need to tell you for the moment, and as soon as I receive your letters (which must surely have arrived at Pisa by now where the Bocchineri gentlemen are) I will write again. Meanwhile I send you the greetings of my heart together with our usual friends, and particularly Suor Arcangela, Signor Rondinelli and Doctor Ronconi, who begs me for news of you every time he comes here. May the Lord God bless you and keep you happy always.

*From San Matteo, the 26th day of February 1633.**

Most affectionate daughter,

S. M. Celeste Galilei

Signor Rondinelli, having this very moment returned from Florence, tells me he spoke to the Chancellor of the Advisors and learned that the 6 scudi must be paid to Vincenzio Landucci and not be deposited, and this will be done . . .

---

*On the Florentine calendar, the new year started on 25 March.

DOCUMENT SIX

INQUISITORS GENERAL

The Sentence of Galileo
(1633)

Galileo's trial and sentence was a dramatic moment in intellectual history. What were the crimes and sins committed in the eyes of the Holy Inquisition? What was his original sentence? Did Sagredo's predictions come true (Document Two)?

. . . We say, pronounce, sentence, and declare that you, the above-mentioned Galileo, because of the things deduced in the trial and confessed by you as above, have rendered yourself according to this Holy Office vehemently suspected of heresy, namely of having held and believed a doctrine which is false and contrary to the divine and Holy Scripture: that the sun is the center of the world and does not move from east to west, and the earth moves and is not the center of the world, and that one may hold and defend as probable an opinion after it has been declared and defined contrary to Holy Scripture. Consequently you have incurred all the censures and penalties imposed and promulgated by the sacred canons and all particular and general laws against such delinquents. We are willing to absolve you from them provided that first, with a sincere heart and unfeigned faith, in front of us you abjure, curse, and detest the above-mentioned errors and heresies, and every other error and heresy contrary to the Catholic and Apostolic Church, in the manner and form we will prescribe to you.

Furthermore, so that this serious and pernicious error and transgression of yours does not remain completely unpunished, and so that you will be more cautious in the future and an example for others to abstain from similar crimes, we order that the book *Dialogue* by Galileo Galilei be prohibited by public edict.

We condemn you to formal imprisonment in the Holy Office at our pleasure. As a salutary penance we impose on you to recite the seven penitential Psalms once a week for the next three years. And we reserve the authority to moderate, change, or condone wholly or in part the above-mentioned penalties and penances.

This we say, pronounce, sentence, declare, order, and reserve by this of any other better manner or form that we reasonably can or shall think of.

So we the undersigned Cardinals pronounce:

Felice Cardinal d'Ascoli.
Guido Cardinal Bentivoglio.
Fra Desiderio Cardinal di Cremona.
Fra Antonio Cardinal di Sant'Onofrio.
Berlinghiero Cardinal Gessi.
Fabrizio Cardinal Verospi.
Marzio Cardinal Ginetti.

Chapter 1
The Scientific
Revolution:
Galileo Galilei
(1564–1642) and
Sister Maria
Celeste (née
Virginia Galilei,
1600–1634)

DOCUMENT SEVEN

GALILEO GALILEI

Recantation
(1633)

What did Galileo confess to believing? Why did he recant?

Galileo's Abjuration (22 June 1633)

I, Galileo, son of the late Vincenzio Galilei of Florence, seventy years of age, arraigned personally for judgment, kneeling before you Most Eminent and Most Reverend Cardinals Inquisitors-General against heretical depravity in all of Christendom, having before my eyes and touching with my hands the Holy Gospels, swear that I have always believed, I believe now, and with God's help I will believe in the future all that the Holy Catholic and Apostolic Church holds, preaches, and teaches. However, whereas, after having been judicially instructed with injunction by the Holy Office to abandon completely the false opinion that the sun is the center of the world and does not move and the earth is not the center of the world and moves, and not to hold, defend, or teach this false doctrine in any way whatever, orally or in writing; and after having been notified that this doctrine is contrary to Holy Scripture; I wrote and published a book in which I treat of this already condemned doctrine and adduce very effective reasons in its favor, without refuting them in any way; therefore, I have been judged vehemently suspected of heresy, namely of having held and believed that the sun is the center of the world and motionless and the earth is not the center and moves.

Therefore, desiring to remove from the minds of Your Eminences and every faithful Christian this vehement suspicion, rightly conceived against me, with a sincere heart and unfeigned faith I abjure, curse, and detest the above-mentioned errors and heresies, and in general each and every other error, heresy, and sect contrary to the Holy Church; and I swear that in the future I will never again say or assert, orally or in writing, anything which might cause a similar suspicion about me; on the contrary, if I should come to know any heretic or anyone suspected of heresy, I will denounce him to this Holy Office, or to the Inquisitor or Ordinary of the place where I happen to be.

Furthermore, I swear and promise to comply with and observe completely all the penances which have been or will be imposed upon me by this Holy Office; and should I fail to keep any of these promises and oaths, which God forbid, I submit myself to all the penalties and punishments imposed and promulgated by the sacred canons and other particular and general laws against similar delinquents. So help me God and these Holy Gospels of His, which I touch with my hands.

I, the above-mentioned Galileo Galilei, have abjured, sworn, promised, and obliged myself as above; and in witness of the truth I have signed with my own hand the present document of abjuration and have recited it word for word in Rome, at the convent of the Minerva, this twenty-second day of June 1633.

I, Galileo Galilei, have abjured as above, by my own hand.

Radical Politics in Seventeenth-Century England: John Lilburne (1615?–1657) and Elizabeth Dewell Lilburne (161?–166?)

▓ SETTING THE STAGE

The seventeenth century in England opened with a new royal family, the Stuarts, occupying the throne. Both the century and the dynasty inherited a legacy of dramatic political, social, economic, and religious changes from the previous era, as well as the many unresolved conflicts and tensions that those changes had produced. Reli-gious and political settlements resulting from the Protestant Reformation in England had established that all subjects of the crown were part of a unified political body whose secular arm was the commonwealth, its spiritual arm, the church. Thus, it was logical to consider challenges to the church as the same as political opposition, and therefore possibly treasonous. The last Tudor ruler, Elizabeth I (r. 1558–1603) had weathered parliamentary claims to power, threats from foreign states, the pressures of colonial expansion, and varied demands for additional religious reform that often bordered on rebellion. Her skillful management and successful efforts at compromise had avoided wholesale violence as a means of resolving vastly differing interests and views of the world. But many issues that had been simmering under Elizabeth's watchful eye boiled over during the reign of her successors James I and Charles I. Neither of these monarchs possessed the political savvy and personal adeptness of their predecessor, and the level of revolt was rising as well.

In the early decades of the seventeenth century, the power of both the English monarchy and the Established Church of England (Anglican Church) were increasingly challenged by individuals and groups who sought to limit and reform the authority of both. The intersections of religion and politics were hardly new and were not confined to England. In the previous century, monarchs' efforts to enforce religious uniformity had often provoked civil rebellion and warfare. Similarly, claims to individual freedom of conscience and autonomy of spiritual communities began to expand explicitly into demands for political rights and freedoms. At the century's turn, the ties that connected rulers and people, or that linked citizens to each other, were re-imagined by secular philosophers. Armed with the new weapons of science and reason, they argued that there was a con-

tract between monarch and people, and that obedience to rulers was conditional and not absolute. These views of authority and responsibility could be applied to both church and state. At issue was the question of power or sovereignty. Who should rule and on what grounds, and were there limits to the exercise of power?

The difficulty of finding universally accepted answers to these questions is reflected in the crises and confrontations of seventeenth-century England. In that century, various constitutional experiments redefined the powers of government and of the people, and popular movements characterized by political consciousness, concrete objectives, and secular as well as religious ideals were begun.[1] None of this occurred peacefully: as 190,000 people died in a decade of civil war, the king was executed, a republican government was established, and eventually the monarchy was restored in a "glorious" revolution.

Between 1640 and 1660, competing claims to truth and visions of a better world produced dramatic and revolutionary events. These developments were not always planned systematically. Political alliances shifted and eroded, and different actors with competing goals and interests walked on and off the military, religious, and political fields of battle.

---

1. Brian Manning, *The English People and the English Revolution, 1640–49* (London: Heinemann, 1976), p. 261. Manning's works, as well as those by Christopher Hill, are essential studies of the civil war and revolution. The figure for deaths resulting from the civil war is from Alison Plowden, *Women All on Fire: The Women of the English Civil War* (Gloucestershire, U.K.: Sutton Publishing Ltd., 1998), p. 163.

Chapter 2
Radical Politics
in Seventeenth-
Century England:
John Lilburne
(1615?–1657)
and Elizabeth
Dewell Lilburne
(161?–166?)

By focusing on two of the actors in this drama, John and Elizabeth Lilburne, and the community in which they operated, we can gain insight into what drove men and women to risk all to challenge the existing order, what they hoped to achieve, and the successes and failures of their actions. Spiritually, the Lilburnes were part of a growing group of English people who were dissatisfied with the Anglican Church and hoped to "purify" it of its Roman Catholic remnants, including elements of both ritual and doctrine. Socially, the Lilburnes were typical of the newer gentry and manufacturing classes, and their personal relationship and family life represented prescribed gender roles. Politically, they were unusual because they were central figures in a radical political movement labeled the Levellers by their opponents, who accused them of attempting to level England politically and economically. The Levellers eventually argued for individual rights, equality before the law, and elected representative government with powers determined by the governed. For these reasons, they clearly fell on the radical end of the political spectrum and in many ways were ahead of their time. Because they were moving into uncharted waters, they often did not agree on questions of social equality and the limits of democracy. Nevertheless, the vantage point of individuals like Elizabeth and John Lilburne and their contributions to events illuminate the political world of the era and tell us a great deal about how one of the earliest popular, secular political movements took shape.

▪ THE ACTORS:

JOHN LILBURNE AND
ELIZABETH DEWELL LILBURNE

John Lilburne was born in 1615 (probably) near Newcastle, in the northernmost part of England. His father Richard was lord of a small manor in Durham Country, while his mother Margaret's family had held positions at the royal palace in Greenwich, near London.[2] He spent some time at one of the royal grammar schools established during the sixteenth century to re-place monastic education, and he learned some Greek and Latin, but most of his learning came from self-teaching and his own reading (often during frequent imprisonments later in life). In customary fashion, his older brother Robert was entitled to inherit the family estate, and thus, as a teenager, John was sent to be a trade apprentice to a London wholesale wool merchant. He had been raised to accept puritan ideas, and in London he was caught up in the currents of more radical puritan reform that began to question all sorts of centralized authority, whether spiritual or political. To this point, John's experience is not unlike that of other young men identified as of "the middling sort," which included new gentry and inde-

2. For information on John Lilburne, see Pauline Gregg, *Free-born John* (London: Harrap, 1961) and M. A. Barg, *The English Revolution of the 17th Century Through Portraits of Its Leading Figures* (Moscow: Progress Publishers, 1990).

pendent small farmers, tradespeople and merchants, skilled workers, and professionals. By the time John moved to London, many of these people had less and less confidence in the monarchy to protect or promote their interests and they resented the economic and political privileges of older elites.

At the end of 1637, John Lilburne was arrested for the first time. At this point, extensive censorship laws controlled what could be printed and by whom, and John was charged with distributing an illegal puritan tract that attacked the Anglican church and its hierarchy. John was found guilty and his punishment was a public flogging (500 lashes), after which he was locked in a public pillory for two hours. His treatment drew sympathy from the London crowd, and his case became a cause célèbre when, after his punishment, he refused to recant. Not only did he insist that he had committed no crime and would not submit as long as he had breath in his body, but he launched a fervent attack on the Anglican bishops. This outrageous behavior was sufficient to return him to prison, but also earned him the popular title "Freeborn John." He remained in prison until November 1640, during which time he managed to obtain writing materials and to produce several pamphlets and petitions that were smuggled out of prison and kept his name before the public eye.

Punishment for religious nonconformity was not unusual in this era. Neighbors and communities, as well as government and church officials, often targeted puritans of all sorts for their beliefs and goals. The puritans hoped to press on with reform of the Anglican Church, and they rejected rituals and ceremony as well as the hierarchical authority of state-appointed bishops and clergy. Although they did not necessarily agree on the organization and structure of religious communities, or on the independence of congregations and individual believers alike, they all objected to state-enforced religious conformity, and many spent time in prison or were forced to emigrate because of their beliefs. Some recognized that political success was a necessary precondition for religious reform and thus believed that Parliament was a venue for expressions of their views. By the time Lilburne was arrested for the first time, supporters of parliamentary authority had challenged royal power on several issues and some of them had also spent time in prison.

In 1640, the differences between the king and his political opponents were sharpened after Charles I (r. 1625–1649) was forced to call a meeting of Parliament to raise money to deal with rebellion in Scotland and unrest in Ireland. Moderation and compromise evaporated as the king asserted his royal prerogatives and Parliament expanded claims to govern. Popular protests in London over various issues added fuel to the fire of this contest. In November 1640, the House of Commons ordered the arrest of two of the king's key advisers, Archbishop William Laud and Sir Thomas Wentworth, the Earl of Strafford, both of whom were symbols of tyranny and arbitrary use of power. Charged with treason, these two men were later executed. Almost simultaneously, parliamentary member Oliver Cromwell, a

Chapter 2
Radical Politics
in Seventeenth-
Century England:
John Lilburne
(1615?–1657)
and Elizabeth
Dewell Lilburne
(161?–166?)

puritan reformer, made a speech pointing to another symbol of arbitrary rule—the unjustly imprisoned John Lilburne. Shortly thereafter, Lilburne was released from prison. Freeborn John now was connected to the politics of protest of the London crowd but was also linked to the community of parliamentary rebels.

After his release from prison, John Lilburne briefly re-entered civilian life, managing an uncle's brewery in London, and sometime in 1641 marrying Elizabeth Dewell, whom he had known for several years. Her father was a merchant, but beyond that we know very little of her background, and no sources document either her birthday or death date. John's age at marriage would fall within the usual range and one might assume the same for Elizabeth. The average age at marriage for men and women at this time was between approximately 26 and 28. Much of what we know of her and of their marriage comes from references in political documents, petitions, and comments by others. Although it is possible to trace their joint and separate activities in the years under consideration, it is much harder to determine exactly how the tumultuous political world in which they lived altered their personal lives, and how each felt about the results. Elizabeth, like John, was literate, as is evident in her political petitions. Given her frequent public exchanges with political figures, often on John's behalf, we can also speculate that she was articulate, with some public presence. John, in fact, always spoke admiringly of his wife, referring to her as his devoted ally and remarking that "though a feminine [she was] yet of a gallant and true Masculine Spirit."[3] Over the course of their marriage, they had ten children, only four of whom outlived their father. Elizabeth's life of frequent pregnancies, several miscarriages, and infant deaths was not extraordinary for this time period.

Several general points can be made about the careers of these two people. First, John Lilburne was fearless and charismatic and quickly became a well-known and popular political leader. He also lived by his ideals and principles, often to Elizabeth's chagrin because the results were one imprisonment after another. Theoretically and ideologically, Elizabeth was John's apprentice or lived in his shadow, but she was capable of organizing support for him and his cause. As we shall see, Leveller women were politically active as organizers, demonstrators, and petitioners, so Elizabeth had a community in which she operated. She also often negotiated with authorities for John's release or for financial support for the family. Again, many women during the civil war and in the Commonwealth lobbied on behalf of their husbands and struggled to maintain themselves financially. But it is critical to keep in mind that the world of seventeenth-century politics was by law and by practice the world of men. In 1632, a 400-page guide to women's legal position, "The Lawes Resolutions

3. Quoted in Patricia Higgins, "The Reactions of Women, with Special Reference to Women Petitioners," in Brian Manning (ed.), *Politics, Religion and the English Civil War* (London: Edward Arnold, 1973), p. 180. Useful information on women's experience in this period can be found in Anne Laurence, *Women in England, 1500–1760* (New York: St. Martin's Press, 1994).

of Women's Rights," had stated clearly that women had no voice in Parliament, and could not make, consent to, or abrogate any laws. Married women had few property rights, and all women were under the protection of a male guardian and had few opportunities to act as autonomous individuals. The fact that women did act publicly for political reasons is therefore even more remarkable. Obviously this is explained in part by the political upheavals of the time, and the civil war did break down many traditional means of controlling individual behavior and maintaining public order. It is also important to remind ourselves that while Protestant religious tradition mandated that women obey their husbands, it also encouraged men *and* women to follow their consciences.

ACT I:

THE FIRST CIVIL WAR

By the summer of 1642, Parliament had presented to the king several documents listing their demands, many of which would have severely limited royal authority. Charles refused any changes and on one occasion even went to Parliament intending to arrest its leaders, but they went into hiding before he could do so. He also began gathering an army; sent his queen, Henrietta Maria, to France; and on August 22, 1642, raised the royal standard as a declaration of war against the treasonous, parliamentary rebels. Many people throughout England opposed such a civil conflict and feared the outcome. Deep division in the country is evident in the fact that when the civil war began, 225 members of parliament sided with the king, 380 were for Parliament. Those who supported Parliament certainly hoped to end arbitrary government and to weaken the power of the Anglican Church, but beyond that major differences existed. As moderate and radical religious and political reformers fought side by side in the civil war, their differences became clearer, and their confrontations more frequent and violent.

The civil war also mobilized many men and women who were outside the existing political structures but who had interests and a stake in the conflict. Women and men alike expressed dissatisfaction with economic and social conditions, and acted out of political and religious motives. In their writings and spoken words, women addressed the men in power and were willing to argue with them on numerous issues. At the same time as they expected their voices to be heard, their religious freedoms guaranteed, and their other interests protected, they did not claim political rights equal to those of men. But both men and women discovered, as the war progressed and power centers shifted, that not all their principles and goals were supported by rebel military and political leaders. John Lilburne, other Leveller leaders, and thousands of their supporters learned this fairly quickly. Calling for freedom, reason, justice, and common

Chapter 2
Radical Politics
in Seventeenth-
Century England:
John Lilburne
(1615?–1657)
and Elizabeth
Dewell Lilburne
(161?–166?)

equity, they found that Parliament and its leaders could be as resistant to change as the king.

When the civil war began in 1642, John Lilburne quickly volunteered to fight for Parliament and became a captain of an infantry regiment made up mostly of apprentices like himself. At that time, it was quite common for wives to accompany husbands who enlisted, and apparently Elizabeth shared quarters with John. In November 1642, he was captured by royalist [Cavalier] forces and charged with treason against the king, a crime punishable by death. Elizabeth, who was then pregnant, hurried off to the House of Commons in London to beg them to save John. They adopted a resolution warning that if anything happened to John (and several other captives), they would retaliate by killing several captured royalists they were holding. With the resolution in hand, Elizabeth returned to Oxford to negotiate the release and actual exchange of the prisoners. Such a scenario was fairly common during the next decade. In prison, John faced execution, while Elizabeth on the outside did whatever she could to secure his release. She was often pregnant during these periods of crisis, and, of course, somehow had to feed and maintain her family. Much later, in 1655, John wrote to Elizabeth from Dover prison thanking her for her fidelity, faith, and love; apologizing to her for the years of uncertainty and poverty she had endured; and reminding her that suffering was a condition of being Christian.

Released from captivity in 1643, John returned to London and a hero's welcome. By then Elizabeth had also negotiated a government position for him that paid £1,000 a year, but John refused the post, insisting that "he must rather fight for eightpence a day till he saw the liberties and peace of England settled."[4] With the help of Oliver Cromwell, Lilburne was given the rank of lieutenant colonel and returned to fight with the Roundheads (the forces of Parliament), and once again Elizabeth and their child accompanied him. The lives of these two important men in the civil war continued to be linked as they fought side by side in the major victory at Marston Moor in July 1644.

Several significant events during 1643–1645 altered the course of the war, reshaped political issues, and directly affected the lives of individuals like John and Elizabeth Lilburne. First, during these years, Oliver Cromwell created an effective parliamentary fighting force, the New Model Army. The recruits for this force came from rural and urban "middle sort of men"—rich and smaller independent farmers, manufacturers and tradesmen, and apprentices with experiences like John Lilburne's. Cromwell intended to create an "army of the godly" fighting for religion and reform, or as he said, the "felicity of state and church."[5] This army had a political character and fought for more than pay and plunder. Obviously, this appealed to Lilburne. But another important development at the time would cause him significant problems.

4. Quoted in Plowden, p. 183.
5. Quoted in Manning (ed.), p. 249.

In November 1643, at a point when the military forces of Parliament were not very effective, political leaders had signed an agreement known as the Solemn League and Covenant with their counterparts in Scotland. Presbyterianism held sway in Scotland and, while opposed to "papist" Anglicans and the authority of bishops, had its own mechanism for church order and discipline in councils of elders or presbyters. The agreement, which essentially established the Presbyterian church structure in England, gave the Scots a subsidy for fighting with Parliament and created a joint committee of both kingdoms to fight the war. This agreement was a blow for Lilburne and for others who believed in independent church congregations and the right to believe and organize as one wished. Adopting Presbyterianism was not what they had in mind. In fact, when Lilburne was offered a higher rank in the New Model Army, he refused because taking an oath to the covenant was a precondition. In Lilburne's eyes, conformity was the same whether it was enforced by the Anglican or by the Presbyterian Church. His concerns were broader, however, because he felt that Parliament itself was overstepping its authority and ignoring the consent of the governed. In April 1645, Lilburne gave up his command, declaring that he "would dig for carrots and turnips before he would fight to set up a power to make himself a slave."[6] The year 1645 thus marked a turning point for John because he continued to insist on religious freedom,

but he now increasingly questioned the authority of Parliament and defined the basis, functions, and limits of government in new terms.

His ideas fell on increasingly fertile ground as more and more men and women outside either parliamentary or royalist circles responded to the religious and political upheavals. They had three basic avenues of action and protest. They could demonstrate inside and outside government chambers, they could present petitions reflecting their concerns to the powers that be, and they could publish and distribute pamphlets and other forms of literature. Censorship had been in the hands of the king and the church prior to 1642, but during the civil war, for a time control over the press lapsed.

The London crowd often acted as a lobbying or pressure group because large numbers of men or women chose to express their interests through these three avenues. Approximately 300,000 to 400,000 people probably inhabited the city of London and its suburbs in 1640. England had a long tradition of popular demonstrations and riots, and the right to petition the king or Parliament was a recognized claim of the people. As a result, crowd activity in the city of London was increasingly common in 1641 and 1642. Even before formal war was declared, a group of women had presented a petition to Parliament complaining of the economic hardships they faced because of the "distractions and distempers" of the state.[7] Additional petitions addressed issues of religious freedom, and by 1643 they focused on the

---

6. Quoted in Barg, p. 221.

7. Quoted in Manning (ed.), p. 185.

Chapter 2
Radical Politics
in Seventeenth-
Century England:
John Lilburne
(1615?–1657)
and Elizabeth
Dewell Lilburne
(161?–166?)

hardships of the war itself. The number of women involved in these actions was anywhere from 400 to 3,000 or more.

In early August 1643, a large crowd of women came to Parliament, wearing white ribbons and calling for peace. For several days, they camped on the doorsteps of the House, making it difficult for the representatives to get in and out of the building, and threatened to use violence against those members who were enemies of peace. Some women even entered the building and filled the stairs so that no one could move up or down. Apparently a man at the top of the stairs then drew his sword, and with its flat side, struck some of the women, breaking up the crowd. The next day, the crowd of women numbered between 3,000 and 5,000 women, according to different accounts. Once again, their actions were militant as they cried for peace and for the safety of sweethearts, husbands,

and families. At this point, the protestors were probably not committed to either side but genuinely interested in ending the war. The response of Parliament to these actions was mixed. Members certainly were willing to use force against the intruders, but at times they would acknowledge that they had received and read the petitions. Newspaper reporters were usually more critical, calling the women "whores, Bawdes, Beggar and Irish women," seeing them as menacing and their actions dangerous to society and the kingdom. As the *Parliament Scout* noted, "thus we see, to permit absurdities is the way to increase them; tumults are dangerous, swords in women's hands do desperate things; this is begotten in the distractions of civil war."[8] By 1646, the protests were more partisan and often reflected Leveller ideas or were on behalf of imprisoned Leveller leaders, like John Lilburne.

■ ACT II:

THE HEIGHT OF LEVELLER POWER

Although John Lilburne returned to civilian life in 1645, he did not withdraw from public affairs. Because Parliament now stood a good chance of victory, he focused on the future political structure of England. Who would rule? What powers should government have, and what were the rights of individuals? Lilburne was not alone in confronting these questions. His answers and those of men like Richard Overton and William Walwyn constituted the fundamental principles of the Levellers. Lilburne was among the most

popular leaders of the London crowds. He was fearless in his attacks on authority; as already shown, he usually disdained threats against him, and during his frequent imprisonments, he turned his own experience into a symbol of everyone's rights and struggle.

Because of his critiques of Parliamentary leaders, he was imprisoned from August to November 1645. Once again, Elizabeth was pregnant, and although we have no documents to tell her story, one can assume she was

8. Quoted in Higgins, p. 198, from August 1643 report.

struggling to make ends meet, perhaps through the kindness of friends or help from family. While in prison Lilburne wrote, "England's Birth-Right Justified," a pamphlet that challenged church tithes, proposed property rather than excise taxes (because the latter affected all citizens equally), and called for annual parliamentary elections. From this point forward, although his ideas and those of the Levellers continued to be grounded in demands for religious liberty, their attacks increasingly targeted the rich and powerful, whoever they might be. They saw the answer to England's economic and political problems in constitutional reforms that would not destroy wealth or property but would dissociate wealth and property from political power.

In May 1646, Charles I surrendered to the Scots, thus ending the first civil war. While the battlefields were quiet for a time, the political arena was even more heated as debates raged about what to do with the king, where political authority should reside, and how much religious freedom should be granted to the people of England. In Parliament and in the New Model Army, lines were drawn among those who thought the king had learned his lesson and could be restored, those who favored additional reforms to guarantee the newly won power of Parliament, and those who saw this as the opportunity for sweeping reforms to create a government based on popular sovereignty delegated to elected representatives. Outside Parliament, Lilburne and the Leveller movement, now numbering some 10,000 men and women, served as an important pres-

sure group and an influential force that could not be ignored in the face of divisions and indecision within the government and the army.

True to form, Lilburne was unwilling to compromise with more moderate factions and consistently pressed his issues. As a result, he was also brought to court frequently, charged with various crimes, and imprisoned. From June 1646 until August 1648, Lilburne suffered various degrees of imprisonment—from strict confinement in the Tower of London to periods of semifreedom when he could leave his cell during daylight hours or at least meet with people from the outside. Ironically, these were also the years of greatest Leveller power, and in part that underscores his ability to capitalize on his experiences and to make his personal drama the center of a political movement.

Incarceration did not stop the activity of recognized leaders, and outside the prison their followers continued to agitate and express dissent through distributing literature, obtaining signatures on various manifestos, demonstrating outside Parliament, and presenting petitions to that body. Elizabeth Lilburne was involved in such activity. In September 1646, she and a small group of "gentlewomen" presented a petition to the "Chosen and betrusted Knights, Citizens and Burgesses" of the high court of Parliament on behalf of her husband (Document One). She reminded them that they were the representatives chosen to maintain law and liberty, the "common Birth-right of English-men who are born equally free and to whom the law of the land is an equal inheri-

*Chapter 2
Radical Politics
in Seventeenth-
Century England:
John Lilburne
(1615?–1657)
and Elizabeth
Dewell Lilburne
(161?–166?)*

tance." She then argued that Lilburne was arrested unjustly and had never received appropriate compensation for his military service or for the previous occasions when he was incarcerated but never found guilty, and that all of this was bringing ruin to her, to John, and to their children. John reinforced this argument with his own petition in October, and this document also entered the popular political world.

The nature of Leveller politics and organization is illustrated in this pattern of publication, arrest, demonstration, and petition. A Leveller leader would write and publish a pamphlet that denounced or threatened certain persons in Parliament; he or she would be arrested, charged (the offending pamphlet was often burned publicly), and imprisoned (not always with a full trial). Then petition drives, large and small, would be organized on behalf of the prisoner(s). Petitions were usually distributed throughout London, through wards and religious congregations, and thousands of signatures were thus obtained. As evident in the example of Elizabeth's petition, these documents were themselves political statements and served to broaden popular knowledge of the issues as well as to garner support for the imprisoned Leveller leaders. By 1647, Lilburne and his associates had an organization with branches far outside London. Agents traveled between the capital and the counties, and each county had representatives who communicated with towns and villages.

Imprisonment of Leveller leaders did not halt their political activity because they managed to obtain writing materials, prepare political tracts, and smuggle them out of prison for publication at several of their illegal presses. Some of the most famous of their essays were penned in prison. John's "Freeman's Freedome Vindicated" (Document Two) was written about five days following his arrest in June 1646 and clearly sets forth two fundamental and radical claims: (1) that all men and women are created equal, and (2) that no one can exercise power or rule without the consent of the governed. The following year (October 1647), the thoughts and hands of several prisoners (John included) produced the first Agreement of the People, in essence a proposed constitution for England. Rule by law, defined powers for parliament, and the rights of citizens are set forth in this document. Of particular importance is the insistence that neither poverty nor wealth should determine one's rights. (Document Three). The Levellers attacked the idle rich and the idle poor, and were consistently critical of unequal taxes, economic exploitation, and wealth gained in illegal ways. While they supported equality before the law, however, they did not advocate equal voting rights for all. Levellers generally believed that autonomy and self-sufficiency were a prerequisite for political power. Anyone dependent on another person could not be expected to make decisions freely, and that meant that wage earners, servants, beggars, and women, in particular, were excluded from the franchise. At least some minimal amount of property was the prerequisite for political independence.

This document saw the light of day

for somewhat different reasons. In the fall of 1647, members of Parliament were struggling to create a government structure and laws for its operation. But they still were deeply divided over questions of religious freedom, who would sit in Parliament, how members of Parliament would be elected, and what their authority might be. The New Model Army was an important political player, and many of its members were religious Independents (favoring individual congregational authority), and in favor of a much broader franchise; elected, representative government; and popular rights and freedoms. To resolve some of these questions, meetings were held at Putney (outside London), from October 28 to November 11, and one of the proposals discussed (Document Four) was derived from the Agreement of the People. In fact, prior to the meeting, Elizabeth had been carrying messages between John (who was still imprisoned) and army radicals, and during the meetings John himself was allowed to confer with the agitators.

At the Putney debates, the radical members of the Army and the Levellers hoped to establish a more equitable social contract. They failed to do so, perhaps because all the factions of Parliament had other issues on their minds. In November 1647, Charles I had escaped from prison and gone to Scotland, where he signed a mutually beneficial agreement with the Scots. Cromwell and his forces once again prepared for battle, thus beginning the second civil war in May 1648. By November, Cromwell was victorious and the king was taken into custody. In the meantime, Lilburne had been released from prison again; perhaps between 10,000 men and women citizens of London petitioned that he be set free or have a legal trial. But the bigger question of the moment was not the treatment of Lilburne, but what to do with the king? By then patience had worn thin, the belief that reconciliation was possible had evaporated, and Cromwell and his loyal officers were anxious to find a solution that would restore peace and order and allow them to construct the godly kingdom they envisioned.

ACT III:

THE LEVELLERS AND THE COMMONWEALTH

Complex political and military maneuverings characterized the next six months or so. Within fairly short order, Parliament was purged of "disloyal" members, the king was tried and executed, and in February 1649 the monarchy was abolished and replaced by a council of state, as England became a republic. Health and family issues had prevented Lilburne from participating in the second civil war, but he was a participant in the negotiations and planning for a new government. In February 1649, when the new state council was created, he and his closest associates were offered seats. The honeymoon between Lilburne and his Leveller colleagues, and Cromwell and his supporters in the army and Parliament was short-lived.

Chapter 2
Radical Politics
in Seventeenth-
Century England:
John Lilburne
(1615?–1657)
and Elizabeth
Dewell Lilburne
(161?–166?)

Once again, Freeborn John felt that the new government organization was only a cover for the rich and powerful. He turned down the offered position, insisting that he would not lend his name to "so unjust and illegal a fabric as an everlasting Parliament purged twice by force of Arms," and also insisting that he would not live on income produced by unjust taxes or "the sweat of other people's brows."[9] His words took on added meaning because the 1648 harvest had been abysmal, prices skyrocketed, and many citizens faced famine and starvation.

In the next few years, Cromwell and his allies solidified their control of England, Scotland, and Ireland, using force where necessary to establish order and stability. Although they supported certain religious freedoms and the rule of law, in truth the new government rested heavily on the success of the army, which became a more reliable instrument for Cromwell and his political allies as radicals (like those who had debated at Putney) were purged from its ranks. Lilburne and the Levellers would not accept this outcome of England's hard-fought rebellion and openly criticized Cromwell and friends.

On February 26, 1649, Lilburne arrived at the House of Commons to deliver a pamphlet, "England's New Chains Discovered." Here, he accused the new government of abandoning the goals of freedom for which they had fought. Instead of free speech and press, freedom of conscience, and government by consent, oppression and authority were the rule of the day. Other pamphlets and petitions followed on the heels of Lilburne's tract. Many were published and read widely in the Leveller newspaper, *The Moderate*. Within a month, the House arrested Lilburne and three other Leveller leaders, charged them with treason, and imprisoned them in the Tower yet again. The popular response to this action was immediate and widespread. Between April and October 1649, hundreds of people demonstrated outside Parliament, and petitions with thousands of signatures flooded the House.

In this cycle of protest, women petitioners were highly visible once again. But in this round of activity, their political claims and rights as citizens were stated more forcefully, and they were directly rejected by the authorities. For three days in April 1649, hundreds of women pushed at the doors of Parliament, wearing on their chests the Leveller symbol, sea-green ribbons. They called for the release of the prisoners, complained of food shortages and unemployment, charged Parliament with acting tyrannically, and justified their petition on the grounds that they had "an equal share and interest with men in the Commonwealth."[10] The House eventually considered their petition and responded by telling them to go home, look after their own business, and not to meddle in affairs of state, which were really beyond their understanding. The women did not give up, and even though they were called all sorts of names, from "brave Viragos" to

9. Quoted in Barg, p. 263.

10. Quoted in Higgins, p. 217.

"Ladys errant of the Seagreen Order," to gossips and meddlers, they produced another petition presented to Parliament in early May.

This document was probably the work of Leveller Katherine Chidley, who by then was well known for her public statements and actions. Chidley was married to a London haberdasher. She herself was a seller of stockings, and her son was a treasurer for the Levellers. Apparently, her husband supported her activities, and she collaborated with her son. She was one of "the most rational and assertive of all preaching women, who organized debates with ministers, led her own Independent congregation, and wrote extensively on social and political issues."[11] In this petition from "Divers Well-Affected Women," they made clear that the affairs of the kingdom were as important to them as to the men, they had the right to have their petitions heard, and they did not want answers transmitted through husbands and friends (Document Five). While never claiming equal political rights, these women did claim an interest in the welfare of their kingdom, and the legal rights and privileges of citizens. Chidley was often seen as brazen and audacious, but she was in the company of other women who were prepared to leave their homes and move into public forums, whether or not their husbands or fathers approved.

11. Phyllis Mack, "Talking Back: Women as Prophets During the Civil War and Interregnum, 1640–55," in Robert Shoemaker and Mary Vincent (eds.), *Gender and History in Western Europe* (London: Arnold, 1998), p. 253.

Meanwhile, in prison, the leaders produced additional documents setting forth their demands and goals. In "A Manifestation" of April 14, they reiterated their beliefs in human freedom but also reassured their critics that they had no intention of abolishing private property, or leveling men's estates (Document Six). This document served to separate them from the Diggers, a group of even more radical Levellers or, as they liked to call themselves, the "True" Levellers. These Diggers held that the English civil wars had been fought against the king and the great landowners; now that Charles I had been executed, land should be made available for the very poor to cultivate. Led by Gerrard Winstanley, they wanted economic as well as political democracy, and they argued that human dignity was possible only when land was held and used collectively. These claims were frightening to large landowners and the wealthy, but they also were not acceptable to the gentry, to manufacturers, or to the "middling sort" of people like John Lilburne.

A final constitutional proposal, "An Agreement of the Free People of England, Tendered as a Peace-Offering" on May 1, was the last and most complete statement of Leveller principles. While insisting on popular sovereignty and limiting governmental authority, this document also makes economic independence a criterion for voting and outlaws any public interference with private property.

During the summer of 1649, yet another disaster hit the citizens of London in the form of a smallpox epidemic. The outbreak was particularly

Chapter 2
Radical Politics
in Seventeenth-
Century England:
John Lilburne
(1615?–1657)
and Elizabeth
Dewell Lilburne
(161?–166?)

tragic for the Lilburne's because two of his sons died, while Elizabeth and a daughter barely managed to survive. These blows pushed Elizabeth to the limit. For years she had supported John, delivered his literature and been arrested for it, spent time in prison with her husband, and lived in constant financial insecurity. In 1649, she desperately pleaded with John to end the struggle, which in this case meant acknowledging the legitimacy of the current government and being tried by its court. Perhaps by then John was also worn down by the years of activism or persuaded by his wife's pleas; he agreed to a trial, which took place in October 1649. After three days, a jury found that Lilburne was not guilty of treason, and the next month he and his colleagues were released. By the end of 1649, the era of major Leveller influence was over. John retired from public life for a time and did not publish a word for the next eighteen months. He worked as a soap boiler for a time, but finally in September 1651, Parliament paid him long-awaited compensation for his military service and the injuries suffered under the monarchy. He bought some property in London and, using the knowledge of the law he had gained in his years in prison, became a legal consultant.

By early 1650, Cromwell was more firmly in the seat of authority, continuing to rely on the army, of course. Those who had gained from the changes of the previous decade were now willing to compromise, but it should not be forgotten that, although the Levellers spoke for the ordinary citizen, the leaders were, after all, men of the middle sort, men of substance. They had certainly hoped to revolutionize government and to guarantee basic rights and freedoms, but they did not intend to turn the world upside down. Perhaps other citizens were simply tired of warfare and conflict, perhaps they felt the worst of government's abuses had been corrected or needed the martyrdom of their leaders to motivate them. Whatever the case, the Leveller movement was hard-pressed to confront many of the dramatic changes of 1649, to continue to challenge the military authority of Cromwell and Parliament, or to steer the process of state building and law in the next few years. Their movement and political strategy, the energies generated by the relationship between vocal, often imprisoned leaders and the crowds who responded to them, were no match for the show and use of force, purges, coups, a constantly changing game of "constitutional" chess, and a more determined Cromwell.

▨ FINALE

What then happens to John and Elizabeth Lilburne? John would not have been himself if he had stopped fighting injustices. In December 1651, one

of his legal cases got him in trouble again. In a public pamphlet, he accused a wealthy landowner who had friends in Parliament of obtaining his estates illegally. Parliament found John's claim false and malicious, fined him, and sentenced him to perpetual banishment or the death penalty as a felon. Obviously, for many, Freeborn John was still a dangerous man, a threat to public order, and a disturbing public conscience. Lilburne left for Holland in January 1652, once again leaving Elizabeth to keep the family afloat. She did so by selling or mortgaging most of their property to support herself and the children. In May 1653, Elizabeth visited him in exile. By then, Cromwell had been named Lord Protector and a new Parliament had been selected. John hoped that perhaps this new government would be based on principles of reason, freedom, and justice, and thus decided (against all of Elizabeth's arguments) that he would return to England. Once again, and for the last time, he was sent to prison, even though he challenged the legality of his banishment. And once again, his Leveller supporters sprang into action, producing petitions on his behalf.

In July 1653, Katherine Chidley's last public act was to go to Parliament with a contingent of women presenting a petition on Lilburne's behalf. As in previous years, the petition contained a variety of claims. They insisted Lilburne's imprisonment was unjust and revealed their fear that what was done to him could be done to all. They warned members of Parliament against acquiring apparel, food, housing, "Fantastique Fashions," and coaches, or advancing their estates, families, and relations while they continued to tax the people heavily. A member came out and told them that the House did not recognize their petition, "because they were women,

and many of them wives, the Law took no notice of them."[12] This appears to be the last of the identifiable Leveller women's petitions. Women, like men, had been caught up in the economic and political crises of this era, formulated their own views on events, put forth their own claims, and justified their political activities. But they did not challenge the gender order and recognized that, as "the weaker sex," their public position and role were different from men's.

In the 1650s, occasional conspiracies and plots were uncovered that were linked to Leveller members, and as far as the authorities were concerned, John remained a potential source of opposition. By then, however, both his physical and mental health had been weakened by lengthy periods of solitary confinement, hunger, and prison conditions. Elizabeth continued to communicate with the authorities, asking for his release. As a condition for this, she tried to convince John to sign a document saying that he would give up permanently any kind of public actions. He refused. He did experience a new conversion in these years and joined the Society of Friends, or Quakers. This newly formed religious group was fast becoming a strong voice for individual freedom of conscience and behavior, and was just as quickly becoming the target of government control. John was temporarily released from prison in 1656 and died at home with Elizabeth and his family on August 29, 1657, before he could

12. Quoted in Higgins, p. 211.

*Chapter 2
Radical Politics
in Seventeenth-
Century England:
John Lilburne
(1615?–1657)
and Elizabeth
Dewell Lilburne
(161?–166?)*

become embroiled in yet another stream of political controversy.

His funeral was attended by 400 people who acknowledged his legacy of courage and convictions. Elizabeth inherited his reputation *and* his debts. Eventually, Cromwell provided her and her remaining children with a small pension. We can only speculate, but perhaps he admired her tenacity and strength, even if John had been one of his most trying opponents. Cromwell himself died in September 1658, and his son Richard, his successor, continued to pay the pension to Elizabeth. We lose sight of her in 1660. By then, amiable but weak Richard Cromwell had retired, and a newly elected Parliament declared the true government of England to be by King, Lords, and Commons. By May 1660, the monarchy was reestablished in the person of Charles II, and together with Parliament, the process of restoration began. The civil war and republican experiment were over.

As a result of developments between 1640 and 1660, England was pushed along the road of religious pluralism or toleration, Parliament's claim to limit the power of the monarchy was realized, the meanings of popular sovereignty were issues of public debates, and human rights and freedoms had been defined more concretely. It would take several more decades, and another much less bloody crisis, the Glorious Revolution of 1688, to translate many of these changes into concrete legal form. Often the political center, or generally agreed-upon principles, solidifies because of pressure or agitation at the margins. In such a scenario, radicals

like the Levellers in the English civil war and Commonwealth play an important role, even though many of their ideas were unrealized or misunderstood. Certainly the Levellers helped to build the bridge between religious dissent, with its emphasis on individual conscience, and the right of political rebellion and inalienable human rights. They also helped to redefine the legitimate political community by insisting that great wealth was not the only basis for power and by bringing into the picture small property owners who were nevertheless free men of substance capable of independent judgments in the interests of the commonwealth. The events of these decades also illustrate that politics takes different forms, running the gamut from petitioning for husband and family, to demonstrations and claims to more abstract and general rights, to voting and sitting in a decision-making body. And politics can be found in churches, the streets, covert publishing houses, places of business and taverns, and prisons, as well as in the halls of government and the chambers of elected officials.

In 1646, in the middle of the civil war, as more of the spotlight focused on the Levellers, a popular ballad published as a broadside was entitled, "The World Turned Upside Down." A song with the same name was popular in the eighteenth century, and supposedly a similar tune was played when Cornwallis surrendered to the American revolutionaries at Yorktown in 1781.[13] Whether this legacy is really

13. See Christopher Hill, *The World Turned Upside Down* (New York: Viking Press, 1972), p. 307.

true or not, it *is* true that the promises of Leveller ideas lived on. If all are born equal, why should there be limits on some and not on others? If one has rights, why shouldn't these rights be extended to all? The men of the seventeenth century had begun to formulate some answers to these questions. Women also took to the streets and the halls of Parliament to articulate their concerns and interests. Often criticized and belittled, not always heard, and certainly not granted rights equal to men's, they did not give up. By the end of the seventeenth century, more women were ready to convince others of their visions of freedom, justice, and equity.

▧ QUESTIONS

1. How were the goals of religion and politics intertwined during the upheavals of the seventeenth century? What motivated John Lilburne to begin to challenge English political authorities? How does he become a recognized political leader?

2. Although Elizabeth Lilburne is connected to the Leveller movement because of her marriage to John, in what ways does she have her own political roles in the movement? What are those roles?

3. What are the most important Leveller goals and ideals? How successful are the Levellers in realizing these goals and ideals?

4. How are men's and women's experiences in seventeenth-century English politics similar? How are they different?

5. Did the window of opportunity for radical groups, and possibly women, close after the world was turned right-side up again?

6. What is the legacy of Leveller ideology? Do their ideas resonate in the next centuries?

▧ DOCUMENTS

DOCUMENT ONE

ELIZABETH LILBURNE

"To the Chosen and Betrusted Knights, Citizens and Burgesses, Assembled in the High and Supreme Court of Parliament" (September 1646)

Even though the first phase of the war is over, John Lilburne is in prison again, and Elizabeth and some supporters present this petition to Parliament asking for

Chapter 2
Radical Politics
in Seventeenth-
Century England:
John Lilburne
(1615?–1657)
and Elizabeth
Dewell Lilburne
(161?–166?)

his release. In her humble petition, Elizabeth Lilburne uses claims to rights and justice to ask for John's freedom, but she also makes some quite practical appeals based on John's participation in the civil war and on their family's material conditions. What are the arguments she makes to Parliament in this petition? Would you consider this a political document? Why or why not? Is she speaking as a wife? As a citizen?

That you only and alone are chosen by the Commons of England to maintain their laws and liberties, and to do them justice and right . . . You confess in your Declaration of 23 October 1642 [that] it is your duty to use your best endeavors that the meanest of the Commonalty may enjoy their own birth-right, freedom and liberty of the laws of the land, being equally entitled (as you say) with the greatest subject, the knowledge of which, as coming from your own mouths and pen, emboldened your Petitioner, with confidence to make her humble address to you, and to put in mind, that her husband, more than two months ago, made his formal and legal appeal to you . . . which you received, read, committed and promised him justice in: But as yet no report is made of his business . . . which is no small cause of sorrow to your Petitioner, and many others, that her husband, who hath adventured his life, and all that he had in the world . . . be so slighted and disregarded by you, . . . which neglect has hastened the almost utter ruin of your Petitioner, her husband and small children. . . . The cruel jailers all that time refusing to let your Petitioner, or any of his friends, to set their feet over the threshold of his chamber door or to come into the prisonyard to speak with him or to deliver to his hands either meat, drink, money or any other necessaries. A most barbarous and illegal cruelty so much complained of by yourselves in your Remonstrance to the King, December 1641. [Citing at length from legal commentaries on the Magna Carta, Elizabeth argues that] [n]o man shall be in any sort destroyed unless it be by the verdict and judgment of his peers, that is, equals or by the law of the land. . . . and that you would without further delay give us relief by doing us justice. [Elizabeth then details the service John provided to the army, and reminds the Court of his previous imprisonments by the royalists and that he had not received payments promised him for his service.] For which, according to law and justice he ought to receive reparations; but he never had a penny. All which particulars considered, do render the condition of your Petitioner, her husband and children to be very near ruin and destruction, unless your speedy and long-expected justice prevent the same. Which your Petitioner does earnestly entreat at your hands as her right, and that which in equity, honor and conscience cannot be denied her.

DOCUMENT TWO

JOHN LILBURNE

"The Freeman's Freedome Vindicated"
(June 19, 1646)

By the time this document was written, the first phase of the civil war was over,
but John Lilburne was in prison again for criticizing parliamentary authority.
Written while in prison, here he sets forth some basic Leveller principles. What
basic ideas are expressed about individual rights and the power of government?

God, the absolute sovereign lord and king of all things in heaven and earth, the
original fountain and cause of all causes; who is circumscribed, governed, and
limited by no rules, but doth all things merely and only by His sovereign will
and unlimited good pleasure; who made the world and all things therein for
His own glory; and who by His own will and pleasure, gave him, His mere creature, the sovereignty (under Himself) over all the rest of His creatures (Genesis
1: 26, 28–9) and endued him with a rational soul, or understanding, and thereby
created him after His own image (Genesis 1: 26–7; 9: 6). The first of which was
Adam, a male, or man, made out of the dust or clay; out of whose side was
taken a rib, which by the sovereign and absolute mighty creating power of God
was made a female or woman called Eve: which two are the earthly, original
fountain, as begetters and bringers-forth of all and every particular and individual man and woman that ever breathed in the world since; who are, and
were by nature all equal and alike in power, dignity, authority, and majesty—
none of them having (by nature) any authority, dominion or magisterial power,
one over or above another. Neither have they or can they exercise any but
merely by institution or donation, that is to say by mutual agreement or consent—given, derived, or assumed by mutual consent and agreement—for the
good benefit and comfort each of other, and not for the mischief, hurt, or damage of any: it being unnatural, irrational, sinful, wicked and unjust for any man
or men whatsoever to part with so much of their power as shall enable any of
their parliament-men, commissioners, trustees, deputies, viceroys, ministers,
officers or servants to destroy and undo them therewith. And unnatural, irrational, sinful, wicked, unjust, devilish, and tyrannical it is, for any man whatsoever—spiritual or temporal, clergyman or layman—to appropriate and assume
unto himself a power, authority and jurisdiction to rule, govern or reign over
any sort of men in the world without their free consent. . . .

Chapter 2
Radical Politics
in Seventeenth-
Century England:
John Lilburne
(1615?–1657)
and Elizabeth
Dewell Lilburne
(161?–166?)

DOCUMENT THREE

JOHN LILBURNE AND OTHERS

"An Agreement of the People"
(October 1647)

As Lilburne and others continued to push for more popular participation in government, and for individual rights and freedoms, they sought allies among radical members of the New Model Army. This document was directed to these radical members. What does this agreement say about how a government is created and the extent of its powers? How does it reflect what some felt they were fighting for in the civil war?

1. That the people of England being at this day very unequally distributed by counties, cities and boroughs for the election of their deputies in parliament, ought to be more indifferently proportioned according to the number, place, and manner, are to be set down before the end of this present parliament.

2. That to prevent the many inconveniences apparently arising from the long continuance of the same persons in authority, this present parliament be dissolved upon the last day of September, which shall be in the year of our Lord, 1648.

3. That the people do of course choose themselves a parliament once in two years, viz. upon the first Thursday in every second March, after the manner as shall be prescribed before the end of this parliament, to begin to sit upon the first Thursday in April following at Westminster or such other place as shall be appointed from time to time by the preceding representatives, and to continue till the last day of September then next ensuing, and no longer.

4. That the power of this and all future representatives of this nation is inferior only to theirs who choose them, and doth extend, without the consent or concurrence of any other person or persons, to the enacting, altering, and repealing of laws; to the erecting and abolishing of offices and courts; to the appointing, removing, and calling to account magistrates and officers of all degrees; to the making war and peace; to the treating with foreign states; and generally, to whatsoever is not expressly or impliedly reserved by the represented to themselves.

Which are as follows:

1. That matters of religion and the ways of God's worship are not at all entrusted by us to any human power, because therein we cannot remit or exceed a

title of what our consciences dictate to be the mind of God, without wilful sin. Nevertheless the public way of instructing the nation—so it be not compulsive—is referred to their discretion.

2. That the matter of impressing and constraining any of us to serve in the wars is against our freedom; and therefore we do not allow it in our representatives; the rather, because money (the sinews of war) being always at their disposal, they can never want numbers of men apt enough to engage in any just cause.

3. That after the dissolution of this present parliament, no person be at any time questioned for anything said or done in reference to the late public differences, otherwise than in execution of the judgements of the present representatives (or House of Commons).

4. That in all laws made or to be made, every person may be bound alike; and that no tenure, estate, charter, degree, birth, or place do confer any exemption from the ordinary course of legal proceedings whereunto others are subjected.

5. That as the laws ought to be equal, so they must be good and not evidently destructive to the safety and well-being of the people.

These things we declare to be our native rights; and therefore are agreed and resolved to maintain them with our utmost possibilities against all opposition whatsoever: . . .

Postscript

Gentlemen,

We desire you may understand the reason of our extracting some principles of common freedom out of those many things proposed to you in the *Case of the army truly stated* and drawing them up into the form of an agreement. It's chiefly because for these things we first engaged against the king. He would not permit the people's representatives to provide for the nation's safety—by disposing of the militia, and other ways, according to their trust—but raised a war against them; and we engaged for the defence of that power and right of the people in their representatives. Therefore these things in the agreement, the people are to claim as their native right and price of their blood, which you are obliged absolutely to procure for them.

And these being the foundations of freedom, it's necessary that they should be settled unalterably, which can be by no means but this agreement with the people.

Chapter 2
Radical Politics
in Seventeenth-
Century England:
John Lilburne
(1615?–1657)
and Elizabeth
Dewell Lilburne
(161?–166?)

DOCUMENT FOUR

"The Putney Debates"
(1647)

In these debates among army leaders at Putney, October to November 1647,
Henry Ireton, son-in-law of Oliver Cromwell and a high-ranking officer in the
army, and Thomas Rainsborough,* a colonel of an infantry regiment, were key fig-
ures.. The debate begins with a consideration of the first paragraph of "An agree-
ment of the people" (Document Three). A key issue in these debates is the extent
and significance of property rights. What do Rainsborough and Ireton say about
property rights? What are the differences in their views? How do these debates re-
flect Leveller principles and goals?

The Paper called the Agreement read:
The first article is, "That the people of England, being at this day very unequally
distributed by Counties, Cities, and Burroughs, for the election of their
Deputies in Parliament ought to be more indifferently proportioned, according
to the number of the Inhabitants; the circumstances whereof, for number, place,
and manner, are to be set down before the end of this present Parliament."

COMMISSARY IRETON: The exception that lies in itt is this. Itt is said: "The people
of England" etc. . . . they are to bee distributed "according to the number of
the inhabitants;" and this doth make mee thinke that the meaning is, that
every man that is an inhabitant is to bee equally consider'd, and to have an
equall voice in the election of the representors, those persons that are for the
Generall Representative; and if that bee the meaning then I have somethinge
to say against itt.

MR. PETTY, A SOLDIER: Wee judge that all inhabitants that have nott lost their
birthright should have an equall voice in Elections.

COL. RAINBOROW: I desir'd that those that had engaged in itt [should speak] for
really I thinke that the poorest hee that is in England hath a life to live as the
greatest hee; and therefore truly, Sir, I thinke itt's cleare, that every man that is
to live under a Governement ought first by his owne consent to putt himself
under that Government; and I doe thinke that the poorest man in England is
nott att all bound in a stricte sence to that Governement that hee hath not had
a voice to putt himself under; and I am confident that when I have heard the
reasons against itt, an Englishman or noe that should doubt of these thinges.

COMMISSARY IRETON: That's [the meaning of] this ["according to the number of
the inhabitants."]
    Give mee leave to tell you, that if you make this the rule I thinke you must
flie for refuge to an absolute naturall Right, and you must deny all Civill

* Modern spelling of the name.

Right; and I am sure itt will come to that in the consequence. For my parte I thinke itt is noe right att all. I thinke that noe person hath a right to an interest or share in the disposing or determining of the affaires of the Kingdome, and in chusing those that shall determine what lawes wee shall bee rul'd by heere, noe person hath a right to this, that hath nott a permanent fixed interest in this Kingedome; and those persons together are properly the Represented of this Kingdome, and consequentlie are to make uppe the Representors of this Kingedome, who taken together doe comprehend whatsoever is of reall or permanent interest in the Kingedome. And I am sure I cannott tell what otherwise any man can say why a forraigner coming in amongst us—or as many as will coming in amongst us, or by force of otherwise setling themselves heere, or att least by our permission having a being heere—why they should nott as well lay claime to itt as any other. Wee talke of birthright. Truly [by] birthright there is thus much claime. Men may justly have by birthright, by their very being borne in England, that wee should nott seclude them out of England, that wee should nott refuse to give them aire, and place, and ground, and the freedome of the high wayes and other thinges, to live amongst us; nott [to] any man that is borne heere, though by his birth there comes nothing at all to him that is parte of the permanent interest of this Kingedome. That I thinke is due to a man by birth. Butt that by a man's being borne heere hee shall have a share in that power that shall dispose of the lands heere, and of all thinges heere, I doe nott thinke itt a sufficient ground . . .

COL. RAINBOROW: Truly, Sir, I am of the same opinion I was; and am resolved to keepe itt till I know reason why I should nott. Therfore I say, that either itt must bee the law of God or the law of man that must prohibite the meanest man in the Kingdome to have this benefitt as well as the greatest. I doe nott finde any thinge in the law of God, that a Lord shall chuse 20 Burgesses, and a Gentleman butt two, or a poore man shall chuse none. I finde noe such thinge in the law of nature, nor in the law of nations. . . .

I doe [think] and am still of the same opinion; that every man born in England cannot, ought nott, neither by the law of God nor the law of nature, to bee exempted from the choice of those who are to make lawes, for him to live under, and for him, for ought I know, to loose his life under. . . .

COMMISSARY GEN IRETON: . . . Now I wish wee may all consider of what right you will challenge, that all the people should have right to Elections. Is itt by the right of nature? If you will hold forth that as your ground, then I thinke you must deny all property too, and this is my reason. For thus: by the same right of nature, whatever itt bee that you pretend, by which you can say, "one man hath an equall right with another to the chusing of him that shall governe him"—by the same right of nature, hee hath an equal right in any goods hee sees: meate, drinke, cloathes, to take and use them for his sustenance. Hee hath a freedome to the land, [to take] the ground, to exercise itt, till itt; he hath the [same] freedome to any thinge that any one doth account himself to have any propriety in.

Chapter 2
Radical Politics
in Seventeenth-
Century England:
John Lilburne
(1615?–1657)
and Elizabeth
Dewell Lilburne
(161?–166?)

COL. RAINBOROW: To the thinge itt self propertie, I would faine know how itt comes to bee the propertie [of some men, and not of others]. As for estates, and those kinde of thinges, and other thinges that belonge to men, itt will bee granted that they are propertie; butt I deny that that is a propertie, to a Lord, to a Gentleman, to any man more then another in the Kingdome of England.

DOCUMENT FIVE

KATHERINE CHIDLEY (PROBABLY)

"To the Supreme Authority . . . A Petition of Divers Well-Affected Women" (May 1649)

The arrest of Lilburne and other Leveller leaders in the spring of 1649 had provoked demonstrations and further petitions, including this petition by a group of women. What are the grievances they describe in this petition? What sorts of rights are they claiming, and on what grounds?

We are assured . . . also of a proportionable share in the Freedoms of this Commonwealth, we cannot but wonder and grieve that we should appear so despicable in your eyes as to be thought unworthy to Petition or represent our grievances to this Honorable House. Have we not an equal interest with the men of this Nation, in those liberties and securities contained in the Petition of Right, and other good Laws of the Land? Are any of our lives, limbs, liberties or goods to be taken from us more than from Men? And can you imagine us to be so sottish or stupid, as not to perceive, or not to be sensible when daily those strong defenses of our peace and welfare are broken down?

. . . Would you have us keep at home in our houses, when men . . . as the four prisoners . . . are . . . forced from their Houses to the affrighting and undoing of themselves, their wives, children and families? Are not our husbands, our selves, our children and families by the same rule as liable to the like unjust cruelties as they?

. . . [A]nd must we keep at home in our houses, as if we our lives and liberties and all, were not concerned? . . . must we show no sense of their sufferings . . . nor bear any testimony against so abominable cruelty and injustice?

No . . . Let it be accounted folly, presumption, madness or whatsoever in us, whilst we have life and breath, we will never cease to importune you . . .

And therefore again, we entreat you to review our last petition . . . For we are no whit satisfied with the answer you gave unto our Husbands and Friends, but do equally with them remain liable to those snares laid in your declaration . . ."

DOCUMENT SIX

"A Manifestation from Lieutenant Colonel John Lilburne, William Walwyn, and Others, Commonly (Though Unjustly) Stiled Levellers"
(April 14, 1649)

By the date of this declaration, divisions among the Levellers were apparent. They did not agree on definitions of equality. Should it be absolute and include social and economic rights as well? In this document some of the imprisoned Leveller leaders defend themselves against popular charges and stereotypes held against them. They also hope to distance themselves from some more radical political factions. What are the misconceptions held about them that they want to correct? In setting the record straight, what do they claim as their true identity and principles?

. . . [O]ur silence gives encouragement to bad Rumors of us; so that in all places they are spread, and industriously propagated as well amongst them that know us, as them that know us not, the first being fed with Jealousies that there is more in our designs then appeares, that there is something of danger in the bottom of our hearts, not yet discovered: that we are driven on by others, that we are even discontented and irresolved, that no body yet knowes what we would have, or where our desires will end; whilst they that know us not are made believe any strange conceit of us, that we would Levell all mens estates, that we would have no distinction of Orders and Dignities amongst men, that we are indeed for no government, but a Popular confusion; and then againe that we have bin Agents for the King, and now for the Queen; That we are Atheists, Antiscripturists, Jesuites and indeed any thing, that is hatefull and of evill repute amongst men. . . .

First, Then it will be requisite that we express our selves concerning Levelling, for which we suppose is commonly meant an equalling of mens estates, and taking away the proper right and Title that every man has to what is his own. This as we have formerly declared against, particularly in our petition of the 11 of Sept. so do we again professe that to attempt an inducing the same is most injurious, unlesse there did precede an universall assent thereunto from all and every one of the People. Nor doe we, under favour, judge it within the Power of a Representative it selfe, ...

We profess therefore that we never had it in our thoughts to Level mens estates, it being the utmost of our aime that the Common-wealth be reduced to such a passe that every man may with as much security as may be enjoy his propriety [ownership]. . . .

Whereas its said, we are Atheists and Antiscripturists, we professe that we beleeve there is one eternall and omnipotent God, the Author and Preserver of

Chapter 2
Radical Politics
in Seventeenth-
Century England:
John Lilburne
(1615?–1657)
and Elizabeth
Dewell Lilburne
(161?–166?)

all things in the world. To whose will and directions, written first in our hearts, and afterwards in his blessed Word, we ought to square our actions and conversations. And though we are not so strict upon the formall and Ceremonial part of his Service, the method, manner, and personall injunction being not so clearly made out unto us, nor the necessary requisites which his Officers and Ministers ought to be furnished withall as yet appearing to us in any that pretend thereunto: yet for the manifestation of Gods love in Christ, it is cleerly assented unto by us; . . . .

. . . That we aim not at power in our selves, our Principles and Desires being in no measure of self-concernment: nor do we relie for obtaining the same upon strength, or a forcible obstruction; but solely upon that inbred and perswasive power that is in all good and just things, to make their own way in the hearts of men, and so to procure their own Establishment. . . .

Lastly, We conceive we are much mistaken in being judged impatient, and over-violent in our motions for the publick Good. To which we answer, That could we have had any assurance that what is desired should have otherwise, or by any have been done; and had not had some taste of the relinquishment of many good things that were promised, we should not have been so earnest and urgent for the doing thereof. . . .

And thus the world may dearly see what we are, and what we aym at: We are altogether ignorant, and do from our hearts abominate all designes and contrivances of dangerous consequence which we are said (but God knows, untruly) to be labouring withall. Peace and Freedom is our Designe; by War we were never gainers, nor ever wish to be; and under bondage we have been hitherto sufferers.

Enlightened Reformers: Maria Theresa (1717–1780) and Joseph II (1741–1790) of the Habsburg Monarchy

▩ SETTING THE STAGE

Monarchy, absolutism, and the Enlightenment ideas of reason, natural law, and natural rights characterize politics and society from 1715 to 1789. At this time, most European states were ruled by monarchs who believed that the sovereign power or ultimate authority in the state rested in their hands. Rulers before had claimed the right to make laws, tax, administer justice, control the state's administrative system, and determine foreign policy because God had ordained monarchs to do so. In the eighteenth century, monarchs sought justification for their rule not only in divine right or royal absolutism, but in utilitarian arguments as well. The sovereign

Chapter 3
Enlightened
Reformers:
Maria Theresa
(1717–1780)
and Joseph II
(1741–1790) of
the Habsburg
Monarchy

identified with the state and at the same time regarded him- or herself as its first servant. Yet what principles should guide this first servant?

In the early 1700s, educated men and women were greatly excited by the discoveries of the Scientific Revolution and by the concepts of reason and natural law. These intellectuals, or philosophes, believed that one could apply reason and use the scientific method not only to discover truth and knowledge about the universe but to improve human society and government. At the center of the philosophes' discussion of rule and government were natural rights, which were thought to be inalienable human privileges that should not be withheld from any person. In theory, these natural rights included equality before the law; freedom of religious worship; freedom of speech and the press; and the right to assemble, hold property, and pursue happiness. Any good government would be one that protected these rights. But what was the best form of government to accomplish these goals?

Voltaire, one of the most famous of the philosophes, argued that society needed to be directed from above, by an enlightened ruler. The absolute monarch must absorb and apply Enlightenment principles to the rule of state. Only strong monarchs were capable of overcoming the entrenched interests of religious institutions, the landed nobility, town councils, and provincial estates and improving the lives of their subjects. To what extent the reforming monarchs of the eighteenth century followed the prescriptions of French, Italian, or Austrian enlightened thinkers is debated by historians. Historians do agree that the eighteenth century was a century of reform when monarchs and their advisers pushed to modernize bureaucracies and legal and fiscal systems, sponsored and encouraged commercial and economic development, attacked the power of the Catholic Church, questioned and abolished the institution of serfdom, and established the basis for universal education. The motivation and influence of each reform or renovation must be understand in its proper context.

The lives of Maria Theresa and her son and co-regent Joseph II of the Habsburg monarchy reveal how personal experience and interest, Enlightenment philosophy, family, gender, and education influenced each monarch's attempt to address the social, commercial, economic, and political problems of their ethnically and socially diverse empire. To what extent each monarch was "enlightened" will be one focus of this chapter. Another focus is to determine how gender may have affected their ascension and their direction and retention of power.

▪ THE ACTORS:

MARIA THERESA AND JOSEPH II

Maria Theresa's ascension to the Habsburg throne was unprecedented. Never before had a woman ruled over the collection of lands that constituted the Habsburg monarchy. The Habsburgs not only ruled over diverse lands but for three hundred years had held the elective office of Holy Roman Emperor. Tradition and law blocked a daughter's inheritance because only males were recognized as legal heirs of the Habsburg monarchy. In addition, the Holy Roman Empire's charter prohibited women from that office. Worried that he would have no male heirs, Maria Theresa's father, Charles VI (r. 1711–1740), prepared the way for a female heir. Charles did not expect his daughters to be capable rulers when he sought to place one of them on the throne. He simply wished to preserve his family's patrimony of land and power. The Habsburg family or the "House of Habsburg" was in fact an extended familial community whose collective interests were threatened by the absence of a male heir. In 1713, Charles VI drafted a document known as the Pragmatic Sanction to ensure that the House of Habsburg's power could be inherited by a female. The Pragmatic Sanction confirmed the indivisibility of the Habsburg possessions and, in default of male heirs, that they should pass to Charles's female heirs. Until his death in 1740, Charles VI worked hard to persuade the individual estates of the empire to accept the succession. He also campaigned in all the major European capitals for similar recognition.

Queenship was not unknown to the major European states. Elizabeth I of England (r. 1558–1603), Christina of Sweden (r. 1633–1654), and two contemporaries of Maria Theresa's, Elizabeth I of Russia (r. 1741–1762) and Catherine II of Russia (r. 1762–1796), all had inherited the right to rule. The inherited right to rule was a system of transferring power from one generation to the next. In France, tradition mandated that inherited rulership descend from male to male. In Russia, Sweden, and England, the order of ascension was much more flexible. Preference was given to any direct male heir first, no matter the age, then to female heirs. This system of inheritance reflected a successful gender ordering that existed at all levels of society. The royal families of Europe (the Bourbons in France, the Tudor-Stuarts and Hanoverians in England, the Romanovs in Russia, the Hohenzollerns in Prussia, and the Habsburgs in Central Europe) and their inherited power depended on each family's ability to reproduce itself in the next generation. Of course, inherited rulership worked only as long as this system of transferring power was accepted by the society over which the monarch ruled.

Maria Theresa ascended to the Habsburg throne upon her father's death in October 1740. Despite his efforts, her inheritance was immediately challenged by the rulers of Prussia, France, Spain, Bavaria, and Saxony. Frederick II of Prussia (r. 1740–1786) and his army quickly defeated a poorly equipped and meager Habsburg army and occupied Silesia, the wealthiest province of the

Chapter 3
Enlightened
Reformers:
Maria Theresa
(1717–1780)
and Joseph II
(1741–1790) of
the Habsburg
Monarchy

Habsburg lands. Frederick's easy victory and quick occupation of a Habsburg province emboldened France and Bavaria to join the fray. In 1741, the young female monarch had only a tenuous hold over all of the Habsburg lands, especially over its Hungarian possessions. The Hungarian nobility had accepted the Pragmatic Sanction, but memories of earlier clashes with their Habsburg rulers still resonated. Understanding the Hungarian nobility's fear of losing privileges and liberties under a new monarch, Maria Theresa immediately recognized the Hungarian nobility's traditional rights. She also sought out Count István Pálffy, one of the leaders of the Hungarian nobility, as one of her early advisers. As a result of her political acumen, Maria Theresa won the Hungarians' support for her rule as well as specific pledges of men and horses to fight the war.

Maria Theresa's successful maneuvering in the dangerous and intimidating political world of eighteenth-century Europe and her fortitude in the wake of Prussia's attack on her inheritance obviously surprised many contemporary observers. They attributed her success to her beauty, youth, and maternity. Myth has often clouded the history of Hungary's pledge of support to Maria Theresa. Voltaire, in his *Short History of the Century of Louis XV*, recounts a now famous story of Maria Theresa with the infant Joseph II cradled in her arms pleading for help from the Hungarian nobility (Document One). It is true that she did address the Hungarian nobility in September 1741, but she

did not go as a cowering princess. She appealed to the Hungarian nobility as an equal, someone whom they could trust to protect their rights and privileges. She described her speech to the Hungarian nobles in her *Political Testament*. While emphasizing the monarchy's need for the nobles to take action and to protect the "very existence of the kingdom of Hungary, of our own person, of our children, and our crown," she made it clear to the assembled that they would be rewarded. She continued, ". . . the faithful states and orders of Hungary shall experience our hearty cooperation in all things, which may promote the pristine happiness of this ancient kingdom, and the honor of the people."[1] The Hungarian aristocracy acted in its own self-interest and not on some chivalric notion of protecting the honor of the young female ruler, as Voltaire dramatically and romantically asserted. Maria Theresa had proven herself to be both a politician and talented actress.

Maria Theresa had not been trained in the art of statecraft. Despite his legal preparations for the possibility that his daughter might ascend the throne, Charles VI had not schooled her in this art (Document Two). Maria Theresa recalled in her Testimony: "It never pleased my father's Majesty to have me present when he transacted business, domestic or foreign. Neither did he ever tell me what had been

1. William McGill, Jr., *Maria Theresa* (New York: Twayne Publishers, Inc., 1972), p. 38. Quoted from William Coxe, *History of the House of Austria* (London, 1882), III, pp. 269–270.

transacted."[2] He assumed that Maria Theresa would marry and then surrender power to her husband. In 1736, she married Francis Stephen of Lorraine, but when her father died four years later, she kept the reins of power for herself.

With the outbreak of the War of the Austrian Succession (1740–1748), Maria Theresa resolved to resist her enemies and preserve the integrity of the empire for her newborn son. One historian argues that Joseph II's birth, not Maria Theresa's steadfastness and alacrity, restored the popularity of the monarchy among the people. "The infant male was greeted as the guarantor of the imperial dignity of the Habsburgs. Scornful warnings directed at Frederick abounded, 'The enemy has lost his chance/For Austria now wears pants.'"[3]

The loss of Silesia and the attack on her patrimony deeply affected how Maria Theresa conducted the affairs of state during her long rule. The desire to avenge the loss of Silesia to Prussia provoked her to reorganize the non-Hungarian parts of the empire. Maria Theresa had inherited a state in which a landed aristocracy controlled most of the land, kept private armies, and paid no taxes; ministers of the imperial household wielded immense power; serfdom existed; and the Roman Catholic Church possessed immense wealth. Surrounding herself

with talented and able advisers, especially Friedrich Wilhelm Count Haugwitz and Prince Wenzel Anton Kaunitz, Maria Theresa embarked on a series of reforms from 1746 to 1756 that reorganized the central administration, abolished private armies and established an imperial army, and improved the administration of finances. By 1756, Maria Theresa's domestic reforms had strengthened the empire sufficiently to allow her contemplation of another war with Frederick the Great's Prussia. But before doing so, Maria Theresa had to reconfigure her diplomatic alliances.

Maria Theresa and her advisers believed that they could not withstand the forces of both France and Prussia. In the War of the Austrian Succession, the monarchy had faced both powers. In 1756, the conditions existed for a reconfiguring of European alliances. In that year, France agreed to come to Austria's aid in the event of an attack by Prussia, on the condition that Austria remain neutral in the French and English war being waged in North America. This new alliance eventually led to Maria Theresa promising that her youngest daughter and fifteenth child, Marie Antoinette, would marry the heir to the French throne, Louis XVI. Marriage to advance the goals of the state or to cement alliances between families was a common practice (Document Three).

The Habsburg's war against Prussia, the Seven Years' War (1756–1763), ended as the War of the Austrian Succession had ended, with Prussia firmly in control of Silesia. An economically important province and

2. J. Kallbrunner, ed., *Kaiserin Maria Theresias Politisches Testament* (Munich, 1952), p. 30. Quoted in Robert Pick, *Empress Maria Theresa* (New York: Harper and Row, 1966), p. 52.

3. Ibid., p. 75.

Chapter 3
Enlightened
Reformers:
Maria Theresa
(1717–1780)
and Joseph II
(1741–1790) of
the Habsburg
Monarchy

part of the Habsburg hereditary lands had been lost and Maria Theresa finally accepted this fact. Despite the loss, the reforms implemented to wage this war had strengthened the Habsburg state and centralized its administration at the expense of provincial interests. Maria Theresa had wielded power absolutely to wage war against Prussia. After 1763, absolutism still reigned, albeit more efficiently, and in the second part of her rule, more humanely.

Maria Theresa's husband, Francis Stephen of Lorraine, died soon after the Seven Years' War. In love with her husband despite his infidelity, Maria Theresa would mourn her husband's death until her own in 1780. With his death, Maria Theresa accepted as coregent her oldest son Joseph II. Their coregency (1765–1780) was fraught with the tensions and contradictions of the day. Maria Theresa's rulership reflected her early experiences as empress, making her pragmatic and cautious. In addition, Christian concern for her subjects often informed her actions and deeds. She was openly hostile to the ideas of the Enlightenment, and she ordered the royal censors to keep writings on rationalist doctrine and religious indifference out of the hands of her subjects. She strongly believed in social hierarchy and in Catholicism, and that God had ordained her to rule for the benefit of her people. In contrast, Christian humanism had little impact on her son's sense of responsibility for his subjects. He insisted that his duty was to promote the well-being of his subjects based on the rational notion of the "general good" or "general best," a

trait he shared with Prussia's Frederick the Great (Documents Four and Five).

Born in 1741, Joseph II's upbringing differed greatly from that of his contemporaries. Louis XVI of France (r. 1774–1793) and George III of England (r. 1760–1820) had lost their parents at the ages of 12 and 13, respectively. Paul of Russia (r. 1796–1801) suffered physical abuse at the hands of his drunken father, Peter III (r. 1762), and the contempt of his German mother, Catherine II (r. 1762–1796). Frederick II of Prussia (r. 1740–1786) survived the beatings, ugly rebukes, and threats of his father, Frederick William I (r. 1713–1740). Joseph II grew up in the warm embrace of both his parents and benefitted from their careful and thoughtful management of his education and training. Joseph once told his mother how lucky he was not to have the sort of relationship with her that Paul of Russia had with his mother, Catherine II.

Joseph's education was the focus of much discussion. His parents, ministers, and tutors wrote copious notes and memoranda about Joseph's program, progress, and prospective for further study. In contrast to his mother's and his sisters' education, Joseph II's education included formal religious instruction, theology, Latin, law, literature, mathematics, music, and physical training. By his eighteenth year, Joseph had proven himself to be an outstanding student of a fairly conservative course of study. His education owed little to the French philosophes, whose works were relatively new or not yet written. Joseph read these works after his formal education. The education of Joseph's four younger brothers followed a similar pattern. Maria Theresa's daughters did not receive the same education as her sons. Their education focused on basic literacy, French language and literature, religious instruction, some geography and history, and the domestic arts of sewing, needlework, and the like.

■ ACT I:

MOTHER AND SON RULE TOGETHER (1765–1780)

Joseph emerged from his studies, married the Infanta Isabella of Parma in 1760, and as Joseph describes, "was employed soon afterwards in attending the councils of the different departments."[4] Maria Theresa was determined that her son gain the experience and responsibility in rulership that her father had not seen fit to give her. Joseph II was ready to rule, but he would have to wait until his thirty-ninth year to rule alone. During the coregency, his mother often resisted her son's attempts at radical change. Joseph aimed to perfect the administration of the empire by strengthening the bureaucracy and weakening the privileges of the church and the landed nobility; eliminating the differences in language, custom, class, and habit that existed among regions; and making the monarchy dominant among the European powers.

Frederick the Great, Catherine the Great, and Maria Theresa shared many of Joseph II's aspirations. However, Joseph II wished to go further than his mother and his contemporaries. He wanted to alter fundamentally the political, social, and economic relationship between lord and peasant; he wanted to abolish serfdom. He believed that the institution of serfdom was inhuman and economically damaging to the state. His mother was not blind to the inhumanity of serfdom, but she preferred to lead by example. She also did not wish to alienate the Austrian and Hungarian nobilities, who were adamantly opposed to serfdom's abolition. On the lands owned by the Habsburg royal house, Maria Theresa granted her serfs freedom of movement, marriage, and choice of profession. After his mother's death, Joseph would extend these freedoms, and more, to lands owned by the nobility. Although he was loathe to admit it, many of his reforms were simply radical extensions of his mother's policies.

Both Maria Theresa and Joseph were devout Roman Catholics, but both also believed in firm state control of ecclesiastical matters outside the strictly religious sphere (Document Six). Early in her reign and with the intention of improving the economy, Maria Theresa ordered restrictions on religious holidays and prohibited the taking of ecclesiastic vows before the twenty-fourth birthday. Maria

---

4. "Memorandum of 1765," in Alfred von Arneth, *Maria Theresia und Joseph II, Ihre Correspondenz* (Vienna, 1867), p. 336. Quoted in Derek Beales, *Joseph II: In the Shadow of Maria Theresa, 1741–1780* (Cambridge: Cambridge University Press, 1987), p. 69.

Chapter 3
Enlightened
Reformers:
Maria Theresa
(1717–1780)
and Joseph II
(1741–1790) of
the Habsburg
Monarchy

Theresa also noted that the church owned sufficient land but used it poorly and administered it badly. She proposed that the acquisition of land by the church be controlled by the government. In addition, Maria Theresa sought to break up the monopoly that the Jesuit order had over education and censorship. In 1759, she removed some Jesuits from their chairs at the University of Vienna and from their places on the censorship commission. Her rationale was that clerics had to be subject to the jurisdiction of the state in nonecclesiastical matters.

Joseph's and Maria Theresa's adviser, Prince Kaunitz, argued for further reform. At the beginning of the coregency, Joseph proposed in a memorandum that the monarchy had to address the issue of religious toleration, the number and wealth of monasteries and their usefulness, the weakness of education controlled by the church, and the oppressiveness of the censorship system. Joseph's attitudes toward the Roman Catholic Church, Prince Kaunitz's endorsement of the philosophes' positions on the corruption and immorality of the church, and Maria Theresa's anger at Rome for appointing bishops without her consent led to a series of edicts. These edicts taxed church lands; prohibited the clergy from acquiring land; required monasteries to send details of membership, resources, and incomes to the state; dissolved a number of religious houses; brought state control over education; and finally in 1773, expelled the Jesuits from Austrian lands.

While mother and son could agree on the need to limit the influence of the Catholic Church throughout the monarchy and in secular affairs, Maria Theresa could never embrace Joseph's desire to tolerate other religions. Maria Theresa regarded Protestants as heretics and Jews as the embodiment of the antichrist. She considered Jews an "evil plague" who "reduce others to beggary through greed, deceit, and usury. . . ." In this respect, Maria Theresa personally and officially practiced the anti-Semitism of her most recent predecessors. In 1669, Leopold I (1640–1705) banished Jews from Vienna and two years later from Austria. Maria Theresa continued this ban, and Jews were allowed into Vienna only with her written permission. In addition, she required Jews to pay a toll upon entering the city and to wear a yellow patch, subjected them to higher taxes, forbade them to be out in public on Sundays or Christian holidays, and prohibited the building of synagogues. In stark contrast to his mother, Joseph respected other Christian denominations and believed Jews did good service for the state.

▪ ACT II:

THE SON RULES ALONE

Soon after his mother's death in 1780, Joseph enacted two edicts on religious toleration, the Edict of Toleration for Protestants (1781) and the Edict of Toleration for Jews (1782) (Document Seven). The edicts and the legislation attached to them gave Lutherans, Calvinists, and Orthodox near-equality with Roman Catholics and gave Jews the right to enter various trades as well as permission to study at universities. Joseph had practical as well as enlightened reasons for issuing these edicts. First, persecuted minorities, the Protestants and Jews, would be transformed into useful subjects, and costly religious conflict would decrease. Second, Joseph had adopted the Enlightenment stance that humans had an inalienable right to worship according to their own beliefs. By the end of his reign, Joseph had established the supremacy of the state over the church.

With the Edict of Toleration of the Jews (1782), Joseph ended the policy of official anti-Semitism in the Habsburg monarchy. This did not mean that anti-Semitism disappeared. In 1782, there were about 70,000 Jews in Bohemia, Moravia, and Silesia; 80,000 in the vast Hungarian Kingdom; and 215,000 in the territory of Galicia, acquired through the first partition of Poland in 1772. No Jews lived in Austria proper, with the exception of several hundred families whom Leopold I had allowed to return to Vienna after his ban in 1669. Joseph's policies fundamentally changed the conditions and lives for the monarchy's Jewish population. Jews gained greater access to opportunities in education and business, and were allowed to move out of their ghettos and into other parts of the monarchy's cities. The 550 Viennese families who had been permitted to settle in the capital now began to integrate into Viennese society. Assimilation and integration of Jews had been one of Joseph's goals. He required that Jews adopt German names and write all bills and contracts in German. In the monarchy's major cities, Prague, Vienna, and Budapest, assimilated Jews became important forces in urban culture, politics, and society in nineteenth- and twentieth-century Central Europe.

Joseph did not stop at reducing the Catholic Church's influence in religious affairs by offering official toleration to the monarchy's other religions. He also sought to reduce its influence over education. He once again took the policies that his mother had begun and radicalized them. The state, under Maria Theresa's direction, was gradually taking control of education away from the church and private individuals. Maria Theresa's reforms had been modest, primarily emphasizing the importance of training nobles for government service. Joseph II was more ambitious in his goals. He sought reform of the curriculum, much of it religious; the establishment of a system of state schools where children would be trained for future service to the state; and the introduction of education for women. Compulsory primary schooling was established, though only for short periods of the year. The state mandated basic qualifications for teachers, textbooks, generous salaries to attract men of talent to the teaching ranks, primary education in the local language, and separate schools for girls where they would be taught domestic skills. At the secondary and university level, Joseph argued that education must emphasize practical subjects, like medicine, law, and engineering. Foreign languages, music, and other impractical subjects would no longer be studied.

Another target of Joseph's reforming zeal was the social and economic

Chapter 3
Enlightened
Reformers:
Maria Theresa
(1717–1780)
and Joseph II
(1741–1790) of
the Habsburg
Monarchy

relationship between lord and peasant. He believed that this feudal relationship, known as serfdom, stood in the way of the creation of an ideal state. He wanted to improve the legal and economic position of the peasants thus boasting their productivity and taking away the nobles' control over their labor and income. Soon after his mother's death, Joseph II issued the Patent to Abolish Serfdom (1781), which freed serfs to marry as they wished, leave the manor and seek employment elsewhere, and learn trades and professions, and abolished the peasants' labor obligation to the lord (robot). Labor service required of a peasant's children was abolished, except for orphans. These new freedoms applied initially only to the lands of the Bohemian crown, but over the next few years they were applied to the other Austrian lands and in 1785 to Hungary, the land that had been exempt from most reforms during his mother's reign.

To prevent the lords from circumventing these reforms, Joseph ordered that peasants could appeal directly to the central government if they had a grievance. The nobility traditionally addressed all grievances between lord and peasant, and Joseph feared that the nobles could sabotage these reforms by issuing decisions against peasants who wanted to exercise their new rights. In one of his final attacks on the nobilities' privileges, Joseph proclaimed in 1789 that all land, whether held by nobleperson or commoner, would be taxed at the same rate.

Time and energy for many of these reforms came from his unhappy personal life. Unlucky in marriage, his first

wife Isabella died in 1763. Joseph's second wife, Josepha of Bavaria, was a woman of breathtaking ugliness and he did not disguise his disgust for her. When asked why there was no heir, he responded, "I would try to have children, if I could put the tip of my finger on the tiniest part of her body that is not covered with boils."[5] After Josepha's death in 1767, Joseph rejected marriage and family life and dedicated all his energy to rule.

A man of few pretensions, he despised the etiquette, privilege, snobbery, and pageantry of the Habsburg court, believing that his status was due to an accident of birth. "At birth we inherit nothing from our parents but animal life. Thus king, count, burgher or peasant, there is not the slightest difference."[6] During his reign, he prohibited the kneeling before the emperor or the kissing of his hand, believing that these servile practices were not compatible with the dignity of humans. Other enlightened monarchs also shed some of the pomp and circumstance of royal custom, but none went as far as Joseph. Joseph wanted to know his subjects and he traveled extensively throughout the empire, not as emperor but as an ordinary man. Often disguised, he stayed at hotels, roadhouses, and inns and participated in and observed the ordinary lives of his subjects. His travels, conversations, and observations informed his views on human dignity, equality, and reform.

5. T. C. W. Blanning, *Joseph II and Enlightened Despotism* (London: Longman, 1970), p. 44.
6. Ibid.

Joseph wished to rule his state by reason and to eliminate all useless conventions and privileges that did not serve the interests of all. He wished to "unite all parts of the monarchy in a joint enterprise, namely the contributing towards its common good." Believing that all individuals, from the lowliest serf to the wealthiest noble, were selfish, only the monarch could do what was best for the people. Joseph's political philosophy reflected Enlightenment ideas of the social contract, utilitarianism, and reason. The monarch was granted the right to rule by society through the social contract. However, the monarch could use this power only for the benefit of his or her people and the state. No individual or group, like the clergy, nobles, or town councils, had the right to oppose the "enlightened" commands of the ruler. To enforce royal decrees, an army of officials, or bureaucrats, had to be trained and deployed throughout the state. Joseph justified this concentration of power in the hands of the monarch and his officials by arguing that it was their duty to promote the welfare of the subjects. His writings as a youth, *Reveries*, revealed this thinking. In them he wrote, "I believe we must strive to convert the provinces and make them feel how useful the short-term despotism, which I propose, would be to them. For this purpose I should want to make an agreement with the provinces requesting full power for ten years to do everything for their good without consulting them."[7]

Joseph's reforms not only reflected the ideas of contemporary writers of the Austrian and French Enlightenment but also built on the earlier reforms of his mother, a fact that he did not like to acknowledge. After his mother's death in 1780, Joseph II embarked on an impressive ten-year period of reform. From his desk in Vienna, he issued over two decrees per day to streamline and create a more efficient government. He subjected Hungary, which was essentially independent, to the same reforms his mother had decreed for the other parts of the Habsburg monarchy several decades earlier. Joseph II desired to have complete administrative control over every nook and cranny of the empire.

During his reign, Joseph attempted to overcome the entrenched interests of religious institutions, the landed nobility, town councils, and provincial estates and to create a strong centralized state that served the interests of the greatest number of his subjects through the use of reason, royal decree, and force of his will. He refused to compromise or to allow opposition to his ideas from any quarter, and this uncompromising, take-it-or-leave-it attitude makes him a despot. This attitude was reflected in his abolition of official censorship in 1781 and its reinstatement in 1786.

In 1781, Joseph issued a decree to ease official censorship, which had been a characteristic of his mother's rule. His immediate purpose was to generate support for his religious policies by unleashing those popular writers eager to condemn Roman Catholic clericalism and especially the pope. And for the first few years he was not

7. Nicholas Henshall, *The Myth of Absolutism: Change and Continuity in Early Modern European Monarchy* (New York: Longman, 1992), p. 193.

*Chapter 3
Enlightened
Reformers:
Maria Theresa
(1717–1780)
and Joseph II
(1741–1790) of
the Habsburg
Monarchy*

disappointed. Joseph soon found out, however, that easing censorship meant that journalists, social critics, and others could write about anything they wished. They soon turned their attention to Joseph and began finding fault with his reforms. He reinstated censorship and in 1786 he issued secret instructions to the police to concentrate their attention on monitoring public opinion at all levels of society. By the late 1780s, the police reports contained news on agitators and potential unrest, and he was well aware of the growing dissatisfaction with his reforms and rule.

Joseph II's ten years of reform by decree met enormous resistance from those whose privileged position he attacked. In 1788, due to ill health, a disastrous war against the Ottoman Empire, a poor harvest, opposition from the nobles, and the rebellion of the peasants, Joseph postponed or withdrew many of his reforms. A year later, he delayed a tax reform on noble land, withdrew the abolition of peasant labor obligations (robot), and recognized the Hungarian nobility's right to control their lands and peasants. At the time of his death, Joseph believed that he had failed to bring about significant change in the empire. He ordered his tombstone to read, "Here lies Joseph II who failed in everything he attempted."[8]

▓ FINALE

Maria Theresa and Joseph II represent two sides of the same coin. Both wished to lay the foundations for a wealthy, strong, and humane centralized state; to build a formidable army; and to reduce the power of the noble estates, town councils, and the Roman Catholic Church. Maria Theresa and her ministers had laid the groundwork and worked tirelessly, if cautiously, in this direction. Her son proved to be much more impatient, arrogant, and unrealistic in many of his reforms. He had once boasted to his mother, "To do things by halves does not agree at all with my principles,"[9] implying that she was far too compromising and accommodating in her efforts. Joseph failed because, unlike his mother, he was too coldly rational, distant, and uncompromising. He did not try to gain support from the bureaucrats, who were to implement his reforms, or from the middle class and intellectuals, who viewed him as despotic. Instead he alienated the most powerful in his realm, the nobility. He did not try to appeal to his subjects as a father figure or even as a compassionate man. He lacked tact and diplomacy, skills that both monarchs and others saw as crucial to the legitimacy and credibility of any ruler.

By contrast, Maria Theresa was able to capture the imagination and the hearts of her subjects. She was able to transform the image of a young mother in distress to that of a robust, dignified, and powerful woman whose sixteen pregnancies came to

8. Walter Oppenheim, *Europe and the Enlightened Despots* (London: Hodder and Stoughton, 1990), p. 115.

9. Ibid.

represent the bountiful and prosperous Habsburg monarchy. She also moved cautiously, cultivating the goodwill of the nobility, and never supplanted the underpinnings of their power: control over their lands and peasants. Her approach to reform was pragmatic and, unlike her son, she believed that her reforms had created a politically stable state and had improved the lives of her subjects.

Maria Theresa and her son Joseph illustrate the complexities of classifying rulers as "enlightened." Maria Theresa, motivated to reform because of the threat to the Habsburg patrimony, embarked on administrative, judicial, educational, religious, fiscal, and social reforms that extended beyond the scope and impact of some of the reforms of her enlightened contemporaries, like Catherine the Great and Frederick the Great. Unlike Catherine and Frederick, Enlightenment principles did not inform her reforms, thoughts, or actions. Her son is often judged as enlightened because of his acknowledged debt to writings of the philosophes, as well as his temporary abolition of serfdom and the issuing of edicts on religious toleration. Yet many of his reforms did not suc-

ceed because he chose to wield power absolutely, alienated the nobility, and had very little support from other classes for his reforms. When open hostility and resistance to his reforms grew and threatened the stability of the empire, Joseph II retreated. Not to do so was to invite chaos, and above all, absolute monarchs sought stability and the strengthening of the state, not social revolution. Increasing the power of the state vis-à-vis other powerful constituencies was always part of the program for enlightened rulers. They did not intend to give up that power without a fight.

Maria Theresa's rule as a member of the House of Habsburg first and as a woman second illustrates one of the ways that women during the eighteenth century had access to power and to politics. Other ways were through marriage, as the reign of Catherine the Great of Russia demonstrated, or through more informal avenues, as Louis XV's mistress, Madame Du Berry illustrated. Royal privilege and absolutism would come under fire, however, during the French Revolution, and with it would come challenges to a woman's right to participate in the political arena.

■ **QUESTIONS**

1. How was political power transferred in the eighteenth century? Why did Charles VI draft the Pragmatic Sanction?

2. What principles and ideas guided and inspired the rule of Maria Theresa, Frederick the Great, and Joseph II?

3. How was Maria Theresa judged as a woman versus as a ruler? How

*Chapter 3
Enlightened
Reformers:
Maria Theresa
(1717–1780)
and Joseph II
(1741–1790) of
the Habsburg
Monarchy*

did Maria Theresa portray herself? Why?

4. What type of training and education did the royal children receive? For what purposes?

5. What were Joseph's attitudes toward the influence of the Roman Catholic Church in the Habsburgs land? How did they differ from his mother's? What were his views on religious toleration? What actions did he take to reduce the influence of the church? Why did he take these actions?

6. How did Joseph's views on social equality and religious toleration differ from his mother's?

7. What were the motivations for Maria Theresa's reforms? What were Joseph II's motivations? On what basis can we assess whether they are enlightened?

8. Did gender affect the direction and governance of Maria Theresa, Joseph II, Frederick the Great, and Catherine the Great? Did Enlightenment ideals encompass women as well as men?

▓ DOCUMENTS

DOCUMENT ONE

VOLTAIRE

"Brave Young Queen"
(1741)

In his Short History of the Century of Louis XV, *Voltaire recounts the now mythical story of Maria Theresa appealing to the Hungarian nobility for help against Prussia and its allies in the War of the Austrian Succession. Describe Maria Theresa's demeanor in front of the Hungarian nobility. Contrast this description with her portrayal in Document Three. Is Maria Theresa a woman and mother first or a ruler? Why does it matter?*

(September 11, 1741) The more the ruin of Maria Theresa appeared inevitable, the more courage she revealed; she had departed from Vienna and threw herself into the arms of the Hungarians, treated so severely by her father and ancestors. Having assembled the four orders of the parliament at Pressburg, she appeared there holding in her arms her young son, barely out of the cradle. Speaking in Latin, a language in which she expressed herself well, she addressed them in words similar to the following: "Abandoned by my friends, persecuted by my enemies, attacked by my closest relatives, I have no other resources than your loyalty, your courage, and my steadfastness; I place in your hands the daughter and son of your king who rely on you for their safety." Pulling their swords from their scabbards, all the attending nobles and their friends cried out *"Moriamur pro rege nostro"* (We will die for our king Maria Theresa). They always give the title of king to their queen, and no princess has been more deserving of this title. They shed tears in declaring the oath to defend her; she alone retained her composure, but when she had retired with her women of honor, she allowed to fall in abundance those tears that her strength had held back. She was pregnant at that time, and shortly afterward she wrote to the duchess of Lorraine, her mother-in-law, "I did not even know if a village would remain to me where I could deliver my baby."

Under these circumstances, she excited the zeal of her Hungarians; she inspired England and Holland in her favor, and they gave her financial assistance. She won support within the [Holy Roman] Empire; she negotiated with the king of Sardinia, and his provinces gave her soldiers.

All the English nation responded in her favor. This people is not one that waits for the opinion of its master in order to express itself. Some people proposed to present a gift to this princess. The duchess of Marlborough, widow of the Marlborough who had fought for Charles VI, assembled the important ladies of London; they promised to furnish one hundred thousand pounds sterling, and the duchess herself deposited forty thousand. The queen of Hungary had the grandeur of soul not to accept this money that had so generously been offered to her; she wished only that which she received from the whole nation assembled in Parliament.

DOCUMENT TWO

MARIA THERESA

On-the-Job Training, Principles of Rule

In 1749–1750, Maria Theresa dictated to her secretaries her reflections on the first ten years of her rule. These "testimonies" evaluate her successes and failures in regard to the War of the Austrian Succession (1740–1747), her preparation for rule, the state of the Habsburg Empire, and her attempts at reform. The following two excerpts discuss her training and the guiding principles of her rule. How was Maria Theresa prepared for queenship?

[ON-THE-JOB TRAINING]

The unexpected tragic death of my lord father of holy memory filled me with great grief because not only did I love and honor him as a father, but like the least of his subjects, considered him my sovereign. Furthermore, I felt double the loss and pain because I possessed so little familiarity with affairs of state

Chapter 3
Enlightened
Reformers:
Maria Theresa
(1717–1780)
and Joseph II
(1741–1790) of
the Habsburg
Monarchy

and so little knowledge necessary to rule such extensive and diverse lands, and my father had never been inclined to instruct me as to the discharge of either foreign or domestic affairs. Consequently, I saw myself stripped all at once of money, soldiers, and advice.

At that time, having had no practice in selecting councilors and being timid and insecure because of it, I had great difficulty assessing the suggestions and instructions offered to me. In the last ten unfortunate years of my father's reign, I had only heard, like any private person, the misfortunes and laments that reached the public, without knowing their origins or why they came. At that time, unlike today, everything was not revealed openly to all the ministers, but kept secret. I resolved, therefore, not to conceal my ignorance but to listen to each official in his own department and thus inform myself correctly. Count [Louis Philip] Sinzendorf, the court chancellor [responsible for foreign affairs], was a great statesman and I realized his loss only later, but at that time I did not fully trust him. Count [Gundaker Thomas] Starhemberg [minister of finance] possessed my complete confidence, and I revered him very much, although he lacked the great political insight of Sinzendorf. From the beginning, the court chancellor prepared me and informed me of everything, but Starhemberg enjoyed my thorough trust. This situation continued quite smoothly until the arrival of [Philip Joseph] Kinsky [Bohemian court chancellor], who, albeit with the best intentions, caused me such confusion and perplexity that I lost my even temper and became greatly depressed.

[PRINCIPLES OF RULE]

From the beginning I decided that, as my principles, I would depend upon my own forthright intentions and prayers to God; I would remove myself from all minor worries, arrogance, personal ambition, and other emotions—which I have on occasion observed in myself—and I would undertake all the necessary business of government resolutely and without passion. These maxims, with the help of God, have sustained me in my great difficulties and have made me stand firm by my decisions. In all my acts—those done and those left undone— I have chosen as my highest rule a trust in God, who, without regard to my own desires, has chosen me for this position and will make me worthy of it through my deeds, principles, and intentions. Thus I felt able to solicit His help and win His almighty protection for myself and my subjects; I recalled this truth daily and it reminded me that I was responsible not only to myself but to my people.

Having each time tested my ideas by these standards, I undertook everything thereafter with complete confidence, sustained mightily and yet so calmly in my soul even in great emergencies, as if they did not affect me personally. With complete tranquillity and pleasure, I would have even abandoned my whole right to rule and surrendered to my enemies, had Divine Providence so willed and had I believed it my duty or the best policy for my lands. And even though I love my heritage and my children and would spare no diligence, worry, concern, or work for them, still, when convinced in my own mind or by general conditions that it is necessary, I would always put the general welfare of my lands first because I am the foremost and universal mother of all my subjects.

In these circumstances, I found myself without money, without credit, without an army, without experience or knowledge, and finally without advice because every counselor wanted to wait and see what would happen. Such were the conditions when my lands were attacked by the king of Prussia. This monarch's sweet words and vigorous promises convinced each of my ministers that he would avoid opening hostilities. This belief—cherished by my ministers, especially Sinzendorf—plus my own inexperience and good faith were the main reasons why defensive preparations in Silesia were neglected, even to the point of failing to muster nearby regiments, and the king of Prussia was given a free hand to conquer the duchy within six weeks.

DOCUMENT THREE

Maria Theresa

Rules for the Wife of a Prince
(1770)

Maria Theresa's daughter Marie Antoinette married the heir to the French throne, Louis XVI, in 1770 at the age of fifteen. In the following passage, Maria Theresa instructs her daughter on the proper way to behave. Note Maria Theresa's warning about subversive literature. The correspondence between mother and daughter was written in French, which was the most civilized of all languages in the eighteenth century. What are the proper ways for the "wife of a prince" to behave?

Maria Theresa to Marie Antoinette, 21 April 1770

[Rules to be read once a month]

This twenty-first of April, day of your departure.—When you wake up, you will immediately upon arising go through your morning prayers on your knees and read some religious text, even if it is only for six or seven minutes without concerning yourself about anything else or speaking to anyone. All depends on the right beginning for the day and the intention with which you begin it, for it may change even indifferent actions into good, even praiseworthy ones. You must be very strict about this, for it depends on you alone and your temporal and spiritual happiness may depend upon it. The same is true for the evening prayers and the review of the day's actions. . . . You will always write me and tell me which book you are using. You will pray during the day as often as you

*Chapter 3
Enlightened
Reformers:
Maria Theresa
(1717–1780)
and Joseph II
(1741–1790) of
the Habsburg
Monarchy*

can, especially during the celebration of Holy Mass. I hope you will attend it every day in the proper spirit, and twice on Sunday and holidays, if such is the custom at your Court. Much as I wish you to pray and read good books, however, you must always conform to French customs and never try to introduce anything new. You must not do anything unusual, nor cite our customs, nor ask that they be imitated; on the contrary, you must absolutely lend yourself to what the Court is accustomed to doing. Go, if you can, after dinner, and especially every Sunday to Vespers and to the *salut*. I don't know whether the French normally have the angelus rung; but pray at that time—if not in public, then at least in your heart. The same is true for the evening, or for when you pass a church or cross, without, however, behaving in ways other than the customary ones. . . .

. . . [D]emand that they tell you how, as a foreigner who wants to please your new country, you must behave; let them tell you sincerely whether there is anything that needs emending in your attitudes, your speeches, or the rest. Answer everyone pleasantly, with grace and dignity: you can if you want to.

. . . The Queen of Naples* wants to hear from you, I see no difficulty there. She will tell you only reasonable and useful things; her example should serve you as a model and an encouragement, her situation having been in everything and being still much more difficult than yours. She used her intelligence and a respectful manner to overcome many great obstacles; she has given me much pleasure and is well thought of everywhere: you may thus write her, but let everything be such that it can be read by anyone. Tear up my letters; it will allow me to write you more freely. I will do the same with yours. Do not expect to hear about domestic affairs here: they consist of nothing but uninteresting, boring facts. About your family you will speak truthfully but tactfully: even though I am seldom wholly pleased with them, you may find that others are worse, that there is simply childishness and jealousy about trifles, but that elsewhere it is about more important matters. One more point about the Jesuits. Say nothing, either for or against them. You may quote me and say I told you to speak neither good nor evil of them, that you know I respect them, that in my lands they have done much good, that I would be sorry to lose them, but that if the Pope decides to dissolve the order, I will do nothing to stop him; that I have always spoken well of them, but that even in my private circle I have never liked to talk about this wretched business.†

*Marie Carolina, Marie Antoinette's sister.

†Joseph II, unlike his mother, favored the dissolution of the order, which was finally ordered by the Pope in 1772.

DOCUMENT FOUR

FREDERICK II OF PRUSSIA

"Essay on the Forms of Government"

Frederick II of Prussia is often described as an "enlightened despot." According to his essay, what are the duties and responsibilities of a sovereign? Does he or she have absolute authority over their subjects?

A sovereign must possess an exact and detailed knowledge of the strong and of the weak points of his country. He must be thoroughly acquainted with its resources, the character of the people, and the national commerce. . . .

Rulers should always remind themselves that they are men like the least of their subjects. The sovereign is the foremost judge, general, financier, and minister of his country, not merely for the sake of his prestige. Therefore, he should perform with care the duties connected with these offices. He is merely the principal servant of the State. Hence, he must act with honesty, wisdom, and complete disinterestedness in such a way that he can render an account of his stewardship to the citizens at any moment. Consequently, he is guilty if he wastes the money of the people, the taxes which they have paid, in luxury, pomp, and debauchery. He who should improve the morals of the people, be the guardian of the law, and improve their education should not pervert them by his bad example.

Princes, sovereigns, and kings have not been given supreme authority in order to live in luxurious self-indulgence and debauchery. They have not been elevated by their fellow-men to enable them to strut about and to insult with their pride the simple-mannered, the poor, and the suffering. They have not been placed at the head of the State to keep around themselves a crowd of idle loafers whose uselessness drives them towards vice. The bad administration which may be found in monarchies springs from many different causes, but their principal cause lies in the character of the sovereign. A ruler addicted to women will become a tool of his mistresses and favourites, and these will abuse their power and commit wrongs of every kind, will protect vice, sell offices, and perpetrate every infamy. . . .

The sovereign is the representative of his State. He and his people form a single body. Ruler and ruled can be happy only if they are firmly united. The sovereign stands to his people in the same relation in which the head stands to the body. He must use his eyes and his brain for the whole community, and act on its behalf to the common advantage.

If we wish to elevate monarchical above republican government, the duty of sovereigns is clear. They must be active, hard-working, upright and honest, and concentrate all their strength upon filling their office worthily. That is my idea of the duties of sovereigns.

*Chapter 3
Enlightened
Reformers:
Maria Theresa
(1717–1780)
and Joseph II
(1741–1790) of
the Habsburg
Monarchy*

DOCUMENT FIVE

JOSEPH II

Letters

Taking up his duties as coregent in 1765, Joseph II drafted a confidential memorandum to his mother and her advisers. In this memo, Joseph details his principles for rule. Several years later, Joseph writes to his brother and eventual successor, Leopold of Tuscany, describing his enthusiasm and passion for rule. From these excerpts, can it be said that Joseph II was both enlightened and an absolutist?

CONFIDENTIAL MEMORANDUM FROM JOSEPH II TO MARIA THERESA

1765

Everything in the world can be good if one rids it of its faults and adds to its advantages. The greatest prejudice of all and the least pardonable is to fail to dare to attack or infringe prejudices. It requires great courage, and, still more, patriotism, to be an innovator in this day and age. Nothing is easier, no illusion is easier to instill, adopt and follow that of leaving things as you found them, without thinking further ahead. We shall make account one day of the good that we ought to have sought and accomplished . . . Great things should be done suddenly. All changes arouse controversy. It is better to publicize your intentions once for all, and, once your mind is made up, to refuse to listen to any opposition and to persist in carrying out unhesitatingly what you have determined on. Those who set only parts of a policy, cannot and must not criticize it. The aim of every measure is to have a total view, every action being related to the overall view, which only the monarch and his closest associates should share and pursue.

LETTER FROM JOSEPH II TO LEOPOLD OF TUSCANY

25 July 1768

Fortunately I have neither a wife nor any other distraction; and so, free from private cares or worries, I can attend to my duties. Patriotism, the welfare of the monarchy, these, dear brother, are my only passion, and they would inspire me to do anything. I am so preoccupied with them that I can never be at ease mentally or physically, unless I am sure of the welfare of the monarchy and the effectiveness of the measures we take. Nothing strikes me as too trivial or insignificant in this important task; every aspect interests me equally; I am just as concerned with the army as with finances.

DOCUMENT SIX

JOSEPH II

Abolishing the Mendicant Orders

Joseph II sought to control and reform the Roman Catholic Church and to rid the empire of contemplative orders. According to Joseph II, why should these orders be abolished?

LETTER FROM JOSEPH II TO MARIA THERESA

13 November 1771

In Bohemia alone . . . the clergy owns one seventh of all the real property of the kingdom; and in Moravia the religious foundations may perhaps own still more, mostly in return for the singing of masses (though it would be impossible to read so many masses, without confusing the times and the days); they nevertheless every day take money for over eight million masses and foundations—obviously fraudulently. What a wealth of reasons for abolishing the mendicant orders and for establishing a proper hierarchy for the furtherance of religion, befitting the true dignity of our most perfect Creator and Redeemer— what funds would be available for the holiest foundations, for increasing vicarages and schools, for building seminaries for priests and deserving church establishments, and lastly for foundlings' homes, orphanages, correctional institutions, workhouses, penitentiaries and hospitals, in which young people would be brought up as true Catholics and members of the State, foundling and orphans would be provided for, the idle removed from society, the wicked punished and rehabilitated and finally the weary and aged provided for.

This will certainly come closer to the perfection of God than the present idle and noisy life of most of the foundations and monasteries and even of the bishops and clergymen. They are all servants of God, as we are—but they are also servants of the State. . . . Recently, the following took place in the city of Prague: in last year's famine it is certain that five or six persons actually died in the streets, and many others fell ill and the holy sacraments were administered to them, also in the street; finally the townsfolk and others took them inside their own houses out of charity and relieved the starving persons or at least let them die peacefully. But though there is a wealthy archbishop there, an important capital, numerous religious foundations, three Jesuit palaces and innumerable monks, there is not one known example of their taking in a single one of the wretched people lying in front of their doors.

*Chapter 3
Enlightened
Reformers:
Maria Theresa
(1717–1780)
and Joseph II
(1741–1790) of
the Habsburg
Monarchy*

DOCUMENT SEVEN

Joseph II

Tolerance

Unlike his mother, the subject of religious toleration stirred Joseph II deeply. Shortly after Maria Theresa's death, Joseph II issued the Charter of Toleration in 1781. The first excerpt is a letter from Joseph to his mother explaining his views. The second excerpt is the charter. Why should the Habsburg state tolerate Protestantism? What rights are Protestants granted?

LETTER FROM JOSEPH II TO MARIA THERESA

20 July 1777

God forbid I should think it of no importance whether subjects turn Protestant or remain Catholic, still less whether they do not believe or at any rate do not observe the religion handed down by their fathers. I would give all I have to see all the Protestants in the country become Catholic. For me, tolerance simply means that in purely secular matters, I would, without considering their religion, employ those who were capable of it and who would bring profit or industry to the country, and allow them to own land, join the professions and be enfranchised. Those who, unfortunately, follow a false creed are much less likely to be converted if they remain in their own country than if they move to one where they see and hear the palpable truths of the Catholic faith. Likewise the peaceful exercise of their religion makes them better subjects and makes them avoid irreligion, which is more liable to seduce our Catholics than the observance by non-Catholics of their own religion. . . . I should be proud to present myself after death before that venerable judgement-seat which will decide my eternal fate. Certainly, no-one would become Lutheran or Calvinist; there would be fewer impieties in all religions and the State would greatly profit; and I cannot believe that all this would make me guilty in the eyes of God; at any rate this does not strike me as compatible with His perfection or the task which He has laid on me by placing me at the service of some fifteen million people.

CHARTER OF TOLERATION

20 October 1781

Faithful and beloved subjects! Convinced, on the one hand of the harmfulness of any coercion in matters of conscience, and on the other hand of the great benefit to religion and the State that derives from true Christian tolerance, we have been moved to grant to the Lutheran and Calvinist faiths and to the non-Uniate Greek faith a proper right to the private exercise of their religion, everywhere, whether or not this was previously customary or prescribed by law. The Catholic faith alone shall retain the privilege of the public exercise of religion, but for both of the Protestant faiths and the existing non-Uniate Greeks, in every locality where the number of persons and the resources of the inhabitants, as defined below, make it practicable, and non-Catholics do not already enjoy the public exercise of their religion, the private exercise of their religion shall be permitted. In particular we grant the following: . . .

Henceforth non-Catholics are to be permitted under a dispensation to purchase houses and property, to acquire municipal domicile and work as master-craftsmen, to receive academic degrees and to take up appointments in the civil service, and shall not be required to take any form of oath that is contrary to their religious principles, or to attend processions or functions of the dominant religion, unless they themselves wish to. No distinction on grounds of religion shall be made in the selection of awards of official appointments (this is standard practice in any case in the army and has proved to be without inconvenience and of great advantage). Appointments shall be made after proper consideration of the character and ability of the candidates and also their Christian and moral way of life.

Conflicting Ideals and the Promises of the French Revolution: Olympe de Gouges (1748–1793) and Maximilien Robespierre (1758–1794)

■ SETTING THE STAGE

A complex mix of volatile conditions, events, and people produced a revolution in France in the late eighteenth century. Economic pressures, ongoing contests over political power, social privilege and a rigid social order, and religious intolerance were all part of this mix. As many of these situations became critical, voices of popular protest were heard more often, and solutions to the problems were articulated more forcefully by educated and "enlightened" members of society.

The increasingly well-educated middle classes, or bourgeoisie, along with many members of the nobility, expressed their views and wishes with zeal and confidence. Intellectual exchange and a common political and cultural world were fostered by increased publication of books and newspapers and by the expansion of the numbers of eighteenth-century intellectual salons, often organized and sponsored by women of the upper bourgeoisie or nobility. Such social clubs, institutes, and academies dotted the landscape and provided forums for sharing new knowledge. The principles informing the debates and discussions in these settings had been laid in the previous century and included belief in the power of human reason and the application of rational principles to social, political, economic, and moral issues. By the eighteenth century, the search for natural laws was accompanied by general acceptance of the possibility of change or progress and by the desire for reforms to improve the lot of humanity. Calls for specific reforms in areas such as schools and prisons were accompanied by broader demands for individual freedoms of speech, press, assembly, and religious belief, and insistence that government itself should be based on reason, equitable procedures, and the consent of the governed.

In Europe, denunciations of tyranny, injustice, and privilege and calls for liberty and equality were even louder in the wake of the American War for Independence. The revolutionary forms of citizenship and representative government resulting from that conflict provided the concrete examples for ideals of transformation and progress. At the center of those changes was the individual citizen with rights and responsibilities. Similar ideas had taken root in France by the 1780s, and although conflicting ideas about what should be changed and by whom certainly existed, in general the energy and enthusiasm for reform multiplied.

France was governed by a monarchy whose absolute claims to power had been articulated by Louis XIV in the mid-seventeenth century. In theory, eighteenth-century rulers upheld those claims, but faced with the conditions described above, and with no other solution at hand, Louis XVI in 1788 agreed to call the Estates General to address the most pressing problems of the day. This action marked the beginning of the most radical, complex, and perhaps influential political movement of the time, the French Revolution.

By the spring of 1789, municipalities throughout France held elections for representatives to the Estates General. Simultaneously, in all the regions, lists of grievances and recommendations were solicited, collected, and given to the delegates to take with them to Paris. All the representatives were male, but women from various regions and social groups exercised their traditional right to petition and put forward their grievances as well. Multiple interests were thus represented when the Estates General began meeting in May 1789. Few people had long-term plans or a precise agenda for the meeting; there were no organized political parties and very few recognized national leaders. The agenda of the revolution was invented and changed as events unfolded. Leadership and political alliances shifted, constitutions and laws were written and rewritten, and diverse groups of people gathered together to rush onto the historical stage. It is impossible to describe all

Chapter 4
Conflicting Ideals
and the Promises
of the French
Revolution:
Olympe de
Gouges (1748–
1793) and
Maximilien
Robespierre
(1758–1794)

the political twists and turns or to hear all the voices, but by following two people who came to symbolize and embody the revolution and its goals— rightfully or not—we can begin to grasp the passions and practices of this great revolution that opened the modern era of politics.

Olympe de Gouges and Maximilien Robespierre were devoted to ideas of liberty and equality, and they believed that the revolution could and should produce a society of equal and virtuous citizens committed to the common good. Thus, for many, they represented the promises and potential of the revolution, for both good and bad. De Gouges and Robespierre were never allies and were often opponents. Whether they ever confronted each other face to face we will probably never know. But they certainly knew of each other. In the summer of 1793, de Gouges wrote a public essay in which she denounced Robespierre for corruption and aspirations to power. He was a member of the government that arrested her and then voted for her execution later that year. They disagreed politically, but in their fearless and public pursuit of radical goals, they became objects of attack and even ridicule. Typical in some ways of their fellow citizens, in others they were absolutely unique. Their lives, philosophies, and practices thus shed some light on the dynamics, controversies, and contradictions of the revolutionary experience.

▓ THE ACTORS:

OLYMPE DE GOUGES
AND MAXIMILIEN ROBESPIERRE

Marie Gouze was born in 1748 at Montauban in southern France. Her father, Pierre Gouze, was a butcher, and her mother, Olympe Mouisset, a trinket peddlar. Marie married Louis Yves Aubry, a restaurant owner, in 1765, and within a year their son Pierre was born.[1] This was not a particularly happy marriage, and when Yves died, Marie swore never to remarry, redesigned her name to Olympe de Gouges, and left her place of birth. By the 1770s, she and Pierre had moved to Paris, where her sister lived. Olympe perhaps had a small pension from her husband, but she also earned a living as a playwright and occasional actress.

1. For information on de Gouges, see Nupur Chaudhuri, "Olympe de Gouges' Perception of Marriage and Motherhood," in *The Consortium on Revolutionary Europe, 1750–1850: Proceedings to Commemorate the Bicentennial of the French Revolution* (Tallahassee, Fla.: Institute on Napoleon and the French Revolution, Florida State University, 1990), pp. 815–821; appropriate chapters in Catherine Montfort (ed.), *Literate Women and the French Revolution of 1789* (Birmingham, Ala.: Summa Publications Inc., 1994); Joan Scott, "'A Woman Who Has Only Paradoxes to Offer': Olympe de Gouges Claims Rights for Women," in Sara Melzer and Leslie W. Rabine (eds.), *Rebel Daughters: Women and the French Revolution* (New York: Oxford University Press, 1992), pp. 102–120; and Candice E. Proctor, *Women, Equality and the French Revolution* (Westport, Conn.: Greenwood Press, 1990). Also very useful is the introduction to the two-volume collection of her works by Olivier Blanc, *Écrits Politiques, 1788–93,* 2 vols. (Paris: Cote-femmes, 1993).

In eighteenth-century France, educational opportunities expanded but were not equal for girls and boys. Overall, the majority of the population was not literate, but illiteracy rates were highest among women. There is evidence that some working-class women could read newspapers and sometimes dictated their interests or grievances for the public record. Wages and work were determined by gender, and women had to struggle for any measure of economic independence. As in other parts of Europe, women had fewer property and inheritance rights than men, and wives were subject to their husbands' authority. Marriage was controlled by the church and divorce was almost impossible.[2] Olympe de Gouges's life reflects most of these conditions. She was self-taught and somewhat familiar with the writings of various Enlightenment thinkers. She apparently was not entirely comfortable with writing, but she was verbally eloquent, even inspired, and often dictated her plays and essays. De Gouges was certainly familiar with marital and economic inequities. Before the revolution she wrote, "Woman is in [men's] eyes a being useless in society," and complained that women were denied "the means to rise and to procure for themselves useful and durable resources."[3] She was a wife and a mother, but also an "emancipated woman" who supported herself as best she could and who deviated in many ways from the eighteenth-century standards of behavior for women. This was a contradiction that she lived, but also one that appeared in her writings.

After arriving in Paris, she stated, "I was obsessed by the desire to write, and also to publish," but had to struggle to do so.[4] Eventually ten of her plays were published and four were performed. They dealt with themes such as religious conformity, inequities in marriage, double standards of sexuality, and the injustices of slavery. A prolific writer—between 1788 and 1793, she produced seventy political pamphlets—she always wrote under her own invented name and refused to be called the widow Aubry. She also consistently argued for the creation of a second national theater where women's plays could be performed. In 1788 and early 1789, de Gouges made public her belief in the need for social and economic reform. In two pamphlets, she advocated a luxury tax structure to help solve some of France's fiscal problems and also proposed a program of social assistance for the unfortunate, the elderly, and children, and the building of a new maternity hospital. In the next four years, more and more of her energy focused on issues of citizenship and government, with particular emphasis on equal rights for women.

2. For conditions on the eve of the revolution, see Ruth Graham, "Loaves and Liberty: Women in the French Revolution," in R. Bridenthal and C. Koonz (eds.), *Becoming Visible*, 1st. ed. (Boston, Mass.: Houghton Mifflin, 1977); see also Darline Gay Levy and Harriet B. Applewhite, "A Political Revolution for Women? The Case of Paris," in R. Bridenthal, S. Stuard, and M. Wiesner (eds.), *Becoming Visible*, 3rd ed. (Boston, Mass.: Houghton Mifflin, 1998).

3. From essays in 1788 and 1789, quoted in Proctor, pp. 49 and 79.

4. Cited in Montfort, p. 23.

Chapter 4
Conflicting Ideals
and the Promises
of the French
Revolution:
Olympe de
Gouges (1748–
1793) and
Maximilien
Robespierre
(1758–1794)

Maximilien Robespierre's background and upbringing were quite different from those of Olympe de Gouges. He came from a long line of lawyers, including his grandfather and father, while his mother was the daughter of a successful brewer and innkeeper in the northern town of Arras, where Maximilien was born in 1758.[5]

At the time, the French society of about 25 million people included 250,000 nobles and 2.3 million bourgeois, or members of the middle classes, which included merchants, lawyers and other professionals, and skilled artisans. While it was possible to move up socially, the lines between the three social orders, or Estates, were clearly defined by specific status and privileges. The rigid social order did not create cohesion or unity in the individual ranks because of variations in economic and political power, education, and claims to longevity or tradition. In fact, values and goals were often shared across the estates, thus creating the possibilities for diverse social interactions and alliances. Maximilien and his family, as educated and economically comfortable members of the Third Estate, operated within such a social milieu.

Maximilien had a sister Charlotte (1760–1834) and a brother Augustin

(1763–1794) who survived childhood. Their mother died in childbirth in 1764, and their father was deeply affected by her death and the subsequent death of the child. In 1765, he abandoned his children to be raised by relatives and left Arras. He died in 1777. Maximilien and Augustin attended the local college of the Oratorians, while Charlotte was sent away to a convent school. In 1769, Maximilien won a coveted scholarship to the Louis-le-Grand school in Paris. At this combination secondary school and university he was a brilliant student and upon graduation in 1780, he received a prize that he used to set up a law practice in Arras. (He was also permitted to pass his scholarship on to Augustin.) In the meantime, Charlotte had been learning to read and write and had received instruction in religion and homemaking. The latter proved of use when Maximilien returned to Arras and set up a household with Charlotte in charge. His law practice was successful but not spectacular. Nevertheless, in the 1780s, several other developments pointed to things to come.

First, although raised in a conventional Catholic tradition and educated at schools with compulsory religious services, Maximilien seemed to abandon this training, ceased to be a practicing Catholic, and by the 1780s had become a confirmed deist. Second, both in his legal practice and in some of his early writings, he became a defender of the underprivileged and began to express interest in political reform. In 1785, he wrote an essay for an academic competition in which he demonstrated an intellectual debt to

5. For Robespierre's life and that of his family, see Colin Haydon and William Doyle (eds.) *Robespierre* (Cambridge, U.K.: Cambridge University Press, 1999); John Hardman, *Robespierre* (New York: Longman, 1999); J. M. Thompson, *Robespierre*, 3rd ed. (New York/Oxford: B. Blackwell, 1988), and Marilyn Yalom, *Blood Sisters: The French Revolution in Women's Memory* (New York: Basic Books, 1993) for Charlotte and her memoirs of her brothers.

Montesquieu and Rousseau by reflecting on the importance of political virtue. He stated, "The essential mainspring of republics is virtue . . . that is to say political virtue, which is no other thing than love of the laws and of the *patrie*; their very constitution requires that all particular interests, all personal ties, unceasingly give way to the general good."[6] Finally, while practicing law he also maintained an active social life, joining the local academy, participating in a literary society, and socializing with the town elite. He might even have had a brief engagement to his cousin at this time. But the pleasures of society and personal life were not his focus. Charlotte

later noted that, although he worked hard, he was also popular with the ladies and might have married "if the call of his co-citizens had not carried him away from the sweetness of private life and launched him upon a political career."[7] In a sense, just as Charlotte was devoted to her brother, he would be married to the revolution. When the call for the Estates General went out, Robespierre decided he would run, and he launched a vigorous and successful campaign to represent the Third Estate from his province, Artois. By May 1789, he had taken up residence in Paris and, like Olympe, was embarked on a career that would make him famous.

▪ ACT I:
MAY 1789–SEPTEMBER 1792

The summer of 1789 was tense and chaotic as representatives of the Third Estate declared themselves the National Assembly and prepared to create a new set of laws for France. Protests in Paris and in communities throughout France expressed popular fears that the king was about to use force against the Assembly to restore royal authority. On July 14, Parisians took to the streets and some citizens stormed the Bastille, a symbol of royal tyranny. Faced with the threat of rebellion, the king moved to embrace the popular movement, thereby legitimating the new political order that was emerging in France. The Assem-

bly was hard at work by August 1789, specifically attacking old feudal privileges and the special position of the church, and on August 26 it issued the Declaration of the Rights of Man and the Citizen (Document One). This document forcefully stated principles that would be fundamental to the revolution: the existence of natural human rights, the responsibility of government to uphold and protect these rights, equality before the law for all citizens, and popular sovereignty.

These were principles that both de Gouges and Robespierre believed in fervently. Over the next years, de Gouges would be dedicated to extending these rights to women as well

6. Quoted in Marisa Linton, "Robespierre's Political Principles," in Haydon and Doyle (eds.,) p. 44.

7. Quoted in *Memoires de Charlotte Robespierre sur ses deux frérès précèdes d'une introduction par Laponneraye* (Paris: Présence de la Revolution, n.d.) p. 39.

Chapter 4
Conflicting Ideals
and the Promises
of the French
Revolution:
Olympe de
Gouges (1748–
1793) and
Maximilien
Robespierre
(1758–1794)

as to men, while Robespierre's goals and actions always rested on the need to defend the declaration and its promises.

As an elected member of the new government, Robespierre frequently participated in floor debates on constitutional matters, calling for universal suffrage, for opening of military ranks to merit, for an end to all abuses of power, and for the rights of Jews and black slaves. Modestly dressed, living an orderly and frugal life, he gained a reputation for honesty and integrity, and by 1790 was known as "The Incorruptible." He was a shrewd tactician with good parliamentary skills. He argued persuasively in abstract, moral terms, and he articulated his revolutionary ideology in a consistent fashion. As he wrote, "before starting out, you must know where you want to end up and what routes you must take." He certainly could never control events as much as that statement advises, but as a colleague said of him: "He will go far, he believes everything he says."[8]

As Robespierre became more accomplished in his political role, he also developed a strong sense of his audience, and his colleagues often remarked that he spoke to the galleries (and even beyond to "the people") as much as he spoke to them. Olympe de Gouges at this time often attended sessions of the Assembly and proba-

bly heard him speak. She kept up with legislative developments and became more and more political as she published a deluge of pamphlets and nailed pamphlets to walls throughout Paris. Changes in marriage and divorce laws and in property and inheritance rights continued to be central issues for her. But above all, she believed in women's abilities to contribute to the betterment of society and in the goals of the revolution. As she wrote in 1791, "All is possible in this century of light and philosophers."[9]

Other developments in these years shaped the course of the revolution and provided the context within which de Gouges and Robespierre lived and acted. France had a long tradition of rural and urban uprisings. Such popular protests continued and became more frequent and influential. While they often were responses to economic pressures, the protestors also demanded rights as citizens of the nation.

On October 5, 1789, 6,000 to 7,000 Parisian women marched twelve miles to the royal palace at Versailles. Bread shortages in Paris prompted the action, but the crowd that arrived in Versailles also insisted that government had a responsibility to respond to its citizens' needs. They succeeded in forcing the king, his family, and the National Assembly to move to Paris, where the king agreed to accept the more limited role the constitution defined for him, and the Assembly accepted the popular mandate to govern

8. Quotes are from Patrice Gueniffey, "Robespierre," in Francois Furet and Mona Ozouf (eds.), *A Critical Dictionary of the French Revolution* (Cambridge, Mass.: Harvard University/ Belknap Press, 1989) pp. 305, 301.

9. Quoted in Proctor, p. 43

on behalf of the "nation." The links between subsistence issues and politics were thus forged early on, and the meanings of citizenship were expressed more forcefully. Neither de Gouges nor Robespierre were participants in the October march to Versailles or in succeeding examples of popular protest. But both claimed identities as citizens, and both believed in the bond between individual and nation and in the right of the people to have their voices heard. Instead of physically joining hands with crowds of people in popular protest, de Gouges and Robespierre chose other venues to reach their goals. For Robespierre and many others, membership in newly emerging political clubs became a major component of their public lives. Such clubs had origins in pre-revolutionary associations, but by 1790 their memberships, ideologies, and goals were much more clearly defined.

Almost as soon as he arrived in Paris, Robespierre had joined with like-minded deputies in a group that eventually became known as the Jacobins because they rented a hall in a convent of the Dominicans who were known popularly as the Jacobins. This location in the Rue Saint Honoré was quite near the center of Paris and the halls of government. By April 1790, when Robespierre was elected president of the club, it had established affiliations with many other similar associations through France, and circulars and correspondence kept the groups informed. The major goals of the clubs were to discuss matters being considered by the government and to try to influence government decisions. Once a new constitution was in place and elections were held, the Jacobins also became involved in electoral politics. Robespierre himself quickly saw the opportunities offered in this network of clubs and often publicized his ideas in speeches at the club in Paris. These speeches were then distributed to key provincial affiliates. For example, in the spring of 1791, Robespierre made a speech in the Assembly calling for universal male suffrage. The local press did not report it, so he distributed it widely through the Jacobin network. One of Robespierre's greatest successes was in the building of this national network, which became a center of power that could critique, pressure, and even challenge the existing government.

The Jacobins were not alone, however. In April 1790, the Society of the Friends of the Rights of Man and the Citizen was founded. It met originally in the Franciscan or "Cordelier" monastery, also fairly near the city center. The club had about 300 members drawn from groups of lawyers, journalists, merchants, and master tradesmen and was also connected to clubs outside Paris. They advocated universal suffrage and direct democracy and eventually moved to depose the king. By 1792, they advocated the use of terror against the wealthy, economic measures like price fixing to help the Parisian lower classes, and attacks on counterrevolutionaries. During the course of the revolution, numerous other clubs were formed, most of them less well-known and with shorter lifespans than the two just described. The

*Chapter 4
Conflicting Ideals
and the Promises
of the French
Revolution:
Olympe de
Gouges (1748–
1793) and
Maximilien
Robespierre
(1758–1794)*

Marquis de Condorcet, for example, was an influential member of the Federation of Friends of Truth, an organization that supported equal rights for men and women. De Gouges occasionally attended their meetings, but she never became a formal member of any group. The Jacobins allowed women to attend their meetings and even to address the club, but they had to sit in separate sections and had no vote. The Cordeliers admitted women but limited the number to sixty. Throughout France in these years, mixed sex clubs sprang up where men and women together voted and debated the issues of the day.

Finally, after 1789, women throughout the country who identified themselves as citizens acted in appropriate fashion by coming together to form at least thirty all-women's clubs. They established rules, elected officers, created networks, and read and discussed the actions of the National Assembly. After 1792, the groups became more radical when they sent petitions to the newly formed National Convention. Eventually in May 1793, the most famous of the women's clubs, the Republican Revolutionary Women, began to meet in the library of the Jacobin Club. Their goal was to enable women to act as full citizens of the new republic.

Olympe de Gouges apparently never joined any of these clubs, but her political activism was expressed in her essays and plays. Her verbal eloquence was the tool by which she hoped to influence revolutionary events and to encourage revolutionary leaders to grant to women the equal rights of citizenship that were being promised to men. She did not

stand alone in making these claims. A Dutch woman residing in France, Etta Palm d'Aelders (1743–?) made frequent speeches on women's behalf. One of these speeches, given before Condorcet's political club in December 1790, argued that "justice must be the first virtue of free men, and justice demands that the laws be the same for all beings, like the air and the sun."[10] Théroigne de Méricourt (1762–1817), a singer by profession, was an active revolutionary who founded a political club and participated in public demonstrations. She explained in her memoirs why she had worn trousers at a demonstration in 1789: "I was at ease playing the role of a man because I was always extremely humiliated by the servitude and prejudices under which men's pride keeps our sex oppressed."[11] Other unnamed women wrote letters to male political leaders, published essays in newspapers, and presented the government with petitions, insisting, as one woman put it in 1789, that women were "equally born for liberty."[12]

Some male political leaders expressed similar sentiments. The strongest support for women's rights came from radical liberal Condorcet, who advocated liberty and equality for all, regardless of gender, race, or class. In his 1790 essay, "On the Admission of

10. From Etta Palm d'Aelders, "Discourse on the Injustice of the Laws in Favor of Men, at the Expense of Women, December 30, 1790," in Lynn Hunt (ed.), *The French Revolution and Human Rights* (Boston, Mass.: St. Martins', 1996), pp. 122–123.

11. Yalom, p. 21.

12. Quoted in Proctor, p. 127, from *Motions adressees à l'Assemblée Nationale en faveur du sexe.*

Women to the Rights of Citizenship," he logically and persuasively argued that "either no individual in mankind has true rights, or all have the same ones" (Document Two). Thus, as the revolutionary government drafted a constitution for France, debates about rights and citizenship were commonplace, and various political groups with particular agendas and ideologies emerged, ready to influence or even steer a reformed government.

In September 1791, the new constitution was approved, but the tensions and conflicts beneath the accompanying celebrations pointed to the rocky revolutionary road ahead. Louis XVI and Marie Antoinette had been caught trying to flee France in June and were now seen by many as untrustworthy and not committed to a bonafide, workable, constitutional monarchy. During the summer, Robespierre had accused the king of attempting to undermine the constitutional process, thereby disregarding the sovereignty of the people, while the more radical Cordeliers were calling for abolition of the monarchy.

The new constitution itself was a disappointment to many. Voting was based on property qualifications; thus only about half of all adult men were enfranchised. They, in turn, chose electors whose property qualifications were even higher. Women were not included in the franchise at all. Equally troubling was the fact that freedom of speech and freedom of the press, included in the original Declaration of Rights, were no longer guaranteed. In light of her enthusiasm for the promises of the revolution, Olympe de Gouges was especially disappointed

in this document. Her response was to draft and make public, in September 1791, a Declaration of the Rights of Woman, in which she outlined her ideas of equality quite clearly (Document Three). With this document as her guide, she would insist in the months ahead that the realization of revolutionary goals required that women stand next to men, as equals in rights and responsibilities.

Different revolutionary agendas and distrust or suspicion of the monarchy and its allies plagued the Legislative Assembly when it began its work in October 1791. Food shortages and other economic pressures built support for an organized and more militant popular movement and for leaders who were willing to promote radical change. The government's declaration of war against the Austrian Habsburgs in April 1792 added to the crisis because France was unprepared for such a contest and fears of foreign invasion and retaliation grew. Enemies at home and abroad prompted Jacques Danton (1759–1794), another Jacobin lawyer, to insist later in 1792 that if they were to win the revolution and the war, "we must be bold, still more bold, ever bold, and France is saved."[13]

One person who was willing to be "bold" was Maximilien Robespierre. He did not sit in the Legislative Assembly and, in fact, had helped pass legislation in June 1791 that made sitting deputies ineligible for re-election. Although he returned home for a

13. Quoted in Leo Gershoy, *The French Revolution and Napoleon* (Englewood Cliffs, N. J.: Prentice, Hall, 1964), p. 221.

Chapter 4
Conflicting Ideals
and the Promises
of the French
Revolution:
Olympe de
Gouges (1748–
1793) and
Maximilien
Robespierre
(1758–1794)

vacation in the fall of 1791, this hardly meant his withdrawal from politics. He had been elected to the paying post of public prosecutor in the criminal court of Paris, and he held that position through the summer of 1792. He continued to be a key figure in the Jacobin club, giving at least 100 speeches until August 1792, and he also established a newspaper that became a new forum for his essays and orations. He continued to oppose the monarchy and to call for universal male suffrage. He accused the Marquis de Lafayette (1757–1834), who was the leader of the Parisian National Guard, of wanting to establish a military dictatorship, and he feared war mongering because he felt at that point war would mean defeat of the revolution. At the same time, he extolled the virtues of army volunteers and elevated the common people as representatives of devotion to country and civic morality. In April 1792 at the Jacobin Club, various members claimed to speak for "the people." In the debate that ensued, Robespierre declared his position: "I am not the courtier, nor the moderator, nor the tribune, nor the defender of the people, I am the people myself!"[14] Ironically, in this disciplined, austere, and even priggish man, the moral fervor and passion of the revolution were to be embodied.

Popular protests about economic issues had opened the year 1792. But claims to political rights and citizenship, and patriotic calls to defend the revolution and the nation were heard more often. Between March and June, thousands of armed men and women marched to the assembly hall. Their ac-

tions linked the rights of citizenship with the right to fight for the *patrie*. Women in particular made this claim. On March 6, Pauline Léon appeared before the Assembly to present a petition, signed by 316 women, claiming women's right to bear arms as the natural right of every citizen to defend his or her life and liberty. They insisted, "You cannot refuse us . . . this right which nature gives us, less it is alleged that the Declaration of Rights is not applicable to women and that they must allow their throats to be slit, like sheep, without having the right to defend themselves."[15] Léon (b. 1768) was a Parisian chocolate maker, active in the revolutionary protests since 1789, and a member of the Cordeliers Club since 1791, and in 1793 she was a leader of the Republican Revolutionary Women.

Later in 1792, the last play Olympe de Gouges wrote reflected similar themes. The settings for "L'entrée de Dumourier à Bruxelles ou les Vivandiers" are military camps and battlefields, and women demonstrate their usefulness to the nation in war. The women warriors proclaim that at last men will learn "that women are able to die by their side for the common cause of the country and the destruction of tyrants." In the play, de Gouges imagines the real-life General Dumourier praising the actions of the women, saying that "the men of the French Republic will be no less equitable toward your sex in a natural revolution that must extend to everyone, without distinction."[16]

Women's calls to be included in the

14. Cited in Haydon and Doyle, p. 22.

15. Quoted in Levy and Applewhite, p. 280
16. Quoted in Montfort, pp. 213–214.

citizen forces defending the revolution were not received with enthusiasm by most members of the government. Nevertheless, some women did fight in revolutionary units, and many women participated in the escalating popular protests and militancy of the summer of 1792. During those months, the municipal government of Paris was taken over by more radical representatives of the popular assemblies in the city. The local sections, various political clubs, and particularly the Cordeliers pushed for an end to the monarchy and prepared for the insurrection on August 9, 1792, that ended with the deposition and arrest of Louis XVI. The Legislative Assembly responded by summoning a National Convention, elected by universal male suffrage, that would decide the fate of the king and draw up a new constitution.

During the summer months, Robespierre did not support insurrection, arguing instead that the law was the best weapon for revolutionary change. He did accept the call to end the monarchy and to call a constitutional convention, and on August 12 was elected to the new government of the municipality or Commune of Paris. On September 5, the city chose him as one of its first representatives to the National Convention. Robespierre was now in a position to realize his dream of a revolutionary republic. Over the next two years, Robespierre's influence on the course of the revolution expanded dramatically.

In the meantime, Olympe de Gouges expressed her opposition to the use of violence by *any* party and argued that liberty could not be won by bloodshed. She was also won over to the republican cause after August 10, 1792. But apparently some of her optimism for revolutionary change to grant women equal rights of citizenship was dampened by this time. In one of her essays written that year, she lamented, "Oh, my poor sex, oh women, who have acquired nothing in this revolution . . ."[17] That was not entirely true. By the end of September 1792, marriage was a civil contract and divorce was legal, and over the next year other reforms would give women more equal inheritance and property rights. But the full measures of citizenship—the rights to vote, to sit in government, and to defend the nation—were still denied to women.

ACT II:

SEPTEMBER 1792–JULY 1794

Between September 1792 and the end of July 1794, Robespierre moved from a position of opposition and radical critique of the government to become one of its most influential and powerful political figures. In this span of time, he served as a deputy to the National Convention and occasionally was its chair. On July 27, 1793, he joined the Committee of Public Safety (CPS), which had been created in April to defend the revolution. This body soon became the center of power in the government, initiating many of the "extraordinary" measures taken to preserve the republic and the nation.

17. Quoted in Proctor, p. 128.

Chapter 4
Conflicting Ideals
and the Promises
of the French
Revolution:
Olympe de
Gouges (1748–
1793) and
Maximilien
Robespierre
(1758–1794)

In the spring of 1794, he took over the police bureau. All the while, he maintained his connections with the Jacobins and his popular base in the Paris Commune.

Robespierre did not act alone in these two years and continued to have support in the Convention as late as June 1794, when he was elected its president by a landslide. Robespierre often provided general principles to support specific government actions, and his rhetorical arguments were persuasive. In the Convention's debates about what to do with the king, Robespierre's words were powerful and convincing. He argued that the king was a traitor who stood in the way of revolutionary change and called for a speedy trial and death without delay. His speech on December 3, 1792, was a ringing call to protect the republic and the revolution. In his words, "Louis must die in order that the nation may live" (Document Four). At the conclusion of the trial in January 1793, the Convention voted overwhelmingly to support the charge of treason, a majority supported the death penalty, and Louis was beheaded on January 21. These events solidified the will and position of Robespierre and his followers, but they also drew the lines for a power struggle between Robespierre and his more moderate opponents.

Shortages of necessities and high prices enabled Robespierre to tighten his connection with the Parisian *sans culottes* and the radical leaders of the Commune. Military defeats and betrayal by several leading generals, coupled with uprisings in the countryside, produced a crisis and eventually another popular insurrection in Paris in May 1793. This time, the targets were the moderate republicans, the Girondins, who were also Robespierre's opponents, and he backed their arrests and trials. Eventually twenty-nine people were indicted, and although most of them were able to flee Paris and hide for a time, their removal left Robespierre's Jacobins in charge of the government. Although the Convention continued to meet and adopted a fully democratic constitution, by July power was concentrated in the hands of the CPS and the police, and the "Terror" began. To put out the fires of rebellion, to wage war effectively, and to guarantee the future of liberty, freedom, and civic virtue, Robespierre demanded that they attack counterrevolutionaries and punish traitors.

Robespierre was closely linked with the politics of terror, which became more severe after he joined the CPS. Indeed, he provided a philsophy or a justification for the use of terror and for the suppression of dissent. He saw the world as divided between good and evil, virtue and vice, patriotism and counterrevolution, and he believed that terror in the service of republican virtue was moral. Following the ideas of Rousseau, he fervently hoped the revolution would provide a new kind of citizen, devoted to civic duty and acting for the common good, and he argued that such citizens could be created through education (propaganda) and independence, but also through the example of punishment. On several different occasions, he made eloquent and persuasive speeches in the Convention that linked terror and virtue and provided an ideology of repression (Document Five).

Olympe de Gouges was one of the people caught in this sweep of the revolution's "enemies." Her "sins" were numerous. In the fall of 1792, she directly accused Robespierre of conspiring to create a despotism that would enslave the people, and in the debates over the fate of the king, de Gouges had defended Louis XVI, arguing that execution would make him a martyr and could only lead to more bloodshed. She also believed that the people should decide Louis's fate and thus sided with those who wanted a national referendum on the question. At least informally, this put her within the Girondin camp, and this connection was made stronger when she also spoke against the popular uprising at the end of May. In early June, she published her *Political Testament*—a document in which she called for an uprising against the Jacobins and denounced Robespierre and another radical leader, Marat, as "corrupt and ambitious 'insects' with dictatorial aspirations."[18] She was arrested in July and kept in prison for the next three months. During this time she managed to smuggle out and have printed two pamphlets that exposed prison conditions, accused Robespierre of destroying the nation because of his ambition, and affirmed her loyalty as a French citizen. At her trial, de Gouges's writings were used against her. Her call to end factionalism and warfare in France by letting the people vote for a republic *or* a constitutional monarchy was especially incriminatory (Document Six). This was surprising to her because she had felt if the tribunal examined her body

of work, they would see her devotion to the revolution.

She was given a chance to recant but would not, and she was executed on November 3, 1793. To the end, she claimed a public identity. In her last letter to her son, Pierre, written the day before her execution, she described her herself as "the most virtuous woman of her century," and stated, "I die, my dearest son, a victim of my worship of the nation and the people."[19] Throughout her life, she had demanded equal citizenship and insisted she be treated as a political actor in her own right. The court and her executioners inadvertently recognized this when they punished her for making her political opinions public through her writing.

In a short time, de Gouges and several other visible political women fell victim to the Terror. The queen, Marie Antoinette; Charlotte Corday, the Girondin who murdered Marat; and Madame Roland, wife of an important Girondin leader, were executed, while Etta Palm spent some time in prison and then returned to her home in the Dutch republic. How did Robespierre view these women and their fates? In general, he disliked publicly active women, viewing them as unnatural. As a follower of Rousseau, he believed women's sphere of virtuous action was the home, where they maintained good republican households and raised the future citizens of the republic (Document Seven). Several of the women named above were criticized by other

---

18. Ibid., p. 164.

19. Quoted in Benoite Groult (ed.) *Olympe de Gouges: Oeuvres* (Paris: Mercure de France, 1986), pp. 57–58.

Chapter 4
Conflicting Ideals
and the Promises
of the French
Revolution:
Olympe de
Gouges (1748–
1793) and
Maximilien
Robespierre
(1758–1794)

political leaders for being "femmes-hommes" or "women-men." And a newspaper report of November 19, 1793, accused de Gouges and others of "forgetting the virtues of [their] sex."

While the government of the Convention and the CPS were responsible for a reign of terror, they also passed legislation that reformed the army. The officer-corp was opened to talent and officers were made responsible to their men. The new officer was to be a patriot, a model of courage, devoted to the republic, and a defender against tyranny, and Robespierre wholeheartedly supported this view. General conscription accompanied the plans for reorganization, and all citizens were called to sacrifice for the nation. Most of Robespierre's colleagues agreed that he knew little of military science, but the spirit of this popular army suited his vision. He had no qualms about using the army to put down internal rebellion, and he supported purges of officers who were not loyal revolutionaries.

Robespierre also supported price fixing, which placed a maximum cost on certain basic commodities. He did not favor redistribution of property or workers' demands for better wages, and he was not sympathetic when women, who were working to produce goods for the war, called for a bread allotment. In fact, as early as June 1793, Robespierre and the CPS had begun to attack many radicals, the popular clubs, and the urban sections that had been their strongest supporters in the previous months.

The actions and politics of the Cordeliers and the militant leaders of the Commune and the Society of Republican Revolutionary Women were all scrutinized and condemned in the months that followed. All these actors supported the need to defend the revolution and saw themselves as patriotic citizens. However, they did not necessarily support concentration of power in the hands of a few, and their economic demands went beyond what the CPS was willing to support. The Republican Revolutionary Women committed the additional crime of taking public action and demanding a greater role in the revolutionary process (Document Eight). On October 30, about the same time as de Gouges was facing a revolutionary court, the National Convention heard a report prepared by Jean Baptiste Amar on women's political behaviors and club activities. Accusing them of causing unrest and public disorder that threatened the revolution, the report also prescribed appropriate roles and rights of virtuous women. The Convention then voted to prohibit clubs and popular societies of women, no matter what their politics.

Targeted political leaders protested the efforts to restrict their activities and in the spring of 1794, when acute food shortages in Paris produced a crisis, radical political leaders and working men and women called for an insurrection against the Jacobin government for its failures to provide for the people. As a result, numerous leaders of the Cordeliers and the Commune were executed, and others were arrested and imprisoned. Almost simultaneously, Convention deputies like Danton, who argued for an end to the Terror and the war, were also arrested and executed. Robespierre was a key figure in these developments, fearing on the one hand the militancy of the people, and on the other what he saw as weakness or failure of will among Convention members.

Having eliminated opposing factions, it appeared Robespierre could now concentrate on creating a "Republic of Virtue." The establishment of a new secular religion that would promote civic morality and rest on simple deist principles was a move toward that goal. In early June 1794, a public ceremony celebrated this effort at spiritual and political revival. Robespierre presided over this festival, which was attended by most of the population of Paris, and explained that the supreme being had created both liberty and virtue and that one could not exist without the other. The salvation of the republic, and thereby of mankind, depended on purity and wisdom and a campaign against vice and evil. Perhaps this Festival of the Supreme Being was the happiest day of Robespierre's life.[20] He was taking a public, ceremonial role, but to many he also looked like a head of state, or even a dictator, and this occasion marked both the zenith of his power and the beginning of his decline.

Robespierre had already lost the popular support of many Paris neighborhoods and portions of the working classes. Members of the government ridiculed his new religion, but also increasingly feared what they saw as his desire for power. By mid-June he was quarrelling with members of the CPS, stopped attending their meetings, and focused his energies on the police bureau. Passage of a new law to speed up trials and executions of suspected people brought even more arrests and deaths. Robespierre himself was more disillusioned and bitter as he watched the effects of the Terror and growing desires to end it and to halt the radical momentum of the revolution.

Finally, on July 27, opposition in the Convention coalesced and Robespierre was accused of being a tyrant, an outlaw, and a traitor to the government. The Convention voted for his arrest, along with his closest associates and his brother, Augustin. With little opposition, they were taken into custody and the next evening, July 28 (or 10 Thermidor on the new revolutionary calendar), Maximilien Robespierre was guillotined along with twenty-one others. Within a short time, another eighty-six persons were executed because of their attachment to Robespierre and his ideas.

▓ FINALE

By the time Robespierre was killed, the army of the revolution was winning victories and the frontiers of France were secured. Very quickly, these same forces would take the offensive, spreading revolutionary change to other parts of Europe. This professional army was perhaps one of the most successful creations of the revolution and would be the springboard to power for Napoleon Bonaparte. The fires of internal civil war were also almost

20. Hardman, p. 123.

*Chapter 4
Conflicting Ideals
and the Promises
of the French
Revolution:
Olympe de
Gouges (1748–
1793) and
Maximilien
Robespierre
(1758–1794)*

extinguished, even though working-class protests over economic conditions continued in 1794 and 1795. The Convention still governed France and moved to dismantle the Terror, strip the CPS of its powers, and restrict activities by political clubs and the Paris Commune. Legislation mandating fixed prices was rescinded, as were most of the changes relating to marriage, divorce, and women's property rights.

In May 1795, the Convention specifically decreed that women could not enter its galleries, attend political assemblies, or gather publicly in groups of more than five. On the question of the place of women in the society and in the revolution, Robespierre and his opponents alike agreed with Rousseau's ideas on separate spheres for men and women. The idealization of republican motherhood remained long after 10 Thermidor and provided the basis for denying to women all the rights guaranteed in the Declaration of the Rights of Man and claimed for women by de Gouges in her Declaration in 1791.

This ideology of differences between men and women and the exclusion of women from public politics and conflict was a major legacy of the revolution. During these years of conflict, the very real actions of thousands of individuals had claimed different spaces and capacities for women, and the political writings of people like Condorcet, Palm, and de Gouges had established the principles of natural and equal political rights for all. Belief in universal human rights remained a potent force in European politics as subsequent generations struggled for equal citizenship and access to power.

In addition to radical ideas of liberty, equality, and democracy, the revolution also defined the lines of debate about how those principles should be enacted or guaranteed and by whom. While de Gouges and Robespierre were equally passionate in their defense of revolutionary change, they had quite different perspectives on the use of force to achieve virtuous ends. Nevertheless, de Gouges broke the rules of appropriate behavior for women, and Robespierre's single-minded vision of the new republic was too extreme or frightening for many of his contemporaries. While committed and courageous, neither had the power to save themselves. Later generations would disagree violently about the significance of these two people. De Gouges would be seen as a symbol of liberty and a feminist foremother, or the example of the disasters that occur when women step out of their "natural" place. Robespierre would be the incorruptible model of virtue who epitomized the will to struggle for "the people," or he would be a monster and a warning against further calls for revolution. Given their actual experiences during the revolution, the fact that they are companions in history would probably come as a surprise to both.

■ QUESTIONS

1. Both Robespierre and de Gouges had radical visions of change for France, but they had quite different perspectives on the use of force to achieve those changes. In what ways do they disagree? Why do you think they had such different views?

2. What hopes and goals did Robespierre have for the revolution? Were they realized?

3. What factors made Robespierre a successful leader in the revolution? What factors brought his downfall?

4. During the revolution, different people put forward various ideas about women's nature and demanded different changes in women's status. What were some of these varied opinions and demands? What factors might explain why individuals held certain views or made particular claims? Were any of the desired changes realized?

5. In what ways were men's and women's experiences in the revolution similar? In what ways were they different?

6. What is the legacy of both Robespierre and de Gouges for the postrevolutionary world?

■ DOCUMENTS

DOCUMENT ONE

THE NATIONAL ASSEMBLY

"The Declaration of the Rights of Man"
(August 26, 1789)

After the creation of the National Assembly in June 1789, members of the Assembly began to issue decrees that changed the way power was exercised in France. In their deliberations, they took into account complaints that had been registered by the population of France in the previous years, and they were influenced by Enlightenment ideas of reason, natural law, and freedom. The document that follows was to provide the groundwork for a new government and clearly states the fundamental rights of French citizens. What is the basis for these claims to rights? What are the most important rights set forth in this document? For the time, which of the claims are the most radical? Which seem quite moderate?

The representatives of the French people, organized as a National Assembly, believing that the ignorance, neglect, or contempt of the rights of man are the sole causes of public calamities and of the corruption of governments, have

Chapter 4
Conflicting Ideals
and the Promises
of the French
Revolution:
Olympe de
Gouges (1748–
1793) and
Maximilien
Robespierre
(1758–1794)

determined to set forth in a solemn declaration the natural, inalienable, and sacred rights of man, in order that this declaration, being constantly before all the members of the social body, shall remind them continually of their rights and duties; in order that the acts of the legislative power, as well as those of the executive power, may be compared at any moment with the objects and purposes of all political institutions and may thus lie more respected; and, lastly, in order that the grievances of the citizens, based hereafter upon simple and incontestable principles, shall tend to the maintenance of the constitution and redound to the happiness of all. Therefore the National Assembly recognizes and proclaims, in the presence and under the auspices of the Supreme Being, the following rights of man and of the citizen:

ARTICLE 1. Men are born and remain free and equal in rights. Social distinctions may be founded only upon the general good.

2. The aim of all political association is the preservation of the natural and imprescriptible rights of man. These rights are liberty, property, security, and resistance to oppression.

3. The principle of all sovereignty resides essentially in the nation. No body nor individual may exercise any authority which does not proceed directly from the nation.

4. Liberty consists in the freedom to do everything which injures no one else; hence the exercise of the natural rights of each man has no limits except those which assure to the other members of the society the enjoyment of the same rights. These limits can only be determined by law.

5. Law can only prohibit such actions as are hurtful to society. Nothing may be prevented which is not forbidden by law, and no one may be forced to do anything not provided for by law.

6. Law is the expression of the general will. Every citizen has a right to participate personally, or through his representative, in its formation. It must be the same for all, whether it protects or punishes. All citizens, being equal in the eyes of the law, are equally eligible to all dignities and to all public positions and occupations, according to their abilities, and without distinction except that of their virtues and talents.

7. No person shall be accused, arrested, or imprisoned except in the cases and according to the forms prescribed by law. Any one soliciting, transmitting, executing, or causing to be executed, any arbitrary order, shall be punished. But any citizen summoned or arrested in virtue of the law shall submit without delay, as resistance constitutes an offense.

8. The law shall provide for such punishments only as are strictly and obviously necessary, and no one shall suffer punishment except it be legally inflicted in virtue of a law passed and promulgated before the commission of the offense.

9. As all persons are held innocent until they shall have been declared guilty, if arrest shall be deemed indispensable, all harshness not essential to the securing of the prisoner's person shall be severely repressed by law.

10. No one shall be disquieted on account of his opinions, including his religious views, provided their manifestation does not disturb the public order established by law.

11. The free communication of ideas and opinions is one of the most precious of the rights of man. Every citizen may, accordingly, speak, write, and print with freedom, but shall be responsible for such abuses of this freedom as shall be defined by law.

12. The security of the rights of man and of the citizen requires public military forces. These forces are, therefore, established for the good of all and not for the personal advantage of those to whom they shall be intrusted.

13. A common contribution is essential for the maintenance of the public forces and for the cost of administration. This should be equitably distributed among all the citizens in proportion to their means.

14. All the citizens have a right to decide, either personally or by their representatives, as to the necessity of the public contribution; to grant this freely; to know to what uses it is put; and to fix the proportion, the mode of assessment and of collection and the duration of the taxes.

15. Society has the right to require of every public agent an account of his administration.

16. A society in which the observance of the law is not assured, nor the separation of powers defined, has no constitution at all.

17. Since property is an inviolable and sacred right, no one shall be deprived thereof except where public necessity, legally determined, shall clearly demand it, and then only on condition that the owner shall have been previously and equitably indemnified.

Chapter 4
Conflicting Ideals
and the Promises
of the French
Revolution:
Olympe de
Gouges (1748–
1793) and
Maximilien
Robespierre
(1758–1794)

DOCUMENT TWO

CONDORCET

"On the Admission of Women to the Rights of Citizenship" (1790)

As a member of the French nobility and a participant in revolutionary govern-
ment from 1789–1793, Condorcet was one of the strongest advocates of equal
rights for all French people, regardless of gender, race, or class. In this document,
he addresses the fact that women were excluded from the rights of citizenship and
questions this predicament. What arguments does he use to support his insistence
that men and women should have equal rights?

Now the rights of men result simply from the fact that they are sentient beings, capable of acquiring moral ideas and of reasoning concerning these ideas. Women, having these same qualities, must necessarily possess equal rights. Either no individual of the human species has any true rights, or all have the same. And he who votes against the rights of another, of whatever religion, color, or sex, has thereby abjured his own.

It would be difficult to prove that women are incapable of exercising the rights of citizenship. Why should individuals exposed to pregnancies and other passing indispositions be unable to exercise rights which no one has dreamed of withholding from persons who have the gout all winter or catch cold quickly? Admitting for the moment that men possess a superiority of mind which is not the necessary result of their different education (this is by no means proved, and it should be before women can be deprived of a natural right without injustice), this inferiority can consist only in two points. It is said that no woman has made any important discovery in the sciences, or has given any proof of the possession of genius in the arts, literature, etc.; but it is not pretended that the rights of citizenship should be accorded only to men of genius. It is added that no woman has the same extent of knowledge, the same power of reasoning as certain men. But that only proves that, with the exception of a limited number of exceptionally enlightened men, there is absolute equality between women and the remainder of the men; that this smaller class of men apart, inferiority and superiority are equally divided between the two sexes. Since it would be completely absurd to restrict to this superior class the rights of citizenship and the eligibility for public functions, why should women be excluded from them any more than those men who are inferior to a great number of women?

Will it be said, further, that there exists in the minds and hearts of women certain qualities which ought to exclude them from the enjoyment of their natural rights? Let us first interrogate the facts. Elizabeth of England, Maria Theresa, the two Catherines of Russia, have shown that women lack neither force of character nor strength of mind. . . .

It has been said that women, in spite of much ability, much sagacity, and a power of reasoning carried to a degree equalling that of subtle dialecticians, are never governed by what is called reason.

This observation is not correct. Women are not governed, it is true, by the reason of men. But they are governed by their own reason. Their interests not being the same as those of men through the fault of the laws, the same things not having the same importance for them as for us, they can (without lacking reason) govern themselves by different principles and seek a different goal. It is as reasonable for a woman to concern herself with her personal attractions as it was for Demosthenes to cultivate his voice and his gestures.

It has been said that women, although superior in some respects to men— more gentle, more sensitive, less subject to those vices which proceed from egotism and hardness of heart—do not really possess the sentiment of justice; that they obey their feelings rather than their conscience. This observation is more correct, but it proves nothing. It is not nature, but education, and social existence, that causes this difference. Neither the one nor the other has accustomed women to the idea of what is just. Instead, they have taught women what is "proper." They are excluded from public affairs, from all that is decided according to rigorous ideas of justice or positive laws. The things with which they are occupied and upon which they act are precisely those which are regulated by natural propriety and sentiment. It is therefore unjust to allege, as an excuse for continuing to refuse women the enjoyment of their natural rights, grounds which only have a kind of reality because women do not exercise these rights.

If reasons such as these were admitted against women, it would also be necessary to deprive of the rights of citizenship that portion of the people who, because they are occupied in constant labor, can neither acquire knowledge nor exercise their reason. Soon, little by little, only persons who had taken a course in public law would be permitted to be citizens. If such principles are admitted, we must, as a natural consequence, renounce any idea of a free constitution. The various aristocracies have had nothing but similar pretexts as their foundation or excuse; the very etymology of the word is proof of this.

Neither can the dependence of wives upon their husbands be alleged against their claims, since it would be possible at the same time to destroy this tyranny imposed by civil law. The existence of one injustice can never be grounds for committing another.

Chapter 4
Conflicting Ideals
and the Promises
of the French
Revolution:
Olympe de
Gouges (1748–
1793) and
Maximilien
Robespierre
(1758–1794)

═══════════ **DOCUMENT THREE** ═══════════

OLYMPE DE GOUGES

"The Declaration of the Rights of Woman"
(September 1791)

De Gouges builds her declaration on the previous "Declaration of the Rights of Man" (Document One). Although she addresses the declaration to the queen (Marie Antoinette), does she appear to be an uncritical supporter of the queen? How does de Gouges explain women's subordinate position in society? What rights are claimed or issues raised in this essay that are not in the earlier declaration of 1789? What concerns does she express that do not appear in Condorcet's essay? How do her experiences help to shape the claims she makes?

If the foreigner bears arms into France, you are no longer in my eyes this falsely accused Queen, this attractive Queen, but an implacable enemy of the French. Oh, Madame, bear in mind that you are mother and wife; employ all your credit for the return of the Princes. This credit, if wisely applied, strengthens the father's crown, saves it for the son, and reconciles you to the love of the French. This worthy negotiation is the true duty of a queen. Intrigue, cabals, bloody projects will precipitate your fall, if it is possible to suspect that you are capable of such plots.

Madame, may a nobler function characterize you, excite your ambition, and fix your attentions. Only one whom chance has elevated to an eminent position can assume the task of lending weight to the progress of the Rights of Woman and of hastening its success. . . .

THE RIGHTS OF WOMAN

Man, are you capable of being just? It is a woman who poses the question; you will not deprive her of that right at least. Tell me, what gives you sovereign empire to oppress my sex? Your strength? Your talents? Observe the Creator in his wisdom; survey in all her grandeur that nature with whom you seem to want to be in harmony, and give me, if you dare, an example of this tyrannical empire. . . .

Man alone has raised his exceptional circumstances to a principle. Bizarre, blind, bloated with science and degenerated—in a century of enlightenment and wisdom—into the crassest ignorance, he wants to command as a despot a sex which is in full possession of its intellectual faculties; he pretends to enjoy the Revolution and to claim his rights to equality in order to say nothing more about it.

[108]

DECLARATION OF THE RIGHTS OF WOMAN AND THE FEMALE CITIZEN

For the National Assembly to decree in its last sessions, or in those of the next legislature:

Preamble

Mothers, daughters, sisters [and] representatives of the nation demand to be constituted into a national assembly. Believing that ignorance, omission, or scorn for the rights of woman are the only causes of public misfortunes and of the corruption of governments, [the women] have resolved to set forth in a solemn declaration the natural, inalienable, and sacred rights of woman in order that this declaration, constantly exposed before all the members of the society, will ceaselessly remind them of their rights and duties; in order that the authoritative acts of women and the authoritative acts of men may be at any moment compared with and respectful of the purpose of all political institutions; and in order that citizens' demands, henceforth based on simple and incontestable principles, will always support the constitution, good morals, and the happiness of all.

Consequently, the sex that is as superior in beauty as it is in courage during the sufferings of maternity recognizes and declares in the presence and under the auspices of the Supreme Being, the following Rights of Woman and of Female Citizens.

Article I

Woman is born free and lives equal to man in her rights. Social distinctions can be based only on the common utility.

Article II

The purpose of any political association is the conservation of the natural and imprescriptible rights of woman and man; these rights are liberty, property, security, and especially resistance to oppression.

Article III

The principle of all sovereignty rests essentially with the nation, which is nothing but the union of woman and man; no body and no individual can exercise any authority which does not come expressly from it [the nation].

*Chapter 4
Conflicting Ideals
and the Promises
of the French
Revolution:
Olympe de
Gouges (1748–
1793) and
Maximilien
Robespierre
(1758–1794)*

Article IV

Liberty and justice consist of restoring all that belongs to others; thus, the only limits on the exercise of the natural rights of woman are perpetual male tyranny; these limits are to be reformed by the laws of nature and reason. . . .

Article VI

The law must be the expression of the general will; all female and male citizens must contribute either personally or through their representatives to its formation; it must be the same for all: male and female citizens, being equal in the eyes of the law, must be equally admitted to all honors, positions, and public employment according to their capacity and without other distinctions besides those of their virtues and talents. . . .

Article X

No one is to be disquieted for his very basic opinions; woman has the right to mount the scaffold; she must equally have the right to mount the rostrum, provided that her demonstrations do not disturb the legally established public order.

Article XI

The free communication of thoughts and opinions is one of the most precious rights of woman, since that liberty assures the recognition of children by their fathers. Any female citizen thus may say freely, I am the mother of a child which belongs to you, without being forced by a barbarous prejudice to hide the truth; [an exception may be made] to respond to the abuse of this liberty in cases determined by the law. . . .

Article XIII

For the support of the public force and the expenses of administration, the contributions of woman and man are equal; she shares all the duties [*corvées*] and all the painful tasks; therefore, she must have the same share in the distribution of positions, employment, offices, honors, and jobs [*industrie*].

Article XIV

Female and male citizens have the right to verify, either by themselves or through their representatives, the necessity of the public contribution. This can only apply to women if they are granted an equal share, not only of wealth, but also of public administration, and in the determination of the proportion, the base, the collection, and the duration of the tax. . . .

Article XVI

No society has a constitution without the guarantee of rights and the separation of powers; the constitution is null if the majority of individuals comprising the nation have not cooperated in drafting it.

Article XVII

Property belongs to both sexes whether united or separate; for each it is an inviolable and sacred right; no one can be deprived of it, since it is the true patrimony of nature, unless the legally determined public need obviously dictates it, and then only with a just and prior indemnity.

Postscript

Woman, wake up; the tocsin of reason is being heard throughout the whole universe; discover your rights. The powerful empire of nature is no longer surrounded by prejudice, fanaticism, superstition, and lies. The flame of truth has dispersed all the clouds of folly and usurpation. Enslaved man has multiplied his strength and needs recourse to yours to break his chains. Having become free, he has become unjust to his companion. Oh, women, women! When will you cease to be blind? What advantage have you received from the Revolution? . . .

I take up my text again on the subject of morals. Marriage is the tomb of trust and love. The married woman can with impunity give bastards to her husband, and also give them the wealth which does not belong to them. The woman who is unmarried has only one feeble right; ancient and inhuman laws refuse to her for her children the right to the name and the wealth of their father; no new laws have been made in this matter. If it is considered a paradox and an impossibility on my part to try to give my sex an honorable and just consistency, I leave it to men to attain glory for dealing with this matter; but while we wait, the way can be prepared through national education, the restoration of morals, and conjugal conventions.

FORM FOR A SOCIAL CONTRACT BETWEEN MAN AND WOMAN

We, _____ and _____ , moved by our own will, unite ourselves for the duration of our lives, and for the duration of our mutual inclinations, under the following conditions: We intend and wish to make our wealth communal, meanwhile reserving to ourselves the right to divide it in favor of our children and of those toward whom we might have a particular inclination, mutually recognizing that our property belongs directly to our children, from whatever bed they come, and that all of them without distinction have the right to bear the name of the fathers and mothers who have acknowledged them, and we are charged to subscribe to the law which punishes the renunciation of one's own

Chapter 4
Conflicting Ideals
and the Promises
of the French
Revolution:
Olympe de
Gouges (1748–
1793) and
Maximilien
Robespierre
(1758–1794)

blood. We likewise obligate ourselves, in case of separation, to divide our wealth and to set aside in advance the portion the law indicates for our children, and in the event of a perfect union, the one who dies will divest himself of half his property in his children's favor, and if one dies childless, the survivor will inherit by right, unless the dying person has disposed of half the common property in favor of one whom he judged deserving.

That is approximately the formula for the marriage act I propose for execution. . . .

DOCUMENT FOUR

MAXIMILIEN ROBESPIERRE

"Asking for the Death Penalty for Louis XVI" (December 3, 1792)

In this speech to the National Convention, Robespierre stated his opinion on the fate of the king and argued for the death penalty. What are the reasons he gives for executing the king? This was a radical step to take. Why do you think Robespierre was ready to make this argument?

CITIZENS! Without its knowledge, the Constituent Assembly has been turned aside from its proper task. The point is not merely that of trying the King. Louis is not the accused. You are not the judges! You are—you cannot be other than statesmen, the representatives of the nation. You have not to give a judgment for or against an individual; on the contrary, you must adopt a measure of public welfare, achieve an act of national wisdom. In a republic, a dethroned king is a source of danger; he will either endanger the safety of the state and attempt to destroy liberty, or he will take steps to consolidate both.

Now, I maintain that your deliberations hitherto directly oppose this end. What, after all, is the attitude prescribed by sound policy in order to strengthen the infant republic? Our object should be to engrave deep in the hearts of men a contempt for royalty, and to terrify all the King's supporters. Now, if you will present his crime to the world as a problem, his cause as the object of the most imposing, most painstaking, most difficult discussion that could engage the attention of the representatives of the French people, if you will thus place a great, incommensurable distance between what once he was, and the dignity of a plain citizen, you will have discovered the true secret of permitting him to remain a danger to liberty.

Louis was King and the Republic was founded. The question before you is disposed of by these few words alone. Louis was dethroned by his crimes.

Louis denounced the French people as counterrevolutionaries; to conquer them he summoned the armies of the tyrants, his brothers. The victory and the masses have decided that it was he who was the rebel. Louis cannot be judged. He is already condemned, or we have no republic.

Louis must die in order that the nation may live. In more peaceful times, once we have secured respect and have consolidated ourselves within and without, it might be possible for us to consider generous proposals. But to-day, when we are refused our freedom; to-day, when, after so many bloody struggles, the severity of the law as yet assails only the unhappy; to-day, when it is still possible for the crimes of tyranny to be made a subject of discussion; on such a day there can be no thought of mercy; at such a moment the people cries for vengeance. I request you to come to a decision at once concerning the fate of Louis.

DOCUMENT FIVE

Maximilien Robespierre

"Report on the Principles of Public Morality" (February 5, 1794)

Robespierre made this speech to the National Convention at a time when France was engaged in a foreign war and during the period of the Terror. In this document, he justifies the extreme measures taken to protect the revolution. In what situations and for what purposes is the use of terror acceptable? How is the use of terror tied to Robespierre's broader visions of a society of just and virtuous citizens?

What is the purpose, what is the goal for which we strive? We wish a peaceful enjoyment of freedom and equality, the rule of that eternal justice whose laws are graven not in marble or in stone, but in the hearts of all men. We wish a social order that shall hold in check all base and cruel passions, which shall awaken to life all benevolent and noble impulses, that shall make the noblest ambition that of being useful to our country, that shall draw its honorable distinctions only from equality, in which the generality shall safeguard the welfare of the individual, and in which all hearts may be moved by any evidence of republican spirit. . . . We want morality in the place of egotism, principles in the place of mere habit, the rule of reason in the place of the slavery of tradition, contempt for vice in the place of contempt for misfortune, the love of glory in the place of avarice. Honest men instead of "good society," truth instead of empty show, manly greatness instead of the depravity of the great, a sublime, powerful, victorious and happy people!

[113]

Chapter 4
Conflicting Ideals
and the Promises
of the French
Revolution:
Olympe de
Gouges (1748–
1793) and
Maximilien
Robespierre
(1758–1794)

You are surrounded beyond the boundaries; at home, all the friends of the tyrants conspire, and will continue to conspire, so long as treason still has a hope. We must stifle the domestic and foreign enemies of the Republic, or we must be destroyed with the Republic. And therefore, under the present circumstances, the principle of our Republic is this: to influence the people by the use of reason, to influence our enemies by the use of terror.

In times of peace, virtue is the source from which the government of the people takes its power. During the Revolution, the sources of this power are virtue and terror: virtue, without which terror will be a disaster; and terror, without which virtue is powerless. But terror is nothing more nor less than swift, severe and indomitable justice. . . .

It is impossible for you to conceive of all the devious ways pursued by all these sowers of discord, these spreaders of false rumors, who disseminate every possible kind of false report, which is not unprofitable in a country in which, as in ours, superstition is still so widespread. . . .

The domestic situation of our country demands your entire attention. Remember that it is our duty simultaneously to make war against the tyrants of all Europe, to keep fed and equipped an army of 1,200,000 men, and that the government is obliged ceaselessly to keep down with due energy and caution all our internal foes, as well as to repair all our defects. . . .

DOCUMENT SIX

OLYMPE DE GOUGES

"The Three Ballot-Boxes, or the Salvation of the Nation" (July 19, 1793)

This essay appeared as a public bill or placard on July 19, 1793. Its framework is a worldwide, aerial journey by an imaginary figure who is observing the errors and crimes of humankind. Among these are the most recent events in France. But a solution for France's problems is then proposed. In her public trial, de Gouges was accused of violating a law that proclaimed no one could speak against the one and indivisible republic, and this document was used as proof. What does she propose in this document? Does this seem to be enough justification for her arrest, imprisonment, and execution?

It is time that death rest, and anarchy return to the underworld. . . .

Several departments [in France] are dissatisfied and lean toward federalism; the royalists are in force within and without the country; the constitutional government, one and indivisible, is in a minority, but courageous. Blood flows everywhere; that strife shocks my eyes! It is time that the fighting cease. . . .

I would like the Convention to enact the decree that I am going to dictate to you. The Convention, affected by great suffering, seeing France divided by opinions and principles about the form of government that should save the nation, proposes at first, in the name of humanity, to stop the warfare [internal and external] for a month to allow the whole nation the time to judge among the three forms of government that divide it. It will direct all the departments to call primary assemblies: three ballot boxes will be placed on the table by the President of the assembly, each will carry one of these inscriptions: Republican government, one and indivisible; federal government; monarchy.

The president will proclaim, in the name of the endangered nation, the free and individual choice for one of the three governments. . . . The government which obtains the majority of the votes, will be preceded by a universal and solemn oath of respect by each of the citizens individually. A great celebration will accompany that solemn act and is the means, both humane and conclusive, that will calm passions, destroy the parties . . . the rebellion will dissipate; powerful enemies will demand peace; and the World [that for such a long time] has observed the dissensions in France, will exclaim: The French are invincible!

DOCUMENT SEVEN

JEAN JACQUES ROUSSEAU

Émile, or a New System of Education
(1762)

Although this essay was written long before the outbreak of the revolution in France, Rousseau's ideas found avid supporters in some of the most radical leaders of the revolution. In other of his writings, Rousseau had called for equal citizenship for all men and had advocated a government by the "General Will," or the will of the majority acting in the interests of the good of society. Rousseau hoped for a new body of virtuous citizens who could act in this fashion. The education system he proposes in Émile is designed to meet that goal. He did not think the world of public politics was the appropriate sphere for women. Rousseau does acknowledge, however, that Émile will need a "helpmeet," and he describes this ideal companion in Book V, "Sophy, or Woman." What does he see as woman's nature and her social function? Why does he oppose women taking an active role in politics? How might his ideas have influenced the way that Robespierre felt about someone like Olympe de Gouges?

[115]

*Chapter 4
Conflicting Ideals
and the Promises
of the French
Revolution:
Olympe de
Gouges (1748–
1793) and
Maximilien
Robespierre
(1758–1794)*

We have reached the last act of youth's drama; we are approaching its closing scene.

It is not good that man should be alone. Emile is now a man, and we must give him his promised helpmeet. That helpmeet is Sophy. . . .

Sophy should be as truly a woman as Emile is a man, i.e., she must possess all those characters of her sex which are required to enable her to play her part in the physical and moral order. Let us inquire to begin with in what respects her sex differs from our own.

But for her sex, a woman is a man; she has the same organs, the same needs, the same faculties. The machine is the same in its construction; its parts, its working, and its appearance are similar. Regard it as you will the difference is only in degree.

Yet where sex is concerned man and woman are unlike; each is the complement of the other; the difficulty in comparing them lies in our inability to decide, in either case, what is a matter of sex, and what is not. General differences present themselves to the comparative anatomist and even to the superficial observer; they seem not to be a matter of sex; yet they are really sex differences, though the connection eludes our observation. How far such differences may extend we cannot tell; all we know for certain is that where man and woman are alike we have to do with the characteristics of the species; where they are unlike, we have to do with the characteristics of sex. Considered from these two standpoints, we find so many instances of likeness and unlikeness that it is perhaps one of the greatest of marvels how nature has contrived to make two beings so like and yet so different. . . .

I am quite aware that Plato, in the *Republic,* assigns the same gymnastics to women and men. Having got rid of the family there is no place for women in his system of government, so he is forced to turn them into men. That great genius has worked out his plans in detail and has provided for every contingency; he has even provided against a difficulty which in all likelihood no one would ever have raised; but he has not succeeded in meeting the real difficulty. I am not speaking of the alleged community of wives which has often been laid to his charge; this assertion only shows that his detractors have never read his works. I refer to that political promiscuity under which the same occupations are assigned to both sexes alike, a scheme which could only lead to intolerable evils; I refer to that subversion of all the tenderest of our natural feelings, which he sacrificed to an artificial sentiment which can only exist by their aid. Will the bonds of convention hold firm without some foundation in nature? Can devotion to the state exist apart from the love of those near and dear to us? Can patriotism thrive except in the soil of that miniature fatherland, the home? Is it not the good son, the good husband, the good father, who makes the good citizen?

When once it is proved that men and women are and ought to be unlike in constitution and in temperament, it follows that their education must be different. Nature teaches us that they should work together, but that each has its own share of the work; the end is the same, but the means are different, as are also the feelings which direct them. We have attempted to paint a natural man, let us try to paint a helpmeet for him. . . .

All the faculties common to both sexes are not equally shared between them, but taken as a whole they are fairly divided. Woman is worth more as a woman and less as a man; when she makes a good use of her own rights, she has the best of it; when she tries to usurp our rights, she is our inferior. It is impossible to controvert this, except by quoting exceptions after the usual fashion of the partisans of the fair sex.

To cultivate the masculine virtues in women and to neglect their own is evidently to do them an injury. Women are too clear-sighted to be thus deceived; when they try to usurp our privileges they do not abandon their own; with this result: they are unable to make use of two incompatible things, so they fall below their own level as women, instead of rising to the level of men. If you are a sensible mother you will take my advice. Do not try to make your daughter a good man in defiance of nature. Make her a good woman, and be sure it will be better both for her and us.

Does this mean that she must be brought up in ignorance and kept to housework only? Is she to be man's handmaid or his helpmeet? Will he dispense with her greatest charm, her companionship? To keep her a slave will he prevent her knowing and feeling? Will he make an automaton of her? No, indeed, that is not the teaching of nature, who has given women such a pleasant easy wit. On the contrary, nature means them to think, to will, to love, to cultivate their minds as well as their persons; she puts these weapons in their hands to make up for their lack of strength and to enable them to direct the strength of men. They should learn many things, but only such things as are suitable. . . .

The children's health depends in the first place on the mother's, and the early education of man is also in a woman's hands; his morals, his passions, his tastes, his pleasures, his happiness itself, depend on her. A woman's education must therefore be planned in relation to man. To be pleasing in his sight, to win his respect and love, to train him in childhood, to tend him in manhood, to counsel and console, to make his life pleasant and happy, these are the duties of woman for all time, and this is what she should be taught while she is young. The further we depart from this principle, the further we shall be from our goal, and all our precepts will fail to secure her happiness or our own.

Chapter 4
Conflicting Ideals
and the Promises
of the French
Revolution:
Olympe de
Gouges (1748–
1793) and
Maximilien
Robespierre
(1758–1794)

DOCUMENT EIGHT

"The Regulations of the Society of Revolutionary Republican Women" (July 1793)

The Society of Revolutionary Republican Women was an organization connected to the Paris sections and to members of the Cordeliers Club. They were strong supporters of the republic and of more radical policies in the National Convention. This document describes their organization and its goals. How do their goals compare to the demands made by de Gouges in The Declaration of the Rights of Woman (Document Three)? How do their ideas reflect the views of people like Robespierre or other leaders of the Terror? By the fall of 1793, the Convention would vote to ban this women's group and all other such women's organizations. Given the political goals they state here, why do you think they were banned?

Convinced that there is no liberty without customs and principles, and that one must recognize one's social duties in order to fulfill one's domestic duties adequately, the Revolutionary Republican *citoyennes* have formed a Society to instruct themselves, to learn well the Constitution and laws of the Republic, to attend to public affairs, to succor suffering humanity, and to defend all human beings who become victims of any arbitrary acts whatever. They want to banish all selfishness, jealousies, rivalry, and envy and to make good their [Society's] name.

But besides the spirit and principle of a Society, there still must be a particular rule which lays down all the conditions of the Society; consequently they [the Revolutionary Republican *citoyennes*] have drawn up the following regulations:

ARTICLE I

The Society's purpose is to be armed to rush to the defense of the Fatherland; *citoyennes* are nonetheless free to arm themselves or not. . . .

[ARTICLE] XII

The Society, believing that people should join together only for mutual honor, support, and encouragement in virtue, has decreed that it will receive in its midst only those *citoyennes* of good habits; it has made this the most essential condition for admission and has resolved that the lack of good habits is one of the principal reasons for exclusion. . . .

[ARTICLE] XV

All newly received *citoyennes* will be summoned by the President, in the name of the Society, to take the following oath: "I swear to live for the Republic or die for it; I promise to be faithful to the Rule of the Society as long as it exists." . . .

[ARTICLE] XIX

All the members of the Society make up a family of sisters, and since an arbitrary act against one of its members must attack the whole Society, the one who suffered the violation of the laws is urged to inform the Society, which will obtain justice for her. . . .

[ARTICLE] XXVI

Believing that no member can be denied the right to speak and that young *citoyennes* could, with the best of intentions, compromise the Society with ill-considered motions, the Society decrees that one must be eighteen years old to be received as a member; however, mothers may bring children younger than eighteen, but they will have no right to deliberate.

National Politics and Industrial Society in the Nineteenth Century

The Passions of Nationalism: Giuseppe Mazzini (1805–1872) and Giuditta Bellerio Sidoli (1804–1871)

■ SETTING THE STAGE

After the defeat of the French Empire and the end of the era of revolution in 1815, the victorious powers at the Congress of Vienna set about restoring the geographic and political map of Europe. While they were able to re-create boundaries and reinstate "legitimate" authorities, they could not erase the legacy of the revolution. The idea that free and equal citizens should choose their leaders and govern themselves, combined with the desire for freedom from foreign controls, produced powerful constitutional and national aspirations. The nineteenth century was marked by contests between conservative, even reactionary governments seeking to maintain their power and movements fighting for freedom and national independence.

Chapter 5
The Passions
of Nationalism:
Giuseppe Mazzini
(1805–1872)
and Giuditta
Bellerio Sidoli
(1804–1871)

The peninsula of Italy was in turmoil after 1815. The French imperial occupation had brought constitutional change, legal reforms, and possibilities of economic development to many areas. It also had fostered anti-French, antiforeign sentiments and the beginnings of a sense of Italian national identity. At the Congress of Vienna, Italy was divided into several small political states dominated by monarchs, the nobility, the military, and church authorities. Among these were the kingdoms of Naples and Sicily in the south; the Papal States, stretching from Rome to the north and east and ending around Bologna; the duchies of Modena, Parma, and Tuscany that had familial ties to the Habsburgs; the territories of Lombardy and Venetia directly under Habsburg control; and the kingdom of Piedmont-Sardinia, governed by the House of Savoy, the only rulers without foreign ties or controls.

To varying degrees in each of these areas, competing economic interests and social groups emerged as the result of developments in agriculture, industry, and commerce. Though the propertied and educated classes constituted barely 2 percent of the total population, many of them had ideas and goals that conflicted with the ideology of restoration. Popular unrest and sporadic rebellions added to an increasingly volatile mix of forces competing for change in Italy. In 1820 and 1821, a revolt in the south, an up-

rising in the Piedmont, and agitation in Lombardy and Venetia were crushed fairly easily by reactionary conservative elites. Although generally the rebels had called for independence and a constitution, they lacked popular support, precise plans of action, or concrete political aims. However, the overall consequences of their actions were, on the one hand, even harsher controls or repression, and on the other, the emergence of new leaders and movements with more clearly defined goals.

As the histories of other revolutionary traditions have shown, the process of creating such movements is difficult, the odds against their success seem unsurmountable, and the costs for individuals involved are great. Nevertheless, men and women chose to take the necessary risks. Many people in Italy in the nineteenth century were willing to dedicate their resources and their lives to altering the worlds in which they lived. Exemplary models of such activism and leadership are the partners and patriots, Giuseppe Mazzini and Giuditta Bellerio Sidoli. Both of them dreamed of a unified Italian nation based on principles of equality and freedom; both were fired by romantic ideas of progress for all humanity. The courses of their lives were shaped, although in dramatically different ways, by the events and struggles that resulted in the unification of Italy in 1870.

■ THE ACTORS:

GIUSEPPE MAZZINI AND GIUDITTA BELLERIO SIDOLI

Mazzini and Sidoli were born and grew up in the era of French occupation and influence in Italy, and after 1815 witnessed the results of the restoration of traditional governments. Giuseppe's birthplace, Genoa, was attached to the kingdom of Piedmont; Giuditta's home was in Milan in Lombardy, and this area was returned to the Austrian Habsburgs at the Congress of Vienna. Both of them were acquainted at an early age with revolutionary ideas of liberty and freedom, but they were also exposed to vague notions of Italian identity that emerged in response to foreign intervention in the peninsula.

Mazzini's father, Giacomo, was a professor of medicine at the University of Genoa. Mazzini senior believed in the democratic ideals of the French Revolution and was not enthusiastic about the 1815 restorations. At the same time, he was not terribly political and did not encourage such activism in his son. Maria Mazzini was more ardent about politics than her husband and was firmly convinced that God had some great mission for her son. Giuseppe was clearly a precocious child, apparently learning to read by the age of four; early on he studied Latin classics and concluded that a republic, a commonwealth, or a government by the people was superior to monarchy.[1] After an excellent

early private education, Giuseppe's father pushed him to study medicine, but that avenue was not successful because Mazzini was squeamish about dissections. Between 1822 and 1827, he studied law at the university, but this course of study bored him. Instead he loved literature, history, and politics. He read widely and by 1830 had published several literary articles in which he began to talk about a "common European consciousness," but he also argued that desires for Italian unity could be traced back to Dante's love of country.

As a teenager, in 1820–1821, Mazzini witnessed the cycle of failed revolutions that called for constitutional governments and the eviction of the Austrians from Italy. From this he learned that people could and did sacrifice themselves for political ideals. By 1829, he had joined the Genoese branch of the *carbonari*, secret societies with widespread connections throughout Europe that originally had been created to fight the French. By the 1820s, they advocated struggle against the restoration governments and espoused vaguely defined goals of personal freedom and political independence for Italy. Their equally vague visions of nationality appealed to Mazzini, but he was disappointed because instead of debates about political issues with

1. There are many sources on Mazzini's life. Among the most recent and useful are Roland Sarti, *Mazzini: A Life for the Religion of Politics*

(Westport, Conn.: Praeger Press, 1997), and Denis Mack Smith, *Mazzini* (New Haven, Conn.: Yale University Press, 1994). Also useful in placing Mazzini's life in the context of the history of Italian national movements are Harry Hearder, *Italy in the Age of the Risorgimento, 1790–1870* (London: Longman, 1983), and Spencer Di Scala, *Italy From Revolution to Republic* (Boulder, Colo.: Westview Press, 1995).

Chapter 5
The Passions
of Nationalism:
Giuseppe Mazzini
(1805–1872)
and Giuditta
Bellerio Sidoli
(1804–1871)

like-minded patriots, he found he was simply supposed to take orders from other secret conspirators.

Disappointment turned to disaster in November 1830 when he was betrayed to Piedmontese authorities by a companion and subsequently imprisoned. Three months later, for lack of evidence, he was released but he faced further surveillance and was now even more motivated to promote revolutionary change. He went into exile in France. Ironically, Mazzini, who would spend his entire life and most of his energy and resources fighting for Italian unity and independence, by 1830 had lived only in Genoa and had visited Tuscany twice. For the next forty years, he would live abroad, mostly in England or Switzerland, often under threat of expulsion or sought by authorities. When he did return to Italy, he usually traveled under a false name and lived in hiding. Not surprisingly in these conditions, one of his great weapons was his pen. Eventually ten thousand or more of his letters were collected in one-hundred published volumes, but it is estimated that hundreds of thousands of other epistles simply disappeared. Among his many letters are those addressed to Giuditta Bellerio Sidoli, whom Mazzini referred to as his great personal and intellectual passion.

Giuditta Bellerio came from a prominent aristocratic family in Milan. Her father held various administrative posts and in 1809 had been named baron of the Kingdom of Italy by Napoleon I. Although the title probably did not survive the restoration of Austrian control in the duchy of Milan, the Bellerio family certainly maintained its elite social position, and for five years Giuditta attended a prestigious girl's school in Milan, where she received a good classical education.[2] In 1820, she married Giovanni Sidoli (?1795–1828), whose family had considerable landed and commercial interests in Reggio, in the nearby duchy of Modena. Such a marriage arrangement would have been quite common at the time, even though she was much younger than he.

Giovanni Sidoli, raised in a world of patriotic ideals, was apparently a member of the *carbonari* and involved in the uprisings of 1820–1821. Those actions failed and the co-conspirators fled to Switzerland to avoid arrest (and in Giovanni's case, the death penalty). Giuditta was pregnant at the time, but once her daughter Marietta was born, she left her with the Sidoli grandparents and joined her husband in Switzerland in the summer of 1823. For the next five years, the Sidolis lived in exile, surrounded by their political companions. Giuditta helped create a community, a "little Italy" in exile, and began to demonstrate the intelligence and charisma that others noted throughout her life. As one

2. No biography of Giuditta Sidoli exists in English. In Italian, see Adriano Bassi, *Le eroine del Risorgimento: Amore e politica femminile* (Brescia: Zanetti Editore, 1996). Most of the information that follows is derived from primary materials. See, for example, Gabriella Marini (ed.), *Nuovi documenti su Giuditta Sidoli* (Pisa: Domus Mazziniana, 1957); Emilio del Cerro (pseud. for Nicola Niceforo), *Giuseppe Mazzini e Giuditta Sidoli* (Turin: S.T.E.N., 1909); Livio Pivano, *Mazzini e Giuditta Sidoli* (Modena: Guanda, 1936); and Giuseppe Mazzini, *Lettere d'amore,* introduced and edited by Gaetano Gasperoni (Turin: Union tipografico-editrice torinese, 1927).

companion remarked, she had "none of the defects common to women . . . She was one of those personalities who leaves a trail of light wherever she goes."[3] She and Giovanni had three children in those years. Life in exile became more difficult when Giovanni was taken ill, and even a move to a warmer climate in southern France did not help. He died in February 1828, and Giuditta had little choice but to return to her in-laws in Reggio (Modena). It appears that the elder Sidolis maintained close connections to the Austrian administration in Modena and were not patriots or sympathetic to their son's politics.

On the other hand, Giuditta's political consciousness was awakened by her husband's fate and the years of exile, and upon returning to Italy she felt she had to continue her husband's struggle. Her brother Carlo was also a patriot and a conspirator, and that might have strengthened her resolve. In 1830, she joined a network of revolutionary committees throughout Italy that was organized by the Modenese liberal, Ciro Menotti, who hoped for independence, union, and liberty for Italy under a representative monarchy. Once again, in 1830–1831, revolutions erupted in Italy, and once again they failed. While the idea of unification and independence certainly seemed to have taken root, how this would be achieved and the form it would take were not clear. Menotti and some of his comrades were arrested and executed. Giuditta had participated in the rebellion in Reggio by taking to the streets and waving the patriot's flag of red, white, and green. As a result, she was banned from the duchy and once again left Italy, leaving her children in the custody of their grandfather, Bartolomeo Sidoli. Carlo also had to flee, and together the siblings arrived in Marseilles in the late summer of 1831. By then, large numbers of Italian political radicals had taken up residence in that city, and Giuseppe Mazzini was among them. There he would establish his first political organization, enunciate the principles of Italian unity that inspired a generation of patriots, and meet Giuditta Sidoli, with whom he formed an intense romantic relationship and a political partnership.

■ **ACT I:**

THE CREATION OF A MOVEMENT, 1830–1848

By 1831, Giuseppe Mazzini was familiar with the writings of most of the prominent revolutionary figures in Europe. The program and ideology he developed thus had roots in an intellectual tradition that preceded him. But he was able to blend those ideas into a plan for national union and a national revolution in both politics and morals. The country he hoped to create would be a fellowship of free and equal men and women bound together by common principles and goals. For him, association was both a

3. Quoted in Del Cerro, p. 41.

Chapter 5
The Passions
of Nationalism:
Giuseppe Mazzini
(1805–1872)
and Giuditta
Bellerio Sidoli
(1804–1871)

human right *and* a duty. Through such connections, individual persons became a people. He acknowledged "God's finger on the pages of History," but insisted that in his era the actors in the divine plan were the people, united in nations, and nations, united in a human commonwealth defined by justice and freedom. Human progress was inevitable in such a plan, and inequalities of class or sex would disappear as social and economic problems were solved through political means. Instead of class warfare, or antagonisms produced by gender inequity, Mazzini foresaw cooperation in a common human endeavor. Just as individuals would associate for the general welfare, so would nations cooperate for the progress of humanity.

Mazzini provided the inspiration for several generations of Italians struggling for independence and unity; but he did more than encourage others to dream—he also insisted on action. In his own life and in the organizations and plans he produced, he gave form and structure to more abstract ideals. Most scholars agree that he cemented the ideals of the *Risorgimento* (or national revival), and fanned the flames of insurrection. Always dedicated to a unified Italian republic free of foreign influences, Mazzini also insisted that Italians, on their own, could achieve this goal if they gathered together in associations dedicated to revolution and unity.

In August 1831 in Marseilles, he founded a movement named "Young Italy." Although at first he decreed that all members had to be under forty, he quickly changed his mind, acknowledging that youth was defined by spirit and commitment, not calendar years. Young Italy would operate in the light of day; it would attempt to reach out to the people through both education and insurrection. Guerilla bands would be the instruments of change to form "the military education of the people and [consecrate] every foot of native soil by the memory of some warlike deed" (Document One). Popular warfare would create the patriots/citizens who would eventually form the government of the new nation.

The organization of Young Italy was quite modern. A central group, which included Mazzini and his closest associates, headed the movement, while every Italian province had a three-person committee that appointed organizers for their regions. Members who possessed both courage and intellect would help to initiate or educate those who had the "heart" but not yet the "mind" for the business of militant revolution. By 1832, Mazzini's organization had spread to several Italian regions, particularly the Piedmont (including Genoa), Lombardy, and the city of Naples, and by 1833, its membership was estimated to be between 50,000 and 60,000 people. The organization published a newspaper of the same name, *Young Italy*, which was closely controlled by Mazzini. Funding for the movement and its publications was always a challenge and came from wealthy Italian supporters of unification, foreigners who also believed in the cause, and from Mazzini himself. Although his family was not wealthy, they did provide him with a stipend; in 1850, he received a small legacy from an aunt, and his mother left him a small annuity after her death in 1852. (She put it in the trust of a Genoese banker so Mazzini would not give it all away at once; it was common for him to support other political refugees.)

By the fall of 1831, Giuditta and Carlo Sidoli were also in residence in Marseilles, and their home was the center of the community of exiled patriots from Modena, many of whom were charter members of Young Italy. When Sidoli and Mazzini met, the attraction was mutual. He was a charming, enthusiastic, honest young man, romantically dressed in black with long, curly black hair and a black beard, and he played the guitar and loved to smoke cigars. Her personal charm and magnetism matched his, and her beauty and intelligence were notable. Although there were other women in the activist community, most of them were married to co-conspirators. Giuditta thus stood out as a single woman of independent means because her family continued to provide her with support, even while in exile and traveling on a Swiss passport. As Mazzini wrote to a friend two years later, "when I saw her, I swore to myself never to love another person in the world."[4] In the next year, they established a personal and working relationship because Giuditta often handled the finances for Young Italy and was privy to the plans for insurrections. She was also the interme-

diary for Mazzini's correspondence as well as communication with his friends, particularly by 1832, when his reputation as a clever and dangerous conspirator was blossoming, and the Austrian, Piedmontese, and papal governments were putting pressure on the French to expel him.

In August 1832, Giuditta gave birth to a son, Adolphe, whose father, to the best of our knowledge, was Mazzini. They did not publicly acknowledge the birth because such recognition would have harmful consequences. Sidoli's father-in-law still had custody of her four children and she feared his reaction if he knew about her relationship with Mazzini. Similarly, for Mazzini, the possible scandal could have destroyed his cause. At about the time Adolphe was born, the new French government of Louise Philippe (r. 1830–1848) ordered the conspirators to leave the country. Complicating matters even more, by early 1833 several of Young Italy's conspiracies in northern Italy had been discovered. Brutal reprisals, executions, and the forced emigration of many of the participants followed. Among the latter was Giuseppe Garibaldi (1807–1882), a member of Young Italy who took part in a failed uprising in Genoa and then fled from Italy, not to return for twelve years. With the police closing in on them, Mazzini and Sidoli departed from France in July 1833, leaving Adolphe behind in the care of one of Mazzini's closest French friends. Mazzini never saw his son again; he apparently sent some money for his support, but Adolphe died in February 1835, possibly the victim of a cholera epidemic in southern France.

---

4. Quoted in Alessandro Galante, "Ancora il figlio di Mazzini," *Il Ponte* (1961): 724. The works by this author are important because they provide the evidence of the birth of Mazzini and Sidoli's child in August 1832.

Chapter 5
The Passions
of Nationalism:
Giuseppe Mazzini
(1805–1872)
and Giuditta
Bellerio Sidoli
(1804–1871)

After leaving Marseilles, Mazzini, Sidoli, and the core group of their movement set up shop in Geneva, Switzerland, in an isolated, walled hotel that became their political headquarters. By October 1833, Sidoli decided to leave Switzerland and returned to Italy via France (possibly to see her son). She was driven by the determination to be reunited with her four children, who were living with their grandparents in Reggio. Mazzini was devastated by her departure, writing to a friend, that "I am beside myself for her. I am a man, after all, per Dio." He also wrote to his mother that though he loved Giuditta, he could not make her happy, and then wondered if it was in his destiny to make anyone happy. Although they saw each other again only rarely, their lives remained linked because they remained loyal to each other and to the same cause—a united, republican Italy. His love for her became almost legendary. Long after his death, a dear friend and political ally, Jessie Mario White, wrote an article in the *Nation* (1895) entitled "Mazzini's Love Story," in which she confirmed his great love for Sidoli. For Giuditta, the link to Mazzini, when added to her own political history, was a huge liability because she would be considered a "dangerous" woman wherever she traveled in Italy, and this burden was a major obstacle in her unfailing quest to be reunited with her children.

Giuditta's first stopping point on her return to Italy was in Florence, where she had influential friends who were able to protect her for a time. Her ultimate goal was to create a home where her children could join her; failing that, she hoped at least to gain the right to visit them in the duchy of Modena. This was extremely difficult because the ruler there would not let rebels into his territory, and her father-in-law had control over the children as well as over any familial inheritance.

Giuditta's reputation as a patriot and close friend of Mazzini's, as well as her own public professions of liberal ideas, meant that the Florentine authorities had her under surveillance and in fact forced her to rent a room in the home of a police official, where they could keep an eye on her. Sidoli felt very alone at this time and began to think she was not a worthy mother, having abandoned her children for what seemed to be an unsuccessful cause. By the fall of 1834, several of Young Italy's planned uprisings had failed, and Mazzini was discouraged, too. He was living in Geneva, and Sidoli decided she would join him there. The fact that she was traveling on a false passport was discovered at the Tuscan frontier, and she was expelled from Florence in October 1834. For the next two years, she traveled to Naples, Rome, Bologna, even Genoa. She ended up being "wanted" in most of these states; she was banished from France, did not have enough money to travel to England, and held only a Swiss passport. Eventually she settled in Parma in 1837. The Habsburg ruler there, Maria Luisa (r. 1798–1857), was quite indulgent toward liberal patriots and did not harass them. Giuditta's children had to remain in Reggio until their education was complete. They did have occasional visits, although only if the authorities agreed that Giuditta could travel. Their primary communication was through frequent letters, many of which were saved and constituted a crucial source of comfort for her in these years. This arrangement—the children in Reggio and she in Parma—lasted for the next eight years.

Mazzini had stayed in Switzerland until late 1836, continuing to plan insurrections and to spread his ideas, including a proposal for a "Young Europe" movement that would do for all of Europe what he hoped Young Italy would do for his own country. Living with a death sentence on his head and with Swiss authorities less welcoming, he left for England, arriving there with several Italian comrades in January 1837. For the next three decades, while he devoted all his energy and resources to the unity and freedom of his country and its citizens, he was a man without a permanent home. The freedom he had in England was balanced by his loneliness and longing for Italy. He referred to his exile as a "slow, lingering death . . . a consumption of the soul," the only cure for which was returning home. Sadly, that happened infrequently, and then only occasionally out in the open, in the light of day.

During his years of exile, Mazzini lived with a community of other Italians but also met and moved in the circles of an English intellectual elite made up of writers, political leaders, and philosophers. Among such acquaintances were Elizabeth Barrett Browning, Charles Dickens, and Thomas and Jane Carlyle. Though they did not all agree with Mazzini's politics, they were singularly impressed with the man. As Thomas Carlyle wrote, ". . . whatever I may think of his practical insight and skill in worldly affairs, I can testify that he, if I have ever seen one such, is a man of genius and virtue, a man of sterling veracity, humanity and nobleness of mind, . . ."[5] Life in exile was not easy for Mazzini. He never adapted well to the English climate, and his financial situation was always precarious. Shortly after his arrival in England, John Stuart Mill asked him to write an essay for his radical journal, the *Westminster Review,* and Mazzini made a little money from writing.

Mazzini often seemed oblivious to his own conditions and health; instead, he focused on gaining support for a free, independent, democratic Italy. And many English liberals and radicals did became converts to his cause. The Italian/English Jewish family, the Nathans, was one such "clan" closely connected to Mazzini and all of his causes. Sara Levi Nathan (1819–1882), the matriarch of the family, was born in Modena, then married and moved to England; her twelve children were dedicated Mazzinians, and she came to represent the Mazzinian ideal of the "citizen-mother." Mazzini referred to her as "the best Italian friend I have, one of the best women I know, pure, virtuous, sweet, devoted to all that is beautiful and good."[6] Later, Sara's son Ernesto Nathan directed one of Mazzini's

5. Quoted in Mack Smith, p. 43, from an article in *The Times,* 15 June 1944.

6. Judith Jeffrey Howard, "Patriot Mothers in the Post-Risorgimento: Women After the Italian Revolution," in Carol Berkin and Clara M. Lovett (eds.), *Women, War and Revolution* (New York: Holmes and Meier Pub., 1980), p. 248.

Chapter 5
The Passions
of Nationalism:
Giuseppe Mazzini
(1805–1872)
and Giuditta
Bellerio Sidoli
(1804–1871)

newspapers; her daughter Janet married an Italian, and their home in Pisa was a place Mazzini visited whenever he could. As we have seen in other revolutionary movements, families with common politics, and political movements resembling large families, were not uncommon in all the nations of Europe in the early modern and modern worlds.

Mazzini and Sidoli continued to communicate with each other, but usually through his mother in Genoa or through friends because it was dangerous for her to receive any letters from him. He continued to express his affection for her, writing to a friend in April 1837: "I love Sidoli, always. I will never see her again. For some time she has sacrificed me to her duty to her children—and she had to do it, I myself exhorted her to it."[7] Sidoli wrote to her children regularly; sent them gifts of clothing, musical instruments, books, and sweets; and visited them when the authorities allowed it. In 1837, when cholera broke out in Italy, she was terribly worried about her children and eventually wrote to the duke of Modena, telling him she was going to visit her children and he could arrest her if he wished (Document Two). She made the trip without incident.

Throughout this period, Sidoli remained committed to instilling republican, liberal ideals in her children. In a letter to her daughter Elvira in 1838, Giuditta wrote, "it is your duty to occupy yourself in your studies in the best way you know . . . *Virtue* and *knowledge* are the only true things of distinction in this world" (Document Three). She also warned Elvira that becoming virtuous was more difficult for women because of their social condition and the limits of their education.

In her sentiments and her behavior, Giuditta fulfilled Mazzini's idea of the "citizen-mother." He believed that women should participate in the divine plan for human progress as individuals equal to men, *and* as mothers raising children committed to the commonwealth. He thus argued for abstract equal rights but separate spheres and natures for men and women. He often expressed concern about women who obliterated their own personalities for their husbands and families and thus were unable to commit to progress and the republican revolution. His ideal mother would reject the patriarchal church and the monarchy, and work for humanity and the republic.[8] Later, in 1860, in an essay to working-class men, Mazzini would insist that they "Love and respect woman . . . Cancel from your minds every idea of superiority over woman. You have none whatsoever" (Document Four).

Bartolomeo Sidoli died in 1839 and by the mid-1840s, Giuditta's daughters had finished school and joined her in Parma. At some point, Maria Luisa heard of the intelligence and charm of

7. Quoted in Luisa Gasparini, "Il dramma materna di Giuditta Sidoli," (Part 1) *Il Risorgimento* 14:1 (1962): 20.

8. The best discussion of Mazzinian ideals regarding women is in Judith J. Howard, *The Woman Question in Italy, 1861–80* (Dissertation, University of Connecticut, 1977; University Microfilms International, 1978), especially Chapter Two, "The Mazzinian Woman."

these young women and their mother, and after seeing them at the theater had invited them to come to her court. Supposedly Sidoli declined, saying that the widow and daughters of Giovanni Sidoli, who had been condemned by a prince for his political beliefs, could not set foot in any monarch's court. Throughout this period, Giuditta remained republican, committed to unity and Mazzinian ideals. At the same time, correspondence between them was irregular, as Mazzini often lamented. No matter where Sidoli lived in the next years, her home remained a center for patriot meetings and discussions.

Although Mazzini was forced to live in exile, he continued to direct and encourage ongoing conspiracies, publicize his ideas, and broaden his network of supporters. Without doubt by the mid-1840s, he had a reputation as an important revolutionary leader feared by many of the existing rulers in Italy and the Habsburg lands. While his fame spread, within Italy, the breadth and strength of the overall movement for Italian unity and independence was growing. The nationalist movement in Italy became more varied and complex in the 1840s, particularly as individuals and groups more willing to compromise and more moderate in their aims gained support and put forth their strategies for realizing Italian unity and independence. By the late 1840s, the three major centers for unification efforts appeared to be the "people," the pope, or the rulers of the kingdom of Piedmont/ Sardinia. Mazzini consistently opposed the latter two, writing in 1847 that he did not think deliverance could ever come to Italy by means of a "Prince, a King or a Pope."

▪ ACT II:

REVOLUTION AND REPUBLIC, 1848–1849

In 1848, revolutions broke out in Italy and throughout Europe. The causes were increased economic hardship and social inequalities, and rising expectations on the part of people who wanted political reform, representative and constitutional government, and national independence. Italian hopes had been raised in 1846 by the election of a new pope, Pius IX (r. 1846–1878), who appeared to be more liberal and seemed sympathetic to the goals of unity. Similarly, Charles Albert (r. 1831–1849), the ruler in the Piedmont, also gave indications that he might consider a constitution for his kingdom and led efforts to expel the Austrians from the northern areas. The revolution first exploded in Palermo, in the south, on January 8, 1849. It spread quickly to other regions, and by March constitutions had been granted in Naples, Tuscany, the Piedmont, and even in Rome. The Habsburg powers held on in their northern duchies, producing bloody street fighting in the "Five Days of Milan," (March 18–22). Eventually, the Austrian commander withdrew from the city, and Charles Albert moved troops

Chapter 5
The Passions
of Nationalism:
Giuseppe Mazzini
(1805–1872)
and Giuditta
Bellerio Sidoli
(1804–1871)

into Lombardy in preparation for battle with the Austrians.

The unfolding of these momentous events gave Mazzini the opportunity to return to Italy. He apparently agreed to support Charles Albert in his struggle against the Austrians, asking in return that the king agree to fight to unify all of Italy. The Piedmontese army was beaten by the Austrians, and on the heels of defeat, the king abdicated and went to Portugal, leaving the kingdom of Savoy in the hands of his son Victor Emmanuel II (r. 1849–1878). None of these events helped Mazzini. Some would argue that he had "sold out" his republican principles, and others pointed to these events as proof that Italy could not achieve independence on its own.

The events of 1848 forced Sidoli to leave Parma because Austrian troops were sent in to occupy the area. She once again moved to Florence, where for several months one of her old political friends was in charge of the government. On his return to Italy, Mazzini stopped in Florence for what he reported as a joyful visit with Giuditta after sixteen years of enforced separation. But his real goal at this time was to reach Rome, where the pope's declaration that he would not support war against the Austrians had provoked uprisings that forced him to withdraw from the city in November 1848. Elections were held quickly for a constitutional assembly, and a republic was declared in February 1849. Sidoli had evidently trained her children well because Achille, her son, went to Rome to defend the republic. One month later, Mazzini arrived and for the first and only time in his life became involved in the operations of government.

Shortly after his arrival in Rome, Mazzini was chosen as one of three leaders of the new republican government. He acquitted himself well in this new role, proving himself a good organizer and an enlightened administrator capable of winning popular support. A wide range of reforms were enacted in the next one-hundred days: freedom of the press and religious toleration were established; the death penalty and the Inquisition were abolished; some church property was confiscated, often to house the poor; secular courts and schools replaced church courts and schools; a new tax code provided some relief for poorer citizens; and efforts were made to eliminate tariffs that hindered trade. Mazzini proved himself a man of the people in other ways as well. He lived modestly in a single room, did not take the salary attached to his position, ate his meals in a workers' *trattoria*, and kept his office accessible to all. Many foreign supporters of the Italian cause had flocked to Rome. The American writer Margaret Fuller was among them, and she judged Mazzini "a man of genius, an elevated thinker . . . in action, decisive and full of resource as Caesar."[9]

Freedom fighters from all over Italy also came to Rome and were eventually grouped together in a make-shift army, largely under the leadership of Garibaldi. Their presence was critical because, by April 1849, French troops had landed in Italy and had begun a

9. Quoted from her writings in Mack Smith, p. 68.

siege of Rome to restore the papacy and the church. Garibaldi met them in the field and was able to drive them back. This victory, of course, added to his heroic stature. When troops from Naples advanced on Rome, Garibaldi was able to hold them off as well. In May, Garibaldi once again brilliantly defended Rome against a French assault, but the result was that the French decided to bombard the city and cut off its food and water supplies. By early July, it was clear that the republicans could not hold out; Garibaldi led the remainder of his forces into the hills, and the French occupied Rome. Mazzini fled to the west coast and escaped by sea to Marseilles; he stayed in Switzerland for a time but by 1851 was back in England and his experience in political office was over.

Although the Roman Republic was short-lived, it became a symbol for those who dreamed of a unified Italy governed by the people. It also helped to create heroic images of its supporters and defenders, particularly Mazzini and Garibaldi. The latter also had returned to Italy in 1848 after his years of exile, many of them spent supporting independence struggles in Latin America. In more practical ways, the Republic also provided ammunition for Mazzini's detractors, who feared this experiment in popular government and spread all sorts of rumors about his role in the revolution. Finally, the Roman experience made clear that Mazzini and Garibaldi, though both great patriots, were not necessarily political soul mates. Garibaldi was a soldier fighting for freedom on the battlefield; Mazzini was an intellectual, an idealist, and thus they were not always able to agree on priorities and day-to-day actions.

By the time the Republic of Rome collapsed, traditional governments had been restored throughout Italy, and constitutions and reforms granted in the first heat of revolution had been rescinded—with one exception, the constitution (or *statuto*) in the Piedmont. This was not a particularly radical document; it provided only limited suffrage and maintained considerable power in the hands of the monarch. But it did provide for the most liberal government in Italy, and it increased support for those moderates who saw the Piedmont as the logical focus for Italian unification. The revolutions of 1848 persuaded many that Mazzini's "people's war" was unrealistic and perhaps even hindered progress toward Italian national independence. While he might remain the idealistic father of unification, his insurrectionary plans seemed less and less practical. Similarly, many recognized that Italian forces alone could not defeat the Austrians and began to look for foreign help. Finally, for others, the idea that Italy could be unified around the papacy was also discredited by the events of 1848–1849.

The Piedmont emerged from these tumultuous years as the model for Italian unification. Its forces, however unsuccessfully, had taken on the Austrians; it had a moderate, constitutional ruler, and its economy seemed the most dynamic and modern in all of Italy. It also produced a new kind of leader in the pragmatic Count Camillo di Cavour (1810–1861), who was

Chapter 5
The Passions
of Nationalism:
Giuseppe Mazzini
(1805–1872)
and Giuditta
Bellerio Sidoli
(1804–1871)

named prime minister in 1852. He built a solid alliance among moderates from the left and right, thus strengthening the center of the movement, and convinced many people that they should stop debating about the form of future government and concentrate on unification. If Mazzini had provided the spiritual and intellectual blueprint for the country, Cavour in many ways was the builder of the new nation.

▨ ACT III:

NATIONAL SUCCESS, PERSONAL FAILURE, 1850–1860

Like many Italian citizens, Sidoli's life was shaped by the outcome of the 1848 revolutions. With the restoration of ducal government in Tuscany, she and her two younger, unmarried daughters returned to their former residence in Parma. Unfortunately for them, the more benign Maria Luisa had died and was succeeded by a new ruler who proved much less tolerant of liberal, national activists. Nevertheless, patriots from other regions of Italy continued to gather in her home, she continued to correspond with many leaders (including Mazzini), and she had in her home copies of his newspapers and other incriminating publications. She was under surveillance for a time, and in January 1852, police entered and searched her home, and found the letters, papers, and hundreds of tricolored cockades. She was arrested and spent about a month in prison. When Sidoli was released, she and her daughters were taken from Parma and transported to Milan, and from there they were expelled to Switzerland. Her sojourn there was brief because she had decided that she would make Turin, the Piedmontese capital, her new home. Although she always considered this "exile" because it was not her native region of Lombardy, she also recognized that it was a territory in which she could talk openly about freedom and Italy's future. Her home in Turin, as had been true elsewhere, served as a salon for patriots expounding a wide range of political views. Perhaps it was there that her daughters Elvira and Corinna met the young liberal exiles they eventually married.

Throughout the 1850s, Mazzini spent most of his time in England, with various trips to Switzerland and clandestine journeys into Italian territory. In fact, in 1856 he visited Giuditta in Turin. Mazzini did not give up his attempts to mobilize support for Italian unification. He created an Italian National Committee in London in 1850, renamed it the National Party, and then renamed it the Party of Action. Mazzini saw this party as a collection of affiliated groups from all over Europe, that were devoted to popular sovereignty and to helping to build a community of free European nations. He and his associates, a smaller circle by then, continued to plan insurrections in various Italian regions, but none was successful. In these years, Mazzini also appeared more willing to compromise with the constitutional monarchy in the Piedmont and was less insistent on the creation of republican government. Finally, he continued to raise funds in England from the 800 or so members of the Friends of Italy Society.

Mazzini had always been interested in reforms that benefitted the lower classes, and in the 1850s he articulated these ideas more clearly and encouraged programs and groups that were working to similar ends. Since the 1840s, as part of Young Italy, Mazzini had created organizations of Italian workers in London for the purpose of educating and building community among the workers. While well versed in the ideas of Karl Marx and other socialists, Mazzini always rejected their philosophy. He acknowledged class differences and criticized the middle classes for selfish pursuit of their own interests, but he also hoped to reduce class conflict, not increase it. He consistently defended property ownership and open market competition while insisting that workers should enjoy more of the fruits of their own labor. Above all, he objected to the materialism of Marxism, arguing that material well-being never could be substituted for moral goals and progress. He often proclaimed that one of the aims in his life was to "save the working classes from the [First] International and other evil influences"[10] (Document Five).

In the meantime, Cavour's plans to unify Italy were moving ahead. The Italian National Society, formed in 1857, subordinated every other idea of reform to unification and independence and built a peninsulawide network of male and female supporters who helped publicize the cause, influence popular opinion, and call up volunteers for unity. Special women's committees raised large sums of money for the cause and provided another avenue into the public sphere for "patriot mothers." Cavour eventually convinced Napoleon III (r. 1852–1870) to help expel the Austrians from Italy, and successful warfare in 1859 freed Lombardy. During that conflict, Giuditta went to Lombardy to help nurse the wounded. Other insurrections throughout Italy created assemblies that declared their desire to be annexed to the Piedmont. By March 1860, a new Chamber of Deputies was elected for an enlarged Piedmont, and Cavour could claim victory. For Giuditta, these developments meant that, for the first time since 1823, she could visit Reggio freely. After this wish was fulfilled, she returned to her new home in Turin.

Mazzini had agreed with Cavour that Austria was their foremost enemy, but he was critical of the end result. Cavour had dealt with a tyrant, Napoleon III, and had given away precious territory, thus giving the impression that Italy was dependent on foreign power. To regain some role for republican initiatives in the unification process, Mazzini sent several of his followers to southern Italy to help prepare for an uprising there against the Bourbon rulers of Naples and Sicily. After a series of complicated preparations and contested plans, Garibaldi eventually led the famous expedition of the Thousand Red Shirts

10. From a September 1871 letter written from Italy to friends in England, in E. F. Richards (ed.), *Mazzini's Letters to An English Family*, Vol. 3 (London: John Lane Co., 1920–1922), p. 289.

Chapter 5
The Passions
of Nationalism:
Giuseppe Mazzini
(1805–1872)
and Giuditta
Bellerio Sidoli
(1804–1871)

to Sicily in May 1860. Mazzini had planned to join Garibaldi but reached Genoa too late to sail with him. Instead, he arrived in Naples in September after various successful battles had freed much of the south. His sojourn in Naples itself was unique because it was the first time since 1849 that he could live openly in Italy. Although free to move about publicly and to meet with friends and comrades, at this point Mazzini was really more of an observer than a leader in the struggle for unification. By the end of 1860, Cavour and Garibaldi were the acknowledged leaders, the Austrians held only Venice, and the papal territories had been reduced to Rome and its environment. Mazzini and his party condemned the process of unification and continued to dream of a democratic republic for Italy, but they were in the minority and had no forces to back their demands. In fact, Mazzini had returned to England before March 17, 1861, when a new parliament officially proclaimed the independence of the Kingdom of Italy under the leadership of Victor Emmanuel II.

▓ FINALE

Cavour died unexpectedly in June 1861, and various other, less adept political leaders assumed the reins of the new government. Some of Mazzini's followers gained seats in parliament in those years, and Mazzini himself was elected three times. Initially denied his seat because he was a "convicted criminal," national and international outcry caused enough embarrassment that the government eventually granted him his seat, but Mazzini refused it because he could not in good conscience swear allegiance to the king. Mazzini continued his pattern of living—moving from England to Switzerland, where he usually stayed with Sara Nathan, a wealthy widow by that time, and to Italy, where he often visited with one of Sara's daughters in Pisa. He continued to write, publish newspapers, raise money, and plan additional insurrections that would liberate Venice and Rome. Neither his health nor his personal finances were particularly good at this point in his life, but he pressed ahead. Giuditta still lived in Turin and although at heart still a republican, she felt that there were advantages to the constitutional monarchy. She continued to correspond with Mazzini, and their letters combined political with personal news and comments (Document Six). She occasionally sent him small packets of chocolate or other items that he treasured.

In the 1860s, structures of a new government, including a revised legal code for all of Italy, began to emerge. Even in Mazzini's absence, his ideas had an impact on proposals for reform and a new civil code for Italy. He continued to hope for republican democracy and was always critical of the fact that most Italians still did not have the right to vote. Mazzini had always assumed that associationism, which served as an avenue into political life, applied to women as well as to men, and numerous women had participated in the struggles of the *Risorgimento*. Some were like Sidoli and had suffered exile and deprivation for their political beliefs. Others accompanied Garibaldi and his forces and served as nurses and support staff for the soldiers. These experiences and the mood and challenges of the *Risorgimento* disrupted the existing order and promised a new one. Many women expected their own emancipation to accompany Italian unity and independence.

Anna Mozzoni (1837–1920) was one of these women. She came from an upper-class family in Milan who were followers of Mazzini. She was familiar with his ideas and was also influenced by the writings of John Stuart Mill, some of which she translated into Italian. She challenged convention by having an illegitimate daughter and delayed marriage until she was forty years old. In the 1860s, she joined an organization dedicated to women's rights that Mazzini had helped to inspire and wrote for a feminist paper *La Donna* (Woman). She was one of the first to confront the issue of women's legal equality in the new Italy. In 1864, her essay *Woman and Her Social Relations* attacked the Roman Catholic Church and criticized the proposed legal code. Although the new code proclaimed the principle of sex equality before the law, declared that women were citizens, and gave single women most property rights, women were denied the right to vote and to hold public offices. Mozzoni was equally concerned with the fact that wives were still controlled by husbands and that the authority of the father in the household remained virtually untouched. Mozzoni argued that indeed if the family was considered the province of women, then they should have power in that sphere[11] (Document Seven).

She was not alone in her concerns. Mazzinian deputy Salvatore Morelli took up the same causes in the new government and introduced bills that would give women the right to vote, access to careers, and the right to divorce. None of these became law in this era. Nevertheless, growing demands for women's rights and increased political consciousness on the part of many women were results of the movement for nationhood, and Mazzini was an important figure in this process. He had written in favor of women's equality and always insisted that women could not understand the rights of citizenship and instill them in their children if they were excluded from them by law. He appreciated the counsel and ideas of numerous Italian, British, French, and American feminists of the time and appeared to be attracted to independent, resourceful women like Sidoli and Sara Nathan. In an 1870 letter to a female friend, he wrote that he could not safely claim his own rights and duties if he did not warmly believe in hers as well.

11. For information on women's rights issues in the new state, see Judith Jeffrey Howard, "Visions of Reform, Visions of Revolution: Women's Activism in the New Italian Nation," in Frances Richardson Keller (ed.), *Views of Women's Lives in the Western Tradition* (New York: The Edwin Mellen Press, 1990): 432–450.

Chapter 5
The Passions
of Nationalism:
Giuseppe Mazzini
(1805–1872)
and Giuditta
Bellerio Sidoli
(1804–1871)

Mazzini's final campaigns were to acquire Rome and Venice, but through Italian efforts, not diplomatic maneuvers. Although he had no cohesive forces to accomplish his goals, he did help to set the agenda for other leaders. As he had written a friend, "We have constantly acted as the spur: we worked, fought and bled for Italy, the Cavour cabinet constantly opposing, then reaping the results...."[12] When war broke out between Prussia and France in July 1870 and French troops began to leave Rome, Mazzini headed for Italy once again with a final plan for rebellion and the establishment of another republic in Rome. He was eventually arrested by the Italian authorities in August and imprisoned for the first time since 1830. But ironically his plan succeeded. Victor Emmanuel and his ministers would have preferred to leave Rome outside the new kingdom, given the position of the church, but to save the throne and prevent another republican uprising, troops took control of the Papal States in late September. Both inside and outside Italy, these events were proclaimed as a victory for Mazzini, who even in prison seemed to be able to chart the course of Italian unification. With the proclamation of a general amnesty in October, Mazzini was released from prison, but he still refused to recognize Victor Emmanuel and left Italy once more.

Mazzini lived the remaining months of his life as he always had, moving from England to Switzerland, and to Pisa and occasionally Genoa. He continued to write articles for newspapers and letters to his friends. His health was not good, but neither was Sidoli's. She had been weakened by typhus in 1868, and she suffered from pulmonary ailments after that and died of pneumonia on March 28, 1871. Mazzini was at Sara Nathan's home in Lugano then and, knowing of Sidoli's illness, wrote to her just before she died: "...I have never stopped thinking of you, of valuing you and loving you as one of the finest spirits I have known in my life ... you should not be afraid of that which men call death, it is nothing but a transformation. One day you will meet again those you love and who love you."[13] The epitaph on her grave marker in Milan read: "She did not live for herself, but for her children and her country."

In the year before his death on March 10, 1872, Mazzini was increasingly frail and suffered from constant coughs and colds. He admitted being discouraged about Italy's future. According to him, Italy at that point had a body but lacked a soul. Where was the Italy of his dreams? "Italy the great, the beautiful, the moral Italy of my soul? I thought to evoke the soul of Italy, and I see before me only the corpse."[14] But he continued to write articles arguing for revolution and social transformation that led to human progress. And above all, he insisted that action and commitment to a cause had to accompany ideas. He never

12. Quoted in Mack Smith, p. 145.

13. Letter from Lugano, 3 March 1871, in *Lettere d'amore* (Introduction by Gaetano Gasperoni, translation by Jane Slaughter, pp. LIV–LV.

14. Quoted in Stringfellow Barr, *Mazzini: Portrait of an Exile* (New York: Henry Holt, 1935): 260.

strayed from the belief that "life is not a question of happiness or unhappiness; it is a question of duty to be fulfilled, a mission to be attempted; nothing else."[15]

Mazzini was buried in Genoa. Thousands of people accompanied the funeral procession and popular demonstrations in Rome and other cities honored his memory. The Italian government, however, gave no formal recognition of his death and refused to honor him with a memorial like those constructed for Cavour and Garibaldi. Finally, eighteen years after Mazzini died, the government allocated money for a monument to him, but it was not built for another fifty years. Mazzini's search for justice, equality, and a spiritual community of all humanity had obviously frightened some people. But he probably inspired many more and above all helped to shape Italian and European political movements in the years that followed.

◼ QUESTIONS

1. Why did most political groups in the 1820s and 1830s operate underground? What motivated Italian men and women to join secret societies? At what costs?

2. What were Mazzini's goals for Italy? Why is Young Italy considered a revolutionary group as well as a modern political organization?

3. Were Mazzini and Sidoli unusual in their politics and ideologies in mid-nineteenth century Europe? Who sympathized with them and why?

4. Why did Mazzini reject the ideas of Karl Marx? Why is this consistent with his ideals about freedom and association?

5. Mazzini is often considered the intellectual father of unified Italy, but Cavour is considered its architect. Why?

6. What makes Sidoli an unusual woman in the nineteenth century? What conditions might she have in common with many other Italian women at the time? What role did women play in the movement for unification and national liberation? Did they receive political and social emancipation? Why or why not?

15. Letter from London, March 1839, in Bolton King (ed.), *Mazzini's Letters* (London: J.M. Dent and Sons, Ltd., 1930): 63.

Chapter 5
The Passions
of Nationalism:
Giuseppe Mazzini
(1805–1872)
and Giuditta
Bellerio Sidoli
(1804–1871)

■ **DOCUMENTS**

<hr>

DOCUMENT ONE

<hr>

GIUSEPPE MAZZINI

"Instructions to Young Italy"
(1832)

In 1832, Mazzini founded a society known as Young Italy, which was designed to help create an Italian republic by appealing to the patriotic instincts of the people. In the following excerpt, Mazzini sets forth the principles and new ideals of the organization. What are Young Italy's goals? How will those goals be reached? Why should Italy be a republic and not a monarchy? Why is Young Italy in favor of unity and not federation?

LIBERTY—EQUALITY—HUMANITY—INDEPENDENCE —UNITY

Young Italy is a brotherhood of Italians who believe in a law of *progress* and *duty,* and are convinced that Italy is destined to become one nation, convinced also that she possesses sufficient strength within herself to become one, and that the ill success of her former efforts is to be attributed not to the weakness, but to the misdirection of the revolutionary elements within her,—that the secret force lies in constancy and unity of effort. They join this association with the firm intention of consecrating both thought and action to the great aim of reconstituting Italy as one independent sovereign nation of free men and equals. . . .

The aim of the association is *revolution;* but its labors will be essentially educational, both before and after the day of revolution; and it therefore declares the principles upon which the national education should be conducted, and from which alone Italy may hope for safety and regeneration. . . .

Young Italy is *republican* and *unitarian,*—republican, because theoretically every nation is destined, by the law of God and humanity, to form a free and equal community of brothers; and the republican government is the only form of government that insures this future: Because all true sovereignty resides essentially in the nation, the sole progressive and continuous interpreter of the supreme moral law; . . . because the monarchical element being incapable of sustaining itself alone by the side of the popular element, it necessarily involves the existence of the intermediate element of an aristocracy,—the source of inequality and corruption to the whole nation; because both history and the nature of things teach us that elective monarchy tends to generate anarchy, and hereditary monarchy tends to generate despotism; . . . .

[142]

Young Italy is *unitarian,* because, without unity there is no true nation; because, without unity there is no real strength; and Italy, surrounded as she is by powerful, united, and jealous nations, has need of strength above all things; because federalism, by reducing her to the political impotence of Switzerland, would necessarily place her under the influence of one of the neighboring nations; because federalism, by reviving the local rivalries now extinct, would throw Italy back upon the Middle Ages; . . . because federalism, by destroying the unity of the great Italian family, would strike at the root of the great mission Italy is destined to accomplish for humanity; because Europe is undergoing a progressive series of transformations, which are gradually and irresistibly guiding European society to form itself into vast and united masses; because the entire work of internal civilization in Italy will be seen, if rightly studied, to have been tending for ages toward unity.

The means by which Young Italy proposes to reach its aim are education and insurrection, to be adopted simultaneously and made to harmonize with each other. Education must ever be directed to teach, by example, word, and pen, the necessity of insurrection. Insurrection, whenever it can be realized, must be so conducted as to render it a means of national education. Education, though of necessity secret in Italy, will be public outside of Italy. . . .

Insurrection, by means of guerrilla bands, is the true method of warfare for all nations desirous of emancipating themselves from a foreign yoke. This method of warfare supplies the want—inevitable at the commencement of the insurrection—of a regular army; it calls the greatest number of elements into the field, and yet may be sustained by the smallest number. It forms the military education of the people and consecrates every foot of the native soil by the memory of some warlike deed. Guerrilla warfare opens a field of activity for every local capacity, forces the enemy into an unaccustomed method of battle, avoids the evil consequences of a great defeat, secures the national war from the risk of treason, and has the advantage of not confining it within any defined and determinate basis of operations. It is invincible, indestructible. The regular army, recruited with all possible solicitude and organized with all possible care, will complete the work begun by the war of insurrection.

Chapter 5
The Passions
of Nationalism:
Giuseppe Mazzini
(1805–1872)
and Giuditta
Bellerio Sidoli
(1804–1871)

DOCUMENT TWO

GIUDITTA SIDOLI

Letters

While Sidoli lived in Parma, her children were in school in Reggio. She wrote to them frequently and also made every effort to visit them. Given the events of the time and Sidoli's place in them, the letters appear quite ordinary and certainly not political. Why might this be the case? What can we learn from these letters? What conclusions might you draw from the last letter from the police in Reggio?

[FROM SIDOLI IN PARMA, TO HER CHILDREN; 28 JUNE 1837]

My dearest children—

This heat makes me think about your health, my dearest children. After Elvira had fevers without my being informed, at any little thing, the fear is born in me that any one of you could be sick again, and I would not know about it. Relieve me of this uncertainty, writing to me immediately that you are well, and promising me for the future, that any accident, however small it might be, . . . you will endeavor through any means possible to notify me very quickly. I also write to Achille [he is in a different school than his sisters], that you take care, and to you others, I repeat, eat little, and do not drink too much; above all, abstain from cold drinks. . . . Cherries are healthy, other fruit not so much, even less for greens and vegetables. . . .

Assure me that none of you have any ailments, no pains, coughs, sore throats, and you have my blessing and my warmest embrace, my dear children.

your Mother

[FROM SIDOLI IN PARMA, TO HER CHILDREN; 20 APRIL 1841]

My dear children—

I hope that you were notified that my trip there is again delayed for a few days, for reasons that should not worry you in the least, because my health is very good and nothing disastrous has happened to me. The time I chose was not agreeable to the police, probably because of a holiday that I did not know fell on Thursday. All of that is not of great concern, only the thought of the uneasiness that came to you in those hours in which you were probably waiting for me, worries me. Have patience. I hope that next week nothing will thwart me. Meanwhile, I embrace you with the greatest tenderness, and I bless you, my delightful children.

your Mother

[Excerpt from a letter from the Minister in Charge of Police in Reggio, to the Counsellor of State of the Government of Modena; 14 December 1839]

. . . [O]n the ninth, current, she [Sidoli] arrived in Reggio at 9:30 and was taken to visit her children; that same evening she spent the night in the suburban Villa de San Pellegrino, returning to the city the following morning, the tenth, at 9 o'clock, and made a new visit to the aforesaid children, resuming at 1:45 P.M. the trip to return to Parma, leaving . . . at 3:30 P.M. As a result of the usual careful surveillance of these very same actions, I have no reservations with which to charge her.

DOCUMENT THREE

Giuditta Sidoli

Letters Educating Her Children

In these letters, written to her children while they are in school in Reggio, Sidoli expresses her views of education and attempts to impart values and ideals to them. What does she say about the importance of education? Why is education especially important for her daughters? What does she say to guide her daughters as they grow up? How do her ideas fit with those of Mazzini?

[Letter from Sidoli in Parma, to Her Daughter Elvira; 7 February 1838]

[Dearest Elvira—]

. . . It is very important to me that you enjoy yourself, but I hope that this does not prevent the customary close attention to your studies, and to your duties, and that you do not stop, my dearest Elvira, applying yourself to your studies in the best way and as much as you can. *Virtue* and *knowledge* are the only things of distinction in this world, and since the means of learning are at last becoming very common because of the great benefit of publishing, it is an absolute duty to study a great deal, and to know very little is shameful. Indeed . . . for women, because of their limited intellectual education and their social condition, are doubly obliged to educate their hearts and souls to virtue. A bad woman is a misfortune; great goodness often makes ignorance tolerable, but it never happens that vice and wickedness are forgiven because of great knowledge. To obtain the improvement of the heart and the intellect is the beautiful moral end to which we should always aspire. . . .

Your Mother

Chapter 5
The Passions
of Nationalism:
Giuseppe Mazzini
(1805–1872)
and Giuditta
Bellerio Sidoli
(1804–1871)

[Letter from Sidoli in Parma, to her daughter Elvira; 12 March 1841]

[Dearest Elvira—]

My delightful Elvira—I think that I owe you a letter, my dear daughter; excuse my delay. Every day I waited to have some good news to tell you, but it didn't happen, and I don't want to prolong the silence. . . .

I know, my dear Elvira, that you make every effort, even for that which I have told you about writing, but have patience, and you will see that you likewise will improve your letters as Marietta [her older sister] also has done. Another thing that I recommend, not just to you, but to all three of you, to review frequently, and to learn by heart some Italian grammar. Believe me, these are things it is absolutely necessary to learn at your age in order always to know them well. For the education of mind and heart, the present time in your lives is precious time.

Your Mother

DOCUMENT FOUR

Giuseppe Mazzini

"On the Duties of Man" (1860)

In this essay, written in 1860, Mazzini articulates his view that women not only could participate in the Risorgimento, but that they were its "fiercer patriots." Why does he make this claim? Mazzini argues that women and men are both equal and different. How does he combine what might seem to be opposites? How does this passage illustrate the democratic climate of the 1848 revolutions?

Chapter VI. Duties Towards the Family.

. . . This Angel of the family is Woman. Whether as mother, wife, or sister, woman is the caress of existence, the soft sweetness of affection diffused over its fatigues, a reflex on the individual of that loving Providence which watches over Humanity. She has in her a treasure of gentle consolation sufficient to soothe every sorrow. Moreover, she is for each of us the Initiatrix of the future. The child learns its first lesson of love from its mother's kiss. In the first sacred kiss of the beloved one, man learns the lesson of hope and faith in life, ...

I have said even more than the Fatherland. Distinctions of country—sacred now—may possibly disappear whenever man shall bear the moral law of Humanity inscribed upon his own heart, but the family will endure while man himself endures. It is the cradle of Humanity. Like every other element of human life, it is, of course, susceptible of progress, and from epoch to epoch its tendencies and aspirations are improved, but it can never be cancelled. Your mission is ever more to sanctify the family, and to link it ever more closely with the country. That which the country is to Humanity, the family must be to the country. Even as the scope and object of our love of country is, as I have told you, to educate you as *men*, so the scope and object of the family is to educate you as *citizens*. The family and the country are the two extreme points of one and the same line. . . .

Love and respect Women. Seek in her not merely comfort, but a force, an inspiration, the redoubling of your intellectual and moral faculties.

Cancel from your minds every idea of superiority over Woman. You have none whatsoever.

Long prejudice, an inferior education, and a perennial legal inequality and injustice, have created that *apparent* intellectual inferiority which has been converted into an argument of continued oppression.

But does not the history of every oppression teach us how the oppressor ever seeks his justification and support by appealing to a *fact* of his own creation? The feudal castes that withheld education from the sons of the people, excluded them on the grounds of that very want of education, from the rights of the citizen, from the sanctuary wherein laws are framed, and from that right of vote which is the initiation of their social mission. The Slaveholders of America declare the black race radically inferior and incapable of education, and yet persecute those who seek to instruct them. For half-a-century the supporters of the reigning families in Italy have declared the Italians unfit for freedom, and meanwhile, by their laws, and by the brute force of hireling armies, they close every path through which we might overcome the obstacles to our improvement, where such really exist, as if tyranny could ever be a means of educating men for liberty.

Now, we men have ever been, and still are, guilty of a similar crime towards woman. Avoid even the shadow or semblance of this crime: there is none heavier in the sight of God, for it divides the human family into two classes, and imposes or accepts the subjugation of one class to the other.

In the sight of God the Father there is neither *man* nor *woman*. There is only the *human* being, that being in whom, whether the form be of male or female, those characteristics which distinguish humanity from the brute creation are united— namely, the social tendency, and the capacity of education and progress.

Wheresoever these characteristics exist, the *human* nature is revealed, and thence perfect equality both of rights and of duties.

Like two distinct branches springing from the same trunk, man and woman are varieties springing from the common basis—Humanity. There is no inequality between them, but, even as is often the case among men, diversity of tendency and of special vocation. Are two notes of the same musical chord unequal or of different nature? Man and woman are the two notes without which the Human chord is impossible.

Chapter 5
The Passions
of Nationalism:
Giuseppe Mazzini
(1805–1872)
and Giuditta
Bellerio Sidoli
(1804–1871)

DOCUMENT FIVE

GIUSEPPE MAZZINI

"On Materialism"
(1869)

Mazzini spent his whole life battling for a unity and association that was moral and spiritual in nature. In this passage, written in 1869, Mazzini sums up his views on those who forsake ideals for a more pragmatic, material solution. In Mazzini's opinion, what does materialism deny the individual?

There are *materialists*—illogical, and carried away by the impulses of a heart superior to their doctrines—who do feel and act upon the worship of the ideal; but *materialism* denies it. Materialism only recognizes in the universe a finite and determinate quantity of matter, gifted with definite properties and susceptible of modification, but not of progress; in which certain productive forces act by the fortuitous agglomeration of circumstances not to be predicted or foreseen, or through the succession of causes and effects—inevitable and independent of human action. Materialism admits neither the intervention of creative intelligence, divine initiative, nor human free-will.

Recognizing no higher historic formula than the alternation of vicissitudes, it condemns humanity to tread eternally the same circle, being incapable of the conception of a spiral path of progress upon which mankind traces its gradual ascent towards an ideal beyond.

Strange contradiction! Men whose aim it is to combat the egotism instilled by tyranny, to inspire a sacred devotion to the fatherland, to make of the Italian people a great nation, present as its first intellectual food a theory the ultimate consequences of which are to establish egotism upon a basis of right.

The same men who urge upon people the duty of shedding their blood for an idea, begin by declaring to them: There is no hope of any future for you: faith in immortality—the lesson transmitted to you by all past humanity—is a falsehood; a breath of air, or a trifling want of equilibrium in the animal functions, destroys you wholly and for ever. There is even no certainty that the results of your labours will endure: there is no providential law or design, consequently no possible theory of the future: you are building up to-day what any unforeseen fact, any blind force or fortuitous circumstance may overthrow to-morrow.

They teach these brothers of theirs, whom they desire to elevate and ennoble, that they are but dust; an unconscious secretion of I know not what material substance; that the thought of a Kepler or Dante is dust, or rather phosphorous; that genius, from Prometheus to Jesus, brought down no divine spark from heaven; that the moral law, free-will, merit, and the consequent progress of the *ego* [beyond this one earth-phase of existence] are illusions; that events are successively our masters, inexorable, irresponsible, and insuperable by human will.

DOCUMENT SIX

GIUSEPPE MAZZINI

Letter to Giuditta Sidoli
(May 14, 1864)

After the initial stage of the unification process ended in 1861, many of Mazzini's associates had decided to support the constitutional monarchy and drop the fight for a republic. Even Sidoli seemed willing to compromise. In this letter, what does Mazzini say about such a position? Why does he refuse so adamantly to compromise with the monarchy? Why is he disappointed with his former colleagues?

My Giuditta,

Don't think that my silence comes from lack of concern: it comes simply from this, that writing pains me, that unfortunately, every day, I have things to write that are necessary for our business, and I don't have the energy to go on. At midday I am tired and obliged to pace back and forth in the room, like a hyena in a cage. I received the chocolate and am grateful to you from my heart. And I have the line in your letter that sounded to me almost like a reproach and an appeal. To the reproach—if it was such—I will not respond with anything. I know two things: one is that I couldn't, for love of country, conduct myself in any other way; the other is that the republicans have abandoned me, not I them. The party, that I have tried to spiritualize, was and is materialist and a worshipper of success and power to its very marrow. But to the appeal, I will say: that . . . I know how to work for our republican ideals. They can do what they want. Italy will be a Republic, as certain as it is united, not because mankind deserves it, but because of the logic of things and events. And that thought directs what I do; . . . .

For the rest, I would like all the republicans to follow my behavior. [To yield to the national will] but to do it with sadness . . . to persist with my "with the monarchy, without it and against the monarchy"; not to bind oneself, not to take oaths, not to beg, not ever to attach your name to anything that carries "Long live Victor Emmanuele" and so forth. I am free as before, and the monarchical party cannot ascribe a single word to me that chains my freedom. And if an act of government will be such that it rouses a logical sense in the young people, and opens a possible path that doesn't take the Party to the ridiculous, I will affirm it, if I am alive.

How are you? How are your daughters? What do you hope for and what do you fear? Snatch a convenient moment and write to me. And believe that I am always yours.

Giuseppe

Chapter 5
The Passions
of Nationalism:
Giuseppe Mazzini
(1805–1872)
and Giuditta
Bellerio Sidoli
(1804–1871)

DOCUMENT SEVEN

ANNA MARIA MOZZONI

"Women and Their Social Relations"
(1864)

Anna Mozzini was Italy's most well-known feminist. Imbued with Mazzini's ideas about associationism, she connected Italians' emancipation with women's rights in the new state. In this passage, she discusses the qualities that women will bring to national life. What are these qualities? How do her ideas compare with Mazzini's?

Since [natural] rights (*il diritto*) are based on attributes common to the human race and not on individual attributes, and since [natural] rights are perceived as the legitimate claim of every person to the development of characteristic human faculties, and to the fulfillment of all the functions that allow him to attain his goals [in life], I will not hesitate to demonstrate that woman, as a human being, has no fewer rights than man, so long as privilege does not usurp the sacred name of rights.

I will say only that all jurists, even though they do not formulate their opinions according to any philosophical basis of [natural] rights, perceive the will to justice and reason as lying in the notion that rights should be extended to every human being. Yet, since they find themselves unable to deny that woman belongs to the human race, they all begin to contradict themselves whenever they introduce inequality between man and woman. And thus does justice cut with a two-edged sword; while it denies a right to one, it grants a privilege to the other.

So it is that, of all the charges brought against woman with the intention of justifying the iniquitous ways she is treated by the laws—charges sanctioned neither by nature nor by reason, but only by the passions—none can be upheld in the face of a very few observations and in view of the true basis of [natural] rights.

[The jurists] say: woman is unfit to exercise rights.

But it is impossible to deny the intelligence of many women, any more than one can refuse to recognize the imbecility of many men. But [natural] rights are not based on individual intelligence.

They say: woman is weak.

But it is impossible to deny the power and strength of many women, just as it is impossible to deny the puniness and chronic illness of many men.

But [natural] rights are not based on strength and good health.

You object to the nature of her social roles?

It is impossible to demonstrate and to prove that maternity, running a household, often teaching, trade, industrial production, are less necessary and less noble occupations than those of the ragpicker, street cleaner, or the liveried servant. But [natural] rights are not based on social roles.

Radical Reformers in Victorian Britain: Annie Wood Besant (1847–1933) and Charles Bradlaugh (1833–1891)

▓ SETTING THE STAGE

When Queen Victoria ascended the throne in 1837, British society was in the middle stages of unparalleled political, social, and economic transformation. The Reform Act of 1832 had just granted political representation to the industrial middle class; the Chartist movement was gaining momentum in working-class quarters; parliamentary committees had begun to investigate working conditions in Britain's factories, mines, and mills; Britain's urban populations were exploding; and British middle-class men and women were setting new rules and norms for their "Victorian" society. Men and women of Britain's middle classes wished to remake society in their own image. The society that emerged and took its name from Queen Victoria embraced laissez-faire economic principles, the desire for

Chapter 6
Radical
Reformers in
Victorian Britain:
Annie Wood
Besant
(1847–1933) and
Charles
Bradlaugh
(1833–1891)

order and security of property and person, abolition of the special privileges of the aristocracy and clergy, consumption of the new products of the industrial age, the separation of home and work, and a domestic culture based on age, class, and gender difference and hierarchy. Victorian ideology attacked aristocratic or lower-class idleness, sexual promiscuity, and drunkenness, and valued individual responsibility, hard work, judgment of an individual based on achievement and not birth, sexual morality, and female modesty and obedience. By mid-century, the Victorians claimed the ascendent role in British politics, culture, and the economy.

Men and women of the middle classes would not be left alone to remake society according to their own interests and desires. The industrial transformation, which had spawned them, had given birth to another class, the industrial working class. By the middle of the nineteenth century, more than half of Britain's manual laborers worked in industry. Men, women, and children of the laboring class worked ten-hour days and a six-day week; earned subsistence-level wages, enough to keep them alive; and lived in overcrowded and unsanitary slums. They could not afford to purchase the goods that they produced and engaged in few leisure activities.

Men, women, and children engaged in different types of industrial work. Iron and steel industries, mines, and mills requiring "skilled" laborers employed men. Women, who made up one-third of the industrial work force, worked in factories, textile mills, laundries, retail shops, and do-

mestic service. In industries where machines supplied the strength, male skilled labor operated the machinery, and where dexterity and nimbleness of finger were required, women and children were the majority. Employers used child labor in their factories, mills, and mines. In mines, boys and girls opened and closed the vents that controlled the supply of air underground and hauled wagons and baskets of coal to the surface. In factories and mills, they were often given the jobs that required small hands and a small body. Chimney sweeps used small prepubescent boys to climb inside chimneys and sweep the toxic coal dust out, much to the detriment of their growth and health. Some of the first legislation passed by the British Parliament in the 1840s regulated a child's age of employment, working hours, and work breaks and prohibited the employment of children in certain occupations such as mining and chimney sweeping.

Men and women of the working class experienced conditions similar to that of their children. Their health was damaged by coal or cotton dust; metal fragments; crippling chemicals, such as lead in pottery and sulfur and phosphorus in matchmaking; repetitive movements; poor ventilation; heat; dampness, which often led to tuberculosis; and countless other hardships associated with unregulated labor practices. Living conditions in Britain's swelling industrial cities rivaled the workers' employment conditions. Often the oldest parts of cities were giant slums. Many working-class families lived in single rooms in rundown houses, built one on top of the other because there was very little space to build. The air was foul, stale, and choked with the poisonous fumes and smoke from coal. Unpaved streets were saturated with rotting garbage and human and animal refuse, and every type of germ and pestilence thrived in these conditions.

Traditional family relations and the patriarchal family unit were recast as a result of this new type of work and labor mobility. Young women as well as children, male and female, left parental control and authority when they moved away from home for factory work. In addition, women and children became integral to the family's financial well-being, subverting a father's or husband's status. Benjamin Disraeli, future prime minister of Great Britain, in his industrial novel *Sybil* (1845) depicted this loss of male status and authority. Two of his characters were an underemployed handloom weaver, who lost his job to a machine, and his newly employed daughter, who moved out of the house, earned a wage, and left patriarchal control.

When depression hit Great Britain in the 1840s, the worst in the nineteenth century, it drew attention to the human cost of industrialization, urbanization, and governmental policies unfavorable to the working class. Industrialists, landowners, and middle-class Victorians had to address Britain's hungry, desperate, and sick working-class population before armed insurrection broke out. The working class had already shown large-scale political activism in the 1830s, when some of its members organized a petition drive to present a "People's Char-

ter" to Parliament. This drive, known as the Chartist movement, called for annual parliaments, voting rights for all adult men, an end to the property qualifications for members of the House of Commons, voting by secret ballot, equal electoral districts that would represent the new urban and industrial centers, and salaries for members of Parliament so that men without private wealth could afford to run and be elected. In 1839, Parliament, controlled by the landed and industrial elites, rejected the first petition, signed by over 1.2 million men.

Trying to stem the tide, Parliament in the 1840s passed several pieces of legislation to ease the crisis. In 1846, it repealed the Corn Laws,[1] which made food cheaper for the working classes. The Factory Act of 1847 restricted the hours of labor for women and children. The group leading the charge for the repeal of the Corn Laws was the Anti-Corn Law League, a middle-class voluntary society that believed not only in the tenets of free trade but also that high food prices would drive the working class to greater desperation and anger. The campaign and the subsequent repeal secured a place for voluntary associations pushing for social and economic reform in British political life. From the decade of the 1840s emerged a new type of Victorian, the middle-class reformer, male or female, who would fight for "the moral and intellectual improvement and the general social welfare of the

---

1. A tariff barrier erected against the import of cheaper foreign grain, resulting in high prices for the staple of the worker's diet, bread, and profits for British landowners.

Chapter 6
Radical
Reformers in
Victorian Britain:
Annie Wood
Besant
(1847–1933) and
Charles
Bradlaugh
(1833–1891)

laboring classes." As reformers attacked the political, social, and economic problems and ills of Victorian Britain, they brought with them their own Victorian values and ideas.

By midcentury, middle-class reformers contended with conflicts and movements that centered on civil liberties and political rights, liberalism and socialism, work and poverty, religion and science, marriage and sex, and motherhood and birth control. Few Victorians escaped contact with at least one of these concerns because these issues began to occupy the public and private spaces of Victorian Britain. In this chapter, we will examine the remarkable lives of two-middle class radical reformers, Annie Besant and Charles Bradlaugh, who were never far from the center of these conflicts. Bradlaugh and Besant challenged and at times threatened the Victorian order. Bradlaugh fought to remove restrictions on free speech, an issue he passionately argued for in his newspaper, *The National Reformer,* and to secure the right of workers and those who held unorthodox religious views to participate in British public and political life. Annie Besant joined Bradlaugh in his fight for political rights and his defense of the Freethought movement.

Freethought followers or "freethinkers" of the Victorian era had deep roots in the political traditions of the French Enlightenment, the writings of Thomas Paine, the American Revolution, Owenite Socialism, English radicalism, and the Protestant legacy of private reflection on one's faith. The Freethinkers were not a unified group or movement, but they shared some common beliefs: first, established Christian institutions and orthodoxy were contrary to freedom and democracy; second, the Church of England's privileged position in society often stood in the way of social justice and change; and third, alternative moral and societal belief systems would replace those traditionally provided by the church. They espoused "secularism," an alternate belief system that placed its faith in science, humanism, morality, and progress. The general reading public was suspicious of Freethought; not only did they believe it preached against religion, but in the mid-1840s, "the mass of nominally educated men" perceived Freethought to be a threat against the social and political order.

Bradlaugh and Besant were first linked in history as the leaders of the Freethought movement: two articulate and fiery orators and defenders of secularism, intimate friends, and radical reformers of existing social and political structures. Their notoriety grew when they became co-defendants in one of the most spectacular and titillating trials of the nineteenth century, where the prosecutor accused them of corrupting the morals of youth, of inciting "indecent, obscene, unnatural, and immoral practices." Their crime was the publication of a book on birth control. Their lives dramatize the dynamic and contentious atmosphere of a modernizing industrial society; the methods that each employed to transform their world; and the penalties inflicted for upsetting Victorian political, religious, social, and moral sensibilities and norms.

■ THE ACTORS:

*CHARLES BRADLAUGH AND ANNIE
WOOD BESANT*

Charles Bradlaugh was born on September 26, 1833, in a rented four-room
terrace house on a newly built street in
London's growing East End. His father,
Charles, was a law clerk and a literate
and educated man. His mother, Elizabeth Trimby, was a nursemaid and she
bore seven children, two of whom died
in early childhood. The Bradlaughs
moved often. The homes they inhabited grew smaller, more dilapidated,
and more expensive as population
pressures and profit drove landlords to
divide and redivide houses and tene-
ments and raise the rents. Their final
family home, a rented, four-room,
dingy terrace house in an area of artisan dwellings and railway junctions
known as Bethnal Green was one degree above a slum. Charles would be a
familiar figure in London's working-
class East End for his entire life.

During his childhood, he witnessed
his father's struggle to make ends meet.
Charles senior worked in the evenings
for a few extra shillings but continued
to lose the fight against poverty as his
family grew, inflation worsened, and
rents increased. The district of Charles's
childhood, Bethnal Green, was known
for its political activism, radicalism, and
militant support for the Chartist movement. Charles junior's political awakening apparently came early. At the age
of ten, "after much hesitation, and with
great trepidation, he crept into a chan-
dler's shop and bought a copy of the
Charter with a precious halfpenny."[2]

2. S. Headingley, *Biography of Charles Bradlaugh*
(New York: The Freethought Press, 1933), p. 3.

Charles was more fortunate than
boys whose fathers worked in the factories, mines, and mills of nineteenth-
century Britain. His father was a clerk,
one of the lowest economic positions
within the British middle class, but
his father was literate and schooled
and made sure that his eldest son
would have some education as well.
Between the ages of seven and eleven,
Charles attended a school, but his
family's increasing impoverishment
forced Charles to stop attending and
to enter the work force as an errand
boy for his father's employer. He continued his education by attending
Sunday school at a nearby Anglican
Church, Saint Peter's.

Charles, a curious, earnest, studious, and intelligent boy, soon caught
the eye of the Reverend John Graham
Packer, who appointed him a student
teacher. During his studies and preparations, Charles noticed that the
gospels of Matthew, Mark, Luke, and
John contained discrepancies, and he
asked the reverend for help and further explanations. Packer became so
unhinged at the thought of having to
explain theology to a young student
that he called him an "atheist" and
suspended him from teaching Sunday
school for three months. This incident
in 1848 so embarrassed and disgraced
Bradlaugh that he shunned going to
services during this suspension as
well. Bradlaugh and his followers portray this suspension as fortuitous. He
now spent his free Sundays listening
to political and "Freethought" speakers at the famous open air meeting
place in Bethnal Green, Bonner's Field.

Bonner's Field and its orators had a
poor record with the British authorities,

Chapter 6
Radical
Reformers in
Victorian Britain:
Annie Wood
Besant
(1847–1933) and
Charles
Bradlaugh
(1833–1891)

who viewed the field as a breeding ground for political and religious dissent. Chartist meetings had been held there during the contentious years of that movement and now, and especially on Sundays, Freethought orators dominated the stage. At 15, young Bradlaugh stood mesmerized and awed by the speakers, the atmosphere, and the intellectual banter. At times, he engaged the speakers and defended passionately and eloquently the Anglican Church and its doctrine against their attacks. Soon the impressionable and soul-searching youth was deeply involved in the movement, much to the chagrin of Reverend Packer. To address Bradlaugh's heresy, the reverend convened a meeting with the youth's father and employer and gave Bradlaugh an ultimatum: give up his new friends and ideas or lose his job and home. Bradlaugh left home at sixteen. During the next few years, Bradlaugh sharpened his oratory skills and knowledge of Freethought and its proponents.

After a brief stint in the army, Bradlaugh, at the age of twenty, had developed a deep desire and zeal to fight for ideas, causes, and movements that promoted human welfare, progress, and freedom. Returning to London after his military term in Ireland, he sought the freethinkers of his youth and discovered that the community that had intellectually nurtured and excited him had changed. Many of his fellow freethinkers had emigrated to America after years of harassment by the local religious and civil authorities, and the revolutionary fervor of 1848 had diminished. The London movement was in the process of reinventing

itself. It adopted the name of the London Secular Society and was guided by George Holyoake. Holyoake continued Freethought's involvement in radical and republican politics, and young Bradlaugh was excited at the prospect of not only addressing religious questions but social and political ones as well.

Bradlaugh quickly readjusted to civilian life; he found a position as an errand boy in a lawyer's office and soon rose to the position of managing clerk. Bradlaugh also struck up an acquaintance with a fellow freethinker, Abraham Hooper, and his family. Bradlaugh began courting the eldest daughter, Susannah, who shared some of Bradlaugh's views and was known for her "kindness of heart and gentility of nature." On June 5, 1855, Susannah and Charles were wed and settled in the district of their childhood, Bethnal Green.

Bradlaugh worked to expand his grasp of contemporary social, political, and philosophical problems during the 1850s and 1860s (Document One). He threw himself wholeheartedly into the secular movement, and his every spare moment was spent on a speaking circuit that took him to tiny, obscure halls and rooms where two or three people were assembled. In these venues, he expounded on the inconsistencies and self-contradictions found in the Bible, the impossibility of miracles, the unreliability of divine revelation, and Christianity and its institutions as deterrents to human progress. He preached about the power of human reason and secularism as the way to promote human welfare by material means; about measuring human welfare by utilitarian rules, that is, the greatest happiness for the greatest number; and "making the service of others a duty of life." Bradlaugh's views on social reform were derived from the utilitarianism of Jeremy Bentham and the liberalism of John Stuart Mill. The works of Bentham and Mill appealed to Bradlaugh because they used ethical theory and moral theorizing to assess the rightness of acts, policies, decisions, and choices and their potential to promote the happiness of those affected by them.

Bradlaugh's lectures appealed primarily to the working class because he preached the message that reason, common sense, self-education, self-help and challenges to convention and tradition could earn the artisan, the small businessperson, the trade unionist, and the skilled worker a place in British society and a stake in the riches of the empire. This message resonated with working men and women because many of them suspected that middle-class churchgoers were hypocrites and snobs. Their views were often reinforced by their daily experiences with and observations of this hypocrisy, such as Parliament's attempt in 1855 to restrict any type of trade or business transaction on Sunday, or "the Lord's Day." During this series of protests over the passage of the Lord's Day laws, Bradlaugh gained greater public recognition in the community.

According to its critics, the Lord's Day laws placed an onerous burden on working-class people because Sunday was often the only day on which to run errands. Working-class leaders and others, such as Charles Dickens, immediately pointed out the hypocrisy of the act and decided to take action. The central London park, Hyde Park, was the site of several demonstrations. On a designated Sunday, thousands of working-class men, women, and children lined the streets to jeer at members of Parliament riding in their carriages driven by coachmen, who were obviously working on the Lord's Day. The second of the demonstrations attracted Bradlaugh and when this demonstration became disorderly, he came to the defense of a man who was being beaten by the police. Bradlaugh's defiance of the police, his eventual defense of his action in court, his intimidating physical presence, and his zealotry made him the ideal spokesperson for the secular movement that often invoked ferocious and riotous opposition. By 1859, the London Secular Society recognized his talent and drive and it elected him president.

Bradlaugh clearly understood the antagonism that "respectable" society directed at the secularists and freethinkers. When he became president of the society, he took special pains to change his cockney accent and appearance. Dressed in dark grey or black broadcloth, matching waistcoat, starched collar, and black neckcloth, Bradlaugh could have easily been mistaken for an Anglican minister. He fought battles with his voice, presence, power of personality, and pen against the Victorian "establishment." His crusades against the establishment did not mean class struggle; he believed in the classes working together for total reform, each recognizing the responsibility of the other for

Chapter 6
Radical
Reformers in
Victorian Britain:
Annie Wood
Besant
(1847–1933) and
Charles
Bradlaugh
(1833–1891)

achieving the greater good. After all, Bradlaugh was a Victorian who believed in self-education, hard work, and self-help. He strictly observed commitments to marriage and family, even after he separated from his wife because of her incurable alcoholism, and opposed any form of indulgence and excess. His extreme respectability, appearance, and nonviolent creed made it difficult for his critics to claim that the spokesperson for the secular movement was immoral, decadent, and violent.

Soon after becoming president of the society, Bradlaugh founded the paper, *The National Reformer,* which in the 1860s became the platform to support various causes: parliamentary and electoral reform; a republican form of government, which meant abolishing the British monarchy; improved standards for housing and sanitation; temperance; birth control; population control; and free speech. In his campaign for parliamentary reform, Bradlaugh advocated universal suffrage: giving the vote to all men and women. Eventually this broad-based movement culminated in the Disraeli- and Conservative-backed Reform Bill of 1867, which enfranchised 1 million new voters, most of them skilled workers. Disappointed with the limited nature of the reform, Bradlaugh fought until the end of his life for the enfranchisement of women and unskilled male workers.

With the expansion of the franchise to artisans, Bradlaugh decided to become a candidate for Parliament. He chose a district (borough) with a large number of newly enfranchised voters and a tradition of radical politics.

Bradlaugh, the candidate, championed compulsory national education, land reform, wealth and land taxation, removal of the Anglican Church from public life, courts of arbitration between capital and labor, and one issue that was influenced by his years in Ireland as a soldier—the representation of minorities in Parliament (Document Two). He muted his secularism, believing that it would complicate his chances for winning. His platform proved too radical, and the district elected two Liberals to the House of Commons.

Bradlaugh's personal life did not thrive in the same way his public life did. He made his living in the legal profession until 1863, when he went into private business as a broker. The early years of his marriage were happy, and he and Susannah had three children, Alice (b. 1856) , Hypatia (b. 1858), and Charles (b. 1859). Susannah tried hard to participate in her husband's activities; she entertained her husband's political friends and, when possible, she accompanied her husband on his speaking tours. During this period, Susannah began to drink, and her drinking grew worse as Bradlaugh's public life became more and more demanding and controversial. His infamy caused many of his clients to leave and he neared bankruptcy. As pressures mounted, Susannah turned to the bottle. Charles, long a supporter of the temperance movement, tried to find a treatment for Susannah's alcoholism, but she eventually succumbed to the disease and died in 1877.

In the contentious, volatile political climate of the late 1860s and 1870s, Bradlaugh used his increasing popularity to fight for social reform and *The National Reformer* to popularize many of the great intellectual and political ideas of the day—feminism, Darwinism, comparative religion, biblical criticism, and new sociological, anthropological, and archaeological studies. He also endorsed practical and often controversial political issues such as women's suffrage, extension of the suffrage to all working men, creation of an Irish republic, and the replacement of the monarchy with a republic.

Both the Conservative and Liberal governments in the 1860s tried to close down Bradlaugh's mouthpiece by invoking the Security Laws. These laws targeted "Pamphlets and printed Papers containing observations upon Public Events and Occurrences, tending to excite Hatred and Contempt of the Government and Constitution of these Realms as by Law established, and also vilifying our holy Religion."[3] Bradlaugh successfully argued in the courts that the laws did not apply to his paper. Winning in court did not help Charles financially; his political notoriety ruined his business. Companies shied away from using him as a broker and he noted in 1870, "I find it is utterly impossible to remain in business in the City in the face of the strong pressure excited against me on political and religious grounds."[4] Bradlaugh's debts forced him to sell the house and its furniture, and the family split up. Susannah and the girls

moved to the country, young Charles went away to school, and Bradlaugh moved to a set of rooms filled with the least desirable furniture from the sale. He sacrificed his own and his family's comfort to devote himself solely "to the movement."

Bradlaugh was a significant force in national politics by 1874. In that year, Annie Besant joined the National Secular Society and was presented her certificate of membership by the forty-one-year-old Bradlaugh. Besant had gained a bit of local notoriety: she was a woman of twenty-seven, a mother of two, the separated wife of an Anglican minister, and a disbeliever. Annie's life to this point had not foreshadowed such a radical break with Victorian norms. She had been brought up by her parents to believe that "women ought to be religious" and the "lightest breath of dishonor was to be avoided."[5] How then did Annie Wood Besant become one of the most unconventional, radical, and vilified woman of the Victorian era?

On October 1, 1847, William Burton Perrse Wood and Emily Roche Morris welcomed the birth of their second child and only daughter, Annie Wood. Annie's father William was the poor relation to a prominent and well-to-do English family. Half Irish, William spent his early life in Ireland earning a medical degree. He put his medical career on hold when a relative offered him a position in commerce in London. He married Emily Roche Morris, the daughter of middle-class Irish parents. Encouraged by both her parents,

3. *The National Reformer*, 17 April 1870, and *The National Reformer*, 22 May 1870, quoted in David Tribe, *President Charles Bradlaugh, M.P.* (London: Elek Books, 1971), p. 115.

4. Ibid.

5. Annie Besant, *Autobiography* (London: T. Fisher Unwin, 1893), p. 34.

*Chapter 6
Radical
Reformers in
Victorian Britain:
Annie Wood
Besant
(1847–1933) and
Charles
Bradlaugh
(1833–1891)*

Annie learned to read at an early age. In her autobiography, Annie recalls her father's influence on her intellectual and religious development. William Wood was a religious skeptic, not subscribing to any particular religion, and was "deeply read in philosophy." He did not recommend that his daughter adopt his skepticism. He believed that women should have a religious upbringing and that "men had a right to read everything and think as they should."[6] Annie would later reject both these opinions. Her mother balanced her husband's skepticism with a deep religious piety and devotion to Anglicanism. When her husband died of consumption in 1852, Emily Wood was left to raise her children and earn a respectable living. Being an in-law to a genteel, prominent, and well-to-do family, Emily took the respectable job of managing a boardinghouse in the town of Harrow for boys of middle-class families attending Harrow public school. This position allowed her to enroll her eldest son, Harry, in the school and give him a proper education. Annie's education was more problematic.

At this point in the 1850s, the education of middle-class girls depended upon the opinions and circumstances of the parents. Few schools existed for girls and even if a young girl was privileged enough to attend one of them, they did not necessarily receive a serious and intellectually rigorous education. Middle-class norms dictated that a girl's education emphasize the social graces, domestic arts, and academic subjects fitting for a woman, such as

languages, music, art, geography, and history. In many families, a girl's early education was left to governesses and then later to male tutors. Annie's mother could afford neither, and her education was left to fate.

Fate was kind to Annie in this instance. Ellen Marryat, a woman known to take an interest in and educate children coming from poor but respectable families, lived in Harrow. Marryat took Annie under her wing and from the age of eight until sixteen, Annie attended Marryat's private academy. Under Marryat's tutelage, Annie learned to be a scholar. She noted how Marryat never gave them "dry questions" and "answers lazy teachers so much affect; how geography was learned by painting skeleton maps, and how 'Auntie' abhorred children learning by rote things they did not understand."[7] Marryat's unconventional views about female education raised a few eyebrows, but she deflected the criticism through a deep belief in a strictly religious upbringing. By the time Annie returned to her mother's house at sixteen, she had embraced Marryat's piety and religious devotion, as well as Marryat's passion for scholarship and independent thinking.

Annie's years with Marryat never diminished her love and affection for her mother, a woman she deeply respected because of her pride; gentle, womanly ways; and fortitude in the face of adversity. Annie spent the next few years of her life helping her mother with the boardinghouse; entertaining young men; and continuing

6. Ibid.

7. Ibid., p. 50.

to study literature, philosophy, and theology. At this point in her young life, still deeply influenced by Marryat, her studies led her deeper and deeper into religious belief. This same inquisitive mind would eventually lead her to disbelief, atheism, secularism, and finally into theosophy.

During this phase of religious intensity and fervor, Annie met a young Anglican clergyman, Frank Besant. He was attending a mission church in a poor district of Clapham, where her grandfather lived. She later describes her fascination with Frank as an attraction of a young religious girl who is drawn to a priest. Frank believed that he had found the perfect wife and soon after their acquaintance asked Annie to marry him. In summer 1866, Annie was eighteen and in love with the idea of being a priest's wife and not with Frank. They were married in December 1867. Annie knew little about her husband, his opinions about marriage, and the physical and emotional demands of matrimony (Document Three).

Annie's life with Frank was miserable from the start. She found her husband domineering, expecting total submission and obedience from his wife. Annie relates that her wedding night was terrifying and shocking, and from this time forward she never reconciled herself to this wifely duty. Frank was known to be cool, formal, humorless, and conscientious, and a man with a temper. Annie posed quite a challenge to Frank, who found her willful, undisciplined, and too proud to talk with his colleagues' wives about babies, servants, and household management. Their marriage was a mismatch, and even the birth of their

two children, Arthur Digby (b. 1869) and Mabel (b. 1870), did not reconcile Annie to the marriage and Frank's demands for his matrimonial rights. Annie's discomfort with sex led her first to consult her doctor about physiology and sex; he told her to consult the work of Chavasse, "on the ground that it was better for a woman to read the medical details than it was for her to have to apply to one of the opposite sex to settle matters which did not need to be dealt with by the doctor."[8]

The reference to Chavasse referred to a popular guide for women written by Henry Pye Chavasse and published in 1843 under the title *Advice to wives on the management of themselves.* Chavasse's advice manual, along with many other advice books of the time, outlined the responsibilities of marriage, child rearing, and household management. Annie found little in Chavasse's manual that discussed the issue that would later propel her to fame, restriction of marital fertility. Annie's discontentment with her marriage propelled her to seek consolation in religious study and meditation. Yet the comfort she sought would not be found in her bible study. Like Bradlaugh, she found many discrepancies in the gospels and could not believe that a loving God would subject children, especially her daughter, who was a sickly and weak child, to the agonies of sickness.

Frank noticed his wife's increasing disbelief and her reluctance to take communion. He grew increasingly concerned that his doubting and rebellious wife would ruin his career. In

---

8. Ibid., p. 84.

*Chapter 6
Radical
Reformers in
Victorian Britain:
Annie Wood
Besant
(1847–1933) and
Charles
Bradlaugh
(1833–1891)*

the context of the time, a vicar's wife publicly affirming her doubt and withdrawing from communion because of this doubt could be interpreted as a minister's inability to tend to the spiritual needs of his parish. Annie's unhappiness and willfulness and Frank's frustration and anger combined to create a volatile mix in the Besant household, occasionally leading to physical violence.

Whenever she could, Annie escaped to London, where her mother and brother now lived. In London, Annie began to seek the company of people who, like her, possessed unorthodox beliefs. In the early 1870s, London possessed many circles of secularists, atheists, and unbelievers, and Annie soon ingratiated herself into these circles through her intellect, charm, and beauty. Returning to Sibsey, the town where her husband's vicarage was, Annie busied herself with the charitable and organizational duties expected of a vicar's wife. But noncompliance with religious duties was noticed, and by the summer of 1873, her husband gave her an ultimatum: if she refused to attend the communion service, she would have to leave home. After con-

sultation with her brother Henry, she separated from Frank and struck out on her own, with Mabel in tow. She had to leave Digby with his father as part of the separation agreement.

Ever conscious of her mother's position, Annie refused to live with her and her brother because of the shame it would bring to their household. Instead, she took a job as a governess for a year, but she resigned from this position when her mother became terminally ill. When her mother died in 1874, she turned for help to one of the freethinkers whom she had met in London. Thomas Scott, a publisher of monthly pamphlets that attacked the dogmas of the Anglican Church, offered the job of writing these pamphlets to Annie. She leapt at the opportunity to flex her intellect and opine about the divinity of Jesus and other subjects. She welcomed what she called her release from "bondage" and delighted in her independence, work, and writing, and in the development of her daughter.[9] It was simply a matter of time before Annie met Charles Bradlaugh while she traveled in this circle of influential freethinkers.

▨ ACT I:

THE TRIAL(S) OF BESANT
AND BRADLAUGH

In 1874, a friend persuaded Annie to visit the sacred site of secularism in Britain, Bradlaugh's Hall of Science. She had recently decided to join the National Secular Society, not as an atheist but as a sympathetizer. Within

a few months of her membership, she was a committed atheist. When Annie entered the hall, she was struck by the electricity and tension of the moment as the crowd waited for Bradlaugh to speak. After the meeting, Bradlaugh

9. Roger Manvell, *The Trial of Annie Besant and Charles Bradlaugh* (London: Elek/Pemerton, 1976), p. 17.

approached her and immediately recognized her drive, intellect, passion, and beauty. He encouraged Annie to discuss her beliefs with him and by the end of their first session together, she came away knowing she was an atheist. Bradlaugh remarked that "you have thought yourself into Atheism without knowing it."[10]

Bradlaugh invited Besant to write for *The National Reformer,* and within a few months she had proven that she could write with equal facility about religion, science, economics, literature, agricultural reform, marriage, and the status of women. She threw herself fully into the mission of *The National Reformer* and augmented her writing with public lecturing. Soon she was a regular on a lecture circuit that promoted Freethought, republicanism, political rights for women, and social reform (Document Four). Of course, her meteoric rise in the ranks caused tongues to wag. Bradlaugh and Besant indeed had become very close. How close they were is the cause of contemporary as well as historical speculation. Most biographers believe that Bradlaugh was in love with her and in other circumstances, if she had been able to obtain a divorce from her husband, he would have asked Annie to be his wife. Most likely because of her abysmal physical relationship with her husband and their high moral standards, they never consummated their deep love and affection for one another. Annie commented on the cruel scrutiny and speculation about their relationship. She wrote: "It will be a good thing for the world when a friendship between a man and a woman no longer means a protective condescension on one side and helpless dependence on the other, but when they meet on equal ground of intellectual sympathy, discussing, criticizing, studying, and so aiding the evolution of stronger and clear thought-ability in each."[11] Their friendship and professional and intellectual partnership incited accusations of "free love" and immorality.

The relationship between Besant and Bradlaugh upset many sacred middle-class Victorian norms and values. Besant rejected the domestic ideology that required women to remain at home; create a safe and tranquil haven for husband and children; and cultivate moral rectitude, religious faith, and discipline. Besant stepped outside this private sphere into the rough and tumble of British public life. Her public speaking and promotion of secularism and science, republicanism, and women's suffrage was an affront to those who believed women should not participate in public debate. When women did venture outside the home into the public sphere in midcentury, Victorian society expected them to engage in charity work. This work was deemed natural because women could use their natural talents of nurturing, motherhood, and religiosity to tend to the sick, poor, and unfortunate. Annie defied this model and instead took radical, subversive political positions not appropriate for her gender.

Annie was not alone in her defiance

10. Ibid., p. 18.

11. Rosemary Dinnage, *Annie Besant* (London: Penguin, 1981), p. 26.

Chapter 6
Radical
Reformers in
Victorian Britain:
Annie Wood
Besant
(1847–1933) and
Charles
Bradlaugh
(1833–1891)

of Victorian convention. Quite a few Victorian women ventured beyond charity work that simply tried to alleviate misery. Some women wanted to reform society so that political, social, and economic inequalities and injustices no longer existed. These efforts were multidirectional and included parliamentary reform, reform of working and living conditions, and the temperance movement. Some reformers campaigned publicly on the behalf of women's interests. Women's health and rights concerning children and marriage, a married woman's property rights, equality in education and employment, laws prohibiting or limiting prostitution, and women's suffrage all were issues fought for in this era. Early reforms often appealed for legal changes based on a woman's "natural" position in society as a mother. Later reforms, such as education, property rights, and suffrage, were based on women's right to be treated equally compared to men. Women who took very public positions were often judged according to their comportment in these public debates. Those who talked about subjects unbecoming a woman, like Josephine Butler discussing the need to repeal the Contagious Diseases Act, which required prostitutes to be tested for venereal diseases, or those like the militant suffragette, Emmeline Pankhurst, were called "wild," "shrieking," or "troublesome" (Document Five). Annie earned the right to be called all three as she waded into the fight for universal suffrage (men's and women's), the promotion of birth control, and compulsory education with a zeal few of her contemporaries possessed.

Annie's notoriety finally reached national status when she and Bradlaugh embarked upon another political and social cause—the publication of a pamphlet on birth control. In 1877, Bradlaugh and Besant decided to reissue a pamphlet on birth control written by a Boston freethinker, Charles Knowlton. Knowlton's *The Fruits of Philosophy: The Private Companion of Young Married People* had been in print for almost forty years and was widely available in secular and Freethought circles. Knowlton's book was as much a philosophical discussion of why birth control was necessary as it was a manual on how to practice birth control. A year earlier Charles Watts, an influential English member of the Secular Society and publisher of *The National Reformer*, had decided to issue a new edition. Bristol and London authorities arrested and prosecuted him for selling "obscene" material. Watts consulted Bradlaugh and Besant, and after much debate among the three, Watts decided to plead guilty and agreed to pay a fine. During their discussions about legal strategies, Annie had argued that the pamphlet was defensible as a medical work. She was especially outraged that the authorities were attempting to silence discussions about birth control. She emerged from the debates determined to reissue the pamphlet under her and Bradlaugh's new publishing venture, the "Freethought Publishing Company."

In March 1877, Annie and Charles reissued *Fruits of Philosophy* with a preface of their own. In the preface, Bradlaugh and Besant stated that the public had the "fullest right" to discuss freely the great social questions of the day, including population control. They endorsed the "scientific checks" promoted by the book and argued: "We think it more moral to prevent the conception of children than, after they are born, to murder them by want of food, air, and clothing or by abortion." Bradlaugh had long subscribed to Thomas Malthus's prediction that the world risked running out of resources for its ever increasing population and that a discussion of ways to prevent this was necessary. Both wanted a confrontation with Victorian authorities, and the London police obliged by arresting them on the day of publication. The police charged that they had unlawfully and wickedly devised to corrupt the morals of the young and other subjects of the queen, and to incite them to obscene, unnatural, and immoral practices by publishing an indecent, lewd, filthy, bawdy, and obscene book.[12]

The publication of the pamphlet and the resulting police action attracted the attention of the press and the curiosity of the public. In the days leading up to, during, and immediately after the trial, the subject of limiting family size through birth control was brought into Victorian homes through newspapers. Curiosity about the content of the book spurred sales and in 1877, 125,000 copies were sold, 124,300 more than the year before. This trial was one of many private and public discussions taking place around birth control. At the time of the trial, the average family size in England was 6.6; by 1900, this number fell below 6; and by the 1920s and 1930s, the average family size fell to slightly more than 2 children.

The trial of Annie Besant and Charles Bradlaugh commenced on June 18, 1877, and lasted four days. Annie opened for the defense and testified for two days. Bradlaugh testified less, but both of them defended themselves and spoke on behalf of all the oppressed and inarticulate poor. As they had expounded in the preface, they asserted in court the Malthusian view that the only existing check on overpopulation was the dreadful rate of infant mortality among the poor. In their estimation, the fight was not only about birth control but the socioeconomic conditions of poor men and women (Document Six). After their individual testimony, their defense team called medical witnesses to confirm their assertions about the suffering of the working class under repeated pregnancies; the diseases caused by excessive child bearing, especially prolapse or "falling of the womb"; and the fact that children of the poor died three times more often than children of the rich. Their defense was so persuasive that the judge presiding over the trial spoke of the injustice of the state prosecutors bringing Besant and Bradlaugh to trial. When Annie and Charles left the court, they believed their case was won.

Politics and prevailing sensibilities proved too powerful for the jury to return with a verdict of not guilty. The foreman of the jury was Arthur Walter, the son of the owner of *The Times*. He took the editorial position of his father's paper and argued vehemently for a guilty verdict. Walter persuaded

12. Manvell, p. 61.

Chapter 6
Radical
Reformers in
Victorian Britain:
Annie Wood
Besant
(1847–1933) and
Charles
Bradlaugh
(1833–1891)

the jury to find that the book in question was calculated to deprave public morals, but he had to settle for his fellow jurors' opinion that Besant and Bradlaugh did not have corrupt motives in publishing it. Faced with a split verdict, the judge had no choice but to pronounce the two guilty. After an appeal, the verdict was dismissed on a technical point. In principle, Besant and Bradlaugh won by advancing the cause for birth control and free speech. Besant's own pamphlet on birth control, *The Law of Population: Its Consequences and Its Bearing Upon Human Conduct and Morals* (1877) was published immediately after the trial, and she was not prosecuted for its content. It sold 175,000 copies.

Despite these public victories, Besant lost a personal battle. Ever since Annie had won custody of their daughter Mabel, Frank had been trying to have her custodial privileges revoked. He had tried in 1875, claiming that Annie's atheism made her an unfit parent and that she was corrupting her daughter by not giving her a religious education. Annie persevered in 1875 but after the highly public trial, the court awarded Frank custody of Mabel and limited Annie to occasional visits (Document Seven). Only when Digby and Mabel came of age could they return to their mother, which they did almost immediately.

Annie's fight for her daughter did result in something positive. English courts became increasingly reluctant to remove a child from a parent because he or she did not practice a religion. Legally, British society was slowly accepting secularism in the public realm. The case that solidified

this position involved the other half of the secular team, Charles Bradlaugh. Bradlaugh had had his eye on a seat in Parliament for some time and in 1880, after three attempts to be elected from Northampton, he finally won a seat as a Liberal.

When Bradlaugh arrived at Parliament, he requested that he make a solemn affirmation or declaration of allegiance instead of taking an oath to God. Partly he believed it would be an affront to members of Parliament who solemnly swore to God and knew of his atheism. He also wished to establish the same precedent that he had established during his various trials in court—to allow individuals the right to chose an affirmation over an oath. His request to make an affirmation was denied and he could not take his seat. Bradlaugh fought for six years to take his seat in Parliament. During this time, Bradlaugh became the focus of vehement and ugly attacks. Members of Parliament called him "an infidel," "a blasphemer," "a moral monster," and "the Cerberus of Atheism, treason, and filth."[13] Conservatives and supporters of the monarchy also pointed out that he was a republican who "would be willing to overthrow the Throne and the Constitution." Bradlaugh's persistence, integrity, and defiance endeared him to his constituents, and they reelected him again and again during this six-year ordeal. When he officially took his seat in 1886, Bradlaugh had gained the respect of his colleagues because he was

---

13. Walter Arnstein, "The Bradlaugh Case: A Reappraisal," *Journal of the History of Ideas* 18:2 (April 1957), p. 260.

an honest and articulate politician whose once radical positions did not seem so radical and extreme anymore, especially when compared to the socialists. His sense of public decorum, always one of his greatest assets; his respect and knowledge of constitutional law; and his attacks upon socialism also helped him earn the respect of his colleagues.

■ ACT II:
SEPARATE ROADS

After the Knowlton trial, Annie and Charles began to drift apart personally and politically. Annie continued to pay the cost for her radical views and her scathing denunciations of the position of women in Victorian society. After losing custody of her daughter, Annie's feminism hardened and she began promoting legal equality in both marriage and divorce for women and the cause of women's suffrage, among many other causes. Concurrently, she and Bradlaugh's daughters, Hypatia and Alice, were among the first women allowed to study for degrees at London University. All three studied for degrees in the sciences and by 1880 Annie had certificates qualifying her to lecture on chemistry, botany, mathematics, physiology, and basic physics. She successfully passed her first B.S. and the Preliminary Science exams with honors, but the college refused to list her as one of their successful examinees because they feared contributors would balk if they saw her name. The college eventually refused to grant her a degree because they argued that she had not performed well on her practical chemistry exam. It is possible that the examiners failed her on purpose.

During the early 1880s, Annie began to seek different male companionship, first becoming involved with Dr. Edward Aveling, a lecturer in science, and then with the young and not yet famous George Bernard Shaw. At the same time, she sought new political ideas and social issues. Annie's intellectual rigor and curiosity often led her to consider and study new ideas, trends, and ideologies. By the mid-1880s, she was "listening, reading, and thinking much, but saying little" about the political ideology of socialism. She hesitated at first to declare her allegiance to this "ism" because she would "bring herself into collision with the dearest of my friends" and "strain the strong and tender tie so long existing."[14] Despite this tie and Bradlaugh's dislike of socialism, Annie took up the socialist cause in words, deeds, and spirit.

Annie became a member of the Fabian Society, which was composed of London intellectuals who encouraged the working class to fight for the right to vote and then pass legislation that would improve their condition. For the next few years, Annie fought passionately for this type of evolutionary socialism and worker causes. Annie's new crusade led her to form an important partnership with the investigative journalist and publisher, W. T. Stead. Stead's paper, *The Pall Mall Gazette*, carried stories on government and police intimidation of

14. Besant, p. 302.

*Chapter 6
Radical
Reformers in
Victorian Britain:
Annie Wood
Besant
(1847–1933) and
Charles
Bradlaugh
(1833–1891)*

workers, parliamentary scandals, worker demonstrations and actions, and industrial abuses. He and Annie founded *The Link*, a halfpenny weekly that published exposés on sweated labor, extortionate landlords, unhealthy workshops, child labor, and prostitution. In 1888, Annie wrote a story, "White Slavery in London," exposing the horrendous working conditions of girls working in Byrant and May's match factory (Document Eight).

Owners of match factories had long employed unskilled girls and women in this unhealthy and dangerous work. Besant's article revealed well-known abuses and practices and generated public sympathy for and outrage over the match workers' plight. Annie took advantage of the publicity and organized a strike. The match workers struck for adequate wages, abolition of a punitive system of fines that reduced their pay, and for healthier and safer working conditions. Particularly horrifying to the public was the debilitating and mutilating deformity of the jaw caused by inhalation of phosphorous, commonly known as "phossy jaw." Public opinion sided with the workers, and they returned to work at a slightly higher wage, with a guarantee of improved working conditions and continuation of the union. Besant had organized and executed the labor action with the help and courage of the 1,400 match workers. This was the first successful strike of unskilled workers and led to labor activism by unskilled workers during the 1890s.

Annie's activism and journalism led her to observe and participate in the lives of the London poor. One issue captured her interest more than

any other, the plight of London's poor children. She could not escape the images of "children lying about on shavings, rags, anything; famine looking out of babies' faces, out of women's eyes, out of the tremulous hands of men" and she decided to campaign for a seat on the London School Board in 1888. Her network of socialists and freethinkers in London's East End gave her the opportunity to address meetings about her program of free secular education, and health services and meals in schools. "If we insist on these children being educated, is it not necessary that they shall be fed?"[15] Besant topped the polls with over 3,000 votes more than the runner-up. During her time on the board, Besant laid the foundations for medical school services and school meals. She also pushed the board to insist that contractors hired to operate the schools had to pay their workers a fair wage.

By the end of the 1880s, Bradlaugh and Besant had carved out separate political paths: he as a respected member of Parliament who supported radical Liberal positions, women's suffrage, and Irish independence, and she as a prominent social reformer. Charles died in 1891 content with his social and political accomplishments. Besant, however, was growing increasingly disenchanted with the slow pace of reform and began to ponder the question of whether people's lives could be made better by focusing on their material conditions. Always a seeker of truths, Annie gravitated

15. Anne Taylor, *Annie Besant: A Biography* (New York: Oxford University Press, 1992), p. 216.

toward theosophy and its guru, Madame Blavatsky. As practiced by Blavatsky's Theosophical Society, theosophy stated that God is the source of all spirit and matter and that humans can attain insight into the nature of God and the spiritual nature of the universe. Mixing Buddhism and Brahminism, the theosophists believed in reincarnation, occult knowledge and powers, and the practice of yoga. Much speculation has revolved around the reasons why Besant adopted theosophy. George Bernard Shaw argued that the Fabians were too intellectual and sophisticated for her and took too little action, that she needed something to stir the passions in her. Others speculate that it was the mysticism of her youth returning. Whatever the reasons, Annie stayed a committed theosophist until her death in 1933.

From the 1890s to the 1930s, Annie turned her political attention to India. She felt a particular affinity for the country because it was the home of the Theosophical Society. Moving to India in 1893, she campaigned for the establishment of schools for girls, Indian home rule, and later for India's independence. She became such a powerful supporter of Indian causes that the Indian National Congress elected her president in 1917, most likely as a snub to the British authorities because the government had interned her as a dangerous subversive, an extraordinary compliment for this seventy-year-old woman. Until she died in 1933, Annie continued to work for the alleviation of human misery and suffering. Maybe her son Digby described her best. At the ceremony for the centenary of her birth, he simply described her as "Mother."

▨ FINALE

The paths Charles Bradlaugh and Annie Besant took were varied and controversial. Separately and together, they saw that all was not right in this new industrial society and Victorian world, and they asked what could be done to improve the political and socioeconomic lives of their fellow citizens. Bradlaugh answered this question by focusing on the institutional and religious structures that he believed restricted an individual's right to think and act freely. He fought for a society free from religious prescriptions and dogma; class and gender privilege; and restrictions on freedom

of thought, expression, and religion (irreligion). His work and dedication were not without costs. He was reviled by many in Victorian society. Despite his notoriety, which affected his personal and family life, Bradlaugh felt it was his calling to destroy idols and to fight for the promise of social and political justice. By the time of his death, he was celebrated for this fight.

Annie Besant would also be celebrated at the end of her long life for fighting for the weak and the oppressed. Fifty years earlier, she would not have been honored because she was a "troublesome" woman then. She had left a marriage that was emotionally and intellectually unsatisfactory;

Chapter 6
Radical
Reformers in
Victorian Britain:
Annie Wood
Besant
(1847–1933) and
Charles
Bradlaugh
(1833–1891)

entered into equal partnerships with men; explored numerous political, intellectual, and scientific ideas that could possibly solve a woman's and child's suffering and misery; and fought against economic and social injustices. She endured all that Victorian society threw at her because of her political and intellectual positions. It accused her of being a harlot and a whore, an unfit mother, and an unnatural woman; many attacks upon her centered on her inabilities and inadequacies as a woman. She remarked how her critics often liked to accuse her of "feminine" inconsistency for her many different stands. She wrote, "The moment a man uses a woman's sex to discredit her arguments, the thought-ful reader knows that he is unable to answer the arguments themselves. But really these silly sneers at woman's ability have lost their force, and are best met with a laugh at the stupendous 'male self-conceit' of the writer."

Like Bradlaugh, Besant adopted causes because of thoughtful reading and introspection, and a commitment to the improvement of Victorian society and experience. Unlike Besant, Bradlaugh was privileged in these causes and fights because, as a man, he was granted the right to work within existing political, social, and legal structures. Besant was not so privileged. As a result, the price she paid for her radical reform work was higher.

■ QUESTIONS

1. Describe the early influences on Charles Bradlaugh's life and his decision to become an atheist, reformer, and feminist. Describe the early influences on Annie Besant's life and her decision to become an atheist, reformer, and feminist.

2. Charles Bradlaugh, like John Stuart Mill, believed that the state had no right to suppress ideas, no matter how unpopular they were. What unpopular ideas did Bradlaugh and Besant promote?

3. Reflecting on John Stuart Mill's *The Subjection of Women* (1869), how did Besant's life mirror his observations on the subjection of women? What qualities did Besant's husband wish her to have? According to Mill, what qualities in general have men sought in women?

4. According to Bradlaugh, Besant, Mill, and Eliza Lynn Linton, should women enter into the public arena and have equal political rights and duties?

5. Describe the avenues and methods that Bradlaugh and Besant, together and separately, used to reform Victorian society. Did they have equal access? Why or why not?

6. Did Bradlaugh reject Victorian society and ideology completely? Did Besant?

7. Did gender influence the types of reform that Bradlaugh and Besant each advocated?

8. What were the consequences for Bradlaugh and Besant when they challenged Victorian values and attitudes? How do these challenges affect our understanding of Victorian society?

■ **DOCUMENTS**

▰▰▰▰▰▰▰▰▰▰▰ **DOCUMENT ONE** ▰▰▰▰▰▰▰

CHARLES BRADLAUGH

A Plea for Atheism
(1864)

Bradlaugh fought his whole life to allow atheists to profess their beliefs without fear of societal and state prosecution and prejudice. In the late 1870s, Bradlaugh wrote this answer to the critics of Freethought and atheism. What are his arguments in favor of atheism?

This essay is issued in the hope that it may succeed in removing some of the many prejudices prevalent, not only against the actual holders of atheistic opinions, but also against those wrongfully suspected of Atheism. Men who have been famous for depth of thought, for excellent wit, or great genius, have been recklessly assailed as atheists by those who lack the high qualifications against which the malice of the calumniators was directed. Thus, not only have Voltaire and Paine been, without ground, accused of Atheism, but Bacon, Locke, and Bishop Berkeley himself, have, amongst others, been denounced by thoughtless or unscrupulous pietists as inclining to Atheism, the ground for the accusation being that they manifested an inclination to push human thought a little in advance of the age in which they lived.

It is too often the fashion with persons of pious reputation to speak in unmeasured language of Atheism as favouring immorality, and of atheists as men whose conduct is necessarily vicious, and who have adopted atheistic views as a desperate defiance against a Deity justly offended by the badness of their lives. Such persons urge that amongst the proximate causes of Atheism are vicious training, immoral and profligate companions, licentious living, and the like. Dr. John Pye Smith, in his *Instructions on Christian Theology,* goes so far as to declare that "nearly all the atheists upon record have been men of extremely debauched and vile conduct." Such language from the Christian advocate is not surprising, but there are others who, while professing great desire for the spread of Freethought and having pretensions to rank amongst acute and liberal thinkers, declare Atheism impracticable, and its teachings cold, barren, and negative. Excepting to each of the above allegations, I maintain that thoughtful Atheism affords greater possibility for human happiness than any system yet based on, or possible to be founded on Theism, and that the lives of true atheists must be more virtuous—because more human—than those of the believers in Deity, the humanity of the devout believer often finding itself neutralised by a faith with which that humanity is necessarily in constant collision.

[171]

Chapter 6
Radical
Reformers in
Victorian Britain:
Annie Wood
Besant
(1847–1933) and
Charles
Bradlaugh
(1833–1891)

DOCUMENT TWO

CHARLES BRADLAUGH

"Northampton Election Address, 1868"

After the Reform Act of 1867, Bradlaugh put himself forward as a candidate for Parliament in the borough of Northampton, north of London. Who or what is the focus of his attacks? How does he propose improving the conditions of his constituents? What influences him to take these stands?

In seeking your suffrages for the new Parliament, I am encouraged by the very warm feeling exhibited in my favour by so many of the inhabitants of your borough, and by the consciousness that my own efforts may have helped in some slight degree to hasten the assembly of a Parliament elected by a more widely extended franchise than was deemed possible two years ago.

If you should honour me by electing me as one of your representatives, I shall give an independent support in the new Parliament to that party of which Mr. Gladstone will probably be chosen leader; that is to say, I shall support it as far as its policy and action prove consistent with the endeavour to attain the following objects, which I hold to be essential to the progress of the nation:—

1. A system of compulsory National Education, by which the State shall secure to each child the opportunity of acquiring at least the rudiments of a sound English education preparatory to the commencement of the mere struggle for bread.

2. A change in our land laws, commencing with the abolition of the laws of primogeniture and entail, diminishing the enormous legal expenses attending the transfer of land, and giving greater security to the actual cultivator of the soil for improvements made upon it.

3. A thorough change in our extravagant system of national expenditure, so that our public departments may cease to be refuges for destitute members of so-called noble families.

4. Such a change in the present system of taxation that for the future the greater pressure of Imperial taxes may bear upon those who hold previously accumulated wealth and large tracts of devised land, and not so much upon those who increase the wealth of the nation by their daily labour.

5. An improvement of the enactments relating to capital and labour, so that employer and employed may stand equal before the law, the establishment of conciliation courts for the settlement of trade disputes, and the abolition of the jurisdiction in these matters of the unpaid magistracy.

6. A complete separation of the Church from the State, including in this the removal of the Bishops from the position they at present occupy as legislators in the House of Lords.

7. A provision by which minorities may be fairly represented in the legislative chambers.

8. The abolition of all disabilities and disqualifications consequent upon the holding or rejection of any particular speculative opinion.

9. A change in the practice of creating new peerages; limiting the new creations to life peerages, and these only to be given as rewards for great national services; peers habitually absent from Parliament to be deprived of all legislative privileges, and the right of voting by proxy in any case to be abolished.

10. The abolition as a governing class of the old Whig party, which has long since ceased to play any useful part in our public policy. Toryism represents obstructiveness to Radical progress, but it represents open hostility. Whiggism is hypocritical; while professing to be liberal, it never initiates a good measure or hinders a bad one. I am in favour of the establishment of a National party which shall destroy the system of government by aristocratic families, and give the members of the community born poorest fair play in their endeavour to become statesmen and leaders, if they have genius and honesty enough to entitle them to a foremost place.

In order that my competitors shall not have the right to object that I unfairly put them to the expense of a contest, I am willing to attend a meeting of the inhabitants of your borough, at which Mr. Gilpin and Lord Henley shall be present, and to be governed by the decision voted at such a meeting as to whether or not I persist in my candidature.

In asking your support I pledge myself, in the event of a contest, to fight through to the last moment of the Poll a fair and honest fight. It would give me special pleasure to be returned as the colleague of Mr. Gilpin, whom I believe to be a thoroughly honest and earnest representative; and if you elect me I shall do my best in the House of Commons for the general enfranchisement and elevation of the people of the United Kingdom.

DOCUMENT THREE

ANNIE BESANT

Autobiography
(1893)

In these passages from her autobiography, Annie describes her marriage. What is her view on marriage? Whom or what does she fault for its failure?

. . . So I married in the winter of 1867 with no more idea of the marriage relation than if I had been four years old instead of twenty. My dreamy life, into which

Chapter 6
Radical
Reformers in
Victorian Britain:
Annie Wood
Besant
(1847–1933) and
Charles
Bradlaugh
(1833–1891)

no knowledge of evil had been allowed to penetrate, in which I had been guarded from all pain, shielded from all anxiety, kept innocent on all questions of sex, was no preparation for married existence, and left me defenceless to face a rude awakening. Looking back on it all, I deliberately say that no more fatal blunder can be made than to train a girl to womanhood in ignorance of all life's duties and burdens, and then to let her face them for the first time away from all the old associations, the old helps, the old refuge on the mother's breast. That "perfect innocence" may be very beautiful, but it is a perilous possession, and Eve should have the knowledge of good and evil ere she wanders forth from the paradise of a mother's love. Many an unhappy marriage dates from its very beginning, from the terrible shock to a young girl's sensitive modesty and pride, her helpless bewilderment and fear. Men, with their public school and college education, or the knowledge that comes by living in the outside world, may find it hard to realise the possibility of such infantile ignorance in many girls. None the less, such ignorance is a fact in the case of some girls at least, and no mother should let her daughter, blindfold, slip her neck under the marriage yoke. . . .

. . . We were an ill-matched pair, my husband and I, from the very outset; he, with very high ideas of a husband's authority and a wife's submission, holding strongly to the "master-in-my-own-house theory," thinking much of the details of home arrangements, precise, methodical, easily angered and with difficulty appeased. I, accustomed to freedom, indifferent to home details, impulsive, very hot-tempered, and proud as Lucifer. I had never had a harsh word spoken to me, never been ordered to do anything, had had my way smoothed for my feet, and never a worry had touched me. Harshness roused first incredulous wonder, then a storm of indignant tears, and after a time a proud, defiant resistance, cold and hard as iron. The easy-going, sunshiny, enthusiastic girl changed—and changed pretty rapidly—into a grave, proud, reticent woman, burying deep in her own heart all her hopes, her fears, and her disillusions. I must have been a very unsatisfactory wife from the beginning, though I think other treatment might gradually have turned me into a fair imitation of the proper conventional article. Beginning with the ignorance before alluded to, and so scared and outraged at heart from the very first; knowing nothing of household management or economical use of money—I had never had an allowance or even bought myself a pair of gloves—though eager to perform my new duties creditably; unwilling to potter over little things, and liking to do swiftly what I had to do, and then turn to my beloved books; at heart fretting for my mother but rarely speaking of her, as I found my longing for her presence raised jealous vexation; with strangers about me with whom I had no sympathy; visited by ladies who talked to me only about babies and servants—troubles of which I knew nothing and which bored me unutterably—and who were as uninterested in all that had filled my life, in theology, in politics, in science, as I was uninterested in the discussions on the housemaid's young man and on the cook's extravagance in using "butter, when dripping would have done perfectly well, my dear"; was it wonderful that I became timid, dull, and depressed?

All my eager, passionate enthusiasm, so attractive to men in a young girl, were doubtless incompatible with "the solid comfort of a wife," and I must have been inexpressibly tiring to the Rev. Frank Besant. And, in truth, I ought never to have married, for under the soft, loving, pliable girl there lay hidden, as much unknown to herself as to her surroundings, a woman of strong dominant will, strength that panted for expression and rebelled against restraint, fiery and passionate emotions that were seething under compression—a most undesirable partner to sit in the lady's armchair on the domestic rug before the fire. . . .

DOCUMENT FOUR

JOHN STUART MILL

The Subjection of Women
(1869)

Besant's challenge to Victorian ideas about marriage was part of a larger debate about the treatment of women in Victorian society. John Stuart Mill, now a member of Parliament, supported the nascent woman's suffrage movement and wrote this essay to argue against male dominance over women. Harriet Taylor, Mill's wife, is said to have had tremendous influence on this essay. How does Mill portray women's position in society?

CHAPTER I

The object of this Essay is to explain as clearly as I am able grounds of an opinion which I have held from the very earliest period when I had formed any opinions at all on social or political matters, and which, instead of being weakened or modified, has been constantly growing stronger by the progress of reflection and the experience of life. That the principle which regulates the existing social relations between the two sexes—the legal subordination of one sex to the other—is wrong in itself, and now one of the chief hindrances to human improvement; and that it ought to be replaced by a principle of perfect equality, admitting no power or privilege on the one side, nor disability on the other. . . .

. . . In early times, the great majority of the male sex were slaves, as well as the whole of the female. And many ages elapsed, some of them ages of high cultivation, before any thinker was bold enough to question the rightfulness, and the absolute social necessity, either of the one slavery or of the other. [*Mill*

*Chapter 6
Radical
Reformers in
Victorian Britain:
Annie Wood
Besant
(1847–1933) and
Charles
Bradlaugh
(1833–1891)*

discusses how slavery was then abolished.] . . . [W]hen so many other things which came down from the same odious source have been done away with. And this, indeed, is what makes it strange to ordinary ears, to hear it asserted that the inequality of rights between men and women has no other source than the law of the strongest.

. . . But, it will be said, the rule of men over women differs from all these others in not being a rule of force: it is accepted voluntarily; women make no complaint, and are consenting parties to it. In the first place, a great number of women do not accept it. Ever since there have been women able to make their sentiments known by their writings (the only mode of publicity which society permits to them), an increasing number of them have recorded protests against their present social condition: and recently many thousands of them, headed by the most eminent women known to the public, have petitioned Parliament for their admission to the Parliamentary Suffrage. The claim of women to be educated as solidly, and in the same branches of knowledge, as men, is urged with growing intensity, and with a great prospect of success; while the demand for their admission into professions and occupations hitherto closed against them, becomes every year more urgent. Though there are not in this country, as there are in the United States, periodical conventions and an organized party to agitate for the Rights of Women, there is a numerous and active society organized and managed by women, for the more limited object of obtaining the political franchise. Nor is it only in our own country and in America that women are beginning to protest, more or less collectively, against the disabilities under which they labor. France, and Italy, and Switzerland, and Russia now afford examples of the same thing. How many more women there are who silently cherish similar aspirations, no one can possibly know; but there are abundant tokens how many *would* cherish them, were they not so strenuously taught to repress them as contrary to the proprieties of their sex. It must be remembered, also, that no enslaved class ever asked for complete liberty at once. . . . It is a political law of nature that those who are under any power of ancient origin, never begin by complaining of the power itself, but only of its oppressive exercise. . . .

All causes, social and natural, combine to make it unlikely that women should be collectively rebellious to the power of men. They are so far in a position different from all other subject classes, that their masters require something more from them than actual service. Men do not want solely the obedience of women, they want their sentiments. All men, except the most brutish, desire to have, in the woman most nearly connected with them, not a forced slave but a willing one, not a slave merely, but a favorite. They have therefore put everything in practice to enslave their minds. The masters of all other slaves rely, for maintaining obedience, on fear; either fear of themselves, or religious fears. The masters of women wanted more than simple obedience, and they turned the whole force of education to effect their purpose. All women are brought up from the very earliest years in the belief that their ideal of character is the very opposite to that of men; not self-will, and government by self-control, but submission, and yielding to the control of others. All the moralities tell them that it is the duty of women, and all the current sentimentalities that it is their nature, to live for others; to make complete abnegation of themselves, and to have no life but in their affections. And by their affections are meant the only ones they are allowed to have—those to the men with whom they are connected, or to the children who constitute an additional and indefeasible tie between them and a man. When we put together three things—first, the natural attraction between opposite sexes; secondly, the wife's entire dependence on the husband, every privilege or pleasure she has being either his gift, or depending entirely on his will; and lastly, that the principal object of human pursuit, consideration, and all objects of social ambition, can in general be sought or obtained by her only through him, it would be a miracle if the object of being attractive to men had not become the polar star of feminine education and formation of character. And, this great means of influence over the minds of women having been acquired, an instinct of selfishness made men avail themselves of it to the utmost as a means of holding women in subjection, by representing to them meekness, submissiveness, and resignation of all individual will into the hands of a man, as an essential part of sexual attractiveness. Can it be doubted that any of the other yokes which mankind have succeeded in breaking, would have subsisted till now if the same means had existed, and had been so sedulously used, to bow down their minds to it?

DOCUMENT FIVE

Eliza Lynn Linton

"The Wild Women"
(1891)

Eliza Lynn Linton was one of the first women to earn her living as a journalist. She wrote for the Saturday Review, Macmillan's Magazine, *and* Nineteenth Century. *Linton supported women's education, property rights, and right to their children. She was against women's suffrage and political rights and coined the phrase "shrieking sisterhood" for those who opposed her on this issue. Below are excerpts from her series on "wild women" in* Nineteenth Century. *What bars women from being political beings?*

All women are not always lovely, and the wild women never are. As political firebrands and moral insurgents they are specially distasteful, warring as they do against the best traditions, the holiest functions, and the sweetest qualities of their sex. Like certain 'sports' which develop hybrid characteristics, these

*Chapter 6
Radical
Reformers in
Victorian Britain:
Annie Wood
Besant
(1847–1933) and
Charles
Bradlaugh
(1833–1891)*

insurgent wild women are in a sense unnatural. They have not 'bred true'—not according to the general lines on which the normal woman is constructed. There is in them a curious inversion of sex, which does not necessarily appear in the body, but is evident enough in the mind. . . .

Be it pleasant or unpleasant, it is none the less an absolute truth—the *raison d'être* of a woman is maternity. For this and this alone nature has differentiated her from man, and built her up cell by cell and organ by organ. The continuance of the race in healthy reproduction, together with the fit nourishment and care of the young after birth, is the ultimate end of woman as such; and whatever tells against these functions, and reduces either her power or her perfectness, is an offence against nature and a wrong done to society.

The cradle lies across the door of the polling-booth and bars the way to the senate. We can conceive nothing more disastrous to a woman in any stage of maternity, expectant or accomplished, than the heated passions and turmoil of a political contest; for we may put out of court three fallacies—that the vote, if obtained at all, is to be confined to widows and spinsters only; that enfranchised women will content themselves with the vote and not seek after active office; and that they will bring into the world of politics the sweetness and light claimed for them by their adherents, and not, on the contrary, add their own shriller excitement to the men's deeper passions. Nor must we forget that the franchise for women would not simply allow a few well-conducted, well-educated, self-respecting gentlewomen to quietly record their predilection for Liberalism or Conservatism, but would let in the far wider flood of the uneducated, the unrestrained, the irrational and emotional—those who know nothing and imagine all—those whose presence and partisanship on all public questions madden already excited men. We have no right to suppose that human nature is to be changed for our benefit, and that the influence of sex is to become a dead letter because certain among us wish it so. What has been will be again. In the mirror of the prophet, which hangs behind him, the Parisian woman of the Revolution will be repeated wherever analogous conditions exist; and to admit women into active participation in politics will certainly be to increase disorder and add fuel to the fire of strife.

DOCUMENT SIX

ANNIE BESANT

"Defense of Dr. Knowlton's *The Fruits of Philosophy*" (June 18, 1877)

In 1877, Besant and Bradlaugh were put on trial for publishing Knowlton's trea-
tise on birth control. In open court, Besant defended her actions. For whom does
Besant wage her defense? For what reasons?

. . . It is not as defendant that I plead to you today—not simply as defending myself do I stand here but I speak as counsel for hundreds of the poor, and it is they
for whom I defend this case. My clients are scattered up and down through the
length and breadth of the land; I find them amongst the poor, amongst whom I
have been so much; I find my clients amongst the fathers, who see their wage
ever reducing, and prices ever rising; I find my clients amongst the mothers
worn out with over-frequent child-bearing, and with two or three little ones
around too young to guard themselves, while they have no time to guard them.
It is enough for a woman at home to have the care, the clothing, the training of a
large family of young children to look to; but it is a harder task when oftentimes
the mother, who should be at home with her little ones, has to go out and work
in the fields for wage to feed them when her presence is needed in the house.

I find my clients among the little children. Gentlemen, do you know the fate
of so many of these children?—the little ones half starved because there is food
enough for two but not enough for twelve; half clothed because the mother, no
matter what her skill and care, cannot clothe them with the money brought
home by the breadwinner of the family; brought up in ignorance, and ignorance
means pauperism and crime—gentlemen, your happier circumstances have
raised you above this suffering but on you also this question presses; for these
overlarge families mean also increased poor rates, which are growing heavier
year by year. These poor are my clients . . . , mothers who beg me to persist in
the course on which I have entered—and at any hazard to myself, at any cost
and any risk—they plead to me to save their daughters from the misery they
have themselves passed through during the course of their married lives.

Gentlemen, I may perhaps say one word for myself before I go right into my
case. The learned Solicitor-General has had the kindness to say that he does not
impute bad intent to us in publishing this work. What bad intent could there be? I
had nothing to gain in publishing this work—I had much to lose. It is no light thing
for a woman, whose ambition is bound up in the name which she hopes to make,
to have the imputation thrown upon her of publishing indecent books and of disseminating obscenity amongst the young. I risk my name, I risk my liberty; and it
is not without deep and earnest thought that I have entered into this struggle. . . .

Chapter 6
Radical
Reformers in
Victorian Britain:
Annie Wood
Besant
(1847–1933) and
Charles
Bradlaugh
(1833–1891)

. . . Do you, gentlemen, think for one moment that myself and my co-defendant are fighting the simple question of the sale or publication of this six-penny volume of Dr Knowlton's? Do you think that we would have placed ourselves in the position in which we are at the present moment for the mere profit to be derived from a sixpenny pamphlet of 47 pages? No, it is nothing of the sort; we have a much larger interest at stake, and one of vital interest to the public, one which we shall spend our whole lives in trying to uphold. The question really is one of the right to public discussion by means of publication, and that question is bound up in the right to sell this sixpenny pamphlet which the Solicitor-General despises on account of its price. We are not fighting simply to obtain your verdict for the sake of selling this work. I, personally, don't care, if your verdict is in my favour, to sell another copy. I sell it so long as the detective police spies and secret agents of a society calling itself a Vice Society resort to the practices that they do to get respectable booksellers into trouble; so long as that goes on, so long shall we endeavour to uphold those principles which we maintain with reference to the right of public discussion, by fighting this great battle until we win ultimate success.

This pamphlet is valuable to us just as is the piece of silk to the soldier who wins the battle for his country: it is the flag which represents the cause we have at stake. It is with that feeling—and that feeling alone—that we stand here today to uphold the right to publish this pamphlet, and I fight that I may make here the right of open and free discussion on a great and important social subject. There are various rights of speech which the public enjoy. The right of discussion in theology is won; the right of publicly discussing politics is won, but as to discussion on social subjects, there is at present no right. There will be this day week, if your verdict is in our favour, because, you may depend upon it, that verdict once given no one will ever go against it; everyone will then feel free to discuss a point of vital interest to society; but till that verdict, that right is not one which can be exercised with impunity. However much you may disagree with Dr Knowlton's theories—and I don't pretend to agree with him on all his points—however much I say you disagree, that is no reason why you should brand his book as obscene.

Difference of opinion is not to be taken as proof of obscenity against any particular subject, and the more you may differ in opinion from Knowlton so much the more jealously should you guard his right of discussion. If it were only to gain your sympathies with Dr Knowlton's work, I would not waste your time or mine here today; but it is because I want you, by your verdict, to lay down this great and just principle—that opinion, honestly given opinion, honestly expressed opinion, freely and fairly published, shall not be prevented public expression because a police officer does not agree with the opinion so expressed upon matters in which probably he is not at all informed.

I have in my hand the opinion of Mr John Stuart Mill, in which he treats of the right of free discussion: he says, in his Essay on Liberty: "If all mankind, minus one, were of one opinion, and only one person were of the contrary opinion, mankind would be no more justified in silencing that one person than he, if he had the power, would be justified in silencing mankind."

DOCUMENT SEVEN

ANNIE BESANT

Autobiography
(1893)

What are the arguments for taking Besant's daughter away from her?

. . . I received notice in January, 1878, that an application was to be made to the High Court of Chancery to deprive me of the child, but the petition was not filed till the following April. Mabel was dangerously ill with scarlet fever at the time, and though this fact was communicated to her father I received a copy of the petition while sitting at her bedside. The petition alleged that, "The said Annie Besant is, by addresses, lectures, and writings, endeavouring to propagate the principles of Atheism, and has published a book entitled 'The Gospel of Atheism.' She has also associated herself with an infidel lecturer and author named Charles Bradlaugh in giving lectures and in publishing books and pamphlets, whereby the truth of the Christian religion is impeached, and disbelief in all religion inculcated."

[THE DECISION]

. . . The judge stated that I had taken the greatest possible care of the child, but decided that the mere fact of my refusing to give the child religious instruction was sufficient ground for depriving me of her custody. Secular education he regarded as "not only reprehensible, but detestable, and likely to work utter ruin to the child, and I certainly should upon this ground alone decide that this child ought not to remain another day under the care of her mother."

DOCUMENT EIGHT

ANNIE BESANT

"White Slavery in London"
(1888)

In this excerpt, Besant describes the conditions of the match workers. What are the conditions under which they labor? What are the remedies suggested by Besant?

Let us see how the money is made with which these monstrous dividends are paid. . . .

[181]

Chapter 6
Radical
Reformers in
Victorian Britain:
Annie Wood
Besant
(1847–1933) and
Charles
Bradlaugh
(1833–1891)

The hour for commencing work is 6.30 in summer and 8 in winter, work concludes at 6 P.M. Half-an-hour is allowed for breakfast and an hour for dinner. This long day of work is performed by young girls, who have to stand the whole of the time. A typical case is that of a girl of 16, a piece-worker; she earns 4s. a week, and lives with a sister, employed by the same firm, who "earns good money, as much as 8s. or 9s. per week." Out of the earnings 2s. is paid for the rent of one room; the child lives on only bread-and-butter and tea, alike for breakfast and dinner, but related with dancing eyes that once a month she went to a meal where "you get coffee, and bread and butter, and jam, and marmalade, and lots of it." . . . The splendid salary of 4s. is subject to deductions in the shape of fines; if the feet are dirty, or the ground under the bench is left untidy, a fine of 3d. is inflicted; for putting "burnts"—matches that have caught fire during the work—on the bench 1s. has been forfeited, and one unhappy girl was once fined 2s. 6d. for some unknown crime. If a girl leaves four or five matches on her bench when she goes for a fresh "frame" she is fined 3d., and in some departments a fine of 3d. is inflicted for talking. If a girl is late she is shut out for "half the day," that is for the morning six hours, and 5d. is deducted out of her day's 8d. One girl was fined 1s. for letting the web twist around a machine in the endeavor to save her fingers from being cut, and was sharply told to take care of the machine, "never mind your fingers." Another, who carried out the instructions and lost a finger thereby, was left unsupported while she was helpless. The wage covers the duty of submitting to an occasional blow from a foreman; one, who appears to be a gentleman of variable temper, "clouts" them "when he is mad."

One department of the work consists in taking matches out of a frame and putting them into boxes; about three frames can be done in an hour, and $\frac{1}{2}$d. is paid for each frame emptied; only one frame is given out at a time, and the girls have to run downstairs and upstairs each time to fetch the frame, thus much increasing their fatigue. One of the delights of the frame work is the accidental firing of the matches: when this happens the worker loses the work, and if the frame is injured she is fined or "sacked." 5s. a week had been earned at this by one girl I talked to.

The "fillers" get $\frac{3}{4}$d. a gross for filling boxes; at "boxing," *i.e.* wrapping papers round the boxes, they can earn from 4s 6d. to 5s. a week. A very rapid "filler" has been known to earn once "as much as 9s." in a week, and 6s. a week "sometimes." The making of boxes is not done in the factory; for these $2\frac{1}{4}$d. a gross is paid to people who work in their own homes, and "find your own paste." Daywork is a little better paid than piecework, and is done chiefly by married women, who earn as much sometimes as 10s. a week, the piecework falling to the girls. Four women day workers, spoken of with reverent awe, earn—13s a week.

A very bitter memory survives in the factory. Mr. Theodore Bryant, to show his admiration of Mr. Gladstone and the greatness of his own public spirit, bethought him to erect a statue to that eminent statesman. In order that his workgirls might have the privilege of contributing, he stopped 1s. each out of their wages, and further deprived them of half-a-day's work by closing the factory, "giving them a holiday." ("We don't want no holidays," said one of the girls pathetically, for—needless to say—the poorer employees of such a firm lose their wages when a holiday is "given.") So furious were the girls at this cruel plundering, that many went to the unveiling of the statue with stones and bricks in their pockets, and I was conscious of a wish that some of those bricks had made an impression on Mr. Bryant's conscience. Later on they surrounded the statue—"we paid for it" they cried savegely—shouting and yelling, and a gruesome story is told that some cut their arms and let their blood trickle on the marble paid for, in very truth, by their blood. . . .

Such is a bald account of one form of white slavery as it exists in London. With chattel slaves Mr. Bryant could not have made his huge fortune, for he could not have fed, clothed, and housed them for 4s. a week each, and they would have had a definite money value which would have served as a protection. But who cares for the fate of these white wage slaves? Born in slums, driven to work while still children, undersized because underfed, oppressed because helpless, flung aside as soon as worked out, who cares if they die or go on the streets, provided only that the Bryant and May shareholders get their 23 per cent, and Mr. Theodore Bryant can erect statues and buy parks? Oh if we had but a people's Dante, to make a special circle in the Inferno for those who live on this misery, and suck wealth out of the starvation of helpless girls.

Failing a poet to hold up their conduct to the execration of posterity, enshrined in deathless verse, let us strive to touch their consciences, *i.e.* their pockets, and let us at least avoid being "partakers of their sins," by abstaining from using their commodities.

7

The Project of Empire: George Nathaniel Curzon (1859–1925) and Mary Leiter Curzon (1870–1906)

HON. MRS. CURZON (MISS MARY LEITER).

THE HON. G. N. CURZON, M.P.

Photo by Alice Hughes, 52, Gower Street.

Photo by Russell and Sons, Baker Street.

MARRIAGE OF THE HON. G. N. CURZON AND MISS MARY LEITER.

■ SETTING THE STAGE

In late nineteenth-century Britain, Lord Salisbury, the conservative prime minister, spoke to the conservative Primrose League and divided the nations of the world into "the living and the dying." In a similar fashion, his newly appointed viceroy of India, Lord Curzon, described the Ottoman Empire, Persia, Morocco, Egypt, China, and Korea as "those countries which must inevitably have attracted the attention of Europe, partly from increasing infirmity, but more for the opportunities suggested by their latent though neglected sources of strength."[1] Both statesmen spoke in the parlance of late nineteenth-century imperialists. Imperialists like

1. G. P. Gooch, *History of Modern Europe, 1878–1919* (New York: Cassell and Company, 1923), p. 369.

Curzon and Salisbury believed that states and their societies were dynamic, living organisms, some of which were fitter, more superior, and more robust than others. Curzon pointed to the "infirmity" of states in Asia and Africa and the duty of Europeans to tap their "neglected" potential.

Salisbury and Curzon were not alone in their attitudes about the states and nations of Asia and Africa. Beginning in the 1880s, Europeans embarked upon a new phase of imperial conquest and domination, commonly referred to as "new imperialism." Armed with ideas of racial and national superiority; new industrial technologies such as the steamboat, railroads, the telegraph, and medicines; and a competitive spirit, Europeans dashed madly around the globe to hoist their national flags over the territories that they hoped would bring profits and prestige back home. By 1914, the Asian and African continents were patchworks of European and American imperial territories and interest.

Armed with their new "tools of empire," Europeans transformed the societies that they colonized in ways that early imperialists could not. Steamboats and railways transported Europeans deeper into the interior of Africa and Asia. Once there, they could fight malaria with quinine; communicate via telegraph; meet native resistance with improved weaponry; and navigate the terrain with bridges, roads, tunnels, and canals. In the late nineteenth century, European men and women could stay longer, live less isolated lives, and have a greater impact on the landscape, culture, and society of the regions they colonized than earlier imperialists. Of course, each encounter varied according to the ambitions and desires of the imperial state and the ability of the colonized society to resist European penetration, modification, and transformation of their political and socioeconomic systems.

From 1756 to 1858, the British had ruled in parts of India informally through the private trading company known as the East India Company. In 1857, the Indians rebelled against the company's rule. After a year, the British, with the help of loyal Indian troops, suppressed the revolt. In response to the rebellion, the British Parliament placed India directly under its rule, proclaimed Queen Victoria "Empress of India," and appointed the first viceroy, Lord Canning. India was now an imperial possession and Indians were the queen's subjects.

India was "the jewel in the imperial crown." Britain considered India vitally important to the wealth, prestige, and power of its overseas empire. Situated along the shipping routes linking Europe with the Far East, the British extracted raw materials for export to its manufacturing industries at home and used India as a market for British manufactured goods and as a port for its goods being shipped further east. India was also a proving ground for 250,000 British soldiers and the young bureaucrats of the Indian Civil Service. Directing, guiding, and watching over all Indians and Anglo-Indians (that is, the British in India) and their political, social, and economic activity for the British government was the government of India, which was headed by the viceroy. The viceroy of India was appointed by the British prime minister

Chapter 7
The Project
of Empire:
George Nathaniel
Curzon
(1859–1925)
and Mary Leiter
Curzon
(1870–1906)

to a four-year term and reported to the secretary of state for India in the British Cabinet. The viceroy not only represented Britain's political and economic interests in India, but also represented the moral and ethical codes that governed late Victorian society. Pomp and circumstance were symbols of Britain's right to rule in India, and elaborate social decorum and manners were symbols of Britain's civilizing mission. Upon his arrival in 1898, George Nathaniel Curzon (1859–1925), the new viceroy of India, and his wife Mary Leiter Curzon (1870–1906) rose to the occasion.

Lord Curzon is the archimperialist whose reign as viceroy (1898–1905) coincided with the climax of British rule in India. His views on British imperial policy, race, class, and relationships between men and women, both Indian and British, influenced his policies and ambitions in India. His reign overlaps with the period when imperialists and British-educated Indians debated the methods and aims of British rule in India. During the late nineteenth and early twentieth century, middle- and upper-class Indians transformed disparate reactions and resistance to British rule into a well-articulated political and cultural nationalist organization, the Indian National Congress (1885).

Mary Curzon's life as the wife of a colonial official and British imperialist demonstrates a phenomenon associated with the new imperialism. In the second half of the nineteenth century, more and more colonial and business professionals and administrators brought their families to India and established Victorian homes in communities segregated from Indian society. The British in India replicated Victorian social orders, mores, and customs. The introduction of women into colonial society caused the imperial, paternal state to worry about encounters between indigenous men and colonial women, especially women missionaries who often lived among the Indians.

When British men and women stepped outside these enclaves, as administrators, tourists, hosts, teachers, missionaries, and adventurers, and encountered Indian society and customs, they judged each encounter according to Victorian notions about race, the proper place of men and women in society, class, and religion. Anglo-Indians, male and female, were expected to follow a strict code of moral and sexual conduct and self-control during encounters with indigenous men and women, and these encounters occurred daily because of the nature of rule and lifestyle. At its peak, 170,000 British citizens lived in India, but this was not sufficient to administer a country of 300 million people. Legions of Indian servants, soldiers, police officers, junior officials, and laborers were employed by the British. Mary Curzon observed such encounters, and she wrote to her American family about her impressions of India, Indians, Anglo-Indian life and society, and its most energetic, ambitious, and forceful viceroy. To help you understand the ways in which colonial encounters affected the colonizer and the colonized, this chapter focuses on the British in India and the lives of one of its viceroys, George Nathaniel Curzon, and his American wife, Mary Leiter Curzon.

▩ THE ACTORS:

GEORGE NATHANIEL CURZON AND MARY LEITER CURZON

George Nathaniel Curzon was born at his family's estate, Kedleston, in 1859. Curzon's family had come to England with William the Conqueror in 1066 and had occupied a corner of Derbyshire ever since. One of eleven children, George portrayed his early childhood as miserable, primarily due to the strict regime of the governess, Miss Paraman, and the aloofness of his father. Sent to boarding school (public school) at the age of ten, Curzon, like other boys of his age and class, hated his school days and wrote bitterly of homesickness, sadistic schoolmasters, brutal beatings, and bleak surroundings. Later in life, Curzon came to appreciate Eton, one of Britain's most elite "public schools," and the traits that Eton and its schoolmasters had instilled in him and his peers. He believed that Eton had not only given him the education necessary to succeed in an age of accelerated change and government service (a facility with modern languages, geography, and history), but the petty tyrannies of Eton and a regime of physical sport had instilled in him strength of character, duty to queen and country, and loyalty to his peers. Reflecting on his school days while viceroy of India, he believed that institutions such as Eton and its alumni were pillars of British civilization.

In 1878, at the age of twenty, Curzon entered Balliol College, Oxford. During his four years at Balliol, Curzon pursued a course of study and extracurricular activities that prepared him for a life of politics. He chose Classics as his course of study, believing that this subject would prepare him for a political career. In 1878, the evidence was in his favor; seven of the fifteen current government's ministers had studied Classics. He joined and then later was elected president of the elite debating club, the Oxford Union, a position that two future prime ministers, Henry Asquith and Alfred Milner, had held. In addition, he joined the Oxford Canning Club, a club dedicated to the articulation of the principles of the British Conservative party (Tory Party). Curzon used both as venues to hone his debating skills, express and craft his political views, and level criticism at political opponents.

After he graduated from Balliol, he applied to and was chosen as one of two fellows at All Souls College in the fall of 1883. Fellowships at All Souls were based on the idea that the fellow, after seven years in residence, would serve God in church and in state. The attraction of an All Souls fellowship lay in the responsibilities, or lack of responsibilities, of each fellow. All Souls did not have undergraduates who required instruction; therefore, the fellows dedicated themselves to scholarship. All Souls attracted young men who parlayed their academic posts to positions in the world of politics. "As a place of scholarship, not of teaching, it combined the amenities of a country house or of a London club with the intellectual stimulus of a learned society."[2] Curzon used this opportunity to

2. Kenneth Rose, *Superior Person: A Portrait of Curzon and His Circle in Late Victorian England* (New York: Weybright and Talley, 1969), p. 101.

Chapter 7
The Project
of Empire:
George Nathaniel
Curzon
(1859–1925)
and Mary Leiter
Curzon
(1870–1906)

master the intricacies of current politics, to travel abroad, and to prepare himself for public life.

While still a fellow at All Souls, Curzon reasoned that his best chances for winning a seat in Parliament lay not in his home district, but in Southport, Lancashire. He negotiated with Southport's local Conservative party to be its candidate in the 1886 parliamentary elections. He agreed to pay for the cost of the election, £600, and to give the association an annual donation of £50. The Conservative party of Southport never regretted their investment. Curzon won a seat in Parliament and remained in that position until 1898, when he was appointed Viceroy of India.

As we already know, Curzon had prepared himself for a life of Tory politics. He and other members of his class were not immune to the political and social problems that plagued British society in the late nineteenth century. While still supporting crown and church, the imperial project, and social hierarchy, the Conservatives proved themselves to be pragmatists. In the era of an expanding franchise, the Tories knew that they had to broaden their base if they were to remain a political factor. This meant attracting the newly enfranchised workers to their cause, and they could do so only if they used the power of government to enact social legislation.

The Tories of the 1880s and 1890s modified their views on what role the state should play in addressing Britain's social ills. Unlike the case of the Liberal party, the role of the state posed fewer intellectual problems for them. The Liberals had long loathed the idea of state interference to alleviate misery, to correct inequities, or to modify the nation's economy. When the idea of state action began to gain currency with some Conservatives, it collided head-on with traditional laissez-faire principles favored by the Liberals. Conservatives had long held the belief that they, as the landed class, were best equipped to protect the working classes against the worst abuses of manufacturers and industrialization. In fact, much of Britain's mid-nineteenth-century social legislation regulating child labor, improving work conditions, and limiting work hours was passed under Conservative governments. The Conservatives did not wish to give up their political power, but they were willing to support social legislation designed to improve the conditions of the poorer classes. This type of social reform without class warfare appealed to Curzon.

Curzon's training for a political life extended beyond his comfortable rooms at Oxford and London. He wished to experience Britain's empire and its territorial interests up close. Beginning with his fellowship at All Souls and continuing through his years as a member of Parliament, Curzon traveled extensively throughout North America, the Far East, and India. He visited India twice (1887–1888 and 1892), Russia and the Caucasus (1888–1889), and Persia (1889–1890). As result of his journeys and the subsequent publication of *Russia in Central Asia, Persia and the Persian Question* (2 vols.), and *Problems of the Far East*, Curzon established himself as a leading expert on Britain's interests in

Asia, especially Britain's need to defend India's borders from an aggressive Russia. Curzon also reflected on Britain's civilizing mission: "The strength and omnipotence of England everywhere in the East is amazing. No other country or people is to be compared with her. We control everything, and are liked as well as respected and feared." When Curzon was appointed to the viceroyalty, he not only brought with him an aggressive national pride, but a belief that the British had a mission in India and the right to rule because "if we were to withdraw, the whole system of Indian life and politics would fall to pieces like a pack of cards."[3] Curzon was expressing the views of his contemporaries. They did not believe that Indians could govern themselves. There were so many conflicting religions, languages, and peoples that only the British could hold the country together.

Until the age of 35, Curzon lived a bachelor's life. His work and travel left him little time for women, whom he considered his inferiors. Curzon was a staunch antifeminist, opposed female suffrage, and believed that women should remain in the domestic sphere and ease the trials and tribulations faced by men in the public world. In an era of contested social and gender roles, he subscribed to the belief that men and women lived in separate spheres, and never should one venture into the other's domain. His attitudes on this subject are revealed throughout his courtship and subsequent marriage to Mary Leiter, heiress to an American fortune. Cur-

zon expressed his views in a letter to his fiancé: "Give me a girl who knows a woman's place and does not yearn for trousers. Give me, in fact, Mary."[4] In fact, Levi Z. Leiter gave away his daughter in marriage to George on April 22, 1895, five years after they had met at a London social gathering.

Mary Victoria Leiter was born on May 27, 1870, to Mary Theresa (Carver) Leiter and Levi Z. Leiter. Levi Z. Leiter was a wealthy Chicago businessman who had acquired his fortune by selling dry goods with his partner Marshall Field and by speculating in real estate. In 1881, Leiter sold his half of the now famous Marshall Field department store, packed up his family, and moved to Washington, D.C. Mary's mother, Mary Theresa Carver, had encouraged the move because she wished to live in a more cosmopolitan city and associate with a better class of people. At the age of eleven, Mary Victoria and her three siblings were being groomed to enter into a more prestigious and powerful social circle.

Mary grew up in a world of American social privilege that only money could buy. Tutors and governesses schooled her in French, German, literature, chemistry, arithmetic, and history. She spent summers in Chicago, visited friends in the fashionable upper-class enclave of Newport, Rhode Island, and traveled to Europe. Finally, at the age of 18, all of her mother's ambitions came true when her coming out ball and her debut social season was a rousing success. Mary's beauty was accompanied by

3. Rose, p. 202.

4. Nigel Nicolson, *Mary Curzon* (London: Weidenfeld and Nicolson, 1977), p. 34.

Chapter 7
The Project
of Empire:
George Nathaniel
Curzon
(1859–1925)
and Mary Leiter
Curzon
(1870–1906)

her wit, poise, character, modesty, and her father's fortune. The *Boston Herald* noted Mary's grace and beauty on the occasion of her visit to Newport, Rhode Island, in the summer of 1889: "The chief sensation was the appearance of Miss Mary Leiter, the Washington belle whose beauty is by this time celebrated, even the buds of last winter dwindling into insignificance before her. . . . Miss Leiter represents exactly the sort of American girl who we should send over to England with pardonable pride."[5] These words could not have been more prophetic. The *Boston Herald* was commenting on a new phenomenon in American society—transatlantic marriages.

■ ACT I:

MARRIAGE AND POLITICS

In the latter part of the nineteenth century, heirs to British hereditary titles married wealthy American women, allowing the holders of these titles access to American fortunes. The income or inheritance from their wives allowed the English nobles to pursue career avenues that required wealth in addition to status. As an example, the marriage of George Curzon to Mary Leiter placed him in a much better economic position vis à vis his ambitions. As he advanced in the Conservative party ranks, appearances had to be considered. A cabinet minister or an undersecretary could not live in bachelor chambers with a new bride. A house in London and one in the country were necessary for any aspiring politician. Curzon's yearly income of £1,000 from his father, Lord Scarsdale, would not cover such expenses. When George married Mary, her father bestowed upon her a settlement of £700,000, and he also awarded to his new son-in-law an annual income of £6,000.

In April 1895, George Nathaniel Curzon and Mary Victoria Leiter married in Washington, D.C. The two had first met five years earlier at the Duchess of Westminster's ball, Mary's invitation coming through a connection cultivated through the transatlantic marriage network. At the ball, she caught Curzon's eye when she danced the first dance with Edward, the Prince of Wales and heir to the throne. After a three-year courtship and two years of a secret engagement, George traveled to Washington and married his American heiress. After their marriage, they returned immediately to London. In June 1895, all of George's education, training, travel, political connections, class position, and ambition paid off. The leader of the Conservative party, Lord Salisbury, became prime minister and appointed George the undersecretary of state at the Foreign Office.

For the next three years, George worked night and day, and Mary languished in the role of wife. He shared nothing of his interests or work with her; he dismissed her or left the room when his friends and colleagues came to the house in London to discuss current politics. He did not even permit her the satisfaction of decorating their

5. Ibid.

home in London or choosing the household staff. Mary's time in the limelight appeared to be over. She was the American wife of an undersecretary, and she had no friends and little to occupy her time. The years between 1895 and 1898 were brightened only by the birth of the first two of her children, Irene and Cynthia, and occasional visits from her parents. In 1898, Mary's dull and dreary life in London came to a quick end when Lord Salisbury appointed her husband the viceroy of India.

■ Act II:

Viceroy and Vicereine in India

On December 30, 1898, the Curzons arrived in an India that had been in the throes of a famine for three years. Close to 1 million people had perished, and the famine had drained the resources of the British Raj. This prolonged crisis revealed the grinding poverty that covered the land and the failure of leadership on the part of previous viceroys. George Curzon arrived in India determined to improve the efficiency of British rule; he believed that the imperial mission needed to be rehabilitated. In a letter to the colonial secretary, Alfred Lyttelton, Curzon wrote, "The English are getting lethargic and they think only of home. Their hearts are not in this country. The big problems had been systematically shirked by every Viceroy for thirty years."[6] Curzon quickly identified important reforms to be undertaken to solve these problems. These included administrative reform within the Indian Civil Service, irrigation reform, preservation of ancient monuments, education reform, reform of the "rotten police system," and "a policy towards the Native States and their rulers to make them worthy partners in government."[7]

Curzon spent his seven years as viceroy pushing through many of these reforms himself, and his years in India are marked by his arrogance, impatience, and autocratic ways. Curzon viewed Indians as schoolchildren and he as their schoolmaster who needed to teach them perfect obedience, no questions asked. He summed up his attitudes thus, "From his [the Viceroy's] lips the Indian people look to learn how and wherefore they are governed."[8] In addition, he crushed many initiatives recommended by his own bureaucracy, the Indian Civil Service. He lavished his contempt on all those who disagreed with him.

Curzon's authoritarianism and arrogance, his contempt for the social responsibilities of the office, and his impatience propelled Mary into the social spotlight. She first had to master the intricate social protocol that had evolved over the last fifty years. In the

---

6. Robin J. Moore, "Imperial India, 1858–1914," in Andrew Porter, ed., *The Oxford History of the British Empire* (New York: Oxford University Press, 1999), vol. 3, p. 435.

7. Ibid.

8. Marian Fowler, *Below the Peacock Fan: First Ladies of the Raj* (New York: Viking, 1987), p. 262.

Chapter 7
The Project
of Empire:
George Nathaniel
Curzon
(1859–1925)
and Mary Leiter
Curzon
(1870–1906)

early years of the Raj, etiquette had been less rigid, and the viceroy was seen as the first among equals. But now, in the late Raj, Mary observed how "the lot of a Viceroy is one of absolute aloofness and everyone is in mortal funk of the august being. Being a Yankee I can't understand it but I manage to assume the necessary amount of awful respect for his Excellency when we appear in public"[9] (Document One). Mary adjusted very quickly to the intimate and cloistered world of Anglo-Indian society, and she soon learned the contrived and pretentious protocols of its inhabitants and how much it cost to maintain this exalted stature. To cover the costs of setting up the household, Mary turned to her father for help in defraying the costs. In a June 1899 letter to her father, she described the expenses: ". . . neither George nor I have made one single expenditure of a personal nature and the whole of this sum has been the public expense of our coming. We were told by our predecessors that the outlay in starting would not be less than £10,000 and it has proved true. Other people who have come here have had capital to draw upon but we had only our income. . . . If the £2,000 are more than you can help us out at present of course you will tell me."[10]

The British, like other Europeans, took great pains to erect barriers between themselves and the native populations and to bring as much as possible of their home country's customs, habits, foods, and morality to the colony. In India, the Anglo-Indians clustered their families, businesses, and leisure activities into "little Englands." Clubhouses, churches, schools, private bungalows, offices, playing fields, parade grounds, and army barracks became standard features in these enclaves. The interiors of each structure were designed to remind the visitor or inhabitant of home. Mary Curzon's first impression of the viceroy's residence, Government House, in Calcutta reminded her of her husband's ancestral home, Kedleston.

The British in India made very few concessions to life in the tropics. British women, or *memsahibs,* as the Indians called foreign women, insisted on wearing the standard Victorian costume: corsets, petticoats, stockings, starched long sleeved shirts, and wool skirts. British men's, or *sahibs',* garb, suits, starched collars, and ties, was equally as unyielding to the climate. The British looked upon Indian cuisine with suspicion and insisted on traditional British fare. Anglo-Indians passed their leisure time fox hunting, horse racing, and playing cricket, card games and billiards. On Sundays, the entire community attended church services, and on holidays, they watched military parades. The British in India believed, as Curzon did, that they were there to civilize the Indians, to demonstrate the superiority of British civilization, and to set an example. Transgressions, in either dress or behavior, were treated with suspicion and accusations of going "native."

One concession that many Europeans did make was to flee to higher

9. Fowler, p. 258.

10. John Bradley, *Lady Curzon's India: Letters of a Vicereine* (London: Weidenfield and Nicolson, 1985), p. 41.

and cooler ground during the hottest part of the year. For the British in India, this meant packing up the government and fleeing to Simla, a British community situated in the foothills of the Himalayas. Like other British enclaves, Simla and its privileged inhabitants observed a strict set of social protocols and customs. Upon reaching Simla, Mary once again noted the privilege awarded to the viceroyalty and the intensity of the social activity. George found Simla a tiresome place, given the intense pace of social obligations and the pettiness of its inhabitants. In Simla, as in "little Englands" elsewhere, Anglo-Indians not only adopted rigid notions about racial separation and hierarchy but they also maintained strict boundaries between social classes. These boundaries were erected as soon as someone boarded the steamship bound for India and they never came down. At the top of the social hierarchy stood the members of the Indian Civil Service (ICS), an institution numbering 1,300 men.

When George arrived in late December 1898, he wanted to improve the administrative efficiency and creativity of the ICS, whose Anglo-Indian members served in the chief administrative positions of the Raj. Three years later, Curzon chastised their narrowness, snobbery, pompousness, and ineptitude in a letter to Lord Hamilton, the secretary of state for India. Curzon believed that the ICS was contributing to Britain's faltering rule in India. He also pointed to the "undisciplined passions of the inferior class of Englishmen in this country." Curzon drew his conclusions based on numerous court cases brought against British planters and soldiers who had beaten or maimed Indian workers or merchants. Many cases had ended in acquittal. As viceroy, he initiated reinvestigation of similar incidents that the military or civilian authorities had ignored, dismissed officers who tolerated "ruffian racism," and punished entire regiments for rampages against natives. He believed that this type of undisciplined violence, motivated by blind racism, tarnished Britain's imperial reputation as a wise and benevolent schoolmaster. Commenting on a case where the officers of the elite corps, the 9th Lancers, refused to identify a suspect in the death of an Indian cook, Curzon noted that it was only natural for "white men to side with the white skin against the dark. But I also know, and have acted throughout on the belief, that it is the duty of statesmanship to arrest these dangerous symptoms and to prevent them from attaining dimensions that might even threaten the existence of our rule in the future."[11] Curzon declined to grant the entire regiment leave for six months. He was denounced for currying favor with the Indians in army messes and civilian clubs. The final insult came at the celebration for Edward VII's coronation. When the 9th Lancers entered the arena, they were resoundingly cheered by the Europeans present. Curzon sat stonily on his horse, feeling a "certain gloomy pride in having dared to do the right."[12]

Curzon's actions and reforms reflected British attitudes toward social

11. Nicolson, p. 163.
12. Ibid., p. 164.

Chapter 7
The Project
of Empire:
George Nathaniel
Curzon
(1859–1925)
and Mary Leiter
Curzon
(1870–1906)

hierarchy that many middle- and upper-class British men and women brought to India. The behavior of the British lower classes, workers and enlisted soldiers, had to be regulated and their actions policed. Curzon abhored their undisciplined racial violence and believed they could not control their sexual urges. Evidence for this was found in the reported rapes and by soldiers' attempts to marry Indian women. To prevent racial mixing and sexual violence, Curzon introduced military prostitution. The Raj would supply enlisted men with lower-caste women who were housed on military bases.[13]

Curzon railed against more than the recalcitrance of the ICS, the ignorance of the British lower classes, and the arrogance of the military. He also laid blame for Britain's faltering rule in India on the incompetence and corruption of the Indians themselves, and he was loathe to promote Indians for service in the bureaucracy. He opined, "We cannot take the Natives up into the administration. They are crooked-minded and corrupt. We have got to therefore go ruling them and we can only do it with success by being both kindly and virtuous. I daresay I am talking rather like a schoolmaster; but after all, the millions I have to manage are less than schoolchildren."[14]

Curzon's contempt for the inhabitants of the Indian subcontinent extended to the Hindu and Muslim

princes who continued to govern almost 500 native, or princely, states within British India (Document Two). These rulers were nominally autonomous, but they were forbidden to wage war on each other, and the viceroy kept a British agent at each court to advise the ruler. Official British policy dictated that the internal affairs of these states was solely in the hands of each native prince and that the viceroy was to honor their rule. Curzon had distinctly political reasons for embracing the rule of these princes; he preferred their presence in public life to that of the Indian National Congress, which sought constitutional reforms and concessions. During the celebration at Delhi to mark the coronation of Edward VII, he wanted to accentuate their role as a pillar of British rule in India and made them leading actors in the pageantry. When he spoke to them about their duty, he wanted them to no longer be "architectural adornments of the Imperial edifice" but "pillars that help sustain the main roof."[15] To many middle-class Indian reformers, like Mohandas Karamchand Gandhi (1869–1848), this pageantry only reinforced India's subservience to Britain (Document Three).

While paying lip service to the importance of the native princes and their states in ruling India, Curzon often lectured the princes about the necessity of emulating British efficiency and rooting out corruption and oppression in their states (Document

13. Scott B. Cook, *Colonial Encounters in the Age of High Imperialism* (New York: Harper Collins College Publishing, 1996), p. 128.

14. Rose, p. 345.

15. Moore, p. 437.

Four). Curzon could not see or did not wish to see how British rule itself contributed to India's poverty, corruption, and religious and ethnic cleavages. Curzon believed that Indians of all castes, genders, religions, and ethnic groups benefitted from the benevolent, judicious, and competent rule of a strong alien presence, one that could be the impartial broker of India's local, regional, class, and historical conflicts. Without Britain, India would descend into chaos and strife (Document Five).

Most British and some Indians shared Curzon's view that India was not capable of self-rule and that the British were a stabilizing force (Document Six). By the end of the nineteenth century, however, an increasing number of middle-class Indians, many of whom were educated in the British system, began to examine the consequences of military occupation, the exploitation of India's human and natural resources, social and racial segregation, and British political hegemony. Coupled with this reexamination was a renewed pride in India that resulted in an Indian cultural and intellectual renaissance. This cultural renaissance helped to fuel the fire of those who argued that British rule had deepened India's problems and had to end for Indians to restore their traditional values, institutions, and dignity and to build a modern state. British recalcitrance toward greater Indian participation in administration and governance and their smug racial attitudes drove many moderate middle-class Indians to rethink their earlier modest demands for greater representation in the Civil Service and local self-government.

By the time Curzon left in 1905, Indian national consciousness, desire for self-rule, and criticism of British rule was growing among middle-class Indians. Some Anglo-Indians and British men and women also agreed with these sentiments. Some like Annie Besant, who moved to India in 1893, supported Indian Home Rule. Yet Besant wanted assurances that an India free of the British would address many of the social and religious inequalities before all ties were severed. As she did in Britain, Annie fought for improving the conditions and status of women in Indian society (Document Seven). The calls for an independent India would only grow stronger, longer, and more numerous throughout the twentieth century. It would take Great Britain until 1947, however, to listen to them.

Curzon's attempts to bring order, efficiency, and reform to India were greatly aided by the efforts of the vicereine. Seven years in India had transformed Mary from a young, shy, and compliant wife into a staunch ally and important adviser to her husband. Social duties and obligations brought her into contact with Anglo-Indians and Indians alike, and she could assess people's opinions of her husband and his reforms. The vicereine also entered into more formal political arenas. By convention, the viceroy never left India during his term in office and therefore was unable to go to Britain to present and argue for key policy initiatives. Wives could return, however, and in 1901

Chapter 7
The Project
of Empire:
George Nathaniel
Curzon
(1859–1925)
and Mary Leiter
Curzon
(1870–1906)

Mary returned to London with her children for six months. During these months, Mary acted as mediator and conciliator for her husband. She met with high-ranking government officials charged with Indian affairs and was able to counter rumors about George's health, his popularity, and his autocratic methods. In return, she listened to these officials give advice and warnings to George that could not be transmitted in letters or cables (Document Eight). What struck her about many of these exchanges was the ignorance about India in the Cabinet and among the British in general.

Upon her return to India, the secretary of state for India, Lord George Hamilton and others charged with Indian affairs wrote to Mary and appealed to her to temper some of George's ambitions and pride. The trust that others had put in Mary and her success at currying favor with his superiors gradually persuaded him to discuss matters of policy with her. Mary's knowledge of India came from a highly privileged and exalted position, and she never ceased to remark upon the preparations and pageantry that accompanied the viceroy wherever he went. She was not blind to the poverty, misery, and deprivations that the best landscaping and draping of flags, canopies, and drapes sought to hide. She also could not help noticing the tasteless transgressions of the British, who sometimes erected symbols of colonial power beside graceful and beautiful buildings from India's past. She was particularly contemptuous of British efforts in Delhi: "All the other conquerors have beautified Delhi but the British have disfigured existing beauty and invited the most frightful iron and brick modernities to stand alongside the splendor and beauty of the past...."[16] George shared her opinions on the majesty and beauty of India's past, and his greatest legacy in India was the preservation and restoration of its ancient buildings and monuments.

▨ FINALE

Curzon's viceroyalty in India was a stormy one. He had some spectacular successes, ranging from historic preservation to irrigation projects, to improved cotton cultivation and cattle breeding. However, Curzon's haughtiness and extravagant living invited criticism in India and Britain. His decision to partition Bengal into two provinces, thus encouraging the aspirations of the Muslims, smacked of a policy of divide and rule and worsened Hindu-Muslim antagonisms. The British government at home rejected one of his pet projects, frontier expansion and activity at the expense of the Russians. The final straw was Curzon's well-publicized dispute with the Boer War hero, Lord Kitchener, who was now the commander in chief of the Indian army. Curzon argued that the Indian army should remain under the control of civil power.

16. Bradley, p. 46.

Kitchener argued this control was cumbersome and requested that the administration as well as the military planning be placed in his hands. The Conservative party cabinet sided with the popular war hero, and Curzon resigned.

Until his dying breathe, Curzon believed in the British mission in India. "I believe in the future of this country," he said, "and the capacity of our own race to guide it to goals that it has never hitherto attained." But Indian aspirations were becoming too strong to be brushed aside by notions of British superiority. These notions died slowly, however, and Indians would have to wait until 1947 for British rule to end.

On December 3, 1905, George and Mary arrived in London after almost seven years in India. Not a single member of the government met them at the train station. There seemed to be little for them in England, and they immediately left for the south of France to rejoin their three daughters, who had remained there on the Curzons' trip back from India. The stay in France was precipitated by Mary's declining health and George's disgrace. Mary had come close to death in 1904 when she contracted severe peritonitis, phlebitis, and pneumonia after the birth of their third daughter. The cumulative effect of these illnesses may have weakened her heart. On July 18, 1906, Mary died from a heart attack.

After Mary's death, George abstained from the career that he had spent his entire life pursuing and retreated into the learned communities of his youth. He first became chancellor of Oxford University, then president of the Royal Geographic Society, and devoted patron of England's aristocratic past. During World War I, George reentered politics primarily as an expert in foreign affairs and finally became foreign minister for one year in 1923. In March 1925, he died at the age of sixty-six.

George and Mary Curzon's lives illustrate the multiple tensions at play in late nineteenth-century imperial Britain and its colonial possessions. George gained his position through a class system that rewarded hereditary, but he needed to marry a wealthy American for the funds necessary to further his political ambitions. He preferred a wife who knew not to wear trousers, but who had the education, intelligence, and grace to politic for him when he could not. He respected the majesty of India's past but adhered to the belief that Indian culture and society had deteriorated to such an extent that Indians could no longer care for this legacy and their state. He was aggressively paternalistic and imbued with a civilizing ethos that extended beyond Indians to include British lower classes. Mary enjoyed the privileges of the viceroyalty but was constantly critical of the snobbery, pretensions, and excess of the British in India. She accepted and defended the virtues of the Victorian woman but moved in political circles that few women entered. The Curzons ordered their world according to fixed notions about gender, race, and class. Even with the contradictions, they continued to believe in Europe's civilizing mission, racial and gender exclusivity, and European superiority.

Chapter 7
The Project
of Empire:
George Nathaniel
Curzon
(1859–1925)
and Mary Leiter
Curzon
(1870–1906)

■ QUESTIONS

1. Define the new imperialism. What is the "white man's burden"?

2. What are British attitudes toward India? What are British goals in India?

3. What are the avenues to political power in late nineteenth-century Britain? Did George and Mary Curzon follow the same political paths as Charles Bradlaugh and Annie Besant. Why or why not?

4. Does Mary Curzon engage in political activity? Why or why not? How does she compare to Annie Besant?

5. How does George rule in India? What role does Mary play?

6. What is life like for Anglo-Indians in India? What types of relationships do they have with the Indians? What influence does race, class, and gender have on British India?

7. What are Indian attitudes toward the British Raj? Is Indian response to British rule uniform?

8. What aspects of Victorian society do Mary Curzon, Annie Besant, George Curzon, and Charles Bradlaugh accept and reject?

■ DOCUMENTS

DOCUMENT ONE

MARY CURZON

Letter to Her Father
(January 17, 1899)

Mary Curzon wrote extensive letters to her family in the United States about the ceremony of the viceroyalty. In the excerpt below, she describes her first few weeks in India. Note her surprise at how George is treated and at the opulence of the viceroy's residence. Describe the ceremony surrounding the viceroyalty and Mary's responsibilities as vicereine.

GOVERNMENT HOUSE
CALCUTTA

My precious darling Papa:

I received a beloved letter from you which has made me so happy. I feel such a long way off from everybody as we only have one post a week, and then my letters are limited to yours and Mamma's, as the world is a busy place and only my own think constantly of me and write faithfully, friends write once in six months! I am getting used to the new life—and it is all very wonderful. George is treated *exactly* like a reigning sovereign. Everyone bows & curtseys—ADCs [government officials] precede him—the only difference is that he has a great deal more power than most kings, and ruling India is no sinecure—and a Viceroy has it in his power to be a *very* great force, or he can be a cypher. Great things are expected of G. as ever since the days of Lord Dalhousie there have been good but not great Viceroys and the whole of India has awakened to the belief that G. will do great things. The Hindu is very superstitious, and many things which have happened since our arrival have meant prosperity. Firstly rain fell all along our journey from Bombay & the weather is cooler than it has been for many years. Secondly in many places the crops have been splendid. Thirdly in Bombay two little cows—you know they are worshipped by the Hindu—joined our procession and ran in front of the state carriages, & this incident was very popular. Then we look so young & happy & bow & smile unceasingly when we are out & this pleases everybody. The other day a soldier in the fort had his arm blown off by a cannon firing a salute to one of the native rajahs who came to see George and we went to the Military Hospital to see him and this pleased everybody, so that now when we go out there are crowds & cheers everywhere. The Elgins were quiet shy people who never did anything so all our doings are in direct contrast to theirs, consequently popular. On Saturday we went to the races in State. Body Guard outriders & five state carriages, we drove up the course in state like Ascot, got out and went to our Royal box from which we looked at the racing & were stared at the whole afternoon. There were five [*sic*] English guests staying with us: Mr and Mrs Verney, Lord De Brooke's eldest son, & Lady Cecilie, & Mr Goff & a Mr Green. They with all our staff made up the procession. When we left the races they cheered us & gave me a special cheer. Last Thursday we held a drawing room—at 9.30 we were escorted to 'God save the Queen' into the throne room where all the high officials were grouped either side of the throne—the throne was covered with a perfectly *magnificent* solid gold carpet which was laid over it, the ends coming far out on the carpet of the room—on the dais [?] were two immense chairs, one of silver with gold tigers behind G. A smaller one for me. We stood in front of them and all the entree ladies filed past making two curtseys—they then took their places to the left of the throne beside their husbands who were already there—as each lady came up her name on a card was given to the ADC who handed it to the Military Secretary & he called out her name—she then proceeded to curtsey to G. who bowed solemnly & then another curtsey to me & I bowed & smiled. We did not shake hands with anyone—just bowed—the ladies were beautifully dressed and did their bows far better than I should have done them—trains & feathers are optional, but *many* wore them. After all the entrée ladies had passed the public entrée were admitted, all the ladies looked very well dressed and it took the private & public entrée just an hour to pass; after they had all passed we marched upstairs to the Great ball room preceded by the staff and followed by the private entrée who had remained throughout the drawing room in the throne room. The rooms were crowded as all the husbands of the ladies had joined them upstairs and there ensued a kind

Chapter 7
The Project
of Empire:
George Nathaniel
Curzon
(1859–1925)
and Mary Leiter
Curzon
(1870–1906)

of evening party, we sitting in big chairs which were arranged in a semi-circle & in about three-quarters of an hour ADCs bringing up a steady stream of people for G. & me to talk to. When the time came to go we marched out of the room & retired to well earned bed. . . .

[DESCRIPTION OF GOVERNMENT HOUSE, CALCUTTA]

. . . I never knew a more inconvenient house than this—and the distances are perfectly awful, you know the plan so you can imagine the distance between my room in one wing, and the children's at the other end of the square. . . . Sunday morning we all went up the river on a launch to Barrackpore—it took us $1^1/_2$ hours and we landed at a little pier and walked a long way under a bamboo arbour up to the house which is very like an English country house—and the park—which alas! is open to the public who pour into it and destroy all privacy—is lovely. Lord Canning made a rolling country out of a flat plain and planted perfectly splendid trees so that with a stretch of imagination we could imagine ourselves in an English park afflicted by drought as the grass is all brown. After lunch I took G. to drive in a tiny little pony carriage drawn by wee little ponies—the body guard had to go with us and you can't imagine anything funnier than two immense horsemen carrying lances, then a pony trap in which sat the Viceroy, entirely filling it—I perched up driving two little specks of ponies—sitting up behind were two red liveried servants, and riding behind more immense body guards—we felt that this cortège was so absurd that we drove once round the park in a cloud of dust & then slunk home by a garden path & saw Lady Channing's* tomb, which is beautifully placed by the river. Luncheon & tea we had under an enormous banyan tree, and as huge kites swoop down and carry off all the food on your plate native servants stand about with great sticks wh. they wave at them. Monday morning we came back to Calcutta by launch, all—especially Irene—having loved our Sunday, and rested for all our labours this week.

Darling—I finish this in pencil as I have not been well. Chill & headache, but shall be better long before you receive this.

I will write all about our State ball. The weather is *better* and I brought *no* warm clothes. The babies flourish bless their hearts.

Goodnight my beloved

Yr loving Mary

*Charlotte (1817–61), the devoted wife of Lord Canning, 'Clemency Canning' (1812–62), Governor-General during the Mutiny of 1857; she died a characteristically swift Indian death. Canning, who survived his wife by only seven months, kept a daily vigil at her graveside, where a light constantly burned. Her early death is the more poignant when it is recalled that Lady Canning bravely endured a period of estrangement during an earlier time in their marriage.

DOCUMENT TWO

GEORGE NATHANIEL CURZON

Letter to Lord Hamilton
(August 26, 1900)

Despite his words of praise for the princes in public, Curzon was contemptuous of them in private. In this letter to the secretary of state for India, Lord Hamilton, Curzon dismisses the princes as schoolboys. Compare this private view with the public proclamations. Describe Curzon's opinions of the native princes.

With reference to what you say about the Native Princes, I do not at all deprecate the remark that to a large extent we act as their schoolmasters. It is not only true, but it is inevitable. For what are they, for the most part, but a set of unruly and ignorant and rather undisciplined school-boys? What they want more than anything else is to be schooled by a firm, but not unkindly, hand; to be passed through just the sort of discipline that a boy goes through at a public school in England, but which they have never had out here; and to be weaned, even by a grandmotherly interference from the frivolity and dissipations of their normal life. I cannot conceive a more fatal policy than to leave them alone to go their own way, so that they may be an object-lesson to their people why do their people want an object-lesson at all? What good will it do to them? Already they are beginning to protest against the extravagance and tyranny of many of these rulers, and it is to us that they turn and ask for security and protection. I am always looking ahead in India. There is not a day of my life in which I do not say to myself, 'What is going to happen in this country 20 years, or 50 years hence?' And I say with the profoundest conviction that any Viceroy, or any Government, that adopted the attitude of letting all these Princes and Chiefs run to their own ruin, would be heaping up immeasurable disaster in the future. We have embarked since the Mutiny upon the policy of sustaining the Native States and Princes. We do so, not so much in the interests of the Princes themselves, who are often quite undeserving of the compliment, as in the interests of the people, who are supposed to like the old traditions and dynasties and rule. But supposing we allow the confidence of the people in their rulers to be sapped; supposing we allow Native India to be governed by a horde of frivolous absentees who have lost the respect and affection of their own subjects—what justification shall we have in such a case for maintaining the Native States at all? No, in my judgment. So long as Lord Canning's policy is adhered to; so long as we regard the Native States and their Chiefs as an integral factor in our system; so long as we guarantee to them a security enjoyed by no other potentates in the world; so long are we bound to train and discipline, and control them, and so to fit them for the unique position which we have placed within their grasp.

Chapter 7
The Project
of Empire:
George Nathaniel
Curzon
(1859–1925)
and Mary Leiter
Curzon
(1870–1906)

Believe me that the matter is looked at in India by all thinking men, whether European or Native, from this point of view; the best Native papers are continually arguing it, and I shall be very much surprised, if there is anything but approbation in them for the policy that I have shadowed out. The sense of duty and responsibility is growing in them under the influence of our teaching; they are beginning to see that Princes cannot afford, any more than Viceroys, to live exclusively in palaces, but that they must be out, and about, setting an example among their fellow-creatures. Any severity that I may show to the ill-doers will be more than compensated by my encouragement of the few and exceptional shining lights; and I hope, by adhering to the principles which I have laid down, and which I first foreshadowed in my speech at Gwalior last year, amid the enthusiastic acceptance of the Press, both English and Native, to do something towards raising the whole tone and standard of the life of Native Princes in my time, and thereby to place their own future existence upon more durable foundations.

DOCUMENT THREE

MOHANDAS KARAMCHAND GANDHI

Gandhi's Autobiography: The Story of My Experiments with the Truth (1948)

Mohandas Karamchand Gandhi (1869–1948) was born in Gujarat, where his father served as an adviser to one of the "native princes." In India, there were over 500 kingdoms, principalities, and states that were allowed autonomy in domestic and internal affairs and were ruled by a local prince. His position of privilege allowed Gandhi not only to observe firsthand British rule through these rulers but also to be educated in England.

After acquiring a law degree, Gandhi returned to India only to find few opportunities. In 1891 he moved to South Africa, where he lived for the next twenty years, with periodic visits to India. In India, England, and South Africa, Gandhi became aware of the frightening force and fury of European racism, and how far Indians were from being considered full human beings.

One of his many visits to India to participate in the meetings of the Indian National Congress corresponded with the celebration, or darbar, *for the coronation of Edward VII. In this passage, Gandhi relates his discussion with some of the native princes who have assembled for the* darbar. *What must they wear to the ceremony? Why? What do they believe this type of dress reveals about their place in a British-ruled India? Is this the same attitude as Curzon?*

The Congress was over, but as I had to meet the Chamber of Commerce and various people in connection with work in South Africa, I stayed in Calcutta for a month. Rather than stay this time in a hotel, I arranged to get the required introduction for a room in the India Club. Among its members were some prominent Indians, and I looked forward to getting into touch with them and interesting them in the work in South Africa. . . .

I shall record here an incident in the India Club. . . .

Lord Curzon held his darbar about this time. Some Rajas and Maharajas who had been invited to the darbar were members of the Club. In the Club I always found them wearing fine Bengalee *dhotis** and shirts and scarves. On the darbar day they put on trousers befitting *khansamas*† and shining boots. I was pained and inquired of one of them the reason for the change.

'We alone know our unfortunate condition. We alone know the insults we have to put up with, in order that we may possess our wealth and titles,' he replied.

'But what about these *khansama* turbans and these shining boots ?' I asked.

'Do you see any difference between *khansamas* and us?' he replied, and added, 'they are our *khansamas*, we are Lord Curzon's *khansamas*. If I were to absent myself from the *levee*, I should have to suffer the consequences. If I were to attend it in my usual dress, it would be an offence. And do you think I am going to get any opportunity there of talking to Lord Curzon? Not a bit of it!'

I was moved to pity for this plainspoken friend.

This reminds me of another darbar.

At the time when Lord Hardinge laid the foundation stone of the Hindu University, there was a darbar. There were Rajas and Maharajas of course, but Pandit Malaviyaji specially invited me also to attend it, and I did so.

I was distressed to see the Maharajas bedecked like women—silk *pyjamas* and silk *achkans*, pearl necklaces round their necks, bracelets on their wrists, pearl and diamond tassels on their turbans and, besides all this, swords with golden hilts hanging from their waist-bands.

I discovered that these were insignia not of their royalty, but of their slavery. I had thought that they must be wearing these badges of impotence of their own free will, but I was told that it was obligatory for these Rajas to wear all their costly jewels at such functions. I also gathered that some of them had a positive dislike for wearing these jewels, and that they never wore them except on occasions like the darbar.

I do not know how far my information was correct. But whether they wear them on other occasions or not, it is distressing enough to have to attend viceregal darbars in jewels that only some women wear.

How heavy is the toll of sins and wrongs that wealth, power and prestige exact from man!

---

*[A cloth of considerable length and fullness that is tucked between the legs and at the waistband. Ed.]

†i.e., waiters.

Chapter 7
The Project
of Empire:
George Nathaniel
Curzon
(1859–1925)
and Mary Leiter
Curzon
(1870–1906)

DOCUMENT FOUR

GEORGE NATHANIEL CURZON

Efficiency of Rule
(1902)

The viceroy of India, appointed by the crown, ruled directly only in the provinces of British India. Hindu and Muslim princes continued to govern almost 600 native, or princely, states within British India. These states were nominally autonomous, but the princes were forbidden to wage war on one another, and the viceroy kept a British agent at each court to advise the ruler. Under Curzon, British intervention in the internal affairs of the states reached its peak. One of the viceroy's duty was to visit the various states. Curzon spoke on the occasion of his visit to Jaipur in November 1902 about efficiency in government. What are Curzon's goals for the Indians? What are his views on the rule of the native princes?

. . . Your Highness has reminded me that three years ago I claimed the Indian Chiefs as my colleagues and partners in the task of Indian administration. It is as such, as fellow-workers in their several exalted stations, that I have ever since continued to treat and to regard them. On many occasions I have discussed with them the conditions and circumstances of their own government, and on others, as Your Highness knows full well, I have sought and obtained their co-operation and advice. I have often recapitulated the benefits which in my view the continued existence of the Native States confers upon Indian society. Amid the levelling tendencies of the age and the inevitable monotony of government conducted upon scientific lines, they keep alive the traditions and customs, they sustain the virility, and they save from extinction the picturesqueness of ancient and noble races. They have that indefinable quality, endearing them to the people, that arises from their being born of the soil. They provide scope for the activities of the hereditary aristocracy of the country, and employment for native intellect and ambition. Above all, I realise, more perhaps in Rajputana than anywhere else, that they constitute a school of manners, valuable to the Indian, and not less valuable to the European, showing in the person of their chiefs that illustrious lineage has not ceased to implant noble and chivalrous ideas, and maintaining those old-fashioned and punctilious standards of public spirit and private courtesy which have always been instinctive in the Indian aristocracy, and with the loss of which, if ever they be allowed to disappear, Indian society will go to pieces like a dismasted vessel in a storm.

It sometimes seems to be thought, because the British Government exercises political control over these States—which is the reverse side of the security that we guarantee to them,—that we desire of a deliberate purpose to Anglicise the Feudatory States in India. That is no part of my idea, and it has most certainly been no feature of my practice. We want their administration to be conducted upon business principles and with economy. We want public works to be developed and the education and welfare of the poorer classes considered. We want to diminish the openings for moneygrabbing, corruption, or oppression. We want a Native State, when famine comes, to treat it both with method and with generosity. In so far as these standards have been developed by British rule in this country, may they be called English. But if any one thinks that we want to overrun Native States with Englishmen, or to stamp out the idiosyncrasies of native thought and custom, then he is strangely mistaken. Englishmen are often required to start some public undertaking or to introduce some essential reform. In industrial and mineral development, and in scientific work in general, outside enterprise is in many cases absolutely indispensable, since the resources of the State might otherwise remain unutilised and unexplored . . . accordingly, whenever I lend a British officer administratively to a Native State, one of his main functions in my view should be to train up natives of the State to succeed him; for there is no spectacle which finds less favour in my eyes, or which I have done more to discourage, than that of a cluster of Europeans settling down upon a Native State and sucking from it the moisture which ought to give sustenance to its own people.

Similarly, if a Native State is ruled well in its own way, I would not insist that it should be ruled a little better in the English way. A natural organism that has grown by slow degrees to an advanced stage of development has probably a healthier flow of life-blood in its veins than one which is of artificial growth or foreign importation. Therefore it gives me pleasure to visit a part of India where these old fashions still survive as in Rajputana, and still more to be the guest of a Chief like Your Highness, whose State is ruled efficiently and well, but ruled upon native lines. The British in this country have already rendered a great service to Rajputana in the past; for it was by their intervention in the first twenty years of the last century that the Rajput principalities were saved from ruin just when they were in danger of being overwhelmed by the mercenary hordes of the Mahrattas and the Pathans. But for the action of Lord Wellesley and Lord Hastings and for the treaties that they made, Rajputana, as a distinct political unit, would have been wiped out of existence. For that service the Rajput Chiefs have always been profoundly grateful, and they have repaid it by unswerving loyalty to the British Crown. But it would be a thousand pities if, having thus saved Rajputana from the break-up of war and rapine, we were now see this aristocratic structure and these ancient institutions go to pieces under the scarcely less disintegrating influences of prosperity and peace. I would fain hope that this ancient society, which was never absorbed by the Moghul, and which has stood the strain of centuries of conflict and siege, may learn so to adapt itself to the conditions of the age as to find in the British sovereignty the sure guarantee of its liberties and traditions, as well as a trustworthy guide on the pathway of administrative progress and reform.

Chapter 7
The Project
of Empire:
George Nathaniel
Curzon
(1859–1925)
and Mary Leiter
Curzon
(1870–1906)

Your Highness knows also that I have made no concealment of what are my views as to the character and duty of native Chiefs. Those views have not always been popular, and I have often seen them misrepresented or misunderstood. My ideal has never been the butterfly that flits aimlessly from flower, to flower, but the working bee that builds its own hive and makes its own honey. To such a man all my heart goes out in sympathy and admiration. He is dear to his own People, and dear to the Government whom I represent. Sometimes I cast my eyes into the future; and I picture a state of society in which the Indian princes, trained to all the advantages of Western culture, but yet not divorced in instinct or in mode of life from their own people, will fill an even ampler part than at present in the administration of this Empire. I would dearly like to see that day. But it will not come if an Indian Chief is at liberty to be a spendthrift or an idler or an absentee. It can only come if, as Your Highness has said, he remains true to his religion, his traditions, and his people.

DOCUMENT FIVE

George Nathaniel Curzon

Convocation Speech at Calcutta University
(1902)

In a speech to the convocation of Calcutta University in 1902, Curzon reaffirmed the necessity of British rule in India. Why should Britain rule?

. . . And now to all of you together let me address these concluding words. The spirit of nationality is moving in the world, and it is an increasing force in the lives and ideals of men. Founded upon race, and often cemented by language and religion, it makes small nations great, and great nations greater. It teaches men how to live, and, in emergencies, it teaches them how to die. But, for its full realization, a spirit of unity, and not of disintegration, is required. There must be a sacrifice of the smaller to the larger interest, and a subordination of the unit to the system. In India it should not be a question of India for the Hindus, or India for the Musulmans, or descending to minor fractions, of Bengal for the Bengalis, or the Deccan for the Mahratta Brahmans. That would be a retrograde and dissolvent process. Neither can it be India for the Indians alone. The last two centuries during which the British have been in this country cannot be wiped out. They have profoundly affected the whole structure of national thought and existence. They have quickened the atrophied veins of the East and the life-blood of the West. They have modified old ideas and created new ones. . . .

Out of this intermingling of the East and the West, a new patriotism, and a more refined and cosmopolitan sense of nationality, are emerging. It is one in which the Englishman may share with the Indian, for he has helped to create it, and in which the Indian may share with the Englishman, since it is their common glory. When an Englishman says that he is proud of India, it is not of battlefields and sieges, nor of exploits in the Council Chamber or at the desk that he is principally thinking. He sees the rising standards of intelligence, of moral conduct, of comfort and prosperity, among the Native peoples, and he rejoices in their advancement. Similarly, when an Indian says that he is proud of India, it would be absurd for him to banish from his mind all that has been, and is being, done for the resuscitation of his country by the alien race to whom have been committed its destinies. Both are tillers in the same field, and both are concerned in the harvest. From their joint labours it is that this new and composite patriotism is springing into life. It is Asian, for its roots are embedded in the traditions and the aspirations of an Eastern people; and it is European, because it is aglow with the illumination of the West. In it are summed up all the best hopes for the future of this country, both for your race and for mine. We are ordained to walk here in the same track together for many a long day to come. You cannot do without us. We should be impotent without you. Let the Englishman and the Indian accept the consecration of a union that is so mysterious as to have in it something of the divine, and let our common ideal be a united country and a happier people. (Loud and continued cheers).

DOCUMENT SIX

C. Sankaran Nair

Influence of the British Raj
(1897)

In December 1897, a year before the beginning of Curzon's viceroyalty in India, the thirteenth session of the Indian National Congress met and its newly elected president, C. Sankaran Nair, delivered the following address about the influence of the British Raj. What have been the advantages and disadvantages of British rule?

We are well aware of the disordered state of this country when it passed, with its insecurity of person and property, under British Rule, of the enormous difficulties our rulers had to overcome in introducing orderly administration without any help from the then existing agencies. We recognise that the association of the people in the government of the country, except to a very limited extent, was then impossible. We also know that British rule cleared the way to progress

Chapter 7
The Project
of Empire:
George Nathaniel
Curzon
(1859–1925)
and Mary Leiter
Curzon
(1870–1906)

and furnished us with the one element, English education, which was necessary to rouse us from the torpor of ages and bring about the religious, social, and political regeneration which the country stands so much in need of. We are also aware that with the decline of British supremacy, we shall have anarchy, war and rapine. The Mahomedans will try to recover their lost supremacy. The Hindu races and chiefs will fight amongst themselves. The lower castes who have come under the vivifying influence of Western civilisation are scarcely likely to yield without a struggle to the dominion of the higher castes. And we have Russia and France waiting for their opportunities. The ignorant masses may possibly not recognize the gravity of the danger attendant on any decline of England's power in the East. But it is ridiculous to suggest that those who have received the benefit of English education are so shortsighted enough not to see and weigh that danger. While, however, full of gratitude for what Great Britain has done to India—for its Government which secures us from foreign aggression and ensures security of person and property—it should not be forgotten for a moment that the real link that binds us indissolubly to England is the hope, the well-founded hope and belief, that with England's help we shall, and, under her guidance alone, we can attain national unity and national freedom. The educational policy of the Government, a policy which combines beneficence with statesmanship, justified such hopes in us. Those hopes were confirmed by various pledges. Those pledges were followed by the creation of institutions by which we were admitted to a share in our ordinary Government which must surely, though slowly, lead to the full fruition of our ambitions.

Just look for a moment at the training we are receiving. From our earliest school-days the great English writers have been our classics, Englishmen have been our professors in Colleges. English history is taught in our schools. The books we generally read are English books, which describe in detail all the forms of English life, give us all the English types of character. Week after week, English newspapers, journals and magazines pour into India for Indian readers. We, in fact, now live the life of the English. Even the English we write shows not only their turns of thought but also their forms of feeling and thinking. It is impossible under this training not to be penetrated with English ideas, not to acquire English conceptions of duty, of rights, of brotherhood. The study and practice of the law now pursued with such avidity by our people, by familiarising them with reverence for authority and with sentiments of resistance to what is not sanctioned by law, have also materially contributed to the growth of mental independence.

Imbued with these ideas and principles, we naturally desire to acquire the full rights and to share the responsibilities of British citizenship. We have learnt that in the acquisition of those rights and in the recognition of the principles on which they are based, lie the remedy for the evils affecting our country, evils similar to those from which England herself once suffered.................It is the hope that one day we may be admitted as equal sharers in this great inheritance, that we shall have all the civil rights associated with the English Government, that we shall be admitted as freely as Englishmen themselves to worship in this temple of freedom—it is this hope that keeps India and will keep her always attached to the British. This hope is sustained by pledges solemnly made; and the sentiment of loyalty to the British connection created by repeated declarations that we shall be gradually allowed the full rights of English citizenship is already in full force. Such a pledge was made in 1833 when Parliament solemnly declared that race or religion or colour shall not be a disqualification for holding any appointment. This declaration of policy in a time of peace has been solemnly affirmed after the Mutiny. Already, the pledge has been in part redeemed. We have been admitted, as it were, into the outer precincts of the temple of freedom. The Press has been enfranchised. Partially elected members sit in our local and legislative councils. We can enter the Civil Service through the open door of competition. These blessings are no doubt now coupled with conditions which unfortunately detract from their rule. But these great and healthy principles have nurtured and consolidated a sentiment of affection. All that England has to do is to persist resolutely in the line of policy she has initiated and thereby deepen that feeling of loyalty which makes us proud of our connection with England. I myself feel that there is very little reason to fear that England will reverse the past...........Thus, the only condition requisite for the fruition of our political aspirations is the continuance of the British Rule. The fond hope that India may one day take her place in the confederacy of the free English-speaking nations of the world can be realised only under England's guidance with England's help. Years must elapse, it is true, before our expectations can be realised, before we get representative institutions on the models of those of the English-speaking communities. Slavery we had under our old rulers, Hindu and Mahomedan; we may again get it under any despotic European or Asiatic Government. But we know that real freedom is possible only under the Government of the English Nation, nurtured in liberty, hating every form of tyranny, and willing to extend the blessings of representative Government to those capable of using it wisely in the interests of freedom and progress.

Great as is the necessity of British Rule for the political emancipation of our country, even greater is the necessity for social and religious reform. In the present circumstances of India, inhabited as it is by followers of various religions, various sects, classes, very often with antagonistic interest, any Government which is not strictly secular and absolutely impartial must be disastrous to the best interests of the country..........We want in brief to eliminate, if necessary, from our system all that stands in the way of progress. We desire to absorb and assimilate into our own what appears good to us in Western civilisation.

Chapter 7
The Project
of Empire:
George Nathaniel
Curzon
(1859–1925)
and Mary Leiter
Curzon
(1870–1906)

DOCUMENT SEVEN

ANNIE BESANT

The Education of Indian Girls
(1913)

Annie Besant left England to move to India in 1893. In India, she continued her commitment to social justice and equality for women and began a new role as critic of the British imperial enterprise. In 1913, she gave a series of lectures focusing on the need of the Indians and the British to improve women's education, and to abolish child marriage, the caste system, and the status of Indian industries. Ironically, the matchstick industry moved to India in the twentieth century and many of the abuses Besant noted in her exposé, "White Slavery in London," continued in India until the 1970s. Besant believed in Indian Home Rule but only after Indians themselves addressed social, religious, and gender inequalities. In the following excerpt, Besant argues for the education of upper-class Indian girls.

What role does Besant advocate for Indian women in the new state? How does this role differ from European women's roles in their own societies? To what extent do Besant's ideas reflect imperialist attitudes?

. . . I have been trying to urge upon you the reasons why you should do something, because the *wish* to raise women is the thing which is most wanted. Suppose you are with me on that, let us see what sort of education shall be given to Indian girls. Clearly it must be one which will not denationalise them. It is bad enough to denationalise your men. It would be a thousand times worse to denationalise your girls, for that would be the death-knell of India. The first thing you will have to recognise is that you cannot give the same education to all the women of the cultivated classes. You must give some of them education, as our chairman suggested, which will enable the great lack of teachers in girls' schools to be supplied. That of course means University education. But that, I think, will never be the education of the great number, the great mass, of educated women in India.

. . . But as your [India's] system is changing and as your young men are no longer willing to live in the joint family, and as they are taking up the western system of separate independent homes, so that each family shall be an isolated unit, there comes the absolute necessity, with the breaking up of the older system, to adapt yourself to it by training widows properly, so that they may perform their ancient duties but perform them in a way suited to modern conditions. That is the secret, of course, of national growth. You cannot bring back the old system which the people have outgrown, and which you are no longer willing to follow. But you can take what you had of good in the old and adapt it to the conditions of the new; and so I submit that you ought to have

Widows' Homes everywhere, where this higher University education should be given, and where technical education for skilled nursing as well as for medical women should be provided. That is a clear line so far marked out for the great widow population.

   . . . How then will you educate the wife and the mother? Religion is clearly a part of her education; religion and morals must be a part of the education. Morals, I think, come almost instinctively to her.

   . . . I say educate your women in religion, not to diminish their devotion but to render it more intelligent, so that they may prevent the boy from growing into a sceptic, and that he may learn at his mother's knee a religion of which he need never be ashamed.

Outside religion and morals, literary education. What should that be? I submit it should include first a thorough literary knowledge of the vernacular, the vernacular of the family to which the girl belongs. That is fundamental, so that the great vernacular literature may be studied by her to the enrichment of her life.

   . . . I plead next for knowledge of English, and I will tell you quite frankly why. English is the language here of politics, of social matters, of discussions among the men. You cannot discuss these things in the vernaculars conveniently, because the vernaculars are so different.

Outside religious, moral and literary education, I will ask you to give her a simple scientific education, so that she shall know the laws of sanitation; that she shall know the laws of hygiene as her grandmother knew them; that she shall know the value of foodstuffs, so that she may know how to build up the bodies of her children, . . .

The only other point in girls' education that I would add to this, is physical education. I have said religious, moral, literary, scientific and artistic. They are all very big names. Lastly I come to physical. Do not forget the bodies of the girls. Let them have plenty of exercise which shall develop and strengthen them. . . .

What you want most in this country is that practical spirit of self-sacrifice, that public spirit which looks on the interests of the country as greater than the interests of the individual. You can learn this from women. They sacrifice themselves every day and every night for the interests of the home; they realise the subordination of the one to the benefit of the larger self of the family. Learn that from your women and then you will become great, and India will become great; for if you carry into public life the self-sacrifice of women, then the redemption of India will be secured. But you will do it best, if you will go with them into the world hand in hand, men and women together. The perfect man is made up, remember, of the man, the wife and the child, and not the man alone. If such men become citizens of India, then her day is not far off.

Chapter 7
The Project
of Empire:
George Nathaniel
Curzon
(1859–1925)
and Mary Leiter
Curzon
(1870–1906)

DOCUMENT EIGHT

MARY CURZON

Letter to George
(May 18, 1901)

In 1901, Mary returned with her children to London for six months. During these months, Mary was Curzon's eyes and ears in government circles and she dutifully reported to George (Pappy) encounters with cabinet members, government officials, and gossip about his rule in India. In this lengthy letter, Mary summarizes a week's worth of dinners, gatherings, and meetings. What is Mary's "private role" in George's public career?

WESTGATE-ON-SEA

Darling Pappy:

Yesterday the babies and I came here from Victoria Station, Evey seeing us off, and I am enchanted to find the nice lodgings in a rundown sort of cottage not half bad . . . but tomorrow I shall be offing to London and not be back until next week when I come from Panshanger.* Now I must begin where my last left off, Thurs. I think or up to late on Friday when Lord Roberts came to see me. He said he was perfectly delighted with the success of the tribal levies—greatly approved of frontier—also of your hope to improve & develop the young princelings—he said he strongly backed *your* scheme though he had not before been sanguine of accomplishing much. He spoke most warmly of Kitchener and said he had improved in two years and acquired greater leniency in dealing with men, & his only fear for India was his attitude to native troops, but this he meant to talk to him about before he went out. His coming to India is a 'secret de Polichinelle'. Arthur, St John, George Wyndham and Lord Roberts & Mr Dawkins have all talked about it, though they say 'of course no one knows yet'. I did *not* think Lord Roberts enthused about St John's reforms, which met him in print at Madeira on his return from South Africa.

Mr Dawkins came while Lord Roberts was there. . . . He said he thought that people's ignorance & indifference about India was growing. They recognized a great personality in *you* but he constantly heard 'Well, if a man like Lord Elgin, who had returned to what he was eminently fitted to be, a County Councillor in his Scotch town, could govern India successfully there couldn't be much required to be a success out there.' He says you have aroused interest in the intelligent but nothing will create intelligence in the ignorant. He was rather gloomy

---

*One of the country seats of the 7th Earl Cowper. With his wife's death in 1913 Panshanger was inherited by 'Ettie', Lady Desborough, her niece. The house was demolished in 1952.

about things in general, & said he was struck by the hollowness of peoples' interests or convictions, & no one *cared* about anything, and the King only wanted to play cards with Sir Ernest Cassel* at private dins. at the latter's house. . . .

[Mary continues.]

Wednesday. Evey allowed me to ask Sir Win Nicholson,† Miss Turner, Miss Myers & Mr Fanshawe to lunch—she then proceeded to ask Lady Savile, Capt. B.-Carr, Mrs Batleman and Lord Berkeley Paget, and this odd mixture of 'monde' amused me immensely as I heard Lord B. Paget say to Lady Savile 'Who on earth are these people?' 'Lady Curzon's Indians' said she. I had a great talk with Sir Wm Nicholson—and I must try to repeat it coherently. First he had heard from Sir Power Palmer, who thought he had been *so* badly treated, & said 'Lady Curzon thought so highly of my wife's *social* talents that I had hoped to be permanently appointed'!!!!!! Did you ever hear such a ground for being made C.-in-Chief. I then turned him on to Kitchener—he said when Lord Roberts went to South Africa he was indignant at the praise of Kitchener in the press and the general impression that though Roberts was C.-in-C. Kitchener was the man who was going to conduct operations—so as soon as Roberts arrived in South Africa he proceeded to send Kitchener off on all sorts of odd and undistinguished jobs and Lady Roberts would have nothing to say to him. Kitchener caught on to the Roberts' dislike—and proceeded to entirely efface himself, was never mentioned in the telegrams—and acted the part of a modest & retiring self-effacing uncomplaining small swell—& this continued for 9 months—until Lady Roberts suddenly discovered that Lord Kitchener was quite a different man to what she & Bobs had expected—hence sudden promotion to command at Paardeburg, eventually followed by whole Command etc. Nicholson said 'I have worked for two years with Kitchener; he is not a clever man—can't write a despatch—his knowledge of administration is *puerile* and his only quality to praise is his relentless determination to advance himself; in that he is the best worker I have ever known.' All soldiers blackguard each other, so Nicholson on Kitchener was no more [than] proof of the disloyalty of soldiers. He said Kitchener did not know the elementary rules of administration & his telegrams which had to go through Nicholson were quite astoundingly ignorant, unmethodical or clear-brained. I hope all this is a lie. I have written his exact words. Nicholson is really miserable not to have got Military Member in India & hates his War Office work. Can't endure St John, says he is a shocking bad speaker and his speech in House of Commons was a stupid statement, neither lucid or able. This is the soldier's view of old St John.

Kinge has been nearly killed on *Shamrock*, where it is believed he went with Favourite [Alice Keppel]; he went off the day after Queen's return. Neither has

*(1852–1921), Cassel was born and educated in Cologne. Financial advisor to Edward VII, Cassel fitted easily into the ruling circles for his recreations—aside from making money—were racing, hunting and shooting. . . .

†(1845–1918), a career soldier of distinction who served in the Afghan and South African wars and in India.

Chapter 7
The Project
of Empire:
George Nathaniel
Curzon
(1859–1925)
and Mary Leiter
Curzon
(1870–1906)

taken the smallest notice of me, though Charlotte Knollys§ wired me from Sandringham saying Queen wished soon to see me. You will have read of accident on *Shamrock*—mast breaking & crashing but hurting no one on board. Perhaps Kinge was in bed below! . . .

Darling I hope you can make out my voluminous letters, & that all the tittle tattle doesn't bore you. My thoughts never, ever leave you and I find that my whole interest in people is what they may tell me which will interest you. . . .

[She finishes with a discussion of a visit from Lord Hamilton, secretary of state for India.]

G. Hamilton came to see me yesterday. He complained of the rise of mediocrity in the last ten years—& how in Indian Civil Service & English public life mediocrity came to the front! It was not so when he entered public life. I gasped assent but felt that he was the crowning illustration of his own theory.

He grudges much praise—speaks of *his* policy of frontier! I never knew such a hopeless dotard or such a small-minded, ferret-faced roving-eyed mediocrity. He took the line that it was such a mistake for you to talk of your programme of twelve reforms as then everyone's back rose in hostility & anticipation. He said your princeling scheme came before Cabinet today. I buttered the grim [?] idiot by saying you appreciated his capital letters. He was delighted. Fancy that fool being Sec. of State. . . .

Time is scampering & this must go beloved. All my whole heart of love.

Loving loving
(unspoilt unhead turned)
Kinkie

I would give a world to kiss you.

§ (1835–1930), Woman-of-the-Bedchamber to Queen Alexandra. The 'inevitable Charlotte' was in 1901 by royal warrant raised to the rank of 'the daughter of a Baron of the United Kingdom'.

Revolutionary Lives:
Vladimir Ilyich (Ulyanov) Lenin
(1870–1924) and
Nadezhda K. Krupskaya (1869–1939)

■ SETTING THE STAGE

In the second half of the nineteenth century, calls for revolution and fears of such upheavals continued to characterize European society as its people grappled with an increasingly complex modern world. Political leaders and intellectuals confronted their changing worlds by investigating social and economic problems, debating causes of the problems, and proposing solutions. For some, evolutionary reform was the answer; for others, only fundamental transformation or revolutionary change could produce a just and equal society and end social misery. Major players in this political

*Chapter 8
Revolutionary
Lives: Vladimir
Ilyich (Ulyanov)
Lenin
(1870–1924) and
Nadezhda K.
Krupskaya
(1869–1939)*

world were the socialist parties and workplace organizations that emerged in the latter decades of the century.

Well-defined socialist organizations appeared in the 1890s in Europe and Russia. Although they all rested theoretically on Marx's philosophy and vision, socialism was hardly monolithic because the parties and their leaders interpreted Marx's ideas and adapted them to particular national conditions. In some cases, leaders argued that an egalitarian and progressive society could be created gradually. Others insisted that only violent revolution would have the desired results. At the same time, all of these emerging socialist groups stressed working-class unity, sought to mobilize the lower classes, and hoped to free both working-class men and women. By comparison with other contemporary political groups, more women responded to the recruitment efforts of and became involved in socialist politics. Socialist theory not only held out the promise of a bright future but also contained a systematic analysis of women's oppression and the preconditions for women's emancipation.

By the 1880s, the writings of Karl Marx, Friedrich Engels, and August Bebel had set forth basic premises of socialist ideology concerning women. All accepted the fact of women's subordination in society and found the origin of this inequality at that point in prehistory when private property and the monogamous family appeared and "mother right" ended. Engels referred to this as "the world historic defeat of the female sex." A pattern of oppression thus unfolded

in the family, where "the wife became the head servant, excluded . . . from public production and unable to earn." Modern bourgeois marriage added the concept of individual sex love, a romantic notion that was in direct contradiction to the reality of the relationship between husband and wife. Given this analysis of the origins of inequality, the socialists argued that the emancipation of women could occur only with the socialist revolution, the destruction of private property, women's entry into the public world of work, and the disappearance of traditional marriage and the family.[1] Of course, theoretical statements are not always borne out in practice and from the beginning, women's involvement in socialist politics was marked by contradictions and controversy.

Although Russia was a vast and potentially prosperous realm in the nineteenth century, it was only slowly entering the modern age. At midcentury, over 70 million people lived in the Russian empire; the majority of them were poor peasants whose discontent erupted sporadically in agrarian revolts. A rigid social hierarchy defined by law was presided over by a powerful emperor, his secret police, and a stagnant and corrupt administrative system. Censorship, control over the universities, a poor educational system, and limits on foreign travel both constrained intellectual development and produced dissent

1. See Introduction to *European Women on the Left*, edited by Jane Slaughter and Robert Kern (Westport, Conn., Greenwood Press, 1981), pp. 4–8, for a discussion of the basic theory and the contradictions within socialism for women.

among those who were educated. Throughout the nineteenth century, the Russian educated elite, the intelligentsia, questioned the status quo; sought to create a Russian identity; and envisioned a future that involved economic, social, and political reform. On occasion, their intellectual challenges became political rebellion.

By midcentury, Tsar Alexander II (r. 1855–1881) became convinced of the need for some reforms, the most dramatic of which was the emancipation of the serfs in 1861. Although peasants were technically "free" after 1861, problems remained because their lives were controlled by village communes, the agricultural system remained outdated and unproductive, and rural poverty deepened. In 1864, Alexander also introduced county or provincial elected assemblies (*zemstvos*), which became the first step to representative government. Nevertheless, the emperor retained extraordinary political powers that limited their autonomy.

Russian women of all social classes were under the rule of their fathers, who controlled their finances, education, travel, and social or political activities. In the 1860s, a group of Moscow women had begun campaigning for admission to higher education, which was finally achieved in 1876, when universities were allowed to offer separate courses for women. But changes such as this seemed only a taste of what might be, and it is not surprising that among educated Russians—the sons and daughters of landowners, military officers, and professionals—desires for change continued to grow and became more militant. In 1881, in fact, Alexander II

was assassinated by a terrorist group, and his successor, Alexander III (r. 1881–1894), a believer in orthodoxy, autocracy, and nationalism, began a crackdown on reform and revolutionary activity. Most of the recently established women's courses were shut down; any progressive view was seen as suspect; and censorship and educational control, and even surveillance of libraries, increased in this era of reaction.

George Plekhanov (1857–1918) introduced the ideas of Marx into this setting in the 1880s. Plekhanov, an intellectual and former populist revolutionary, stressed Marx's systematic analysis of economics and history and, through both propaganda and study groups, convinced others of his belief that a democratic revolution and transition to socialism would inevitably occur in Russia after the growth of capitalism. His ideas found a welcoming audience among a generation of men and women who desired political, economic, and social change in Russia. Among them were women like Vera Zasulich (1849–1919), a radical activist who had attempted the assassination of the governor of St. Petersburg in 1878. In 1881, she corresponded with Marx and two years later willingly joined with Plekhanov as she accepted "scientific" socialism, and Marxism, as the solutions for Russia's problems. She was not alone; as she stated, "In the 1870s women revolutionaries ceased to be exceptional phenomena. In their persons, ordinary women—a whole network of such women—achieved . . . the possibility of acting in the capacity not of inspirers, wives and mothers of men,

*Chapter 8
Revolutionary
Lives: Vladimir
Ilyich (Ulyanov)
Lenin
(1870–1924) and
Nadezhda K.
Krupskaya
(1869–1939)*

but in complete independence, as equals with men in all social and political activities."[2]

By the 1890s, there were twenty marxist groups in St. Petersburg alone. Participating in such groups was dangerous and could result in imprisonment or exile. Nevertheless, revolutionary circles grew and Vladimir Ilyich Ulyanov (1870–1924), better known as Lenin, and Nadezhda Krupskaya (1869–1939), the woman he eventually married in 1898, were among the radical reformers attracted to marxist socialism in these years. They and many others like them would build a revolutionary movement that took shape in the early twentieth century and eventually took power in October 1917. Examining their experiences through 1917, watching as friendships and alliances developed, and tracing their steps to political power provide insights into the motives, activities, and goals of revolutionaries.

■ THE ACTORS:

VLADIMIR ILICH (ULYANOV) LENIN AND NADEZHDA K. KRUPSKAYA

Lenin and Krupskaya actually met in early 1894 at a pancake (bliny) party, the pretext for a meeting of Marxists in St. Petersburg. By the time Lenin moved to that city in 1893, he was already well versed in Marxism and had earned a reputation as a revolutionary thinker. Lenin was born April 23, 1870, in the small provincial capital, Simbirsk. His father Ilya, trained as a mathematics professor, was by then the director of the school system for the province. Maria Blank, his mother, was the daughter of a German doctor, but she received no formal university training and instead was educated by an aunt. Ilya had received honors from the emperor and through service rose to a rank that conformed with hereditary nobles. He was a self-described liberal, a humanist, and a democrat, but he certainly was no revolutionary. He died unexpectedly in 1886, and thereafter Maria used his pension and rent from some property to keep the family going.

In 1887 the police arrested Lenin's older brother Alexander, a gifted university student, in St. Petersburg for his membership in a group of conspirators who planned to use terror to unseat the autocracy. Alexander was convicted but refused to recant and, with other of his co-conspirators, was eventually hanged in May 1887. This execution profoundly shocked the Ulyanov family. Lenin, in particular, who was about to begin his law studies at Kazan University, concluded that while terror could be a radical act, Alexander and his comrades had followed the wrong path to effect change. In the fall of 1887, as the government clamped down on the universities, student protests erupted and Lenin was among those arrested briefly and then expelled from the university. Lenin returned to his fam-

2. Quoted in Jane McDermid and Anna Hillyar, *Midwives of the Revolution: Female Bolsheviks and Women Workers in 1917* (Athens, Ohio: Ohio University Press, 1999), p. 30.

ily's country home in Samara, along with his older sister Anna. She had been living in St. Petersburg with Alexander and also had been arrested for a short time with her brother. In this period, as Lenin sought to understand history and the process of change, he broadened his reading and began to study seriously the writings of Karl Marx. The historical framework appealed to him, and Marx's critique of industrial capitalism and his ideas of class struggle and the eventual dictatorship of the proletariat during the course of revolution made sense to Lenin.[3]

Lenin eventually was given permission to sit for law school exams in St. Petersburg and thus moved there in 1893. He was always regarded as a scholar of the first order, but the other qualities for which he would be known—his keen, analytical intellect; his tactical and strategic abilities; and his single-minded pursuit of his political goals—would be developed in the next decades. Lenin had little patience or tolerance for those who did not accept his blueprint for revolution and was capable of subjecting his opponents, even those within his circle, to biting sarcasm and verbal humiliation. Krupskaya became aware of this at their first meeting in 1894. At the time, she was teaching evening classes to workers and was part of a revolu-

tionary committee promoting literacy as a means of enabling the working class to improve its own conditions. At the meeting, when someone stressed the importance of the illiteracy campaign, Krupskaya remembers that "Lenin laughed, and his laughter sounded rather harsh. 'Well, if anyone wants to save the country by working in the Illiteracy Committee,' he said, 'let him go ahead'."[4]

Krupskaya was born in February 26, 1869, in St. Petersburg. Both her parents were part of the hereditary nobility, though they were never wealthy. Her father, Konstantin Krupsky, was a military officer, and her mother, Elizaveta Tistrova, orphaned when she was nine, was enrolled in a government institute, where she was trained as a governess. They married in 1867, and shortly after Nadezhda was born, they moved to Warsaw in Russian-governed Poland, where Krupsky was made head of an administrative district. Apparently in that capacity, he attempted to administer in an enlightened manner: opening a hospital, combatting persecution of Jews in the province, and establishing a system of regulation of hired labor. There are even hints that he might have had contact with revolutionaries in the area. At the very least, he was a man of radical sentiments, critical of the political and social regime in which he lived. For this, the government issued charges against him and

3. There are numerous biographies of Lenin. Quite useful are Robert Service, *Lenin: A Biography* (Cambridge, Mass.: Harvard University Press, 2000); and Robert Payne, *The Life and Death of Lenin* (New York: Simon and Schuster, 1964). The quite critical and revisionist work by Dmitri Volkogonow, *Lenin: A New Biography* (New York: Free Press, 1994) is also interesting.

4. From N. K. Krupskaya, *Reminiscences of Lenin* (New York: International Publishers, 1970), p. 13. The best-known biography of Krupskaya is Robert H. McNeal, *Bride of the Revolution* (Ann Arbor, Michigan: University of Michigan Press, 1972).

Chapter 8
Revolutionary
Lives: Vladimir
Ilyich (Ulyanov)
Lenin
(1870–1924) and
Nadezhda K.
Krupskaya
(1869–1939)

he was eventually tried and demoted. He died a few years later, in 1883, leaving Krupskaya and her mother in difficult economic circumstances.

Krupskaya attended a prestigious female gymnasium in St. Petersburg from 1881–1887, and then gave lessons, helped her mother with boarders, and earned money writing envelopes for business firms. Her lifelong desire was to be a teacher, and she was convinced of the importance of education in social reform, especially for women. Like her future partner Lenin, Krupskaya was considered a brilliant student, and she too appears to have been single-minded. A friend at school remembered that "earlier than any of us . . . more unyieldingly than any of us, she had defined her views, had set her course. She was one of those who are forever committed, once they have been possessed by their thoughts or feelings. . . ."[5] By the late eighties and early nineties, Krupskaya had moved beyond her earlier attraction to liberal/romantic fiction and was reading revolutionary writings and had even tackled Marx's *Capital*. His vision of inevitable revolution appealed to her desires for social and economic justice. As she remembered later, "Marxism meant the greatest happiness. To know where you have to go, to be sure about the happy ending of the cause with which your life is from now on linked."[6] Thus, when Lenin and Krup-

skaya met, they were both committed revolutionaries. Their family backgrounds and education, combined with events in their personal lives, made them aware of the repressive politics, rigid social order, and harsh economic conditions of late nineteenth-century Russia, and both were committed to changing those conditions.

In the year after they met in 1894, Lenin and Krupskaya spent a great deal of time together. He listened to her talk about education and her firsthand experiences teaching workers, and was impressed with her considerable organizing and administrative skills. She was drawn to his knowledge, intellectual incisiveness, ambitions, and strength of will. She became convinced, rightly so as it turned out, that Lenin was the person who could lead the revolution that would realize her dreams and those of other Russian radicals at the time. In 1895, Lenin traveled to Europe for the first time, meeting with various Russian radicals in exile, including Plekhanov. Upon his return, he and Krupskaya planned to publish a newspaper for workers. They were both under police surveillance at the time, and in 1897 the police arrested them. Lenin was sentenced to a three-year exile or house arrest at Shushenskoe in southern Siberia; Krupskaya was sent to exile at Ufa in the north. Some sources indicate that prior to their separate exiles, Lenin had asked her to marry him. More certain is the fact that in 1898 he requested permission to have his fiancée join him at Shushenskoe, and Krupskaya applied for transfer on the grounds that she planned to marry Lenin. She and her mother moved to

5. Ariadne Tyrkova quoted in McNeal, p. 19.

6. Quoted in Beate Fieseler, "The Making of Russian Female Social Democrats, 1890–1917," *International Review of Social History* 34:2 (1989), p. 221.

the south in April of 1898. A modest wedding ceremony took place in July and was witnessed by her mother, two local peasants, and a few of their exile-friends.

The first years of their marriage laid the groundwork for the patterns that Lenin and Krupskaya would follow in later years. Lenin was writing a book on the development of capitalism in Russia, and Krupskaya helped him choose materials, listened as he read chapters aloud, and helped to rewrite passages. They also enjoyed the same kinds of literature and spent time working together in their garden. And he taught her how to fire a revolver. Mutual respect, affection, and common values and ideals bound them together in what was probably one of the most successful political marriages of the time.

ACT I:

THE EMERGENCE OF A REVOLUTIONARY PARTY

Meanwhile, in 1898, a small group of marxist activists had met to create a national revolutionary party that eventually took the name Russian Social Democratic Labor party (RSDLP). By the turn of the century, their well-known leaders, people like Plekhanov, Zasulich, or Yuli Martov, were in exile and the second party congress was held on foreign soil in 1903. When Lenin's term of exile ended in 1900, he returned to St. Petersburg, was arrested again and briefly detained, and in December decided to leave Russia for self-imposed exile. When Krupskaya was released in 1901, she also left Russia to join Lenin. By April 1902, they and Krupskaya's mother were living together in London in a small two-room flat. They took English lessons, attended the theater, and continued their revolutionary writing and organizing. Before leaving Russia, Krupskaya had written an article that addressed the terrible pay and working conditions of women, and (possibly with Lenin's encouragement) Zasulich published the essay in the party paper.

A more earth-shaking publication that appeared in 1902 was Lenin's influential essay entitled, "What Is to Be Done?" (Document One). In this piece, Lenin provided his blueprint for a successful revolutionary party made up of a limited number of professionally trained revolutionaries. Other Social Democratic leaders like Martov disagreed, arguing that the party should be comprehensive and open to all who believed in their goals. Adding to the intellectual fires that year was Lenin's influence on the drafting and publishing of the program for the party's Second Party Congress, to be held in 1903 in London (Document Two). All these factors produced heated debates at the congress. Lenin's followers had a slight voting majority and hence were named the Bolsheviks (men of the majority); minority opponents became the Mensheviks. Leon Trotsky attended the congress and was shocked and even indignant about

*Chapter 8
Revolutionary
Lives: Vladimir
Ilyich (Ulyanov)
Lenin
(1870–1924) and
Nadezhda K.
Krupskaya
(1869–1939)*

Lenin's willingness to confront and challenge the respected older leaders of the party. He remembered older members asking, "'Where, then, did he get that supreme self-confidence? Where did he get the nerve?' But Lenin had the nerve. . . . Lenin was not merely a remarkable party worker, but a leader, a man with every fibre of his being bent on one particular end. . . ."[7] For the next several years, the party was in conflict, even though party members continued to meet together and pursue the general goal of revolution. Lenin meanwhile fought to gain control of the party, and hoped he could direct it using Krupskaya's skills and experience.[8] Nadya at least was the secretary for the Bolshevik wing of the party and was kept busy as chief accountant and bursar for the organization, as well as reading proofs of Lenin's writings and insuring that all his works were collected for library or archival purposes. Two strong dimensions of Lenin's character emerged in these years: first, his obsession with silence and order when he was working, and second, his insistence on his plan for revolution without the possibility of compromise.

In the meantime, changes in Russia, for both good and ill, were creating energy and frustration that would lead to an explosion in 1905. Under the new tsar, Nicholas II (r. 1894–1917), efforts were made to attract foreign investment and to expand industrial output, which in the 1890s achieved one of the highest growth rates anywhere in the world. Conditions in the countryside were not improved, however, and political rights and freedoms were still nonexistent. While the Social Democrats in exile and underground in Russia continued to spread propaganda and to organize mostly among the urban lower classes, the efforts of other groups added fuel to the fires of revolution. The Social Revolutionaries, with a largely peasant constituency, also advocated terrorism and assassinated several provincial governors and three government ministers between 1901 and 1904. Moderate liberalism, with demands for constitutional reform and representative government, also grew from its base in provincial *zemstvos* to include broader membership and foreign support. In general, demands for change became louder, even in the face of imperial repression, and in 1905, both economic difficulties and a disastrous war with Japan produced an explosion that started with a factory workers' strike in St. Petersburg in January. By the end of the summer, other strikes, agrarian revolts, and acts of terrorism became a revolution that enabled those around the tsar to convince him that reform was necessary.

Beginning in 1906, the state enacted various promising political reforms that broadened fundamental liberties and created a national legislative assembly, the Duma. People's hopes were raised because it looked like Russia was developing into a more open, constitutional monarchy. Over the next decade, however, the tsarist government succeeded in diluting the power of the Duma, and radical political groups ceased to play a role in that body. It remained as a political institu-

7. Leon Trotsky, *My Life* (New York: Pathfinder Press, 1970), p. 163.

8. McNeal, pp. 114, 124.

tion until 1917, led generally by a bloc of moderate liberals. Economic reforms to improve agriculture were also enacted in this time period, with the results that more peasants controlled land and agricultural production improved. Ironically, the poorest peasants often sold their plots and used the money to move to the cities, where they increased the numbers of a potentially volatile proletariat.

Lenin, Krupskaya, and other Social Democrats had returned to Russia in 1905, but the situation clearly was not one that they could exploit effectively (or safely) for revolutionary goals. By 1907, they were once again in exile in Europe. From that point forward, they remained in Europe until revolution broke out in Russia in 1917. To understand the nature and significance of their lives in exile, it is important to look at the development of a revolutionary community in and outside Russia in those years, and to consider how other men and women of the time entered political life and perhaps Lenin and Krupskaya's revolutionary circle.

▪ ACT II:

The Making of Revolutionaries

Lenin and Krupskaya were unique personalities with an unusual commitment to politics. His creative intellect and her administrative and organizing skills combined to make them the centripetal force for a generation of revolutionaries with whom they shared common backgrounds and goals. Building an organization and setting a course for revolution would take time. In the early years of the twentieth century, a solid network of leaders in exile, clandestine organizers, and underground activists in Russia kept in touch through letters and secret travels, and spread their message in pamphlets and a newspaper, *Iskra*. By 1905, the revolutionary party, the RSDLP, counted approximately 12,300 members, 15 percent of whom were women.[9]

The overwhelming majority of those people who formed the core of revolutionary leadership came from families of the lesser nobility or had parents who were teachers, merchants, or provincial administrators or other bureaucrats. Almost universally, the leaders were well-educated, and often their parents were at least sympathetic to movements for reform in Russian society. As young people, they frequently saw firsthand the problems of the lower classes in their society, developed a political consciousness, and became determined "to do something." In the course of their work, they often found companions whom they married. Particularly in the case of those who went into exile, their political allies became a kind of surrogate family because they lived, traveled, and worked together.

Dermid and Anna Hillyar, *Midwives of the Revolution: Female Bolsheviks and Women Workers in 1917* (Athens, Ohio: Ohio University Press, 1999).

9. Fieseler, p. 195. An excellent recent study of women in the history of the party is Jane Mc-

Chapter 8
Revolutionary
Lives: Vladimir
Ilyich (Ulyanov)
Lenin
(1870–1924) and
Nadezhda K.
Krupskaya
(1869–1939)

Lev Kamenev (1883– 1936) and Grigory Zinoviev (1883–1936) and their wives, Olga Davydovna (1881–1936) and Liliana Ionovna (1882–1929), respectively, illustrate this situation. From the same generation as Lenin and Krupskaya, they were all reasonably well educated, generally joined the RSDLP in the early twentieth century, but then were forced to leave Russia for exile in Europe. There they met Lenin and Krupskaya and, like many others, traveled back and forth to Russia on behalf of the party.

Lives like these illustrate that both men and women in the party shared similar ideals and heroes, and politics and personal lives were easily intertwined. Although their goals and purposes might not have wavered, their lives were uncertain; for security reasons, their social circles were limited and having an equally committed partner was both practically and emotionally advantageous. That sense of shared danger and the same visions would also foster a strong network of revolutionary friendships during the long years of underground activity and exile.

As might be expected, the lives of the men and women were different in some dimensions. For the women, marriage was one of the few ways they could escape the control of their fathers. In fact, in some rather notable instances, revolutionary women married and then left their husbands and families in order to devote themselves to revolutionary politics. What they hoped for, what they assumed women's role in the movement should be, and how they saw women's emancipation

were often quite different. Zasulich, for example, chose not to focus on women's issues nor in working with women. Krupskaya was interested in improving the conditions of working women, their families, and their children and would often write about such issues and support legislation to assist women. At the same time, she, perhaps under Lenin's influence, did not think women should be organized separately because this could disrupt working-class unity.

More radical in both their personal lives, their willingness to challenge male political leaders, and their goals for women were Alexandra Kollontai (1872–1952) and Inessa Armand (1874–1920). These two women are connected in their revolutionary roles because both came to radical politics out of concern for women's status, shared similar views of women's emancipation, helped to organize women, and eventually, after the October Revolution, first Armand and then Kollontai served as leaders of the *Zhenotdel* (Women's Department) of the Communist party.[10] Paris-born Inessa Stephane was assimilated into Russian society when she moved to Moscow in 1879 with a maternal aunt, who was the governess for the family

10. For information on these women, see R. C. Elwood, *Inessa Armand: Revolutionary and Feminist* (Cambridge: Cambridge University Press, 1992); Barbara E. Clements, *Bolshevik Feminist: The Life of Alexandra Kollontai* (Bloomington, Ind.: Indiana University Press, 1979). Another important source of information about them and other women active at the time is Richard Stites, *The Women's Liberation Movement in Russia* (Princeton, N. J.: Princeton University Press, 1978).

of wealthy textile manufacturer, Evgenii Armand. Alexandra Mikhailovna Domontovich was born into the nobility, and her father was an imperial general. Both women were raised to be cultured and educated ladies of the leisure classes, and both married men of their social standing. Inessa married Alexander Armand, the second oldest son of the family, and Alexandra married a distant cousin, an engineer, Vladimir Kollontai. Inessa had five children, Alexandra one.

Like other women of her social position, Inessa engaged in charity work and in 1899 helped establish the Moscow Society for Improving the Lot of Women. The society hoped to "render women moral and material support, to promote the spread of women's education and technical training; to establish shelters and refuges for fallen women, and for juveniles who have sunk into the vice of depravity; . . . ."[11] While doing this work in Moscow, Inessa was introduced to the social and political circles of her brother-in-law Vladimir, who was a university student and involved in left-wing organizations. While her husband was certainly a liberal thinker, it was Vladimir whom Inessa recognized as helping to make her a Marxist. In 1908, she wrote to him that "Marxism for me is not youthful enthusiasm, but the culmination of a long evolution from right to left."[12] As she moved into the mainstream of revolutionary politics, Armand also traveled to Europe and eventually left her husband to live in a "free union" with Vladimir until he died in 1909. Inessa and Alexander continued to share in the raising of their children, and he provided her with material and emotional support throughout her life. She joined the RSDLP in 1904, spent time in prison, escaped and fled to Europe in 1907, and met Lenin in Paris two years later.

Kollontai's life was equally dramatic. She claimed her consciousness first was raised in 1896, when she accompanied her husband to an engineering project at a nearby factory and witnessed the terrible living conditions of the workers. Two years later, she sympathized with a strike by textile workers, but she recognized that, while such emotions were commendable, they would do little to bring understanding or change. In 1898, she left Russia to study at the university in Zurich, where she became familiar with Marx's revolutionary ideas. Upon her return to Russia in 1903, she taught in worker's circles and organized female workers. In 1906, she joined the Menshevik wing of the party, and after attending a feminist congress in 1908 and publishing a book in favor of socialism, she fled Russia (and her family) as she was about to be arrested. Germany was her primary residence in exile, and she eventually joined the German Social Democratic party. Perhaps that party appealed to her because it was the largest, most influential Socialist party in Europe and had an active women's section. She first corresponded with

11. Ellwood, p.28.
12. Ibid., p. 38.

Chapter 8
Revolutionary
Lives: Vladimir
Ilyich (Ulyanov)
Lenin
(1870–1924) and
Nadezhda K.
Krupskaya
(1869–1939)

Lenin after war began in Europe in 1914 because she found his interpretation of the causes of the war and his denunciation of nationalism compelling. She remained in Europe until the revolution began in 1917. Later, in her autobiography, Kollontai described her life's purpose: "To go my way, to work, to struggle, to create side by side with men, and to strive for the attainment of a universal human goal, . . . but, at the same time, to shape my personal, intimate life as a woman according to my own will and according to the given laws of my nature."[13] The fact that Armand and Kollontai both shaped their lives according to their wills perhaps can be attributed to their privileged backgrounds, their intelligence and education, and to a resulting sense of confidence and independence.

Although Kollontai and Armand corresponded and worked together on women's issues while in exile and in Russia after October 1917, they were not particularly good friends. But both women had a special relationship to Lenin. Kollontai and Lenin first met in 1905, but the fact that she did not join him politically until the outbreak of the World War I, and that she later would disagree and oppose him, made their relationship rather prickly. Sometime after, when Maxim Gorkii wrote his *Reminiscences of My Youth*, he remembered "how gaily and how long Lenin laughed when some-

where he read Martov's utterance, 'There are only two communists in Russia, Lenin and Kollontai'."[14]

Armand and Lenin were closely connected intellectually and emotionally, and she was one of the few people with whom he ever used the familiar form of address (ty). Historians continue to debate whether their relationship was more than a platonic friendship. He trusted her and respected her intellect and her ability to articulate Bolshevik ideas. One biographer refers to her as Lenin's "cudgel [who] beat wavering Bolsheviks back into line, delivered uncompromising messages to his political opponents, and carried out uncomfortable missions which Lenin himself preferred to avoid."[15] She also argued with him and occasionally refused to carry out his orders. Inessa was also a close friend of Krupskaya's, but the real spark was between her and Lenin. As one of his comrades observed at Armand's funeral in 1920: "I never saw such torment; I never saw any human being so completely absorbed by sorrow, by the effort to keep it to himself, to guard it against the attention of others, as if their awareness could have diminished the intensity of his feeling."[16]

Although Armand and Kollontai are significant historical actors be-

13. Alexandra Kollontai, *The Autobiography of a Sexually Emancipated Communist Woman*, foreword by Germaine Greer (New York: Schocken Books, 1975), p. 4.

14. Quoted by Iring Fetscher in the afterword to *The Autobiography of a Sexually Emancipated Woman*, p. 105.

15. Ellwood, p. 125.

16. From Angelica Balabanoff, *Impressions of Lenin* (Ann Arbor, Michigan: University of Michigan Press, 1964), p. 14.

cause of their visibility and their feminist ideas and politics, they are probably not typical of the majority of the revolutionary women who joined the RSDLP. Their female comrades certainly arrived at political consciousness from their background and experiences as women, but most did not join the party because of its inclusion of the "woman question" and women's emancipation in its program. The work that they did was essential but often hidden or not discussed. They organized, administered, maintained communication, and helped to build a revolutionary party, and many of them wrote pamphlets and essays dealing with issues of work, family, education, and culture. In many ways, Anna Elizarova (1864–1935), Lenin's older sister, fits this profile more accurately.

Anna Ulyanova had been able to take advantage of the women's university courses offered in the 1880s and, like her brothers, was drawn into revolutionary politics. In 1887, her studies were ended when she was implicated in the conspiracy for which her brother Alexander was arrested and then executed. Anna taught and wrote pamphlets in the 1890s, joined the RSDLP in 1898, and then spent two years in Europe working on the party newspaper, *Iskra*. She collaborated with Lenin and was his confidante, but she was also a revolutionary in her own right, responsible for propaganda activity and organization in Russia when the more visible leaders were in exile. In 1913, when Armand convinced the party that they should publish a journal specifically for women, *Rabotnitsa*, Anna was assigned the hands-on job of editor, even though by then she was frequently on the move or in hiding. All the while, she kept a home for her mother and her husband, Mark Elizarov, also a revolutionary. During the events of 1917, she continued to work with the press, and Lenin and Krupskaya lived with the Elizarovs for a time after their return to Russia.

Becoming a radical could be a dangerous choice for both men and women, and it was fairly common for all to be imprisoned periodically. Nevertheless, rebellion meant different things for men and women because women had fewer social options than men and "had to challenge not only the state, but the patriarchal family structure and traditional notions of femininity and women's role."[17] Even so, unusually high percentages of women participated in all of the nineteenth-century Russian reform, radical, and revolutionary movements. Whether male or female, the revolutionary cadres might well have shared a moment of truth like Kollontai's: "Since childhood I liked the 'all goes well with me' feeling. [But now] I pace from one corner of the room to the other and torment myself with the thought: how can one so arrange the scheme of things so that 'all goes well' with everybody?"[18]

17. McDermid and Hillyar, p. 81.
18. From an interview quoted by Fetscher, p. 107.

*Chapter 8
Revolutionary
Lives: Vladimir
Ilyich (Ulyanov)
Lenin
(1870–1924) and
Nadezhda K.
Krupskaya
(1869–1939)*

▪ ACT III:

REVOLUTIONARY WORK IN EXILE

Between 1907 and 1917, Lenin and Krupskaya lived a peripatetic life, beginning with a year in Switzerland, moving to France for several years and then to Austrian Poland, and finally returning to Switzerland when war began in 1914. Although they had no children, they were rarely alone. Krupskaya's mother was with them, and they often shared rented apartments or small houses with their closest colleagues, or at least they all were neighbors. Lilina and Grigorii Zinoviev were either housemates or resided nearby most of this time, and Inessa Armand also lived in close proximity after she fled Russia and met Lenin in Paris in 1909. Lev Kamenev moved in and out of their lives as he traveled back and forth to Russia on party business (Document Three). Although Krupskaya and Lenin were never destitute, they were not economically secure either. She had received a small inheritance from an aunt, and Lenin's mother also sent money from his father's pension and from interest gained when she sold the small family estate. The party had a fund to support its members and Lenin was paid a salary sporadically. He also received donations from benefactors and earned small sums for his writings and for lecturing. When times were especially difficult, Krupskaya returned to addressing envelopes for local businesses.

During these years, Lenin was reading and writing, talking with colleagues, and attending international Socialist meetings and party congresses. Krupskaya also wrote several pieces on education and sometimes accompanied Lenin to meetings, but she was kept busy with party organization and administration. As Trotsky remarked, "She was at the very center of all the organization work; she received comrades when they arrived, instructed them when they left, established connections, supplied secret addresses, wrote letters, and coded and decoded correspondence"[19] (Document Four). In 1911, Lenin, Krupskaya, Armand, and the Zinovievs moved to a small town outside Paris, where they set up a Bolshevik school for Russian workers who had been imprisoned and then emigrated west. Lenin lectured on the agrarian question and the theory and practice of socialism, Armand on political economy, and Krupskaya on how to set up an underground newspaper. When the settings were suitable, they also enjoyed their favorite pastimes: hiking, swimming, and taking long (70-kilometer) bike rides.

The differences between Lenin and his socialist colleagues did not lessen in these years and, in fact, were heightened with the coming of war in Europe in 1914. In 1915, Lenin, with the help of Zinoviev, wrote *Socialism and War*, which formed the basis for discussions among socialists at several meetings in Switzerland. Lenin insisted that the war was imperialist and motivated by capitalist gain, and that revolutionaries must use the opportunity to turn soldiers against their rulers and governments and to convince them to quit fighting their brother workers across the "enemy" lines. Many socialists found this "de-

19. Trotsky, p. 152.

featism" unacceptable and preferred to remain neutral or to support their national efforts. Lenin also used this opportunity to denounce the followers of the Second International for abandoning the goals and practices of revolutionary Marxism, and for cooperating with bourgeois governments and their interests. Early in 1917, Lenin focused specifically on the economic processes and the significance of imperialism in one of his most famous pamphlets, "Imperialism, the Highest Stage of Capitalism."

Within Russia, the war weighed heavily on all aspects of life. By early 1917, government ineptness and confusion, problems of organization and transport within the military, and economic pressures and food shortages combined to set the stage for revolution. Strikes and demonstrations became common, but on February 23 (March 8 of the new calendar), 1917, one such protest began in St. Petersburg, spearheaded by women demanding bread and coal. The tsarist authorities summoned soldiers garrisoned in the city to help the police in crushing the revolt. The soldiers refused to fire at the crowds and shortly thereafter joined with the protestors, sharing weapons and ammunition. A few days later a council of workers' and soldiers' deputies (to be known as the Petrograd Soviet) was formed, the Duma persuaded the tsar to abdicate, and a provisional government was created. The door was now open for reform, or more dramatically, for revolution.

▩ FINALE

Lenin, Krupskaya, the Zinovievs, Armand, and others returned to Russia by April and found a world in upheaval. In the next month, the Provisional Government enacted political and legal reforms, but continued the war and was unable to meet the basic economic needs of the population. Strikes and protests continued, and more workers' organizations were established, often with Bolshevik encouragement and leadership. Kollontai had returned to Russia in March and threw herself into winning over lower-class women by recognizing their economic grievances, resulting from food shortages and low wages in particular. Forty thousand laundresses went on strike in May 1917, and Kollontai was there to encourage and support them. She continually advised the party that it should organize women separately.

Upon her return to Russia, Krupskaya's revolutionary activity changed. In exile, she had served as the secretary of the party, but back at home someone else held that position and Lenin thought it important not to disrupt the organization. This also meant that they did not work together as they always had. Krupskaya's matter-of-fact account of these shifts perhaps hides feelings of some isolation. She noted that her current job was "nothing like the secretarial job I had done abroad or that of 1905–07 when I had done rather important work on my

Chapter 8
Revolutionary
Lives: Vladimir
Ilyich (Ulyanov)
Lenin
(1870–1924) and
Nadezhda K.
Krupskaya
(1869–1939)

own under Ilyich's direction."[20] But this was, after all, her revolution as much as Lenin's, and Krupskaya quickly returned to grass-roots organizing. She took over the running of the Committee for the Relief of Soldiers' Wives in the Vyborg district of St. Petersburg, and throughout the summer of 1917 continued to work in that working-class neighborhood, "observing what was happening and listening to what was being said on the streets, playing especially close attention to what women, youth and teachers had to say"[21] (Document Five). In this regard, she too remained true to the issues that had interested her for decades.

Shortly after he returned to Russia, Lenin had presented to the Bolsheviks his views of and plans for the revolution. These were published and referred to as the "April Theses" (Document Six). His plans caught many of his colleagues off guard, even Krupskaya apparently, but he was a person who often kept his own counsel. He also thoroughly angered his opponents because Lenin insisted that the Bolsheviks should not cooperate with the provisional government. Instead, he argued that the hour for proletarian revolution had arrived, and that they must push for peace immediately and support a government based on the revolutionary Soviets, which were springing up all over Russia. With hindsight, this approach makes sense because the Bolsheviks clearly were

influential in the Soviets and because the provisional government, refusing to sue for peace and slow to deal with workers' and peasants' demands, became increasingly weak without a cohesive constituency to support it. Lenin's plans also help to explain why the Bolsheviks spent considerable effort in organizing lower-class men *and* women. Although without doubt the dominant image of a rank-and-file revolutionary was still an industrial worker, the number, militancy, and tenacity of women like the laundresses and other service workers did not escape the attention of the Bolshevik leaders.

A failed military offensive in late June, another round of popular demonstrations and strikes in July, and an unsuccessful attempt at military takeover in August seemed to lend credibility to Lenin's predictions and ultimately weakened the government to the extent that, when the Bolsheviks finally staged their coup d'état in October, the revolution was almost bloodless. Lenin and Krupskaya were reunited by then, and she had been an important source of support during the previous months when "the frantic political pace put him under unrelieved pressure."[22] Although Lenin issued decrees on land and peace, began the process of drawing up a constitution in November, and initiated peace talks with Germany that resulted in the signing of a treaty in March 1918, the hard work had only begun.

All the members of the revolution-

---

20. Quoted in McNeal, p. 170.

21: McDermid and Hillyar, p. 65. Her account of the revolution in Petrograd in 1917 is most illuminating.

22. Service, p. 276, describes the toll these months took on Lenin.

ary "family" had important roles to play in the building of the new socialist society. Krupskaya, for example, was quickly made a Deputy Commissar of Enlightenment (essentially of the Ministry of Education and Culture), and in the 1920s headed the Political Education Administration of that ministry. The broad goals of this agency were to build something one might call working-class culture or identity, to raise consciousness, and to promote basic education. Krupskaya believed she now had the opportunity to provide better education for women, which she felt would help them get better jobs. In the meantime, Kollontai had been elected to the Party Central Committee; she continued to organize working women, and in October 1917 she was named Commissar for Social Welfare, a position she held for about a year. The party finally agreed to form a separate women's department, the Zhenotdel, headed by Armand until her death in 1920 and then by Kollontai. While the party assumed the organization would be a way to bring revolutionary goals to women, raising their consciousness and drumming up support for the Bolsheviks, Kollontai assumed it would bring issues of women's everyday lives to the party and help to influence state policy. In this view, as on several other issues, she soon found herself in opposition to the party.

Single-mindedness became ruthlessness as resistance to the new regime turned into a full-scale civil war that started in 1919 and lasted for two years. As revolutionaries were transformed into rulers, priorities shifted and new skills and talents were needed.

In building a revolutionary party, underground and in exile, organization, administration, and communication were paramount to Bolshevik success. But after October 1917, institutional structures, hierarchy, and a streamlined party provided the means for retaining power. In 1918, Lenin's "State and Revolution" was published. This essay helped to define Bolshevik strategies and to solidify his position as the true leader of the party. He forcefully asserted the importance of the dictatorship of the proletariat, the legitimacy of coercion to force others to adapt, and increased centralized power, especially in the hands of the core of the party leadership. This piece, combined with actual practice, made it clear that for Lenin, actions should be judged only by how they promoted the revolution. Like leaders of other revolutions, Lenin believed that individual rights could be suspended for the greater good, and that use of force, even civil war, could be appropriate instruments for revolutionary transformation. As the flexibility and even spontaneity of the earlier period disappeared, the visibility of women colleagues lessened and their work was considered less critical.[23] Although women would remain important as workers and supporters, and although they held positions of leadership in agencies responsible for family and social welfare or education, they were rarely involved in the highest levels of decision making.

23. McDermid and Hillyar provide an excellent discussion of these changes in their conclusion; see pp. 187–201. Also see Stites, especially pp. 326–328.

Chapter 8
Revolutionary
Lives: Vladimir
Ilyich (Ulyanov)
Lenin
(1870–1924) and
Nadezhda K.
Krupskaya
(1869–1939)

By 1920, Kollontai had spelled her own demise by criticizing centralization and advocating greater worker authority and democratization of the political structures. She also insisted that the revolution should produce a "new" woman who had multiple roles and identities beyond motherhood, and that it should attack double standards of sexual behavior and objectification of women. This was clearly too radical for both the party leaders and the rank and file (Document Seven). As if to give substance to her ideas, she divorced her new husband in 1922, telling him, "I am not the wife you need. I am a person before I am a woman." In her 1926 autobiography, she wrote, "Over and over again, the man always tried to impose his ego upon us and to adapt us fully to his purposes."[24] She was eventually dismissed from her position in the Zhenotdel in 1922. From then until her death thirty years later, she was in virtual exile, serving in various ambassadorial posts in places as diverse as Sweden and Mexico.

In May 1922, Lenin suffered the first of a number of strokes; he died almost two years later on January 21, 1924. Krupskaya had been working to develop public education, but as Lenin became increasingly ill, she devoted herself to supporting and protecting him. She also resumed her role as his political assistant, helping to keep him politically informed and connected when other leaders, like Josef Stalin, were anxious to isolate him and disable

24. Quoted in the Introduction to *Alexandra Kollontai: Selected Writings*, edited by Alix Holt (New York: W. W. Norton, 1977), p. 19.

his political networks. As Lenin's own awareness of the severity of his illness increased, he expressed distress that his work was not yet accomplished. "It's too early to leave. Five more years of training are needed," he said to a friend in 1923. He was particularly worried about who would succeed him in leading the party and the state, and expressed little confidence in most of the possible candidates. Even while ill, however, he could leave his ideas and advice regarding the future strategies and his assessments of those vying to succeed him. He thus dictated a letter to the next party congress that was, in essence, a testament. Five copies of the letter were left in a sealed envelope that only he or Krupskaya, in the event of his death, could open. When he died in January 1924, Krupskaya tried to respect his wishes but she was outmaneuvered by Stalin and dismissed by Trotsky, another contender. The testament of Lenin that eventually was made public ironically was a revised version. Even though Krupskaya was absolutely opposed to the plan, the party decided to embalm Lenin and permanently display his body in a Red Square mausoleum. Although she hated the public display, in the decades that followed she actively propagated an image of Lenin that was heroic and unblemished—the perfect revolutionary man, thinker, and husband.

She survived Lenin, the contests for power, and the brutality of the Stalin years, and she continued her work in the ministry of education. She also continued to address Russian women, but the model she promulgated was that of the mother-worker, an image that would fit well within various Stalinist plans for industrialization and modernization in Russia. Once again, women were asked to "do it all" and to sacrifice for their children and families. The revolution, in its initial stages, had legislated equality and promised women opportunities in work and education, but by the end of the 1920s, many provisions regarding freedom in marriage and divorce were rescinded or altered. The Zhenotdel became less and less an advocate for women's interests and eventually was abolished with a party reorganization in 1930. Material conditions tended to deteriorate, causing hardships for women and men, and if there were more women working it was probably because that was the only way a family could survive. Women were party members, but they did not occupy decision-making positions. As one woman noted in 1928, "In the family life of women, the old way of life is retained in almost all its totality. All of the burdens of the organization of domestic life in the present period lie completely, fully and exclusively on women."[25] While Soviet women might have been freed from the older constraints of private, familial patriarchy, they now were controlled by a "patriarchal" state that limited their personal choices and insisted that they had dual responsibilities: to produce healthy children and maintain private morality, and to serve the state directly as workers and in social assistance efforts (Document Eight).

In the 1930s, Krupskaya seemed to be reconciled to the Stalinist version of a socialist society, and while continuing to work for women's education, its purpose was the political one of creating loyal citizens who did not question state or party. When purges of Stalin's opponents began, she occasionally tried to use her influence to protect old Bolshevik comrades. Not surprisingly, she was unable to affect broader politics, even though she did serve on the Party Central Committee several times in these years. Perhaps she convinced herself that Stalin was simply continuing a strategy that Lenin had set forth. Or perhaps she was enough of a pragmatist to recognize that she could save herself but not a different view of the revolution. She continued to promote Lenin's memory, and even his detractors would agree that at the very least he had helped to change the history of Russia and the world. But now it is also clear that "he would not have risen to historical eminence without the support of Krupskaya and the other women" who helped him and were devoted to him.[26] Eventually both Lenin and his partner, Krupskaya, became mythical figures: he as the great champion of humankind, she as the tender, solicitous mother of the Soviet people.

25. Quoted in Carol Eubanks Hayden, "The Zhenotdel and the Bolshevik Party," *Russian History* 3:2 (1976), p. 170. For additional information on revolutionary developments for women in the 1920s and 1930s, see Wendy Z. Goldman, *Women, the State and Revolution, 1917–1936* (Cambridge: Cambridge University Press, 1993). Finally, a good discussion of the different ideals of Kollontai and Krupskaya can be found in Norma Noonan, "Two Solutions to the Zhenskii Vvopros [the Woman Question] in Russia and the USSR—Kollontai and Krupskaia: A Comparison," *Women and Politics* 11:3 (1991), pp. 77–99.

26. Service, p. 493.

*Chapter 8
Revolutionary
Lives: Vladimir
Ilyich (Ulyanov)
Lenin
(1870–1924) and
Nadezhda K.
Krupskaya
(1869–1939)*

◼ **QUESTIONS**

1. Compare and contrast Lenin's and Krupskaya's paths into revolutionary activity, their roles in building a revolutionary movement, and their positions once the revolution took place.

2. How did the concrete historical conditions of the late nineteenth century produce Bolshevik ideology? The Bolshevik party was formed in exile and underground. How did such circumstances affect the organization and the definition of its goals?

3. In attempting to bring revolutionary change to Russia, Lenin faced some of the same problems and decisions that other leaders of earlier revolutions had confronted. What are some of the common issues they faced? How did earlier leaders and Lenin answer the question: Do the ends justify the means?

4. Why is motherhood a central issue for revolutionary leaders in Russia and also for previous radical leaders like Mazzini or Robespierre? How do the Russian revolutionary women like Kollontai and Krupskaya contribute to debates over this issue?

5. Compare and contrast the experiences and attitudes of both men and women toward the Bolshevik party and the revolution.

6. Assess women's gains for political equality in the French and Russian revolutions.

◼ **DOCUMENTS**

DOCUMENT ONE

V.I. LENIN

What Is to Be Done? Burning Questions of Our Movement (1902)

For some time throughout Europe, socialists had debated about who should be members of the party and what the role of the party would be. These became particularly important issues for the Russian socialist leaders in exile. Some felt that the party should be loosely organized and open to all. In this document, originally published in 1902, Lenin spells out his views on how to organize a revolutionary party, and who should be included. What does he recommend as the best party organization and membership? What does he say about the charges that he is "antidemocratic"?

. . . I could go on analysing the Rules, but I think that what has been said will suffice. A small, compact core of the most reliable, experienced, and hardened workers, with responsible representatives in the principal districts and connected by all the rules of strict secrecy with the organisation of revolutionaries, can, with the widest support of the masses and without any formal organisation, perform *all* the functions of a trade union organisation, in a manner, moreover, desirable to Social-Democracy. Only in this way can we secure the *consolidation* and development of a *Social-Democratic* trade union movement, despite all the gendarmes.

It may be objected that an organisation which is so *lose* that it is not even definitely formed, and which has not even an enrolled and registered membership, cannot be called an organisation at all. Perhaps so. Not the name is important. What is important is that this "organisation without members" shall do everything that is required, and from the very outset ensure a solid connection between our future trade unions and socialism. Only an incorrigible utopian would have a *broad* organisation of workers, with elections, reports, universal suffrage, etc., under the autocracy.

The moral to be drawn from this is simple. If we begin with the solid foundation of a strong organisation of revolutionaries, we can ensure the stability of the movement as a whole and carry out the aims both of Social-Democracy and of trade unions proper. If, however, we begin with a broad workers' organisation, which is supposedly most "accessible" to the masses (but which is actually most accessible to the gendarmes and makes revolutionaries most accessible to the police), we shall achieve neither the one aim nor the other; we shall not eliminate our rule-of-thumb methods, and, because we remain scattered and our forces are constantly broken up by the police, we shall only make trade unions of the Zubatov and Ozerov type the more accessible to the masses. . . .

"A dozen wise men can be more easily wiped out than a hundred fools." This wonderful truth (for which the hundred fools will always applaud you) appears obvious only because in the very midst of the argument you have skipped from one question to another. You began by talking and continued to talk of the unearthing of a "committee," of the unearthing of an "organisation," and now you skip to the question of unearthing the movement's "roots" in their "depths." The fact is, of course, that our movement cannot be unearthed, for the very reason that it has countless thousands of roots deep down among the masses; but that is not the point at issue. As far as "deep roots" are concerned, we cannot be "unearthed" even now, despite all our amateurism, and yet we all complain, and cannot but complain, that the *"organisations"* are being unearthed and as a result it is impossible to maintain continuity in the movement. But since you raise the question of *organisations* being unearthed and persist in your opinion, I assert that it is far more difficult to unearth a dozen wise men than a hundred fools. This position I will defend, no matter how much you instigate the masses against me for my "anti-democratic" views, etc. As I have stated repeatedly, by "wise men," in connection with organisation, I mean *professional revolutionaries*, irrespective of whether they have developed from among students or working men. I assert: (1) that no revolutionary movement

*Chapter 8
Revolutionary
Lives: Vladimir
Ilyich (Ulyanov)
Lenin
(1870–1924) and
Nadezhda K.
Krupskaya
(1869–1939)*

can endure without a stable organisation of leaders maintaining continuity; (2) that the broader the popular mass drawn spontaneously into the struggle, which forms the basis of the movement and participates in it, the more urgent the need for such an organisation, and the more solid this organisation must be (for it is much easier for all sorts of demagogues to side-track the more backward sections of the masses); (3) that such an organisation must consist chiefly of people professionally engaged in revolutionary activity; (4) that in an autocratic state, the more we *confine* the membership of such an organisation to people who are professionally engaged in revolutionary activity and who have been professionally trained in the art of combating the political police, the more difficult will it be to unearth the organisation; and (5) the *greater* will be the number of people from the working class and from the other social classes who will be able to join the movement and perform active work in it. . . .

DOCUMENT TWO

V. I. LENIN

"Draft Programme of the Russian Social-Democratic Party" (1902)

Prior to the Second Party Congress to be held in London in 1903, a program of goals for the party was prepared. Lenin managed to revise it according to his own wishes and this draft appeared in the party paper Iskra *in 1902. How is this document like other declarations of rights you have read? What claims and goals are unusual?*

[B]
XIII. The tsarist autocracy is the most outstanding of these remnants of the serf-owning system and the most formidable bulwark of all this barbarism. It is the bitterest and most dangerous enemy of the proletarian emancipation movement and the cultural development of the entire people.
[C]
For these reasons the Russian Social-Democratic Labour Party advances as its immediate political task the overthrow of the tsarist autocracy and its replacement by a *republic* based on a democratic constitution that would ensure:

    1) the people's sovereignty, i.e., concentration of supreme state power in the hands of a legislative assembly consisting of representatives of the people;

2) universal, equal, and direct suffrage, both in elections to the legislative assembly and in elections to all local organs of self-government, for every citizen who has reached the age of twenty-one; the secret ballot at all elections; the right of every voter to be elected to any of the representative assemblies; remuneration for representatives of the people;

3) inviolability of the person and domicile of citizens;

4) unrestricted freedom of conscience, speech, the press and of assembly, the right to strike and to organise unions;

5) freedom of movement and occupation;

6) abolition of social-estates; full equality for all citizens, irrespective of sex, religion or race;

7) recognition of the right to self-determination for all nations forming part of the state;

8) the right of every citizen to prosecute any official, without previously complaining to the latter's superiors;

9) general arming of the people instead of maintaining a standing army;

10) separation of the church from the state and of the school from the church;

11) universal, free, and compulsory education up to the age of sixteen; state provision of food, clothing, and school supplies to needy children.

[D]

To protect the working class and to raise its fighting capacity, the Russian Social-Democratic Labour Party demands:

1) that the working day be limited to eight hours for all wage-workers;

2) that a weekly rest period of not less than thirty-six consecutive hours for wage-workers of both sexes employed in all branches of the national economy be established by law;

3) that all overtime be prohibited;

4) that night-work (from 9 P.M. to 5 A.M.) in all branches of the national economy be prohibited, with the exception of those branches in which it is essential for technical reasons;

5) that employers be forbidden to employ children under the age of fifteen;

6) that female labour be forbidden in industries specifically injurious to the health of women;

7) that the law establish employers' civil liability for workers' complete or partial disability caused by accidents or by harmful working conditions; that the worker should not be required to prove his employer's responsibility for disability; . . . .

Chapter 8
Revolutionary
Lives: Vladimir
Ilyich (Ulyanov)
Lenin
(1870–1924) and
Nadezhda K.
Krupskaya
(1869–1939)

━━━━━━━━━━━━━━━ **DOCUMENT THREE** ━━━━━━━━━━━━━━━

Nadezhda Krupskaya

Reminiscences of Lenin

In this writing, Krupskaya describes her memories of her and Lenin's years in ex-
ile in Europe. What does this memoir tell you about her activities and life with
Lenin, and the importance of the political community to which they were con-
nected?

. . . Inessa Armand arrived in Paris from Brussels in 1910 and immediately became an active member of our Paris group. Together with Semashko and Brit-
man (Kazakov) she was elected to the presidium of the group and started an
extensive correspondence with the other groups abroad. She had a family of
two little girls and a boy. She was a hot Bolshevik, and before long our whole
Paris crowd had gathered round her.

Our Paris group, as a matter of fact, was steadily gaining strength. It was becoming ideologically welded too. The trouble was that many of us were hard
up. The workers managed somehow to make a living, but the intellectuals were
in dire straits. They could not always become workers. To live at the expense of
the political emigrants' benefit fund and feed on credit at the emigrants' restaurant was humiliating in the extreme. I remember several sad cases. One comrade became a furniture polisher, but it was a long time before he learned the
job, and he had to change his place of work. . . .

It was decided to organize the school in the village of Longjumeau, fifteen
kilometres from Paris, a locality in which there were no Russians or summer
residents. Longjumeau was a straggling French village stretching along the
highroad along which carts with farmers' produce for *le ventre de Paris* rolled
endlessly all through the night. There was a small tannery there, and all around
lay fields and orchards. The arrangements were these: the students rented
rooms in the village, while Inessa Armand rented a house, in which a canteen
for the students was organized. We and the Zinovievs moved to Longjumeau
too. All the housekeeping was done by Katya Mazanova, the wife of a worker
who had been in Siberian exile together with Martov (in Turukhansk) and later
had worked illegally in the Urals. Katya was a good housekeeper and a comrade. Things went swimmingly. . . .

Inessa's house was thus occupied entirely by our own crowd. We lived at the
other end of the village and took our meals in the common dining room, where
it was pleasant to chat with the students, ask them about all kinds of things, and
discuss current topics with them.

We took two rooms in a small two-storey brick house (all the houses in
Longjumeau were brick-built) tenanted by a tannery worker, and were able to

observe at firsthand the life of a small-factory employee. He went to work early in the morning and came home in the evening dog tired. The house did not have a bit of garden round it. Sometimes a table and chair would be carried outside, and he would sit there for hours, resting his tired head on his toil-worn arms. . . .

Ilyich liked Cracow very much. It reminded him of Russia. The new surroundings and the absence of emigrant squabbles tended to soothe his nerves. Ilyich closely observed the everyday life of the Cracow population, its workers and its poor. I liked Cracow, too. I had lived in Poland once when I was a child from the age of two to five, and I had still retained some memories of it. I liked the open wooden galleries in the courtyards; they reminded me of those on whose steps I used to play with the Polish and Jewish children; I liked the little gardens—*ogródki*, where they sold *kwaśne mleko z ziemniakami* (sour milk and potatoes). My mother, too, was reminded of her young days. As for Ilyich, he was glad to have escaped from Paris at last; he cracked merry jokes, and praised both the *kwaśne mleko* and the Polish *mocna starka* (strong liquor).

Lilina knew more Polish than any of us. I knew it poorly; I remembered a little from my childhood days and had studied it a bit in Siberia and Ufa, and now I was obliged to make immediate use of the language along domestic lines. The housekeeping there was much more difficult than in Paris. There was no gas, and we had to light a wood fire in the kitchen. I tried asking for meat without bones at the butcher's, the way they used to sell it in Paris. The butcher looked at me and said: "The Lord God has created cows with bones, so how can I sell you meat without bones?" . . .

. . . In Berne we lived in Distelweg, a clean, quiet little street adjoining the Berne woods, which stretched for several miles. Inessa lived across the road, the Zinovievs a five-minute walk from us, and the Shklovskys a ten-minute walk. We used to roam for hours along the woodland paths, which were bestrewn with yellow leaves. Mostly the three of us went on these walks together—Vladimir Ilyich, Inessa and myself. Vladimir Ilyich spoke about his plans of struggle along international lines. Inessa was very enthusiastic about it all. She had begun to take a direct part in the rising struggle—she carried on correspondence, translated various of our documents into French and English, collected material, talked with people, etc. Sometimes we would sit for hours on a sunny wooded hillside, Ilyich jotting down notes for his articles and speeches, and polishing his formulations, I studying Italian with the aid of a Toussaint textbook, and Inessa sewing a skirt and basking in the autumn sunshine—she had not quite recovered yet from the effects of her imprisonment. In the evening we would all gather in Grigory's (Zinoviev's) tiny room—the three of them, Grigory, Lilina and their little boy Styopa, lived in a single room—and after playing about with little Styopa before he went to bed, Ilyich would make a number of concrete proposals. . . .

*Chapter 8
Revolutionary
Lives: Vladimir
Ilyich (Ulyanov)
Lenin
(1870–1924) and
Nadezhda K.
Krupskaya
(1869–1939)*

━━━━━━━━━━━━ **DOCUMENT FOUR** ━━━━━━━━━━━━

LEON TROTSKY

My Life: An Attempt at Autobiography

Trotsky eventually became one of Lenin's closest revolutionary comrades. In his autobiography, he gives another view of Krupskaya and Lenin during the years of underground activity and exile. How does Trotsky describe the role of Krupskaya in the party? What does he say about disagreements in the party and how Lenin responded to such conflicts? What does he admire most in Lenin?

. . . Lenin concentrated all connections with Russia in his own hands. The secretary of the editorial board was his wife, Nadyezhda Konstantinovna Krupskaya. She was at the very centre of all the organization work; she received comrades when they arrived, instructed them when they left, established connections, supplied secret addresses, wrote letters, and coded and decoded correspondence. In her room there was always a smell of burned paper from the secret letters she heated over the fire to read. She often complained, in her gently insistent way, that people did not write enough, or that they got the code all mixed up, or wrote in chemical ink in such a way that one line covered another, and so forth.

Lenin was trying, in the every-day work of political organization to achieve a maximum of independence from the older members and above all from Plekhanov, with whom he had had many bitter struggles, especially in the drafting of the party programme. Lenin's original draft, submitted as a counter-proposal to Plekihanov's, received from the latter a sharply unfavorable estimate, in the jesting and superior manner characteristic of Geórgy Valentinovitch on such occasions. But of course Lenin could not be confused or intimidated by such methods. The struggle took on a very dramatic aspect. Zasulitch and Martov acted as intermediaries; the former on behalf of Plekhanov, the latter of Lenin. Both intermediaries were in a most conciliatory mood, and besides this, they were friends. Vera Ivanovna, according to her own account, once said to Lenin: "George [Plekhanov] is a hound—he will shake a thing for a while, and then drop it; whereas you are a bulldog—yours is the death-grip." When she repeated this conversation to me later, Vera Ivanovna added: "This appealed to Lenin very much—'a death-grip,' he repeated, with obvious delight." As she said this, she good-naturedly mimicked Lenin's intonation and accent. (He could not pronounce the sound of "r" clearly)

All these disagreements took place before I arrived from Russia. I never suspected them. Nor did I know that the relations among the editors of the *Iskra* had been aggravated even more by my coming. . . .

The seriousness of the conflict which blazed up at the congress, apart from the impact of principles, which was still very incipient, was also caused by the failure of the older ones to recognize the stature and importance of Lenin. During the congress and immediately after, the indignation of Axelrod and others on the board at Lenin's conduct was coupled with amazement: "How could he have the nerve to do it?

"Was it so long ago that he came abroad as a mere pupil and behaved as a pupil?" the older ones argued. "Where, then, did he get that supreme self-confidence? Where did he get the nerve?"

But Lenin had the nerve. All he needed was to be convinced that the older ones were incapable of assuming direct leadership of the militant organization of the proletarian vanguard in the revolution which was clearly approaching. The older ones—and they were not alone—erred in their judgment; Lenin was not merely a remarkable party worker, but a leader, a man with every fibre of his being bent on one particular end, one who finally realized that he was himself a leader after he had stood side by side with the elders and had been convinced that he was stronger and more necessary than they. In the midst of the still vague moods that were common in the group that upheld the *Iskra* banner, Lenin alone, and with finality, envisaged "to-morrow," with all its stern tasks, its cruel conflicts and countless victims.

At the congress, Lenin won Plekhanov over, although only for a time. At the same time, he lost Martov; this loss was for ever. Plekhanov apparently sensed something at the congress. At least he told Axelrod, in discussing Lenin: "Of such stuff Robespierres are made." . . .

DOCUMENT FIVE

NADEZHDA KRUPSKAYA

Reminiscences of Lenin

In this excerpt, Krupskaya describes conditions and her activities after her return to Russia in March 1917. How does she react to the situation in Russia? What work does she feel is most important for the Bolsheviks? Now that the revolution has begun, has her role in the party changed?

I was becoming tired of my job at the Secretariat, and wanted to get into real work among the masses. I also wanted to see more of Ilyich, about whom I was getting very anxious. He was being hounded more and more. Going down the street in the Petrograd District you could hear the women saying to each other: "What's to be done with this Lenin fellow who's come from Germany? He ought to be drowned in a well, if you ask me." There was no doubt as to the

*Chapter 8
Revolutionary
Lives: Vladimir
Ilyich (Ulyanov)
Lenin
(1870–1924) and
Nadezhda K.
Krupskaya
(1869–1939)*

source from which all those rumours about bribery and treachery came, but they did not make pleasant hearing nevertheless. It was one thing to hear the bourgeoisie talk like that, but quite another to hear it from the masses. I wrote an article for *Soldatskaya Pravda* about Lenin under the title "A Page from the History of the Party." Vladimir Ilyich looked through the manuscript and made some corrections, and the article was published in No. 21 of *Soldatskaya Pravda* for May 13, 1917.

Vladimir Ilyich used to come home tired, and I did not have the heart to question him about affairs. But both of us felt a need to talk things over the way we were used to doing—during a walk. We sometimes managed to go for a walk along the quieter streets of the Petrograd District. . . .

. . . This work in the Vyborg District taught me a great deal. It was an excellent school of Party and Soviet work. To me, who had lived abroad for so many years and had never had the pluck to address even a small meeting or write a single line for *Pravda*, such a school was very necessary.

The Vyborg District had a strong and active Bolshevik membership, who enjoyed the confidence of the masses of workers. Shortly after assuming office I took over the business of the Vyborg District branch of the Committee for Relief of Soldiers' Wives from my old friend and school chum Nina Gerd (Struve's wife), with whom we had taught together at the Sunday School, and, who, in the early years of the working-class movement, had been a Social-Democrat. Now we held opposing points of view on political matters. In handing over to me, she said: "The soldiers' wives don't trust us. No matter what we do they are never satisfied. They believe only in the Bolsheviks. Well then, take things into your own hands, perhaps you'll make a better job of it." We were not afraid to tackle the job, believing, that with the active cooperation of the workers, we would succeed in getting things going with a swing. . . .

DOCUMENT SIX

V. I. LENIN

"April Theses"

These theses were published in Pravda *on April 17, 1917, and they begin by describing how the Bolsheviks should respond to the provisional government created as a result of the uprising the previous month. For his position, Lenin was accused of starting a civil war in the midst of a democratic revolution. What actions did he propose for the Bolsheviks? Why were his proposals so controversial or frightening?*

1) In our attitude towards the war, which under the new government of Lvov and Co.* unquestionably remains on Russia's part a predatory imperialist war owing to the capitalist nature of that government, not the slightest concession to "revolutionary defencism" is permissible.

The class-conscious proletariat can give its consent to a revolutionary war, which would really justify revolutionary defencism, only on condition: (a) that the power pass to the proletariat and the poorest sections of the peasants aligned with the proletariat; (b) that all annexations be renounced in deed and not in word; (c) that a complete break be effected in actual fact with all capitalist interests.

In view of the undoubted honesty of those broad sections of the mass believers in revolutionary defencism who accept the war only as a necessity, and not as a means of conquest, in view of the fact that they are being deceived by the bourgeoisie, it is necessary with particular thoroughness, persistence and patience to explain their error to them, to explain the inseparable connection existing between capital and the imperialist war, and to prove that without overthrowing capital *it is impossible* to end the war by a truly democratic peace, a peace not imposed by violence.

The most widespread campaign for this view must be organised in the army at the front.

Fraternisation.

2) The specific feature of the present situation in Russia is that the country is *passing* from the first stage of the revolution—which, owing to the insufficient class-consciousness and organisation of the proletariat, placed power in the hands of the bourgeoisie—to its *second* stage, which must place power in the hands of the proletariat and the poorest sections of the peasants.

This transition is characterised, on the one hand, by a maximum of legally recognised rights (Russia is *now* the freest of all the belligerent countries in the world); on the other, by the absence of violence towards the masses, and, finally, by their unreasoning trust in the government of capitalists, those worst enemies of peace and socialism.

3) No support for the Provisional Government; the utter falsity of all its promises should be made clear, particularly of those relating to the renunciation of annexations. Exposure in place of the impermissible, illusion-breeding "demand" that *this* government, a government of capitalists, should *cease* to be an imperialist government.

4) Recognition of the fact that in most of the Soviets of Workers' Deputies our Party is in a minority, so far a small minority, as against *a bloc of all* the petty-bourgeois opportunist elements, from down to the Popular Socialists and the

---

*["Lvov and Co." refers to Prince G. Lvov, premier of the Provincial Government after March 1917; he continued to support the war effort. Ed.]

*Chapter 8
Revolutionary
Lives: Vladimir
Ilyich (Ulyanov)
Lenin
(1870–1924) and
Nadezhda K.
Krupskaya
(1869–1939)*

Socialist-Revolutionaries† down to the Organising Committee (Chkheidze, Tsereteli, etc.), Steklov, etc., etc., who have yielded to the influence of the bourgeoisie and spread that influence among the proletariat.

The masses must be made to see that the Soviets of Workers' Deputies are the *only possible* form of revolutionary government, and that therefore our task is, as long as *this* government yields to the influence of the bourgeoisie, to present a patient, systematic, and persistent *explanation* of the errors of their tactics, an explanation especially adapted to the practical needs of the masses.

As long as we are in the minority we carry on the work of criticising and exposing errors and at the same time we preach the necessity of transferring the entire state power to the Soviets of Workers' Deputies, so that the people may overcome their mistakes by experience.

5) Not a parliamentary republic—to return to a parliamentary republic from the Soviets of Workers Deputies would be a retrograde step—but a Republic of Soviets of Workers', Agricultural Labourers' and Peasants' Deputies throughout the country, from top to bottom.

Abolition of the police, the army and the bureaucracy.‡

The salaries of all officials, all of whom are elective and displaceable at any time, not to exceed the average wage of a competent worker.

6) The weight of emphasis in the agrarian programme to be shifted to the Soviets of Agricultural Labourers' Deputies.

Confiscation of all landed estates.

Nationalisation of *all* lands in the country, the land to be disposed of by the local Soviets of Agricultural Labourers' and Peasants' Deputies. The organisation of separate Soviets of Deputies of Poor Peasants. The setting up of a model farm on each of the large estates (ranging in size from 100 to 300 dessiatines, according to local and other conditions, and to the decisions of the local bodies) under the control of the Soviets of Agricultural Labourers' Deputies and for the public account.

7) The immediate amalgamation of all banks in the country into a single national bank, and the institution of control over it by the Soviets of Workers' Deputies.

---

†The Popular Socialists split off from the Right Socialist-Revolutionaries in 1906; their demands were moderately democratic and did not go beyond a constitutional monarchy. The Popular Socialists rejected the Socialist-Revolutionaries' programme for the socialisation of the land and recognised the payment of compensation for socialised lands. After the February Revolution the Popular Socialists gave the Provisional Government their active support.

The Socialist Revolutionaries, (S.R.s) emerged in the late 1901–early 1902 when a number of Narodnik groups and circles joined forces (the Union of Socialist-Revolutionaries, the Party of Socialist-Revolutionaries and others). Their official publications were the newspaper *Revoliutsionnaya Rossiya* (*Revolutionary Russia*) (1900–1905) and the journal *Herald of the Russian Revolution* (1901–1905).

‡I.e., the standing army to be replaced by the arming of the whole people. [*Lenin*]

8) It is not our immediate task to "introduce" socialism, but only to bring social production and the distribution of products at once under the *control* of the Soviets of Workers' Deputies.

9) Party tasks:
  (a) Immediate convocation of a Party congress;
  (b) Alteration of the Party Programme, mainly:
      (1) On the question of imperialism and the imperialist war;
      (2) On our attitude towards the state and *our* demand for a "commune state";§
      (3) Amendment of our out-of-date minimum programme.
  (c) Change of the Party's name. ‖

10) A new International.

We must take the initiative in creating a revolutionary International, an International against the *social-chauvinists* and against the "Centre."

This peculiar situation demands of us an ability to adapt ourselves to the *special* conditions of Party work among unprecedentedly large masses of proletarians who have just awakened to political life.

DOCUMENT SEVEN

Alexandra Kollontai

Writings by Alexandra Kollontai
(1921)

Both these documents appeared in 1921, at a time when Kollontai was becoming critical of the party for several reasons. "The Workers' Opposition" was a paper to be presented at the next party congress; it focused on both party organization and also the place of the workers in the revolution. The second was an article published in Kommunistka, *the journal of the Zhenotdel. What are the basic criticisms she makes of the party in the "Workers' Opposition"? What aspects of the theses on morality seem to fit within existing Bolshevik ideology? Which ideas seem much more radical? Why might these writings and her ideas more generally seem threatening to the Bolshevik leadership?*

§ I.e., a state of which the Paris Commune was the prototype. [*Lenin*]

‖ Instead of "Social-Democracy," whose official leaders *throughout* the world have betrayed socialism and deserted to the bourgeoisie (the "defencists" and the vacillating "Kautskyites"), we must call ourselves the *Communist Party.* [*Lenin*]

Chapter 8
Revolutionary
Lives: Vladimir
Ilyich (Ulyanov)
Lenin
(1870–1924) and
Nadezhda K.
Krupskaya
(1869–1939)

THE WORKERS' OPPOSITION

. . . The masses are not blind. Whatever words the most popular leaders might use in order to conceal their deviation from a clear-cut class policy, whatever the compromises made with the peasants and world capitalism, and whatever the trust that the leaders place in the disciples of the capitalist system of production, the working masses feel where the digression begins.

The workers may cherish an ardent affection and love for such personalities as Lenin. They may be fascinated by the incomparable flowery eloquence of Trotsky and his organising abilities. They may revere a number of other leaders as leaders. But when the masses feel that they and their class are not trusted, it is quite natural that they say: "No, halt! We refuse to follow you blindly. Let us examine the situation. Your policy of picking out the middle ground between three socially opposed groups is a wise one indeed, but it smacks of the well-tried and familiar adaptation and opportunism. Today we may gain something with the help of your sober policy, but let us beware lest we find ourselves on a wrong road that, through zigzags and turns, will lead from the future to the débris of the past."

Distrust of the workers by the leaders is steadily growing. The more sober these leaders get, the more clever statesmen they become with their policy of sliding over the blade of a sharp knife between communism and compromise with the bourgeois past, the deeper becomes the abyss between the "ups" and the "downs", the less understanding there is, and the more painful and in-evitable becomes the crisis within the party itself.

The third reason enhancing the crisis in the party is that, in fact, during these three years of the revolution, the economic situation of the working class, of those who work in factories and mills, has not only not been improved, but has become more unbearable. This nobody dares to deny. The suppressed and widely-spread dissatisfaction among workers (*workers*, mind you) has a real justification. . . .

What then is it that the Workers' Opposition wants? What is its role?

Its role consists in raising before the party all the perturbing questions, and in giving form to all that heretofore was causing only a subdued agitation in the masses and led the non-partisan workers ever further from the party. It clearly and fearlessly shouted to the leaders: "Stop, look and think! Where do you lead us? Are we not going off the right road? It will be very bad for the party to find itself without the foundation of the dictatorship. The party will be on its own and so will the working class. In this lies the greatest danger to the revolution."

The task of the party at its present crisis is fearlessly to face the mistakes and lend its ear to the healthy class call of the wide working masses. Through the creative powers of the rising class, in the form of industrial unions, we shall go forwards towards reconstruction and the development of the creative forces of the country; towards purification of the party itself from elements foreign to it; towards correction of the activity of the party by means of going back to democracy, freedom of opinion, and criticism inside the party. . . .

Theses on Communist Morality in the Sphere of Marital Relations

. . . Once the family has been stripped of its economic functions and its responsibilities towards the younger generation and is no longer central to the existence of the woman, it has ceased to be a family. The family unit shrinks to a union of two people based on mutual agreement.

In the period of the dictatorship of the proletariat, the workers' state has to concern itself not with the economic and social unit of the family, since this unit dies as the bonds of communism are consolidated, but with the changing forms of marital relations. The family as an economic unit and as a union of parents and children based on the need to provide for the material welfare of the latter is doomed to disappear. Thus the workers' collective has to establish its attitude not to economic relationships but to the form of relationships between the sexes. What kind of relations between the sexes are in the best interests of the workers' collective? What form of relations would strengthen, not weaken, the collective in the transitional stage between capitalism and communism and would thus assist the construction of the new society? The laws and the morality that the workers' system is evolving are beginning to give an answer to this question. . . .

Each historical (and therefore economic) epoch in the development of society has its own ideal of marriage and its own sexual morality. Under the tribal system, with its ties of kinship, the morality was different from that which developed with the establishment of private property and the rule of the husband and father (patriarchy). Different economic systems have different moral codes. Not only each stage in the development of society, but each class has its corresponding sexual morality (it is sufficient to compare the morals of the feudal landowning class and of the bourgeoisie in one and the same epoch to see that this is true). The more firmly established the principles of private property, the stricter the moral code. The importance of virginity before legal marriage sprang from the principles of private property and the unwillingness of men to pay for the children of others.

Hypocrisy (the outward observance of decorum and the actual practice of depravity), and the double code (one code of behaviour for the man and another for the woman) are the twin pillars of bourgeois morality. Communist morality must, above all, resolutely spurn all the hypocrisy inherited from bourgeois society in relationships between the sexes, and reject the double standard of morality.

In the period of the dictatorship of the proletariat, relations between the sexes should be evaluated only according to the criteria mentioned above—the health of the working population and the development of inner bonds of solidarity within the collective. The sexual act must be seen not as something shameful and sinful but as something which is as natural as the other needs of healthy organism, such as hunger and thirst. Such phenomena cannot be judged as moral or

Chapter 8
Revolutionary
Lives: Vladimir
Ilyich (Ulyanov)
Lenin
(1870–1924) and
Nadezhda K.
Krupskaya
(1869–1939)

immoral. The satisfaction of healthy and natural instincts only ceases to be normal when the boundaries of hygiene are overstepped. In such cases, not only the health of the person concerned but the interests of the work collective, which needs the strength and energy and health of its members, are threatened. Communist morality, therefore, while openly recognising the normality of sexual interests, condemns unhealthy and unnatural interest in sex (excesses, for example, or sexual relations before maturity has been reached, which exhaust the organism and lower the capacity of men and women for work).

As communist morality is concerned for the health of the population, it also criticises sexual restraint. The preservation of health includes the full and correct satisfaction of all man's needs; norms of hygiene should work to this end, and not artificially suppress such an important function of the organism as the sex drive. Thus both early sexual experience (before the body has developed and grown strong) and sexual restraint must be seen as equally harmful. This concern for the health of the human race does not establish either monogamy or polygamy as the obligatory form of relations between the sexes, for excesses may be committed in the bounds of the former, and a frequent change of partners by no means signifies sexual intemperance. . . .

As regards sexual relations, communist morality demands first of all an end to all relations based on financial or other economic considerations. The buying and selling of caresses destroys the sense of equality between the sexes, and thus undermines the basis of solidarity without which communist society cannot exist. Moral censure is consequently directed at prostitution in all its forms and at all types of marriage of convenience, even when recognised by Soviet law. The preservation of marriage regulations creates the illusion that the workers' collective can accept the "couple" with its special, exclusive interests. The stronger the ties between the members of the collective as a whole, the less the need to reinforce marital relations. Secondly, communist morality demands the education of the younger generation in responsibility to the collective and in the consciousness that love is not the only thing in life (this is especially important in the case of women, for they have been taught the opposite for centuries). Love is only one aspect of life, and must not be allowed to overshadow the other facets of the relationships between individual and collective. The ideal of the bourgeoisie was the married couple, where the partners complemented each other so completely that they had no need of contact with society. Communist morality demands, on the contrary, that the younger generation be educated in such a way that the personality of the individual is developed to the full, and the individual with his or her many interests has contact with a range of persons of both sexes. Communist morality encourages the development of many and varied bonds of love and friendship among people. The old ideal was "all for the loved one"; communist morality demands all for the collective.

Though sex love is seen in the context of the interests of the collective, com-

munist morality demands that people are educated in sensitivity and understanding and are psychologically demanding both to themselves and to their
partners. The bourgeois attitude to sexual relations as simply a matter of sex
must be criticised and replaced by an understanding of the whole gamut of joyful love-experience that enriches life and makes for greater happiness. The
greater the intellectual and emotional development of the individual the less
place will there be in his or her relationship for the bare physiological side of
love, and the brighter will be the love experience. . . .

DOCUMENT EIGHT

V. I. LENIN AND NADEZHDA KRUPSKAYA

Documents on Women and the Bolshevik Revolution

*The excerpts that follow, though not written at the same time, provide examples of
the Bolshevik Party's view of women in the revolution and in the new socialist society. What ideas do they hold in common? What are their visions of the future for
Soviet women? What are the bases for women's emancipation, as described here?
How do their views differ from the arguments Kollontai makes in her theses on
morality (see Document Seven)?*

LENIN, ON INTERNATIONAL WORKING WOMEN'S DAY

Capitalism combines formal equality with economic and, consequently, social
inequality. That is one of the principal features of capitalism, one that is deliberately obscured by the supporters of the bourgeoisie, the liberals, and is not
understood by petty-bourgeois democrats. This feature of capitalism, incidentally, renders it necessary for us in our resolute fight for economic equality
openly to admit capitalist inequality, and even, under certain conditions, to
make this open admission of inequality the basis of the proletarian statehood
(the Soviet Constitution).

But even in the matter of formal equality (equality before the law, the "equality" of the well-fed and the hungry man, of the man of property and the prop-
ertyless), capitalism *cannot* be consistent. And one of the most glaring
manifestations of this inconsistency is the *inequality* of women and men. Complete equality has not been granted even by the most progressive republican
and democratic bourgeois states.

The Soviet Republic of Russia, on the other hand, at once swept away *all*

[249]

Chapter 8
Revolutionary
Lives: Vladimir
Ilyich (Ulyanov)
Lenin
(1870–1924) and
Nadezhda K.
Krupskaya
(1869–1939)

legislative traces of the inequality of women *without exception,* and immediately ensured their complete equality before the law.

It is said that the best criterion of the cultural level is the legal status of women. This aphorism contains a grain of profound truth. In this respect only the dictatorship of the proletariat, only the socialist state could attain, and has attained, the highest cultural level.

The new, mighty and unparalleled upsurge in the working women's movement is therefore inevitably associated with the foundation (and consolidation) of the first Soviet Republic—and, in addition to and in connection with this, with the Communist International.

Since mention has been made of those who were oppressed by capitalism, directly or indirectly, in whole or in part, it must be said that the Soviet system, and only the Soviet system, guarantees democracy. This is clearly shown by the position of the working class and the poor peasants. It is clearly shown by the position of women.

But the Soviet system is the last decisive struggle for the *abolition of classes,* for economic and social equality. Democracy, even democracy for those who were oppressed by capitalism, including the oppressed sex, *is not enough for us.*

The chief task of the working women's movement is to fight for economic and social equality, and not only formal equality, for women. The chief thing is to get women to take part in socially productive labour, to liberate them from "domestic slavery", to free them from their stupefying and humiliating subjugation to the eternal drudgery of the kitchen and the nursery.

This struggle will be a long one, and it demands a radical reconstruction both of social technique and of morals. But it will end in the complete triumph of communism.

[Pravda,] *March 4, 1920*

KRUPSKAYA, WOMAN—FRIEND, COMRADE AND MOTHER

. . . One of these survivals of the past is the cultural backwardness of women. This backwardness greatly hinders our women and girls in their work and their social activities. They could not go to school before because they were overburdened with housework and caring for the children. Girls used not to be allowed to go to school, since they were wanted at home to help with the housework and to nurse the children.

Universal compulsory education is playing a part of exceptional importance in this respect. Only we must see that it is really applied, that girls are not kept home for all kinds of "weighty" reasons, that their school work is not interfered with by housework, and so on.

But the question does not touch on the schoolgirls alone—they live under conditions which are already incomparably better than those of previous times.

The problem of disseminating knowledge is still an acute one as regards our young women, especially in the countryside.

Every girl knows the words of Lenin to the effect that every cook must learn to govern the state. But one must study how to do this; one must know how to do it; one has to know a great deal, much more now than formerly.

We must do away with illiteracy. But merely to be literate no longer satisfies the masses. At the level of economic and social life which our Land of Soviets has now reached, the masses need knowledge that will open up the road to independent creative work, that will raise their qualifications. . . .

Our changing life has confronted us point-blank with the problems of the family, the relations between husband and wife, between parents and children; it has confronted us with the problem of bringing up the new generation.

These are the problems that particularly concern our young people now. The correct solution can be found only on the basis of communist morality. Here we meet with great difficulties, and the chief difficulty is that very often the old views dress up in new, fashionable attire. We need great vigilance in this respect, especially against petty-proprietor morality, petty-proprietor views of the family and the upbringing of children.

Marx and Engels wrote that only in the depths of the proletariat could new marital relations be born—marriage based not on material considerations, but on mutual attraction, mutual love, mutual confidence and common views.

In the Soviet Union the conditions for emancipating women from the burdensome old forms of marriage relations have been created.

But there are still survivals of the old in personal life. Petty-proprietor psychology often attempts to creep in through all sorts of cracks, disguising itself in new attire.

Women are still sometimes regarded as playthings. Philandering, dissoluteness, an irresponsible attitude towards women—do we not find these even among League members? We'll fool around and have a good time, but it's not time to get married yet—that is the attitude. A girl is made pregnant—well, what of it? Let her have an abortion. This is not love; it is the old way of regarding a woman—not as a human being but as a toy, a plaything. . . .

. . . This it is that every day new strength, is gained by the new family based on profound mutual confidence, on a similarity of ideas, on a natural attraction which develops into the boundless joy of love.

And finally, the question of upbringing.

Every woman is a mother or a potential mother. She has a strong maternal instinct. This instinct of motherhood is also a great force and a source of great joy.

The mother is the natural person to bring up her children. Her influence on her children, particularly when they are still young, is very great. And we know that a person's whole character, his whole development bears the impress of his earliest years. The whole point is how children are to be brought up.

One may bring one's daughter up in slavish obedience, one may make her a

Chapter 8
Revolutionary
Lives: Vladimir
Ilyich (Ulyanov)
Lenin
(1870–1924) and
Nadezhda K.
Krupskaya
(1869–1939)

petty-bourgeois young lady who takes no interest in the seething events of life around her; or one may make her a collective-minded, active builder of socialism, a person who takes joy in concerted labour, in the struggle for our great goal—one may make her a real communist.

It all depends on what the mother is like, what her views are.

Frederick Engels, the friend of Marx and one of the great founders of Marxism, wrote: "But if the ideas are true for which we, children of new times, are struggling, then the time is not far off when women's hearts will beat for the ideal of modern times as ardently as they now beat for the religious faith of their fathers—and the new spirit will be victorious only when the younger generation imbibes it with their mothers' milk." . . .

Krestyanka Magazine, 1936.

PART

III

The Challenges of Modernity in the Twentieth Century

World War I and Its Aftermath: Käthe Schmidt Kollwitz (1867–1945) and Erich Maria Remarque (1898–1970)

▪ SETTING THE STAGE

On November 12, 1918, Europeans awoke with the knowledge that their four years of war had been a destructive, costly, and all-consuming event. Four years earlier, enthusiastic civilians had prophesied that the war would be over by Christmas and volunteers queued at recruiting offices to enlist. The majority of Europeans in 1914 welcomed the war, perhaps as a release from the tension that had been developing over the previous ten years. States quickly mobilized their citizens for war: men to the military front, women to war work. Little did they realize how many would fight and die over the next four years. Only a few realized the terrible nature of the

Chapter 9
World War I and
Its Aftermath:
Käthe Schmidt
Kollwitz
(1867–1945) and
Erich Maria
Remarque
(1898–1970)

conflict that the European countries had brought upon themselves. Sir Edward Grey, a British diplomat whose hopes of peace had been shattered, was one such man. On the evening of the first day when Great Britain declared war, Grey went to an upper-story window and watched the London street lamps flicker off. Darkness crept over the city. He observed to a friend, "The lamps are going out all over Europe. We shall not see them lit again in our lifetime."

World War I and the revolutions it spawned changed irrevocably the political, social, economic, and cultural world of Europeans. The 8.3 million soldiers and 8 million civilians dead, the 20 million wounded, and another 21.5 million who died during the deadly flu epidemic of 1919 meant that few men and women escaped the war's shock and aftershocks. The high casualty rates and the war's destructiveness ensured widespread loss and devastation. Families not only lost family members, but communities watched as messengers passed through their streets searching for the correct house to deliver the news that the neighborhood cobbler, metalworker, student, nurse, teacher, or bully had died. Those unfortunate enough to have lived along the warfront or to have experienced invasion and occupation returned to the charred and battered remains of their towns and villages, desperately searching for some remnant of their former lives. The men and women returning from the war often wondered if their families, friends, and neighbors understood the real war and what was lost. Harry Crosby, an American who vol-

unteered for ambulance service in France, wrote, "We who have known war must never forget war. And that is why I have a picture of a soldier's corpse nailed to the door of my library."[1] Gone were the romantic images of young heroes coming home with stories of honor and glory demonstrated on the battlefield. If anyone was willing to listen, they heard instead about the misery, despair, and desperation of young men and women who had faced the new weapons and tactics of Europe's first "total war." The returning combatants *and* their loved ones asked the question, Why did we fight?

Much has been written of World War I and its effects on European society. Historians and other scholars continue to wrestle with its significance for the political, socioeconomic, and cultural developments of the 1920s and 1930s. The lives of Erich Maria Remarque and his older contemporary, Käthe Kollwitz, reveal how two Germans from different backgrounds and generations experienced the coming of war, combat, the homefront, loss of life, and the war's aftermath. Like others, Remarque had enthusiastically greeted the coming of war because it was a chance to prove Germany's honor and prowess. Kollwitz stood aside and watched her two sons enlist and wondered if the world had gone mad. Despite their varied experiences, both Remarque and Kollwitz emerged from the war commit-

---

1. Modris Ekstein, *Rites of Spring: The Great War and the Birth of the Modern Age* (New York: Anchor Books, 1989), p. 275.

ted to expressing the desolation, isolation, and grief that each felt.

Remarque's and Kollwitz's Germany had lost 2 million dead, far more than any other state except Russia. Eventually they became pacifists and spent the remainder of their lives searching, as did many other Europeans of all nations, ages, and genders, for the meaning behind the war and concluded that another "total war" had to be avoided at all costs.

Not everyone in Germany was convinced of this point of view. Some believed that the German army, though on the retreat, had not been defeated when the armistice came. In fact, they argued that the soldiers had been betrayed by the politicians. Thus, Erich's and Käthe's artistic and literary expression during the 1920s and 1930s became part of a larger debate within Germany about the nature of World War I and its impact.

■ THE ACTORS:

ERICH MARIA REMARQUE AND KÄTHE SCHMIDT KOLLWITZ

When *All Quiet on the Western Front* appeared in Germany in 1929, one of its critics wondered if its author, Erich Maria Remarque, really existed. Its antimilitaristic, antiwar tone and instant popularity posed a problem for Germans who claimed that Germany's defeat came at the hands of politicians and not the army. Nationalist parties and sympathizers immediately tried to discredit the author and his background, to such an extent that they claimed Remarque was the pen name for a Jew named Kramer, or Remark (the German spelling) spelled backward. What the novel's critics did not want to acknowledge was that the author was a most ordinary young German by the name of Erich Paul Remark.

On June 22, 1898, Peter Franz and Anna Maria (Stallknecht) Remark celebrated the birth of their second son, Erich Paul Remark, in Osnabruck, Westphalia. The Remarks were a poor,

Catholic, middle-class family. Peter was a bookbinder for a local firm in Osnabruck and, by all accounts, he was a colorless, humorless man who often moved his family from house to house in Osnabruck to save money. Paul's mother, Anna, fought bout after bout with cancer and finally succumbed to the disease in 1917. Erich had an older brother, who died in 1901, and two sisters, Elfriede and Erna. The Nazis would murder Elfriede in 1943 in part because of her brother's writings.

Erich's childhood was quite ordinary. His parents sent him to Catholic grammar and high schools with the hope that their bright, artistic, and musical son would secure a position as a schoolteacher. This was one of the few professions that a young man from his background could enter. Early in his childhood, Erich showed great promise as a musician and learned to play both the piano and organ. In addition, the young Remark showed a flair for painting and for the natural sciences. While attending a teacher-training seminar for

Chapter 9
World War I and
Its Aftermath:
Käthe Schmidt
Kollwitz
(1867–1945) and
Erich Maria
Remarque
(1898–1970)

elementary schoolteachers, Erich began to associate with a group of young, aspiring artists, writers, and musicians known as the *Traumbude* (the Dream Circle or Dream-Den) and became quite fond of its poet-painter leader, Fritz Horstemeier (1882–1918). The name for the group was derived from Horstemeier's attic rooms, where the group discussed the literature and art of an offshoot of the art nouveau movement in Europe, *Jugendstil* (Youth style). Like the leading representatives of the movement, the Viennese artist Gustav Klimt; the architects Otto Wagner, Josef Hoffmann, and Adolf Loos; and the painters Oskar Kokoschka and Egon Schiele, Erich's group believed that art could transform the drab reality of their world into an idealized world of beauty.

The *Traumbude* longed to escape from the ordinariness of their daily lives and participate in something extraordinary. At the root of such attitudes lay a fear of boredom typical of middle-class youth, but these attitudes also resulted from a certain restlessness and opposition to what seemed to them a petrified, bourgeois, Victorian society. When war broke out in 1914, they embraced this opportunity to remake their world. Erich Remark also saw the war's regenerative possibilities, even two years into the conflict. In his first published piece in 1916, Remark tried to capture the meaning of the war before ever setting foot on the battlefield. He described the euphoria of leading a patrol of his fellow classmates in a training exercise: "A feeling of strength overwhelms one, such a sunny, splendid feeling of strength, that the ancient Ti-

tanic defiance of the Germans is born anew, a defiance which, trusting only in itself, obliterates one world and builds a new one."[2] Imbued with the spirit of his generation, he believed that the war would bring about fundamental change, fulfilling the dreams of youth like himself, and creating new men who would put an end to bourgeois complacency, tyranny, and hypocrisy. Five months after this article appeared, Erich and his classmates were drafted into the real war.

In the summer of 1917, after several months of training and some time at home to attend to his seriously ill mother, Remark joined a sapper unit stationed along the front, first near Arras and then Flanders in Belgium. The duty of these units was to construct and maintain fortifications along the front. Units such as these laid barbed wire; built gun emplacements, bunkers, and dugouts; and were instrumental in the construction and maintenance of over 12,000 miles of German trenches. Remark's tour of duty amounted to seven weeks before he was wounded by fragments from English long-range artillery shells on the first day of the Third Battle of Ypres, a British offensive launched on the muddy fields of Flanders on July 31, 1917.

What would Remark have seen or heard in these fifty days of war? Later his critics, seeking to discredit the authenticity of Remark's experiences, claimed that he did not have front-line experience. His duty as a sapper could be interpreted as one

2. Julie Gilbert, *Opposite Attraction: The Lives of Erich Maria Remarque and Paulette Goddard* (New York: Pantheon Books, 1995), pp. 11–12.

that did not lead him into direct conflict with the enemy, but certainly his work brought him within easy range of enemy gunfire and artillery. The ten days of artillery barrage leading up to battle were certainly some of the most horrific seen along this front. Remark was stationed not far from the main objective of the British offensive, the village of Passchendaele. On July 21, more than 2,300 British guns began a ten-day artillery bombardment that claimed 30,000 German casualties.

A month earlier, the British had begun softening up the line around Ypres and Flanders by igniting 600 tons of high explosives with nineteen mines under the German first-line defenses at Messines Ridge, a bit south of Ypres. The earth moved visibly as far as thirty miles away and Vera Brittain, a young Englishwoman, felt the tremor in England. The British then followed this explosion with a ferocious artillery barrage of the same 2,300 guns that would lay siege to the German trenches a month later at Passchendaele. The landscape that Remark encountered in July 1917 was truly a wasteland, and the marshlands surrounding Ypres did not help matters (Images One and Two). The trenches built along this salient were often muddy, flooded, and crawling with nature's worst pestilence: lice and rats (Document One). This was the front that Remark encountered, a front that was continuously pounded and fought over, and one that he would highlight in his novel, *All Quiet on the Western Front*. For men along the Western Front, Ypres and its wet, marshy hinterland, Flanders was one of the worst tours of duty, rivaled only

by those at Verdun and the Somme River.

Remark sustained wounds in the neck, the left leg above the knee, and the right forearm. From a field hospital behind the lines, he was transported to an army hospital in Duisburg. His wounds kept him in convalescence until November 1918, when his battalion physician cleared him to return to the front. Knowing that his convalescence was converging with the end of the war, Remark described his ambivalence at the prospect of peace in his diary entry of October 13, 1918:

> There is peace now! People are not exactly exultant about this. I guess one got used to [the war]. It was a cause of death just like other diseases. A bit worse than pulmonary tuberculosis—. I'm not really happy either—why, I don't know. I had reconciled myself to the thought of having to go into the field. Now I'm annoyed that there's nothing. Oh, who knows, perhaps it's not working out after all. On the other hand, I'm also looking forward to peacetime. And I also worry about it: everything so different, Fritz [Horstemeier died in early 1918] dead, no real relationship with another human being—everything out of whack, displaced, broken—that's how one resumes a life one once left so serenely and happily. Lonely and torn.[3]

Remark built on these sentiments in the final pages of *All Quiet on the West-*

3. *A Time to Live: The Life and Writings of Erich Maria Remarque* (New York: Fales Library, New York University, 1998), p. 4.

Chapter 9
World War I and
Its Aftermath:
Käthe Schmidt
Kollwitz
(1867–1945) and
Erich Maria
Remarque
(1898–1970)

ern Front when he wrote of his protagonist's despair at having to return home. Within days of his return to the front, Germany signed the armistice on November 11, 1918. The war was over. Among the dead was Peter Kollwitz, Käthe Kollwitz's youngest son. Her other son, Hans, had survived all four years of war and joined Remark among the ranks of Germany's war veterans.

In August 1914, Kollwitz watched the younger of her two sons, Peter, and his friends volunteer for the war and wondered, "Where do all the women [German women] who have watched so carefully over the lives of their beloved ones get the heroism to send them to face the cannon?"[4] (Document Two). That Kollwitz would ponder these ideas is not surprising because mourning and the death of children had been important themes in her etchings for the previous ten years. On October 22, 1914, her art became life when Peter was killed two days after his arrival in Belgium. Kollwitz would now use her talent to express her own grief and give meaning to her son's death. Her fame throughout the European art world and her well-developed social consciousness meant that her views and opinions about the war and its consequences were noted and recorded by herself and others.

Käthe Kollwitz was forty-seven when her son died. By then, she had reached a position in the European art world that few women have been able

to emulate. Prior to the war, she was known for etchings that realistically portrayed Germany's poorer classes and their social ills. She used an expressive, naturalistic style that captured the misery, poverty, and despair of Berlin's poor. Her work depicting gaunt mothers and exploited workers attracted the attention of the Berlin art world. By the late 1890s, her reputation was firmly established with the exhibition of her three lithographs and three etchings on the German Weavers' Revolt of 1844. From this time forward, Kollwitz was a fixture in the Berlin Secession, a group of artists who had seceded from the Association of Berlin Artists in 1893, and was an instructor of Graphics and Nude Studies at the Berlin School of Art for Women.

Kollwitz had come to Berlin in 1891 at the age of twenty-four with her doctor husband, Karl Kollwitz, and a fierce determination to become an artist. She was born on July 8, 1867, in the East Prussia town of Königsberg (now Kaliningrad, Russia) to Karl Schmidt and his wife Katharina (Rupp). Käthe, the fifth of six children, lived a life of middle-class privilege and comfort. Her father had taken a degree in law but preferred to become a mason, successful master builder, and owner of a building yard. Her mother, Katharina Rupp, grew up under the tutelage of her father, Julius, who founded a dissident religious group, the Free Religious Congregation, whose members were persecuted by the Prussian authorities. Julius, Käthe's grandfather, believed in educating his daughters, and her mother was widely read in German and En-

---

4. Hans Kollwitz, *The Diaries and Letters of Käthe Kollwitz* (Chicago, Ill.: Henry Regnery, 1955), pp. 62–63.

glish and was especially fond of Shakespeare, Shelley, and Byron. Her mother not only passed on her love of literature and learning to her children, but the courage of her convictions as well. Despite a deep respect for her mother, Käthe saw her as aloof and stoic. Käthe explained this distance in her diary. Her mother had lost her first two children before the birth of her older brother, Konrad, and Käthe claimed that "although she [her mother] never surrendered to the deep sorrow of those early days of her marriage, it must have been her years of suffering which gave her for ever after the remote air of a madonna."[5] Kollwitz witnessed and felt this suffering when her younger brother, Benjamin, died of meningitis at the age of one. Besides her two brothers, Konrad and Benjamin, Kollwitz had two older sisters, Julie and Lisbeth (Lise).

The surviving Schmidt children were encouraged to develop their artistic and intellectual talents. Käthe and her sisters endured what she called a mediocre education at a private school. However, her parents encouraged the children to pursue self-education according to their interests and talents. The children could read any book from the family bookcases, roam around the town, and take the ferry across the Pregel to the docks without parental supervision. Years later, Käthe argued that these "casual expeditions" through the busy commercial district "teeming with work" contributed to her fascination with workers.

Karl Schmidt recognized his daughter's artistic talent and when she was fourteen, he commissioned Rudolph Mauer, an engraver, to help develop this talent. In her diary, Kollwitz interpreted her father's support. "By now my father had long since realized that I was gifted at drawing. The fact gave him great pleasure and he wanted me to have all the training I needed to become an artist. Unfortunately I was a girl, but nevertheless he was ready to risk it. He assumed that I would not be much distracted by love affairs, since I was not a pretty girl; and he was all the more disappointed and angry later when at the age of only seventeen I became engaged to Karl Kollwitz."[6] Käthe's engagement to the dear friend of her older brother lasted for six years, during which she explored new intellectual and creative horizons in Berlin and then in Munich.

In 1885, at the age of seventeen and newly engaged, Kollwitz left her home to study in Berlin. Shepherded around Berlin by her older brother, Konrad, who had been studying in the city for several years and was by this time an active socialist, Kollwitz absorbed the sounds, smells, and images of a Berlin bursting under the pressures of industrialization, political unrest, and a great depression. Her art teacher, Karl Stauffer-Bern, introduced her to the prints of Max Klinger. From this time forward, she explored the artistic possibilities of the graphic arts (drawing, etchings, and lithographs). Returning home at the end of her first year, Käthe was deter-

5. Ibid., p. 18.

6. Ibid., p. 23.

Chapter 9
World War I and
Its Aftermath:
Käthe Schmidt
Kollwitz
(1867–1945) and
Erich Maria
Remarque
(1898–1970)

mined to return to Berlin the following year, but the death of her teacher changed her plans. The following year, she remained in Königsberg, studying privately with Emil Neide because the art academy in Königsberg did not admit women. At this time, Neide was an up-and-coming artist, not because of his technique but because his paintings focused on criminal and underworld subjects. Neide's own training had been in Munich, which was a bustling mecca for young artists and thinkers in the 1880s. In 1888, her father enrolled her at the Women's Art School in Munich. Gender segregation in art was the norm. The moral standards of the day would not permit young women to look upon a nude model, even in their own segregated art classes.

In Munich, she continued to dabble in painting, but the graphic arts and drawing were for her the best medium to express the stark realities of urban life. Already pegged as a Social Democrat (the German version of a socialist) by her fellow students, Kollwitz gravitated to the writings of authors who commented critically on the position of workers and women. She read Henrik Ibsen, Leo Tolstoi, Émile Zola, and the political writings of Germany's Social Democrats, Karl Kautsky and August Bebel. Zola's novel, *Germinal*, about the miners of northern France and their struggle against exploitation and oppression, proved so powerful for her that she produced an etching on this very theme in 1894.

During her studies, she continued her courtship with Karl Kollwitz. When he received his medical school diploma and took a position as a workers' health insurance doctor in a working-class district in Berlin, they finally married. In 1891, she and her new husband moved to a typical working-class tenement, gray, somber, and damp, in a suburb north of the city. Kollwitz was now an intimate observer of workers' daily lives. In her husband's office, which was attached to their apartment, she witnessed sickness, unemployment, hunger, despair, and death. In her drawings and etchings, she began to sketch the bitter daily struggle to survive. If Käthe had not been totally committed to etching and drawing before her move to Berlin, the cramped apartment pushed her firmly into these techniques because there was no room for a painting easel and no money to rent a studio.

Shortly after the birth of Hans (1892), she saw a production of Gerhart Hauptmann's play, *The Weavers*, which explored the 1844 revolt of Silesian weavers. Because of its incendiary theme, Wilhelm II soon prohibited public performances. Kollwitz abandoned her study of Zola's *Germinal* and immediately went to work on three etchings and three lithographs about the revolt. She worked on this project for almost five years. Not only did the research slow her down—she read everything available about the revolt—but the birth of her second son, Peter, in 1896 interrupted her work. She finally exhibited her study at the Berlin Lehrter Station exhibition hall in 1898, and the show was a stunning success. The jury recommended the study for an award, but Wilhelm II rejected the jury's endorsement, not because of Kollwitz's talent but because he despised art with this type of social message, calling it "gutter art."

After this initial success, Kollwitz continued to use drawings, etchings, and lithographs to narrate the plight of the downtrodden. She was often labeled a "socialist artist," and certainly she was influenced by the politics of socialism (Document Three). However, she explained her choice of subjects not in political and economic terms but because there was beauty, grace, dignity, and meaning in the bodies, motions, and expressions of workers. Other groups, like the middle class, seemed unreal, stiff, and boring to her. Deeply influenced by her neighborhood, she began to concentrate even more on representing the realities of the working men and women she encountered at her husband's practice.

Kollwitz's multiple roles as wife, mother, and artist were unusual in the early twentieth century. Her decision to marry Karl was not a hasty one. She and her fellow students at the Women's Art School in Munich often debated the question of marriage and whether it was possible to be an artist, wife, and mother. Kollwitz's choice of Karl as her husband enabled her to do both. Karl and his sister Lisebeth were orphans living with a family in Königsberg when they became friends with Käthe's older brother Konrad. Konrad, Karl, and another friend of theirs, Hans Weiss, would spend hours discussing the political ideas of the German Social Democratic party (SPD). August Bebel, the cofounder of the SPD, and his ideas were favorite topics of discussion. Bebel not only criticized the Bismarckian system for its exploitation of workers but he championed the fight for women's rights. In his pioneering work, *Woman and Socialism* (1879), he argued for the equality of men and women in the new German state and the removal of "all barriers that make one human being dependent upon another, which includes the dependence of one sex upon another."[7] He demanded "the release of woman from her narrow sphere of domestic life, and her full participation in public life and the missions of civilization."[8] Käthe debated these ideas with her brother's friends and found in Karl a kindred spirit.

Their six-year engagement survived Käthe's doubts about the compatibility of marriage and art for a woman, and in 1891 they were married. Karl had just obtained a position as one of a handful of doctors chosen to participate in a new plan of social and medical insurance for workers. As a socialist, Karl was elated. He would be able to participate in Europe's first health-insurance system, which covered accident, sickness, and old age expenses through a fund based on contributions from workers, employers, and the state. Käthe shared his enthusiasm and politics, and both of them saw Karl's post as an opportunity to realize their dreams, both separately and collectively. Their commitment to this working-class community lasted a lifetime. Despite Käthe's many successes and her inter-

7. August Bebel, *Women and Socialism*, Meta Stein, trans. (New York: Socialist Literature Company, 1910), p. 7.

8. Ibid, p. 238.

Chapter 9
World War I and
Its Aftermath:
Käthe Schmidt
Kollwitz
(1867–1945) and
Erich Maria
Remarque
(1898–1970)

national acclaim, the Kollwitzs would remain in the same noisy, bustling tenement for fifty years.

Käthe's ability to work as an artist depended on many variables. Because of their unconventional religious convictions, political beliefs, and faith in Käthe's talent, her family and husband supported Käthe's passion. Karl Kollwitz accepted his wife's help in his clinic but understood the importance of his wife's work and that it often came first. Their position as middle-class people also played a significant role, particularly because they were able to hire a live-in housekeeper, Lina Makler, to keep house and watch the children. Housekeeping duties for unmarried working-class women like Makler allowed them to escape factory work and to live in better, if imperfect, conditions with a middle-class family. Makler would remain with the Kollwitzs until the end of her life.

Käthe's class position, her husband's and family's support, and her ambition and talent allowed her to become an artist. Very few women of her era could depend on such support. Käthe was in a unique position to make a lasting impression on art and to contribute, through her art, to debates concerning the conditions of the men and women of the German working class at the beginning of the twentieth century. As an established and respected artist, Kollwitz also put this talent to work to articulate the grief, anguish, and sorrow of losing her son in World War I.

Both sons, Hans and Peter, had volunteered immediately for the war. Each was intoxicated with the mood of 1914, and the elder Kollwitzs could not deny their own convictions that Germany needed each individual, even themselves, to contribute to the homeland. Hans pointed out that his mother was caught up in the enthusiasm of the moment and the emotions of her sons, but she was also frightened by the realities of war. Kollwitz's nascent pacifism was not only borne of her intellectual reservations but because of her youngest son's death on October 22, 1914, near Diksmuide, Belgium. Like so many parents, Karl and Käthe grieved deeply for their son and tried to find ways to ascribe meaning to his death. In late 1914, Käthe dedicated the remainder of her life and work as an artist to her son Peter. As a result of his death, she reexamined her position on war and concluded that the youth in Germany and elsewhere had been betrayed. There was no justification for Peter, or any youth from any country, to have sacrificed his life for honor and glory.

Her diary and letters from this period voiced grief and longing for Peter, and she searched for reasons why she should continue to live and work (Document Four). As she had done in her childhood, she sought the answer in literature and art. Peppered throughout her diary at this time was an expression from the nineteenth-century German author and poet, Johann Wolfgang von Goethe: "Seed for planting must not be ground." Peter and his generation were the seeds for the future. She as well as other mothers had carried and nurtured this seed, only to have it destroyed by war. This thought—that seed set aside to be sown must not be destroyed—inspired her pacifism and her work through the interwar period and into the next "total" war.

Vowing to continue to cultivate her talent, Kollwitz began work at the end of 1914 on a memorial for her son. She originally conceived the memorial as a sculpture of Peter's body stretched out horizontally, with a mother figure standing at his feet and a father figure at his head, but Käthe had difficulty completing the design until she decided the memorial must be for all the war dead. She decided to sculpt only the mourning parents and worked on a monumental headstone for the entire cemetery where her son was laid to rest. The memorial symbolized bereaved parents everywhere. The finished work consisted of two sculptures, "The Mother" and "The Father" (Image Three). However, the completed memorial was not placed at the Roggevelde cemetery in Belgium until July 1932. Like Erich Paul Remark, Käthe was caught up in the political storms of post–World War I Germany.

ACT I:

REMARQUE AND ALL QUIET ON THE WESTERN FRONT

After his discharge from the army, Remark planned to return to the life he had been leading before the war: to the Catholic Seminary for Teachers to continue his preparation for a teaching career. Erich and other veterans returning to their studies found that postwar German society was unwilling to accommodate them. The teachers at the seminary could not adjust to the fact that, at the front, young men had gained another type of knowledge, "harsh, bloody, cruel, inexorable" and forced them to adhere to insulting, belittling institutional routines designed for teenagers. Remark would write about his experiences and the problems of displacement, adjustment, and treatment in his fourth published novel, *The Road Back*. In an interview shortly after the publication of *All Quiet on the Western Front* in 1929, Remark explained his intentions for his novel: "In my next book, which I am now writing, I describe the way back to life; how a young man like myself—and Paul Baumer—experienced war as a youth, who still carries its scars, and who was then grabbed up by the chaos of the postwar period."

Remark found the profession that he had decided upon prior to the war no longer suited him and after three temporary teaching posts between 1919 and 1920, he began to pursue his writing career in earnest. In 1920, Remark published his first novel, *Die Traumbude*, several poems, and an essay, but 1920 was not a year to launch a literary career. Unemployment was widespread, inflation in Germany was running wild, and Remark had very few marketable skills. From 1920–1922, he eked out a living selling clothes and tombstones, and playing an organ for Sunday religious services in an insane asylum, where at least he received a good meal with wine. By 1922, his

Chapter 9
World War I and
Its Aftermath:
Käthe Schmidt
Kollwitz
(1867–1945) and
Erich Maria
Remarque
(1898–1970)

connections at the stone-cutting and gravestone company translated into a post at the Continental Rubber Company in Hannover, where he became editor of the company magazine, *Echo-Continental,* and publicity manager. During his three years of employment there, Remark continued to write and submit stories to literary magazines and publishers. One notable submission was to the *Hannover Kurier* under the pen name "Erich Maria Remarque."

Erich's talent did not go unnoticed in the world of publishing. His articles for the *Echo-Continental* were exceptionally clever and original; they linked Continental's product—rubber—with biking, cars, and racing. By 1925, he used his contacts to secure a job as the picture editor of *Sport im Bild* (*Sports in Pictures*) in Weimar Germany's cultural and political capital, Berlin. Remark thrived in the intellectual, cultural, and permissive atmosphere of 1920s Berlin. His writing during these years was dedicated mostly to the thrilling new sport of car racing and to cars. His second novel, *Station am Horizont* (*Station on the Horizon*), was serialized in *Sport im Bild* and focused on the world of auto racing and the beautiful people in that world. After this endeavor, he sat down in the autumn of 1927 and began writing a story about the war. Six weeks later he completed *All Quiet on the Western Front*. In an interview with an American reporter, Remarque, now using his pen name as his preferred name, claimed that he sat down to write this novel because he, like many of his friends, was experiencing depression and "violent attacks of despair." *All Quiet on the Western Front*

was an attempt to exorcize some of his feelings of restlessness, despair, and hopelessness (Document Five). He prefaced his story by stating: "This book is to be neither an accusation nor a confession, and least of all an adventure, for death is not an adventure to those who stand face to face with it. It will try simply to tell of a generation of men who, even though they may have escaped its shells, were destroyed by the war."[9]

Remarque took his title from a commonly used expression in German war communiqués. He meant the irony to be clear to all because his protagonist, Paul Baumer, is killed on a day when it was reported to be "all quiet on the Western Front." Remarque used his given middle name for his main character, Paul, and he drew not only on his experiences but on those of friends and other soldiers. In the novel, Paul was "everyman," and Remarque purposefully avoided mentioning battles by name or giving exact dates and locations because he wished his readers to identify with the experiences and characters in the novel, not actual events. As a result of this strategy, *All Quiet on the Western Front* consisted of several vignettes that "described typical war experiences such as food disbursements, artillery barrages, gas attacks, furloughs, watch guards, patrols, visits to a comrade in the army hospital, rats, and latrines." In addition, the novel targeted incompetent military and government leaders, war profiteers, and misguided, chauvinis-

9. Erich Maria Remarque, *All Quiet on the Western Front* (New York: Fawcett Crest Books, 1975), preface.

tic teachers who deceived Remarque and his classmates into fighting for honor and glory.

Paul was neither hero or warrior. He and his student/soldier cohort quickly ceased fighting for ideals preached to them by their pompous, bombastic schoolmaster. Instead, they defended themselves from annihilation at the hands of both their enemies and the German officers who moved them around like pawns and sent them again and again into perilous and murderous situations. Directly or indirectly, the novel indicted the older generation, whom Remarque saw as responsible for the senseless slaughter and destruction of his generation, "a lost generation." In its closing pages, Remarque expressed these sentiments:

> Had we returned home in 1916, out of the suffering and the strength of our experience we might have unleashed a storm. Now if we go back we will be weary, broken, burnt out, rootless, and without hope. We will not be able to find our way any more.
>
> And men will not understand us—for the generation that grew up before us, though it has passed these years with us already had a home and a calling; now it will return to its old occupations, and will be forgotten—and the generation that has grown up after us will be strange to us and push us aside. We will be superfluous even to ourselves, we will grow older, a few will adapt themselves, some others will submit, and most will be bewildered;—the years will pass by and in the end we shall fall into ruin.[10]

10. Ibid., pp. 253–255.

All Quiet on the Western Front was originally published in serialized form and appeared weekly from November to December 1928. It appeared in book form on January 31, 1929, and by the end of the year, it had been translated into twelve languages and a million and a half copies were sold. The number of copies sold doubled in 1930. The success of *All Quiet on the Western Front* irrevocably changed Remarque's life. He went from being an obscure journalist to a world-famous author almost overnight and was relentlessly pursued by the public and media alike. Such success invited scrutiny and criticism. One group that was particularly critical of Remarque's novel were the National Socialists (Nazis).

The National Socialist German Workers' Party (NSDAP) had been founded in Munich in 1920. After the abortive putsch of 1923, the Nazis descended into political obscurity during the prosperous years of the Weimar era. The intimidation of its paramilitary arm, the SA (Storm Troopers) or Brownshirts, and the targeting of scapegoats such as the Jews and the Weimar politicians and foreign powers who imposed the Versailles Treaty on Germany won little popular support for the party in the mid-1920s. In 1930, Germany was once again in the throes of an economic and political crisis that began with the Wall Street crash of October 1929 and quickly led to a worldwide economic depression. Germany was particularly hard hit because of its dependence on American loans. To meet domestic and international obligations, the Weimar government followed a rigidly orthodox policy of cutting government expenditures, and

Chapter 9
World War I and
Its Aftermath:
Käthe Schmidt
Kollwitz
(1867–1945) and
Erich Maria
Remarque
(1898–1970)

unemployment rose steadily to a peak of 6 million in 1933. National income declined by 40 percent and foreign trade by more than one-half; a severe financial crisis in 1931 led to the suspension of reparations payments by international agreement. In the midst of this crisis, the ruling coalition in the German parliament (Reichstag) disintegrated and new elections had to be held. In September 1930, the public went to the polls and supported parties on the political extremes: the Nazis increased their seats from 12 to 107, and the Communists, from 54 to 77. Germany was quickly becoming a divided society.

Violence, intimidation, nationalist rhetoric, and verbal attacks on the "enemies" of Germany became common in late Weimar Germany, which was the arena into which Remarque's *All Quiet on the Western Front* entered. The novel became a favorite target of the Nazis and other nationalist groups because of its antiheroic and antimilitaristic message. The Nazis accused Remarque of creating "caricatures of frontline soldiers" and "corroding the Volk spirit." His depiction of the fight for survival of a small group of students challenged the Nazi myth of individual heroism and unselfish sacrifice for Germany. An honorable and glorified war experience was essential to the Nazi's narrative about war because they regarded the experience as the fire in which the iron spirit of National Socialism had been forged (Document Six). Paul Baumer's death was not glorious; it was not even noticed by anyone. His death was not the hero's death so often and readily glorified by the Nazis. Such criticism be-

wildered Remarque, in part because he had not written the book with specific political motives in mind. He maintained that "it is unpolitical. And at first the impression it made was entirely non-political. Only through its success was it drawn into the political debating arena. I think it was more the number of copies sold than the book itself which was the object of attack."[11]

The firestorm over *All Quiet on the Western Front* continued to rage with the German premiere of the American-made movie in Berlin in December 1930. At this time, Joseph Goebbels, the soon-to-be-famous propaganda minister for the Nazis, was the head of the Berlin party as well as commander of Berlin's brownshirted thugs. He ordered the Brownshirts to infiltrate the crowd and, when the lights went down, to release hundreds of white mice, set off stink bombs, and throw beer bottles to disrupt the premiere. The Brownshirts succeeded in having the event cancelled, despite heroic efforts by the theater's management and some members of the audience to collect the mice, calm the crowd, and resume the movie. In the end, the Brownshirts prevailed. The mélée at the theater prompted two regional governments in Germany to ban the film in their regions, and eventually the film was forbidden throughout Germany. Earlier in 1930, the Nazis had come to power in the large central German state of Thuringia, and the new minister of education, Wilhem

11. Christine R. Barker and R. W. Last, *Erich Maria Remarque* (New York : Barnes and Noble Books, 1979), p. 18. From A. Eggebrecht, "Gesprach mit Remarque," *Die literarische Welt*, June 14, 1929.

Frick, announced that *All Quiet on the Western Front* had been banned in all schools because it was "pacifist, Marxist propaganda."

The increasing hostility toward his novel and person forced Remarque to leave for Switzerland in 1931. Later in life, he explained his reasons: "In the year 1931 I had to leave Germany, because my life was threatened. I was neither a Jew nor orientated towards the left politically. I was the same then as I am today: a militant pacifist."[12] When the Nazis came to power in 1933, they banned *All Quiet on the Western Front* and his next novel, *The Way Back*. Both novels were included in a well-coordinated book-burning ritual held in nearly all German university cities on the evening of May 10, 1933. The Nazis selected books written by "degenerate and Jewish litterateurs" and containing material of a "non-German spirit." Slogans chanted as cartloads and truckloads of books were thrown into the fire included "No to decadence and moral corrup-

tion! Yes to decency and morality in family and state!" "I consign to the flames the writings of Heinrich Mann, Ernst Glaeser, Erich Kästner!" At the book-burning frenzy in Berlin, one of the speakers picked up *All Quiet on the Western Front* and shouted, "Against literary betrayal of the soldiers of the World War, for the education of the nation in the spirit of the truthfulness, I consign to the flames the works of Erich Maria Remarque."[13] After the book-burning incident, the Nazi government embarked upon a campaign against democratic and left-wing literature and its authors. It used the Weimar republic's "Law to Protect Youth from Filth and Trash Writings" to censor and ban politically disagreeable books. Measures against the offending writers were immediately intensified: they lost their teaching posts and were ejected from professional associations and public service. Little opposition to the book burnings or bans arose in Germany.

▨ ACT II:

KOLLWITZ AND ARTISTIC EXPRESSION

Käthe Kollwitz's work during the 1920s also reflected the tumult of the times and her strongly held political views. Her "Memorial for Karl Liebknecht" expressed her sorrow and sympathy for the slain founder of the German Communist party, who was brutally murdered by the predecessor

to the Nazi Brownshirts, the reactionary, nationalist Free Corps. She produced numerous posters for leftist and pacificist causes such as International Workers Aid, the International Trade Union Federation, and antiwar and youth day events. She admitted that these posters were among her

12. Ibid.

13. Hans Wagener, *Understanding Erich Maria Remarque* (Columbia, S.C.: University of South Carolina Press, 1991), p. 6. From Joseph Wulf, *Literatur und Dichtung im Dritten Reich: Eine Dokumentation* (Gütersloh: Sigbert Mohn, 1964), p. 45.

Chapter 9
World War I and
Its Aftermath:
Käthe Schmidt
Kollwitz
(1867–1945) and
Erich Maria
Remarque
(1898–1970)

most political and powerful compositions. She wrote, "Everyone must work as he can. I agree that my art has purpose. To be effective in this time when people are so helpless and in need of aid." The posters "Help Russia," "Vienna is Dying! Save her Children!" "Germany's Children are Hungry!" "Bread," "The Survivors," and the powerful and often reprinted "Never Again War!" utilize the stark, tragic, austere power and beauty of her draftsmanship to depict the hunger, degradation, and injustice of the period (Image Four).

Between 1919 and 1933, Kollwitz's reputation as an artist continued to grow and be recognized. She became the first women elected to the Prussian Academy of Arts and received the coveted title of professor in 1919. During the 1920s, her work was shown in numerous European capitals and in the United States. In 1927, she and her husband traveled to Moscow at the invitation of the Soviet government for the tenth anniversary of the Russian Revolution. Despite the exhibitions, the recognition, and her international reputation, Kollwitz earned very little, maybe $500 annually. Finally, in 1928, the state of Prussia made her a civil servant and she began to supervise students in graphics for the Prussian Academy of Arts. She hoped this appointment would ease the burden on her husband. In 1929, she won the highest Prussian public award, *Pour le Mérite,* which was given for outstanding merit in the arts and sciences.

Like Remarque, Kollwitz watched as Germany descended into economic depression and political and social chaos. In 1930, she noted that the

Nazis were quickly ascending to power, symbolized by their victory in Thuringia and their significant number of seats in the Reichstag. Their numbers in the Reichstag made them the second largest party. Reflecting on the year's events, Kollwitz wrote, "Evil reaction is creeping into all areas," including liberal, permissive Berlin with the ban against the film, *All Quiet on the Western Front.* Not intimidated by the atmosphere, Kollwitz spoke out against the violence and coercion that soon became the hallmark of German political life in the 1930s. She lent not only her talent but her name to petitions, manifestos, and letters that warned against, protested, and appealed for resistance to the brutal, intolerant, and violent tactics of the Nazis.

When the Nazis came to power in 1933, one of their first steps was to purge literary and artistic organizations and institutions of leftists or those unsympathetic to the Nazis and their views. The new Nazi minister of education, Dr. Bernhard Rust, forced Kollwitz to resign from the roster of notables at the Prussian Academy of Arts because she had signed a manifesto calling for unity among the left during the Reichstag elections in March 1933. Ironically, Kollwitz had originally been praised by the National Socialists as a "strongly expressive depicter of big-city misery." However, her commitment to national and international humanitarian and pacifist organizations, her known leftist sympathies, and the fact that German socialists regarded Kollwitz as the illustrator of their aims and ideals earned her the new regime's hostility.

Kollwitz could have been of some use to the Nazis, but she refused to trade on her fame to escape their wrath. She realized that her open opposition to the Nazis prior to their seizure of power and her deep socialist roots would mean "a slapping down." Her opportunity to exhibit new works diminished and the few pieces she had hanging in public galleries all but disappeared by late 1936, right before she and other German artists were declared "degenerate."

The Nazis sought to put art and the artist in the service of the state, and they proclaimed that the artistic work of Kollwitz, Max Beckmann, Otto Dix, Paul Klee, and others was "degenerate" and must be banned. The art classified as "degenerate" was mostly expressionist, dadaist, or abstract art and anything that had socially critical content. The Nazis asserted that this type of art had "a spiritually destructive impact" on society because the artists imposed their "unbridled individualistic tyranny" on the viewer and "propagated a subhuman culture."[14] In the summer of 1937, the president of the Reich Chamber of Fine Arts, Adolf Ziegler, put together an exhibition in Munich under the title "Degenerate Art." This show exhibited paintings, graphics, and sculpture of Germany's most prominent artists of the 1920s and 1930—Klee, Dix, Emil Nolde, Beckmann, and Oskar Kokoschka. The exhibit captioned their art works with phrases such as "the monstrous products of madness and arrogance," "mockery of Christianity," "defilement of German womanhood," "slander of German heroes," and "Jewish art." Noticeable in its absence was Kollwitz's work. The Nazis had not dared place her in the exhibition because of her popularity. Their only recourse was to condemn her to obscurity.

Kollwitz and her family shared the fate of many other families who were on the wrong side of the political fence. Her husband and her son, also a doctor, briefly lost their positions early in the Nazi period. The Kollwitzs were watched and at times visited by the Nazi secret police, the Gestapo. Käthe was even threatened with internment in a concentration camp if she did not repudiate a newspaper interview that she had given to a journalist writing a piece on how well-known artists were faring under Hitler. She wrote a retraction but refused to divulge the name of the third person who had attended the interview. Years later, the third person, Otto Nagel, wrote of her courage.

Kollwitz suffered indignity after indignity. Her beloved sculpture of "The Mother," which had been placed at the entrance of the Belgian cemetery where her son was buried, was mocked in the Nazi Party's central newspaper: "Thank God a German mother does not look like this." The Nazis found the sculpture to be an affront to all that they were espousing for the proper role of mothers in this new state. Mothers of German soldiers had to celebrate the loss of their brave sons for the Fatherland; this sculpture depicted the senselessness and devastation of this loss.

14. Martha Kearns, *Käthe Kollwitz: Woman and Artist* (New York: The Feminist Press, 1976) p. 187. From *Deutsche Kultur-wacht* 2 (1933).

Chapter 9
World War I and
Its Aftermath:
Käthe Schmidt
Kollwitz
(1867–1945) and
Erich Maria
Remarque
(1898–1970)

▪ FINALE

Given her international reputation and standing, Kollwitz certainly could have fled abroad. An American patron offered her and Karl refuge in the United States, but fearing reprisals against their family, they chose to remain and wait out the war without ever openly confronting the Nazis again. The Kollwitzs even went so far as to submit their family tree to the Nazis to prove that their family was free of Jewish blood. Kollwitz joined the appropriate government guilds to continue working. In 1942, she produced her last piece. Living through her second world war, Kollwitz's last work, "Seed for the planting must not be ground," is a living testament to her ideals. Shortly after completing this work, her family persuaded her to leave the apartment where she and Karl had lived for fifty years because the Allied bombing had made this industrial suburb unfit to live in. (Karl had died in July 1940). Their family home, with its memories and many of Kollwitz's remaining pieces of art work, was bombed in late 1943. Soon after, her son's home, with an equal number of valuable works, was also destroyed. In 1945, Kollwitz noted, "the war accompanies me to the end." It certainly did: on April 22, 1945, Käthe Kollwitz died.

Erich Maria Remarque would face none of the hardships and moral choices presented to Kollwitz. With few responsibilities or ties to his father and two sisters, Remarque decided to go into exile in Switzerland in the early 1930s. Like so many of Germany's foremost writers, he watched much of the Nazi terror and persecu-

tions from a distance. From 1931 to 1939, Remarque remained in Switzerland and enjoyed the life of an internationally renowned author and playboy. During this time, he remarried his first wife, Jeanne "Jutta" Zambona, whom he divorced in 1930, most likely to get her out of Germany and into Switzerland. After the war, he remained married to her until 1957 to enable her to emigrate to the United States. Unable to persuade one of Germany's most distinguished authors to return to Germany, the Nazis revoked his German citizenship in 1938. He was a man without a country, and in 1939, he became involved in a demanding and torrid affair with the German-born film star, Marlene Dietrich. Remarque set sail for the United States in that same year with a Panamanian passport on the last peacetime voyage of the Queen Mary.

At first glance, Remarque's life in Hollywood and then in New York appeared to be free of the distractions of war in Europe. In 1943, however, the Nazis beheaded his younger sister, Elfriede, for what they claimed was "many months of unfettered, hateful, defeatist, rumor-mongering." Many assume, and the German judge's own words confirm, that her death was in part a result of the Nazis' animosity toward her brother. Roland Freisler, the judge presiding over the case, explained to her during the trial that "because her brother was beyond the control of the court she would have to atone for his guilt." Many years later, Remarque hired a lawyer to find documented material related to the court hearings and to get the case reopened. The high court in Berlin eventually refused to reopen the case of Elfriede Scholz, born Remark.

Remarque never returned to Germany to live. His citizenship had been revoked by the Nazis and he felt that since he did not apply for his rights to be taken away, he should not have to ask for them back. He bluntly argued, "As far as I know, none of the mass murderers of the Third Reich have been deprived of their citizenship. The emigrants, therefore, are far worse off than they are." Until his death in 1970, Remarque returned to Germany only briefly to collect materials for new novels, receive awards, or attend premieres of movies made from his books. He divided his time between the United States—he became a U.S. citizen in 1947—and Switzerland with his second wife, the screen legend, Paulette Goddard.

None of Erich Maria Remarque's other twelve novels received the acclaim and attention that *All Quiet on the Western Front* did, though many were bestsellers and some were made into Hollywood movies. Remarque left a legacy not because of the literary genius of his novel but because he made himself a spokesperson for an entire generation. Those who read it saw an antimilitaristic, antinationalistic, and pacifist statement of the first order. They also saw a novel that rejected the ideologies and philosophies of the old generation and blamed them for the war and its deleterious effects on the young people who were forced to fight it. It was not just a story about German soldiers but about soldiers of all nations who had experienced the horrors of war and did not want the experiences to be repeated.

The Nazis vilified Remarque because he did not glorify the war or see its regenerative force and energy. There were writers on all sides who depicted their time in the trenches as sacred, their comrades as members of a fraternity to be revered and honored, and the experience of "real war" as marking them off from the rest of society. The Nazis embraced this view and directed their appeal of love of state and the nation, comradeship as sacred, loyalty and military courage to the veterans of the Great War and Germany's youth. Remarque's best selling novel contradicted this view.

Käthe Kollwitz's last piece, the lithograph, "Seed for the planting must not be ground," depicts a mother shielding sixteen-year-old boys with her coat, and the boys are about to break free. She wrote of this lithograph, "the old mother who is holding them together says, 'No! You stay here! For the time being you may play rough and tumble with one another. But when you are grown up you must get ready for life, not for war again'."[15] Kollwitz rooted her pacifism and art in her experience as a mother and a mother's right to protect her children and prepare them for life, not death. She appealed to women as wives and mothers to halt the slaughter. Nazi propaganda also appealed to women as wives and mother, but they wished to persuade women to teach their sons to love the fatherland, to sacrifice their sons for the German nation, and to endure the sacrifice. Kollwitz's last piece told German women that they had had a choice.

15. Ibid., p. 217.

Chapter 9
World War I and
Its Aftermath:
Käthe Schmidt
Kollwitz
(1867–1945) and
Erich Maria
Remarque
(1898–1970)

▄ QUESTIONS

1. How do Remarque and Kollwitz greet the war? What do each contribute to the German war effort?

2. How do their backgrounds influence their views about the coming of World War I? Why does their initial enthusiasm and the enthusiasm of other Europeans evaporate?

3. Why do Remarque and Kollwitz question the meaning of war? How do they express their opinions?

4. What are the public responses to their artistic expressions?

5. Compare and contrast the nationalist/Nazi interpretation of World War I and that of Remarque and Kollwitz. Who or what groups are attracted to these different views? Why?

6. Why do the Nazis burn Remarque's book and ban exhibitions of Kollwitz's work? Why does art matter?

7. What messages and ideas run through the images that you have examined in this chapter?

▄ DOCUMENTS

DOCUMENT ONE

ERICH MARIA REMARQUE

All Quiet on the Western Front (1929)

Remarque published All Quiet on the Western Front *in 1929. He attempted to universalize the experience of soldiers and never placed his characters in a specific place. Although this is fiction, did Remarque get the soldiers' experiences right? Why or why not?*

. . . Killing each separate louse is a tedious business when a man has hundreds. The little beasts are hard and the everlasting cracking with one's fingernails very soon becomes wearisome. So Tjaden has rigged up the lid of a boot-polish tin with a piece of wire over the lighted stump of a candle. The lice are simply thrown into this little pan. Crack! and they're done for.

We sit around with our shirts on our knees, our bodies naked to the warm air and our hands at work. Haie has a particularly fine brand of louse: they have a red cross on their heads. He suggests that he brought them back from the hospital at Thourhout, where they attended personally on a surgeon-general. He says he means to use the fat that slowly accumulates in the tin-lid for polishing his boots, and roars with laughter for half an hour at his own joke. . . .

. . . We must look out for our bread. The rats have become much more numerous lately because the trenches are no longer in good condition. Detering says it is a sure sign of a coming bombardment.

The rats here are particularly repulsive, they are so fat—the kind we all call corpse-rats. They have shocking, evil, naked faces, and it is nauseating to see their long, nude tails.

They seem to be mighty hungry. Almost every man has had his bread gnawed. Kropp wrapped his in his waterproof sheet and put it under his head, but he cannot sleep because they run over his face to get at it. Detering meant to outwit them: he fastened a thin wire to the roof and suspended his bread from it. During the night when he switched on his pocket-torch he saw the wire swing to and fro. On the bread was riding a fat rat.

At last we put a stop to it. We cannot afford to throw the bread away, because then we should have nothing left to eat in the morning, so we carefully cut off the bits of bread that the animals have gnawed.

The slices we cut off are heaped together in the middle of the floor. Each man takes out his spade and lies down prepared to strike. Detering, Kropp, and Kat hold their pocket-torches ready.

After a few minutes we hear the first shuffling and tugging. It grows, now it is the sound of many little feet. Then the torches switch on and every man strikes at the heap, which scatters with a rush. The result is good. We toss the bits of rat over the parapet and again lie in wait.

Several times we repeat the process. At last the beasts get wise to it, or perhaps they have scented the blood. They return no more. Nevertheless, before morning the remainder of the bread on the floor has been carried off.

In the adjoining sector they attacked two large cats and a dog, bit them to death and devoured them. . . .

At night they send over gas. We expect the attack to follow and lie with our masks on, ready to tear them off as soon as the first shadow appears.

Dawn approaches without anything happening—only the everlasting, nerve-wracking roll behind the enemy lines, trains, trains, lorries, lorries; but what are they concentrating? Our artillery fires on it continually, but still it does not cease.

We have tired faces and avoid each other's eyes, "It will be like the Somme," says Kat gloomily. "There we were shelled steadily for seven days and nights." Kat has lost all his fun since we have been here, which is bad, for Kat is an old front-hog, and can smell what is coming. Only Tjaden seems pleased with the good rations and the rum; he thinks we might even go back to rest without anything happening at all.

It almost looks like it. Day after day passes. At night I squat in the listening-post. Above me the rockets and parachute-lights shoot up and float down again. I am cautious and tense, my heart thumps. My eyes turn again and again to the luminous dial of my watch; the hands will not budge. Sleep hangs on my

Chapter 9
World War I and
Its Aftermath:
Käthe Schmidt
Kollwitz
(1867–1945) and
Erich Maria
Remarque
(1898–1970)

eyelids, I work my toes in my boots in order to keep awake. Nothing happens till I am relieved;—only the everlasting rolling over there. Gradually we grow calmer and play skat and poker continually. Perhaps we will be lucky.

All day the sky is hung with observation balloons. There is a rumour that the enemy are going to put tanks over and use low-flying planes for the attack. But that interests us less than what we hear of the new flame-throwers.

We wake up in the middle of the night. The earth booms. Heavy fire is falling on us. We crouch into corners. We distinguish shells of every calibre.

Each man lays hold of his things and looks again every minute to reassure himself that they are still there. The dug-out heaves, the night roars and flashes. We look at each other in the momentary flashes of light, and with pale faces and pressed lips shake our heads.

Every man is aware of the heavy shells tearing down the parapet, rooting up the embankment and demolishing the upper layers of concrete. When a shell lands in the trench we note how the hollow, furious blast is like a blow from the paw of a raging beast of prey. Already by morning a few of the recruits are green and vomiting. They are too inexperienced.

Slowly the grey light trickles into the post and pales the flashes of the shells. Morning is come. The explosion of mines mingles with the gun-fire. That is the most dementing convulsion of all. The whole region where they go up becomes one grave.

The reliefs go out, the observers stagger in, covered with dirt, and trembling. One lies down in silence in the corner and eats, the other, an older man of the new draft, sobs; twice he has been flung over the parapet by the blast of the explosions without getting any more than shell-shock.

The recruits are eyeing him. We must watch them, these things are catching, already some lips begin to quiver. It is good that it is growing daylight; perhaps the attack will come before noon.

The bombardment does not diminish. It is falling in the rear too. As far as one can see spout fountains of mud and iron. A wide belt is being raked.

The attack does not come, but the bombardment continues. We are gradually benumbed. Hardly a man speaks. We cannot make ourselves understood.

Our trench is almost gone. At many places it is only eighteen inches high, it is broken by holes, and craters, and mountains of earth. A shell lands square in front of our post. At once it is dark. We are buried and must dig ourselves out. After an hour the entrance is clear again, and we are calmer because we have had something to do.

Our Company Commander scrambles in and reports that two dug-outs are gone. The recruits calm themselves when they see him. He says that an attempt will be made to bring up food this evening.

That sounds reassuring. No one had thought of it except Tjaden. Now the outside world seems to draw a little nearer: if food can be brought up, think the recruits, then it can't really be so bad.

We do not disabuse them; we know that food is as important as ammunition and only for that reason must be brought up.

But it miscarries. A second party goes out, and it also turns back. Finally Kat tries, and even he reappears without accomplishing anything. No one gets through, not even a fly is small enough to get through such a barrage.

We pull in our belts tighter and chew every mouthful three times as long. Still the food does not last out; we are damnably hungry. I take out a scrap of bread, eat the white and put the crust back in my knapsack; from time to time I nibble at it.

The night is unbearable. We cannot sleep, but stare ahead of us and doze. Tjaden regrets that we wasted the gnawed pieces of bread on the rats. We would gladly have them again to eat now. We are short of water, too, but not seriously yet.

Towards morning, while it is still dark, there is some excitement. Through the entrance rushes in a swarm of fleeing rats that try to storm the walls. Torches light up the confusion. Everyone yells and curses and slaughters. The madness and despair of many hours unloads itself in this outburst. Faces are distorted, arms strike out, the beasts scream; we just stop in time to avoid attacking one another.

The onslaught has exhausted us. We lie down to wait again. It is a marvel that our post has had no casualties so far. It is one of the less deep dug-outs.

A corporal creeps in; he has a loaf of bread with him. Three people have had the luck to get through during the night and bring some provisions. They say the bombardment extends undiminished as far as the artillery lines. It is a mystery where the enemy gets all his shells.

We wait and wait. By midday what I expected happens. One of the recruits has a fit. I have been watching him for a long time, grinding his teeth and opening and shutting his fists. These hunted, protruding eyes, we know them too well. During the last few hours he has had merely the appearance of calm. He had collapsed like a rotten tree.

Now he stands up, stealthily creeps across the floor hesitates a moment and then glides towards the door. I intercept him and say: "Where are you going?"

"I'll be back in a minute," says he, and tries to push past me.

"Wait a bit, the shelling will stop soon."

He listens for a moment and his eyes become clear. Then again he has the glowering eyes of a mad dog, he is silent, he shoves me aside.

"One minute, lad," I say. Kat notices. Just as the recruit shakes me off Kat jumps in and we hold him.

Then he begins to rave: "Leave me alone, let me go out, I will go out!"

He won't listen to anything and hits out, his mouth is wet and pours out words, half choked, meaningless words. It is a case of claustrophobia, he feels as though he is suffocating here and wants to get out at any price. If we let him go he would run about everywhere regardless of cover. He is not the first.

Chapter 9
World War I and
Its Aftermath:
Käthe Schmidt
Kollwitz
(1867–1945) and
Erich Maria
Remarque
(1898–1970)

Though he raves and his eyes roll, it can't be helped, we have to give him a hiding to bring him to his senses. We do it quickly and mercilessly, and at last he sits down quietly. The others have turned pale; let's hope it deters them. This bombardment is too much for the poor devils, they have been sent straight from a recruiting-depot into a barrage that is enough to turn an old soldier's hair grey. . . .

DOCUMENT TWO

KÄTHE KOLLWITZ

Diary and Letters
(August and September 1914)

Kollwitz's diary entries at the beginning of the war reflect a "frightful melancholy." Why is she critical of the "heroic stiffness" of war? If war is so "ghastly and insane," why do young men, like her son and his friends, fight?

August 27, 1914

In the heroic stiffness of these times of war, when our feelings are screwed to an unnatural pitch, it is like a touch of heavenly music, like sweet, lamenting murmurs of peace, to read that French soldiers spare and actually help wounded Germans, that in the franc-tireur villages German soldiers write on the walls of houses such notices as: Be considerate! An old woman lives here.— These people were kind to me.—Old people only.—Woman in childbed—And so on.

A piece by Gabriele Reuter in the *Tag* on the tasks of women today. She spoke of the joy of sacrificing—a phrase that struck me hard. Where do all the women who have watched so carefully over the lives of their beloved ones get the heroism to send them to face the cannon? I am afraid that this soaring of the spirit will be followed by the blackest despair and dejection. The task is to bear it not only during these few weeks, but for a long time—in dreary November as well, and also when spring comes again, in March, the month of young men who wanted to live and are dead. That will be much harder.

Those who now have only small children, like Lise her Maria, seem to me so fortunate. For us, whose sons are going, the vital thread is snapped.

September 30, 1914

Cold, cloudy autumnal weather. The grave mood that comes over one when one knows: there is war, and one cannot hold on to any illusions any more.

Nothing is real but the frightfulness of this state, which we almost grow used to. In such times it seems so stupid that the boys must go to war. The whole thing is so ghastly and insane. Occasionally there comes the foolish thought: how can they possibly take part in such madness? And at once the cold shower: they *must, must!* All is leveled by death; down with all the youth! Then one is ready to despair.

Only one state of mind makes it at all bearable: to receive the sacrifice into one's will. But how can one maintain such a state?

[Peter Kollwitz was killed on October 22, 1914.]

DOCUMENT THREE

KÄTHE KOLLWITZ

Diary and Letters
(1909 and 1922)

Hans Kollwitz, Käthe's oldest son, asked his mother after World War I to "set down an account of her." In 1922, his mother acquiesced and she wrote an account of her childhood, early youth, and her year in Munich. The first selection is a passage from this memoir; the second is excerpted from her diary. What are her motivations for choosing the subjects she does?

[ON BEING A "SOCIALIST" ARTIST, 1922]

I should like to say something about my reputation for being a "socialist" which clung to me from then on. Unquestionably my work at this time, as a result of the attitudes of my father and brother and of the whole literature of the period, was in the direction of socialism. But my real motive for choosing my subjects almost exclusively from the life of the workers was that only such subjects gave me in a simple and unqualified way what I felt to be beautiful. For me the Koenigsberg longshoremen had beauty; the Polish *jimkes* on their grain ships had beauty; the broad freedom of movement in the gestures of the common people had beauty. Middle-class people held no appeal for me at all. Bourgeois life as a whole seemed to me pedantic. The proletariat, on the other hand, had a grandness of manner, a breadth to their lives. Much later on, when I became acquainted with the difficulties and tragedies underlying proletarian life, when I met the women who came to my husband for help and so, incidentally, came to me, I was gripped by the full force of the proletarian's fate. Unsolved problems such as prostitution and unemployment grieved and tormented me, and contributed to my feeling that I must keep on with my studies of the lower classes.

Chapter 9
World War I and
Its Aftermath:
Käthe Schmidt
Kollwitz
(1867–1945) and
Erich Maria
Remarque
(1898–1970)

And portraying them again and again opened a safety-valve for me; it made life bearable.

Then, too, my temperamental resemblance to my father strengthened this inclination in me. Occasionally even my parents said to me, "After all there are happy things in life too. Why do you show only the dark side?" I could not answer this. The joyous side simply did not appeal to me. But I want to emphasize once more that in the beginning my impulse to represent proletarian life had little to do with pity or sympathy. I simply felt that the life of the workers was beautiful. As Zola or someone once said, "Le beau c'est le laid."

["THE *TYPICAL* MISFORTUNE"]

September 1909

Frau Pankopf was here. She had a bad black eye. Her husband had flown into a rage. When I asked her about him, she said he had wanted to be a teacher, but had become a worker in tortoise-shell and was well paid for his work. His heart became enlarged, and at the same time he had his first attacks of extreme restlessness. He went for treatment and then tried to work again. It wouldn't do; he tried to get other work; and last winter went about with a hurdy-gurdy. His feet swelled, and the longer it went on the more he suffered from melancholy and nervousness. Wailed continually that he longed for death, could not support his family, and so on. When their next to the last child died, he remained in a state of hysterical misery much longer than his wife. Six of the children are living. Finally he started to have fits of rage and was taken to Herzberge.

The more I see of it, the more I realize that this is the *typical* misfortune of workers' families. As soon as the man drinks or is sick and unemployed, it is always the same story. Either he hangs on his family like a dead weight and lets them feed him—cursed by the other members of the family (Schwarzenau or Frank), or he becomes melancholy (Pankopf, Goenner), or he goes mad (likewise Frank), or he takes his own life. For the woman the misery is always the same. She keeps the children whom she must feed, scolds and complains about her husband. She sees only what has become of him and not how he became that way.

DOCUMENT FOUR

KÄTHE KOLLWITZ

Diary and Letters
(October 11, 1916)

The following excerpts from her diary express Kollwitz's grief for her son and his generation. Does her grief become political?

["THIS FRIGHTFUL INSANITY"]

October 11, 1916

Everything remains as obscure as ever for me. Why is that? It's not only our youth who go willingly and joyfully into the war; it's the same in all nations. People who would be friends under other conditions now hurl themselves at one another as enemies. Are the young really without judgment? Do they always rush into it as soon as they are called? Without looking closer? Do they rush into war because they want to, because it is in their blood so that they accept without examination whatever reasons for fighting are given to them? Do the young want war? Would they be old before their time if they no longer wanted it?

This frightful insanity—the youth of Europe hurling themselves at one another.

When I think I am convinced of the insanity of the war, I ask myself again by what law man ought to live. Certainly not in order to attain the greatest possible happiness. It will always be true that life must be subordinated to the service of an ideal. But in this case, where has that principle led us? Peter, Erich, Richard, all have subordinated their lives to the idea of patriotism. The English, Russian and French young men have done the same. The consequence has been this terrible killing, and the impoverishment of Europe. Then shall we say that the youth in all these countries have been cheated? Has their capacity for sacrifice been exploited in order to bring on the war? Where are the guilty? Are there any? Or is everyone cheated? Has it been a case of mass madness? And when and how will the awakening take place?

I shall never fully understand it all. But it is clear that our boys, our Peter, went into the war two years ago with pure hearts, and that they were ready to die for Germany. They died—almost all of them. Died in Germany and among Germany's enemies—by the millions.

When the minister blessed the volunteers, he spoke of the Roman youth who leaped into the abyss and so closed it. That was one boy. Each of these boys felt that he must act like that one. But what came of it was something very different. The abyss has not closed. It has swallowed up millions, and it still gapes wide.

[281]

Chapter 9
World War I and
Its Aftermath:
Käthe Schmidt
Kollwitz
(1867–1945) and
Erich Maria
Remarque
(1898–1970)

And Europe, all Europe, is still like Rome, sacrificing its finest and most precious treasure—but the sacrifice has no effect.

Is it a breach of faith with you, Peter, if I can now see only madness in the war? Peter, you died believing. Was that also true of Erich, Walter, Meier, Gottfried, Richard Noll? Or had they come to their senses and were they nevertheless forced to leap into the abyss? Was force involved? Or did they want to? Were they forced? . . .

DOCUMENT FIVE

Cyrus Brooks

"Herr Remarque Shuns Literary Honors"
(September 22, 1929)

The following is an interview with Erich Maria Remarque that was printed in The New York Times Magazine. *What are the reasons why Remarque wrote* All Quiet on the Western Front? *What are his views on war? What is the value of an interview for a historian?*

. . ."How did you come to write your book?"

He looked at me. Apart from his eyes, Herr Remarque might be any one of tens of thousands of healthy young men to be found in the capitals of Europe, but his eyes have an alertness, a power, a penetration which reveal the mind and character behind them.

"Coming back to Germany after the war," he said, "was a terrible experience for every one of us. After the strain and hardships and horror of the war we returned to find the country in a state of disintegration, everywhere hunger, depression and bereavement. My own homecoming was overshadowed by the loss of my mother, which was a great blow to me. I had entered the army as a mere boy and was not one of the few lucky ones with a job to come back to, so I had to turn my hand to whatever offered—school teacher, handworker, journalist. I could not settle down to anything, there was a continual restlessness and dissatisfaction that drove me from one job to another."

He stopped and for a moment, his lips grim and tight.

"The truth was," he went on,"there was something on my mind—the weight of horror and suffering I had seen during the war years. It was still there, unexpressed and chaotic, robbing one of peace of mind, making it impossible to settle down to the ordinary avocations of civilian life. At last—I was on the editorial staff of a Berlin illustrated weekly at the time—I realized that I had to get these things straight in my own mind, to get them into focus once for all.

[282]

"The idea of my book came as a sort of safety valve. I came home one night from my work and started to write it. For obvious reasons I adopted the fiction form, but what I put down was the truth. I was not writing for any wide audience; my object was to see clearly the experiences I had been through, and therefore I wrote with the utmost simplicity and integrity as though I were telling the story to an intimate friend. I avoided all panegyric and let the terrible facts speak for themselves. In six weeks the book was finished—it had written itself—and I called it 'Im Westen Nichts Neues'—'All Quiet on the Western Front.'"

"A superb piece of irony," I said.

"When my readers have finished the book," he agreed, "they close it and read the title again—'All Quiet'—such were the things that were happening—when officially all was quiet!"

"And, of course, the publishers jumped at it?"

"No. Two publishers read it and turned it down. They admired it, but said it would never sell. Then a friend of mine went and talked to one firm and they made me an offer. Fifteen minutes after the contract was signed the second firm telephoned to say they had reversed their decision."

"How does it feel," I asked, "to be the author of the world's bestseller?"

The smile vanished from his face.

"As far as possible," he said, "I avoid feeling it at all. I don't think I have read a review since the first two or three notices of the German edition. As for what they call fame, I don't want it. It comes between a man and reality. As soon as you become a celebrity you lose touch with humanity, with life. That is why I live so quietly and keep out of the limelight. I must keep in touch. Otherwise I cannot write simply and directly for the minds and hearts of ordinary men and women. I like to keep close to natural things, trees and flowers. I want to have a little place in the country and breed dogs."

I thought of the third-floor flat in a quiet street in Wilmersdorf where I had found Herr Remarque the day before. It is a flat he reserves as his workshop and even there amid piles of books and papers he had introduced a reminder of the quiet countryside—a reminder that at first sight appeared bizarre—a large glass tank where little fish were swimming among water plants.

"But you like Berlin?" I asked.

"I like Berlin. But not the literary and social functions. I find what I want when I talk to ordinary folk in the streets and cafés, the simple people who are doing the world's work and not theorizing about it. Do you know what gives me the greatest pleasure?—the letters I get from common soldiers, men whom my book has helped to get the war into focus, to see the thing again as it was. In my future work my aim is to go on helping the ordinary man to face and solve the problems of life, and for that a man must try to live truly and simply."

There was no pose in Herr Remarque's modesty. He spoke in a low voice, slightly embarrassed by his self-revelation. He was not pleased when I called him modest. Indeed, it is difficult to get him to talk of himself. He is possessed by a passion to help. He desires to use his gifts of mind and heart for the re-

Chapter 9
World War I and
Its Aftermath:
Käthe Schmidt
Kollwitz
(1867–1945) and
Erich Maria
Remarque
(1898–1970)

moval of the misery, stupidity and cruelty which still exist, active or latent, in this post-war world. Success is welcome as a proof that men's ears are open to the words he speaks to them.

Turning to more general matters I asked him: "What do you consider the great positive result of the war?"

"An immense increase in world-will toward peace. Every one realizes today that war is a horror and an anachronism that must be avoided wherever humanly possible. This realization is not the monopoly of any political section; it is common to all classes, even to the soldiers themselves, and with this realization humanity must and will find methods by which war can be avoided." . . .

. . . "Germany has been through a period of terrific upheavals; it needs much more than ten years before the face of the new Germany can be truly seen. Almost the entire adult population has lived under two completely different sets of circumstances—pre-war and post-war. The new poor cannot find their bearings. They cannot forget the fact that they were well off; they cannot accept hard work. Hence our violent political differences. But the young men and women have accepted the new conditions. They love work and orderly progress, and therefore they love peace, for without peace progress is impossible. Only the coming generations will show the true face of Germany, but my hopes for the moral and cultural future of my country are very high."

DOCUMENT SIX

ERNST JÜNGER

The Storm of Steel
(1920)

Ernst Jünger joined the German army in 1914 at the age of nineteen and served with the 73rd Hanoverian Fusiliers until the end of the war. During his four years of service, Jünger fought with his platoon of "shock troops" in some of the bloodiest battles in northern France and Flanders. He was wounded seven times and received the highest German military award. During the war, he kept a diary and in 1920 it was published as The Storm of Steel.

In his memoir of the war, Jünger explores many of the themes Remarque writes about in All Quiet on the Western Front. *Both express the dehumanizing effect of the war on the soldiers, but they also have an aesthetic appreciation of the war. However, Jünger's work was embraced by the Nazis and ultranationalists for his belief that war is a steel bath, a storm of steel that tests character and forges a new man. Compare the passage below with Remarque's closing pages of* All Quiet on the Western Front. *How do these two views of the war's aftermath differ?*

. . . After fourteen days I was lying on the feather mattress of a hospital train. Once again a German landscape flitted by me, tinged this time with the first dyes of autumn, and once again, as on that time at Heidelberg, I was gripped by the sad and proud feeling of being more closely bound to my country because of the blood shed for her greatness. Why should I conceal that tears smarted in my eyes when I thought of the end of the enterprise in which I had borne my share? I had set out to the war gaily enough, thinking we were to hold a festival on which all the pride of youth was lavished, and I had thought little, once I was in the thick of it, about the ideal that I had to stand for. Now I looked back: four years of development in the midst of a generation predestined to death, spent in caves, smoke-filled trenches, and shell-illumined wastes; years enlivened only by the pleasure of a mercenary, and nights of guard after guard in an endless perspective; in short, a monotonous calendar full of hardships and privation, divided by the red-letter days of battles. And almost without any thought of mine, the idea of the Fatherland had been distilled from all these afflictions in a clearer and brighter essence. That was the final winnings in a game on which so often all had been staked: the nation was no longer for me an empty thought veiled in symbols; and how could it have been otherwise when I had seen so many die for its sake, and been schooled myself to stake my life for its credit every minute, day and night, without a thought? And so, strange as it may sound, I learned from this very four years' schooling in force and in all the fantastic extravagance of material warfare that life has no depth of meaning except when it it is pledged for an ideal, and that there are ideals in comparison with which the life of an individual and even of a people has no weight. And though the aim for which I fought as an individual, as an atom in the whole body of the army, was not to be achieved, though material force cast us, apparently, to the earth, yet we learned once and for all to stand for a cause and if necessary to fall as befitted men.

Hardened as scarcely another generation ever was in fire and flame, we could go into life as though from the anvil; into friendship, love, politics, professions, into all that destiny had in store. It is not every generation that is so favoured.

And if it be objected that we belong to a time of crude force our answer is: We stood with our feet in mud and blood, yet our faces were turned to things of exalted worth. And not one of that countless number who fell in our attacks fell for nothing. Each one fulfilled his own resolve. For to every one may be applied the saying from St. John that Dostoievski put in front of his greatest novel:

'Verily, verily, I say unto you, except a corn of wheat fall into the ground and die, it abideth alone: but if it die, it bringeth forth much fruit.'

Chapter 9
World War I and
Its Aftermath:
Käthe Schmidt
Kollwitz
(1867–1945) and
Erich Maria
Remarque
(1898–1970)

To-day we cannot understand the martyrs who threw themselves into the arena in a transport that lifted them even before their deaths beyond humanity, beyond every phase of pain and fear. Their faith no longer exercises a compelling force. When once it is no longer possible to understand how a man gives his life for his country—and the time will come—then all is over with that faith also, and the idea of the Fatherland is dead; and then, perhaps, we shall be envied, as we envy the saints their inward and irresistible strength. For all these great and solemn ideas bloom from a feeling that dwells in the blood and that cannot be forced. In the cold light of reason everything alike is a matter of expedience and sinks to the paltry and mean. It was out luck to live in the invisible rays of a feeling that filled the heart, and of this inestimable treasure we can never be deprived.

■ IMAGES

IMAGE ONE

"An Old Gun Position in Sanctuary Wood in the Ypres Sector, 25 October 1917"

The Western Front proved the perfect subject for photography to show its amazing potential to document war. Compare this photography with Paul Nash's painting, The Menin Road. *What does the photograph capture that the painting does not? Can these images be used as evidence that European art was transformed by the experiences of war?*

IMAGE TWO

<small>PAUL NASH</small>

The Menin Road

In 1917, Paul Nash convalesced at home after three years at Ypres on the Western Front. Trained as an artist before the war, Nash sketched his surroundings and life in the trenches. During his convalescence, he produced a series of paintings depicting the surreal, mutilated, and deformed landscape around Ypres.

Chapter 9
World War I and
Its Aftermath:
Käthe Schmidt
Kollwitz
(1867–1945) and
Erich Maria
Remarque
(1898–1970)

IMAGE THREE

KÄTHE KOLLWITZ

"The Mother" and "The Father"

*These two monuments stand in the military cemetery of Roggevelde in Flanders.
Are these war memorials? Why or why not?*

IMAGE FOUR

KÄTHE KOLLWITZ

"Never Again War"

Kollwitz produced this lithograph poster in 1924 for the Central Germany Youth Day held in Leipzig August 2–4, 1924. The young man is swearing the oath, "Never Again War," with an arm raised and two fingers extended in the traditional German manner.

Fascism Between the Wars: Benito Mussolini (1883–1945) and Margherita Grassini Sarfatti (1880–1961)

▓ SETTING THE STAGE

The destruction of material resources, the tremendous loss of human life, disillusionment, and crises of the spirit weighed heavily on the nations of Europe as they struggled to their feet at the conclusion of World War I. Unmet war aims and unresolved fears complicated matters as nationalist sentiments came through the war, not just unscathed, but strengthened. Both the potential and the dangers of modern mass society evident at the century's turn appeared to have taken concrete form in the experiences of a total war fought with varying intensity around the globe. Responses to these conditions were as diverse as the nations and societies experiencing them, ranging from anxiety and a sense of loss to an energetic embrace of new behaviors and beliefs, from apathy and withdrawal to enthusiasm and activism, from uncertainty to excitement, from pacifism to militarism. Such reactions

Chapter 10
Fascism Between
the Wars:
Benito Mussolini
(1883–1945)
and Margherita
Grassini Sarfatti
(1880–1961)

were evident in economic, social, cultural, and political arenas in the two decades after World War I. The fascist movements appearing throughout Europe in the 1920s and 1930s were one such response. They had their roots in the challenges and fears of modernity, and the tumult and crisis that followed World War I.

The word *fascism* comes from the Italian, *fascio,* meaning literally "a bunch" or "a bundle." Its political origins trace back to symbols of office used in ancient Rome. In the twentieth century, the term could be applied to various nationalist and militarist movements that grew out of mass society, depended on technology and economic development, and flourished in an atmosphere of crisis. The contradictions and even flexibility of fascist policies and practices make absolute definition difficult. In general, because of the diversity of their political menus, the movements had large popular support from different social groups. They were elitist and antidemocratic, and they emphasized the role of the leader. They questioned liberalism's focus on individual interests and freedoms, which they saw as motivated by selfish personal desires and advantages. They also promised to replace class struggle with cooperation among all sectors of society. The goals of economic self-sufficiency and state capitalism maintained private ownership but directed production for national needs and were important preconditions for expansionism and empire. Pronatalism or the promotion of population growth and health were necessary to realize these goals. To understand developments in the interwar years, two points

should be emphasized: first, fascism could be both revolutionary and reactionary, using images of both a romantic past and a "new order"; and second, the movements changed over time, shifting their appeals, goals, and constituents as they rose to power and then assumed control.

Italy's fascist movement was one of the oldest in Europe, and the Italian Fascist party (PNF) was the first to take power when Benito Mussolini (1883–1945) was called to form a government in October 1922. In some ways, the Italian movement is the prototype of fascism, with a longer history and more experimentation, expression, and representation of ideology than fascist parties in other areas. The Italian example invites examination because of its complexity, its longevity, and its failure to create an effective totalitarian regime.

At the close of World War I, Italy, with a population of 38 million people, was not fully industrialized.[1] Agriculture still contributed slightly more than 38 percent of national income; industry, 31.4 percent. In the north, however, major industrial development had created a standard of living like most of industrialized Europe; the south lagged far behind. The 1921 census showed that 73 out of 100 Italians were literate, but the figures for the south were much lower. While the nation might have seemed modern on some levels, there were really two Italies and this bifurcation remained a problem well into the twentieth century.

The constitutional monarchy and

1. Consult Spencer Di Scala, *Italy from Revolution to Republic* (Boulder, Colo.: Westview Press, 1995), for a good narrative of these years.

parliamentary system created in the nineteenth century was still firmly in place, but a fairly closed political class tended to serve in government. By the outbreak of World War I, most adult males had the right to vote, but many citizens felt far removed from any decision-making power. Within the institutional political world, politicians often gathered around prominent individuals but were fragmented ideologically, and government thus usually was formed of fairly broad coalitions. The reigning monarch, Victor Emmanuele III (r. 1900–1946), was seen as weak, wavering, and inclined to follow the path of least resistance.

By the 1890s, radical and reformist political tendencies had coalesced around Marxist ideas, and the Italian Socialist party (PSI) emerged in 1892 as the first centralized, disciplined, and modern political party in Italy. In the ensuing years, party unity would be disrupted by various issues; the most important were whether and how the party should participate in government, whether revolutionary or evolutionary processes could best reach socialist goals, and whether the party should support Italian entry into World War I. By 1919, the PSI was the largest party in government, with 156 out of the 508 seats in the legislative body, the Chamber.

Other reformist impulses came from Catholic clergy, who hoped to create a nonconfessional party based on Christian ideals. In 1918, the pope rescinded the ban on Italian Catholic participation in national elections, with the result that an Italian Popular party (PPI) was formed in 1919 and elected 100 deputies to the Chamber.

While the socialists and the *popolari* did not cooperate, they did represent increasing concerns for the welfare of the lower classes in Italy and would begin to challenge the political status quo. They were often joined by a small but dynamic Republican party (whose origins harkened back to the days of Mazzini) and by numerous reform groups outside parliament, like the feminist organizations demanding votes and parity for women.

The impact of World War I on Italy matched that in other European nations. Combat deaths numbered 571,000 and another 452,000 individuals were disabled. Spectacular inflation, a rising cost of living, a fall in real wages, and dislocation in the industrial sector that produced high unemployment increased the pressures on a society already suffering from economic hardships. Italian claims to territories in the Adriatic were not granted in the Paris peace accords, which helped to produce resentment toward the war and a view of the treaties as a "mutilated victory." Facing these problems was a government that was both unresponsive and often unable to deal with the crises. Increasing numbers of people—from nationalist thinkers and business leaders to supporters of a Bolshevik-style revolution—began to question whether the existing parliamentary government could provide the leadership to meet the needs of the people and the nation.

Benito Mussolini emerged in the stormy waters of war and postwar Italy. He was charismatic, charming when he wished to be, ideologically "creative" and eclectic, and above all a believer in struggle and action. He saw

*Chapter 10
Fascism Between
the Wars:
Benito Mussolini
(1883–1945)
and Margherita
Grassini Sarfatti
(1880–1961)*

himself as a modern warrior and helped forge a movement that took the reins of government in 1922. He led Italy for two decades, but not on a linear path and not without challenge and critique from his closest friends, colleagues, and various institutions of power in the country. Margherita Grassini Sarfatti was one of the people who knew him best. Political comrade, counselor, mythmaker, and longtime lover, Sarfatti and her life illuminate the multiple faces of Mussolini, *Il Duce*. As a woman and a Jew, she represents contradictions and diversities in the puzzle of the Italian fascist era.

▣ THE ACTORS:

BENITO MUSSOLINI AND MARGHERITA GRASSINI SARFATTI

Although Mussolini and Sarfatti's dates of birth are quite close, their family backgrounds and childhood upbringing were quite different. Even so, as they moved into the public world of politics, their paths would cross and eventually converge. Mussolini was born outside a small village in the Romagna hillsides. The nearest town of any size was about ten miles away. His father, Alessandro, was a frequently unemployed blacksmith who proclaimed himself a socialist and often read Marx's writings to his family. Perhaps his politics explain why he named his son after Benito Juarez, an important nineteenth-century Mexican revolutionary leader. Alessandro Mussolini was strongly anticlerical, in contrast to Mussolini's mother, Rosa, a devout Catholic and a schoolmistress who basically supported the family. In both the Catholic and secular schools Benito attended, he was disruptive and disobedient, with frequent suspensions for fighting.[2]

2. For biographical detail on Mussolini's life, see Ivone Kirkpatrick, *Mussolini: A Study in Power* (New York: Hawthorne Books, Inc., 1964), and Denis Mack Smith, *Mussolini: A Biography* (New York: Vintage Books, 1983).

Mussolini was not particularly well schooled and is better described as self-educated. He learned some Latin and French, and read (or claimed to have read) a wide variety of political, philosophical, and literary works. His intellectual development was not systematic, and his ideology would later be inconsistent. He was devoted to Marx's ideas but was also struck by the views of Friedrich Nietzsche (1844–1900), who attacked most social and political conventions. Mussolini found especially appealing his assaults on Christian virtues of humility and goodness and his emphasis on the superior individual whose will to act set him apart from the ordinary masses. Mussolini eventually obtained a diploma in 1901 that qualified him to teach school, and he held various teaching posts in the next decade. By then he identified with revolutionary socialism, and those views, combined with anticlericalism and continued aggressive behavior, often resulted in his dismissal.

His sporadic teaching career was mixed with travel to Switzerland, Austria, and France. In Switzerland, he encouraged Italian industrial workers to organize and agitate, and became acquainted with various socialist leaders who often gave him

other nationalists' calls for a cooperative spirit rather than excessive individualism as the means to make the nation great; and, above all, John Ruskin's (1819–1900) ideas on art and culture. Ruskin argued that art in all its forms must have a moral purpose, helping to uplift and define the human spirit. For Margherita, this meant that art was never just for "art's sake" but instead could reveal and reshape national character. She would also conclude that "government had a duty to sponsor artistic creativity and to control the values expressed through art."[5] Margherita was often drawn to ideas, behaviors, and issues that were new and certainly was not afraid of shocking her family and friends with her "modern" attitudes and actions. She rebelled against gender constraints. Later, in her professional life as an art critic, in her feminist and social politics, and in her personal life, she moved far away from traditional models of ideal feminine behavior.

Margherita was striking and intelligent, and had numerous suitors as a young woman. After a courtship that was somewhat secret because of her father's opposition, in 1898 she married Cesare Sarfatti (1866–1924), a lawyer from another Venetian Jewish family who was sixteen years older than she. They had two sons, Roberto, born in 1900, and Amedeo, born in 1902. By that time, probably because of Margherita's influence, husband and wife were committed socialists and decided to move to Milan, where their views would be more acceptable. In Milan, she began to write for both socialist and feminist publications, and for art magazines and journals. She was one of the first women in Italy to pursue successfully a career in art criticism. That career brought her into contact with a wide range of young artists and intellectuals who sought new forms of expression and new aesthetic standards. In particular, she was drawn to an artistic movement known as Futurism, founded in 1909 by poet Filippo Tomasso Marinetti (1876–1944). In their founding manifesto, the Futurists praised technology, speed, and modernity, insisted they were "anti-everything," and argued that "energy and dynamism were born out of struggle." Finally, they glorified war as "the sole hygiene of the world."[6] Margherita often worked on behalf of young artists and writers, and the Sarfatti home in Milan became an intellectual and cultural salon.

Margherita's generous dowry enabled the Sarfattis to live comfortably, and Cesare could take pro bono cases for working-class people. In 1908, her father, Amedeo, died and additional income from his estate meant that the Sarfattis could move to a larger apartment and buy a country home in the mountains near the Swiss border. The farm, named *Il Soldo* (The Penny), remained a crucial refuge and safe haven for Margherita throughout her life. In 1909, their third child, Fiammetta (Little Flame) was born.

5. Cannistraro and Sullivan, p. 32.

6. Di Scala, p. 186.

Chapter 10
Fascism Between
the Wars:
Benito Mussolini
(1883–1945)
and Margherita
Grassini Sarfatti
(1880–1961)

▪ ACT I:

SOCIALISM AND WAR

By 1910, the Sarfattis, like Mussolini, were deeply involved in the activities of the growing Italian Socialist Party. Cesare ran for national office several times, but without success. Margherita wrote articles for various socialist publications, including *Avanti!,* and also for the socialist women's newspaper, *La difesa della lavoratrici* (*The Defense of Women Workers*). In 1910, she supported Anna Kuliscioff (1854–1925), one of the most prominent women socialists in Italy, in her successful efforts to push their party to adopt universal suffrage in the party platform. Sarfatti and Kuliscioff were never close friends, but Margherita always recognized her personal power and magnetism, and learned an important lesson from her political senior. Because women did not have the vote and could not hold office, it was hard for them to exercise influence in the party. One way they could was through association with prominent political men whom they might influence or who might support them.

In addition to women's right to vote, Sarfatti also challenged Italian family law, which gave extraordinary power to fathers and husbands, and the sexual double standard, which, in her view, freed men from sexual responsibilities. While Sarfatti was engaged on these fronts, Mussolini was carving out his own place in the party. They might have seen each other at various party congresses, but they met face to face in December 1912 when she went to the offices of *Avanti!* to offer her resignation as a reporter on artistic issues, "assuming art would not be high on his list of priorities."[7] He asked her to continue to write for the paper, and they had a conversation about Nietzsche. She remembered that she knew Nietzsche's philosophy much better than Mussolini did but chose not to contradict him. Although there was a spark between them, in the early stages of their relationship she called him a "hoodlum," and he, in turn, made remarks about her being cunning and greedy, qualities he identified as Jewish.

World War I would change the personal and political lives of Mussolini and Sarfatti. When conflict began in August 1914, socialists throughout Europe debated whether they should support their nations' war efforts. Mussolini initially argued that the war was a bourgeois concern and encouraged the working classes to rebel against it. By October 1914, however, he recognized that the war had not brought worker revolution and that perhaps intervention could be justified (particularly if Italy was to join the Allies), and he reversed his position. He wrote an article in *Avanti!* advocating Italian involvement in the war. The rest of the party leadership did not back him and he resigned his editorship. Almost immediately, he began to publish another paper, *Il Popolo d'Italia* (*The People of Italy*). Apparently he received financial support from various allied powers and from several Italian industrialists. In the meantime, Margherita had traveled to the French front and was impressed by nationalist appeals to French

7. Cannistraro and Sullivan, p. 94.

women and the patriotic fervor of female volunteers. By 1915, when Italy formally declared war, she too had adopted a prowar stance and was expelled from the socialist party.

Mussolini volunteered for military service and received his orders in August 1915. He was a capable soldier and was promoted to acting corporal. He was wounded in a grenade accident and released from duty in June 1917. By then he was deeply depressed by front-line experience and critical of both the military's and the politicians' conduct of the war. Upon return to civilian life, his articles in *Il Popolo* were increasingly angry and blamed his old socialist allies, military officers, the prime minister, and parliament for Italian losses in the war. He also questioned whether the existing form of government could indeed wage a victorious war. Sarfatti's oldest son, Roberto, had volunteered for duty in 1916 and eventually joined the *Arditi* (the Daring Ones) of his regiment. They were responsible for leading offensives, fighting rear-guard actions, and carrying out reconnaissance. He was killed in an attack in January 1918, and Margherita was devastated. Some speculate that this was the period when Mussolini and Sarfatti fell in love. Because of grief and pain, their doubts about the real meaning of victory, and the sacrifices of soldiers like Margherita's son, they were drawn together. Mussolini would later use Roberto to build a myth of the dedicated young soldier, fervently patriotic and totally committed to the national cause. Margherita became Mussolini's constant companion and began to work at the newspaper. They seemed to have discovered each other, and the outlines of a cause and a plan of action for Italy.

▪ ACT II:

PATHS OF POWER AND PASSION, 1918–1925

Mussolini and Sarfatti were not the only people deeply affected by World War I. As mentioned earlier, hardship, fear, and discontent were widespread in Italy by 1918. Those who had favored the war and espoused nationalist sentiments felt the losses had not brought corresponding rewards and they resented the peace provisions. Economic crisis affected property owners and industrialists as well as workers, and by 1919 labor unrest had produced 1,663 strikes in industry and 208 strikes among agricultural workers. In 1920, this militancy continued as 1 million industrial workers and 1 million peasants went on strike. The socialist party leadership failed to provide direction for a Bolshevik-style revolution and, at the same time, gave up trying to influence the existing political system. A dissident group of young revolutionaries, led by Antonio Gramsci (1891–1937), hoped to build a revolution in factory councils and through workers' control over production and caused even more friction. At the 1921 socialist party

Chapter 10
Fascism Between
the Wars:
Benito Mussolini
(1883–1945)
and Margherita
Grassini Sarfatti
(1880–1961)

congress in Livorno, the divisions took concrete form. Gramsci and others more inclined to a Leninist model of revolution walked out and established the Communist Party of Italy. The results of these divisions were critical: many workers were left disillusioned, the middle classes were frightened by the activism of the "red years," and major economic interests demanded some sort of counteroffensive against labor and the left.

In this scenario of conflict, crisis, and instability, Benito Mussolini decided to launch his own movement because his bridges with the Socialist Party had been burned. His goals, tactics, and strategies were not entirely clear. He still believed in certain socialist principles that would benefit working-class people, and he certainly hoped to expand Italy's fortune and power (as well as his own). A will to power and a belief in the importance of dynamic leadership were also tenets he accepted. By then, out of his political and editorial work, he was developing a leadership style that would be "electric [and] explosive . . . , [as he said] there was no point in rehearsing all the arguments on an issue, because the object was to sweep readers off their feet," not to engage them in debate.[8]

On March 23, 1919, Mussolini called a meeting at a hall in Milan's Piazza San Sepolcro. Between 100 and 300 people turned out to hear him proclaim the founding of the first *Fascio di Combattimento*, or combat group. Among those in attendance were war veterans, ex-*Arditi*, dissident socialists

who had favored the war, futurists and some journalists. The program they adopted called for universal suffrage, an eight-hour workday, a minimum wage, and a graduated income tax, among other things. This program would bear very little resemblance to any of the policies implemented once Mussolini was in power. Even among the "Fascists of the first hour," many thought political programs and strategic planning were a waste of time. Instead they bragged that "the fist is the synthesis of our theory" and that they intended to seize the state and manage it in a new way.[9] Sarfatti was probably one of a handful of women at that meeting and subsequently would work to build support for the *fasci* as well as give Mussolini advice and encouragement. Their personal relationship was deepening at this point, but she tried to keep it hidden for the sake of her husband and her two remaining children. Mussolini continued to have affairs with other women, and Rachele, whom he married in 1915, was known for her jealousy, so this probably suited his needs as well.

When elections were held later in 1919, no fascists were elected to government. In the next two years, the real impetus for what would become an important Fascist movement was located in towns throughout rural Italy.[10] Agrarian Fascist groups

8. Mack Smith, pp. 39–40.

9. R. J. B. Bosworth, *The Italian Dictatorship* (London: Arnold, 1998), p. 39.

10. Alexander De Grand, *Italian Fascism: Its Origins and Development* (Lincoln, Nebraska: University of Nebraska Press, 1982), provides an excellent description of the movement and the regime. Also useful by the same author is *Fascist Italy and Nazi Germany: The "Fascist" Style of Rule* (London/New York: Routledge, 1995).

emerged in 1920. Their members were recruited from business interests and landowners who sought to break the power of the Socialist unions and peasant leagues responsible for what they saw as the disruption or erosion of their power and status in the countryside. In some cases, the leaders of these groups hoped to create their own peasant leagues and to serve as a link between the masses and the ruling political class in Italy. A good example of these provincial bosses, or *ras* (Ethiopian chiefs), as they were often called, was Italo Balbo (1896–1940), the son of schoolteachers in Ferrara, a decorated war veteran, and a member of the Republican Party. He had a university degree and had written a thesis on the economic and social thought of Mazzini, whose nationalist idealism and sense of duty appealed to him. Like Mazzini, he was concerned with selfish materialism and hoped to reconcile class interests and the "spiritual ones of the nation."[11] Balbo turned out to be especially effective at rallying the masses and leading militant squads to crush the "red terror." With Balbo's kind of leadership, violence became more systematic and organized, and financial support for the squads and leagues grew. Among competing leaders, Mussolini probably feared him the most and later referred to him as "a good looking Alpino, a great aviator, but the only one who would have been capable of killing me." The combined efforts of an urban movement,

led by Mussolini, and a vast agrarian reaction paid off because there were 834 *fasci* with 250,000 members by 1921. In the elections of May that year, Fascists gained thirty-five seats in the Chamber, and in November, after much internal debate, the *fasci* formed a unified party, the National Fascist party (PNF).

In the next year, several of Italy's political leaders began to see the Fascists as an inevitable, if temporary, solution to many of their problems. Similarly, members of the royal family and major business interests had decided that the PNF should be included in a government. Some in the party were plotting a March on Rome to seize power, while others thought they could take the reins of government through legal processes. Mussolini probably favored the second avenue, and he proved to be a skilled manipulator of parliamentary procedure, fearful political leaders, and an indecisive king. He also might have been nervous about a military exercise because he was not convinced they could win if the army and police stood against them. Sarfatti apparently pushed him to take the chance, and rumor had it that she was running out of patience with him, insisting, "Either you will die or you will march. But I am sure you will march."[12] Hundreds of black-shirted Fascists showed up in Rome on the last days of October, and the king, fearing a revolt, asked Mussolini on October 29 to form a government (Document One). Rather than a conquest of power, historian Alexander De Grand compares

11. Claudio Segre, *Italo Balbo: A Fascist Life* (Berkeley, California: University of California Press, 1987), p. 30.

12. Cannistraro and Sullivan, p. 260.

Chapter 10
Fascism Between
the Wars:
Benito Mussolini
(1883–1945)
and Margherita
Grassini Sarfatti
(1880–1961)

this victory to winning a high-stakes poker game.

Being named the leader of a coalition government was not the same as exercising total power, and the next three years were difficult for Mussolini as he sought to consolidate his regime. Some have referred to this as the "liberal" phase of Fascism because Mussolini tried to balance multiple forces and interests. Other leaders in the hierarchy of his own party now demanded a real takeover or called for a "second revolution." Some provincial *ras*, like Balbo, published their own newspapers in which they consistently issued criticisms and encouraged dissenting opinions. Another Fascist subgroup was made up of younger, urban people and professionals interested in modernity and technocratic advances. Conservative businesspeople and landowners, the army, the monarchy, and the church hoped for stability and normalization—not more violence and upheaval. Added to this mix was the opposition of Liberal Democrats, Socialists, and Communists who still had seats and a voice in government, and support among many workers.

While Mussolini was in Rome maneuvering among political land mines, Sarfatti remained in Milan and began the propaganda and press activities that would occupy her for the next decade or so. She also began to expand her cultural work from that of art criticism to active influence on the direction of artistic production and on cultural values. She had always believed in the political and moral dimensions of art, and now she had the opportunity to use art in the service of

a political movement that could change society. She had many contacts with artists and intellectuals who were not Fascists (or anti-Fascists), thus giving the "useful impression that Mussolini tolerated intellectual dissent."[13] Her primary responsibility at this point was to establish contacts with the foreign press, and she also played a major role in the publication of the semi-official voice of the Fascist movement, *Gerarchia*. Although the magazine was published under Mussolini's name, she did much of the work and actually ran it from 1925–1933. In January 1924, Cesare Sarfatti died of inoperable appendicitis. He had been silent about Margherita's relationship with Mussolini and certainly had never attempted to curb her independence. His death and family matters took a toll on her, and in May she went to Spain for a vacation.

The year 1924 was a critical one in Mussolini's political life. Would he exercise the energy and will to bring change in society, or would he continue trying to negotiate, build coalitions, and persuade his opponents? The Matteotti Crisis of 1924 clarified these issues. On May 30, Giacomo Matteotti (1885–1924), a respected young socialist deputy, gave a speech exposing and denouncing Fascist fraud and violence (Document Two). Mussolini was angered and indicated he wanted Matteotti punished. On June 10, his opponent disappeared; his body was discovered in August, and several Fascist henchmen were implicated in the murder. Accusations about Mussolini's responsibility exploded,

13. Ibid., p. 252.

and all his opponents took the opportunity to make demands or criticize his behavior and leadership. Sarfatti returned from Spain to find him "weak and confused" and increasingly isolated. In one phone conversation, she advised him "to remain calm, not to let your temper run amok. Don't get carried away by your anger." He responded, "fate has dealt its card in favor of my enemies, and if I lose the game, which is almost certain, there's not even the possibility of saving face."[14] The Matteotti affair clearly shook Mussolini. It also had major repercussions in the history of fascism

in Italy. Mussolini finally made a decision to act forcefully; to support the more extreme elements in his party who wanted to move against the opposition; and to admit that although he had had nothing to do with the murder, as leader of the state he was responsible (Document Three). The way to rectify the situation was to take full power into his own hands. In the days that followed, squads of *fascisti* shut down anti-Fascist organizations, confiscated their newspapers, and attacked and beat their leaders. The foundations for a Fascist regime were in place.

■ ACT III:

IL DUCE *IN POWER*

Beginning immediately in 1925, repressive legislation was introduced to eliminate Fascism's opponents and to control social and political life. A special tribunal for political crimes and the creation of a secret police force, the OVRA, were instituted, with the effect that members of political parties from the center to the left were imprisoned, forced underground or into exile. Antonio Gramsci was one of the targets of these policies. He was arrested in November 1926 and after his trial, he was sentenced to twenty years in prison. Health problems necessitated his transfer to medical clinics, where he eventually died in April 1937. During his imprisonment, he wrote pages of essays and observations that were

eventually collected and published as *Prison Notebooks*. Those opponents who could leave Italy often ended up in France and Switzerland, where they constituted an anti-Fascist opposition in exile.

Mussolini also came to terms with important centers of power in Italy, creating a series of semi-autonomous fiefdoms for conservative institutions like the military, the church, and major industries.[15] The years between 1925 and 1935 were times of experimentation, but they were also times of contradiction and even ambivalence because there did not seem to be a unifying principle or cohesive doctrine for the regime. Legal changes made the prime minister responsible only to the king, and constitutional

14. Ibid., p. 295.

15. Alexander De Grand describes these semi-autonomous centers as fiefdoms in *Italian Fascism*, pp. 20–21.

Chapter 10
Fascism Between
the Wars:
Benito Mussolini
(1883–1945)
and Margherita
Grassini Sarfatti
(1880–1961)

government was dismantled as Italy became a one-party state. Mussolini did assert control over his own party, but even here he was unwilling to eliminate or silence his critics completely. His tendency was to fire rather than to execute dissidents in his own ranks, especially if they were in the upper levels or part of the original *gerarchi*. Mussolini had never really had friends, and after 1925 he became more and more of a loner. This situation was balanced by his relationship with Sarfatti and other affairs he had in the 1930s.

One feature that characterized the regime after 1925 was increased intervention of the state in all aspects of life. In the rhythms of day-to-day existence, and in popular culture and expectations, the Fascists touched the lives of most Italians, regardless of their politics. Educational and cultural institutions, labor unions, and women's organizations were brought under the umbrella of the state. Health programs, maternal and infant care, and paid vacations were supposed to create a prosperous and cooperative society. Goals of technological progress, productivity, and even self-sufficiency were set as the state built roads, oversaw irrigation and land reclamation projects, and invested in major industrial and banking concerns. Ideals and expectations usually outran concrete results, however, and many people received few direct benefits from the regime.

As a result, popular response to the regime was a mixture of enthusiasm or consent, and skepticism. Efforts to shape perceptions and attitudes through imagery, myth and propaganda were one of the most consistent activities of the regime as the role of the leader and personal dictatorship became the mark of Mussolini's power. Sarfatti and others were the architects of the myth of *Il Duce,* but it was one that pleased and even convinced Mussolini himself. Sarfatti had taken a first step in the direction of mythmaking when she began to write his biography in 1924. It eventually was published in 1925 in English as *The Life of Benito Mussolini,* and a year later an Italian edition came out with the title, *Dux* (Latin for *Duce*). The book was an immediate bestseller, went through seventeen editions between 1926 and 1938, and was translated into eighteen other languages. In the book, Sarfatti used some notes and documents but mostly wrote from her own memories and perceptions. She presents Mussolini as "a complex web of ideals and contradictions, an uncommon, exceptional man."[16] The book made money and made Mussolini an international celebrity. Two years later, Sarfatti helped to negotiate and then to influence another biographical production, this time written by a former British ambassador, based on notes provided by Sarfatti and Mussolini's brother, Arnaldo (Document One). By the end of the decade, Sarfatti had arranged contracts for a series of articles that she would write under Mussolini's name and that would be distributed to U.S. newspapers by the United Press. In the 1930s, she negotiated a similar kind of contract for a series of "Mussolini" articles to be published by William

16. Cannistraro and Sullivan, p. 306.

Randolph Hearst, who was an admirer of the Duce. Hearst also agreed to publish several pieces under Sarfatti's own name. In all these activities, Sarfatti was able to shape Mussolini's public persona and the ideas he supposedly held, and to increase her own international exposure and connections with powerful journalists and public figures.

Sarfatti had not given up her interest in art and her broader conviction that culture could influence national values and goals. She was determined to unite art and politics and hoped to give definition to something that could be called Fascist art. She sponsored and inspired a new artistic movement that took the name of *Novecento* (the twentieth century). The *novecentisti* were supposed to make Italy once more a leader of European culture, and in the late 1920s and early 1930s, Sarfatti spent a great deal of time publicizing the movement and planning major exhibitions of their work. Sarfatti never had a monopoly on the world of culture under Fascism. Giuseppe Bottai (1895–1959), one of the original *gerarchi*, was always a major competitor. He was the editor of an important and intellectually respected fascist journal, *Critica Fascista*, and was responsible for reforms in education and in charge of numerous cultural programs. Mussolini actually did not like squabbling over artistic truths and insisted that, while the state would help artists, they must see themselves as servants of the state. Bottai eventually spelled out Fascism's artistic policy—art had to be straightforward, not too abstract; no one style should prevail, and above

all, it had to be useful.[17] This probably did not entirely please Sarfatti, but at least her sense of the social and political functions of art remained.

By the time Mussolini was in a position to launch his personal dictatorship, he was suffering from health problems. By early 1925, he had been diagnosed with a severe gastroduodenal ulcer that often caused him great pain and eventually forced him to follow a mostly liquid diet, sometimes consuming several quarts of milk a day. He had always had the reputation of not being particularly interested in food and usually preferred to eat alone. He also did not drink alcohol and coffee, or smoke. Much of this may have derived from his physical ailments (or lack of confidence in his manners), but his habits became the basis for legends of frugality, abstemiousness, and discipline. He was always interested in physical fitness, was an avid sports fan, and believed in action, no matter the outcome. He told young Fascists that they should "live dangerously," and the motto of the youth organizations was "Believe. Obey. Fight." Mussolini was above all "an actor, an exhibitionist who changed his role from hour to hour [and had the] marvelous facility for playing the most diverse and contradictory parts one after the other."[18] Perhaps that trait made him easier to mythologize, and it certainly would help him maneuver in a complex and potentially dangerous political world.

Looking at some individual responses to Mussolini gives an idea of

17. Mack Smith, p. 135.
18. Ibid., pp. 111–112.

Chapter 10
Fascism Between
the Wars:
Benito Mussolini
(1883–1945)
and Margherita
Grassini Sarfatti
(1880–1961)

his chameleonlike character. For example, one of his oldest friends, a socialist interventionist colleague during World War I, said in 1915 that "he has a soul of steel serving a formidable will. . . . Mussolini has a physical horror of easy options. He never lounges about, savoring and digesting a long lunch." Iste Cagossi (b. 1924) grew up under Fascism and was part of the organizations created for young girls and women. She remembered how proud she was to wear a uniform and show off the various awards pinned to her white blouse. "I imagined adventurous dreams of glory. Often because of my quick response and diabolically clever intuition I saved the beloved Duce from assassination attempts, or accidents of drowning. For every feat there was a solemn ceremony at which

another shining metal cross was pinned on my shirt." Another woman (b. 1898) from the rank and file expressed her views in later years: "Let's be honest—he [Mussolini] did some fine things—because he drained all the marshes, provided us extra bonuses at the end of the year, gave us holidays, took it upon himself to make lots of nurseries for children. . . . [Unfortunately] he always had crooks around him!"[19] Even Bottai, who later was a member of the Fascist Grand Council and voted to remove Mussolini from office, noted nostalgically, "A Chief is everything in the life of a man; beginning and end, justification and scope, starting point and finishing line. . . . I want to refind my Chief, to put him back at the center of my world, to reorder this world around him."

■ ACT IV:

GENDER AND RACIAL POLICIES

By 1926, Sarfatti and her daughter Fiammetta had moved to Rome and eventually took an apartment quite close to Mussolini's quarters. By then, most people in the political and artistic world were aware of their relationship, which certainly enhanced Sarfatti's power because people who wanted favors from him often went to her. But problems began to emerge in 1928 and 1929 that would alter their personal and collegial relationship. First, in November 1928, Italian Zionists held a conference in Milan. Mussolini had said very little publicly about Jews since the forming of the Fascist Party, but several weeks later

he wrote a short article asking whether Jews were a religion or a nation, once again raising the issue of Jewish loyalty to Italy. Shortly thereafter, Sarfatti converted to Christianity. (Both her son Amedeo and Fiammetta would do the same within the next two years.) She also quickly managed to have published several articles by Fascist Italian Jews who proclaimed their na-

---

19. The first account is from Bosworth, p. 60, as is Bottai's remark, p. 58. Cagossi's testimony is in Victoria De Grazia, *How Fascism Ruled Women* (Berkeley, California: University of California, 1992), p. 95, the authoritative source on women and the Fascist regime. The other case is cited in Luisa Passerini, *Fascism in Popular Memory: The Cultural Experience of the Turin Working Class* (Cambridge: Cambridge University Press, 1987), p. 131.

tional loyalties and rejected Zionism. In 1929, Mussolini signed the Lateran Pact with the Catholic Church. This document not only created regular relations between Catholicism and the Fascist state, it also recognized Catholicism as the official religion in Italy. All of these events made Sarfatti uneasy, but she still believed both her own history and the idealized memory of her son Roberto would protect her from any attacks.

Problems were emerging on another front by this time. Fascist ideology had generally been opposed to feminism just as it had rejected other movements based on liberal, egalitarian arguments. Women had been organized in their own Fascist organizations and had their own publications, but by 1925 they were fighting to maintain their autonomy. Fascism had always balanced between ideals of modernity and tradition, and in the early years there were multiple models for women. There were images of a "new" woman, like the new Fascist man, who embraced modernity, was capable of intellectual endeavors and work in the public sphere, and was as energetic and dynamic as the man, and there were models of a sentimental and romantic femininity and the elevation of the roles of wife and mother. By the late 1920s, a version of the latter became more pronounced. This "feminine woman" was not a radical and certainly not "mannish"; she was not passive but dynamic and obedient, with the courage and energy necessary to carry out her special mission (Document Four). Girls and women could indeed go to school, participate in sports, and perhaps

even work, but only in the spheres and activities appropriate to women. Whatever a woman did, her activity should not take energy away from her fundamental mission of wife and mother. The rhetoric of domesticity and maternity escalated with growing unemployment that resulted from the depression, and then with Italy's strident militarism and expansionism in the 1930s.

Sarfatti probably saw herself as a "new" woman, and although she was aware of Mussolini's own deprecating views of women, she felt that she was his equal if not his intellectual superior. Of course, she was also the mother of Roberto, a model of young, male heroism. But Mussolini, as the acknowledged head of state with an international reputation, and having just signed an agreement with the Catholic Church (which certainly did not approve of his relationship with Sarfatti), began to realize that it was important for him to project the image of a happy family man. In 1929, he moved Rachele and his children to Rome. Even though their residences were almost separate, he did try to spend more time with his family. As one might expect, Rachele did not like Sarfatti, but an even greater opponent was Mussolini's daughter, Edda, who had spent time with her father and his lover. Edda resented the fact that Sarfatti had influence over where she went to school and with whom she associated. In 1930, Edda married Count Galeazzo Ciano, giving her an entré to one of Italy's powerful, aristocratic families. The Cianos themselves did not like Sarfatti's connection with Mussolini and hoped for her eclipse.

Chapter 10
Fascism Between
the Wars:
Benito Mussolini
(1883–1945)
and Margherita
Grassini Sarfatti
(1880–1961)

By 1930, Sarfatti was beginning to lose her influential position because of the emerging racial and gender politics of the regime, as well as the growing numbers of her personal enemies. Clinching the breach that had begun to grow between Sarfatti and Mussolini was the fact that the passion and romance in their relationship seemed to be cooling. By 1931, her influence in cultural affairs had begun to shrink.

She stopped writing for Fascist papers, and in 1932, when she was not invited to the opening of an important demonstration of Fascist propaganda, the Exhibition of the Fascist Revolution, word spread that their relationship had ended. In 1932 Mussolini also met Clara Petacci (1908–1945), who would be his companion through the war years and who would be killed with him in April 1945.

▩ FINALE:

WAR, EXILE, AND DEATH

In the 1930s, Mussolini became more focused on his own personal prestige and power. Within Italy, he monopolized more offices of state and dismissed people who either disagreed with him or who proposed creative or different solutions to national problems (Document Five). Typical of this pattern was his choice of Achille Starace (1889–1945) as secretary of the Fascist party from 1931–1939. He was described as "unintelligent, humorless, utterly obedient, an unctuous flatterer, [so] he was someone the Duce could despise yet depend on."[20] Starace insisted on greater conformity in the party and became increasingly unpopular. At the same time, his loyalty to the leader was unquestioned, and he was shot along with Mussolini and Petacci at the close of the war.

Mussolini also became more determined to build an empire and to play the role of power broker in international relations. These efforts were complicated by Hitler's assumption of power in 1933. Initially Mussolini had

ideological differences with Nazism and disliked German claims to be the center of civilization and of an international fascist movement. Hitler visited Mussolini in Venice in 1934, and neither man was particularly impressed with the other. Mussolini hoped to position himself between France and Germany, maintain good relations with the United States and Britain, and appear as a protector for Austria, all of which would enable him to expand in Africa without international criticism. In 1935, his dreams of expansion became a reality when he went to war with Ethiopia, and eight months later announced the existence of an Italian-African empire. Meanwhile, though the relationships between Mussolini and Sarfatti were much diminished, he continued to use her in his relations with foreigners because she had excellent contacts with political leaders and the press (Documents Six and Seven). Her 1933–1934 trip to the United States was intended to smooth the way for Italian expansion. She agreed to go partially because she hoped that stronger U.S.-Italian relations would make an Italo-German alliance less likely.

20. Mack Smith, p. 175.

After 1935, German and Italian intervention in the Spanish civil war, and other aggressive moves by Hitler, brought a shift in alliances. By the time Mussolini made an unprecedented trip to Berlin in 1937, he told his son-in-law, Count Ciano, that he felt at the center of the "most formidable political and military combination that has ever existed."[21] The ties to Germany were not popular among many Italians, and the possibility of Italy developing racial policies similar to those of the Nazis disturbed many.

Sarfatti was not unique as a Jewish Fascist. Probably 10 percent of the Jewish population belonged to the party before 1938—a figure comparable to that for the total population. It was also true that by 1938, about 44 percent of Jews in Italy had non-Jewish spouses.[22] By the early 1930s, as Sarfatti discovered, there was a low-level anti-Semitism among the Fascists, and often the label of Jew was used to attack anti-Fascists as well as to question one's loyalty to the regime. By 1935, Mussolini articulated doctrines of racial superiority more clearly when he justified Italian control of Africans in Libya and Ethiopia, and his trip to Germany in 1937 may have persuaded him of the political usefulness of such ideas. In July 1938, after Hitler had made another trip to Italy with the hope of solidifying their alliance, Mussolini introduced a Charter of Race and the national parliament approved racial laws (Document Eight). The new policies were not welcomed by the population as a whole, and several

Fascist leaders spoke out strongly against them. Italo Balbo, for example, was vociferous in his opposition both in the Fascist Grand Council and in public. Many Italians felt such policies were German and disliked what they saw as Nazi influence in Italy.

By the time of Hitler's visit, Sarfatti was aware that her position, perhaps even her life, was in danger and planned to leave Italy on short notice. Mussolini continued to link Italy to Germany and plans for war proceeded, although it was clear Italy was not prepared for another conflict. Apparently Mussolini did not have Sarfatti under very strict surveillance, possibly because of her extensive foreign connections and the fact that he was afraid she might publish his letters to her. When war finally broke out in Europe in September 1939, Sarfatti was out of the country, as was her son Amedeo. They eventually went to Montevideo, Uruguay, and Sarfatti subsequently divided her time between that city and Buenos Aires. She also avoided any connection with anti-Fascism or resistance activity. Other Jews were not as fortunate. Sara Nathan's grandson, Giuseppe, lost his executive position at the Bank of Rome and his children were unable to attend school. He eventually was imprisoned and scheduled for deportation to Auschwitz, but he was saved by the arrival of the Allies in Rome.

Mussolini dreamed of being a great war leader; he was not, and leadership problems combined with ongoing economic difficulties and lack of military preparedness spelled disaster for the Italians after war was declared in 1940. Popular resistance in Italy grew,

21. Quoted in Mack Smith, p. 217.
22. Zuccotti, p. 27.

Chapter 10
Fascism Between
the Wars:
Benito Mussolini
(1883–1945)
and Margherita
Grassini Sarfatti
(1880–1961)

and so did lack of confidence in Mussolini among the Fascist *gerarchi* and military leaders. When the Allies landed in Sicily in early July 1943, a meeting of the Fascist Grand Council was called, and a majority of Mussolini's colleagues voted "no confidence" in his leadership. The king, never an independent thinker and leader, dismissed Mussolini and replaced him with Marshall Pietro Badoglio (1871–1956), former chief of staff of the armed forces, who began discussions with the English and Americans to end the war.[23] When an armistice was finally signed in September 1943, the Badoglio government fled south, and the Germans moved in to protect their southern flank. Mussolini, whom Badoglio had imprisoned, was rescued in a spectacular German commando operation and set up in a puppet government, under German protection, at Salo on Lake Garda in the north. Some of his Fascist supporters, like Starace, were with him, and a division of Italian Fascist troops did fight on the side of the Germans from 1944–1945. Nevertheless, the days of Fascism, of Mussolini, and of Hitler were numbered. In this desperate situation, violence and brutality toward civilians escalated. More and more Jews were deported, and although the survival rate of Italian Jews was one of the highest in Europe, 7,749 people perished in death camps. Sarfatti's daughter and her family went into hiding after 1943 and survived the war. Mussolini did not.

By April 1945, as most of Italy was

liberated either by partisan or Allied forces, Mussolini appeared uncertain about what to do. Those who saw him in those last days noted that "he lacked energy or will-power, appeared helpless and exhausted. . . . [He] was a broken man."[24] Partisan commanders had already issued orders for his execution as a war criminal, and he saw little advantage to falling into Allied hands. He headed for the Swiss border and on April 28, 1945, fell into the hands of a band of partisans who shot him, along with Petacci, Starace, and several others. They were then taken to Milan, where their bodies were hung by the heels in a public piazza.

Sarfatti had continued writing in exile, and one of her major productions was *Mussolini As I Knew Him*. In this work, she explored her own responsibility for events in Italy and concluded that her sin was believing in Fascism and in writing *Dux*. Her latest work was thus an attempt to revise the heroic portrait of Mussolini that she had painted twenty years before. By the 1930s, she no longer admired him. She eventually returned to Italy in 1947 and again took up residence at her mountain farm. She continued to travel and to write, including her reminiscences, which begin with her life in Venice and document her encounters with important people, including Anna Kulisioff, Albert Einstein, and Franklin and Eleanor Roosevelt. She does not mention Mussolini in this account. These memoirs were published in 1955 in a book entitled *Water Under the Bridge*. Perhaps that was how she saw her

---

23. See Jane Slaughter, *Women and the Italian Resistance, 1943–45* (Denver, Colo.: Arden Press, Inc. 1997), pp. 28–32; De Grand, *Italian Fascism*, p. 126.

24. Mack Smith, p. 318.

years with Mussolini and the Fascist movement. She died at *Il Soldo,* her farmhouse, on October 30, 1961. She was buried in the town nearby, and her headstone has no epitaph. Instead, a sculpture she had obtained in 1919 is affixed to it. The name the artist had given the piece was "Victory."

■ QUESTIONS

1. Why were both Sarfatti and Mussolini initially attracted to socialism and its ideals? Why did they forsake this ideology?

2. What postwar conditions existed in Italy that helped the Fascists come to power? Which people eventually supported Fascism? What appealed to them in the movement?

3. How was Italian Fascism both revolutionary and reactionary? What were its basic tenets?

4. What were Sarfatti's and Mussolini's opinions about the role of the state in people's political, social, and cultural lives? As partners in the Fascist regime, what goals did they share? On what issues did they disagree?

5. How was Fascism's impact on men's and women's lives both the same *and* different?

6. What was the position of Jews in twentieth-century Italy? How does their situation help explain why people like Sarfatti were comfortable joining the Fascist Party? Why did the Italian Fascist state eventually adopt racial laws?

■ DOCUMENTS

DOCUMENT ONE

BENITO MUSSOLINI

My Autobiography

After several biographies about Mussolini were published in the mid-1920s, the former American ambassador to Italy, Richard Washburn Child, convinced Mussolini to write his story in his own words. This autobiography was published first in serialized form in The Saturday Evening Post *and shortly thereafter in book form.* My Autobiography *was actually ghostwritten, but it does give a vivid (though certainly one-sided) portrait of Mussolini and his regime. In this passage, Mussolini describes the March on Rome. What does he say about the way in which he took control of the government? Why didn't he declare a dictatorship? How does he describe his goals? How does he see himself and his role as Italy's leader?*

[311]

Chapter 10
Fascism Between
the Wars:
Benito Mussolini
(1883–1945)
and Margherita
Grassini Sarfatti
(1880–1961)

. . . The atmosphere was pregnant with the possibility of tragedy. I had mobilized three hundred thousand black shirts. They were waiting for my signal to move. They could be used for one purpose or another. I had in the Capital sixty thousand armed men ready for action. The March on Rome could have set tragic fires. It might have spilled much blood if it had followed the example of ancient and modern revolutions. This was for me a moment in which it was more necessary than ever to examine the field with calm serenity and with cold reason to compare the immediate and the distant results of our daring action when directed toward definite aims.

I could have proclaimed a dictatorship, I could have formed a dictatorial ministry composed solely of Fascisti on the type of the Directory that was formed in France at the time of the Convention. The Fascist revolution, however, had its unique characteristics; it had no antecedent in history. It was different from any other revolution also in its capacity to re-enter, with deliberate intent, legal, established traditions and forms. For that reason also, I knew that the mobilization should last the shortest possible time.

I did not forget that I had a parliament on my hands; a chamber of deputies of sullen mind, ready to lay traps for me, accustomed to an old tradition of ambiguity and intrigue, full of grudges, repressed only by fear; a dismayed senate from which I could obtain a disciplined respect but not an eager and productive collaboration. The Crown was looking on to see what I would do, following constitutional rules.

The Pontificate followed the events with anxiety. The other nations looked at the revolution suspiciously if not with hostility. Foreign banks were anxious for news. Exchange wavered, credit was still vacillating, waiting for the situation to be cleared. It was indispensable first of all to give the impression of stability to the régime. . . .

It was necessary to reorganize all civil life, without forgetting the basic need of a supervisory force. It was necessary to give order to political economy, to the schools, to our military strength. It was necessary to abolish double functions, to reduce bureaucracy, to improve public services. It was necessary to check the corrosion and erosion of criticism by the remnants of the old political parties. I had to fight external attacks. I had to refine and improve Fascism. I had to divide and floor the enemies. I saw the vision that I must in every respect work to improve and to give tone to all the manners and customs of Italian political life. . . .

To-day there is no change. I want to be a simple, devoted servant of the state; chief of a party, but, first, worthy head of a strong government. I abandoned without regret all the superfluous comforts of life. I made an exception only of sports which, while making my body alert and ready, succeed in creating healthy and happy intervals in my complex life of work. In these six years—with the exception of official dinners—I have never passed the threshold of an aristocrat's salon, or of a café. I have also almost entirely abandoned the theatre, which once took away from me useful hours of evening work.

I love all sports; I drive a motor car with confidence; I have done tours at great speed, amazing not only to my friends, but also to old and experienced drivers. I love the airplane; I have flown countless times. . . .

No other amusement interests me. I do not drink, I do not smoke, and I am not interested in cards or games. I pity those who lose time, money, and sometimes all of life itself in the frenzy of games.

As for the love of the table; I don't appreciate it. I do not feel it. Especially in these last years my meals are as frugal as those of a pauper. In every hour of my life, it is the spiritual element which leads me on. Money has no lure for me. The only things at which I aim are those which identify themselves with the greatest objects of life and civilization, with the highest interests, and the real and deep aspirations of my country. I am sure of my strength and my faith; for that reason I do not indulge in any concession or any compromise. I leave, without a look over my shoulder, my foes and those who cannot overtake me. I leave them with their political dreams. I leave them to their strength for oratorical and demagogic exertion. . . .

Voting was reduced to a childish game; it had already humiliated the nation for entire decades. It had created a perilous structure far below the heights of the duties of any new Italy. I faced numberless enemies. I created new ones—I had few illusions about that! The struggle, in my opinion, had to have a final character: it had to be fought as a whole over the most diverse fields of action. . . .

DOCUMENT TWO

GIACOMO MATTEOTTI

"The Legality of the Fascists' Majority, Speech of May 30, 1924"

It was not yet clear in early 1924 that Mussolini's Fascist government would become a dictatorship, but in this speech, Matteotti warns of this tendency. What are Matteotti's charges? How do the Fascists react? How is Matteotti's view of politics and the actions of the Fascists different from Mussolini's? Matteotti is subsequently assassinated, and the ensuing crisis created an opportunity for Mussolini to crack down on the opposition.

[We Socialists) maintain that the government's majority list which received a nominal vote of more than 4 million ballots. . . . (*Interruptions.*)
    (*Voices from the center:*) And even more!
    Matteotti: In fact this list did not obtain these votes freely and it is therefore

[313]

Chapter 10
Fascism Between
the Wars:
Benito Mussolini
(1883–1945)
and Margherita
Grassini Sarfatti
(1880–1961)

doubtful that it obtained the percentage necessary (*interruptions; protests*) for it to receive, even according to your law, the two thirds of the seats assigned to it. . . . We do here and now contest the validity of the election of the entire governmental majority. (*Most lively rumblings.*). . . . No voter was free in this election because everyone knew *a priori* that, even if the majority of the voters dared vote against the government, there was a force at the government's disposal that would annul any contrary results. (*Rumblings and interruptions from the right.*). . . . This intention of the government was reenforced by the existence of an armed militia. (*Most lively and prolonged applause from the right and shouts of Long live the militia.*). . . . About 60 of our 100 candidates were not able to move about freely in their constituencies. . . . In 90 per cent of the cases, and in some regions even in 100 per cent of the cases, the supervisory body at the polling places was wholly Fascist, and the representative of the minority list was not allowed to be present during the voting. Except for a few large cities and in some very few provinces, the representative of the minority list who did go to the polling places was met with the violence that had been promised. . . . We recall what occurred especially in the Milanese and Genoese provinces and in several other places where the results were not very comforting to the Fascist list. Newspapers were destroyed, headquarters were devastated, and beatings were administered. . . . In the Po Valley, in Tuscany, and in other regions cited by the President of the Council for their act of loyalty to the Fascist government and where the peasants had previously been organized under Socialist or Popularist auspices, the electors voted under Fascist party controls. . . . The poor peasants knew that any resistance was useless, and for the sake of their families' safety they had to submit to the law of the strongest, the law of the master, by voting for the candidates assigned them by the local boss of the Fascist union or the Fascist club. (*Lively rumblings; interruptions.*). . . .

It is a fact that only a small minority was able to give its vote freely. . . . For all these reasons and for others that I forgo presenting because of your noisy importunings—you know very well what these other reasons are because each one of you was at least a witness to them (*rumblings*)—for all these reasons we request that the election of the majority be annulled in toto. . . . We request that all elections compromised by violence be deferred to the Committee on Credentials. (*Applause from the extreme left; lively rumblings.*)

DOCUMENT THREE

Benito Mussolini

"Speech of October 28, 1925"

In this speech given to an audience in Milan marking the anniversary of the March on Rome, Mussolini defines his regime. What is his idea of the state? What are his intentions of exercising power? What role will Parliament play?

Mussolini Defines his Regime . . .

This is our formula: all within the state, nothing outside the state, nothing against the state. . . . What occurred in October 1922 was not a change of Ministry, it was the creation of a new political regime. I shall be explicit on this matter.

This political regime proceeds from a presupposition that is unassailable and beyond question: the monarchy and the dynasty. *(All present rise and at the shout* "Long live the King" *engage in a great manifestation.)* All the rest are institutions that were far from perfect when they arose and today are even less so than before.

Gentlemen! Italy of 1925 cannot dress in that little costume that was suitable for little Piedmont in 1848.* The day after the promulgation of the *Statuto* Cavour himself said that it was something to be reviewed, modified, and perfected.

From what evil have we been suffering? It is the evil of parliamentary supremacy. What is the remedy? Reduction of this supremacy. Great solutions can never be adopted by assemblies unless these assemblies have been adequately prepared beforehand. A battle is either won by a single general or lost by an assembly of generals. You must always keep in mind that modern life is fast and complex, that it presents continuous problems. When modern nations arose under a liberal regime, they had 10 or 15 million inhabitants. Their political classes were small, restricted, and derived from a limited number of families having a special education. Today the environment is radically changed. The people can no longer wait: they are stirred by their problems and urged on by their needs. These are the reasons why I consider the executive power as the first among all the powers of the state: the executive power is the omnipresent and the omnioperating power in the everyday life of the nation. . . .

The government considers itself the general staff of the nation at work on the civil task of peace. The government never sleeps, because it will not allow the citizenry to be lazy; it is hard, because it feels that the enemies of the state have no right of citizenship in the state (*good!*); it is inflexible, because it feels that in these days of trial only inflexible wills can go forward. . . .

---

*A reference to the *Statuto* (Constitution) of 1848. [Original editors: Clough and Saladino.]

Chapter 10
Fascism Between
the Wars:
Benito Mussolini
(1883–1945)
and Margherita
Grassini Sarfatti
(1880–1961)

DOCUMENT FOUR

THE NATIONAL FASCIST PARTY (PNF)

"The Duties of the *Fasci Femminile*"
(1929)

This document, published in 1929 by the Fascist party, provides a description of women's role in fascism and in the broader society. How would you describe the ideal Fascist woman? What are her primary responsibilities? Why might these ideals and duties appeal to many Italian women at the time?

Few people yet know the duty entrusted by the Party to fascist women, the duty of profound goodness that leads women back to old, revered family traditions, reinstilling in them strength and gentleness, and directing them to the new demands that are manifested much more each day in modern life and that require a competence and profound awareness of the society and the special conditions in which helping activities must unfold.

The problem of the new woman, whose actions are necessarily reflected in all national and social life—as a potent means of improvement or a cause of decadence—was confronted by the Party with the acute vision, and prompt solution that are particularly fascist; it was necessary to oppose masculinization of dress, the false and frivolous direction given to female education; in addition it was necessary to organize all the social and assistance work that gives people the well-being and the possibility of raising themselves morally, and, besides preserving the race from physical decadence, of strengthening and taking care of the next generation.

[To the fascist woman] is given the duty to educate the new generation to the creed of fascist ideals, and the still more complex and arduous duty of organizing social work. . . .

Thus the Program of the Fasci Femminile can be outlined under the following main points:

(1) physical strength and above all the moral health of the next generation.

(2) the reconstruction of the family, the primary base of society, on high moral grounds, developing with the institutions of Domestic Economy and Social Assistance, the creed of the home and of all the activities inherent in it. . . .

Particularly close to housewifely virtues should be caring for moral and spiritual values that in a woman can be the inspiration and the propagandist for all that is beautiful, lofty, great, the sustainer of ideas that have initiated the most noble movement [fascism] that has led Italy to be among the first Nations in the world to oppose the direction of the communists and socialists.

DOCUMENT FIVE

Benito Mussolini
"The Doctrine of Fascism"

In 1932, with the help of Giovanni Gentile, Mussolini wrote an entry for the Italian Encyclopedia *on the definition of Fascism. What are the principles of Fascism? What is the most important factor in Fascism?*

. . . Fascism reaffirms the State as the true reality of the individual. And if liberty is to be the attribute of the real man, not of that abstract puppet envisaged by individualistic Liberalism, Fascism is for liberty. And for the only liberty which can be a real thing, the liberty of the State and of the individual within the State. Therefore, for the Fascist, everything is in the State, and nothing human or spiritual exists, much less has value, outside the State. In this sense Fascism is totalitarian, and the Fascist State, the synthesis and unity of all values, interprets, develops and gives strength to the whole life of the people.

8. Outside the State there can be neither individuals nor groups (political parties, associations, syndicates, classes). Therefore Fascism is opposed to Socialism, which confines the movement of history within the class struggle and ignores the unity of classes established in one economic and moral reality in the State; and analogously it is opposed to class syndicalism. Fascism recognizes the real exigencies for which the socialist and syndicalist movement arose, but while recognizing them wishes to bring them under the control of the State and give them a purpose within the corporative system of interests reconciled within the unity of the State.

9. Individuals form classes according to the similarity of their interests, they form syndicates according to differentiated economic activities within these interests; but they form first, and above all, the State, which is not to be thought of numerically as the sum-total of individuals forming the majority of a nation. And consequently Fascism is opposed to Democracy, which equates the nation to the majority, lowering it to the level of that majority; nevertheless it is the purest form of democracy if the nation is conceived, as it should be, qualitatively and not quantitatively, as the most powerful idea (most powerful because most moral, most coherent, most true) which acts within the nation as the conscience and the will of a few, even of One, which ideally tends to become active within the conscience and the will of all—that is to say, of all those who rightly constitute a nation *by reason of* nature, history of race, and have set out upon the same line of development and spiritual formation as one conscience and one sole will. Not a race, nor a geographically determined region, but as a community historically perpetuating itself, a multitude unified by a single idea, which is the will to existence and to power: consciousness of itself, personality.

Chapter 10
Fascism Between
the Wars:
Benito Mussolini
(1883–1945)
and Margherita
Grassini Sarfatti
(1880–1961)

10. This higher personality is truly the nation in so far as it is the State. It is not the nation that generates the State, as according to the old naturalistic concept which served as the basis of the political theories of the national States of the nineteenth century. Rather the nation is created by the State, which gives to the people, conscious of its own moral unity, a will and therefore an effective existence. The right of a nation to independence derives not from a literary and ideal consciousness of its own being, still less from a more or less unconscious and inert acceptance of a *de facto* situation, but from an active consciousness, from a political will in action and ready to demonstrate its own rights: that is to say, from a state already coming into being. The State, in fact, as the universal ethical will, is the creator of right. . . .

DOCUMENT SIX

JOSEPH B. PHILLIP
"Italy's Heroine of Fascism"
(October 8, 1933)

This article was written by an American journalist and appeared in an American newspaper. It describes Sarfatti. On the basis of this article, what impression do you think readers would have of Sarfatti? How does this story compare to what you know about Sarfatti's politics, personality, and life?

Mussolini's biographer [Sarfatti] had a record of long and close association with the men and forces of the Fascist revolution, but it was a thorough training as a critic which gave her the ability to clarify those complex forces [in her biography of Mussolini]. Years before she felt the influence of Mussolini's leadership, Margherita Sarfatti had made the sacrifices and performed the labor which are the lot of the political rebel. Long before she founded the artistic movement which probably will remain as her especial contribution to Fascist Italy, she had made a reputation as a critic for the most radical and advanced journal in the country. Fascism and Italian art have profited equally from the combination of patriotism and critical perception. . . .

The career which has embraced so much variation actually started from nothing more solemn than a basket of roses. The roses made a political rebel, led to a barnstorming campaign which startled non-feminist Italy, and eventually . . . [led the way] to collaboration with Mussolini and inoculation with the Fascist doctrine.

The roses were intended as a reward, but resulted in punishment. In the days when socialism had just begun to appeal to active minds as a remedy for some of the glaringly unsatisfactory features of national life, a thoroughly conservative Venetian family took their fourteen-year-old daughter to the mountains for a quiet holiday. It was so quiet that the young lady found no companions other than two earnest professors. The outcome was her conversion to socialism. Wishing self-expression the new convert anonymously sent an article to a radical newspaper. One of the proselytizing professors, receiving a clipping, expressed his pleasure with the roses. The aftermath was a parental investigation, reprimands—and a natural strengthening of the new faith. . . .

Even after her marriage, three years later, the duties of the young mother of a growing family did not obliterate an active interest in politics. Her husband, a lawyer and also a convert to socialism, became a candidate for the Chamber of Deputies. Women on the political stump were as rare in Italy then as they would be today. Margherita Sarfatti made from five to fifteen speeches a day on behalf of her husband. . . .

[Sarfatti first saw Mussolini] when he spoke at a [Socialist] party meeting three years before the war. His personality made a tremendous impression. She was art critic for "Avanti" [the Socialist newspaper] when Mussolini became editor, and the memory of the first impression remained with her so vividly that she concluded the best way for a non-essential art critic to keep her job would be to avoid the path of the impetuous editor. Consequently it was not work which was their first introduction, but a mutual desire to see a French actress perform. Friends introduced them between acts. . . .

Years of daily association with the forces of chaos, war and finally directed revolution, with their toll of personal loss, may be the training ground for patriotism. Fascism was ambitious to reach into every corner of the national life. Signora Sarfatti had the unparalleled qualifications of a thorough assimilation of the doctrines of the new governing power and competence to estimate the position of artistic traditions and possibilities in relation to the upheaval which had taken place. . . .

Signora Sarfatti described the frustration felt by Italians: "After the generation of giants which made Italy came the generation of small men. A new note was needed in the national life, a new spiritual aristocracy." The search for new giants began long before Fascism was a power in the land. . . . However the quest was not finished, and the cultural life of Italy still felt desperately the need for orientation and direction. Even today it would take courage to say Fascism has supplied the complete answer, but at least it has made the effort. Peculiar dangers have faced it. Revolutions can suffer as much damage from misdirected enthusiasm as from downright charlatanry. . . .

The change from evening to afternoon hours, however was about the only transformation in the gatherings in the home of Signora Sarfatti when she moved from Milan to Rome. Even on days when she is not receiving, the chairs in her drawing room still are arranged in a conversational circle. Her study may be an editor's confusion of manuscripts, proof-sheets and unexpected volumes anywhere between the encyclopedia and "The Case of Henry Ford," but the salon remains ready for service as a clearing house for artists trying to find themselves in a rapidly changing land and the representatives of forces which are bringing about the change.

Chapter 10
Fascism Between
the Wars:
Benito Mussolini
(1883–1945)
and Margherita
Grassini Sarfatti
(1880–1961)

DOCUMENT SEVEN

Margherita Sarfatti

"Women of Fascism"
(November 8, 1933)

Sarfatti's articles and pieces about her often appeared in various U.S. publica-
tions. In the subheading to this article from the New York Herald Tribune, *the*
editors state that, in this article, Sarfatti is arguing that behind all the things that
Fascism is doing for women "is the realization that women hold the key in Italy's
future." According to this article, what is Fascism doing for women? What place
do women hold in Fascist Italy, according to Sarfatti? Is Sarfatti an advocate for
women's rights? Does she fit the model of the ideal Fascist woman?

. . . It is therefore perhaps useless to talk or write about *woman* when *women* exist. Why do we allude to our Fascist comrades as *men* in the plural, while WE
are alluded to as *woman* in the singular?

Among the many women of this world, Italian women are generally admired
for their high sense of womanhood. Not Italian "woman," but women, in the
plural. There are differences between us, not only as regards individual temperament, but also birthplace, climate, etc. Between a Sicilian woman and her
Piedmontese sister there is about half the latitude of central Europe. . . .

[But] there are common characteristics between us Italians which grow
stronger daily. Woman is taking her full share in the political, moral and intellectual renascence [sic] of her country, chiefly contributing to all that is highest
and most sacred: the religion of family life.

As is well-known, Fascism from a political viewpoint does not regard the citizen as an individual or a cell detached from the great bosom of the state and the
nation. Above all it regards both state and nation as a great collectivity, extending not only in space but also in time—with a mystic, almost liturgical and religious communion between the living and the dead, and between the living and
those who are yet to live—the future citizens. . . .

As a logical result of the ideas and measures adopted by the Fascist government, women inscribed in the Fascist party are encouraged to give their entire attention to the care of maternity and infancy. . . . Charity is, in fact, the order of the
day of the activities of the feminine "Fasci." It is an activity of a social order, but
which indirectly has a most efficacious, political result. The main object is to help
working women, mothers and children in all of the stages of their existence, organizing, through assistance, a campaign against the disintegrating forces of misery and corruption by reinforcing the primeval nucleus of society—the family.

The problems with which woman is faced are naturally not easy, but serious
and arduous in the extreme. Feminists may well remark: "A great deal is demanded of her—what does she get in return? Very little indeed."

To give much and receive little is the common lot of mortals, and one which unfortunately weighs more heavily on women. It is nothing new in feminine existence. But, on the other hand, the Italian woman receives the reward most dear to her heart—namely, the deep, almost religious tribute of respect of the family and of her children. . . .

Italy is the land of *Mater Matuta,* that remote Etruscan divinity carrying a child Madonna-like in its arms. Italy is the land of the Madonna and of the Child Jesus, ... The joyful mysteries and the sorrowful mysteries of the Madonna are symbols of many a mother's life. To love a man and to bear a child; to mourn for one's love or for one's children: these are the ectasies of joy and grief, the thrilling hope and the appalling dread which is at the bottom of every true woman's heart. Perhaps in this elementary sense we may speak of "woman" at large as a separate being from man bound together by the common bonds of wifehood and motherhood, however, different a woman may be from another in every other individual respect.

DOCUMENT EIGHT

DECREE OF THE ITALIAN GOVERNMENT

"Measures for the Defense of the Italian Race" (November 17, 1938)

When the Nazis came to power in 1933, Mussolini's surrogates poked fun at Nazi Germany's pretensions to racial purity. As late as 1938, the Italians maintained that their fascist state had no intentions of persecuting Jews. However by the end of that year, in order to placate its new ally, Nazi Germany, the government passed a number of anti-Semitic decrees. What rights are now denied Italian Jews? What had been their position in Italy prior to 1938?

CHAPTER I. MEASURES REGARDING MARRIAGE

Article 1. Marriage between an Italian citizen of the Aryan race and a person belonging to another race is prohibited.

A marriage contracted in violation of this prohibition is null and void. . . .

CHAPTER II. ON MEMBERS OF THE JEWISH RACE

Article 8. With respect to this law: a) a person is of the Jewish race if born of parents both of the Jewish race, even if he belongs to a religion other than Jewish; b) a person is considered to be of the Jewish race if he is born of parents one of

Chapter 10
Fascism Between
the Wars:
Benito Mussolini
(1883–1945)
and Margherita
Grassini Sarfatti
(1880–1961)

whom is of the Jewish race and the other of foreign nationality; c) a person is considered to be of the Jewish race if born of a mother of the Jewish race and of an unknown father; d) a person is considered to be of the Jewish race if, although born of parents of Italian nationality only one of whom is of the Jewish race, he belongs to the Jewish religion, or is enrolled in a Jewish community, or has in any other fashion made manifestations of Jewishness [*"ebraismo"*].

A person born of parents of Italian nationality only one of whom is of the Jewish race, and who belonged to a religion other than Jewish as of October 1, 1938, is not considered to be of the Jewish race.

Art. 9. Membership in the Jewish race must be declared and entered on the public registers.

All extracts from these registers and related certificates must make express mention of the entry regarding members of the Jewish race. . . .

Art. 10. Italian citizens of the Jewish race may not: a) render military service in time of peace or of war; b) exercise the function of guardian or custodian of minors or disabled persons not of the Jewish race; c) be proprietors or managers in any capacity of enterprises declared to be related to the defense of the country . . . and of enterprises of any nature employing a hundred or more persons; . . . d) be proprietors of lands which altogether have an appraised valuation of more than 5,000 lire; e) be proprietors of urban buildings which altogether have a tax value of 20,000 lire. . . .

Art. 11. A parent of the Jewish race may be deprived of his parental authority over his children if they belong to a religion other than the Jewish and if it is shown that he is giving them an education not corresponding to their religious principles or to national ends.

Art. 12. Members of the Jewish race may not employ Italian citizens of the Aryan race as domestics. . . .

CHAPTER

11

Intellectual Resistance:
Simone de Beauvoir (1908–1986) and
Jean-Paul Sartre (1905–1980)

■ SETTING THE STAGE

On June 22, 1940, Marshal Henri Philippe Pétain, newly appointed premier of France, surrendered to the Nazis after six weeks of resistance. The Germans then occupied two-thirds of France, while Pétain's government ruled the remainder from Vichy, a resort in southern France. With the capitulation of the French, Britain stood alone as the sole European state still at war with Nazi Germany. As one Frenchmen wrote later in the fall, "All of France, all of Europe, is in prison."[1]

Conquered Europeans faced a daunting question: How should they respond to occupation? Some answered this question with quiet acquiescence,

1. Jean Guehenno, *Journal des années noires, 1940–1944* (Paris: Gallimard, 1947), p. 59 (diary entry, November 30, 1949). Quoted in James D. Wilkinson, *The Intellectual Resistance in Europe* (Cambridge, Mass.: Harvard University Press, 1981), p. 25.

Chapter 11
Intellectual
Resistance:
Simone de
Beauvoir
(1908–1986) and
Jean-Paul Sartre
(1905–1980)

others with open cooperation and collaboration, and others with some type of defiance or resistance. Some, like the young French General Charles de Gaulle, vowed to continue the war by any means necessary. He and other Europeans fled to Britain to establish governments in exile and to keep the spirit and the legality of their former states alive. German policies toward many of the conquered people quickly led to the emergence of resistance groups because their freedoms were restricted, daily life was disrupted by the pressures of rationing, and they suffered from petty brutalities, surveillance, and overt violence. Within the occupied territories, resistance groups committed sabotage against the occupiers, gathered intelligence, spread anti-German propaganda, and engaged the Germans in combat. Many of the resistance fighters drew upon their anger, courage, and personal experiences to fight the enemy. Political ideologies such as nationalism, socialism, and/or communism also influenced an individual's choice to resist. In France, a small group of Parisian intellectuals knew that they had ignored the struggle against fascism in the 1930s and their guilt drove them to join the French Resistance. Some intellectuals, like the social historian Marc Bloch, chose to fight France's enemies with a gun, grenade, and grit. Others turned to different weapons—the intellect, the pen, and the voice—and argued the reasons why and defined the means by which to resist the enemy. They were engaged in intellectual resistance, which meant using the power of ideas, illegal and clandestine writings, and speeches and lectures to incite the French people to resist.

Resistance movements in Europe not only fought to drive the occupier out of their countries, they were often also fighting for the right to participate in the reconstruction of their societies after the war. Reconstruction meant the rebuilding of Europe's destroyed cities and built landscapes, but it also included the remaking of political institutions, addressing the social inequalities and injustices prevalent before the war, reexamining the philosophies and ideologies that had brought Europe to the brink of physical and moral destruction, and redefining the role of the individual in society. Members of the French resistance, including the playwright and philosopher Jean-Paul Sartre, claimed that it was their duty to lead the new French state on the road to renewal and reconstruction. Immediately after the war, Sartre, with Simone de Beauvoir and other friends and associates, founded the journal, *Les temps modernes (Modern Times)*. In the first issue, Sartre argued that it was the intellectual's duty, learned through resistance activity, to participate in France's moral and social reconstruction.

Jean-Paul Sartre and Simone de Beauvoir and their writings soon became the center of post–World War II French intellectual life. Their names and lives were consistently linked, not only because of their unconventional relationship but also because of their public images as free thinkers, leaders of the existentialist movement, and supporters of leftist revolutionary values and activities. Sartre and Beauvoir typified a group of French writers born between 1900 and 1915, including Albert Camus, Marguerite Duras, and

André Malraux, whose experiences of war and revolution deeply affected European philosophy and social thought between 1945 and 1970. Controversy often followed this pair. Political historians and critics debate whether they achieved anything political; historians of resistance movements question their resistance credentials; women's historians debate the depth of Beauvoir's feminism; and most historians are still trying to decipher the influence that each had on the other's writing. Beauvoir and Sartre then are the perfect pair to examine the contradictions and complexities of the intellectual, social, and political worlds of postwar Europe.

THE ACTORS:
JEAN-PAUL SARTRE AND SIMONE DE BEAUVOIR

Jean-Paul Sartre was born on June 21, 1905, in Paris. His parents, Jean-Baptiste Sartre and Anne-Marie Schweitzer, had been married the year before in Cherbourg, where Jean-Baptiste, a second lieutenant in the navy, was recovering from a fever contracted during a tour of duty in French Indochina. Jean-Baptiste never fully recovered from this fever and he died in late summer 1906, when Jean-Paul was just 16 months old. Anne-Marie and her son returned to her parents' home on the outskirts of Paris, and Jean-Paul grew up in the home of his elderly grandparents, Charles and Louise Schweitzer. In his autobiographical work devoted to his childhood, *The Words,* Sartre recalled how he grew up in a world of adults and that this world was dominated by his grandfather, whom Sartre portrayed as the most important influence in his early life. In *The Words,* Charles appears as an overbearing patriarch who refers to the bedroom where Sartre and his mother slept as the "children's" room, quarrels with and intimidates his sons, exploits his widowed daughter, and retreats to his study to escape the mundane routine of the household. Sartre's life began in this room amidst his grandfather's books. He wrote, "I began my life as I shall no doubt end it, amidst books"[2] (Document One).

Sartre was a studious child, often shunned by other children because of his small stature and social awkwardness. He could read by the age of four and was soon devouring French literary classics and writing poems. School posed a real challenge for Sartre and his family. None seemed suitable for the gifted boy and he was eleven before his grandfather finally enrolled Jean-Paul permanently in school. At the age of eleven, he met his first real friend, Paul Yves Nizan, who would remain Sartre's dear friend, intellectual counterpart, and confidant until Nizan's death at Dunkirk in 1940. During his high school years, his mother married Joseph Mancy, a civil

2. Jean-Paul Sartre, *The Words* (New York: George Braziller, 1964), p. 40.

Chapter 11
Intellectual
Resistance:
Simone de
Beauvoir
(1908–1986) and
Jean-Paul Sartre
(1905–1980)

engineer and manager of a shipyard in La Rochelle, and they moved to this provincial city. Not only did Sartre have to adjust to a new domestic arrangement where he was no longer the center of attention, but to a new high school. Here Sartre endured the taunts and insults of boys from the provincial middle class whom he considered his intellectual and social inferiors. The humiliations that he suffered at the hands of his classmates and his contempt for his bourgeois stepfather formed the basis of Sartre's lifelong antagonism toward the French middle class.[3] In addition, his loneliness, despair, and position as an outsider moved him to consider the plight of the downtrodden. Sartre's salvation came when his grandfather arranged for him to go to Paris, attend the elite Henri IV High School, and be with his friend Paul Nizan. After his graduation in June 1922, he studied for his entrance exams to the École Normale Supérieure (ENS, the Superior Normal School), which is part of the Sorbonne, and was accepted in the fall of 1924.

The École Normale Supérieure was the most selective educational institution in France. Only twenty-five students in the humanities and an equal number in the sciences were admitted each year. Once admitted, students were encouraged to pursue individual courses of study, and they were helped on occasion by tutors and lecturers. Graduation from the ENS

placed them among France's intellectual elite. At the Sorbonne, Sartre and his friend Nizan, who had also been admitted, found themselves surrounded by some of the future luminaries of postwar French society: Réné Maheu, future director of the United Nations Educational, Social, and Cultural Organization (UNESCO) from 1961 to 1974; Raymond Aron, future social critic and an intellectual rival of Sartre's; Maurice Merleau-Ponty, future existentialist and long-time colleague of Sartre and Beauvoir; Simone Weil, the distinguished Christian philosopher of the postwar period; and of course, Simone de Beauvoir.

Simone - Ernestine - Lucie - Marie Bertrand de Beauvoir was born January 9, 1908, in Paris to Georges de Beauvoir and Françoise Brasseur. The marriage of her parents was not only a love match but also an important alliance between two families. Françoise's family was a prosperous and religiously devout provincial family; her father was a Verdun banker. She was given a typical education for a girl of her background: convent school, where she learned the social graces and religious piety. This education was meant to prepare her for a good marriage.

Georges's family fell on the social scale someplace between aristocracy and the upper middle class (*haute bourgeoisie*). Georges was the youngest of three children, and his social status did not permit him to pursue the career he wanted—acting. Instead, he studied law and became a secretary to a well-established lawyer. His income included a small legacy from his parents, but it was not enough to support

3. Kate Fullbrook and Edward Fullbrook, *Simone de Beauvoir and Jean-Paul Sartre: The Remaking of a Twentieth Century Legend* (New York: Basic Books, 1994), p. 21.

the comfortable and at times extravagant upper-middle-class life to which he and his wife aspired. During World War I, her parents' fortunes fell and the family moved to a small, shabby, cold-water apartment in Paris when Beauvoir was ten. They also lost one of the most important symbols of middle-class respectability: a live-in servant.

Beauvoir wrote about her upbringing and how it influenced her to be a writer in the first volume of her autobiography, *Memoirs of a Dutiful Daughter*. She portrayed her childhood and adolescence as a journey that eventually led her to reject her family's bourgeois values and the important class designation, "dutiful daughter." She narrated how both her parents encouraged her and her younger sister, Hélène, to read and write at an early age. Beauvoir also described how her father nurtured her intellectual side and her mother, the spiritual side. Both parents agreed that it was necessary to send the girls to school and in 1913, at the age of five and a half, Beauvoir was sent to a Catholic girls' school. Beauvoir's education at this institution was inferior to Sartre's. Rote memorization, religious instruction, and outdated materials were the order of the day, and when Beauvoir graduated from this school at sixteen, she had received the equivalent of a junior high school education. This was not enough for Beauvoir; she studied for the baccalaureate, the degree necessary to enter a university, and received it in 1925.

Beauvoir's success as a student served her well. Her father made it clear to both of his daughters that he did not have the dowry necessary to arrange a good marriage and they would have to enter a profession appropriate to their class and sex, such as civil service, librarianship, or private tutoring. Simone wanted to pursue philosophy, but her mother feared this course of study would put her into contact with atheists who would corrupt her soul and stain her good character. A compromise was reached, and Simone began her studies in 1925 at two Catholic institutions of higher learning: the Institut Catholique and the Institut Sainte-Marie.

At the Institut Sainte-Marie, Beauvoir found two excellent role models: the head of the Institut Sainte-Marie and an advocate of women's education, Madame Charles Danielou, who held more degrees than any other woman in France at this time (1925), and Mademoiselle Mercier, who held an *agrégé* in philosophy, the highly competitive degree that granted the holder the right to pursue a professorial position. Beauvoir was also fascinated with an article about a pioneering woman who was single, had a doctorate in philosophy, and adopted a young niece. To Simone, the woman seemed to have "succeeded in reconciling her intellectual life with the demands of female sensibility."[4] As she recalls in her memoirs, Beauvoir had never wanted to be like her mother, and this story and the two intellectual woman at the Institut impressed upon her that she could choose a different path (Document Two).

4. Ibid., p. 48.

Chapter 11
Intellectual
Resistance:
Simone de
Beauvoir
(1908–1986) and
Jean-Paul Sartre
(1905–1980)

At the Institut Catholique, Beauvoir became enamored of Robert Garric, a young lecturer of French literature and an ardent Catholic. Garric was not only an inspiring teacher of literature, he was also a social activist. He had founded a movement known as Les équipes sociales, which dispatched teams of student teachers into working-class quarters to teach the workers about French high culture. This episode with Garric was Beauvoir's first exposure to politics of the left and she, while not directly engaged in specific political struggles until her later years, retained a leftist political orientation her entire life.

Among other influences in her early life was her best friend, Elizabeth Le Coin, or Zaza, whom Simone had met in grammar school. Zaza played the role of intellectual equal, social mentor, rebel, and promoter of her own and Simone's intellectual superiority. In this friend, Simone found someone with whom she could have a real conversation. Zaza's role diminished when Simone chose to continue her studies at the Sorbonne in 1928. Zaza's mother discouraged her daughter's further education and the friendship with Beauvoir for fear that Zaza would become "too intellectual to find a husband."[5]

▪ ACT I:

BEFORE THE WAR

At the Sorbonne, Beauvoir was now among the intellectual elite, and she proved early that she belonged by coming in second to Jean-Paul Sartre in the competitive *agrégation,* or teaching examination, in 1929. She was the youngest of her class at age twenty-one, and this was Sartre's second try: he had failed the exam the year before. Réné Maheu, one of Sartre's best friends at the ENS, introduced Beauvoir into his small circle of friends and to Sartre. Maheu, who was married, and Beauvoir were having an affair, and Sartre became intrigued by his friend's proprietorial interest in the young, beautiful, intellectual woman. Sartre and Beauvoir finally met in a study group arranged by Maheu to prepare all of them for their oral examinations. During this two-week period in 1929, Beauvoir and Sartre recognized that each of them had found their equal. Raymond Aron, a fellow student at the time, described the impact that this meeting had on his relationship with Sartre:

> I think that our relationship changed the day Sartre met Simone de Beauvoir. There was a time when he was pleased to have me as a sounding board for his ideas; then there was that meeting, which resulted in that, suddenly, I no longer interested him as an interlocutor.[6]

5. Axel Madsen, *Hearts and Minds: The Common Journey of Simone de Beauvoir and Jean-Paul Sartre* (New York: William Morrow and Company, Inc., 1977), p. 25.

6. John Gerassi, *Jean-Paul Sartre: Hated Conscience of his Century* (Chicago, Ill.: University of Chicago Press, 1989), p. 91.

Simone de Beauvoir and Jean-Paul Sartre started a conversation in that fateful study group that lasted until Sartre's death in 1980.

Much of what we know about their early years together comes from Beauvoir's memoirs, in which she wrestles with an aspect of their relationship that has been the subject of much speculation: Which one had the superior intellect? When her lover and friend Maheu did not pass his exams and left Paris, Beauvoir noted in her memoirs that Sartre said to her, "From now on I'm going to take you under my wing." In their study group, she also mentioned how "he's marvelous at training intellects."[7] Out of context, these remarks can be interpreted as a master taking on a disciple, the disciple admiring the master. In addition, the story about Beauvoir coming in second to Sartre seems to confirm Beauvoir's "second-place" status. However, the examination team for the agrégation deliberated intensely over which one of the two should be awarded first place. All agreed that she was the "true philosopher." One judge voted for her, but the other two decided that since Sartre was at the more elite institution, the ENS, and a man, he should receive first place.[8] Beauvoir's sister, Hélène, heard rumors to this effect. Whether Beauvoir knew about the rumors or not is unclear, but she spoke confidently and

clearly of her abilities in her autobiography, and there is little doubt that she turned to Sartre not as a disciple but as an equal. At the beginning of their relationship, it was Sartre who pursued Beauvoir, for both her mind and body.

After the exams, Beauvoir spent the summer with her family in the country. She had declined a teaching post in the provinces, the first step toward a university teaching position, and decided that she would return to Paris in the fall and embark on a writing career. At this point, she and Jean-Paul Sartre were not yet lovers and it was not clear that they would be. He followed her to the country, where they spent several weeks immersed in conversation, and then, after their parting, exchanged letters daily. By the end of the summer, each had returned to Paris, Sartre because he was waiting his orders for mandatory military service, and Beauvoir because she planned to move out of her family's apartment, teach part-time, and write. During the summer, they had become lovers and were on their way to a life-long and much debated intellectual, emotional, and sexual relationship. They never married but remained in a free union. Each had different lovers, each accepted the arrangement, and perhaps each contributed to the legend of their "essential love" and "contingent love affairs." Their adult lives where beginning just as storm clouds were slowly forming over Europe.

The depression; social displacement and class conflict; political struggles between the left and the right in France and out; and a climate of anxiety, fear, and despair characterize France of the 1930s. During this

7. Simone de Beauvoir, *Memoirs of a Dutiful Daughter*, trans. James Kirkup (Cleveland: World Publishing Company, 1959), p. 476.

8. Fullbrook and Fullbrook, p. 61. See also Gerassi, p. 91, and Deirdre Bair, *Simone de Beauvoir* (London: Jonathan Cape, 1990), pp. 145–146.

Chapter 11
Intellectual
Resistance:
Simone de
Beauvoir
(1908–1986) and
Jean-Paul Sartre
(1905–1980)

decade, Sartre and Beauvoir ignored the political tensions and international causes that compelled their friend, Paul Nizan, to join the French Communist party. Sartre and Beauvoir lived the lives of independent, single people, unencumbered by family responsibilities, social activism, or political commitment. Neither of them actively engaged in a political movement; they preferred the desk chair and the pen to the streets and the placard. They critiqued an increasingly stagnant and morally bankrupt French bourgeoisie rather than denounce Franco, Mussolini, or Hitler. What interested Sartre and, to some extent, Beauvoir was the nature of being and their own condition. The communist politics of their friend, Paul Nizan, did not interest either of them.

In 1931, after his army discharge, Sartre became a high school philosophy teacher. The teacher whom Beauvoir had recognized during their studies together won the admiration of his students. But Sartre was not happy in this milieu. He was living in the bourgeois world he despised, following its discipline, hierarchies, and rules; teaching its children; and involving himself with its headmasters, colleagues, and parents. In addition, his first posting was in Le Havre, an industrial port city on the Seine 150 miles to the northwest of Paris. The same year, Beauvoir took a job in a girl's high school in Marseilles. Their separation pained both of them, and Sartre proposed marriage so that they could be posted together, Beauvoir declined.

Sartre's unhappiness, loneliness, and disdain for the townspeople of Le

Havre and their bourgeois ways motivated him to begin writing. Later he told interviewers, "It was when I arrived at Le Havre with my scribbling behind me that I told myself, 'This is the moment to begin real writing.'"[9] He felt that he had simply ended up at Le Havre. His life at this point was chance; he had done little to shape or influence his fate. He described this state as "contingent" and believed that, to escape this condition, an individual had to be responsible for what he or she became. He argued that the only thing we can know with the greatest certainty is our inner self and that life was to be grasped and shaped from within. The end result of this thinking and writing and of his disdain for his bourgeois world was his first published novel, the critically acclaimed *La nausée* (*Nausea*) in 1938.

La nausée is a novel in the form of a diary. A fictional provincial scholar, Antoine Roquentin, tells what happens when one accepts contingency. Unhappy with his life, Roquentin comes face to face with what existence is all about. As the novel progresses, Roquentin perceives the hollowness of his life and the lives of his fellow townspeople. Humans, he realizes, exist with no more justification for their presence on earth than a stone or a tree. Roquentin states, "Everything is gratuitous, this garden, this city, and myself. When one realizes this, it turns one's stomach and everything begins to waver. . . ." With this realization he becomes physically sick, nauseated. To Roquentin (a thinly disguised Sartre), the world is un-

9. Madsen, p. 55.

doubtedly a nauseating, empty, and meaningless place more often than not. The only thing that has valid meaning is a sense of nausea. And if you're not one of the sick, you're much worse: you're one of the lost.

In 1938, Sartre found the acclaim that he had been seeking with the publication of *La nausée*. Beauvoir's recommendations, advice, and reading of the novel had contributed to this success. She suggested to Sartre that he take his philosophical musings and turn them into a novel. She read each page carefully and critically, sometimes commenting on how Sartre had overdone his adjectives and comparisons. In contrast to Sartre, Beauvoir's first foray into becoming a writer had not been successful. Her years in Paris after graduation, 1929–1931, were not fruitful. When she left Paris for her teaching post in Marseilles, she left her comfortable, familiar bohemian life and moved to a new setting, where she soon embarked upon a strenuous physical regimen to shake her out of her intellectual malaise.

In Marseilles, she reflected upon her time in Paris and how she had formed close relationships with Sartre and with her friend, Zaza. She concluded that these relationships had resulted in the loss of her self. She had used Sartre to "release her from the burden of supporting the weight of her own life."[10] In the unpublished works of this period, she explored the problem of the "other." This problem arose in personal relationships when caring for the other jeopardized one's self. She believed that this problem of the other had its origins in the family and continued throughout one's life. In 1938, she submitted a collection of short stories to several publishers, but it was rejected. Her stories focused on women's experience, family, relationships, and the biological dimensions of a woman's life and were of little interest to publishing houses. Nevertheless, the themes that she explored during this period came to dominate the body of her later work.

Sartre, Beauvoir, and their circle of friends spent the 1930s in a state of denial about Europe's political situation. Sartre spent 1933–1934 studying and writing in Berlin, aware of but dismissing the Nazi takeover and threat. Prior to his arrival in Berlin, he and Beauvoir traveled to Fascist Italy, taking advantage of the Italian government's reduction of railway fares so that foreign tourists could come to the "Fascist Exhibition." Later in life, both reflected on how their apathy and irresponsibility influenced their thinking and their actions when the Germans invaded France in May 1940.

10. Simone de Beauvoir, *The Prime of Life,* trans. Peter Green (Cleveland: World Publishing Company, 1962), p. 103.

Chapter 11
Intellectual
Resistance:
Simone de
Beauvoir
(1908–1986) and
Jean-Paul Sartre
(1905–1980)

■ ACT II:

RESISTANCE AND THE INTELLECTUAL

Sartre's political awakening and philosophical reorientation came as a result of his experiences as a prisoner of war. Like many Frenchmen, he had been drafted in May 1940 and when France surrendered in June, he was immediately captured and interned in a prisoner of war camp for eight months. During these months, Sartre came to know a world through experience and not observation. He was no longer a schoolboy or schoolmaster absorbed by abstractions; he participated in the mundane routine of a prisoner of war camp (Document Three). Classified as an "artist" in the camp, Sartre escaped working in the fields and was able to continue writing. When possible, he exchanged letters with Beauvoir and planned for his escape from the camp. Instead of escaping, however, he obtained a release by pretending that he was a civilian who had been rejected by the army because of his poor sight and who had been mistakenly captured by the Germans during the surrender. The ruse worked and he returned to Paris in March 1941.

Sartre found Parisians in a defeatist mood, and it pained him that Beauvoir had compromised her moral authority by signing a declaration that she was neither Jewish nor a freemason to keep her teaching post, and by buying and selling on the black market. Beauvoir found that Sartre had undergone a change. He was committed to acting against the German occupation and wanted to form a resistance group. She pointed out that

it was enough to help their friends and themselves survive. He persisted. The time in the prison camp had convinced him to abandon his solitary life and participate in collective political action. For him, resistance was the moral choice.

Sartre's attempts to create a coherent and successful resistance group were sincere but misguided. The "solitary" man had very little political savvy and understanding of clandestine activities. He gathered several former students and friends into the group, "Socialisme et liberté." Beauvoir remarked that this group was like many formed in Paris at the time, all characterized by "their tiny membership and their lack of prudence." This lack of caution ranged from a group member carrying a mimeograph machine down the street in plain view to distribution of anti-Nazi literature by bicycle. Most of the group's energy was spent discussing the political program to be adopted after the war's end. By the end of 1941, Sartre realized that his friends were running the risk of arrest and interrogation because the Nazis began to crack down on such activities, and he abandoned the cause. Groups such as Sartre's were also being eclipsed by the French Communist party's resistance activities. Prior to the German invasion of the Soviet Union in June 1941, the French Communists had watched from the sidelines. Now that the Soviets were no longer allied with the Nazis, they could mount active resistance.

To continue his resistance, Sartre turned his energies to what he did best, writing. During the war, Sartre cemented his reputation as a writer and intellectual. In 1941 and 1942, he worked on the play, *The Flies*, which was eventually performed in 1943, and the philosophical treatise, *Being and Nothingness* (1943). Through symbolism and muted references, both these works contained antiauthoritarian and resistance themes. In *Being and Nothingness,* Sartre conceived humans as beings who create their own world by rebelling against authority and by accepting personal responsibility for their actions, unaided by society, traditional morality, or religious faith. This work eventually established Sartre as one of the late twentieth century's most important philosophers. In one of the most quoted passages, on the problem of freedom and choice, he wrote: "I am engaged in the world for which I carry the entire responsibility, without being able, whatever I do, to escape this responsibility even for a moment. For I am responsible even for my desire to flee my responsibility." While this work was not widely read during the Nazi occupation of France, *Being and Nothingness* would be read by future generations as a call to individual responsibility for action.

Sartre's efforts were noticed by other Parisian intellectuals writing against the Nazi occupation and the collaboration of Vichy France. Membership in various French resistance groups was growing as the Nazi occupation grew more and more brutal. In 1942, the Germans needed more and more resources for their fight against the Soviets, and they began to strip their occupied territories of natural, physical, and human resources. In France, food and fuel became increas-

ingly scarce, and French men and women were deported to Germany as conscript laborers. The Vichy government turned a blind eye to these actions and continued to publish anti-Jewish and pro-Nazi propaganda. To counter Vichy propaganda, underground papers like *Combat, L'humanité,* and *Les lettres françaises* were published. In the fall of 1943, *Les lettres françaises*, a monthly publication, had a circulation of 12,000 but reached many more because readers passed it on. These papers tried to build morale, expose those who had taken positions or honors from the Nazis, and promote ideals necessary for the defeat of fascism. These resistance writers believed that military action was not enough to drive the fascists out of France. French citizens had to be reminded of the freedoms espoused in the "Declaration of the Rights of Man and Citizen"—freedom of expression, freedom of conscience, and the defense of human dignity.[11]

In 1943, the National Committee of Writers, a group of resistance intellectuals, invited Sartre to join their group, and he accepted. Beauvoir watched with envy as Sartre moved into this circle; she had not yet published a book and was lesser known. She would have to wait until later that year to have her first novel, *She Came to Stay*, published. The novel related, in fictionalized form, the relationship among Sartre; one of his lovers, Olga Kosakievicz; and Beauvoir in late 1930s Paris. The novel received the praise and acclaim of the occupation press and Beauvoir was now, along

11. Wilkinson, pp. 45–46.

Chapter 11
Intellectual
Resistance:
Simone de
Beauvoir
(1908–1986) and
Jean-Paul Sartre
(1905–1980)

with Sartre, a literary celebrity. The publication of *She Came to Stay* occurred simultaneously with Beauvoir's new job at the hated German-controlled Parisian national radio. She had taken this job when she lost her teaching post. Later, seeking to explain her choice, Beauvoir consistently maintained that throughout the war years her primary responsibility was to her family, and her salary at the radio station helped her family's circumstances immensely, not to mention Sartre's.

Sartre's and Beauvoir's choices in wartime Paris show a "kind of muted acceptance of the Occupation and a willingness to work in and benefit from it." Both writers, however, suffered many of the deprivations associated with wartime Paris—substandard living quarters and scarcity of food and fuel. Sartre and Beauvoir rejected military engagement and settled on writing as their form of resistance. Other intellectuals made different choices. The world-renowned social historian, Marc Bloch, joined a resistance group and was arrested and shot by the enemy, and Sartre's friend, Nizan, died at Dunkirk (Document Four). Beauvoir and Sartre focused their energies on the moral dimensions of resistance and collaboration and they, along with others, came to the conclusion that the occupation had bred a new class of moral elites who would lead France in the postwar period.

Liberation came to France in August 1944 and with it the leader of the Free French military forces, Charles de Gaulle. De Gaulle had spent the war years outside France fighting the enemy, and on his return he met a rival

for France's postwar reconstruction, the National Council of the Resistance (NCR). The NCR, with de Gaulle's aid, had been established in 1942 and was composed of various resistance groups and prewar France's principal parties and trade unions. De Gaulle had hoped that by placing one of his representatives, Jean Moulin, as president of the NCR, he could dictate the direction of the council's activities. When Moulin was arrested and killed by the Gestapo in June 1943, de Gaulle lost his source of influence.

The NCR drafted a resistance charter that mapped the transition from war to peace and reconstruction, and it assumed that it would share power with General de Gaulle until elections were held. Many within the NCR, especially the Communists, feared that de Gaulle wished to establish some type of authoritarian regime after the war, and they watched the general's every move. De Gaulle had a different role in mind for the Resistance: to enter into the "glorious history of the liberation." He stated, "[It no longer] had reason to exist as an active agency." With liberation in August 1944, de Gaulle became provisional president and remained in this post until October 1945. During this period, he sent his representatives throughout France to assume control of local and regional administration. Often, de Gaulle's officials displaced the NCR's representatives, many of whom were members of the French Communist party. As a result of this displacement, a question arose: What role then should the Resistance, its veterans, and especially its intellectuals play in postwar France?

Albert Camus, director of the underground resistance paper, *Combat*, answered for the intellectuals. He wrote in October 1944, "The men of the Resistance have thought it their duty to continue through word and action what they began in silence because they possess a clear perception of their role as teachers. . . . The Resistance does not wish to dominate; it demands only to be given a hearing."[12]

What the Resistance wanted French men and women to hear was that postwar France should be founded on the principles of freedom, democracy, and social and economic justice, that France should move from "resistance to revolution." The revolution never came. The new French state, the Fourth Republic, was more interested in continuity then revolution.

▪ ACT III:

INTELLECTUAL TRENDSETTERS

Simone de Beauvoir, Jean-Paul Sartre, and Maurice Merleau-Ponty used their credentials as resistance intellectuals to found the monthly periodical, *Les temps modernes,* in 1945. This journal provided the nonaligned left (people who were neither Socialist nor Communist party members) with a platform to comment on anything that seemed important to France's political, social, cultural, or economic reconstruction. In the first issue, Sartre argued that intellectuals had to produce literature that performed a social function, a "literature of engagement." How could this literature result in social change? was a question that was frequently asked. Sartre asserted that an author's words could only stir one's consciousness and it was up to the individual to take action. Individuals had to choose how they would respond to what they read and saw. Freedom, individual choice, engagement, and commitment were the themes that Sartre and others had

focused on before and during the war. By 1945, these themes were coming together into a philosophical system called existentialism.

Existentialism was not Sartre's term or invention. Earlier philosophers and writers like Friedrich Nietzsche (1844–1900) and Sören Kierkegaard (1813–1855) pondered the question of human existence. These two philosophers depicted humans as alone and afraid in a world they never made and that the world is devoid of any meaning. For them, there were no timeless truths (or essences), no fixed human nature, and no god. Sartre, building on these previous philosophical traditions and his experiences, believed that our natures are not given to us but that we make them. He argued that human existence is distinguished by the unique capacity of people for self-awareness and self-concern, and that human existence and what a person becomes cannot be explained by any given essential characteristics. For Sartre, "existence precedes essence"; that is, we first exist in this world and our very being or existence does not have any substance or essence until we

12. Ibid., p. 59.

Chapter 11
Intellectual
Resistance:
Simone de
Beauvoir
(1908–1986) and
Jean-Paul Sartre
(1905–1980)

choose our own ethics and values and define ourselves, outside and separate from any established system of value or meaning (Document Five).

Attempting to bring clarity to this philosophy, Sartre gave a public lecture, "Existentialism Is Humanism," in the fall of 1945. In the lecture, Sartre drew on his previous writings, his wartime experiences, and the moral teachings of the Resistance to give a moral roadmap to postwar Europeans, who were confronting an incomprehensible universe and moral uncertainty. What could humans know in this world? He argued that individuals could know nothing more than their own existence and that they were free to make choices, to shape their own lives, to make themselves. In the lecture, he argued, "Man is nothing else but what he makes of himself. Such is the first principle of existentialism." He recognized that this freedom to act and choose in an absurd, irrational universe was lonely and painful, but it was necessary duty. Humans had to create their own values and give their lives meaning, and the only way to do this was to commit to life. Only through a person's acts can one determine his or her values. In a world torn asunder by war, genocide, and madness, existentialism told individuals, in its basic message, to be true to themselves in a depersonalized and inhuman world.

Sartre and the other famous advocate of existentialism, Albert Camus, developed a philosophical system that drew on people's disillusionment with concrete systems of values, their anxiety with an increasingly depersonalized and technological world, and their despair at their insignificance and isolation. In the immediate postwar years, some French men and women gravitated toward existentialism's dark ethical message, but others rejected it because it preached a message of pessimism, gloom, and despair. By the beginning of the 1950s, France was on the road to recovery, and existentialism's message lost its potency.

In the early years after the war, Sartre became a spokesperson for his time and place; Beauvoir, on the other hand, struggled to find an audience for her writing. Like Sartre, she published prolifically. Her philosophical treatise *The Ethics of Ambiguity,* her resistance novel *The Blood of Others,* and other works did not find an audience nor the critical acclaim that Sartre's works on existentialist themes did, especially the play *No Exit* and two philosophical pieces, *Existentialism is Humanism* and *What Is Literature?* She would have to wait for the publication of *The Second Sex* in 1949 to have her own success.

Beauvoir's decision to write *The Second Sex* was complex. She wanted to write about the woman that she had become and sat down in 1946 to write about this process. Influences that came to bear on this study were existentialist thought, her earlier works that explored the construction of one's self-identity through interpersonal relationships, how social oppression worked, and the notion of the *"other."* She also credited Sartre for pointing her in the direction of a less personal essay and in the direction of a general essay on the condition of women. They had discussed how Beauvoir had not had a boy's childhood. She had not read the same books; she did not grow up with the same myths as boys did; and, as a female, she was somewhat separate from them. Beauvoir protested that being a woman had almost never counted in her success and he responded, "All the same, you weren't brought up like a boy. This is something worth looking into further."[13] In October 1946, Beauvoir started upon the research that led to one of the most important and thorough books about women in the twentieth century.

The Second Sex is a two-volume study that contends society is responsible for a woman's secondary status, that "she is not born a woman, rather one becomes a woman." At the beginning of the work, she noted with irony how a man would never consider writing about the genesis of the male position in society nor try to define what men were. She writes, "There is an absolute human type, the masculine. . . . He is the Subject, he is the Absolute—she is the Other."[14] If one accepts this view, then men are the universal and women are defined by the differences to men and as a result are "the second sex." She states, "What peculiarly signals the situation of woman is that she—a free and autonomous being like all human creatures—nevertheless finds herself living in a world where men compel her to assume the status of the other."[15] Women are compelled to do so, posits Beauvoir, because men have always defined women through myths, science, and male-determined rituals and conventions of family and social life. In subsequent autobiographical works, Beauvoir portrayed herself as having escaped such definitions because she had chosen the difficult road: self-definition and interaction and confrontation with the male Other (Sartre).[16] As a result, she had defined her own identity or essence. Her message was that individual women can liberate themselves by efforts of the mind (Document Six).

The first volume of *The Second Sex* sold 22,000 copies in its first week of publication in June 1948. The second volume appeared in November 1949. This two-volume study was a political and philosophical orphan in many ways because it fell somewhere between political and feminist movements. In 1945, French feminists had finally won their longtime struggle for a woman's right to vote, and it was not until the mid-1950s that French feminists rallied around the movement for women's reproductive rights. *The Second Sex* was a first and invited instant criticism because of envy over its popularity and its status as an instant classic. A 1200-page study blending existential theory, Marxism, anthropology, psychoanalysis, literary criticism, historical analysis, and liberal political ideology certainly could be critiqued from many different quarters. What made many critics uncomfortable was the

13. Madsen, p. 133.

14. Simone de Beauvoir, *The Second Sex,* H. M. Parshley, trans. and ed. (New York: Bantam, 1961), p. xvi. Quoted in Bonnie Smith, *Changing Lives: Women in European History Since 1700* (New York: D.C. Heath, 1989), p. 519.

15. Ibid., p. xxviii.

16. Smith, p. 519.

Chapter 11
Intellectual
Resistance:
Simone de
Beauvoir
(1908–1986) and
Jean-Paul Sartre
(1905–1980)

subject matter: women's physiology, the roots and myths of misogyny, lesbianism, and the call for women to define themselves. Beauvoir, and not her work, became the focus of attacks.

The notoriety and success of *The Second Sex* firmly established Beauvoir's reputation and also made her financially independent. She had finally moved out of Sartre's shadow, if not out of his life. Beauvoir's next book, *The Mandarians* (1954), a portrait of the French Left during the immediate postwar period, won the Prix Goncourt, France's highest literary prize. In 1956, Beauvoir began her autobiographical writings and produced four volumes of memoirs: *Memoirs of a Dutiful Daughter* (1958), *The Prime of Life* (1960), *The Force of Circumstance* (1963), and *All Said and Done* (1972).

By the beginning of the 1950s, Beauvoir and Sartre stood at the center of French intellectual life. They had earned this status not only for their philosophical and theoretical writings but their defense of the international left. Immediately after the war, both Beauvoir and Sartre considered themselves to be left-wing intellectuals who critiqued the French bourgeoisie and committed themselves to a classless society without exploitation, oppression, violence, and hunger.[17] Beauvoir disliked the French Communist party because of its refusal to reject the authoritarianism and abuses of the Stalinist regime in the Soviet Union, and she remained outside organized politics until the early 1980s.

17. Toril Moi, *Simone de Beauvoir: The Making of an Intellectual Woman* (Oxford: Blackwell, 1994), p. 188.

She resented the geopolitical division of the postwar world, where leftists like herself were forced to choose between the Soviet Union and the United States, and concentrated her political efforts on publicizing the exploitative colonialism of the West.

Unlike Beauvoir, Sartre participated in postwar political life. Immediately after the war's end, he called for a united socialist front and then, disillusioned with the fractious nature of leftist politics in France, he tried to set up a neutral, noncommunist leftist party from 1948 to 1949. In the 1950s and 1960s, he often criticized the United States, his own government, and other European governments for resisting and fighting leftist and communist liberation movements in the decolonizing world. In the early 1950s, he flirted with Soviet communism but turned away from it in 1956 when the Soviets invaded Hungary and crushed its nonviolent, anticommunist movement. He continued to view himself as a Marxist and searched for a new Marxist hero who could actually keep the promise of Marxism. He traveled to China, Yugoslavia, and Cuba to meet with their political leaders and intellectuals. By the mid-1960s, he had become a devotee of China's Chairman Mao. Beauvoir often made these trips with Sartre. Together they traveled to Africa (1950), China (1955), Cuba and Brazil (1960), the Soviet Union (1962 and 1963), Japan (1965 and 1966), and the Middle East (1967).

Wherever they traveled, separately or together, they brought the press with them. They were not simply French citizens traveling abroad but international spokespersons for leftist, humanitarian, and human rights causes. Their two most significant causes were publicizing France's brutal repression and war against Algerian rebels, who sought independence from French rule (1954–1962) and the United States' involvement in Vietnam. During the Algerian War, Sartre and de Beauvoir used their international fame and their journal, *Les temps modernes,* to publicize the torture and violation of human rights by French soldiers, police, and intelligence agents against Algerians. In 1960, Sartre met with Frantz Fanon, the Martinique-born doctor who had lived and worked in Algeria since the 1950s and was a member of the Algerian provisional revolutionary government. Fanon had witnessed firsthand the suffering and oppression of Algerians by working in their hospitals, and in 1960 had just completed the now classic study on national liberation struggles in the colonial world, *The Wretched of the Earth* (1961). Deeply influenced by Sartre's recent study, *The Critique of Dialectical Reason,* which attempted to reconcile Marxism and its theory of history with existentialism, Fanon asked Sartre to write a preface to his book. Sartre not only wrote the preface but Fanon's first chapter from *The Wretched of the Earth,* "On Violence," appeared in the June 1960 edition of *Les temps modernes*.

Beauvoir's profile in the politics of the Algerian War was raised with her June 1960 letter to the widely read French daily, *Le Monde*. In this letter, Beauvoir publicized the case of Djamila Boupacha, a young Algerian woman who had been sexually tortured by French soldiers during a military interrogation to determine whether or not she had planted a bomb. Sartre's and Beauvoir's militant support for Algerian independence resulted in a series of bomb threats against them, and one bomb exploded in Sartre's empty Parisian apartment. Finally in 1962, the left's old nemesis, the president of the French Fifth Republic, Charles de Gaulle, ended the Algerian War by granting Algeria independence.

Sartre and Beauvoir did not disappear from the political scene after the end of the Algerian War. Sartre was on the front pages again when he refused the Nobel prize for literature in 1964 on the principle that the prize had been denied to authors who were openly aligned with communism. In a statement to the Parisian daily, *Le Monde,* he stated, "It's regrettable that the prize was given to Pasternak before Sholokhov, and that the only Soviet work to be honored should be published abroad and banned at home."[18] Several years later, in 1967, Sartre and Beauvoir refused an invitation to the Congress of the Soviet Writer's Union because of the Soviets' imprisonment of two Soviet writers who had dared publish outside official channels. Beauvoir's and Sartre's critics have argued that the couple practiced a political dilettantism— looking for a cause on the left to adopt and then abandoning it when its abuses or hypocrisies were revealed. Their critics were able to continue

18. *Le Monde,* October 24, 1964. Quoted in Hayman, *Writing Against: A Biography of Sartre,* p. 373.

Chapter 11
Intellectual
Resistance:
Simone de
Beauvoir
(1908–1986) and
Jean-Paul Sartre
(1905–1980)

such criticism when they lent their fame and talents to the French students' protests of May 1968.

Through their work as editors of *Les temps modernes,* Beauvoir and Sartre had continued to comment on the condition of French society. In 1968, their journal began to report sympathetically on the plight of French university students. French universities had increased enrollment threefold since the 1950s, when only 4.5 percent of young people (123,000) attended university. By 1965, 14.5 percent of young people (651,000) were enrolled, placing tremendous pressures on antiquated classrooms and housing facilities. In addition, students complained of aloof and inaccessible professors; outdated curricula that did not address the social, cultural, intellectual, and politics issues of postwar Europe; and administrators who treated them like children. Adding to the students' discontent was their increasing awareness of the polarization of the world into two camps, Soviet communism and American capitalism, which became symbolized by the Vietnam War. Some students rejected the bipolar cold-war world and explored the ideas and writings of Mao Zedong, Fidel Castro, Che Guevara, and Ho Chi Minh.

Sartre's protests against the Vietnam War were well-known to French students. He was a member of the nongovernmental International Tribunal Against War Crimes in Vietnam. This tribunal had been organized by the English pacificist and leftist, Bertrand Russell, to judge American tactics in Vietnam. Sartre's existentialist ideas, public condemnation of

American involvement, and his public sympathy for the students' grievances made him a hero among the protestors in May 1968. During the May days, he frequently commented on student actions, addressed the students at the Sorbonne, and took over editing a Maoist paper, *La cause de peuple,* which had been banned by the government. Students revered him as one of the intellectual godfathers of the student revolts of 1968. Beauvoir's status as the godmother of a movement did not come until the early 1970s and the second wave of feminism.

In May 1968, French women had actively participated in the meetings, demonstrations, and occupations of university buildings, but their presence was overshadowed by their male comrades, who were not interested in women's subordinate place in the movement and throughout French society. Just as Sartre's works had been read by the students, many young women students embraced *The Second Sex* as their philosophical guide to liberation. Women's groups in universities, workplaces, and neighborhoods sprang up in the late 1960s. The women's movement in France did not receive much publicity until 1970, when ten women laid a wreath at France's holiest secular shrine—the Tomb of the Unknown Soldier. The ribbon enveloping the wreath was addressed to the Unknown Soldier's Wife. The evening papers referred to these women as the representatives of the Mouvement de la Libération des Femmes (MLF); (Women's Liberation Movement). A year later, this coalition of women's groups concerned about reproductive rights, employment opportunities for women, and women's political power had persuaded Beauvoir to join the campaign for reform of French abortion laws.

For the first time in her life, Beauvoir became involved in a cause that Sartre did not join. In 1971, Beauvoir and 342 other women publically signed the MLF's *Manifesto of the 343,* which announced that they had had illegal abortions. This act marked Beauvoir as a committed feminist, a label she had repeatedly rejected (Document Seven). In the 1970s, she

became president of the pro-choice pressure group, *Choisir* (Choice), and a member of the League for Women's Rights. She devoted her editorial talents to the journal, *Questions féministes,* which she founded, and her writing talents to a column on feminist issues in *Les temps modernes.* With the election of the Socialist François Mitterrand as president in 1981, she abandoned her lifelong boycott of political parties and agreed to be the honorary spokesperson for the Commission on Women and Culture.

▪ FINALE

Jean-Paul Sartre died on April 15, 1980; Simone de Beauvoir died exactly six years later on April 15, 1986. The coincidence of Beauvoir dying on the same day as Sartre only added to the mystique of their lives, both as individuals and as a couple. Their deaths in the 1980s caused leading commentators, politicians, and scholars to reflect on the significance of their lives and their relationship. Sartre's contributions to philosophy, his commitment to left-wing thought and revolutionary activity, his devotion to the idea that a book could change its reader if the author practiced "engaged literature," and his association with Simone de Beauvoir are well documented. Sartre's abilities, ideas, and philosophical credentials are not in doubt. His place in European intellectual history is firmly established.

Beauvoir's life is also well documented; in fact, she documented a great deal of it herself. Her autobiographical works reveal Sartre and their relationship; her philosophical works reveal what her examiners at the Sorbonne suspected, that she was a "true philosopher"; and her actions in later life reveal a women committed to improving the lives of women and men. Yet her place in the pantheon of European philosophers is not as secure as Sartre's. Beauvoir's life was as unconventional, committed, productive, and famous as Sartre's. However, she was measured and compared to the universal male and found to be the "other," the life that she had written about in *The Second Sex.* Writing about her life shortly after her funeral, a French conservative daily opined about Sartre's role in Beauvoir's life: "he was her teacher, her father, and her lover." Another French magazine

*Chapter 11
Intellectual
Resistance:
Simone de
Beauvoir
(1908–1986) and
Jean-Paul Sartre
(1905–1980)*

challenged Beauvoir's philosopher credentials and portrayed her life in very traditional terms: "Was Simone de Beauvoir a philosopher? No. Not essentially. Nor was she militant. What remains of her is not action or ideas: she was unaware of too much. It is her passion, for life and for a man. A woman's destiny, in the end." As a woman, she could not possibly leave a legacy of actions and ideas because this destiny was a man's, not a woman's.

What the editorial board of this magazine failed to understand was that Simone de Beauvoir developed the historical, philosophical, and analytical tools to refute such an observation and to question the notion that there is such a thing as a "woman's destiny." Beauvoir argued against the idea of an "eternal feminine" (or for that matter, an "eternal masculine")

which is immutable, eternal, and absolute. She asserted that gender, in all of its complexities, has no eternal essence or absolute but that societal institutions and norms, dominated by men, constructed gender identities. In *The Second Sex*, Beauvoir urged women to resist being swayed by these patriarchal institutions and myths and to forge their different identities through their own actions and choices in the world.[19] Beauvoir made many choices about her life and the choices she made left her life open to much criticism, scrutiny, and speculation because she existed outside traditional, bourgeois norms and values and outside contemporary feminist ideals. Sartre's and Beauvoir's lives and their relationship were too complex to be categorized. However they lived their lives, their ideas proved transcendent.

▦ QUESTIONS

1. How did Sartre and Beauvoir become intellectual leaders?

2. What factors in their earlier lives influenced their intellectual positions? When did they become politically active and why?

3. What was the impact of World War II on Sartre and Beauvoir? How did they each respond?

4. What was the significance of existentialism and Beauvoir's *The Second Sex* in postwar Europe?

5. What do the experiences Beauvoir and Sartre tell us about the connection between intellectual life and politics?

6. What are Beauvoir's contributions to modern feminism and ideas about modern identities?

19. Moi, p. 184.

▨▨▨▨▨▨▨▨▨▨▨▨ **DOCUMENT ONE** ▨▨▨▨▨▨▨▨▨▨▨▨

JEAN-PAUL SARTRE

The Words
(1964)

Jean-Paul Sartre wrote a memoir of his childhood. Like Beauvoir, he delves into his childhood to pinpoint the influences that led him to a life of reading and writing. Reading and writing are the titles of the two sections of his memoir. Who and what are his early influences? Compare and contrast his childhood with Beauvoir's.

I began my life as I shall no doubt end it: amidst books. In my grandfather's study there were books everywhere. It was forbidden to dust them, except once a year, before the beginning of the October term. Though I did not yet know how to read, I already revered those standing stones: upright or leaning over, close together like bricks on the book-shelves or spaced out nobly in lanes of menhirs. I felt that our family's prosperity depended on them. They all looked alike. I disported myself in a tiny sanctuary, surrounded by ancient, heavy-set monuments which had seen me into the world, which would see me out of it, and whose permanence guaranteed me a future as calm as the past. I would touch them secretly to honor my hands with their dust, but I did not quite know what to do with them, and I was a daily witness of ceremonies whose meaning escaped me: my grandfather—who was usually so clumsy that my grand-mother buttoned his gloves for him—handled those cultural objects with the dexterity of an officiant. . . .

Nevertheless, I had to be told about authors. My grandfather told me, tact-fully, calmly. He taught me the names of those illustrious men. I would recite the list to myself, from Hesiod to Hugo, without a mistake. They were the Saints and Prophets. Charles Schweitzer said he worshipped them. Yet they bothered him. Their obtrusive presence prevented him from attributing the works of Man directly to the Holy Ghost. He therefore felt a secret preference for the anony-mous, for the builders who had had the modesty to keep in the background of their cathedrals, for the countless authors of popular songs. He did not mind Shakespeare, whose identity was not established. Nor Homer, for the same rea-son. Nor a few others, about whom there was no certainty that they had existed. As for those who had not wished or had been unable to efface the traces of their life, he found excuses, provided they were dead. But he lumped his contempo-raries together and condemned them, with the exception of Anatole France, and of Courteline, who amused him. Charles Schweitzer proudly enjoyed the

Chapter 11
Intellectual
Resistance:
Simone de
Beauvoir
(1908–1986) and
Jean-Paul Sartre
(1905–1980)

consideration that was shown his great age, his culture, his good looks, his virtues. That Lutheran could not help thinking, very biblically, that the Eternal had blessed his House. At the table, he would sometimes collect his thoughts and conclude off-handedly: "My children, how good it is to have nothing with which to reproach each other." His fits of anger, his majesty, his pride, and his taste for the sublime covered up a timidity of mind that came from his religion, his century, and his academic environment. For that reason he felt a secret aversion for the sacred monsters of his library, out-and-out scoundrels whose books he regarded, in his heart of hearts, as incongruities. I was wrong about that: the reserve which appeared beneath a feigned enthusiasm I took for the severity of a judge; his priesthood raised him above them. In any case, as the minister of the cult would whisper to me, genius is only a loan: it must be merited by great suffering, tested by ordeals that must be accepted modestly and firmly. One ends by hearing voices and writes at their dictation. . . .

DOCUMENT TWO

SIMONE DE BEAUVOIR

Memoirs of a Dutiful Daughter
(1959)

Simone de Beauvoir wrote four volumes of memoirs. In the first, Memoirs of a Dutiful Daughter, *she describes the early influences on her intellectual development. What does Beauvoir emphasize in these passages? What does she remember and why?*

. . . Despite their conformity, my books helped to broaden my horizons; besides, I was charmed to be an apprentice to the sorcery that transmutes printed symbols into stories; and it was natural that I should want to reverse the magical process. Seated at a little table, I would transfer to paper sentences that were winding about in my head: the white sheet would be covered with violet blotches which purported to tell a story. The silence all around me in the room took on an aura of solemnity: I felt I was officiating at a solemn rite. As I did not look to literature for a reflection of reality, I never had the idea that I might write down my own experiences or even my dreams; the thing that amused me was to fit together something with words, as I had once used to build things with blocks; only books, and not life in all its crudity, could provide me with models: I imitated. My first work was entitled *The Misfortunes of Marguerite*. The heroine, from Alsace, and an orphan to boot, was crossing the Rhine with a brood of sisters and brothers in order to escape to France. I learned, to my regret, that the river didn't run where it ought to, and my novel was abandoned. . . .

[END OF SECONDARY SCHOOL]

My school life was coming to an end, and something else was going to begin: what would it be? In *Les Annales* I read a lecture which set me daydreaming; a former student at the women teachers' training college at Sèvres was recalling her experiences there: she described the gardens in which beautiful young women, athirst for knowledge, went walking by moonlight, the sound of their voices mingling with the murmur of fountains. But my mother didn't like the idea of the École Normale Supérieure at Sèvres. And when I came to think about it, I hardly wanted to shut myself up with a lot of women away from Paris. So what should I do? I dreaded having to make an arbitrary choice. My father, who at the age of fifty had the painful prospect of an uncertain future ahead of him, wanted me, above all, to have some sort of security; he thought I should go into the civil service, which would provide me with a fixed salary and a pension on retirement. Someone recommended l'École des Charles (the School of Paleography and Librarianship). I went with my mother for an interview with a lady behind the scenes at the Sorbonne. We went along seemingly endless corridors lined with books; here and there were doors leading to offices full of filing cabinets. As a child I had always dreamed of working in this dusty anteroom of learning, and today I felt as if I were penetrating the holy of holies. The lady we went to see described to us the attractions and also the difficulties of librarianship; I was put off by the thought of having to learn Sanskrit; I wasn't interested in dry-as-dust erudition. What I should have liked was to continue my study of philosophy. I had read in an illustrated magazine an article about a woman philosopher who was called Mademoiselle Zanta: she had obtained her doctorate; she had been photographed, in a grave and thoughtful posture, sitting at her desk; she lived with a young niece whom she had adopted: she had thus succeeded in reconciling her intellectual life with the demands of feminine sensibility. How I should love to have such flattering things written one day about *me!* In those days, the women who had a degree or a doctorate in philosophy could be counted on the fingers of one hand: I wanted to be one of those pioneers. From a practical point of view, the only career that would be open to me if I had a degree in philosophy was teaching: I had nothing against that. My father did not object to this plan; but he wouldn't hear of me giving private tutoring in pupils' homes: I would have to get a post in a lycée. Why not? This solution was very much to my taste, and also set his mind at rest. My mother went in fear and trembling to acquaint my teachers with my decision; their faces went rigid with disapproval. They had given their lives to combating secular institutions and to them a state school was no better than a licensed brothel. In addition, they told my mother that the study of philosophy mortally corrupts

[345]

*Chapter 11
Intellectual
Resistance:
Simone de
Beauvoir
(1908–1986) and
Jean-Paul Sartre
(1905–1980)*

the soul: after one year at the Sorbonne, I would lose both my faith and my good character. Mama was worried. As a degree in classics held out greater possibilities—or so my father thought—and as there was a possibility that Zaza might be allowed to follow a few of the courses, I agreed to sacrifice philosophy for literature. But I was still determined to teach in a lycée. How scandalous! Eleven years of sermons, careful grooming, and systematic indoctrination, and now I was biting the hand that had fed me! It was with complete unconcern that I read in my teachers' eyes their opinion of my ingratitude, my unworthiness my treachery: I had fallen into the hands of Satan.

[ON MAN-WOMAN RELATIONSHIPS]

. . . Why did I insist that he should be superior to me? I don't for one moment think I was looking for a father image in him; I valued my independence; I would have a profession, I would write and have a life of my own; I never thought of myself as a man's female companion: we would be two comrades. Nevertheless the concept I had of our relationship was influenced indirectly by the feelings I had had for my father. My education, my culture, and the present state of society all conspired to convince me that women belong to an inferior caste; Zaza was doubtful about this because she much preferred her mother to Monsieur Mabille; but in my own case my father's prestige had strengthened that opinion: my whole existence was in part founded upon it. If in the absolute sense a man, who was a member of the privileged species and already had a considerable lead ahead of me, did not count more than I did, I was forced to the conclusion that in a relative sense he counted less: in order to be able to acknowledge him as my equal, he would have to prove himself my superior in every way.

On the other hand, I would think of myself, as it were, from within, as someone who was in the process of being created, and my ambition was to progress to the ultimate of perfection; I saw the chosen one from outside, like a complete person; in order that he might always be at my own lofty level, I would provide him from the start with perfections that for me were still unrealized hopes; from the very start he would be the model of all I wished to become: he would, therefore, be superior to me. Yet I was careful not to set too great a distance between us. I could not have accepted a man whose thoughts and work were an enigma to me; love would be a justification, not a limitation. The picture I conjured up in my mind was of a steep climb in which my partner, a little more agile and stronger than myself, would help me up from one stage to the next. I was grasping rather than generous; if *I* had had to drag someone along behind me, I should have been consumed with impatience. In that case, celibacy was preferable to marriage. A life in common would have to favor and not stand in the way of my fundamental aim, which was to conquer the world. The man destined to be mine would be neither inferior nor different, nor outrageously superior; someone who would guarantee my existence without taking away my powers of self-determination.

DOCUMENT THREE

JEAN-PAUL SARTRE

"As a Prisoner of War"

*Sartre was captured on June 21, 1940, in the province of Lorraine. He would
spend the next eight months in German prisoner of war camps. Sartre claimed
that the camps converted him to activism because he realized that his individual
and isolated actions were felt and borne by a large group whose fortunes he shared.
Some have criticized Sartre because he had time to write and in fact "profited"
from his time in camp. In this letter to Beauvoir, whom he addressed as Beaver, her
college nickname, he describes his life in the camps. What are the experiences
Sartre shared with others? What is his attitude toward his work?*

[Written Between October 26, 1940, and December 1940]

My darling Beaver, herewith some brief scrawls, since I mustn't encumber the
mails with my prose, and I also have to write to T., who has received nothing at
all from me, and to my mother. So kindly cut along the lines and give to each her
due. How I love you, my sweet. I want you to know that all your letters are
coming through without delay. But you really mustn't be so submissive. Write
a little note every day, it's not against the law. My dear little Beaver, my love, it
gives me so much pleasure to get your little letters. They're so minuscule, I have
to construct a whole story out of a single word; it's like reading a French history
book. But the concentrated stories seem poetic and mysterious. As when you
say, "Bianca is marrying a young American." It made me laugh till I cried. Aside
from that, our little group appears so unchanged, it's amazing. And you, my
sweet, how wise you seem, how much you love me. You will have to be patient.
In one letter you tell me I'll be set free in a month. I don't believe that at all, reason tells me how slowly these things move; think of a dab of tar stuck to you
ever so slightly, the way it clings from inertia more than anything else and just
won't let go, though eventually it will. I so yearn to see you, to take a walk with
your arm in mine. But, my poor dear Beaver, you'll be very disappointed: I've
come up with no new theories. Only tons of stories. Those I can promise you. At
first, I fell in with an odd group: the camp's aristocrats, in the infirmary. There's
also the powerful plutocracy of the kitchens, and the politicians or barracks
bosses. I was ejected from the infirmary through intrigues and—aiming to
avoid fieldwork, for which, till further notice, I have no great gift—found myself in the unoffending milieu of *artistes*, reminiscent of the cricket* and Racine,

*Referring to the fable of Jean de La Fontaine about the improvident cricket, who sang all summer
while the ant was laying in winter supplies.

*Chapter 11
Intellectual
Resistance:
Simone de
Beauvoir
(1908–1986) and
Jean-Paul Sartre
(1905–1980)*

too, under Louis XIV.† Lots of bowing and scraping, right-minded citizens. Actually they're very appealing. The most appealing I've seen since the war began. They have a regular little theater where they put on shows for the fifteen hundred prisoners in the camp, twice a month on Sundays. And for this service they get paid, can sleep late in the morning, and needn't do a bloody thing the rest of the day. I live with them in a large room crowded with guitars, banjos, flutes, and trumpets hung on the walls, with a piano that some Belgians play throughout the day. The Belgians play swing in the same style as the pianists at the College Inn— this will provide the pretext for a little heartfelt note to T. I write plays for them, which are never presented, and I'm paid too. Aside from that, my usual company is priests. Particularly a young vicar and a Jesuit novice, who actually hate one another and come to blows about Marian theology and have me settle their disputes. Which I do. Yesterday as it turned out, I ruled against Pope Pius IX on the Immaculate Conception. They can't decide between Pius IX and me. And I want you to know that I'm writing my first serious play, and putting all of me into it (writing, directing, and acting), and it's about *the Nativity.* Have no fear, my sweet, I won't end up like Ghéon,‡ not having begun like him. But take it from me, I really do have talent as a playwright. I wrote a scene of the angel announcing Christ's birth to the shepherds that absolutely took everyone's breath away. Tell that to Dullin, and that some had tears in their eyes. I recall what he was like when he directed, and I draw my inspiration from him, but remain much more polite, given that I'm not paying my actors. It will be given on December 24th, with masks, there'll be 60 characters, and it's called *Bariona,* or the Son of Thunder.§ Last Sunday I also acted onstage, with a mask, a comic role in a farce. I get lots of fun out of it all, thanks to loads of other farces funnier still. After this, I will write plays. My love, I'm not bored, I'm very cheerful, I'm waiting patiently, resolved, if the heavens don't help me, to help myself. I do three-quarters of an hour of gymnastics every day with boxers and wrestlers. In addition, since last week I have been charged with organizing a sort of people's university here, and that interests me too. Incidentally, I have lice but, like all natural phenomena, lice have been a disappointment. They don't bite, you just feel them crawling, and they are notable only for being remarkably prolific. My old pipe has arrived. Thank you, that moved me to tears, my sweet, charm of my life. I haven't ceased being bound to you. My love, we prisoners are a little like old men, mulling over old stories, and you're in all of them. How happy you and I have been, and we will be again (but I don't want anything like Tennyson's life ‖). Kisses to you for your little face and little cheeks. I love you.

†Jean-Baptiste Racine (1639–99), retiring from the theater in 1677 and renouncing its promiscuous ways, became a paragon of idle respectability at the court of the Louis XIV.

‡Henri Ghéon, pseudonym of Henri Vauglon (1875–1944), dramatist and poet who converted to Catholicism.

§Published in Paris in a limited edition in 1962; again in *Les Écrits de Sartre,* in 1970; and in English in *Selected Prose: The Writings of Jean-Paul Sartre,* trans. Richard McCleary, Evanston, Ill., 1974.

‖In her letter of October 29 Beauvoir had wished him such a life—absolutely calm and uneventful—by her side (*Letters to Sartre,* p. 345.)

DOCUMENT FOUR

MARC BLOCH

A Strange Defeat
(1940)

Marc Bloch was one of France's most respected and famous social historians when he went off to war for the second time in his life. He had fought in World War I and at the age of fifty-five, he decided that he would fight once again for France. Witnessing the rapid defeat of the French army in the spring of 1940, Bloch wrote this book "in a white heat of rage" and he blames the "strange defeat" on France's military leaders, its citizens, and its intellectuals. Bloch believed that it was his duty to join the Resistance, which he did during the war. In 1944, he was captured by the German Gestapo, tortured, and then executed for his activities.

At the beginning of this statement, he professes his love of and loyalty to France. Is Bloch French? According to Bloch, what are the responsibilities of the French under German occupation? In the last passage, who is to blame for France's defeat? Why? Would Bloch include Beauvoir and Sartre in this indictment? Why or why not?

["I WAS BORN IN FRANCE"]

. . . By birth I am a Jew, though not by religion, for I have never professed any creed, whether Hebrew or Christian. I feel neither pride nor shame in my origins. I am, I hope, a sufficiently good historian to know that racial qualities are a myth, and that the whole notion of Race is an absurdity which becomes particularly flagrant when attempts are made to apply it, as in this particular case of the Jews, to a group of co-religionists originally brought together from every corner of the Mediterranean, Turco-Khazar, and Slav worlds. I am at pains never to stress my heredity save when I find myself in the presence of an anti-Semite. But it may be that certain persons will challenge the evidence which I propose to put on record, and attempt to discredit it on the grounds that I am an 'alien'. I need say no more in rebuttal of such a charge than that my great-grandfather was a serving soldier in 1793; that my father was one of the defenders of Strasbourg in 1870; that both my uncles chose to leave their native Alsace after its annexation by the Second Reich; that I was brought up in the traditions of patriotism which found no more fervent champions than the Jews of the Alsatian exodus, and that France, from which many would like to expel me to-day (and may, for all I know, succeed in doing so), will remain, whatever happens, the one country with which my deepest emotions are inextricably bound up. I was born in France. I have drunk of the waters of her culture. I have made her past my own. I breathe freely only in her climate, and I have done my best, with others, to defend her interests. . . .

Chapter 11
Intellectual
Resistance:
Simone de
Beauvoir
(1908–1986) and
Jean-Paul Sartre
(1905–1980)

["What, After All, *Is* a 'Civilian' in Time of War?"]

. . . Confronted by the nation's peril and by the duties that it lays on every citizen, all adults are equal, and only a curiously warped mind would claim for any of them the privilege of immunity. What, after all, *is* a 'civilian' in time of war? He is nothing more than a man whose weight of years, whose health, whose profession (if it be judged essential to the well-being of his country) prevents him from bearing arms effectively. To find himself thus kept from serving his fellows in the one way that any citizen would wish to do is a misfortune for any man. Why should it confer on him the right to escape from the common danger? In a few years from now I shall be too old for mobilization. My sons will take my place. Am I, therefore, to conclude that my life has become more precious than theirs? Far better, on the contrary, that their youth should be preserved, if necessary, at the cost of my grey hairs. Herodotus said, a long time ago, that the great impiety of war is that it forces fathers to consign their children to the tomb. Should it be a matter of complaint for us that Nature's law has once more come into its own? For the nation at large there can be no worse tragedy than having to sacrifice those very lives on which her destiny reposes. Against the strength of those young bodies we others weigh but lightly in the scale. Nor do I except the women, save only those young mothers whose survival is necessary in the interests of their children. Girls to-day laugh at the swooning habits of their grandmothers. They are right to do so, and I am certain that courage in them is no less natural than in us, nor less a duty. In the days of professional armies the soldier, whether knight or mercenary, shed his blood for his patron, and for this service the non-combatants paid in rents and wages. If he put their safety in peril they had a just ground of complaint, for the contract had been broken. To-day, when every fit man is a soldier, no one in the menaced city can escape the tedium and the risks. To share them is his bounden duty. To maintain otherwise is mere sentimentality—or cowardice.

These self-evident truths are so simple that one feels a certain shame at having to call men's attention to them. But were they generally understood in the course of those months through which we lived but recently? I find it hard to believe. Too many mayors thought it their duty to ask that their towns should not be defended; too many leaders, military as well as civilian, were only too willing to act in accordance with this fallacious conception of the public interest. Truth to tell, such timid souls were not moved solely by the wish—in itself admirable—to human lives. The fearful destruction of property that had accompanied the war of 1914–18 left bitter memories. Everybody knew that the artistic heritage of the country had been cruelly mutilated, and our national prosperity to a large extent compromised. There was a feeling that it would be better to accept any humiliation rather than undergo a second time this twin impoverishment. It was a strange form of wisdom that did not even ask whether, in fact, there could be any worse catastrophe, for our culture or for the system of our economic life, than to let ourselves be conquered by a robber society. . . .

["WE LET THINGS TAKE THEIR COURSE"]

The generation to which I belong has a bad conscience. It is true that we emerged from the last war desperately tired, and that after four years not only of fighting, but of mental laziness, we were only too anxious to get back to our proper employments and take up the tools that we had left to rust upon the benches. So behindhand were we with our work that we set ourselves to bolt it down in indigestible mouthfuls. That is our excuse. But I have long ceased to believe that it can wash us clean of guilt.

. . . Not being prophets we did not foresee the advent of the Nazis. But we did foresee that, in some form or other, though its precise nature was hidden from us, a German revival *would* come, that it would be embittered by rancorous memories to which our foolish ineptitude was daily adding, and that its explosion would be terrible. Had anyone asked us how we thought a second war would end we should, I doubt not, have answered that we hoped it would end in victory. But we should have been perfectly clear in our own minds that if the terrible storm broke again there was grave danger that the whole of European civilization might well suffer irremediable shipwreck. We did realize that in the Germany of that time there were signs, however timid, of a new spirit of goodwill, of an attitude that was frankly pacific and honestly liberal. The only thing wanting was a gesture of encouragement on the part of our political leaders. We knew all that, and yet, from laziness, from cowardice, we let things take their course. We feared the opposition of the mob, the sarcasm of our friends, the ignorant mistrust of our masters. We dared not stand up in public and be the voice crying in the wilderness. It might have been just that, but at least we should have had the consolation of knowing that, whatever the outcome of its message, it had at least spoken aloud the faith that was in us. We preferred to lock ourselves into the fear-haunted tranquillity of our studies. May the young men forgive us the blood that is red upon our hands!

All, or almost all, these things had long been whispered among intimate friends: the weakness that was slowly undermining the robust health of the nation; the intellectual lethargy of our ruling classes, and their bitter grievances; the illogical propaganda which was providing so adulterate but so heady a draught for our workers; the dominance of age, and the unrest in the Army. But how many had the courage to speak their thoughts aloud? I know well enough that we lacked the partisan spirit, and that is something of which we need not be ashamed. Those of us—and they were the exceptions—who let themselves be caught up in one or other of the political parties almost always ended by being its prisoners rather than its guides. It was not to work on electoral committees that our duty should have urged us. We had tongues and brains in our heads and pens in our hands. But we were all of us either specialists in the social sciences or workers in scientific laboratories, and maybe the very disciplines of those employments kept us, by a sort of fatalism, from embarking on individual action. . . .

Chapter 11
Intellectual
Resistance:
Simone de
Beauvoir
(1908–1986) and
Jean-Paul Sartre
(1905–1980)

DOCUMENT FIVE

Jean-Paul Sartre

Existentialism
(1947)

Jean-Paul Sartre was existentialism's main theorist. In this passage, he defines existentialism. What is existentialism and why does this philosophical system arise immediately after World War II?

... What is meant by the term *existentialism?* Most people who use the word would be rather embarrassed if they had to explain it, since, now that the word is all the rage, even the work of a musician or painter is being called existentialist. A gossip columnist in *Clartés* signs himself *The Existentialist,* so that by this time the word has been so stretched and has taken on so broad a meaning, that it no longer means anything at all. It seems that for want of an advance-guard doctrine analogous to surrealism, the kind of people who are eager for scandal and flurry turn to this philosophy which in other respects does not at all serve their purposes in this sphere.

Actually, it is the least scandalous, the most austere of doctrines. It is intended strictly for specialists and philosophers. Yet it can be defined easily. What complicates matters is that there are two kinds of existentialist. ... What they have in common is that they think that existence precedes essence, or, if you prefer, that subjectivity must be the starting point.

Just what does that mean? ...

Atheistic existentialism, which I represent, is more coherent. It states that if God does not exist, there is at least one being in whom existence precedes essence, a being who exists before he can be defined by any concept, and that this being is man, or, as Heidegger says, human reality. What is meant here by saying that existence precedes essence? It means that, first of all, man exists, turns up, appears on the scene, and, only afterwards, defines himself. If man, as the existentialist conceives him, is indefinable, it is because at first he is nothing. Only afterward will he be something, and he himself will have made what he will be. Thus, there is no human nature, since there is no God to conceive it. Not only is man what he conceives himself to be, but he is also only what he wills himself to be after this thrust toward existence.

Man is nothing else but what he makes of himself. Such is the first principle of existentialism. It is also what is called subjectivity, the name we are labeled with when charges are brought against us. But what do we mean by this, if not that man has a greater dignity than a stone or table? For we mean that man first exists, that is, that man first of all is the being who hurls himself toward a future and who is conscious of imagining himself as being in the future. Man is at the start a plan which is aware of itself, rather than a patch of moss, a piece of garbage, or a cauliflower; nothing exists prior to this plan; there is nothing in heaven; man will be what he will have planned to be. Not what he will want to be. Because by the word "will" we generally mean a conscious decision, which is subsequent to what we have already made of ourselves. I may want to belong to a political party, write a book, get married; but all that is only a manifestation of an earlier, more spontaneous choice that is called "will." But if existence really does precede essence, man is responsible for what he is. Thus, existentialism's first move is to make every man aware of what he is and to make the full responsibility of his existence rest on him. And when we say that a man is responsible for himself, we do not only mean that he is responsible for his own individuality, but that he is responsible for all men. . . .

DOCUMENT SIX

SIMONE DE BEAUVOIR

The Second Sex (1949)

Beauvoir published The Second Sex *in 1949. Her basic premise was to destroy the myth of women's inferiority to men. She traces the historical role of women from traditional societies to the present. According to Beauvoir, what is a woman? How does that definition make women subordinate in society?*

. . . If her functioning as a female is not enough to define woman, if we decline also to explain her through "the eternal feminine," and if nevertheless we admit, provisionally, that women do exist, then we must face the question what is a woman?

To state the question is, to me, to suggest, at once, a preliminary answer. The fact that I ask it is in itself significant. A man would never get the notion of writing a book on the peculiar situation of the human male.* But if I wish to define myself, I must first of all say: "I am a woman"; on this must be based all further discussion. A man never begins by presenting himself as an individual of a certain sex; it goes without saying that he is a man. The terms *masculine* and *feminine* are used symmetrically only as a matter of form, as on legal papers. In actuality the relation of the two sexes is not quite like that of two electrical poles, for man represents both the positive and the neutral, as is indicated by the common use of *man* to designate human beings in general; whereas woman repre-

*The Kinsey Report [Alfred C. Kinsey and others: *Sexual Behavior in the Human Male* (W. B. Saunders Co., 1948)] is no exception, for it is limited to describing the sexual characteristics of American men, which is quite a different matter.

Chapter 11
Intellectual
Resistance:
Simone de
Beauvoir
(1908–1986) and
Jean-Paul Sartre
(1905–1980)

sents only the negative, defined by limiting criteria, without reciprocity. In the midst of an abstract discussion it is vexing to hear a man say: "You think thus and so because you are a woman"; but I know that my only defense is to reply: "I think thus and so because it is true," thereby removing my subjective self from the argument. It would be out of the question to reply: "And you think the contrary because you are a man," for it is understood that the fact of being a man is no peculiarity. A man is in the right in being a man; it is the woman who is in the wrong. It amounts to this: just as for the ancients there was an absolute vertical with reference to which the oblique was defined, so there is an absolute human type, the masculine. Woman has ovaries, a uterus; these peculiarities imprison her in her subjectivity, circumscribe her within the limits of her own nature. It is often said that she thinks with her glands. Man superbly ignores the fact that his anatomy also includes glands, such as the testicles, and that they secrete hormones. He thinks of his body as a direct and normal connection with the world, which he believes he apprehends objectively, whereas he regards the body of woman as a hindrance, a prison, weighed down by everything peculiar to it. "The female is a female by virtue of a certain *lack* of qualities," said Aristotle; "we should regard the female nature as afflicted with a natural defectiveness." And St. Thomas for his part pronounced woman to be an "imperfect man," an "incidental" being. This is symbolized in Genesis where Eve is depicted as made from what Bossuet called "a supernumerary bone" of Adam.

Thus humanity is male and man defines woman not in herself but as relative to him; she is not regarded as an autonomous being. . . .

The reason for this is that women lack concrete means for organizing themselves into a unit which can stand to face with the correlative unit. They have no past, no history, no religion of their own; and they have no such solidarity of work and interest as that of the proletariat. They are not even promiscuously herded together in the way that creates community feeling among the American Negroes, the ghetto Jews, the workers of Saint-Denis, or the factory hands of Renault. They live dispersed among the males, attached through residence, housework, economic condition, and social standing to certain men—fathers or husbands—more firmly than they are to other women. If they belong to the bourgeoisie, they feel solidarity with men of that class, not with proletarian women; if they are white, their allegiance is to white men, not to Negro women. The proletariat can propose to massacre the ruling class, and a sufficiently fanatical Jew or Negro might dream of getting sole possession of the atomic bomb and making humanity wholly Jewish or black; but woman cannot even dream of exterminating the males. The bond that unites her to her oppressors is not comparable to any other. The division of sexes is a biological fact, not an event in human history. Male and female stand opposed within a primordial *Mitsein*, and woman has not broken it. The couple is a fundamental unity with its two halves riveted together, and the cleavage of society along the line of sex is impossible. Here is to be found the basic trait of woman: she is the Other in a totality of which the two components are necessary to one another. . . .

DOCUMENT SEVEN

SIMONE DE BEAUVOIR

On Being a Feminist

Later in her life, Beauvoir rethought her position on feminism. The following excerpts are from two different sources. The first is from the last volume of her autobiographical works, All Said and Done. *The second excerpt is from an interview with Alice Schwarzer and published in* Le nouvel observateur. *How did Beauvoir become a feminist?*

ALL SAID AND DONE

. . . The fact is that the status of women has been scarcely changed at all in France during the last ten years. They have been granted an easing of matrimonial legislation. Birth-control has been authorized: but as I have said, scarcely seven per cent of Frenchwomen of child-bearing age make use of it. Abortion is still strictly forbidden. Household tasks are still done exclusively by women. Their claims as workers are stifled. . . .

In their tactics and their forms of action the feminists of today have been influenced, in the USA, by the hippies, the yippies and above all by the Black Panthers, and in France by the events of May 1968: they aim at a kind of revolution other than that of the traditional left, and they are inventing new methods of bringing it about.

I have read the American feminist literature; I have corresponded with their militants; I have met some of them, and learnt with great pleasure that the new American feminism quotes *The Second Sex* as its authority: in 1969 the paperback edition sold seven hundred and fifty thousand copies. No feminist questions the statement that women are manufactured by civilization, not biologically determined. Where they do differ from my book is on the practical plane: they refuse to trust in the future; they want to tackle their problems, to take their fate in hand, here and now. This is the point upon which I have changed: I think they are right.

The Second Sex may be useful to some militants; but it is not a militant book. When I wrote it I thought the state of women and society would evolve together. I wrote, 'By and large, we have won the game. There are many problems that we look upon as more important than those which affect us specifically.' And speaking of women's condition in *Force of Circumstance* I said, 'It depends on the future of labour in the world; it will change only at the price of an upheaval in production. That is why I have avoided confining myself to feminism.' Somewhat later, in an interview with Jeanson,* I said that the most accurate way of interpreting

---

*Francis Jeanson, *Simone de Beauvoir ou L'Entreprise de vivre.*

Chapter 11
Intellectual
Resistance:
Simone de
Beauvoir
(1908–1986) and
Jean-Paul Sartre
(1905–1980)

my opinions would be to stress the feminist component. But I remained on a theoretical plane: I totally denied the existence of a femine [sic] nature. Now when I speak of feminism I mean the fact of struggling for specifically feminine claims at the same time as carrying on the class-war; and I declare myself a feminist. No, we have not won the game; in fact we have won almost nothing since 1950.

ALICE SCHWARZER, *AFTER THE SECOND SEX:* *CONVERSATIONS WITH SIMONE DE BEAUVOIR*

ALICE SCHWARZER: Your analysis of the situation of women is still the most radical we have, in that no author has gone further than you have since your book *The Second Sex* came out in 1949, and you have been the main inspiration for the new women's movements. But it is only now, twenty-three years later, that you have involved yourself actively in women's actual, collective struggle. You joined the International Women's March last November. Why?

SIMONE DE BEAUVOIR: Because I realised that [the] situation of women in France has not really changed in the last twenty years. There have been a few minor things in the legal sphere, such as marriage and divorce law. And the availability of contraception has increased—but it still does not go far enough, given that only seven per cent of all French women take the Pill. Women haven't made any significant progress in the world of work either. There may be a few more women working now than there were, but not very many. But in any case, women are still confined to the low-grade jobs. They are more often secretaries rather than managing directors, nurses rather than doctors. The more interesting careers are virtually barred to them, and even within individual professions their promotion prospects are very limited. This set me thinking. I thought it was necessary for women who really wanted their situation to change to take matters into their own hands. Also, the women's groups which existed in France before the MLF† was founded in 1970 were generally reformist and legalistic. I had no desire to associate myself with them. The new feminism is radical, by contrast. As in 1968, its watchword is: change your life today. Don't gamble on the future, act now, without delay.

When the women in the French women's movement got in touch with me, I wanted to join them in their struggle. They asked me if I would work with them on an abortion manifesto, making public the fact that I, and others, had had an abortion. I thought this was a valid way of drawing attention to a problem which is one of the greatest scandals in France today: the ban on abortion.

†Mouvement de Libération des Femmes.

So it was quite natural for me to take to the streets and to join the MLF militants in the march [in November 1971] and to adopt their slogans as my own. Free abortion on demand, free contraception, free motherhood! . . .

A. S.] The term 'feminism' is much misunderstood. What is your definition of it?

S. de B.] At the end of *The Second Sex* I said that I was not a feminist because I believed that the problems of women would resolve themselves automatically in the context of socialist development. By feminist, I meant fighting on specifically feminine issues independently of the class struggle. I still hold the same view today. In my definition, feminists are women—or even men too—who are fighting women's condition, in association with the class struggle, but independently of it as well, without making the changes they strive for totally dependent on changing society as a whole. I would say that, in that sense, I am a feminist today, because I realised that we must fight for the situation of women, here and now, before our dreams of socialism come true. Apart from that, I realised that even in socialist countries, equality between men and women has not been achieved. Therefore it is absolutely essential for women to take their destiny into their own hands. That is why I have now joined the Women's Liberation Movement.

12

The Politics of Feminism, Ecology, and Peace: Petra Kelly (1947–1992) and Gert Bastian (1923–1992)

▦ SETTING THE STAGE

Two Germanys emerged from one in the aftermath of World War II. In 1949, the United States, Great Britain, and France joined their three zones of occupation to create a new German state, the Federal Republic of Germany (West Germany). The Soviet Union responded by supporting the establishment of the Democratic Republic of Germany (East Germany). Both the United States and the Soviet Union hoped to influence political, economic, and social developments in their respective spheres, and by the 1950s had tethered each of these states to their military alliance systems. The Federal Republic of Germany (FRG) became a member of the North Atlantic Treaty Alliance in 1955. In the same year, the Democratic Republic of Germany (DRG) joined with the other states of Eastern Europe and the Soviet Union to form the Warsaw Pact. In the case of West Germany, postwar attempts to

[358]

rebuild materially and to construct a new, democratic political and civic culture were shaped by the complexities of cold war politics.

For the citizens of the new Federal Republic and their political leaders, visions of the future were also complicated by the meanings they gave to the past. In the half-century after the end of World War II, West Germans "remained divided over the responsibility for the atrocities of the Third Reich."[1] These divisions were often generational, sometimes shaped by pragmatic economic and political interests, and frequently expressed in controversies about re-armament, national and European defense, and the relationship between the military and civil society.

Until the late 1950s, many Germans chose to put questions about the Nazi era on hold. Instead, they focused on the path to security and prosperity that was laid out for them by West Germany's first postwar prime minister, Christian Democrat Konrad Adenauer (1876–1967). His leadership brought unprecedented social stability and economic growth to Germany. Given growing cold war tensions, he recognized that he could trade German re-armament for restored German independence and the re-creation of German national identity. By 1955, when Germany became a member of NATO, the plans for a new German army were set. Ninety-five thousand men would be in uniform that year—a total of 500,000 in three years.[2] Adenauer and his associates insisted that they were creating a new kind of soldier who was first and foremost a citizen defending his country. Nevertheless, the broader issues of the nature of Germany's military institutions and their relationships to state power and society, and fears of militarism and entanglements in a western alliance system, produced criticism and protest.[3] While at first the number of protestors was small, the protestors began to ask, at what price had prosperity and security been obtained? Eventually, a generation of radical students would add their voices to these challenges and insist on both a different vision of the future and a more open assessment of the past.

Protesting everything from the West's materialism to the overcrowded conditions at European universities, from the United States' war in Vietnam to the actions of their own country's police, students in West Germany, the rest of Europe, and the United States sought to remake their parents' world. They marched and campaigned for social justice, civil rights, and peace and protested against crass materialism, capitalism, and militarism. Romantic and idealistic, this gen-

2. Donald Abenheim, *Reforging the Iron Cross: The Search for Tradition in the West German Armed Forces* (Princeton, N.J.: Princeton University Press, 1988), pp. 165–166.

3. See Richard Barnet, *The Alliance* (New York: Simon and Schuster, 1983), pp. 55–58, for Adenauer's politics. A useful discussion of the competing images of German soldiers can be found in "Forum: The 'Remasculinization' of Germany in the 1950s," *Signs* 24:1 (1998): pp. 101–170.

1. Robert Moeller, "War Stories: The Search for a Usable Past in the Federal Republic of Germany," *American Historical Review* 101:4 (October 1996): p. 1017.

Chapter 12
The Politics of
Feminism,
Ecology, and
Peace: Petra
Kelly
(1947–1992) and
Gert Bastian
(1923–1992)

eration was more publicly active than their parents, and they joined mass protests and movements for causes that inspired them. The issues that many young West Germans embraced in the seventies and eighties were the nascent ecology movement, anti-nuclear movement, and women's movement.

Petra Kelly (1947–1992) and Gert Bastian (1923–1992) were like other West Germans who lived during the tumultuous years of West Germany's founding, reconstruction, integration into Europe, and re-emergence as a political heavyweight in European affairs. Their lives demonstrate how men and women of different generations, life experiences, and political starting points ended up in the same place at the end of the 1970s: protesting the deployment of Pershing missiles in West Germany, their government's use of nuclear energy, the degradation of the environment, and the position of women in society. Some, like Bastian, were trying to reconcile West Germany's central position in NATO with their desire to reach out to their eastern neighbors. This uneasiness with American security policy and with American society as a model to be emulated had existed prior to the 1970s, but it was given new life when a growing number of young West Germans began to reject what they saw as American imperialism and capitalism that produced the Vietnam War, deadly nuclear weapons, and ecological damage. Others, like Kelly, wished to embrace social movements that would rethink and refashion political, economic, social, and gender structures. The common ground these disparate groups found paved the way for the West German peace movement of the 1980s and the rise of a new political phenomenon, the Green movement. This chapter examines the lives of two West Germans who became spokespersons and leaders of these movements and how their activism and dedication altered West Germany's and Europe's political landscape in the late twentieth century.

▣ THE ACTORS:

PETRA KELLY AND GERT BASTIAN

Gert Bastian was born in Munich on March 26, 1923, the youngest son of a German mother, Charlotte, and a Brazilian-German father, Alberto Bastian. His paternal grandfather had emigrated to Brazil, where he had made and lost a fortune before he returned to Germany with his family. Gert's father, Alberto Bastian, studied at the university, received his Ph.D. in economics, and then found work as a certified public accountant. When Hitler came to power in 1933, both Alberto and Charlotte supported the Nazis, and Charlotte encouraged her children, Gert, Ruth, and Rüdiger, to become active in the Hitler Youth.[4]

---

4. Biographical information on Bastian has been taken from the following sources: Alice Schwarzer, *Eine Tödliche Liebe: Petra Kelly und Gert Bastian* (Köln: Kiepenheuer and Witsch,

When World War II began, Bastian was fully inculcated in the belief that Germany was surrounded by enemies. Many years later, he remembered his feelings when war broke out: "... we [his classmates and he] were firmly convinced that Germany had been attacked by a malicious and hostile alliance which wished to destroy all the achievements of the past years and they had to be defended."[5] Two years later, in 1941, Bastian volunteered and found himself in a Panzer division on the eastern front. He excelled at being a soldier and within a year was promoted group leader of his battalion. By 1943, he was an officer and continued his steady rise through the officer ranks. Despite being wounded three times, twice in Russia and once in France during the Normandy invasion, Bastian remained committed to Germany and to Hitler. The last injury sustained at Normandy was from six U.S. machine gun bullets in his torso. He survived three days and nights wounded and alone behind enemy lines by pretending to be dead. Once found, he managed to leave Paris on the last German transport train. Perhaps it was his family's connections, one of his mother's closest friends was Hitler's secretary, or the seriousness of his wounds that gained him a place on that train.

During his convalescence, Bastian married Charlotte (Lotte) Baronin von Stipsicz, the daughter of a Hungarian noble whom he had met on a train in 1942. Since Lotte was a non-Aryan and Gert a German officer, he needed special permission to marry her. A few weeks before Germany surrendered, permission was granted by a call from Hitler's headquarters. The couple married on March 8, 1945, and their marriage lasted until Gert's death in 1992. Shortly after the ceremony, Gert returned to the western front, where he was captured and placed in an American prisoner of war camp at Regensburg. There he learned of Germany's defeat. Years later he described his shock: "And when this unavoidable event, the defeat, came about, the imaginary world we had constructed collapsed with a huge bang, and this was a terrible spiritual shock."[6]

Like many Germans of his generation and experiences, Bastian remained reticent about the details of his war years. When he became a spokesperson for the peace movement in the 1980s, he always maintained that he knew little about the atrocities committed against Soviet Jews, the burning of villages and towns along the eastern front, and the building and maintenance of death camps in the east. In the years immediately after the war, Bastian at first did not want to believe the stories of the atrocities or of Hitler's suicide. "[W]e found out that he [Hitler] had committed suicide, and that was just another of those outrageous lies told to soldiers [in the POW camps] right up to the end."[7] Later, upon learning that these

1993) and Sara Parkin, *The Life and Death of Petra Kelly* (London: Pandora, 1994).

5. Parkin, p. 95.

6. Ibid., p. 97.

7. Ibid.

Chapter 12
The Politics of
Feminism,
Ecology, and
Peace: Petra
Kelly
(1947–1992) and
Gert Bastian
(1923–1992)

events were true, he fell into "absolute despair."

As a result, the early postwar years were difficult for soldiers like Bastian. He was torn between shame and disillusionment, and was severely depressed about the things he found out while in captivity. For example, pictures from Auschwitz were shown to all POWs in American camps. This was part of the Allied attempts to re-educate the Germans and to change basic attitudes. The Allies also hoped to remove from positions of authority those people who had served the Nazi regime directly. These policies of denazification did not work because of the need for economic recovery and for qualified personnel to carry out reconstruction plans.[8] For a period of time, however, the Allied demilitarization was effective. Germany pledged not to re-arm, and the responsibility of the German army for past abuses was discussed publicly.

In June 1945, Bastian returned home after having been an American prisoner of war for six weeks and found that his family's apartment in Munich had survived the bombing. Soon seven people were living in this three room apartment: Bastian; Lotte; their baby girl, Eva, born in the summer of 1945; his parents; Bastian's sister; and her son. By the winter of 1945,

these seven people were huddled together around one stove because there were only enough coals to heat one room. They lived like so many Germans did in this first postwar decade: three families for every one house.

Having been a Nazi officer, Bastian was not permitted to attend university and he started an apprenticeship as a bookbinder. After completing his apprenticeship in 1948, he began working in a government office and found the work boring and his colleagues dull. He had such contempt for his peers that he took to playing chess against himself. He was equally dissatisfied with his home life. He, Lotte, and their two children were still sharing the three-room apartment with his parents. His life meandered without purpose for years after the war. A sense of purpose would return to him only when a new army was created, and Bastian was able to reenlist in 1956. As Bastian was trying to find his place in postwar West German society, Petra Karin Lehmann Kelly was among the first generation born after World War II into the realities of a new West German state.

Petra Karin Lehmann (Kelly) was born on November 29, 1947, in a small market town in Bavaria on the banks of the Danube. Her parents, Marianne Birle and Richard Siegfried Lehmann, had married earlier that year. Their courtship was unusual. Lehmann had been held in an American prisoner of war camp and Marianne, a young schoolgirl at the time, had struck up a correspondence with the young soldier from Dresden. When the Americans released Lehmann, they intended to send him back to Dresden, which

---

8. For "denazification" efforts, see Barnet, p. 31; Michael Kater, "Problems of Political Reeducation in West Germany, 1845–1960," *Simon Wiesenthal Center Annual* 4 (1997): pp. 1–20; and David Clay Large, "Reckoning Without the Past: The HIAG of the Waffen-SS and the Politics of Rehabilitation in the Bonn Republic, 1950–1961," *Journal of Modern History* 59:1 (March 1987), pp. 79–113.

was in the Soviet zone of divided Germany. Like many of his fellow prisoners, Lehmann did not want to live in the Soviet sector, so he asked his schoolgirl pen pal and her mother if they could help him. They offered him a room in their home in Günzburg and in a short time, Marianne and Richard were married.

Petra's father was a well-educated man and his facility with language earned him a position at an American army base near their home. Richard's job with the Americans not only brought in a steady income, which was unusual for postwar Germany, but it also familiarized the family with Americans and their way of life. Petra's parents divorced in 1954, but Marianne maintained the link to the American community by working as a saleswomen at the American military base's Post Exchange, a department store exclusively for American military personnel and their families. As a result of her parents' employment, Petra's childhood was more comfortable than most in postwar Germany, and she was among the first of her generation to experience American products such as Coca Cola, jeans, and the comics. She was growing up in a world that promised women citizenship and equal treatment before the law, but simultaneously idealized gender differences and elevated the family.

West German women had entered the work force in unprecedented numbers after the war, but they encountered discrimination in wages, working conditions, and family allowances, which did not recognize female heads of households. Part of West Germany's strategy for social and economic reconstruction depended on the reconstitution of an ideal family headed by a male wage earner whose wife stayed at home and cared for their three or more children. The reality was, however, that almost 60 percent of married couples had only one or two children, and more and more women were working outside the home, even though child-care facilities were inadequate. As women's movements emerged in the late 1960s, their concerns focused on child-care, reproductive rights, and marital relations.

Kelly's grandmother, with whom the family lived and who was Kelly's role model, liked to remind her granddaughter of the hardships of the war. "Omi," a term of endearment that Petra used for her grandmother, had lost her husband in the waning days of the war when the Nazis began drafting older men and young boys. Like all German women, she was "a woman of the rubble," the name given to German women after the war because of their backbreaking and painstaking clearing—by hand—of the debris and rubble left after Allied bombing attacks.

After the departure of her son-in-law and as a result of her daughter's work schedule, Omi devoted herself to her granddaughter and made sure that Petra knew how to read and write before she entered a nearby Catholic school. Omi continued to tutor Petra, even after her formal education had begun. One of their daily rituals was reading about current events from the newspaper. Petra liked to credit her grandmother for her interest in world affairs and antinuclear politics. She often told the story of the time when her

Chapter 12
The Politics of
Feminism,
Ecology, and
Peace: Petra
Kelly
(1947–1992) and
Gert Bastian
(1923–1992)

grandmother explained to her, in 1957, the issues surrounding West Germany's re-armament and the appeal made by several prominent German scientists, the "Göttinger Appell," which argued against giving the German army nuclear weapons. When Kelly entered the political arena as a peace and Green activist in the 1970s and 1980s, her grandmother acted as secretary, confidante, adviser, and companion and was often referred to in the German press as the "Green Granny."

Petra's and her mother's link with the American way of life became much stronger when Marianne met and married an American lieutenant-colonel, John Kelly, in 1958. The next year, Petra, her parents, and her new baby sister, Grace, moved to the United States. Petra had to adjust to the demands of a new country, language, and culture just as Americans were adjusting to a new president, John F. Kennedy, and a rapidly changing social and political landscape. The Kellys were stationed at Fort Benning, near Columbus, Georgia, until 1964. From this vantage point, Petra witnessed the events of the black civil rights movement and became an ardent admirer of Martin Luther King, Jr. The political and intellectual atmosphere of the early 1960s ignited in Kelly a desire to dedicate herself to a higher cause. When she was in Germany, she had believed that this higher purpose meant joining a Catholic religious order. Now, after experiencing the charisma and idealism of Kennedy, the bravery and determination of King, and the social and political injustices of the American South, Petra believed that she was called to politics.

ACT I:

THE MAKING OF AN ACTIVIST (PETRA KELLY)

In the fall of 1966, Petra Kelly (she had taken her stepfather's name) enrolled at American University in Washington, D.C., because, as she noted, "It's the capital, I can just walk down the street and see everyone."[9] Kelly chose American University and its School of International Service not only for its proximity to her parents and her half-sister, Grace, and half-brother John (b. 1960), but because the university provided opportunities to meet members of the government and international community. She met Hubert H. Humphrey in this setting, and when he became the democratic nominee for president in 1968, he personally asked Kelly to join his campaign as a student adviser to help shape his appeals to young Americans. Humphrey lost the election, but Kelly had received, at the age of twenty-one, "valuable lessons about the drudgery, grind, and minutiae of political campaigning

9. Parkin, p. 35.

and that the sparkling moments were few and far between and even these were hard earned."[10]

Kelly took advantage of her time and place. She witnessed firsthand American presidential politics, and she experienced the tumult and absorbed the energy of the time. During the race riots in Washington, D.C., after the assassination of Martin Luther King, Jr., in April 1968, Petra stayed with Walt and Elizabeth Rostow. She questioned the violence of the riots and also the actions of Rostow, who was special security adviser to President Johnson. Late one night, Rostow took a phone call from the president in his study. His wife had prepared a camp bed for Petra in this room, and Petra overheard Rostow and Johnson "coolly, clinically" discuss new bombing targets in Vietnam. In the same year, she stood on the sidelines as students in the United States took their grievances to the streets. She wondered, "How was it that, of all sections of society, students should fail to come up with more imaginative ways of making their protest felt than hurling bricks and stones?"[11] With such sentiments "Petra absorbed and synthesized what was going on, but she was not an activist in the strict sense of the word," recalled one friend.

Leaving the United States for a summer holiday in Europe and a trip with her beloved grandmother to Prague in August 1968 did not mean that Kelly was leaving behind the tumult. She and her grandmother arrived in Prague on the afternoon of August 20, 1968; the following morning, Soviet and Warsaw Pact forces invaded Czechoslovakia. In a postcard to one of her professors on the day of the invasion, she wrote:

> Arrived in "my golden city" yesterday afternoon and was proud of its progress and peoples. Last night I danced with proud and happy Czech peoples—this morning I am terrified. My idealism has dwindled to 0. Russian tanks now pass my window, people cry silent tears. The freedom they now slowly had gained is drowned out by tanks, planes, and shooting.

In a postscript, she added, "... why must might always try to prove right ... ?" Petra and her grandmother spent five days under house arrest in their hotel and then were among the first tourists allowed to leave Czechoslovakia.

Kelly's university years were formative. When she graduated in 1970 with a B.A. cum laude in international relations (West/East European studies), she parlayed her academic, personal, and political experiences into a postgraduate fellowship at the Europa Institut in Amsterdam to study European integration. After a year of study, she moved to an internship position at the European Community (EC) in Brussels. Kelly wondered if the years of the late 1960s, "this unrest and cacophony," heralded the coming of a new age. For Germans and Europeans in general, the new epoch encouraged the exploration of further European

10. Ibid., p. 47.
11. Ibid., p. 48.

*Chapter 12
The Politics of
Feminism,
Ecology, and
Peace: Petra
Kelly
(1947–1992) and
Gert Bastian
(1923–1992)*

integration and cooperation and the establishment of new and better relations with the states of Eastern Europe and the Soviet Union. As a result of her experiences within Europe's political and economic institutions, Kelly's issue became the exclusion of women from the arenas of power.

When Kelly began working as an administrator for the Economic and Social Committee of the European Community shortly after receiving her M.A. at the Europa Institut, she noted the absence of women in decision-making positions, discrimination against them throughout EC institutions, and women's inequality in general. After observing the overwhelming male culture at the EC, in a 1973 staff journal, Kelly noted that "Europe is strictly for males." Soon she was writing and lecturing on making women's rights one of the priorities of the European Community. In a speech in 1975, she argued, "Europe is one big male supremacy bastion—the Church, the political parties, the trade unions, the national bureaucracies, and the European Institutions," and she wanted the European Community to enforce the principle of men's and women's equality guaranteed in Article 119 of the Treaty of Rome (1957).

Kelly was not alone in making such demands. Men's and women's equality also had been guaranteed to all German citizens in the FRG's founding document, the Basic Law (Document One). During the late 1960s, in Germany and elsewhere, young university women joined the student movements and a few of them, as a result of their exclusion from positions

of leadership, began to form their own caucuses. In September 1968, at the national convention of the Student Movement of the FRG, they articulated a program that criticized patriarchy and women's token presence in the new movement. Their concerns, such as legal abortion, free child-care, improvements in women's educational and training opportunities, and better job prospects, were personal interests and grievances and they made them political. By the early 1970s, the European and German women's movement and their demands for greater equality and liberation within their societies forced their governments to examine women's situation in Europe. Kelly was asked by her committee at the EC, the Economic and Social Committee, to conduct the research.

With facts and figures at her disposal, Kelly began to lecture and write extensively on the oppression of and violence against women. For Kelly, the problem could not be solved by women alone. She argued that both men and women had to work together for women's liberation. In 1973, she wrote:

One must in all cases avoid falling into the trap of creating additional barriers between men and women—therefore, the warm parlours of European Women's Liberation movements, women's clubs, and feminist political parties may serve the temporary cause of gathering wood—but they are not the place to start a longlasting fire. The aim is ultimately to confront and meet men on their own ground, namely, politics, and to build an equal partnership with them. . . . It must be remembered that there are no "female questions" which at the same time are not also of importance to the society as a whole . . . *the creation of a new woman of necessity demands the creation of a new man!*[12]

She maintained this position throughout her political career and often admonished her male colleagues within the Green party that they, as a party, had to address women's liberation (Document Two).

Kelly's first foray into the political arena was in feminist politics, but her passion for women's equality was increasingly matched by her growing concern about nuclear energy and the dangers of radiation. Petra's younger sister, Grace, had died in 1970 of sarcoma cancer, which had attacked the tissues around her right eye. The only form of treatment available was radiation, and in a letter to Hubert Humphrey, Kelly described how the radiation was affecting Grace: "The sarcoma cancer has always been successfully burned and dried out by radiation, yet, the complications that have set in through swellings, breathing difficulties and much loss of weight, have complicated it all."[13] Her sister's painful and disfiguring treatment and her slow death had a profound affect on Kelly. Several years later, she set up a foundation in her sister's name to improve care for cancer patients and to research the link between radiation and cancer.

12. Ibid., p. 71.
13. Ibid., p. 57.

The perils of radiation were becoming part of the public discourse in the early 1970s because more and more power companies in the United States and Europe began to explore alternative ways to produce electricity. After Grace's death in 1970, Kelly had the opportunity to attend several meetings concerning nuclear energy, which were organized and led by the leading opponent of nuclear energy, Ralph Nader, the American consumer activist. Kelly represented the Young European Federalists at one of these conferences, "Critical Mass '74." At this meeting, she interviewed several experts on the possible side effects of nuclear radiation and then persuaded the editor of the organization's journal to publish an article based on these interviews. When the editor argued with Kelly over the appropriateness of such an article in a journal dedicated to issues concerning European integration, Kelly asserted that there was an audience for such issues. Demonstrations against nuclear power plants in western Europe had already taken place in France and West Germany in 1971, and nuclear power was now becoming a European issue.

In February 1975, a major protest against the building of a nuclear power plant occurred in Wyhl, a town in southwestern Germany, near the Swiss and French borders, and one of the most polluted areas in this part of Europe. When construction of the power plant was about to begin, several hundred local activists (farmers, housewives, merchants, and students) held a press conference at the construction site and sat down in front of the

Chapter 12
The Politics of
Feminism,
Ecology, and
Peace: Petra
Kelly
(1947–1992) and
Gert Bastian
(1923–1992)

bulldozers. Police cleared the area with water cannons and arrested demonstrators. Nevertheless, some local people stayed there overnight, and soon word spread about the protest. Over the next week, 28,000 supporters from all over Germany and from the border regions of France and Switzerland converged on the scene. Kelly was one of them, and she witnessed firsthand the power of a grass-roots movement. Despite numerous attempts by the police to clear the site, people occupied it for over a year. In 1977, a panel of judges was established to resolve the issue and they eventually ruled against the plant.

Many of the people who had come to Wyhl were members of citizen action groups that had formed during the 1970s in Germany and elsewhere. These groups were organized to protest nuclear installations; pollution, especially acid rain; and commercial and government development. By the time of the Wyhl protest, they had come together in a national organization, the Bundesverband Bürgerinitiativen Umweltschutz (BBU), or the Association of Citizens' Initiatives for the Conservation of Nature, which counted more than 300,000 members and whose power was being felt by West German authorities. During the two years of occupation and court battles, the citizen groups at Wyhl opened a school to educate people on nuclear and environmental issues. These discussions led to broader debates concerning the fragility of the whole ecosystem, the consequences to the health and well-being of those living around plants and factories, and the

reasons why German society and its political institutions were willing to continue industrial development and expansion unabated.

The action at Wyhl and the subsequent antinuclear movement in Germany brought together farmers whose land and livelihood were threatened, young schoolteachers who had been educated during the upheavals of the 1960s, housewives who were concerned for their children's health, leftist radicals who wanted to use the movement to critique existing social and political conditions, and many middle-class people who had grown discontented with social democratic rule in the FRG. The actions and initiative of these citizens at Wyhl impressed Kelly for their consensus, nonviolence, and organization from below. Kelly was soon a committed member of the BBU and in 1977, she was elected to its board. Flushed with its success at Wyhl and at other antinuclear protests, where the crowds often numbered in the tens of thousands, the BBU realized that its various antinuclear and environmental protests had coalesced into a mass ecological movement.

This union of activists around the common theme of ecology can be understood by examining the concerns of many Europeans about nuclear power and nuclear war during the 1970s. During the Cold War, there was always the threat of mass destruction from an all-out nuclear war between powerful nations, and many activists, angered by this possibility, protested the continued arming of the state with weapons of mass destruction. In addition, the threat of nuclear power plants leaking or being hit by missiles and creating massive explosions, as well as issues of nuclear waste disposal, pushed the movement to seek protection for local workers and citizens and their environment. In 1980, the BBU published its position statement:

> Protection of the environment today means more than eliminating or moderating some of the worst effects of the industrial system. This would be dealing with the symptoms only. . . . We are beginning to understand the destruction of the environment, economic inequality, social injustice, and the growing dependence of the individual on the powers of the state are not avoidable side-effects of the system, but are essential features of it. Our interest is not merely in the correction of errors and the elimination of unpleasant side effects. Rather, our goal is a more just, a freer and more humane social order.[14]

The question at the end of the 1970s for many in this new social movement was: What was the best method for attaining these goals: forming a political party or remaining outside formal politics? Kelly believed that the ecology movement had to make itself heard at the parliamentary level and she argued for the creation of a full-fledged political party, the Greens. She

stated, "We can no longer rely on the established parties, and we can no longer depend entirely on the extra-parliamentary road. The [political] system is bankrupt, but a new force has to be created both inside and outside of the parliament."[15]

In 1979, the first German Green party was founded in Frankfurt to run candidates for the upcoming elections for the European Parliament. Kelly was chosen as the first candidate on the Green party list. The party polled 3.2 percent of the vote (900,000 votes), which was not enough to elect any of the candidates to office. Nevertheless, the campaign had given the Greens a nationwide platform and led to the founding of the West German Green party in 1980. In West Germany, the antinuclear and ecology movements had grown into a full-fledged political party, the Greens. Their platform stated, "Our policies are founded on four basic principles: ecology, social responsibility, grass roots democracy, and nonviolence."[16] In their first German parliamentary elections, in October 1980, the Greens polled only 1.9 percent of the vote; they would have to wait until March 1983 for another chance at a national election. In this election, the Greens polled 5.4 percent and won twenty-seven seats. Kelly, who had headed the slate of Green candidates in Bavaria, won a seat in the federal Parliament.

The Greens' transformation from social movement to a legitimate and

14. Werner Hulsberg, *The German Greens: A Social and Political Profile,* trans. Gus Fagan (New York: Verso,1988), p. 62.

15. Ibid., p. 78.

16. Fritjof Capra and Charlene Spretnek, *Green Politics* (New York: E P. Dutton, 1984), p. 30.

Chapter 12
The Politics of
Feminism,
Ecology, and
Peace: Petra
Kelly
(1947–1992) and
Gert Bastian
(1923–1992)

successful political party was aided greatly by NATO's decision on December 12, 1979, to place 108 Pershing II and 464 cruise missiles in West Germany, Italy, Belgium, the United Kingdom, and the Netherlands, beginning in 1983. Mass demonstrations and individual protests immediately broke out (Document Three). In Brussels, the site of the NATO high command, 40,000 people took to the streets, and in Bonn, West Germany, a divisional tank commander, General Gert Bastian, publically criticized the proposed missile deployment and was relieved of his duties.

▪ ACT II:

THE MAKING OF AN ACTIVIST (GERT BASTIAN)

When the Federal Republic of Germany was admitted to NATO in 1955, its leadership had to establish a new army, and Gert Bastian was one of the first men to enlist. The ex-Nazi officer, who had had trouble adjusting to civilian life, was now in the West German army. Many of his colleagues were also experienced former officers and few had any difficulty serving in an army that was created to fight communism because they had fought the Bolsheviks years earlier.[17] Aware that German militarization and unbending military discipline had led to the most devastating of all modern wars, West German leaders drew up plans to create a "citizens' army," whose officers and soldiers would be instructed to follow their own inner and moral compass, even if it went against military orders and protocol. The founders of the FRG military wanted to ensure that no soldier could ever claim as an ex-

cuse for brutality and atrocities that he was "just following orders."[18]

As the Bundeswehr (the FRG's armed forces) approached combat readiness in the mid-1960s, West German society was finally showing signs of facing its Nazi past. Early in the decade, West Germans, old and young alike, consistently and publically encountered literary, journalistic, cinematic, and theatrical representations of the brutality of the Nazi regime: the West German republication of Anne Frank's diary in 1955; the radio play and movie about Frank's life; the publication of "accusatory literature" by young Germans born after the war, who wrestled with "the sins of the fathers"; the 1961 trial of Adolf Eichmann in Jerusalem; and the *Spiegel* affair of 1962. The *Spiegel* affair pitted Adenauer's minister of defense, Franz Joseph Strauss, against the popular weekly magazine, *Der Spiegel*. The magazine had published a series of unflattering and critical articles about Strauss. The government used mea-

17. Schwarzer, p. 121.

18. Gordon Craig, *The Germans* (London: Penguin, 1991), p. 245.

sures reminiscent of the Nazi period, like police intimidation and censorship, to silence the critics. This scandal led to Strauss's resignation and eventually to Adenauer's retirement from politics.

As a newly inducted officer in the Bundeswehr in 1956, Bastian took seriously the army's desire to create *Innere Führung:* "military leadership appropriate to the modern world, enabling a solider to carry out his mission while assuring his rights as a citizen."[19] He joined Franz Joseph Strauss's Christian Social party, the Bavarian version of the Christian Democratic party. When Strauss showed signs of authoritarianism during the *Spiegel* affair, Bastian resigned from the party. Because of these events and public debates about Germany's Nazi past, Bastian became increasingly sensitive to and critical of intolerance, rigidity, and inappropriate military traditions and rituals associated with Nazism. When the Ministry of Defense issued in 1965 a memorandum instructing officers about their duties in a democracy, Bastian embraced the recommendations. One of the sections discussed the importance of political participation for army officers and how an officer's duty extended into the civic sphere: "He who follows a false tradition of the unpolitical soldier and restricts himself to his military craft neglects an essential part of his sworn duty as a soldier in democracy"[20] (Document Four).

19. Abenheim, p. 45.
20. Craig, p. 148.

At the same time, Berlin's charismatic mayor, Willy Brandt, took control of the German Social Democratic party and began a debate within West Germany about increasing democracy everywhere—from political parties to the army. This was a breath of fresh air after the years of Konrad Adenauer's "Chancellor democracy," and Bastian, like many Germans, took to heart Brandt's slogan, "Risk more democracy." Bastian transferred his sympathies and his party membership to the Social Democratic party.

By the time Bastian was promoted to major general in 1976, he was a vocal advocate for increased democratization in the army and civilian control over the military. This advocacy was fueled by his fear that there were still elements within the army that prevented open debates about military protocol, procedure, or policy and that such rigidity could lead to the emergence of neo-Nazism within the army. Acting on his own *Innere Führung* (inner/moral leadership), Bastian stopped the performance of one of Hitler's favorite marches during a military ceremony in 1978. In addition, he intercepted the distribution in his barracks of neo-Nazi literature, which denied the gassings at Auschwitz. His leadership in the arena of democratization of the army and his support of the Social Democratic party led to various speaking engagements.

In March 1979, Bastian attended a discussion sponsored by the youth organization of the Social Democratic party about the "political education and the social standing of the soldier." At this meeting, he responded to a

Chapter 12
The Politics of
Feminism,
Ecology, and
Peace: Petra
Kelly
(1947–1992) and
Gert Bastian
(1923–1992)

question about Chancellor Helmut Schmidt's re-armament plans and argued that no communist offensive need be feared because the Soviet Union, traumatized by Nazi Germany, was only arming itself for self-defense. To deploy the Pershing and cruise missiles in Europe would fundamentally change the NATO policy of "mutually assured destruction." For years, NATO operated on the assumption that a parity of arms between the superpowers would ensure peace because each had the same capability to destroy the other. The deployment of these short-range missiles altered this parity because it gave NATO the advantage of first-strike capability. Not only did this alter parity, it also guaranteed that Europe would be the first line of defense and that the two Germanys would be center stage.

Within days, the general became the center of the debate about deployment. The Social Democrats, already divided over the armament question, were embarrassed; the conservatives, the Christian Democrats and the Christian Social party, started calling him a security risk. Bastian added to his notoriety when, in response to NATO's official announcement in December 1979, he composed a letter of resignation to the minister of defense.

In this letter, he labeled this deployment as "a major and therefore destabilizing escalation in first strike ability."[21] His letter was accompanied by an eight-page memorandum of his arguments against deployment. The ministry refused to grant retirement and thus denied the antinuclear and peace movements a martyr. The government tried to silence Bastian by relegating him to an obscure post in Cologne, but the public and the press protested. Within a week, his letter of resignation and the accompanying memo were published in a Frankfurt daily. All of West Germany could now read the opinion of Major General Bastian, who claimed that the West German people had been cheated out of a proper debate about the dangers of the missile deployment. Bastian's detractors did everything they could to discredit him. Finding nothing in his military record that they could use, they turned to his personal life and discovered that the two-star general was a notorious womanizer. In addition to the public embarrassment, Bastian's chances of ending his military career on a high note of integrity and righteousness faded. In June 1980, Bastian requested early retirement, and this time it was granted to the fifty-seven-year old-major general.

21. Parkin, p. 94.

■ ACT III:

GREEN POLITICIANS

On November 1, 1980, Bastian met Petra Kelly at a conference about women and peace, where they debated the subject of women in the army. Several years earlier, the Ministry of Defense had announced that the army would draft women as well as men for eighteen months of compulsory service. Many women, like Kelly, argued that the army was using the cover of women's rights as yet another ploy for the re-armament and militarization of West German society. At this conference in 1980, Bastian and Kelly agreed on the point that women should not serve in the army, but for very different reasons. Kelly asserted, "The question is not should women become soldiers, but how can men stop being soldiers?"[22] Bastian contended that women by nature were unfit to serve in the armed forces and lacked the physical or mental capabilities for soldiering.

Despite Bastian's views about women, his status as a retired major general gave the peace movement credibility among a broader range of West German citizens. In many ways, he was not very far from Kelly's position. He desired the demilitarization of West German society. He argued that the justifications for the army—defense and protection of citizens—were obsolete because "nothing can be protected in a nuclear war." On November 16, 1980, in conjunction with the peace and antinuclear movements, he started the Krefelder *Appell* (Document Five). This appeal became a nationwide petition drive calling for the Social Democratic government to withdraw approval of the deployment of Pershing II and cruise missiles in Germany. By the end of the three-year petition drive, the *Appell* had more than 5 million signatures and Bastian had become one of the founding members of the international organization, Generals for Peace and Disarmament, which counted among its ranks retired generals from the United States, Canada, Great Britain, and France.

Kelly was in the audience when the appeal was made public. She had accepted Bastian's invitation to attend the ceremony. While recognizing that the general had to be educated about feminism, she was impressed by the fact that he had matched his words with action. His years of experience within the military could teach her a lot about military attitudes and beliefs. The fact that the two were sharing the same stage, and arguing the same points but for different reasons, reveals how feminist, antinuclear, environmental, and peace movements converged into a heterogeneous political movement, the Greens. Kelly and Bastian represented many West Germans who had searched for solutions to questions of women's equality, environmental protections and standards, nuclear disarmament and war in the existing political ideologies of the postwar period and had found that none of the postwar political parties addressed their concerns adequately. The emergence of the Greens signified a new type of politics. Bastian, the former Nazi officer, Bundeswehr general, Christian Social party member, and Social Democrat,

22. Ibid., p. 102

*Chapter 12
The Politics of
Feminism,
Ecology, and
Peace: Petra
Kelly
(1947–1992) and
Gert Bastian
(1923–1992)*

was now a member of the Green party. This transformation exemplified how far West German politics had come in thirty-five years.

On March 6, 1983, the West German Green party gained seats in the German Parliament for the first time: they had polled 5.4 percent of the total vote. Their transformation from a loose alliance of grass-roots civic associations into a parliamentary party was helped by the momentum created by the antinuclear movements. During the early 1980s, West Germans and Europeans took to the streets again and again to protest the deployment of missiles in Western Europe. Their actions included the Krefelder *Appell,* concerts, rallies, anniversary events for the victims at Hiroshima, and a sixty-mile human chain stretching between two U.S. army bases in the FRG. The hundreds of people that partcipated in these actions were not bound by national or geographical concerns and interests but by the wider messages of a nuclear-free Europe, ecology, feminism, and nonviolence. Coordination for these events meant that social activists from various European countries and the United States developed an international network that became the Campaign for Nuclear Disarmament (Document Six). With her contacts at the EC, her linguistic abilities, and her American credentials, Kelly became a pivotal figure in this new transnational movement.

As Kelly's visibility was rising, so too was the Green party's. During regional elections in 1982, the Greens won seats in three parliaments and held the balance of power in several of them. In addition, these victories at-

tracted the attention of Franz Joseph Strauss, the leader of the Christian Social party, who wished to have the party banned on the grounds that it lacked any clearly defined political goals, a prerequisite for official recognition. Kelly herself summarized the public's thinking about the Greens: "We've got back-to-the land romantics, and drop outs, young anarchists, mature Christian pacifists, utopians, socialists, dogmatic conservatives who think animals are more important than people, old aunts who like gardening."[23] For Kelly, this membership was the movement's strength; she wanted the party to be "beyond the politics of the left and right," to reject the politics of compromise, and to be the antiparty party (Document Seven).

Members and supporters of the Green party were repelled by existing politics and political choices. To many of them, ecology encompassed everything from the economy and living conditions to more metaphysical questions such as the place of the individual in an increasingly technological and industrialized society[24] (Document Eight). Such sentiments propelled the Green party into the Federal Parliament in 1983 with twenty-seven seats; two of these seats were occupied by Bastian and Kelly. A few months after the Greens won their victory at the polls, Bastian moved into Kelly's house in Bonn and would remain there until their deaths in 1992.

Bastian and Kelly had begun their intimate relationship in the summer of

---

23. Ibid., p. 119.
24. Hulsberg, p. 10.

1982 after a series of professional and personal encounters. In the months after the launch of the Krefelder *Appell,* they often found themselves sharing the same public platforms. The attraction was mutual. Bastian at first wished to add the passionate, intense, and attractive Kelly to his long list of conquests. Kelly was attracted by the courage of his convictions and by his range of experiences. Kelly often found herself attracted to and in relationships with older men whose political experiences she could learn from and whose political commitments matched her own. Much has been made about these liaisons, but Kelly always explained that she found most younger men boring and politically immature. She looked upon sexual relationships as an extension of deep friendship and community of purpose. Bastian was not always comfortable with Kelly's conviction that when she worked with someone intensely, sleeping with them was as natural as sitting down to dinner. During their decade together, Bastian experienced bouts of jealousy and feelings of inadequacy when Kelly entered into other relationships.

Kelly, Bastian, and other members of the Green party now had to contend with the logistics and politics of being a parliamentary party. They rejected standard party structures, such as professional staffers, party whips, and leaders, and adopted the policy of rotation, which meant that each Green parliamentarian handed his or her seat after two years of service to another. This policy plunged the Green party into almost immediate disarray. The initiatives and policies that they had campaigned for were dying for lack of focus, organization, professional staffing, and leadership. By 1984, Bastian, used to the order and efficiency of military structure, resigned from the Green party but refused to give up his seat. Factionalism was the main characteristic of the Green party's first turn as a parliamentary party, and this factionalism only grew worse after the Green party's second round of Bundestag elections in 1987, when it polled 8.2 percent of the vote.

During their first year in parliament, the Greens had one issue that kept them from imploding: the plan to deploy Pershing and cruise missiles in late 1983. During the summer and autumn of 1983, the Greens and Kelly stood at the center of German politics. Kelly, Bastian, Lucas Beckmann, cofounder of the Green party, and others traveled extensively to promote resistance to deployment (Document Nine). Kelly and the Greens visited East Germany and appeared before the Foreign Relations Committee of the United States Congress. Kelly also appeared on NBC's *Meet the Press,* where she displayed a knowledge about weapons systems and foreign policy that clearly surpassed that of the four panelists, and her performance provoked a round of applause by the television crew.

In the fall, Kelly and the Greens fought on the floor of Parliament and on the streets for the reconsideration of deployment. The West German Parliament, controlled by the Christian Democrats, refused to consider a referendum on deployment and instead insisted that the matter be decided within Parliament. They feared that deployment would lose in a nationwide vote because opinion polls were

Chapter 12
The Politics of
Feminism,
Ecology, and
Peace: Petra
Kelly
(1947–1992) and
Gert Bastian
(1923–1992)

showing that 75 percent of the population opposed the missiles. The public protests, demonstrations, and blockades of the proposed missile barricades eventually forced the Social Democrats to reconsider their position on deployment but did little to alter the outcome. When the vote came to the floor of Parliament, the majority of Social Democrats and the Greens voted against deployment, but their votes were not enough. The governing coalition carried the day.

Kelly's tenure as a Green party member of Parliament was rocky from the start. She was critical of the party's increasing polarization and she refused to give up her position in 1985 when it was time for Green party members to rotate their seats among other members. The Green party had adopted this principal of rotation because it feared that incumbency bred corruption. Its party membership prided itself on purity of principle, and Kelly had broken ranks. She would not be forgiven for this act, her increasing celebrity, or her failure to captivate her Bundestag audience as she had moved hundreds of thousands during protests and mass actions. The person most identified internationally with the West German Green party was now *persona non grata* within the party.

During her tenure as a Green party member, Kelly's parliamentary work rested not on the charisma that she had shown as a social and peace activist, but on the skills and knowledge she had acquired during her years working in Brussels. Her seat on the foreign affairs committee allowed her to work on military and nuclear issues. She and Bastian continued to work for peaceful resistance against nuclear armaments, and for a brief time in 1986 he rejoined the Green party, only to leave again in January 1987. Bastian increasingly followed in Kelly's wake as she used her office to promote equal rights for women throughout the world and to fight for human rights in Tibet and China and for indigenous peoples worldwide. His image in the media as the maverick general was replaced with that of a solicitous and deferential gentleman, a "butler" to the crusading Kelly, as he took on more and more responsibilities for Kelly's travel and work schedule.

Another source of permanent frustration to Kelly was her male colleagues' approach to feminism. She often criticized them for their unwillingness to consider women's liberation and the alleviation of women's powerlessness as primary issues, and she worked unceasingly to bring attention to women's oppression throughout the world. Much of Kelly's parliamentary work focused on women's and human rights, and when she spoke in public, it was often about the relationship between Green politics and women's rights. She was at the forefront of what is now called ecofeminism, a political movement operating on the assumption that ideologies that allow injustice based on gender, race, and class are related to the ideologies that sanction exploitation and degradation of the environment.[25]

25. Noel Sturgeon, "The Nature of Race: Discourses of Racial Difference in Ecofeminism," in Karen J. Warren, *Ecofeminism: Women, Culture, and Nature* (Bloomington, Ind.: Indiana University Press, 1997), p. 261.

In 1990, the Green party's first foray into parliamentary politics was over. The impending reunification of Germany dictated the political discourse and the Greens, still factionalized and leaderless, chose to focus on global ecological problems instead. They failed to reach the threshold of 5 percent of the vote in West Germany and received only 6.1 percent in East Germany. The Greens had to regroup if they were to become successful political players in a united German state. But who would lead the Greens in the next decade? Could an antiparty party become a significant force in German politics?

Kelly wished to remain true to the Green party of the early 1980s, but its membership, goals, and status as an outsider no longer fit the Green party of the 1990s. Many Greens sat in local and regional governments, and they found that building coalitions, com-

promising, and participating in power had its benefits. Kelly refused to accept the changes, and when she stood for party speaker at the Green national convention in 1991, she came in third in the balloting. Her open letter to the party, which had argued for noncompromise and continued collaboration with international organizations like Amnesty International and Greenpeace, did not resonate with the rank and file. They were interested in issues and problems that emerged as a result of the impending reunification, environmental degradation of East Germany, absorption of new regions and constituencies into the body politic, and the need to legitimize the Green agenda in the new Germany. In 1991, Kelly did not represent the future of Green politics in Germany, only its past.

▨ FINALE

On October 19, 1992, the bodies of Gert Bastian and Petra Kelly were found in their home. They had been dead for almost three weeks before anyone noticed they were missing. The cause of death was murder/suicide. Bastian had put a 38-caliber Derringer to Kelly's temple while she was sleeping and shot her. Afterward, he walked out of the bedroom, put the gun to his head, and pulled the trigger. His body was found in the hallway.

What caused Bastian to kill his companion of ten years? Kelly was a demanding and difficult person to live with, and over the ten years of their

relationship, she had come to depend on the general for her professional and daily needs. Their sexual relationship had ended around 1984, and Kelly did little to hide this fact, often announcing during interviews that they were in love with each other intellectually, not physically. Their relationship was based on mutual need. During his months in the spotlight, Bastian had proven to be a stiff and awkward speaker. After the excitement of his resignation and opposition to deployment died down, he seemed to have little to say. Staying close to Kelly and becoming indispensable to her was a way to stay in the limelight and he accepted his role. If

Chapter 12
The Politics of
Feminism,
Ecology, and
Peace: Petra
Kelly
(1947–1992) and
Gert Bastian
(1923–1992)

the role was too demanding and Kelly too difficult to manage, as some have argued, he always had the opportunity to break off the relationship. In the 1989, Kelly met Palden Tawo, a Tibetan physician, during a parliamentary hearing about Tibet and soon the two became lovers. Instead of taking the affair as an opportunity to leave, Bastian continued to travel and live with Kelly until the affair with Tawo ended in 1991.

The months and weeks leading up to the murder/suicide have been examined and reexamined for clues to Bastian's state of mind. In March 1992, Bastian was struck by a taxi and suffered a debilitating leg injury that required seven hours of surgery and extensive physical therapy and rehabilitation. For months, he was in a wheelchair and then on crutches. During these months, he was depressed about his health, concerned about their finances, and possessed with feelings of frailty and mortality. Nevertheless, they kept their usual political schedule. The night before they died, they had returned from a conference on radiation. Bastian had been the first one to rise on October 1, which was their usual pattern. Kelly often worked late into the night and did not rise until the afternoon. Around noon, Bastian made a telephone call to Beckmann concerning the East German's secret police records on Beckmann, Bastian, Kelly, and other activists. The call to Beckmann was the last time anyone heard from him. Earlier in the morning, Bastian had written a letter to his wife Lotte, telling her that he had returned home and that he would not be coming to

Munich before her departure to Crete on October 4. He put the letter into an envelope but did not mail it. He had begun a letter to his lawyer but when police arrived several weeks later, it was left unfinished in the typewriter. Sometime in the early afternoon, Bastian went upstairs, killed Kelly, and then committed suicide.

The gruesome and tawdry details of their deaths should not overshadow their political significance in late twentieth-century Germany. These two people, separated by gender, age, and political ideology, met on the same stage and argued the same points, but for different reasons. Their meeting and the intertwining of their lives revealed how feminist, antinuclear, environmental, and peace movements converged into a heterogeneous political movement, the Greens. Kelly and Bastian were like many West Germans who had searched for solutions to questions of women's equality, nuclear disarmament, environmental protections and standards, and war in the existing political ideologies of the postwar period.

For Kelly, the Greens sought to merge many of the social victories of the last three generations, including those of civil rights, feminism, nuclear disarmament, and global concern for the environment, into a single movement. Kelly believed that the Greens were more than an ecological party; they advocated a nonviolent, nonexploitative society and sought solutions in decentralization, local political autonomy, and direct democracy outside the boundaries of the traditional ideologies of both the right and the left. Kelly added another dimension to this movement: she insisted that "the liberation of women and men from the bonds of patriarchy is essential to the work of building a peaceful, just and ecological society." It seems ironic that she died a violent death at the hands of a man who perhaps was not able to throw off those bonds.

▪ QUESTIONS

1. What was the political and social climate in the Federal Republic of Germany in the 1950s and 1960s? What were the origins for the new social movements that emerged in the 1970s?

2. How did Germany's Nazi past shape postwar military policies and politics?

3. How did Kelly's and Bastian's backgrounds influence their views on nuclear disarmament, the peace movement, and feminism?

4. What were the sources of Europeans' fears about nuclear weapons and nuclear war?

5. What were Kelly's and Bastian's arguments for nuclear disarmament? Why did Kelly and Bastian question the meaning of war? How were their positions similar and different?

6. Why should women and men be both feminists and ecologists? How did these two ideologies come together in Green politics?

7. What is an antiparty party?

8. What comparisons can you draw between Simone de Beauvoir's *The Second Sex* and Petra Kelly's writings on women's liberation and oppression?

9. Was the antinuclear movement specific to a time and place? Why or why not?

*Chapter 12
The Politics of
Feminism,
Ecology, and
Peace: Petra
Kelly
(1947–1992) and
Gert Bastian
(1923–1992)*

■ **DOCUMENTS**

▨▨▨▨▨▨▨▨▨▨▨▨ **DOCUMENT ONE** ▨▨▨▨▨▨▨▨▨▨▨▨

"The Basic Law of the Federal Republic of Germany"
(1949)

*The Federal Republic of Germany came into existence in 1949 and its founding
constitution, "The Basic Law," was envisaged as a temporary document at the
time. The last article of the Basic Law would cease to be in force "on the day on
which a constitution adopted by a free decision of the German people comes into
force." The document, which the occupying powers (France, Great Britain, and
the United States) agreed would not be called a constitution, was a mixture of
conservative political values and political values that reflected advances in social
and civil rights. On what basis are rights claimed by citizens? Who or what en-
joys special protection of the state? Why?*

PREAMBLE

The German People in the Laender, Baden, Bavaria, Bremen, Hamburg, Hesse,
Lower Saxony, North Rhine-Westphalia, Rhineland-Palatinate, Schleswig-
Holstein, Wuerttemberg- Baden and Wuerttemberg-Hohenzollern,

Conscious of its responsibility before God and Men, Animated by the resolve
to preserve its national and political unity and to serve the peace of the World
as an equal partner in a United Europe,

Desiring to give a new order to political life for a transitional period, has enacted, by virtue of its constituent power, this Basic Law of the Federal Republic
of Germany.

It has also acted on behalf of those Germans to whom participation was denied.

The entire German people is called on to achieve by free self-determination
the unity and freedom of Germany.

I. BASIC RIGHTS

Article 1

(1) The dignity of man shall be inviolable. To respect and protect it shall be
the duty of all state authority.

(2) The German people therefore acknowledge inviolable and inalienable
human rights as the basis of every community of peace and of justice in
the world.

(3) The following basic rights shall bind the legislature, the executive and the judiciary as directly enforceable law.

Article 2

(1) Everyone shall have the right to the free development of his personality insofar as he does not violate the rights of others or offend against the constitutional order or moral code.

(2) Everyone shall have the right to life and to inviolability of his person. The freedom of the individual shall be inviolable. These rights may only be encroached upon pursuant to a law.

Article 3

(1) All persons shall be equal before the law.

(2) Men and women shall have equal rights.

(3) No one may be prejudiced or favored because of his sex, his parentage, his race, his language, his homeland and origin, his faith or his religious or political opinions.

Article 4

(1) Freedom of faith and of conscience, and freedom of creed, religious or ideological, shall be inviolable.

(2) The undisturbed practice of religion shall be guaranteed.

(3) No one may be compelled against his conscience to render war service as an armed combatant. Details shall be regulated by a Federal Law. . . .

Article 6

(1) Marriage and family shall enjoy the special protection of the state.

(2) Care and upbringing of children are the natural right of the parents and a duty primarily incumbent on them. The state shall watch over the performance of this duty.

(3) Separation of children from the family against the will of the persons entitled to bring them up may take place only pursuant to a law, if those so entitled fail in their duty or if the children are otherwise threatened with neglect.

*Chapter 12
The Politics of
Feminism,
Ecology, and
Peace: Petra
Kelly
(1947–1992) and
Gert Bastian
(1923–1992)*

(4) Every mother shall be entitled to the protection and care of the community.

(5) Illegitimate children shall be provided by legislation with the same opportunities for their physical and spiritual development and their position in society as are enjoyed by legitimate children. . . .

Article 9

(1) All Germans shall have the right to form associations and societies.

(2) Associations, the objects or activities of which conflict with the criminal laws or which are directed against the constitutional order or the concept of international understanding, shall be prohibited.

(3) The right to form associations to safeguard and improve working and economic conditions is guaranteed to everyone and to all trades and professions. Agreements which restrict or seek to hinder this right are null and void; measures directed to this end are illegal. . . .

DOCUMENT TWO

PETRA KELLY

"Women and Power"
(1994)

In her essays in Thinking Green, *Kelly explores the intersection of environmentalism, feminism, and nonviolence. In this essay, Kelly calls upon her male colleagues in the Green movement to take up the mantle of feminism and overthrow patriarchy. What are Kelly's criticisms of her colleagues? What are the consequences of a world where women do not have power?*

> *"True emancipation begins neither at
> the polls nor in the courts. It begins
> in women's soul."*
> —Emma Goldman*

---

*Emma Goldman, "The Tragedy of Woman's Emancipation," in *The Traffic in Women and Other Essays on Feminism* (Albion, California: Times Change Press, 1970), p. 14.

As a teenager growing up into a young woman, I was enraged when I saw how women have been obliterated from the pages of history and the pages of the Bible. Women were subordinated and dependent on men for their realization and value, always needing men as their path to fulfillment. I began to read Rosa Luxemburg's writings, particularly her prison diaries, and to search through biographies of Alexandra Kollontai, George Sand, Emma Goldman, Helen Keller, and other women who have put their very special stamp on history but have been mostly ignored by male historians and male scholars. I set out to rediscover these brave women. I never had much respect for Marx, Engels, and all the other dogmatic macho men who theorized and philosophized about the working classes and capital while, at the same time, discriminating against their wives and children and leading the lives of "academic *pashas*," always being rejuvenated by their wives and mistresses. They couldn't even cook or clean or sew or take care of themselves. They always needed women for their most basic needs.

Men's domination of women is deep and systemic, and it is accepted around the world by most men and many women as "natural," as something that somehow cannot be changed. But norms of human behavior do change. Because the oppression of women is so deeply embedded in our societies and our psyches, it continues to be invisible, even to those who are working to overcome other forms of injustice. Feminism is considered by many people to be one aspect of social justice, but to me it is a principle in and of itself. To rid the world of nuclear weapons and poverty, we must end racism and sexism. As long as white males hold all of the social and economic power, women and people of color will continue to be discriminated against, and poverty and the military mentality will continue unabated. We cannot just analyze structures of domination and oppression. We must also practice disobedience in our own lives, starting by disobeying all systems of male domination.

The system in which men have more value and more social and economic power than women is found throughout the world—East and West, North and South. Women suffer both from structural oppression and from individual men. Too many movements for social justice accept the assumptions of male dominance and ignore the oppression of women, but patriarchy pervades both our political and our personal lives. Feminism rejects all forms of male dominance and affirms the value of women's lives and experiences. It recognizes that no pattern of domination is necessary and seeks to liberate women and men from the structures of dominance that characterize patriarchy.

Many women are beginning to reject the existing systems and styles of male politics. Whether at Greenham Common, Comiso, Australia, Belau, protecting the Himalayn forests, or working for peace in Eastern Europe, women have been stirred to action. Motivated to act on our own, not only as mothers and nurturers but also as leaders in a changing world, we must stand up as women and become elected to political and economic offices throughout the world, so

Chapter 12
The Politics of
Feminism,
Ecology, and
Peace: Petra
Kelly
(1947–1992) and
Gert Bastian
(1923–1992)

we can change the policies and structures from those of death to those of life. We do not need to abrogate our positive, feminist principles of loving, caring, showing emotions, and nurturing. Every individual has both feminine and masculine qualities. We should not relieve men of their responsibility to transform themselves, to develop caring human qualities and become responsible for childcare, housework, and all other essential support work. We will never be able to reclaim the Earth if men do not give up their privileges and share these basic tasks with women. Children are not just the responsibility of their mothers.

The scientific revolution of the seventeenth century contained in it the seeds of today's oppressive technologies. If we trace the myths and metaphors associated with the conquest of nature, we will realize how much we are under the sway of masculine institutions and ideologies. Masculine technology and patriarchal values have prevailed in Auschwitz, Dresden, Hiroshima, Nagasaki, Vietnam, Iran, Iraq, Afghanistan, and many other parts of the world. The ultimate result of unchecked, terminal patriarchy will be ecological catastrophe or nuclear holocaust.

Feminism is about alleviating women's powerlessness. Women must share half the Earth and half the Sky, on our own terms and with our own self-determined values. Feminism seeks to redefine our very modes of existence and to transform nonviolently the structures of male dominance. I am not saying that women are inherently better than men. Overturning patriarchy does not mean replacing men's dominance with women's dominance. That would merely maintain the patriarchal pattern of dominance. We need to transform the pattern itself. The work of feminist women and profeminist men is to liberate everyone from a system that is oppressive to women and restrictive to men, and to restore balance and harmony between women and men and between masculine and feminine values in society and within each of us. Feminists working in the peace and ecology movements are sometimes viewed as kind, nurturing Earth mothers, but that is too comfortable a stereotype. We are not meek and we are not weak. We are angry—on our own behalf, for our sisters and children who suffer, and for the entire planet—and we are determined to protect life on Earth.

Green women work together with men on issues like ecology and disarmament. But we must also assert women's oppression as a central concern, for our experience is that men do not take women's oppression as seriously as other causes. There is a clear and profound relationship between militarism, environmental degradation, and sexism. Any commitment to social justice and nonviolence that does not address the structures of male domination of women is incomplete. We will work with our Green brothers, but we will not be subservient to them. They must demonstrate their willingness to give up the privileges of membership in the male caste.

There is a saying: Where power is, women are not. Women must be willing to be powerful. Because we bear scars from the ways men have used their power over us, women often want no part of power. To a certain extent, this is good sense. Patriarchal power has brought us acid rain, global warming, military states, and countless cases of private suffering. We have all seen men whose power has caused them to lose all sense of reality, decency, and imagination, and we are right to fear such power. But playing an active part in society, on an equal footing with men, does not mean adopting the old thought patterns and strategies of the patriarchal world. It means putting our own ideas of an emancipatory society into practice. Rather than emulating Margaret Thatcher and others who loyally adapt themselves to male values of hierarchy, we must find our own definitions of power that reflect women's values and women's experience. Jean Baker Miller points out how women, though closed out of male dominions of power, experience great power in the daily work of nurturing others.† This is not power *over* others, but power *with* others, the kind of shared power that has to replace patriarchal power.

Women in the Green movement are committed to fighting the big wars—the destruction of nature, imperial politics, militarism, and the like. But we are just as determined to end the little wars that take place against women every day, often invisibly. Women's suffering seems so normal and is so pervasive that it is scarcely noticed. These restrictions, degradations, and acts of violence are so embedded in our societies that they appear natural, but they are not natural. The system of which these are a part has been constructed over centuries by laws and through institutions that were developed by men and excluded women. We want to end these forms of oppression by doing away with the power and mentality that produced and maintains them.

†Jean Baker Miller, *Toward a New Psychology of Women* (Boston: Beacon Press, 1986. Second edition).

Chapter 12
The Politics of
Feminism,
Ecology, and
Peace: Petra
Kelly
(1947–1992) and
Gert Bastian
(1923–1992)

DOCUMENT THREE

GREENHAM COMMON WOMEN'S PEACE CAMP

"Women for Life on Earth" Letter
(August 1981)

In late August 1981, a group of women marched 120 miles from Cardiff, South Wales in the United Kingdom to the United States Airforce base at Greenham Common Royal in Bekshire. NATO had just recently decided to install cruise missiles at this site. When the women arrived, they presented to the base commander a statement declaring their intent to stop the installation of the missiles. They then set up a "peace camp" outside the main gate of the base. In the days and weeks following the establishment of the first camp, satellite camps sprung up around the nine-mile perimeter fence of the base. The last camp was closed in 1994. On what basis do these women claim the right to protest?

We are a group of women from all over Britain who have walked one hundred and twenty miles from Cardiff to deliver this letter to you. Some of us have brought our babies with us this entire distance. We fear for the future of all our children, and for the future of the living world which is the basis of all life.

We have undertaken this action because we believe that the nuclear arms race constitutes the greatest threat ever faced by the human race and our living planet. We have chosen Greenham Common as our destination because it is this base which our government has chosen for 96 "Cruise" without our consent. The British people have never been consulted about our government's nuclear defence policy. We know that the arrival of these hideous weapons at this base will place our entire country in the position of a front-line target in any confrontation between the two superpowers, Russia and the United States of America. We in Europe will not accept the sacrificial role offered us by our North Atlantic Treaty Organisation (NATO) allies. We will not be the victims in a war which is not of our making. We wish to be neither the initiators nor the targets of a nuclear holocaust. We have had enough of our military and political leaders who squander vast sums of money and human resources on weapons of mass destruction while we can hear in our hearts the millions of human beings throughout the world whose needs cry out to be met. We are implacably opposed to the siting of U.S. Cruise Missiles in this country. We represent thousands of ordinary people who are opposed to these weapons and we will use all our resources to prevent the siting of these missiles here. We want the arms race to be brought to a halt now—before it is too late to create a peaceful, stable world for our future generations.

DOCUMENT FOUR

MINISTRY OF DEFENSE

"New Directive on the Problem of Traditions in the Armed Forces" (1982)

As a career military officer, Gert Bastian often worried about neofascist or neo-Nazi traditions, ideas, or support emerging from the ranks of the German military. This was a sentiment shared by many in the FRG. In 1965, a directive was issued to articulate the proper thinking and behavior for a German soldier. The selection below is a directive issued in 1982, in response to fears about neo-Nazism. What are a soldier's rights, duties, and responsibilities?

I. BASIC PRINCIPLES

1. Tradition is the passing on of values and norms. They are formed through a value-orientated analysis of the past. Tradition binds generations, safeguards an identity, and builds a bridge between the past and the future. Tradition is an essential foundation of man's culture. It presupposes an understanding of the historical, political and social context.

2. The yardsticks for an understanding and preservation of traditions in the German Federal armed forces are the Basic Law and the delegated assignments and duties of the army. The Basic Law is the response to history. It allows much latitude yet entails definite limits.

The portrayal of common, united values and a democratic awareness of the armed forces is the foundation of the preservation of their tradition. . . .

5. Political-historical education contributes decisively to the development of a common understanding of tradition in conformity with the Basic Law and an up-to-date preservation of that tradition. This demands an approach that incorporates the whole of German history and omits nothing.

6. The history of the German armed forces has not been without abrupt changes of a serious nature. The armed forces were both instruments and victims of political abuse during the period of National Socialism. An unjust regime, such as the Third Reich, cannot found a tradition. . . .

15. In the preservation in the German Federal armed forces, such records of conduct and experiences from history should be preserved which, as ethical and constitutional, free and democratic traditions, can serve as examples and are worthy of remembrance today.

16. In the preservation of tradition in the German Federal armed forces, events should be remembered such as those in which soldiers, beyond their mil-

Chapter 12
The Politics of
Feminism,
Ecology, and
Peace: Petra
Kelly
(1947–1992) and
Gert Bastian
(1923–1992)

itary performance, took part in progressive political activities which contributed to the emergence of a mature citizenry and led the way to a free, republican and democratic Germany.

17. In maintaining the tradition of the German Federal armed forces special emphasis should be placed on the following political stances and modes of behaviour:

1) Critical acceptance of German history, love of the homeland and mother country, orientation not only towards success and the successful, but also towards the suffering of the persecuted and the humiliated.

2) Political participation and common responsibility, awareness of democratic values, judgment without prejudice, tolerance, readiness and ability to discuss the ethical aspects of military service, the will for peace.

3) Conscientious obedience and loyal fulfillment of duties in everyday life, comradeship, determination and will to fight when defence is required. . . .

20. The German Federal armed forces preserve their own established traditions, which should be further developed. Those included above all are:

1) The mission to preserve peace in freedom as the foundation of a soldier's commitment.

2) Abstention from creating ideologically-motivated images of an enemy or from cultivating feelings of hatred.

3) Participation in the Atlantic Alliance and comradely cooperation with Allied troops on the basis of common values.

4) The model of 'Citizen in Uniform' and the principles of Innere Führung.

5) The active contribution to the shaping of democracy through the role of the soldier as a citizen.

6) An open-minded attitude to social change and the readiness for contact with the civilian citizen.

7) Assistance to the civilian population in emergency and catastrophe at home and abroad.

These are unchangeable characteristics of the German Federal armed forces.

DOCUMENT FIVE

"Appeal of Krefeld"
(1980)

*In November 1980, Gert Bastian stood in front of the cameras with others calling
for the FDR to withdraw permission to deploy midrange nuclear missiles in central Europe. When this appeal was issued, some accused the general and later the
organization that he founded, Generals for Peace and Disarmament, of being organized by the Soviet Union. By the end of the three-year petition drive, however,
over 5 million Germans signed the petition. What are the concerns of the appeal?
Who is criticized and why?*

NATO RESOLUTION A FATEFUL MISTAKE
EUROPEAN NATIONS SHOULD NOT BE EXPOSED TO UNBEARABLE RISKS

More and more obviously the NATO rearmament resolution of 12 December
1979 is proving to be a fateful mistake. The hope for agreements between the
USA and the Soviet Union over a restriction of Euro-strategic arms systems before a new generation of American middle-range nuclear weapons is stationed
in Western Europe will apparently not be fulfilled.

A year after Brussels, not even the commencement of such talks is in sight.
On the contrary: the newly elected president of the USA frankly declares that he
does not even want to accept the Salt II treaty on the restriction of Soviet and
American strategic nuclear weapons and therefore does not want to pass it on
to the Senate for ratification.

However, the American refusal to ratify the treaty would unavoidably push
the chance of talks on restricting Euro-strategic nuclear arms into the distant future. A suicidal arms race would not be stopped at the last moment; its increasing acceleration together with increasingly specific speculations about the
possibility of limiting a nuclear war necessarily exposes the European nations,
above all, to unbearable risks.

The participants in the Krefeld Talks of 15 and 16 November 1980 therefore
jointly appeal to the Federal government:

> To withdraw their consent to stationing Pershing II rockets and cruise missiles in
> Central Europe; to take an attitude within the alliance which no longer leaves
> room to suspect our country of wanting to be the forerunner of a new nuclear
> arms race which would endanger the Europeans above all.

Worry about recent developments is growing among the general public. The
possibilities of an alternative security policy are being discussed with more and
more determination. Such deliberations are of great importance for the demo-

Chapter 12
The Politics of
Feminism,
Ecology, and
Peace: Petra
Kelly
(1947–1992) and
Gert Bastian
(1923–1992)

cratic process of opinion-forming and can contribute to preventing our nation from suddenly being confronted with a *fait accompli*.

The whole population is therefore asked to support this appeal in order to enforce by unceasing and increasing pressure of public opinion a security policy:

> which does not permit Central Europe to be equipped as a nuclear arms platform for the USA; disarmament is considered more important than deterrent; development of the armed forces is to be orientated to achieve these goals.

Krefeld, 16 November 1980

DOCUMENT SIX

"An Appeal for European Nuclear Disarmament" (1980)

In April 1980, a group of over several hundred peace activists from all over the world stood in the House of Commons in Great Britain and launched an appeal for nuclear disarmament through a petition drive. Among the speakers were politicians like the head of the British Labour Party, Tony Benn; one of the founders of the Campaign for Nuclear Disarmament, Bruce Kent; the Soviet dissent, Zhores Medvedev; and the distinguished historian and longtime leftist thinker, E. P. Thompson. What are the primary concerns of the signatories? What solutions do they pose?

We are entering the most dangerous decade in human history. A third world war is not merely possible, but increasingly likely. Economic and social difficulties in advanced industrial countries, crisis, militarism and war in the third world compound the political tensions that fuel a demented arms race. In Europe, the main geographical stage for the East-West confrontation, new generations of ever more deadly nuclear weapons are appearing.

For at least twenty-five years, the forces of both the North Atlantic and the Warsaw alliances have each had sufficient nuclear weapons to annihilate their opponents, and at the same time to endanger the very basis of civilised life. But with each passing year, competition in nuclear armaments has multiplied their numbers, increasing the probability of some devastating accident or miscalculation.

As each side tries to prove its readiness to use nuclear weapons, in order to prevent their use by the other side, new more 'usable' nuclear weapons are designed and the idea of 'limited' nuclear war is made to sound more and more plausible. So much so that this paradoxical process can logically only lead to the actual use of nuclear weapons.

Neither of the major powers is now in any moral position to influence smaller countries to forego the acquisition of nuclear armament. The increasing spread of nuclear reactors and the growth of the industry that installs them, reinforce the likelihood of world-wide proliferation of nuclear weapons, thereby multiplying the risks of nuclear exchanges.

Over the years, public opinion has pressed for nuclear disarmament and detente between the contending military blocs. This pressure has failed. An increasing proportion of world resources is expended on weapons, even though mutual extermination is already amply guaranteed. This economic burden, in both East and West, contributes to growing social and political strain, setting in motion a vicious circle in which the arms race feeds upon the instability of the world economy and vice versa: a deathly dialectic.

We are now in great danger. Generations have been born beneath the shadow of nuclear war, and have become habituated to the threat. Concern has given way to apathy. Meanwhile, in a world living always under menace, fear extends through both halves of the European continent. The powers of the military and of internal security forces are enlarged, limitations are placed upon free exchanges of ideas and between persons, and civil rights of independent-minded individuals are threatened, in the West as well as the East.

We do not wish to apportion guilt between the political and military leaders of East and West. Guilt lies squarely upon both parties. Both parties have adopted menacing postures and committed aggressive actions in different parts of the world.

The remedy lies in our own hands. We must act together to free the entire territory of Europe, from Poland to Portugal, from nuclear weapons, air and submarine bases, and from all institutions engaged in research into or manufacture of nuclear weapons. We ask the two super powers to withdraw all nuclear weapons from European territory. In particular, we ask the Soviet Union to halt production of the SS-20 medium range missile and we ask the United States not to implement the decision to develop cruise missiles and Pershing II missiles for deployment in Europe. We also urge the ratification of the SALT II agreement, as a necessary step towards the renewal of effective negotiations on general and complete disarmament.

At the same time, we must defend and extend the right of all citizens, East or West, to take part in this common movement and to engage in every kind of exchange.

We appeal to our friends in Europe, of every faith and persuasion, to consider urgently the ways in which we can work together for these common objectives. We envisage a European-wide campaign, in which every kind of exchange takes place; in which representatives of different nations and opinions confer and co-ordinate their activities; and in which less formal exchanges, between universities, churches, women's organisations, trade unions, youth organisations, professional groups and individuals, take place with the object of promoting a common object: to free all of Europe from nuclear weapons.

We must commence to act as if a united, neutral and pacific Europe already

Chapter 12
The Politics of
Feminism,
Ecology, and
Peace: Petra
Kelly
(1947–1992) and
Gert Bastian
(1923–1992)

exists. We must learn to be loyal, not to 'East' or 'West', but to each other, and we must disregard the prohibitions and limitations imposed by my national state.

It will be the responsibility of the people of each nation to agitate for the expulsion of nuclear weapons and bases from European soil and territorial waters, and to decide upon its own means and strategy, concerning its own territory. These will differ from one country to another, and we do not suggest that any single strategy should be imposed. But this must be part of a transcontinental movement in which every kind of exchange takes place.

We must resist any attempt by the statesmen of East and West to manipulate this movement to their own advantage. We offer no advantage to either NATO or the Warsaw alliance. Our objectives must be to free Europe from confrontation, to enforce detente between the United States and the Soviet Union, and, ultimately, to dissolve both great power alliances.

In appealing to fellow Europeans, we are not turning our backs on the world. In working for the peace of Europe we are working for the peace of the world. Twice in this century Europe has disgraced its claims to civilisation by engendering world war. This time we must repay our debts to the world by engendering peace.

This appeal will achieve nothing if it is not supported by determined and inventive action, to win more people to support it. We need to mount an irresistible pressure for a Europe free of nuclear weapons.

We do not wish to impose any uniformity on the movement nor to pre-empt the consultations and decisions of those many organisations already exercising their influence for disarmament and peace. But the situation is urgent. The dangers steadily advance. We invite your support for this common objective, and we shall welcome both your help and advice.

DOCUMENT SEVEN

PETRA KELLY

"Thinking Green"

In this essay, Kelly defines the politics of "thinking Green." How does Green politics differ from previous political parties and movements? What does politics need?

"Never doubt that a small group of thoughtful,
committed citizens can change the world. Indeed, it's
the only thing that ever has."—Margaret Mead

When we founded the West German Green Party, we used the term "anti-party party" to describe our approach to politics based on a new understanding of power, a "counter-power" that is natural and common to all, to be shared by all, and used by all for all. This is the power of transformation, rooted in the discovery of our own strength and ability to be active participants in society. This kind of power stands in stark contrast to the power of domination, terror, and oppression, and is the best remedy for powerlessness.

Using power to dominate humans and nature has brought us to an impasse and can never take us beyond it. We must learn to think and act from our hearts, to recognize the interconnectedness of all living creatures, and to respect the value of each thread in the vast web of life. This is a spiritual perspective, and it is the foundation of all Green politics. It entails the radical, nonviolent transformation of the structures of society and of our way of thinking, so that domination is no longer the primary *modus operandi.* At the root of all Green political action is nonviolence, starting with how we live our lives, taking small, unilateral steps towards peace in everything we do. Green politics requires us to be both tender and subversive. Affirming tenderness as a political value is already subversive. In Green politics, we practice tenderness in relations with others; in caring for ideas, art, language, and culture; and in cherishing and protecting the Earth.

To think Green is to build solidarity with those working for social justice and human rights everywhere, not bound by ideologies. The problems that threaten life on Earth were produced collectively, they affect us collectively, and we must act collectively to change them. We cannot retreat into isolation. The Green vision of a just society is one in which economic, social, and individual rights are guaranteed and protected, and everyone is free from exploitation, violence, and oppression.

Politicians give speeches about these values while working to undermine them. The benefits of the current political and economic systems are reserved for the privileged; therefore, any meaningful movement for social justice must focus on systemic change, on transforming both the oppressive state and economic structures that concentrate wealth and power in the hands of a few. The Green methodology is not to work from the top down, but to begin at the grassroots, empowering ourselves to direct our own destinies through the cultivation of civil space and democratic social forms.

First and foremost, Green politics is grassroots politics. Politics from the top is almost always corrupt and compromised. To bring about change from below is to challenge the moral authority of those who make decisions on our behalf. Through grassroots organization, education, and empowerment, we work to reverse the state-orientation of politics and instead open up a civil space in which we are active subjects, not passive objects of those in power. Substantive change in politics at the top will come only when there is enough pressure from below. The essence of Green politics is to live our values. . . .

Nonviolence, ecology, social justice, and feminism are the key principles of Green politics, and they are inseparably linked. We know, for example, that the wasteful patterns of production and consumption to the industrial North deplete and ravage the environment and furnish the motive and means for the vi-

Chapter 12
The Politics of
Feminism,
Ecology, and
Peace: Petra
Kelly
(1947–1992) and
Gert Bastian
(1923–1992)

olent appropriation of materials from the weaker nations in the South and for the wasteful process of militarization throughout the world. In both capitalist and state socialist countries, human beings are reduced to economic entities, with little or no regard for the human or ecological costs. Politics from the top, the pattern of hierarchical domination, is the characteristic of patriarchy. It is not a coincidence that power rests in the hands of men, benefits accrue first and foremost to men, and that women are exploited at all levels of society.

The Green approach to politics is a kind of celebration. We recognize that each of us is part of the world's problems, and we are also part of the solution. The dangers and the potentials for healing are not just outside us. We begin to work exactly where we are. There is no need to wait until conditions become ideal. We can simplify our lives and live in ways that affirm ecological and humane values. Better conditions will come because we have begun.

We have found so many ways to think each other to death—neutron warheads, nuclear reactors, Star Wars defense systems, and many other methods of mass destruction. We are killing each other with our euphemisms and abstractions. In warfare, we accept the deaths of thousands and millions of people we call our "enemy." When we dehumanize people, devalue nature, and exalt narrowly defined self-interests, destruction is sure to follow. The healing of our planet requires a new way of thinking about politics and about life. At the heart of this is the understanding that all things are intimately interconnected in the complex web of life. It can therefore be said that the primary goal of Green politics is an inner revolution. Joanna Macy calls this "the greening of the self."* . . .

*Joanna Macy, *World as Lover, World as Self* (Berkeley: Parallax Press, 1991), p. 183.

DOCUMENT EIGHT

KONRAD ADENAUER FOUNDATION
FOR SOCIAL SCIENCE RESEARCH

"Value Orientations of Green Supporters Compared to Those of Other Party Supporters (in Percent)" (1984)

The poll below reveals West Germans' attitudes toward their state and society in the early 1980s. What values are shared among West German voters?

I want to live in a society . . .	Population as a whole	CDU/CSU voters	SPD voters	FDP voters	Green voters
in which people are more important than money	51	46	55	47	69
in which law and order are respected	50	59	47	51	19
in which people can get ahead by working hard	30	36	25	34	16
in which tradition is respected	25	29	21	24	6
in which citizens take part in decision-making	25	18	32	18	45
which is open to new ideas and change	18	12	19	26	43

DOCUMENT NINE

HARRY KREISLER
Conversations with History
Interview with Petra K. Kelly and Gert Bastian
(October 23, 1984)

On October 23, 1984, Kelly and Bastian sat down with Harry Kreisler of the Institute of International Studies, University of California, Berkeley, to discuss the European Peace Movement. For the complete interview go to http://globetrotter. berkeley.edu/conversations/KellyBastian/kelly-bastian0.html. In this excerpt, Bastian discusses the reasons why he left the army and why he became an antinuclear activist

Chapter 12
The Politics of
Feminism,
Ecology, and
Peace: Petra
Kelly
(1947–1992) and
Gert Bastian
(1923–1992)

and member of the Green Party. Kelly's comments further explain why people join the peace movement.

TURNING TO THE PEACE MOVEMENT

[KREISLER:] General Bastian, you were an officer in the German army. What set of factors led you to make this dramatic move from the army into the peace movement?

[BASTIAN:] In my time as an active soldier, [I was] always speaking for a necessary defense, but for a defense which is organized on the lowest possible level. It should be organized in a way which does not have a provocative effect on the other side and is not pushing forward the arms race. Such a defense gives not more security but is destroying the existing security, and when the discussion was started regarding Pershing and cruise missiles as an answer to SS-20 on the other side, I came to the conclusion very fast that this is a step in the wrong direction. It brings us not more security in Europe but creates a new danger for a limited nuclear war, which is possible with such new nuclear weapons, and the answer was to expect the Soviet side to respond with the deployment of SS-22s and SS-23s in East Germany and Czechoslovakia. I was not willing to accept this step. I had the wish to protect the soldiers, first, from being misused in such a terrible way. Therefore, I made a lot of protests to my minister of defense, and made the request to leave the army.

NEW WEAPONS CHANGE MILITARY STRATEGY

[KREISLER:] . . . What in particular about these two weapons [Pershing and cruise missiles]? Is it that they are a symbol of an arms race that doesn't stop? What in particular was disturbing about these two weapons?

[BASTIAN:] That's a good question. In my opinion, these two weapons are a significant change in nuclear strategy. In former times, nuclear weapons have been only available to prevent war. Effective deterrence as a revenge potential. Nobody could fire the first shot without a risk of being killed as a result of the second shot. But these new weapons are more accurate and more precise and are mobile, and are deployed in a forward-based European terrain. This is an important fact: it gives the owner a chance to win—to wage and win war in a traditional way, if war is not long avoidable. This makes a new situation for the European allies of the United States. The entrance in a nuclear war is much easier when such weapons are available. . . .

[KREISLER:] You were then not saying that you are opposed to all nuclear weapons. In terms of this decision that led you from being in the military to being in the peace movement, it was the particular quality of the new weapons that were being introduced that was changing the overall strategy behind the weapons.

[BASTIAN:] I think all nuclear weapons are a danger for the whole world, and are no longer useful. But we have been accustomed to the fact that they are existing, and it was possible to accept this situation by thinking, "Nobody is so crazy as to fire the first nuclear weapons, knowing very well that we must die in the second round." But this situation is no longer a given with these new weapons and with the answer of the Soviet Union with new missiles of the same quality. We have come to a new situation, and now these weapons are directed from one side to another in Europe, potentially crossing the Iron Curtain, with a very short fly and warning time. It is easy to understand that nobody will have the time in a situation of increasing crisis and fear to make a second check if the first impression is given that the other side is attacking. Then these weapons must be fired or lost. Therefore the danger that they are fired too early is very much greater than before.

[KREISLER:] The Pershings being a hard-target kill weapon with a time of ten minutes warning.

[BASTIAN:] And that's the purpose. To prevent the other side to start a war, they have the purpose to neutralize, to hit the nerve centers in the military and political leading organizations on the other side, in the Warsaw Pact side. And have a war-waging quality, in my opinion. Our government is saying no, but I have another estimation of the real purpose of these new weapons.

[KREISLER:] And that is, a war-fighting strategy.

[BASTIAN:] Yes, a war-fighting strategy which goes with a new concept of the United States, which is not the official concept of NATO in Europe but is the concept of the United States troops and is another sign that there is an important change going forward. A change which is, that if war is not avoidable, it is not the first objective to have crisis management in which the first missile does not cause the next missile to be fired, but if the first troop is fired on, then the new concept has the objective to make new fronts and to make new offensives and to wage this war until the other side is completely defeated.

[KREISLER:] So you are talking about nuclear weapons not being in place to stop there ever being a war, but rather actively engaged in waging and winning the war. The assumption being that you could, in fact, terminate the war, which is an open question.

[BASTIAN:] Right the other side is completely defeated with these weapons.

ANTI-AMERICANISM AND THE PEACE MOVEMENT

[KREISLER:] Intertwined in all of this and related to these problems is the question of whether the peace movement is anti-American. How do you respond to that question?

[KELLY:] First of all, I think that the peace movement in Europe has probably most of its friends in the American people. At every demonstration that I can remember we've had key speakers from the United States, whether it be Ron Dellums or Mrs. King or Mr. Belafonte. The argument is, of course, a pretty good one. [People] can immediately say that if you're anti-American weapons, then you're anti-American. In fact, all of our whole inspiration coming from people like the Berrigans, many others who've blockaded with

Chapter 12
The Politics of
Feminism,
Ecology, and
Peace: Petra
Kelly
(1947–1992) and
Gert Bastian
(1923–1992)

us, who've been taken and arrested with us, have shown how we're tied together. We also have many friends, of course, in the Eastern Bloc countries,
but they can't travel to us so easily. I think that is completely wrong.

But certainly, throughout the whole population, the criticism is very
strong of Mr. Reagan, of interventionism in Central America, of policies en-
circling the globe, whether it be Mr. Schultz going to New Zealand and saying to Mr. Luntz, "you cannot do this nuclear-free zone," or whether it is in
fact the Americans looking for new bases because the Philippine bases might
go. There is a mistrust of this administration.

There is a deep mistrust that, for example, now we're talking about whose
missiles are being put on U-boats, and we can't even count how many there
are going to be. And this is a mistrust in the population against the [Reagan]
administration, but never against the American people. In fact, every time
there is a big demonstration here, there is a movement to, in a way, be critical. People are very happy in Europe and are in solidarity. I think what worries people most, at the present, is, for example, the problem with Central
America. Because there is a fear that Mr. Reagan's second term might be
more dangerous than the first. And there is a feeling that this administration
does not know historically what has happened, what is going on. [The peace
movement] is always being misinterpreted by the media. I must say the media, the American media, has done so much damage to the peace movement
and to the whole idea, but they are the first ones to call it anti-American.
They will even call a speaker like Mrs. King "anti-American" if she comes to
demonstrations.

[KREISLER:] Is the criticism even-handed? Is the peace movement as critical of,
say, the downing of the KAL flight, without going into what actually happened, or the invasion in Afghanistan? These are important questions for
American audiences because, as you say, this is the way the media frames the
question.

[KELLY:] Well, first of all, it is very clear that, especially with the Green Party,
there has been this non-aligned factor. It's been very critical for both sides.
We were doing the very famous blockade in Moolanda when the KAL air-
liner was downed, and that night there was an incredible reaction of people
who holding special services and making very much protest, including the
day that Ron Dellums had come to a platform where we openly, again, mentioned that we cannot accept this. On the other hand, we have also spoken in
Afghanistan as well as in Nicaragua, and we have Greens traveling to both
Nicaragua and to Afghanistan. What is amazing, though, is that the human
rights issue is so ideologically misused, you will have Americans talk about
Afghanistan until you cannot hear it and will have Russians talk about
Nicaragua until you cannot hear it anymore, because they both misuse their
own backyard, everybody's backyard is so full of bodies and corpses and yet
[each] side always points to the other side. For me the biggest hypocrisy, I
must say, was when we had so much with hope with the Solidarity move-

[398]

ment in Poland, and there was Mr. Reagan suddenly a champion of trade union rights, which he does not in any way support in his own country, but he supports them in Poland. The same in the reverse, Mr. Strauss.

We have, as a peace movement, learned to go beyond ideologies, beyond systems, beyond national borders, and to point out the human rights infringements wherever they happen. That's been the role of the peace movement. For example, with the question of Sakharov, it was the Greens that went to Moscow, and the first thing they asked was the fate of dissidents, not only Mr. Sakharov, but many more. And we would also go to the State Department and ask what happened in El Salvador. But the problem is that, again, this non-aligned attitude is something so new and so special that so many people have not yet comprehended that we look all over the world. That we try to be an Amnesty International, more or less, and we try to do it in a way that it cannot be misused. And so I think that the argument is really wrong.

[BASTIAN:] Can I add something? I am much older than Petra, and for me, another point, very important, is my deep feeling of friendship to the United States and to the United States people. The origin of this feeling was the end of World War II. I was living in Bavaria. I was coming from a prisoner camp of the United States in Bavaria, and have never forgotten, and shall never forget, that the United States was the first which gave us the end and helped us to come back to a normal life after this terrible end of this war and all these crimes which were done by my own country and by all of us. I will never forget it. Therefore, I have such a deep feeling of friendship to the United States and to the United States' soldiers. I am full of respect for the United States' soldiers in Germany. I have had good comrades in the United States army—the division command of General Blanchard, a former high commander of the United States troops in Europe; his successor General Kurzon—[all] have been very fine soldiers and officers. This is the reason that I am so angry. That now, wrong policy gives such a deep shadow to the relationship between Europe and the United States in the Western Alliance. It makes such an unnecessary danger and damage in these relationships. And this is one of the reasons of my protest.

[KREISLER:] General Bastian, when you resigned from the Greens, the *Washington Post* quoted you as criticizing the antiquated politics of class struggle as well as the one-sided anti-American foreign policy of the Greens. Is that quotation correct?

[BASTIAN:] It is correct, but it was only one of many reasons that I left only the Parliamentary group, not the Green Party. I am a member of the Green Party still now. I have written in the paper to the Green friends in the faction in this time, said I am angry at a small group which is a clear minority within the Greens, which came from the former Communist Party and has, in my opinion, old-fashioned Marxist thinking and is very anti-American. Its manipulating the sessions of the board of the Green Party and the faction also, and has more success that is declared than [merited] by the small number of

Chapter 12
The Politics of
Feminism,
Ecology, and
Peace: Petra
Kelly
(1947–1992) and
Gert Bastian
(1923–1992)

members in this group. The reasons that I have written this is to give a warning to my friends to be careful that this minority come not to such an unnecessary success. I think this warning was successful. In the following time, this group was not successful.

It is, of course, a small group of, maybe, 200 members for whom I fought very hard that they will become members, because I don't want to have an anti-communistic Green Party. But they had a long process of integrating. I think it was necessary that sometimes we have to do this. The many different strands in the Green look and vie for influence, that's very clear. You have them in a very big, successful movement, where you have many ideologies coming together. Though we have to also add that what has been frustrating was that, in fact, the Green Party parliamentary group was always worrying about its own problems more than those outside, because of its structure. That was the main reason I left.

That was the main reason. This was so blown out of proportion. That's why I'm shaking my head here. Because the *Washington Post* and *The New York Times* took that little one line, and the letter was two pages, that was one line, and that was a worry that he expressed, and immediately blew it up. That was the typical media style.

I have left the Parliament, at first, on account of the internal problems, not the effective work of the organization. The chaos, the parliamentary people, the succeeders working together in one group was a wrong construction from the first day. This other was only an additional aspect, but not the main point.

[KREISLER:] You both have touched on something that I want to pursue, which is this generational difference of the view of America. Your generation, General Bastian, remembers the American role in World War II, remembers the Marshall Plan, remembers whatever else America achieved in that early rebuilding of Europe. It is said that the successor generation thinks more of America in terms of Watergate, of Vietnam, and so on. How does this resolve itself? What I think I hear both of you saying is that the peace movement is in fact not anti-American, that in fact it is a rejection of particular policies.

[KELLY:] It is a rejection of militarism wherever it may be. I would like to say that rather clearly. I have a stepfather who was in the American military, so I have a rather good insight into it. I could never accept the Vietnam War. It was pure barbarism. To me, this barbarism was the worst kind, which is committed also on the other [Eastern bloc] side. And I think those soldiers were just as misused as German soldiers, as any soldier. The problem, I think, that the peace movement is trying to show is militarism. When you come to a certain degree, then there can be nobody who is a fine general or a fine soldier because they are all being misused or they misuse themselves. At a certain point, the United States had a tradition in Vietnam out of which they should have learned. Now, in fact, they are going back to policies again misusing their soldiers, misusing them completely as a kind of checkmate on a chess board. They are misused in the sense that American soldiers in Europe are becoming worried. They are sending us little slips through the fence saying please continue, because we don't like this here either. I think this is what has to be the warning to all political military leaders in both superpowers, that they cannot continue misusing. Because its not the generals on the front, it's certainly the soldier out there who are going to be using nuclear weapons, who are going to throw them a few miles and hit his own territory and who are going to be misused in all this thinking. This has become the criticism. It is a criticism of militarism and of nuclear policies, nuclear barbarism. No person said it better than Archbishop Hunthausen, when he said it is a time now of nuclear Auschwitz. I think that is the correct wording. It is really, really horrifying. That is what the peace movement is trying to create. Of course, our criticism is very loud against our own protective power, called the United States. . . .

[KREISLER:] Now, there is another set of issues that I want to get into here, and that is the question of German nationalism. To what extent, in the words of *The New York Times* foreign correspondent, Mr. Vincour, is the peace movement a left-wing nationalism, a manifestation of what we experienced?

[KELLY:] I have had a discussion with another commentator who made the same statement, that the peace movement is a very nationalistic movement in West Germany and has as the only objective to make forgotten the crime of Auschwitz in pointing out Hiroshima. It is crazy to speak so. No. This movement is an idealistic movement, not a nationalistic movement, and has more internationalistic input and thinking and has good friends in all other countries and continents, in Japan as well as in Australia, in the United States as well as in Austria and the United Kingdom, and, if it is possible, also on the other side of the Iron Curtain. There is no nationalistic thinking in this movement. I can say that really.

[BASTIAN:] I must add this. Because you know where the misunderstanding came, was when Heinrich Albert, the ex-mayor of Berlin said once, we have a new form of patriotism. What he meant was that Europeans are finally saying, "We are not going to be the slaughterhouse of two superpowers. We are going to be a very sovereign continent that says it doesn't want to die. So we are patriots of our life." Mr. Vincour, whom we followed for several years, is now in Paris doing the same stories, has always said that that sentence of Mr. Albert's, the SPD mayor of Berlin, was very dangerous because it showed that we are nationalistic. It is such a misuse of this movement, because there is no talk of reunification in the peace movement, because it doesn't concern us at this moment, second because nobody wants two German military nations to come together, and third, it is never a discussion because it is not a nationalistic movement whatsoever. . . .

13

Cold War Europe: Václav Havel (1936–) and Olga Šplíchalová Havlová (1933–1996)

■ SETTING THE STAGE

Three years after the Soviet Red Army drove the Nazis from Prague in 1945, Czechoslovakia succumbed to communist rule. On the eve of parliamentary elections in February 1948, the Czechoslovak Communists bullied, intimidated, and manipulated the parliamentary system to gain control of the government. Once in control, the Communists embarked upon the stalinization of the postwar Czecho- slovak state. Under the watchful and threatening eye of the Soviet Union and its leader, Joseph Stalin, the Czechoslovak Communists stalinized by purging newspapers, universities, professional organizations, sports clubs, and civilian and military insti- tutions of any anti-Communists and people opposed to their rule. In addi- tion, they passed a series of laws that nationalized large and midsize industries and business enterprises, collectivized agriculture, and censored any independent thought or action.

By the early 1950s, the Soviets had successfully forced Czechoslovakia and its neighbors to imitate Soviet political, administrative, and cultural institutions and to enter into international agreements with the Soviets that isolated them from the noncommunist world. Stalin now had a bloc of states that would cater to the interests of the Soviet Union. The governments of the Soviet bloc countries obeyed all dictates emanating from Moscow, whether they concerned domestic or foreign policy. With the help of the Soviet Red Army and security forces, Stalin maintained an iron grip on this region until his death in March 1953.

With Stalin's death, moderate Communists in the region began to explore the boundaries of economic, social, and political reform of the Stalinist system. From these experiments in reform came periodic revolts—East Germany in 1953, Poland and Hungary in 1956, Czechoslovakia in 1968, Poland in 1980–1981, and finally most of the Soviet bloc in 1989. These revolts were the result of social discontent and dissatisfaction with the Stalinist system, whether it was workers protesting working conditions and salaries, Communist party officials wishing to replace Stalinist leaders with moderates, students unhappy with living conditions, or intellectuals chafing to be free from censorship. Even when these revolts were brutally suppressed, individuals continued to challenge and subvert the system by associating freely with other like-minded individuals, and they did so in spite of intimidation and harassment by the Communists. Such individuals were often given the name *dissident*. In this chapter, we will examine the lives of two Czechs who became dissidents and how their dissent from the regime eventually contributed to the dismantling and demise of the Czechoslovak communist state.

Václav Havel and Olga Šplíchalová Havlová were members of a generation who survived World War II and the consolidation of communist power as children, learned and matured under Czechoslovak Stalinism as teenagers, and came of age when the Stalinist cloud began to lift. As young adults, this generation put reform of the socialist system on the political and socioeconomic agenda, even when they were quickly thwarted by an ideologically bankrupt communist regime that sought to silence them. This generation knew by middle age that the only way to live free and in truth was to dismantle the system. They had to emerge as the political and moral leaders of a postcommunist Czechoslovakia. Havel's and Havlová's lives show us the dynamic and contentious atmosphere of the building, maintenance, and dismantling of state socialism; their interests, grievances, and aspirations of everyday; the methods that each employed to transform their world; and the consequences visited upon each for challenging socialist practices and norms.

Chapter 13
Cold War Europe:
Václav Havel
(1936–) and Olga
Šplíchalová
Havlová
(1933–1996)

■ **The Actors:**

Václav Havel and Olga
Šplíchalová Havlová

Václav Havel was born on October 5, 1936, in Prague, Czechoslovakia, to well-to-do middle-class parents. Václav's father, Václav M. Havel, had been raised in a bourgeois milieu that he would pass on to his sons. His father spoke of his parents' and grandparents' successful forays into business in nineteenth-century Prague: restaurants, a building firm, and leisure venues for the growing Czech middle class in Prague. Václav's grandfather built the first indoor skating rink and the largest modern entertainment complex in Prague. His father continued his grandfather's work and built a development of large houses for the well-to-do. He eventually built and then managed the Barrandov Terrace, a restaurant of haute cuisine.

When Czechoslovakia became an independent republic in 1918, Václav's father became a firm believer in an individual's duty and need to participate in Czechoslovakia's new democracy: "political activity or inactivity is a question of conscience. We are the state—each of us is therefore responsible for its condition and future."[1] Growing up with such sentiments would influence young Václav's thoughts about politics. His mother's background and family also contributed to Václav's world view. His mother, Božena (Vavrečka) Havlová, was a well-educated woman whose interests ranged from "science, especially astronomy and zoology, to history and the arts." Her father, Hugo Vavrečka, served as the Czechoslovak ambassador to Hungary and Austria and was a minister in one of the last cabinets before the Nazi invasion and dismemberment of Czechoslovakia in 1939. Later in life, Božena, talked about the mistake she had made by not insisting that the family pack their trunks and escape to London when the Nazis invaded.

Václav and his younger brother, Ivan (b. 1938), spent their early lives under Nazi occupation. When he became a target of communist persecution in the 1970s and 1980s, Václav was often accused of coming from a family that had continued to thrive under the Nazi protectorate of Bohemia and Moravia. Václav freely admitted that during the war his father had been interested in preserving his business interests and his uncle, Miloš, continued to be associated with the protectorate's film industry. Havel's family, like Käthe Kollwitz's and Simone de Beauvoir's, walked a tightrope between protecting their interests, livelihoods, and lives and avoiding open collaboration with the Nazis and their supporters. When the Communists seized control of the government in 1948, enough questions about the Havel family existed to cause the communists to harass them and eventually to discredit Miloš Havel in the 1950s. Stripped of his interest in Czechoslovakia's largest film enterprise by the communist government and painted as a collaborator, Miloš fled to the West in 1952.

1. John Keane, *Václav Havel: A Political Tragedy in Six Acts* (New York: Basic Books, 2000), p. 36.

The Havel family weathered the war with their assets intact. When liberation came, initially they did not see the Communists as a threat to their persons or their property. Before World War II, the Czechoslovak Communist party had been a respected and credible one, usually polling 10 percent in interwar elections. After the Nazi invasion of the Soviet Union in 1941, the Czechoslovak Communists became committed anti-Nazis, and after the war they regained the support of the trade unions that had been so important to their success in the interwar period. The Communist party added to their numbers in the first year after the war, when unemployment increased. They agitated for land reform and the dismantling of some of the country's biggest industrial corporations, many of which had survived the war. In postwar Europe, the Czechs and the Slovaks appeared to favor a collective commitment to the nationalization of important assets for the reconstruction and rebuilding of their state. For the first three years, the Communists adhered to the idea of private property and refrained from preaching, in public, the tenets of Marxism-Leninism. Believing themselves and their property safe, the Havels decided to remain in Czechoslovakia and prepared their sons to take prominent positions within the business or political elite of the postwar state. They were, after all, members of the Czech elite and fleeing would mean losing their privileges and assets and joining the millions of refugees traversing Europe after World War II.

Private tutors and their parents supervised Václav's and Ivan's early education. This was typical for members of their class, and it had the added advantage of sheltering the brothers from the nazification of Czech schools. In the fall of 1947, his parents enrolled Václav in a new private school for boys, The King George School of Podebrady, which was founded specifically to educate future leader-citizens. Václav spent three years at Podebrady, where he was exposed to a rigorous academic regimen, including the learning of languages—Czech, Russian, and Latin—and strict discipline. Many of Czechoslovakia's future luminaries (the filmmakers Miloš Forman, Ivan Passer, and Jerzy Skolimowski; the Sesame Street animator Pavel Fierlinger; the politician and general secretary of the Czechoslovak Socialist party, Jan Škoda; and the chairperson of the Czechoslovak Olympic Committee, Milan Jiřasek) attended this academy. However, its avowed educational mission and appearance of class privilege brought the school under the scrutiny of the Communists when they assumed power in 1948.

The Communists closed the school in the 1950s, but not before Václav and his brother were expelled because of their class background. The building of socialism in Czechoslovakia meant that room in such an institution had to be made for the children from less privileged families, that is, the working class. The Havel family had already attracted the attention of the Communists. The state needed to condemn such families as the enemies of socialism, and Václav would now spend a good part of his life branded as a class enemy. Whenever Václav

Chapter 13
Cold War Europe:
Václav Havel
(1936–) and Olga
Šplíchalová
Havlová
(1933–1996)

challenged the system, the Communists often attacked his bourgeois origins and attitudes. The expulsion from school of boys and girls like Václav and his brother, and the expropriation of the property and wealth of families like the Havels were supposed to provide greater opportunities to working-class people like Václav Havel's future wife, Olga Šplíchalová.

Olga Šplíchalová was born on July 11, 1933, in Žižkov, a working-class suburb of Prague. Her father, Šplíchal, was a horsemeat butcher, and he was periodically unemployed during Olga's childhood. Her mother, Anna, worked in a bottling company while Olga was growing up. Olga had two siblings, a sister, Jaruna, eleven years her senior, and a half-brother, Josef, who was born out of wedlock to Olga's mother. Olga's father legitimized the boy and gave him the Šplíchal name, but he and Olga's mother soon divorced, partly because Anna was still in love with her son's father. Olga's humble and slightly tarnished background eventually elicited the disapproval of Václav's mother.

After the divorce of her parents at the age of six, Olga and her siblings lived in Žižkov with their mother. Like many working-class girls, Olga quickly assumed responsibility for her younger brother because of her mother's long shifts at the bottling company. The war compounded the Šplíchals' troubles. Josef's father disappeared and Jaruna's husband left her destitute and with five children. Jaruna was also forced to work long hours to make ends meet, and care of the children was left to Olga.

Unlike boys and girls from Václav's background, Olga remained in Prague for the duration of the war and there she attended elementary school. Although she liked to read on her own, Olga did not care much for school and she specifically remembered despising the German language course that each Czech student was forced to attend under the laws of the Nazi protectorate. In her recollections of the war, she does not dwell on its deprivations. She noted how she saw the whole thing as an adventure. The reports of troop movements and bombings were exciting for her rather than terrifying, and she saw her Soviet "liberators" more as bearers of American-supplied soaps and chocolate than of lost freedom.

Olga's opinion of the Soviet army changed quickly. Soviet troops were quartered in the homes of Czechoslovak citizens during their occupation of Prague and, as Olga later reported, they generally sought out households headed by women. The Šplíchals' flat was such a home. Four Russian soldiers entered the house, and one stood guard with the children as the others took Anna into the bedroom and raped her. No one spoke of the incident for years, but the family's opinion of the Red Army as "liberators" changed dramatically. This incident, however, did not stop Anna from joining the Communist party in 1945.

Like many members of the Czech working class and as a "daughter of Žižkov," Anna Šplíchal felt that she and her family had much to gain from the Communists. She supported the Communists' immediate postwar platform of nationalizing the banks, heavy industry, and large factories because it was in her class interest to do so. She believed that such programs were socially necessary after the deprivations suffered by all Czechs during the war. Her husband's support of the Communists during the interwar period also influenced her position. After the war, Anna joined a Žižkov communist women's group and participated in yearly party demonstrations and celebrations.

Olga and Jaruna challenged their mother's faith in and devotion to the Czechoslovak communist state. As a sixteen-year-old, Olga quarreled with her mother about the trainload of gifts sent by Prague workers to Joseph Stalin, the leader of the USSR, for his seventieth birthday in 1949. She believed that such gifts would be more useful to Czech workers and their families. The next year Olga became even more convinced of the Communists' moral and political corruption. The Czechoslovak Communists, like the other East European Communists, conducted witch-hunts within their party to root out suspected enemies of Stalin, especially those who might have sympathized with the Yugoslav Communist party leader, Josip Broz Tito, who dared break ties with the Soviet Union and Stalin in 1948. Many communists took this opportunity to attack their party rivals or enemies. A series of purges, arrests, trials and executions swept through Eastern Europe. Olga listened to the live broadcast of the trial of Milada Horáková, who was accused of belonging to "the leadership of the subversive conspiracy against the Republic." Horáková was found guilty and executed, but the

transparency of the charges and Anna's support of them caused mother and daughter to quarrel bitterly.

Olga's disagreements with her mother over politics resulted in Olga's desecration and destruction of her mother's icons. In preparation for an upcoming holiday, her mother decorated one of their apartment's windowsills with metal portraits of Edvard Beneš, the president of Czechoslovakia until 1948; Klement Gottwald, one of the leaders of the Czechoslovak Communist party and current president; and Stalin. During an argument, Olga took a hammer and knocked the icons off the sill. Olga also defied her mother by refusing to join the youth organization for the Communist party, the Young Pioneers, and then later the organization for communist teenagers, the Czechoslovak Youth Union. Olga often argued that it was her practical day-to-day experience in the communist system that convinced her it simply did not work. As an adult, she often referred to the Communists as "cheats" and "criminals."[2] Her mother formed a similar opinion when it became apparent that the Communists had failed to make her or her family's life better.

By the 1950s, Anna could no longer deny the profound dissonance between communist myths and reality, and the celebration of International Women's Day was an important example. The communist states promoted March 8 as the day to celebrate women. Working the long hours that she did at the bottling factory and

2. Keane, p. 143.

Chapter 13
Cold War Europe:
Václav Havel
(1936–) and Olga
Šplíchalová
Havlová
(1933–1996)

then coming home to take care of her family, Anna experienced what was called the "double burden." Anna had hoped and believed that the Czechoslovak communist state would relieve some of that burden by providing better social services and improving her family's standard of living. When the easing of this burden did not happen, Anna began to see the holiday as a thinly veiled means of forcing women into factory work and of glossing over the injustices of the double burden.

Anna's experience was not unusual for a woman living in the communist states of Eastern Europe. As the Communists consolidated their power, they wrote new constitutions that guaranteed women's political, civil, and social equality and gave them equal protection under the law, the right to vote for the first time in all countries except Czechoslovakia, and the right to work. In return, the Communists expected women to work when their work was needed by the state, to be politically active, and to reproduce. During the communist period, women's access to education increased and large numbers of women entered the work force. However, traditional norms and ideas about a woman's role in society were difficult to overcome, even among male Communists who considered themselves revolutionaries.

Women often chose or were channeled into educational institutions or employment opportunities that were deemed appropriate for women, such as teaching, medicine, light industrial labor, clerical work, or service jobs. The occupations inhabited by women

paid less and lacked prestige. Women were represented symbolically at all levels of government, but they did not hold real power in the state or in the Communist party. During the early years of communist rule in Czechoslovakia, the Communists pushed for industrialization and the mobilization of the labor force, and women were an integral part of these plans. Women's economic and political equality and the easing of their double burden were placed far down on the list of priorities. The communist regimes did enact protective labor legislation for women, health-care provisions for pregnancy and maternity, short- and long-term maternity leaves, and earlier eligibility for retirement, usually so they could care for elderly parents or grandchildren.

As a member of a working-class family and the daughter of a Communist party member, Olga had good prospects for entering the university after high school. She demonstrated very little interest in school, however, and began working shortly after her high school graduation. Her first job was textile work in the Bat'a shoe factory, but a machine press trapped Olga's fingers, damaging her hand, and she left this job. She soon found a job as a bookkeeper at a secondhand shop in Prague. By the age of twenty, Olga realized that such jobs would be the staple of her life, and she began to seek diversions from the monotony of her daily grind.

Olga tried acting. There is very little in her background that explains this interest other than the fact that her mother had some interest in the theater, always as a spectator, never as a participant. Whatever the reasons, Olga threw herself into this new arena and soon theater work took up most of her time and energies. In 1953, she enrolled in acting classes taught by Paula Wegner (Ludmila Wegenerová), who was a German theater and film star and member of a well-known avant-garde theater company. For the rebellious and noncomforming Olga, Wegner's methods were perfect. They were infused with an originality and creativity that differed from those of the instructors at the state schools. More important, perhaps, were the friendships Olga made in her acting classes. She entered into a new social circle of young people who traveled, went to plays and movies, and spent time at cafés. At one such café, Café Slavia, Olga met Václav Havel for the first time, in 1953.

▪ ACT I:

LIVING UNDER CZECHOSLOVAK STALINISM, 1953–1968

By age seventeen, Václav already had a circle of friends with whom to explore intellectual and artistic ideas. This group was known as the Thirty-Sixers because its members were born in 1936. Its members were children from bourgeois origins and were ostracized by the party because of these origins. This group valued academic achievement, and they believed that knowledge, however it was attained, could be a powerful tool for survival and success in life. Václav's mother, Božena, encouraged her son in this endeavor and often offered the Havels' apartment and summer home for the group's gatherings. Václav emerged as the unofficial leader. With the others, he began to search for the literary and historical traditions of the first Czechoslovak Republic, which had been suppressed by the years of Nazi occupation, total war, and communist rule. Years later, Václav reflected on how they boldly defied the dictates of the new authorities and read forbidden authors, poets, and politicians such as Franz Kafka; Herman Hesse; Anna Akhmatova; Tomáš Masaryk, the first Czechoslovak President, and Edvard Beneš. The Czechoslovak authorities might have control over the schools, but Václav and the Thirty-Sixers grasped the importance of creating their own community outside the purview of the state. For Václav, this would be the first of many such associations.

Václav's class position and his family's contempt for formal education under the Communists resulted in his unorthodox secondary education. At fifteen, he began to train as a carpenter but physical awkwardness and vertigo soon ended this career. Through friends, his parents found him a job as a lab technician at the Institute of Chemical Technology. He took night classes to graduate from high school, then he applied to Charles University with the hope of joining the art department and the film and drama

Chapter 13
Cold War Europe:
Václav Havel
(1936–) and Olga
Šplíchalová
Havlová
(1933–1996)

department. He was rejected by both. He eventually enrolled in the public transportation major at the economics department of the Technical University in Prague, primarily to avoid being drafted into military service. Despite his course of study, Václav followed closely the debates concerning art and literature in the Czechoslovak communist state, which were conducted in the shadow of Nikita Khrushchev's speech to the Soviet Communists in February 1956 denouncing the excesses of Stalin. In a letter to a new journal for young writers, *Kveten,* Václav appealed to the editors to be more open and tolerant of submitted materials that did not fit into a socialist-realist view of the world. His letter received extraordinary attention, and as a result he was invited to a conference for young writers in the fall of 1956.

Václav's first foray into the world of the literary elite was a shock and surprise to those who had invited him. The conference began as a tepid affair. The party functionaries (*apparatchiks*) reinforced the duty of writers to remain in touch with young workers and young farmers, and to write poetry and prose that extolled the virtues of their leaders, the resistance of Czech Communists to the Nazis and to capitalism, and the hard work and daily dedication of Czechoslovak workers. Václav was not impressed with the communist literati, whom he considered party hacks unworthy of admiration. He saw himself as an outsider, prepared to defend the literary traditions of the Czechs prior to the arrival of the Communists, socialist realism, and Stalinism. In a speech to the assembled, Václav pointed out that the editors of *Kveten* offered nothing new to young writers. The editors encouraged them to walk on already familiar terrain and to remain silent about any other Czech aesthetic trends. Václav demanded that the assembled take seriously the thaw offered by Khrushchev months earlier. He stated, "After the Twentieth Congress of the Communist Party of the Soviet Union (CPSU) and the Second Writers' Congress, it is obvious that all restrictions on the freedom to develop different opinions and to express reality can only burden our cultural and national life with the repetition of past mistakes and negative results, in every sense."[3]

Václav challenged the Czechoslovak literary authorities to move beyond dogmatism and embrace the reforms suggested by Khrushchev, just as the Polish and Hungarian Communists had done. His call came as Soviet tanks rolled into Budapest in November 1956, crushing the Hungarian uprising against the Communists. Thus, his pleas fell on deaf ears. He probably escaped serious rebuke because of his youth. In the future, he would not have such a shield.

Václav's age did put him in the state's sight and at the age of twenty-one, in 1957, he was drafted into the Czechoslovak army for his compulsory two years of army service. During his service, Václav would write his first play, *You've Got Your Whole Life Ahead of You.* This drama told the story

3. Keane, p. 128.

of a fictional young private who is promoted to lance corporal under fraudulent circumstances. At the last minute, he refuses the promotion because of moral considerations. Václav wished to dramatize the importance of individual resistance to lies, amorality, and duplicity, themes that dominated his later works.

Prior to his entrance into the university and his military service, Václav Havel met Olga Šplíchalová at Café Slavia in 1953. This café was and still is a well-known Prague establishment catering to well-to-do patrons of the National Theater and young bohemian intellectuals. Olga and Václav were introduced by a friend from her graduating class, who was Havel's coworker at the laboratory. Although younger than the two women (Václav was seventeen and Olga was twenty), he was smart and an interesting conversationalist. Nonetheless, it was not exactly love at first sight. Three years seemed like a big difference to these two at that point in their lives, so Olga and Václav became friends.

Olga and Václav came from and traveled in vastly different social worlds. As the privileged son of one of the First Republic's wealthiest bourgeois families, Václav was able to introduce Olga to new social circles and different values than those held by her own family. Though she seems to have maintained a careful distance from them for a long time, Olga became acquainted with Václav's circle of bohemian friends and shared with them a growing interest in experimental and avant-garde theater. After Václav's discharge from the military in

1959, he tried to enter the Academy of Arts but was refused. His class position was still an obstacle. But Václav's family rescued his ambitions once again.

Václav's father introduced his son to Jan Werich, a leftist performer, entertainer, and playwright who had managed to bridge the artistic gap between the vibrant leftist theater of the 1920s and the dogmatic, socialist-realist theater of the 1950s. Werich was still in a position of authority in the ABC Theater in Prague and offered Václav a job as a stagehand. Participating firsthand in the production of live theater, Václav learned how the theater could create a place where audience and performers interacted outside the official world of the Communist party and its state. Václav's brief association with the ABC Theater convinced him that the theater and playwriting were his calling.

In the winter of 1959–1960, Václav became affiliated with a new theater group, the Balustrade, an experimental, quasi-improvisational theater group begun in December 1958. The Balustrade and its director attracted young people who worked in the theater and who aspired to create new forms of performance, not plays from the past that were produced by older established theaters. The Balustrade threw off the conventions of socialist-realist drama and began to produce absurdist plays (Document One). Václav wrote plays for the theater and by the mid-1960s Václav's association with the Balustrade brought him and the theater a Europeanwide reputation. Olga continued to see Václav

Chapter 13
Cold War Europe:
Václav Havel
(1936–) and Olga
Šplíchalová
Havlová
(1933–1996)

during his early forays into the theater, and as their relationship turned romantic, Václav's mother voiced her displeasure.

To support his playwriting and to stay close to Václav, Olga became an usher at the Balustrade and participated in the oversight of some of his early plays. Olga felt that her membership in the theater group depended on her relationship to Václav. Given her educational and class background, she felt like the outsider and believed that marriage to Václav would somehow ameliorate this situation. Also, she was now in her thirties and was thinking about having children. In July 1964, Václav and Olga married in a civil ceremony two days before her thirty-first birthday.

As was typical of many young couples, Václav and Olga moved in with the elder Havels after their wedding, but soon Václav's growing success at the Balustrade allowed them to find their own apartment and to purchase a weekend cottage at Hrádeček, a secluded locale about thirty kilometers outside Prague. During the 1960s, the cottage acted as a meeting place for young Czech intellectuals, friends of the younger Havels, and members of their theater group. Under Soviet prodding, the Czechoslovak Communist party finally renounced Stalinism, but President Antonín Novotný, a staunch Stalinist, still refused to relinquish the party's control over culture. The Czechoslovak Writer's Union challenged Novotný's recalcitrance. It argued in 1963 that destalinization had not occurred and demanded more freedom to travel and to make contacts with the West. The dispute between the Writer's Union and Novotný's government created a window of opportunity for artists, intellectuals, and writers. In the mid-1960s, a new wave in writing, film, and theater rolled through Czechoslovakia.

Václav, his plays, and his position as a member of the editorial board of a literary monthly for young writers, *Tvář* (*The Face*), typify the cultural and civic politics that emerged during the 1960s in Czechoslovakia. In two of his plays, *The Garden Party* (1963) and *The Memorandum* (1965), Václav wrote of the anti-hero who encounters the depersonalized modern world and reacts with feelings of futility and turmoil. The word play, not the literary structure, was the most significant part of these dramas. Václav wanted to point out to the audience how people had stopped communicating with each other in Czechoslovak society. They had resorted to prefabricated clichés acceptable to the Communists and no longer understood each other. For people in the audience in 1960s Prague, the meaning was clear. They suffered under the doublespeak of Czechoslovak Communism, a leadership that regularly attempted cosmetic reform, only to follow it up with sanctions, bans, and purges.

Václav tapped into a reservoir of generational angst. His and Olga's generation had grown up under state socialism, with its intolerance for any movement or idea not socialist in content and form and sanctioned by the state. By the early 1960s, cultural production in Czechoslovakia was stagnant. Václav and the editorial board of *Tvář* wanted to challenge socialist-realism and redefine the cultural landscape. *Tvář* established an editorial policy that called for publication of what was good writing, regardless of the political message. The move to depoliticize culture led the older, more established writers in the Writers' Union to feel that criticism of their works would lead to their purge from the writers' ranks. To them, literary production was an institution in which the party had installed them, bestowed honors and laurels upon them, and then expelled them from it.[4] They did not understand the function of literature and literary criticism except as dictated by the party bosses. In June 1965, the Writers' Union moved to shut down the journal. The editors decided to fight the decision, and they began to circulate a petition in support of the journal. The 600 signatures did little to influence the union's decision.

This controversy was Václav's first official battle with the party, represented by the Writers' Union, and he suffered attacks on his class background and on his views about the depoliticization of culture, surveillance, and intimidation by the secret police. The state now listed him as an "antisocialist collaborator," criticized him in the official media, and tried to bribe him with the offer of starting his own magazine.[5] He refused and concluded from this experience that a civic initiative such as a petition could be successful within the repressive atmosphere of Novotný's regime.

Challenges from within and without the party sprang up in the mid-1960s. The Slovak Communists, led by Alexander Dubček, professed displeasure with the Slovak underrepresentation in state institutions. Students grew restless as they studied the endless tracts of Marxism-Leninism, lived in squalor in overcrowded dormitories, and chafed under restrictions of travel to the West. The Czech and Slovak legal profession openly discussed the need for protecting the civil rights of citizens, with independent courts and judges. Economists discussed the possibility of less centralized planning, returning production decisions to factory managers, and acceptance of some market mechanisms. In June 1967, the Czechoslovak Writers' Union found its voice and backbone and called for an end to censorship. These pressures from multiple constituencies forced the Czechoslovak Communist party to accept leadership changes. In January 1968, Alexander Dubček, the reformed Slovak Communist, replaced Novotný as first party secretary.

Under his stewardship, Dubček proposed that the Czechoslovak Communists reform the economy, ease party controls of the state and societal organizations, and gain control of the cultural and political renaissance that had captured the imagination of most Czechs and Slovaks. Czechs and Slovaks believed that they were living in a time of rebirth after a long, dark, and dreary winter. The period between January 1968 and August 1968 is referred to as the Prague Spring. During these eight months, the Czechoslovak Communist party, under reformed

4. Eda Kriseova, *Václav Havel: The Authorized Biography* (New York: St. Martin's Press, 1993), p. 60.
5. Keane, pp. 172–173.

Chapter 13
Cold War Europe:
Václav Havel
(1936–) and Olga
Šplíchalová
Havlová
(1933–1996)

leadership, committed itself to creating "socialism with a human face." Dubček firmly believed in the tenets of Marxism-Leninism, the leading role of the party, and meeting all of Czechoslovakia's commitments to its military alliance, the Warsaw Pact. His early stewardship of the reforms aroused little concern from the Soviets, who saw the Prague Spring as a necessary movement for renewal and rearticulation of communism in Czechoslovakia. Dubček could not control the exuberance of the regime's emerging critics, however, and with censorship revoked, the party lost its ability to direct reform.

In June 1968, Czechoslovak intellectuals published a stinging indictment of the twenty years of communist rule. This statement, "2,000 Words," attracted the attention of the Soviet Union (Document Two). In the early summer, the Soviets feared that the Czechoslovak Communists had lost control of the reform movement and, after monitoring the situation closely for eight weeks, ordered the invasion

of Czechoslovakia by Warsaw Pact troops on August 21, 1968.

The Czechs and Slovaks put up massive nonviolent resistance. Civilian efforts were no match, however, for the twenty-nine divisions, 7,500 tanks, and 1,000 planes sent to suppress the Prague Spring, and at least eighty people were killed during the invasion. If the Soviets had not articulated their stand clearly with the crushing of the Hungarian revolt in 1956, they made their position perfectly clear with the invasion of Czechoslovakia. The Soviet Union would not tolerate liberalization of state socialism by its neighbors because any reform of socialism and its state meant the possibility of losing control over society. In a statement in November 1969, the leader of the Soviet Union, Leonid Brezhnev, said that the Soviet Union and its allies had the right to intervene if socialism was threatened in another socialist state. This statement, known as the Brezhnev Doctrine, dictated Soviet policy in the region until 1987.

■ ACT II:

NORMALIZATION AND DISSENT

Under the liberalizing reforms of Dubček in 1968, Václav and Olga enjoyed unprecedented freedom for their generation. Given passports for the first time, they visited the United States and England in May and June 1968. They watched *The Memorandum*

performed in New York and joined antiwar demonstrations there, and in London discussed art and politics on British Broadcast Company (BBC) television. Václav's reputation and the connections that he made while abroad increased his visibility and stature and allowed him the possibility of leaving Czechoslovakia after the invasion. In January 1969, several months after the invasion, he declined several offers to travel abroad. He feared that once he left, he would not be allowed to return. Instead, he chose to remain and resist the impending crackdown.

Between 1969 and 1971, the Communist Party, now under the leadership of Gustáv Husák, embarked upon a series of purges that resulted in the removal of 500,000 party members from its ranks of 1.5 million. In addition, between 250,000 and 750,000 people lost their jobs. No one was spared because of privilege or political connections. Three-quarters of the ministers and all of the top leaders of the government, including Dubček, were dismissed. Leading diplomats, public prosecutors, bank officials, professors, teachers, newspaper and journal editors, journalists, and representatives of worker organizations were removed and prohibited from working in their respective fields. The cultural industry was especially hard hit: 475 of the 590 members of the Writers' Union were removed, and 130 writers, including Václav, were blacklisted and their works removed from public libraries and institutions. Husák wanted any possible reform communist, nonconformist, independent thinker, or dissident marginalized and banished from public platforms and consciousness.

Václav's vocal support of the Prague Spring and his reputation as an independent thinker quickly attracted the attention of the new regime. In early 1969, Olga and Václav discovered listening devices in their house and apartment, and political discussions and debates ceased in their homes (Document Three). Skirmishes with the regime became a regular feature of their lives. At the end of 1969, Václav signed a public declaration against Husák's policies and was threatened with arrest and a trial. The state revoked his membership in the Writers' Union, prohibited the production of his plays, and banned his writings. In addition, the regime attacked the friends and family members of the Havels, and soon old friends shied away from gatherings at Hrádeček. Olga broke ties with her old friends in Žižkov as well. She counted herself lucky that she had not had the children she wanted because the government's measures would have limited their options. While Olga experienced some of the repression directed toward her husband, she did not have his celebrity dissident status. His work of the 1970s and 1980s would not have been possible, however, without her.

The citizens of Czechoslovakia fell into a deep malaise and melancholy. Gone were the political discussions and the creative energies of the 1960s. The regime rewarded those who refrained from political involvement, asked no embarrassing questions, and participated mechanically in everyday life. Preferential treatment in jobs, housing, and the purchase of consumer goods and the tolerance of black market economic activity were awarded to those who conformed. The regime turned a blind eye to theft in the workplace and small-scale corruption. Václav would later argue that millions of his compatriots had taken

Chapter 13
Cold War Europe:
Václav Havel
(1936–) and Olga
Šplíchalová
Havlová
(1933–1996)

the path of least resistance and had dispensed with the values of honesty, truth, and responsibility (Document Four). Olga, Václav, and other intellectuals refused this path.

The intellectual resistance to the Husák regime, its policies of "normalization," and its reinstatement of censorship began in the early 1970s with the first self-published works or journals, *samizdat*. Writers, journalists, poets, and scholars typed their manuscripts and circulated copies of their works among their friends and colleagues. Václav and his intellectual circle met openly, knowing that the secret police were listening and detailing every meeting and who was in attendance. At first, the resistance movement was little more than a small group of writers, most of them male. Wives or female partners often provided editorial comments, clerical skills, household duties, shopping, and bartering to support the men in their efforts, but they gained none of the fame bestowed on their husbands and lovers for their dissent.

Olga was a loyal and supportive wife to Václav during the early 1970s, at a time when many relationships between banned artists and their spouses were failing. She acted as a gracious hostess to his friends and co-conspirators who visited the house, and was often the first editor and critic of her husband's written work. During this time, Václav wrote five plays: *The Conspirators* (1970), *The Beggar's Opera* (1974), *Audience* (1974), *Vernissage* (1974), and *Mountain Hotel* (1976). In addition, his circle of intellectuals formed an independent publishing house in 1973. By 1978, they had published more than 100 books. Each manuscript was painstakingly edited, typed, reproduced, and distributed. In 1975, Václav started his own publishing unit, *Despatch Editions* (*Edice Expedice*) and, with Olga's guidance and help, published fifty titles in four years. These manuscripts would often be smuggled to the West and published. When Václav was arrested in 1979, Olga continued their work. Václav earned royalties from abroad for his smuggled and banned works, but the authorities eventually prohibited their receipt. Desperate for money, Václav went to work in a brewery stacking barrels in 1975. His work at the brewery appeared so subversive to the regime that they planted a listening device in the brewery's lounge to monitor the famous playwright. Václav's truly subversive activity, the production and performance of his latest play, *The Beggar's Opera*, went undetected by the police.

News of the play, which was performed in a restaurant a block away from a Prague police station, infuriated the authorities and Václav was brought in for questioning. The courage that the directors, actors, and audience displayed by supporting the play led Václav to believe Czechs and Slovaks were ready for a challenge to the Husák regime. In April 1975, he wrote a letter to Husák indicting the regime. This 10,000-word letter was widely circulated underground, published abroad, and broadcast to Czechoslovakia by Western radio stations. Václav fully expected to be arrested for this bold act, but the regime continued to follow the policy of tolerating its famous dissident intellectuals.

All of this changed in 1977, when the Czechoslovak authorities reacted to a petition, Charter 77, signed by several hundred prominent Czechoslovak intellectuals and circulated underground.

Charter 77 was a simple text asserting that the Czechoslovak government had signed the International Covenant on Civil and Political Rights at Helsinki in 1975 and that this covenant, known as the Helsinki Accords, bound the regime to respect the rights of Czechoslovak citizens. The charter listed the regime's many infringements of basic human rights. (Document Five). The signatories of the charter denied that they were a political group or that they were engaged in overtly political activity. They were simply a group of citizens coming together in a free, informal, and open association, and anyone who accepted the basic ideas of the charter could join them. The charter called on citizens to organize themselves outside the control of the state. Charter 77 and the organization formed to protect its ideals, the Committee for the Defense of the Unjustly Persecuted (VONS), were the first expressions of an emerging debate about creating a civil society. In the 1980s, many dissidents throughout the Soviet bloc began to form associations that could be used as a tool against the all-encompassing claims of the party-state. Despite the denials of the organizers of Charter 77 and members of VONS that they did not want to play an oppositional political role, the Czechoslovak authorities persecuted the two groups. Of course, Václav was a leading member of both.

On January 14, 1977, Václav was arrested, tried, and sentenced to fourteen months in prison for "damaging the interests of the Republic abroad" and for his part in the declaration of Charter 77. The judge suspended the sentence for three years. He would have to serve the sentence only if he persisted in his political activities. In 1979, the regime's patience with Václav finally came to an end. He was arrested in May for being a cofounder of VONS, and was tried, found guilty, and sentenced to four and a half years in prison for sedition.

▪ ACT III:

LETTERS TO OLGA

Olga's position within the dissident community and of course her relationship to her husband changed dramatically after Václav's imprisonment. Václav was allowed very little contact with the outside world during his imprisonment, and letters to Olga became his lifeline. He was permitted to write one letter a week, and each was subject to censorship. At first, Václav's letters to Olga consisted of demands, requests, tasks to be performed, lists of items to send, directives about their farmhouse (Hrádeček), and concerns about how she would earn a living. His worrying about the details of her everyday life and wanting her to be "sociable" was a code for her to be his eyes and ears outside the prison walls.

Chapter 13
Cold War Europe:
Václav Havel
(1936–) and Olga
Šplíchalová
Havlová
(1933–1996)

He wanted to know about his circle of friends, the underground concerts, the unofficial seminars, the newest *samizdat* books and journals, and the gossip. Later, the letters began to communicate his thoughts on writing, the theater, the prison regime, and himself (Document Six).

The tone of his letters to Olga has generated some controversy because they contained condescension, petty cruelties, put-downs, a lack of warmth, and hints at extramarital affairs. Whatever the nature of their relationship, it is clear that Václav would not have survived the experience if Olga had decided to leave him. Of his decision to publish the letters under the title, *Letters to Olga,* he said, "It's true that you won't find many heartfelt, personal passages specifically addressed to my wife in my prison letters. Even so, I think that Olga is their main hero, though admittedly hidden. That is why I put her name in the title of the book. Doesn't that endless search for a firm point, for certainty, for an absolute horizon that fills those letters say something, in itself, to confirm that?"[6]

While Václav's letters to Olga are well known, Olga's letters to her husband are lost. Václav was not allowed to keep the originals, Olga never made copies of them, and copies presumably made by the Czechoslovak police have never been recovered. All that remains are the memories of Olga's friends with whom she discussed the letters, and according to their reports, the letters probably revealed very little of what she was thinking and feeling during the time. Olga was always a very private person, and she seems to have hated writing to Václav because it reminded her of what was lost. She sent news to Václav of his friends, political developments, their dogs, and her daily routine, but little of her private thoughts and feelings.

Olga remained characteristically quiet about the personal difficulties and harassments that she experienced as a result of her husband's incarceration. The secret police monitored her movements constantly, searched the house numerous times, offered her the promise of emigration to the Federal Republic of Germany, sexually harassed her, and arrested and interrogated her for four days because of her continued work with *Edice Expedice.* She maintained the house at Hrádeček, watched after the dogs, kept up correspondence with Václav's supporters and admirers outside Czechoslovakia, and participated in a reading group with other "straw widows" of jailed dissidents. This group, *Hrobka* (Crypt), argued that it had no real political goal and that its fundamental purpose was to discuss trashy erotic and Gothic novels by banned authors. Despite such protestations, *Hrobka* served several very important functions for Olga. First, it gave her a social space within which she could forget the stressful realities of life under surveillance. Second, it allowed her to develop her own social circles where she could enjoy her membership in her own right, and not merely as the wife of Václav Havel. Third, it gave her the contacts and the confidence

6. Václav Havel, *Disturbing the Peace,* p. 157. Quoted in Keane, p. 302

she needed to begin acting politically on her own. Other straw widows of the jailed leaders of VONS formed similar associations. Anna Šabatová-Uhlová, Petr Uhl's wife, established a group that continued the work of VONS, and Kamila Bendova, wife of Václav Benda, formed a Catholic dissident group to reinforce the tenets of Charter 77.

During Václav's imprisonment, Olga signed political petitions and declarations, including a slew of petitions to the Czechoslovak government asking for the release of jailed dissidents involved in the charter movement. She collaborated in writing a petition to Simone Weil, the chairperson of the European Parliament for the release of yet another group of supporters of the charter. Most important, Olga took over the duties of editor of the *samizdat* publishing association, *Edice Expedice*. In a letter, Václav had instructed Olga in 1979 to find someone to take over this work for him, and she decided that she was the logical choice. While Olga was assisted in her editorial duties by a dedicated staff of assistants, she bore the political responsibility alone. As a result of her activities, Olga was subject to police intimidation, harassment, and arrest. In May 1981, Václav discovered that Olga and his brother, Ivan, had been detained by the Prague police. The Czechoslovak authorities responded to the suppression of the Solidarity movement in Poland by planning a major roundup of the country's remaining dissident activists, and Ivan and Olga were caught in the snare. Police had discovered their names on a list of contacts taken

from two French citizens arrested for trafficking in works by exiled and jailed dissident. Detained for ninety-six hours by the police, Olga received an oral notice that criminal procedures against her would commence, but the written resolution to that effect never arrived. Neither she nor Ivan heard anything more of the matter.

In March 1983, under intense pressure from foreign dignitaries and dissidents, and their own fear that Czechoslovakia's most famous dissident might die in prison from pneumonia, the Czechoslovak authorities released Václav Havel. Olga went immediately to his bedside in the hospital, happy that he was released. But this happiness was short-lived because of his decision to rekindle his affair with Jitka Vodňanská, a psychologist, and the only one of Václav's numerous mistresses who ever posed a threat to their marriage. Fearing the end of their marriage, Olga informed Václav of the affair that she was having with Jan Kašpar, a friend from the Havels' theater circle and twenty years Olga's junior. This affair had begun while Václav was in prison. Olga chose to end her affair and move back with her husband, but he continued to see Vodňanská. They agreed not to divorce and to have an open marriage to maintain a unified front against the regime.

During the mid-1980s, both of them continued with their dissident activities. Charter 77 and VONS remained underground movements, but popular frustration and disaffection in Czechoslovakia was beginning to bubble to the surface. In 1983, the majority of Czechoslovak citizens, including

Chapter 13
Cold War Europe:
Václav Havel
(1936–) and Olga
Šplíchalová
Havlová
(1933–1996)

some industrial workers, signed petitions protesting the deployment of Soviet nuclear missiles in their country. Additional petitions concerning the economy, social issues, and general conditions in the country circulated; *samizdat* publishing associations flourished; underground punk rock groups played; and the Catholic church gained strength daily. Václav continued to write plays and several political tracts exploring how individuals, no matter how insignificant or powerless, can change the world. Many of these writings would eventually be published in *Václav Havel: Living in Truth,* issued on the occasion of his winning the award from the Erasmus Prize Foundation of Amsterdam in 1987.

Olga continued her independent political work after Václav's release. Several projects and issues occupied her during the 1980s. The first was the creation of *The Original Videojournal,* a news and cultural program conceived as a kind of audio-video *samizdat.* Each video depicted the realities of life in socialist Czechoslovakia and was distributed inside and outside the country. The Czechoslovak government paid little attention to such works because it dismissed the power of video. Nonetheless, the journal cap-

tured many of the demonstrations leading up to the 1989 Velvet Revolution and served to notify Western audiences of political developments in the Eastern bloc. The second project, begun in 1985, was a *samizdat* theater journal, *O divadle (On the Theater),* and was intended to inform foreigners about the activities in the Czechoslovak underground theaters.

Olga also became concerned about the burdens and indignities that women endured under state socialism. Women's issues had never interested her husband. In his essay, "The Anatomy of Reticence," he dismissed the idea that women could be opinion formers or opinion makers. Olga herself first derided feminism as a misguided distraction from real political work. During the 1980s, she became more sympathetic when she realized that societal attitudes and obstacles could be just as damaging as state oppression. In November 1988, she participated in a women's demonstration protesting the failures of the Czechoslovak command economy to provide basic necessities, such as sufficient quantities of feminine hygiene products, for its female citizens (Document Seven).

■ FINALE

During the mid-1980s, winds of change were blowing in from the Soviet Union. In March 1985, Mikhail Gorbachev became the leader of the Soviet Communist Party and began to

speak about restructuring the Soviet economy (*perestroika*) and to discuss openly the problems facing the Soviet state and its allies (*glasnost*). The signals from Moscow were that leaders in the Soviet bloc countries should embark on their own policies for reform.

Some countries, like Poland and Hungary, welcomed these calls for the reform of state socialism and moved in this direction as quickly as possible. Husák and the top leadership of the Czechoslovak Communist party shunned glasnost and perestroika, making the case that they had tried reform in 1968 and it had led to chaos. Gorbachev was reluctant to intervene in the internal politics of the bloc's communist parties because it would negate his anti-imperialist stand. If change was to occur in Czechoslovakia, it would have to come at the hands of its own civil society.

Václav was aware that Charter 77 and VONS did not have the support that Solidarity had had in Poland. After ten years in existence, these Czechoslovak movements were still small and elitist and had been successful only in courting students and alienated youth. Unlike the Polish communist leadership, Husák had successfully cultivated the industrial working class, and this class saw little reason to join with intellectuals and students against the regime. For any widespread popular resistance movement to emerge in Czechoslovakia, the workers would have to participate.

Czechoslovakia remained relatively quiet in 1988 and for most of 1989. During these two years, Václav continued his political activity. The public increasingly embraced him as a moral and spiritual leader for the opposition, which meant that Václav was becoming a serious threat to the increasingly fearful and insecure Czechoslovak regime. His appearance at a memorial service for Jan Palach, the young Czech student who had immolated himself in January 1969 as a way to protest the invasion of Czechoslovakia, provoked the authorities. They arrested and imprisoned him in early 1989. National and international indignation about the incarceration forced the state to release him quickly.

Revolution came to Czechoslovakia in November 1989, when the resistance activities of the East Germans, Poles, and Hungarians finally inspired Czechs and Slovaks. After watching East Germans flee to the West and witnessing the destruction of the Berlin Wall in early November 1989, students began to visit factories, explaining to the blue-collar workers why their continued support of the regime would prove to be self-defeating. Responding to the events of their communist neighbors, students, dissidents, and city dwellers took to the streets of Prague in mid-November and refused to retreat, even under brutal police repression. It was finally time for the fragmented opposition to consolidate and create an umbrella organization to coordinate their activities. On November 19, 1989, Civic Forum was founded. Václav and the leaders of the other opposition groups issued a proclamation calling for an investigation into the police action against the demonstrators. With the creation of a united opposition, Václav quickly positioned himself to become its undisputed leader. Momentum was in favor of the opposition, and on November 25, 1989, 750,000 people attended a Prague rally organized by Civic Forum. Its main speaker was Václav Havel. In a matter of weeks, Husák resigned as the country's president, and

Chapter 13
Cold War Europe:
Václav Havel
(1936–) and Olga
Šplíchalová
Havlová
(1933–1996)

Václav was swept into office on the basis of a unanimous vote by the Czechoslovak Federal Assembly on December 29, 1989.

Václav Havel remains president of the Czech republic to this day. The Slovaks and the Czechs ended their political union peacefully in 1993. Olga died in 1996 after a successful and graceful transition from political dissident to first lady, and she continued to be one of Václav's closest and most trusted advisers after the revolution. Václav has often been criticized by Czech and Slovak commentators as being an ivory-tower intellectual, too out of touch with the needs and concerns of ordinary people to govern effectively. This criticism is still levelled at him. On the other hand, Olga was viewed as being one of the people, and her pragmatic, commonsense approach was seen as a much needed corrective to Václav's more elitist and intellectual perspective.

Olga threw herself into the type of nongovernmental work that she had pursued her entire life. In the early 1990s, she founded the Committee of Good Will (*Výbor dobré vůle*). The committee addressed some of the ugliest legacies of the communist era, legacies associated with the lack of social welfare and human services for the country's disabled (Document Eight). New ideas about the care and welfare of the physically disabled had failed to make an impact on the country's communist bureaucrats. Children with disabilities, for example, had been shut up in institutions rather than provided with the rehabilitative therapy that would allow them to integrate into society and to live with their own families. The socialist economy had failed entirely to meet the country's need for wheelchairs, walkers, and prosthetics; in some cases, individuals had to wait three years to get a wheelchair.

The committee raised money and responded to requests to improve the lives of these forgotten citizens. It worked to obtain the supplies necessary for rehabilitation, sponsored new and innovative projects in the sphere of social welfare and health, and led the development of new social-welfare laws. The committee received a good deal of foreign and domestic support and was able to sponsor several important initiatives, including a fourteen-day summer camp in the Austrian Alps for asthmatic children, a campaign to stop the spread of AIDS in the Czech republic, and a program to make medicines, medical instruments, and supplies developed in the West available to Czech and Slovak hospitals. Related organizations were set up in several West European countries and in the United States. As a result of her efforts, Olga was nominated in 1995 as the Czech republic's candidate for European Woman of the Year. Her death in 1996 was mourned by Czechs and Europeans alike.

During the 1990s, Václav used the office of president as a pulpit to examine the conditions of human beings in the modern world, to teach and cajole the citizens of the Czech state to accept democratic institutions, and to keep the office above the political fray. Many criticized him when he married an actress, Daša Veškrnová, in 1997. Daša relished the role of first lady as much as Olga had despised the political and ceremonial trappings of this position. To many around the president, Olga had connected him to the people; his new wife did nothing to check his tendencies toward abstraction, intellectualism, and aloofness. Olga was irreplaceable in political terms. The Czech public had known little about Olga Havlová in 1989 when they supported her husband for president. Ten years later, they realized that they had voted for a political, intellectual, and personal partnership that had led their country out of communism.

▨ QUESTIONS

1. Why did the Havels' class background come under the scrutiny of the Czechoslovak Communists? Did their class position hurt or help them under communism?

2. Compare Olga's family experiences and position with Václav's. What were the advantages and disadvantages of communism for each of them?

3. What was the position of women under state socialism?

4. How did Václav become a playwright and writer?

5. What role did Olga play in the dissident movement? What role did other women play? Why?

6. What was the position of the writer, artist, and intellectual under state socialism? Why did art, poetry, and prose matter to the Communists?

7. What was the relationship of culture to politics in the modern world? Can culture be used as both a tool of the state and an instrument of resistance? Why or why not?

8. Throughout this textbook, we have encountered many spouses or partners, like Elizabeth Lilburne, Nadezhda Krupskaya, Gert Bastian, and Olga Havlová, who were not heralded as the main figure or leader of a movement. How would you assess their historical significance?

Chapter 13
Cold War Europe:
Václav Havel
(1936–) and Olga
Šplíchalová
Havlová
(1933–1996)

■ **DOCUMENTS**

DOCUMENT ONE

VÁCLAV HAVEL

A Conversation with Karel Hvížďala
(1985)

In 1985, Havel wrote answers to over fifty questions submitted to him by Czech ex-ile, Karel Hvížďala. They worked on this "conversation" for over a year, communicating by underground mail. The end result was published by Edice Expedice *in the summer of 1986. In the following passages, Havel explains the reasons for his fascination with theater and its impact in early 1960s Prague. Why are the "small" theaters important for artistic expression? What is their political significance?*

[HVÍŽĎALA:] What was the situation like in theatre in the late 1950s, about the time when the first small theatres began to appear in Prague?

[HAVEL:] In the 1950s there were only the large official theatres—we called them the "stone theatres." Apart from the classics, or the occasional interesting perform-ance, the only kind of thing that genuinely attracted wide audiences was satire. By that I mean more or less superficial critiques of abuses, short comings, hu-man weaknesses (they were called "holdovers from the past"), bureaucracy, and bribery, the kind of satire that had a certain tradition in Soviet drama. In its time, the most popular event of this kind was Jelinek's *Scandal in the Picture Gallery* in the E. F. Burian Theater, which at the time was still called Décká, or "Theatre D." The natural assumption in such satire was that abuses could only be criticized by someone who identified with "all the positive aspects of how our society lives," and who shared the ideals that society was allegedly aspiring to. Such satires were therefore written by communists, people who sincerely identified with the government ideology and who—seeing the contradictions between their ideals and social practice—castigated the evil practices.

The small theatres and cabarets had once had a rich tradition in this coun-try, with theatres like Dada, the Liberated Theatre, the Red Seven, and others like them, but after 1948 they vanished from our theatrical culture. . . .

[Havel describes the atmosphere in the night club, Reduta, where the first well-known rock band played in 1956 and 1957.]

The Theatre on the Balustrade was founded in 1958, when I was in the army. The director Helena Philipová was there from the beginning; in fact, she was the one who came up with the idea; she found the space, and she urged Suchý to write something that could be done onstage and would bring the atmo-sphere of Reduta into the theatre. Suchý got together with Ivan Vyskočil, who was very important for that whole era, and together they wrote *If a Thousand Clarinets*. To be more precise, Suchý wrote it and worked texts by Vyskočil into it. It was with this play that the Theatre on the Balustrade began. There were no professional actors in it. I saw a performance during one of my army leaves; I can't recall whether I liked it or not, but I remember being fascinated by the atmosphere of the theatre. It looked different then. In one corner of the hall there was an enormous old coal-burning stove; the first generation of those little lamps we called *kondelíky* were flickering on the walls. Many of the audience stood on the balcony outside the building and watched performances through the windows (later, when my wife was an usher, she had endless problems with this phenomenon). It was all somewhat reminiscent of a nightclub. (By the way—and I don't know exactly why this is, and someday I'm going to have to give some thought to it—an inseparable part of the kind of theatre I've been drawn to all my life is a touch of obscurity, of decay or degeneration, of frivolity, I don't know quite what to call it; I think theatre should always be somewhat suspect.) No matter how the performance turned out, one thing was certain: it was full of the joy of performance, there was freedom, pure humor, and intelligence in it; it didn't take itself too seriously, and people were delighted. In short, something new and unprecedented was born.

[HVÍŽDALA:] What basic differences were there between the aesthetics of the small theatres of the time and traditional theatre?

[HAVEL:] I've already mentioned one of the differences: the divergence, the non-ideological nature of those theatres. We didn't try to explain the world; we weren't interested in theses, and we had no intention of instructing anybody. It was more like a game—except that the "game" somehow mysteriously touched the deepest nerves of human existence and social life, and if it didn't always do this, at least it did so in its happier moments. The humor was described as pure, as an example of *l'art pour l'art,* as dadaistic, as being an end in itself, but, oddly enough, this humor, which apparently had no connections with "burning events" of the time, as that phrase is conventionally understood, gave expression—strangely and indirectly—to the most urgent matter of all: what man really is. And without necessarily being intellectuals, perceptive members of the audience felt that even the most grotesque escapade by Vyskočil touched something essential in them, the genuine drama and the genuine ineffability of life, things as fundamental as despair, empty hope, bad luck, fate, misfortune, groundless joy.

Another important characteristic of these theatres was the way they worked against illusion. The theatre no longer pretended that it was an "image of life." Psychologically detailed types, characters represented in the kind of relationships they would allegedly find themselves in real life, disappeared from the stage. The small theatres simply wanted to show something, so they showed it; they showed it in all kinds of ways, as it occurred to them, randomly, according to the law of ideas. People were on the stage in their own right; they played with each other and they played with the audience;

[425]

Chapter 13
Cold War Europe:
Václav Havel
(1936–) and Olga
Šplíchalová
Havlová
(1933–1996)

they did not present stories but, rather, posed questions or opened up themes. And—something I considered the most important thing of all—they manifested the experience of absurdity.

━━━━━ **DOCUMENT TWO** ━━━━━

LUDVIK VACULIK

"2,000 Words to Workers, Farmers, Scientists, Artists, and Everyone" (1968)

In June 1968, the novelist, Ludvik Vaculik, composed this indictment of twenty years of communist rule and published it in the Prague literary journal, Literarni listy. *What were the primary sins of the Czech and Slovak Communists? Can they redeem themselves? Why would the Soviet Union denounce this statement as counterrevolutionary?*

. . . First, the life of our nation was threatened by the war. Then came blacker days, which threatened our spiritual and national character. Most of the nation accepted and had faith in the new program of socialism, which was taken over by the wrong people. It would not have mattered so much that they lacked the experience of statesmen, the knowledge of scholars or the training of philosophers, if they had allowed themselves to be replaced by more capable persons.

The communist party betrayed the great trust the people put in it after the war. It preferred the glories of office, until it had those and nothing more. The disappointment was great among communists as well as noncommunists. The leadership of the party changed it from a political and ideological group into a power-hungry organization, attracting egoists, cowards and crooks.

They influenced the party's operations to such an extent that honest people could not gain a foothold without debasement, much less make it a modem political instrument. There were many communists who fought this deterioration but they could not prevent what happened.

The situation in the party led to a similar situation in the state, resulting in the linkage of party and state. There was no criticism of the state and economic organizations. Parliament forgot how to deliberate, the government forgot how to rule and managers how to manage. Elections had no significance and the laws lost their value. We could not trust any of our representatives, and when we could it was impossible to ask them for anything because they were powerless. What made things even worse was that we could not trust each other.

THE DECLINE OF HONESTY

Personal and collective honor deteriorated. Honesty led nowhere, and it was useless to speak of rewards according to ability. As a result, most citizens lost interest in public affairs. They were concerned only with themselves and with accumulating money. The situation got so bad that now one cannot even rely on money. Relations among people were undermined and joy in work was lost. To sum up, the nation was in a morass that threatened its spiritual health and character.

We are all responsible for the present state of affairs, with the greater responsibility on the communists among us. But the prime responsibility lies with those who made up the component parts or were the instruments of uncontrolled power, the power of a dogmatic group placed everywhere by the party apparatus, from Prague to the smallest district and community. The apparatus decided what one could or could not do and directed the cooperatives for the cooperative members, the factories for the workers and the national committees for the citizens. No organization was run by its members, not even the communist party.

The greatest deception of these rulers was that they presented their arbitrariness as the will of the workers. If we believed this, we could now blame the workers for the decline of our economy, for the crimes against innocent people, for the introduction of censorship which made it impossible for all this to be described. The workers would have to be blamed for mistaken investments, for the losses in trade, for the shortage of apartments.

Naturally, no sensible person believes that the workers are guilty of these things. We all know—and each worker knows—that he did not decide anything. Someone else chose the union officials he elected. Power was executed by trained groups of officials loyal to the party and state apparatus. In effect, they took the place of the former ruling class and became the new authority.

In all justice, we can say that some of them did realize what was happening. We know that now because they are redressing wrongs, correcting mistakes, bringing decisions to the membership and the citizens, and limiting the authority and the size of the official apparatus. They no longer support the conservative viewpoint in the party. But there are still many officials opposed to change who exercise the instruments of power, particularly in the districts and in the communities.

Since the beginning of the year we have been in the process of reviving democratization. It began in the communist party. We must say this. And those noncommunists, among us who, until recently, expected no good to come from the communists also know it. We must add, however, that this process could not have begun elsewhere. After twenty years, only the communists had an actual political life; only communist criticism was in a position to assess things as they were; only the opposition in the communist party had the privilege of being in contact with the enemy.

Chapter 13
Cold War Europe:
Václav Havel
(1936–) and Olga
Šplíchalová
Havlová
(1933–1996)

THE BASIS OF DEMOCRATIZATION

The present effort of the democratic communists is only an installment in the re-payment of the debt the entire party owes the people outside the party, who had no political rights. No gratitude is due to the communist party, although it should probably be acknowledged that it is honestly striving to use this last opportunity to save its own honor and the nation's.

The process of revival is not producing anything new. Many of its ideas and recommendations are older than the errors of socialism in our country. These errors should have been exposed long ago but they were suppressed. Let us not now cherish the illusion that these ideas prevail because truth won out. Their victory was decided by the weakness of the old leadership, aggravated by the accumulation of mistakes of 20 years of misrule. All the defects in the ideology of this system were nourished until they matured.

Therefore, let us not overestimate the significance of the criticism from the ranks of writers and students. The source of social change is in the economy. The right word is significant only if it is spoken under conditions which have been duly prepared. "Duly prepared conditions in our country"—unfortunately, this cliché means our general level of poverty and the complete disintegration of the old system of rule, under which certain types of politicians calmly and peacefully compromised themselves at our expense.

Truth does not prevail. It only remains when everything else fails. There is no cause for a national celebration of victory. But there is cause for new hope. We turn to you in this moment of hope, which is still under threat. It took several months for many of us to believe that they could speak out and many still do not believe it.

Yet, we have not spoken up. All we have to do is complete what we started out to do—humanize this regime. Otherwise the revenge of the old forces will be cruel. We turn to those who have been waiting. The days immediately ahead of us will determine our future course for many years to come. . . .

DOCUMENT THREE

Olga Havlová

Interview with Eva Kanturková
(1979)

In 1979, shortly after Václav was imprisoned. Olga talked with Eva Kanturková about her dissident husband, Charter 77, and the police harassment and surveillance of their farmhouse, Hrádeček to which they had been subjected. In this part of the interview, Olga explained the significance of the surveillance. How does police surveillance affect their relationship with their neighbors and friends? Why might an individual be reluctant to act against the state?

[KANTURKOVÁ:] How did people treat you there in the country?

[HAVLOVÁ:] Normally, humanely.

[KANTURKOVÁ:] Bravely?

[HAVLOVÁ:] I wouldn't say bravely. Just humanely, simply humanely. In the beginning, when they didn't know us too well and considered us to be those Prague people in the country, they weren't very interested in us. Only when the police started coming to see us, people would say hi in a friendly way. The police threatened our neighbors and forbade them to see us, we live in the mountains, people live far away from one another and they need each other so such an inhibition seems rather drastic there. I came to see my neighbor and she was crying so hard that I thought some horrible tragedy had happened. In response to the police's inhibition, our neighbor said: "I felt like a beaten dog." Or another example. We couldn't drive our own car so when the neighbor saw me walk to town he gave me a ride. Because of this, the police revoked his driver's license.

DOCUMENT FOUR

VÁCLAV HAVEL

"The Power of the Powerless"
(October 1978)

In this excerpt from Havel's most famous essay, "The Power of the Powerless," he asserts that the "powerless" always contain within themselves the power to liberate themselves from oppression. Why does Václav use a greengrocer to illustrate his point? What types of daily choices must the grocer make under this system? What choices do the Havels make? Are Czechs and Slovaks the ultimate cause of their own subordination? Why or why not?

. . . The manager of a fruit and vegetable shop places in his window, among the onions and carrots, the slogan: 'Workers of the world, unite!' Why does he do it? What is he trying to communicate to the world? Is he genuinely enthusiastic about the idea of unity among the workers of the world? Is his enthusiasm so great that he feels an irrepressible impulse to acquaint the public with his ideals? Has he really given more than a moment's thought to how such a unification might occur and what it would mean?

Chapter 13
Cold War Europe:
Václav Havel
(1936–) and Olga
Šplíchalová
Havlová
(1933–1996)

I think it can safely be assumed that the overwhelming majority of shop-keepers never think about the slogans they put in their windows, nor do they use them to express their real opinions. That poster was delivered to our green-grocer from the enterprise headquarters along with the onions and carrots. He put them all into the window simply because it has been done that way for years, because everyone does it, and because that is the way it has to be. If he were to refuse, there could be trouble. He could be reproached for not having the proper 'decoration' in his window; someone might even accuse him of dis-loyalty. He does it because these things must be done if one is to get along in life. It is one of the thousands of details that guarantee him a relatively tranquil life 'in harmony with society,' as they say.

Obviously the greengrocer is indifferent to the semantic content of the slogan on exhibit; he does not put the slogan in his window from any personal desire to acquaint the public with the ideal it expresses. This, of course, does not mean that his action has no motive or significance at all, or that the slogan communi-cates nothing to anyone. The slogan is really a *sign*, and as such it contains a subliminal but very definite message. Verbally, it might be expressed this way: 'I, the greengrocer XY, live here and I know what I must do. I behave in the man-ner expected of me. I can be depended upon and am beyond reproach. I am obe-dient and therefore I have the right to be left in peace.' This message, of course, has an addressee: it is directed above, to the greengrocer's superior, and at the same time it is a shield that protects the greengrocer from potential informers. The slogan's real meaning, therefore, is rooted firmly in the greengrocer's exis-tence. It reflects his vital interests. But what are those vital interests?

Let us take note: if the greengrocer had been instructed to display the slogan, 'I am afraid and therefore unquestioningly obedient', he would not be nearly as indifferent to its semantics, even though the statement would reflect the truth. The greengrocer would be embarrassed and ashamed to put such an unequivo-cal statement of his own degradation in the shop window, and quite naturally so, for he is a human being and thus has a sense of his own dignity. To overcome this complication, his expression of loyalty must take the form of a sign which, at least on its textual surface, indicates a level of disinterested conviction. It must allow the greengrocer to say, 'What's wrong with the workers of the world uniting?' Thus the sign helps the greengrocer to conceal from himself the low foundations of his obedience, at the same time concealing the low foundations of power. It hides them behind the façade of something high. And that some-thing is *ideology*. . . .

[Havel discusses the significance of the greengrocer's ritual.]

. . . We have seen that the real meaning of the greengrocer's slogan has noth-ing to do with what the text of the slogan actually says. Even so, this real mean-ing is quite clear and generally comprehensible because the code is so familiar: the greengrocer declares his loyalty (and he can do no other if his declaration is to be accepted) in the only way the regime is capable of hearing; that is, by ac-cepting the prescribed *ritual*, by accepting appearances as reality, by accepting the given rules of the game. In doing so, however, he has himself become a player in the game, thus making it possible for the game to go on, for it to exist in the first place. . . .

Because of this, dictatorship of the ritual, however, power becomes clearly *anonymous*. Individuals are almost dissolved in the ritual. They allow themselves to be swept along by it and frequently it seems as though ritual alone carries people from obscurity into the light of power. Is it not characteristic of the post-totalitarian system that, on all levels of the power hierarchy, individuals are increasingly being pushed aside by faceless people, puppets, those uniformed flunkeys of the rituals and routines of power? . . .

[Havel asks the question, Why did "our greengrocer have to put his loyalty on display in the shop window?"]

The greengrocer had to put the slogan in his window, therefore, not in the hope that someone might read it or be persuaded by it, but to contribute, along with thousands of other slogans, to the panorama that everyone is very much aware of. This panorama, of course, has a subliminal meaning as well: it reminds people where they are living and what is expected of them. It tells them what everyone else is doing, and indicates to them what they must do as well, if they don't want to be excluded, to fall into isolation, alienate themselves from society, break the rules of the game, and risk the loss of their peace and tranquility and security.

The woman who ignored the greengrocer's slogan may well have hung a similar slogan just an hour before in the corridor of the office where she works. She did it more or less without thinking, just as our greengrocer did, and she could do so precisely because she was doing it against the background of the general panorama and with some awareness of it, that is, against the background of the panorama of which the greengrocer's shop window forms a part. When the greengrocer visits her office, he will not notice her slogan either, just as she failed to notice his. Nevertheless their slogans are mutually dependent: both were displayed with some awareness of the general panorama and, we might say, under its *diktat*. Both, however, assist in the creation of that panorama, and therefore they assist in the creation of that *diktat* as well. The greengrocer and the office worker have both adapted to the conditions in which they live, but in doing so, they help to create those conditions. . . . Metaphysically speaking, without the greengrocer's slogan the office worker's slogan could not exist, and vice versa. Each proposes to the other that something be repeated and each accepts the other's proposal. Their mutual indifference to each other's slogans is only an illusion: in reality, by exhibiting their slogans, each compels the other to accept the rules of the game and to confirm thereby the power that requires the slogans in the first place. Quite simply, each helps the other to be obedient. Both are objects in a system of control, but at the same time they are its subjects as well. They are both victims of the system and its instruments. . . .

Everyone, however, is in fact involved and enslaved, not only the greengrocers but also the prime ministers. Differing positions in the hierarchy merely es-

Chapter 13
Cold War Europe:
Václav Havel
(1936–) and Olga
Šplíchalová
Havlová
(1933–1996)

tablish differing degrees of involvement: the greengrocer is involved only to a minor extent, but he also has very little power. The prime minister, naturally, has greater power, but in return he is far more deeply involved. . . . What we understand by the system is not, therefore, a social order imposed by one group upon another, but rather something which permeates the entire society and is a factor in shaping it, something which may seem impossible to grasp or define (for it is in the nature of a mere principle), but which is expressed by the entire society as an important feature of its life. . . .

[Havel asserts that living in this system and obeying its rituals force people to live a lie.]

Human beings are compelled to live within a lie, but they can be compelled to do so only because they are in fact capable of living in this way. Therefore not only does the system alienate humanity, but at the same time alienated humanity supports this system as its own involuntary masterplan, as a degenerate image of its own degeneration, as a record of people's own failure as individuals. . . .

. . . Let us now imagine that one day something in our greengrocer snaps and he stops putting up the slogans merely to ingratiate himself. He stops voting in elections he knows are a farce. He begins to say what he really thinks at political meetings. And he even finds the strength in himself to express solidarity with those whom his conscience commands him to support. In this revolt the greengrocer steps out of living within the lie. He rejects the ritual and breaks the rules of the game. He discovers once more his suppressed identity and dignity. He gives his freedom a concrete significance. His revolt is an attempt to *live within the truth.* . . .

DOCUMENT FIVE

Charter 77
(1977)

In 1975, Czechoslovakia signed the Helsinki Accords on human rights. As a result of these accords, Helsinki watch groups were formed to monitor their regime's record on human rights. In 1977, many Czech and Slovak intellectuals drafted and then signed a charter asking their government to honor these accords. The charter also asks Czechoslovak citizens to do what they can in defense of human rights. What human rights abuses does the charter discuss? Is the charter movement a political one? Why or why not? Is the regime threatened by this charter?

In the Czechoslovak Collection of Laws, no. 120 of 13 October 1976, texts were published of the International Covenant on Civil and Political Rights, and of the International Covenant on Economic, Social, and Cultural Rights, which were signed on behalf of our Republic in 1968, were confirmed at Helsinki in 1975 and came into force in our country on 23 March 1976. From that date our citizens have the right, and our state the duty, to abide by them.

The human rights and freedoms underwritten by these covenants constitute important assets of civilized life for which many progressive movements have striven throughout history and whose codification could greatly contribute to the development of a humane society.

We accordingly welcome the Czechoslovak Socialist Republic's accession to those agreements.

Their publication, however, serves as an urgent reminder of the extent to which basic human rights in our country exist, regrettably, on paper only.

The right to freedom of expression, for example, guaranteed by Article 19 of the first-mentioned covenant, is in our case purely illusory. Tens of thousands of our citizens are prevented from working in their own fields for the sole reason that they hold views differing from official ones and are discriminated against and harassed in all kinds of ways by the authorities and public organizations. Deprived as they are of any means to defend themselves, they become victims of a virtual apartheid.

Hundreds of thousands of other citizens are denied that "freedom from fear" mentioned in the preamble to the first covenant, being condemned to live in constant danger of unemployment or other penalties if they voice their own opinions. . . .

Freedom of public expression is repressed by the centralized control of all the communications media and of publishing and cultural institutions. No philosophical, political, or scientific view or artistic expression that departs ever so slightly from the narrow bounds of official ideology or aesthetics is allowed to be published; no open criticism can be made of abnormal social phenomena; no public defense is possible against false and insulting charges made in official propaganda; the legal protection against "attacks on honor and reputation" clearly guaranteed by Article 17 of the first covenant is in practice nonexistent; false accusations cannot be rebutted, and any attempt to secure compensation or correction through the courts is futile; no open debate is allowed in the domain of thought and art. Many scholars, writers, artists, and others are penalized for having legally published or expressed, years ago, opinions which are condemned by those who hold political power today.

Freedom of religious confession, emphatically guaranteed by Article 18 of the first covenant, is systematically curtailed by arbitrary official action; by interference with the activity of churchmen, who are constantly threatened by the refusal of the state to permit them the exercise of their functions or by the withdrawal of such permission; by financial or other measures against those who express their religious faith in word or action; by constraints on religious training; and so forth.

One instrument for the curtailment or, in many cases, complete elimination of many civic rights is the system by which all national institutions and organi-

Chapter 13
Cold War Europe:
Václav Havel
(1936–) and Olga
Šplíchalová
Havlová
(1933–1996)

zations are in effect subject to political directives from the apparatus of the ruling party and to decisions made by powerful individuals. . . .

Further civic rights, including the explicit prohibition of "arbitrary interference with privacy, family, home, or correspondence" (Article 17 of the first covenant), are seriously vitiated by the various forms of interference in the private life of citizens exercised by the Ministry of the Interior, for example, by bugging telephones and houses, opening mail, following personal movements, searching homes, setting up networks of neighborhood informers (often recruited by illicit threats or promises), and in other ways, The ministry frequently interferes in employers' decisions, instigates acts of discrimination by authorities and organizations, brings weight to bear on the organs of justice, and even orchestrates propaganda campaigns in the media. This activity is governed by no law and, being clandestine, affords the citizen no chance to defend himself. . . .

Some of our people—either in private, at their places of work, or by the only feasible public channel, the media—have drawn attention to the systematic violation of human rights and democratic freedoms and demanded amends in specific cases. But their pleas have remained largely ignored or been made grounds for police investigation.

Responsibility for the maintenance of civic rights in our country naturally devolves in the first place on the political and state authorities. Yet, not only on them: Everyone bears his share of responsibility for the conditions that prevail and accordingly also for the observance of legally enshrined agreements, binding upon all citizens as well as upon governments. It is this sense of coresponsibility, our belief in the meaning of voluntary citizens' involvement and the general need to give it new and more effective expression that led us to the idea of creating Charter 77, whose inception we today publicly announce.

Charter 77 is a free informal, open community of people of different convictions, different faiths, and different professions united by the will to strive, individually and collectively, for the respect of civic and human rights in our own country and throughout the world—rights accorded to all men by the two mentioned international covenants, by the Final Act of the Helsinki conference, and by numerous other international documents opposing war, violence, and social or spiritual oppression, and which are comprehensively laid down in the United Nations Universal Declaration of Human Rights.

Charter 77 springs from a background of friendship and solidarity among people who share our concern for those ideals that have inspired, and continue to inspire, their lives and their work.

Charter 77 is not an organization; it has no rules, permanent bodies, or formal membership. It embraces everyone who agrees with its ideas, participates in its work, and supports it. It does not form the basis for any oppositional political activity. Like many similar citizen initiatives in various countries, West and East, it seeks to promote the general public interest. It does not aim, then, to set out its own programs for political or social reforms or changes, but within its own sphere of activity it wishes to conduct a constructive dialogue with the political and state authorities, particularly by drawing attention to various individual cases where human and civil rights are violated, by preparing documentation and suggesting solutions, by submitting other proposals of a more general character aimed at reinforcing such rights and their guarantees, and by acting as a mediator in various conflict situations which may lead to injustice and so forth.

By its symbolic name Charter 77 denotes that it has come into being at the start of a year proclaimed as the Year of Political Prisoners—a year in which a conference in Belgrade is due to review the implementation of the obligations assumed at Helsinki.

As signatories, we hereby authorize Professor Dr Jan Patočka, Václav Havel, and Professor Jiří Hájek to act as the spokesmen for the charter. These spokesmen are endowed with full authority to represent it vis-á-vis state and other bodies, and the public at home and abroad, and their signatures attest the authenticity of documents issued by the charter. They will have us, and others who join us, as their coworkers, taking part in any needful negotiations, shouldering particular tasks and sharing every responsibility.

We believe that Charter 77 will help to enable all the citizens of Czechoslovakia to work and live as free human beings.

DOCUMENT SIX

VÁCLAV HAVEL

Letters to Olga

During Václav's imprisonment between 1979 and 1982, he wrote 144 letters. All but nineteen survived and were first published in samizdat. *Václav's first inclination was to publish only those letters in which he pondered the nature of existence, the theater, the police state, and life in prison. His friends dissuaded him from this impulse, and the original collection includes letters with personal details and lengthy instructions to Olga concerning their homes, their friends, and her verbal parsimony. In this letter, Václav tells his wife to come prepared for his next visit.*

November 8, 1980

Dear Olga,

As you probably already know, our visit is scheduled for Saturday, December 6. First, then, some peripheral remarks:

   1. I've already written you about what I'd like to be included in the parcel; essentially, it should be the same as the one before (basic items: a kilo of

Chapter 13
Cold War Europe:
Václav Havel
(1936–) and Olga
Šplíchalová
Havlová
(1933–1996)

tea, 300 good cigarettes, chocolates, perhaps some other Christmas sweets). Particular items: 3 spolarins, two pairs of warm socks, one large toothpaste. You needn't bring lotion with you (a friend gave me some); if there's some room left for hygienic items, all I need is another soap dish (I have one already, but need another for work) and a stiff sponge for my body. Otherwise, I have everything I need.

2. Please go over some of my earlier letters, which contain a lot of unanswered questions, and prepare replies to compensate for the verbal parsimony of your letters. You should have a systematic report ready and shouldn't rely on my questions—I can't have notes with me, and knowing myself, I am bound to forget many things. The basic thematic areas that interest me are: (a) a detailed description of your life: I have only a very hazy impression of many things—from your movements between Hrádeček and Prague (about who spends time with you at Hrádeček and when; who visits, and how often, who drives you there, etc.) to your life in Prague (how you actually spend your days, whom you see and how frequently, what you are working on, what you think about and how you feel, what cultural events you attend, etc.) (b) Hrádeček—the condition it's in, how it looks, work completed and incomplete, the legal situation. (c) The Prague flat—are you getting rid of the furniture or has it remained only an intention or half-completed? If exchanging the flat isn't an immediate issue (though there's nothing to prevent you from working on it—regardless of the problems surrounding the building inspector's approval of Hrádeček, then it should at least be quickly cleared of those veneered monstrosities and left empty, or rather furnished only provisionally or with what comes to hand. (As I've written you more than once, that middle-class furniture is a burden on my spirit even here and while I'm only condemned to a few years in Heřmanice, I'm horrified at the prospect of a life sentence with that furniture.) d) Social life: I lack news of many friends, those who've emigrated and those who've remained; the outlines of that "particular horizon" I devoted my last letter to are even more shrouded in fog than necessary. (Among many other things, I'd be most interested to know, for instance, how the outside world seems to Otka now that she is out of prison—that might well make some things more vivid to me than information provided by those who have lived continuously in that external world.) e) The outcome of my plays and news about how they were received. . . .

The last visit was almost too improvised; there were clearly many things we wanted to say but time and again we fell silent out of sheer uncertainty as to what we should actually talk about and in what order, how much detail we should go into on various matters, etc. When the visit is only an hour long, you are constantly anxious about wasting precious minutes on less important subjects at the expense of more important ones. In fact you can scarcely say which are more important and which less; occasionally you may even be subconsciously influenced by the feeling that you must rush to get everything in (that applies mainly to me—whence the impression of a certain lack of focus or inadequate attention to particular subjects). I think such dangers can be avoided by taking two measures: (1) we will both try, beforehand, to get ourselves into the most balanced and harmonious frame of mind; (2) prepare yourself well and be somewhat systematic in what you say (you know how I appreciate that), so it won't just be a fountain of individual facts lacking a context (later, one often attributes inappropriate and distorted meanings to those separate bits).

Will Ivan come as well? Naturally I'd be delighted if he could maintain the tradition by coming—perhaps it could be coordinated somehow with the St. Nicholas celebrations. (You'd probably not leave until night, so you could celebrate, in the tradition of my own St. Nicholas Eve two years ago, when—if you remember—I played the angel for a number of families and then, at night, set out on a certain adventurous journey. And by the way: how did you get to Ostrava last time? Weren't you overdoing it just a little, not wanting to tell me anything about it?)

I don't suppose I have to emphasize how much I'm looking forward to the visit and how I cling to the prospect; in any case, it should be clear enough from the above instructions. . . .

As I promised in my last letter, this letter should have been devoted to the question of how I experience being torn out of my home, what I miss most and how, etc. As you can see, there were so many specific things to relate that there's no more room for my intended subject, and frankly I'm just as glad: the more I thought about it during the week, the more the whole thing seemed too complex and difficult to describe. The phenomenon of loss of freedom, as I am only now beginning to realize, is more concealed from direct perception and more mysterious in its structure and consequences than may be apparent on the outside. In some ways the whole experience is better—compared to conventional expectations—in some ways worse; but in any case, it is different and immensely more complicated. With some relief, therefore, I will set the whole subject aside until I've thought it over more carefully.

*Vašek**

---

*[Common nickname for Václav. Ed.]

Chapter 13
Cold War Europe:
Václav Havel
(1936–) and Olga
Šplíchalová
Havlová
(1933–1996)

SLAVENKA DRAKULIĆ

How We Survived Communism and Even Laughed
(1991)

Slavenka Drakulić is a Croatian columnist who wrote a series of vignettes about life under communism for American periodicals in the late 1980s and early 1990s. She often noted how the communist system failed to provide its citizens, especially women, with what she considered the essentials for everyday life. What are communism's failures? Compare these failures with the Havels' lives. How might the combination of grievances contribute to the fall of communism in Eastern Europe?

Drakulić was always critical of Western leftists who refused to recognize the problems of the communist system in Eastern Europe. In the passage called "A Letter from the United States," she describes shocking an audience of mostly men with her observations about the system's failure to provide the basics for women.

PIZZA IN WARSAW, TORTE IN PRAGUE

[On Arriving in Prague in 1990, Immediately After the Velvet Revolution]

. . . One of the things one is constantly reminded of in these parts is not to be thoughtless with food. I remember my mother telling me that I had to eat everything in front of me, because to throw away food would be a sin. Perhaps she had God on her mind, perhaps not. She experienced World War II and ever since, like most of the people in Eastern Europe, she behaves as if it never ended. Maybe this is why they are never really surprised that even forty years afterwards there is a lack of sugar, oil, coffee, or flour. To be heedless—to behave as if you are somewhere else, where everything is easy to get—is a sin not against God, but against people. Here you have to think of food, because it has entirely diverse social meanings. To bring a cake for dessert when you are invited for a dinner—a common gesture in another, more affluent country—means you invested a great deal of energy to find it if you didn't make it yourself. And even if you did, finding eggs, milk, sugar, and butter took time and energy. That makes it precious in a very different way from if you had bought it in the pastry shop next door.

When Jaroslav picked me up at Prague airport, I wanted to buy a torte before we went to his house for dinner. It was seven o'clock in the evening and shops were already closed. Czechs work until five or six, which doesn't leave much time to shop. 'The old government didn't like people walking in the streets. It might cause them trouble,' said Jaroslav, half joking. 'Besides, there isn't much to buy anyway.' My desire to buy a torte after six o'clock appeared to be quite an extravagance, and it was clear that one couldn't make a habit of bringing a cake for dessert. In the Slavia Café there were no pastries at all, not to mention a torte. The best confectioner in Prague was closed, and in the Hotel Zlatá Husa restaurant a waitress repeated 'Torte?' after us as if we were in the wrong place. Then she shook her head. With every new place, my desire to buy a torte diminished. Perhaps it is not that there are no tortes—it's just hard to find them at that hour. At the end, we went to the only shop open until eight-thirty and bought ice cream. There were three kinds and Jaroslav picked vanilla, which is what his boys like the best. . . .

[On Visiting Friends in Sofia, Bulgaria]

. . . In a totalitarian society, one *has* to relate to the power directly; there is no escape. Therefore, politics never becomes abstract. It remains a palpable, brutal force directing every aspect of our lives, from what we eat to how we live and where we work. Like a disease, a plague, an epidemic, it doesn't spare anybody. Paradoxically, this is precisely how a totalitarian state produces its enemies: politicized citizens. The 'velvet revolution' is the product not only of high politics, but of the consciousness of ordinary citizens, infected by politics.

Before you get here [Bulgaria], you tend to forget newspaper pictures of people standing in line in front of shops. You think they serve as proof in the ideological battle, the proof that communism is failing. Or you take them as mere pictures, not reality. But once here, you cannot escape the *feeling* of shortages, even if you are not standing in line, even if you don't see them. In Prague, where people line up only for fruit, there was enough of all necessities, except for oranges or lemons, which were considered a 'luxury.' It is hard to predict what will be considered a luxury item because this depends on planning, production, and shortages. One time it might be fruit, as in Prague, or milk, as in Sofia. People get used to less and less of everything. In Albania, the monthly ration for a whole family is two pounds of meat, two pounds of cheese, ten pounds of flour, less than half a pound each of coffee and butter. Everywhere, the bottom line is bread. It means safety—because the lack of bread is where real fear begins. Whenever I read a headline 'No Bread' in the newspaper, I see a small, dark, almost empty bakery on Vladimir Zaimov Boulevard in Sofia, and I myself, even without reason, experience a genuine fear. It makes my bread unreal, too, and I feel as if I should grab it and eat it while it lasts.

Every mother in Bulgaria can point to where communism failed, from the failures of the planned economy (and the consequent lack of food, milk), to the lack of apartments, child-care facilities, clothes, disposable diapers, or toilet paper. The banality of everyday life is where it has really failed, rather than on the level of ideology. . . .

Chapter 13
Cold War Europe:
Václav Havel
(1936–) and Olga
Šplíchalová
Havlová
(1933–1996)

A Letter from the United States

. . . I was to give a paper on the same subject: women in Eastern Europe. But before I started my speech, I took out one sanitary napkin and one Tampax and, holding them high in the air, I showed them to the audience. 'I have just come from Bulgaria,' I said, 'and believe me, women there don't have either napkins or Tampaxes—they never had them, in fact. Nor do women in Poland, or Czechoslovakia, much less in the Soviet Union or Romania. This I hold as one of the proofs of why communism failed, because in the seventy years of its existence it couldn't fulfil the basic needs of half the population.'

The audience were startled at first; they hadn't expected this, not at a scholarly conference where one could expect theories, analyses, conclusions—words, words, words. Then people started applauding. For me, the sight of a sanitary napkin and a Tampax was a necessary precondition for understanding what we are talking about: not the generally known fact that women wait in long lines for food or that they don't have washing machines—one could read about this in *Time* or *Newsweek*—but that besides all the hardship of living in Eastern Europe, if they can't find gauze or absorbent cotton, they have to wash bloody cloth pads every month, again and again, as their mothers and grandmothers and great-grandmothers did hundreds of years ago. For them, communism has changed nothing in that respect.

But I wasn't sure that my audience grasped this fact, after all: first, because they were mostly men and, by some caprice of Mother Nature, men usually don't have to wash bloody cloth pads every month; second, because they were leftists. I know them, the American men (and women) of the left. Talking to them always makes me feel like the worst kind of dissident, a right-wing freak (or a Republican, at best), even if I consider myself an honest social democrat. For every mild criticism of life in the system I have been living under for the last forty years they look at me suspiciously, as if I were a CIA agent (while my folks, communists back home, never had any doubts about it—perhaps this is the key difference between Eastern and Western comrades?) But one can hardly blame them. It is not the knowledge about communism that they lack—I am quite sure they know all about it—it's the experience of living under such conditions. So, while I am speaking from 'within' the system itself, they are explaining it to me from without. I do not want to claim that you have to be a hen to lay an egg, only that a certain disagreement between these two starting positions is normal. But they don't go for that; they need to be right. They see reality in schemes, in broad historical outlines, the same as their brothers in the East do. I love to hear their great speeches or read their long analyses after brief visits to our poor countries, where they meet with the best minds the establishment can offer (probably speaking English!) I love the way they get surprised or angry when the food is too greasy, there is no hot water in their hotel, they can't buy Alka Seltzer or aspirin, or their plane is late. But best of all I love the innocence of their questions. Sitting in that luncheonette on Seventy-fifth Street with

B, I resented the questions she asked me, the way she asked them, as if she didn't understand that menstrual pads and Tampax are both a metaphor for the system and the reality of women living in Eastern Europe. . . .

Olga Havlová (Havel)

Life Under Socialism and Its Aftermath
(1990)

During the long years of opposition to state socialism, dissidents focused atten-tion on the political oppression and failed socio-economic agendas of their govern-ments. In the next two selections, one a letter written by Olga and the other an interview given to Valerie Grove of The Sunday Times, *Olga details some failed legacies of the communist period. What are these legacies? What does she propose as a solution?*

The interview with Olga Havel was conducted in November 1990, less than a year after Václav Havel became president of the Czechoslovakia. What is the focus of the interviewer's questions? Would you ask different questions of Olga Havel? Why or why not?

Letter to the Editor

The New York Review of Books
June 14, 1990
To the Editors:

The handicapped in our country have been forced into isolation, removed from sight into homes and institutions. There are a million of them in Czechoslova-kia, in a population of only fifteen million. This did not trouble us. The state said they were being looked after, so we chose to believe it.

This was our habit of inhumanity. It would have been inhuman even if the state had been looking after these people well. But it turns out that it has been looking after them badly. There is practically no equipment, no nursing, some-times not even the most basic conditions for living in dignity.

We are now changing the state. But we also need to change our habits. The handicapped must be brought back from the dark and given a place in our lives. In civilized societies the less fortunate are not shut away from the more fortu-

Chapter 13
Cold War Europe:
Václav Havel
(1936–) and Olga
Šplíchalová
Havlová
(1933–1996)

nate. The handicapped are not forgotten and the lucky realize that there is much to be gained from facing up to their obligations toward others. This is the habit of humanity, and we in our country want to acquire it.

But money is needed for equipment for medicines and training, and for many other things which, like the spirit of charity itself, have been in drastically short supply. We are now forming the Czechoslovak Society for the Handicapped, and would welcome your support. All contributions are tax-deductible and should be made out to the Charter 77 Foundation, marked for the account of CSH, and sent to the Charter 77 Foundation, 888 7th Avenue, Room 3301, New York, NY 10106.

Please help us to help those who, through no fault of their own, are unable to help themselves.

Olga Havel

Prague, Czechoslovakia

Interview with Olga Havel

Valerie Grove, *The Sunday Times*

Olga Havel is the antithesis of her husband Václav. Where he is gregarious, she is private; he is convivial and bearlike, she is chilly and spiky and wears a tragic mask. But Olga was the rock in Havel's life when he was the imprisoned playwright, enemy of society: his Letters to Olga became one of the last testaments of oppression. When the world changed, and he became the president of Czechoslovakia, Olga became, after 36 years of wifely obscurity, first lady.

"Don't ask Olga where she met her husband," the interpreter advised me at once. Why ever not? "Everybody wants to see her husband and talk to her husband—and when they meet her the first thing they ask is where did she meet her husband.

"And women write to her and say 'please look after your husband, keep him well for us. And stop him smoking'." . . .

What brought her to London last week, her first visit since the Prague Spring of 1968, was her goodwill committee, Vybor Dobre Vule, or what the Americans insist on calling the Olga Havel Foundation. She has decided to raise some money. During the Havels' state visit to North America, there was a gathering of Czechoslovak exiles. Olga mentioned that the communists had squandered health service money on their own grand houses, leaving the health service in a piteous state. One old Czech who had made a fortune out of taps said: "I'm going to send you $100,000," and Olga realised that she could do something.

"We handed this wonderful first money straight over to a children's hospital at Brno. Unfortunately, to put it into its proper state you would need $3m." The Olga Havel Foundation is still embryonic, but in New York she did the rounds of rich expatriates such as Ivana Trump and her husband's old buddy, Milos Forman. (They are still wondering whether to approach the bounciest of British Czechs, Robert Maxwell.)

The problem at home is that there is no concept of charity. "The communists pretended that handicapped people didn't exist, nobody in a wheelchair was ever allowed to be seen in the street. But there are 1m out of a population of 15m in institutions or shut up at home; our aim is to bring them out." So far they have managed to get the news broadcast in sign language for the deaf, which Olga regards as a great breakthrough.

They still need every form of medical equipment: incubators for newborn babies, kidney dialysis machines, prostheses, wheelchairs, and hard cash.

The regime may nave changed utterly, but the fabric of Prague still crumbles and chaos remains. The Czechoslovakia-born Diana Phipps, née von Sternberg, in whose splendid London house Olga was staying, recalls remarking as they went into a Prague restaurant, how pretty it was. "Pretty? You call this pretty? Look." And Olga banged the spoon on the table so that it bent in half.

Antonia Fraser has written her account of the two contrasting lives of the Havels, before and after last January. The first time the Pinters went to Prague, Havel had just left prison, having been arrested after a demonstration in memory of Jan Palach. They met at the Havels' converted farmhouse in the hilly, wooded countryside of northern Bohemia, a house with books, pictures, open fireplace, and a continual stream of dissidents in sleeping bags. The Pinters slept under white duvets in Havel's study, while the police watched the arrivals from their permanent camp outside the house, in a cabin on stilts which Havel nicknamed Lunochod after the Russian lunar module. Today, that lookout post is still policed, only now it houses the security men who guard President Havel while he is there working on state problems. Olga says he has hardly time to sleep, let alone write a play.

In Prague the Havels scorn to live in the castle's presidential apartments, where the oppressive ambience of communism lingers. Instead they have stayed in their old apartment overlooking the Vlatava River. It was built by Havel's wealthy property developer father and is a modest two and a half rooms in size. Quite enough, Olga says. "As long as there are families with four children who have to live in a room and a half I'm not going to have more myself." Not that she wants to sound like some kind of *communist*, she adds. The tall Victorian house where we sit has eight rooms, all for one person. But Olga believes people must be free to choose where they live. . . .

While her husband was in prison the other dissidents formed a kind of family group. There were always people needing help, being arrested and imprisoned; Havel depended on her to suffer his absence stoically, and to help the others.

Her day always began with the postman, and if there was a letter from Havel, the other dissidents would flock to read it. Then the letters were published in *samizdat*. She was called in for questioning; her letters were withheld from him.

*Chapter 13
Cold War Europe:
Václav Havel
(1936–) and Olga
Šplíchalová
Havlová
(1933–1996)*

"The fight against communism kept us going. It produced adrenaline, excitement, the determination that they weren't going to get us down." I wondered how Olga had felt to have her husband's criticisms of her exposed in the letters. He exhorted her to move house, get a job—as an usherette, he suggested—learn to drive. He implored her to write more often, and more spontaneously, accusing her of "verbal parsimony". "Your letter was sweet but somewhat, telegraphic." "I tend to be sentimental and you don't."

The details of his requests are fascinating: he asked for rose-hip tea, garlic, cigarettes, toothpaste, warm socks and a stiff sponge; he told her about his piles. Every three months she could visit him: he would later ponder on the silences that fell between them. He would remind her constantly to be cheerful and see friends, and then make a comment like: "Your hair has, as you know, a tendency to look like spikes or straw." (While he was in prison she began to let her dyed hair grow white.)

Did she mind all that? A stream of Czech ensued. "As you gather, Olga is a private person. She is not going to say, 'Oh my God I hate my husband'," said the interpreter firmly. All that had been in another land and time, and the old world is dead. The letters will stand as a loving testimony. Havel was never able to tell what hard labour he endured at the prison camp of Hermanice, but wrote philosophical essays that bamboozled his censors who kept inventing rules: "No quotation marks. No exclamation marks. No underlinings. No foreign words. No *thoughts*."

The only time she wrote a long, frank letter, the prison authorities first refused to give it to him, then, allowed him to look at it once before confiscating it again. They were furious when Havel suggested Olga should buy a car, angry she might be able to, with royalties from abroad; and that Havel had the courage to suggest it.

The images he then recalled of their life outside suggest a sybaritic personality: he would dream of barbecuing chicken, sipping white wine and listening to favourite records, of sunning himself on the lawn. Olga has more sparing appetites. When mango is served ("Do you get mango in Prague?" "Mango! You can hardly find a banana") she consumes little. The only hint of self-indulgence about her is her silver nail polish, which she also wears on her toes.

For most women of Prague life goes on as ever: up at 5.30, getting the children to school by 7.30, and themselves to work by 8. They cook, wash, iron; men have not yet been reconstructed, women's rights are an irrelevance, says Olga, when everyone has to queue for bread. It takes a month to get a dress dry-cleaned, half an hour to make a phone call. In the Havel's chaotic office, someone has given them a computer but nobody knows how to programme it. . . .

Olga had told Mrs Thatcher over their lunch together, she said, about the terrible polluted air, the chemical fumes and, acid fog and the water unfit to mix babies' food with; all the detritus of the old regime. "So much damage," she says bleakly. . . .

CREDITS

CHAPTER 1 **Page 3:** *(Left)* Chalk drawing by Ottavio Leoni (c. 1578–1630), Biblioteca Marucelliani, Florence, Italy. Photo Copyright Scala/Art Resource, NY. *(Right)* Portrait by an anonymous artist, 16th Century, Torre del Gallo, Villa Galletti, Arcetri, Florence, Italy. Photo Copyright Aliari/Art Resource, NY. **Document 1, page 22:** From *Discoveries and Opinions of Galileo* by Galileo Galilei, translated by Stillman Drake, copyright © 1957 by Stillman Drake. Used by permission of Doubleday, a division of Random House, Inc. **Document 2, page 24:** Laura Fermi and Gilberto Bernardini, *Galileo and the Scientific Revolution* (New York: Basic Books, Inc., 1961), p. 72. **Document 3, page 25:** Galileo, *The Galileo Affair: A Documentary History,* Maurice A. Finocchiaro, 1989, p. 87–93. **Document 4, page 28:** Mary Allan-Olney, *The Private Life of Galileo, Compiled Principally from His Correspondence and That of His Eldest Daughter, Sister Maria Celeste* (London: Macmillan, 1870), pp. 115–118, 120–121. **Document 5, page 31:** Letter by Sister Maria Celeste, trans. Dava Sobel (1999) from "The Galileo Project," Rice University, <http://es.rice.edu/ES/humsoc/Galileo/MariaCeleste/Letters/077-2_26_33.html>. **Document 6, page 33:** Galileo, *The Galileo Affair: A Documentary History,* Maurice A. Finocchiaro, 1989, pp. 87–93. **Document 7, page 34:** Galileo, *The Galileo Affair: A Documentary History,* Maurice A. Finocchiaro, 1989, pp. 87–93.

CHAPTER 2 **Page 36:** *(Left)* Line engraving, 18th Century. The Granger Collection, NY. *(Right)* The Fotomas Index, London. **Document 1, page 53:** Elizabeth Lilburne, "To the Chosen and Betrusted Knights, Citizens and Burgesses, Assembled in the High and Supreme Court of Parliament," in *Lilburne Tracts/Leveller Tracts,* vol. 1, no. 8 (Minneapolis, Minn.: University of Minnesota, Anderson Rare Books), pp. 66, 70. **Document 2, page 55:** John Lilburne, "The Freeman's Freedome Vindicated," in *The English Levellers,* ed. Andrew Sharp (Cambridge: Cambridge University Press, 1998), p. 31. All the Sharp texts are taken from editions in *The Thomason Tracks* in the British Library and are available on microfilm. **Document 3, page 56:** John Lilburne, et al., "An Agreement of the People," in *The English Levellers,* ed. Andrew Sharp (Cambridge: Cambridge University Press, 1998), pp. 93–95, 100–101. **Document 4, page 58:** "The Putney Debates," in *Sources of the West,* ed. Mark Kishlansky (New York: Harper Collins, 1991), pp. 13–15. First published in William Clarke, *The Clarke Papers,* vol. 1, ed. C. H. Firth (London: Royal Historical Society, 1891), pp. 299–307. **Document 5, page 60:** Katherine Chidley (probably), "To the Supreme Authority . . . A Petition of Divers Well-Affected Women" from Patricia Higgins, "The Reactions of Women, with Special Reference to Women Petitioners," in *Politics, Religion and the English Civil War,* ed. Brian Manning (London: Edward Arnold, 1973), p. 217. Slightly different version of the document also appears in *Not in God's Image,* ed. Julia O'Faolian and Lauro Martines (New York: Harper and Row, 1973), pp. 268–269. Original is from British Library, *The Thomason Tracts.* **Document 6, page 61:** "A Manifestation from Lieutenant Colonel John Lilburne, William Walwyn, and Others, Commonly (Though Unjustly) Stiled Levellers," in *Leveller Tracts, 1647–1653,* ed. William Haller and Godfrey Davis (Gloucester, Mass.: Peter Smith, 1964), pp. 278–279, 281–282, 284. This document is also from *The Thomason Tracts.*

CHAPTER 3 **Page 63:** *(Left)* Portrait by Martin Mytens the Younger, 1744. Photo © Archivo Iconografico, S.A./CORBIS. *(Right)* Portrait by an anonymous artist, 18th Century; Chateaux de Versailles et de Trianon, Versailles, France. Photo Copyright Giraudon/Art Resource, NY. **Document 1, page 76:** Roider, Karl, ed., *Maria Theresa.* Copyright © 1973. Reprinted with permission of the author. **Document 2, page 77:** Roider, Karl, ed., *Maria Theresa.* Copyright © 1973. Reprinted with permission of the author. **Page 78:** Roider, Karl, ed., *Maria Theresa.* Copyright © 1973. Reprinted with permission of the author. **Document 3, page 79:** From *The Secrets of Marie Antoinette* by Olivier Bernier, copyright © 1985 by Olivier Bernier. Used by permission of Doubleday, a division of Random House, Inc. **Document 4, page 81:** Frederick II of Prussia, "Essay on the Forms of Government," in *The Foundations of Germany,* trans. J. Ellis Barker (New York: E. P. Dutton, 1916), pp. 22–23. **Document 5, page 82:** Lentin, Anthony, ed., *Enlightened Absolutism (1760–1790).* Copyright © 1990. Reprinted with permission of the author. **Document 6, page 83:** Lentin, Anthony, ed., *Enlightened Absolutism (1760–1790).* Copyright © 1990. Reprinted with permission of the author. **Document 7, page 84:** Lentin, Anthony, ed., *Enlightened Absolutism (1760–1790).* Copyright © 1990. Reprinted with permission of the author.

CHAPTER 4   **Page 86:** *(Left)* © Phototheque des Musèe de la Ville de Paris/chichè: I. Andreani. *(Right)* Portrait c. 1792. © Archivio Iconographico, S.A./CORBIS. **Document 1, page 103:** The National Assembly, "The Declaration of the Rights of Man," in James Harvey Robinson and Charles Beard, *Readings in Modern European History,* vol. 1 (Boston: Ginn and Company, 1908), pp. 260–262. **Document 2, page 106:** *Condorcet: Selected Writings,* by Keith Michael Baker, © 1976. Reprinted by permission of Pearson Education, Inc. Upper Saddle River, NJ. **Document 3, page 108:** From *Women in Revolutionary Paris, 1789–1795: Selected Documents Translated with Notes and Commentary.* Copyright 1979 by Board of Trustees of the University of Illinois. Used with permission of the editors and the University of Illinois Press. **Document 4, page 112:** *Speeches of Maximilien Robespierre with a Biographical Sketch,* vol. 1 of *Voices of Revolt.* Copyright © 1927 by International Publishers Co. Reprinted with permission. **Document 5, page 113:** *Speeches of Maximilien Robespierre with a Biographical Sketch,* vol. 1 of *Voices of Revolt.* Copyright © 1927 by International Publishers Co. Reprinted with permission. **Document 6, page 114:** Olympe de Gouges, "The Three Ballot-Boxes, or the Salvation of the Nation," in *Olympe de Gouges: Ecrits Politiques, 1792–93,* vol. II, ed. Olivier Blanc (Paris, cote-femmes, 1993), pp. 247–248. Translation by M. Jane Slaughter. **Document 7, page 115:** © Everyman Publishers Plc., Gloucester Mansions, 140a Shaftesbury Ave., London WC2H 8HD. Reprinted with permission of Everyman Publishers Plc. **Document 8, page 118:** From *Women in Revolutionary Paris, 1789–1795: Selected Documents Translated with Notes and Commentary.* Copyright 1979 by Board of Trustees of the University of Illinois. Used with permission of the editors and the University of Illinois Press.

CHAPTER 5   **Page 123:** *(Left)* Undated photograph, © Bettman/CORBIS. *(Right)* Wellesley College, Special Collections. **Document 1, page 142:** Giuseppe Mazzini, "Instructions to Young Italy," in James Harvey Robinson and Charles A. Beard, *Readings in Modern European History* (New York: Ginn and Company, 1909), pp. 115–118. **Document 2, page 144:** *(Letter #1)* Luisa Gasparini, "Il dramma materno di Giuditta Sidoli," Part 1, in *Il Risorgimento* 14:1 (1962): 14–15. Imprint [Milano] Edizioni Comune di Milano, "Amici del Museo del Risorgimento." Translated by Jane Slaughter. *(Letter #2)* Luisa Gasparini, "Così vicina ai suoi figli e così lontana," in *Il Risorgimento* 14:2 (1962): 107. Translated by Jane Slaughter. **Page 145:** *(Letter #3)* Luisa Gasparini, "Così vicina ai suoi figli e così lontana," in *Il Risorgimento* 14:2 (1962): 102. Translated by Jane Slaughter. **Document 3, page 145:** *(Letter #1)* Emilio Del Cerro [Niceforo Nicola], *Giuseppe Mazzini a Giuditta Sidoli: Con Documenti Inediti* (Turin: S.T.E.N., Societa Tipografico-Editrice Nazionale, 1909), pp. 270–271. Translated by Jane Slaughter. **Page 146:** *(Letter #2)* Luisa Gasparini, "Così vicina ai suoi figli e così lontana," in *Il Risorgimento* 14:2 (1962): 106. Translated by Jane Slaughter. **Document 4, page 146:** Giuseppe Mazzini, "On the Duties of Man," in E.A. Venturi, *Joseph Mazzini* (London: Henry S. King, 1877), pp. 319–321. **Document 5, page 148:** Giuseppe Mazzini, "On Materialism," in *Mazzini's Letters to an English Family,* vol. 3, ed. E. F. Richards (London: J. Lane, 1922), pp. 221–222. **Document 6, page 149:** Gabriella Marini, ed., *Nuovi Documenti su Giuditta Sidoli* (Pisa: Domus Mazziniana, 1957), pp. 113–114. Translation by Jane Slaughter. **Document 7, page 150:** Susan Groag Bell and Karen M. Offen, *Women, the Family, and Freedom,* vol. 1. Copyright © 1983 by the Board of Trustees of the Leland Stanford Jr. University. With the permission of Stanford University Press, www.sup.org.

CHAPTER 6   **Page 151:** *(Left)* Photograph c. 1906 © CORBIS. *(Right)* Line engraving, 19th Century. The Granger Collection, NY. **Document 1, page 171:** Charles Bradlaugh, *Champion of Liberty: Charles Bradlaugh,* Centenary Volume (New York: The Freethought Press Association, Inc., 1933), pp. 119–122. **Document 2, page 172:** Charles Bradlaugh, "Northampton Election Address, 1868," in *Champion of Liberty: Charles Bradlaugh,* Centenary Volume (New York: The Freethought Press Association, Inc., 1933), pp. 165–167. **Document 3, page 173:** Annie Besant, *Autobiography* (London: T. Fisher Unwin, 1893), pp. 71, 72, 81, 82. **Document 4, page 175:** John Stuart Mill, *The Subjection of Women* (Cambridge, Mass.: The M.I.T. Press, 1970), pp. 3, 7, 15, 16. **Document 5, page 177:** Eliza Lynn Linton, "The Wild Women," *Nineteenth Century,* July 1891. Excerpt published in Susan Hamilton, ed., *Criminals, Idiots, Women, and Minors* (Orchard Park, N.Y.: Broadview Press, 1995), pp. 188–189. **Document 6, page 179:** Annie Besant, "Defense of Dr. Knowlton's *The Fruits of Philosophy,*" in Roger Manvell, *The Trial of Annie Besant and Charles Bradlaugh* (London: Elek/Pemberton, 1976), pp. 70–71, 79–80. **Document 7, page 181:** Annie Besant, *Autobiography* (London: T. Fisher Unwin, 1893), pp. 213–214, 217. **Document 8, page 181:** Annie Besant, "White Slavery in London," *Link* (June 23, 1888): 2.

CHAPTER 7   **Page 184:** Halftone illustration, 1895. The Granger Collection, NY. **Document 1, page 198:** Copyright 1985 Professor John Bradley, reprinted with permission of Gillon Aitken Associates, Ltd. **Document 2, page 201:** India Office Records, *Hamilton Papers,* vol. 17, no. 38 in *Documents and Speeches on the Indian Princely States,* ed. Adrian Sever (Delhi: B.R. Publishing, 1985), pp. 346–347. **Document 3, page 202:** Mohandas K. Gandhi, *Gandhi's Autobiography: The Story of My Experiments with the Truth.* Copyright © 1948. Reprinted with the permission of The Navajivan Trust. **Document 4, page 204:** Sir Thomas Raleigh, ed., *Lord Curzon in India: Being a Selection from His Speeches as Viceroy and Governor-General of India, 1898–1905* (London: Macmillian, 1906), pp. 242–246. **Document 5, page 206:** *Speeches of Lord Curzon, Viceroy of India* (Calcutta: Government Printer, 1902) in L.R. Gardiner and J.H. Davidson, *British Imperialism in the Late Nineteenth Century* (London: Edward Arnold, 1971), pp. 18–19. **Document 6, page 207:** J. K. Majumdar, *Indian Speeches and Documents on British Rule, 1821–1918* (Delhi: Kanti Publishers, 1987), pp. 151–155. **Document 7, page 210:** Lisa DiCaprio and Merry E. Wiesner, *Lives and Voices: Sources in European Women's History* (Boston: Houghton Mifflin, 2000), pp. 328–332. Originally published in Annie Besant, *Wake Up, India: A Plea for Social Reform* (Philadelphia, Pa.: Theosophical Publishing House, 1913). **Document 8, page 212:** Copyright 1985 Professor John Bradley, reprinted with permission of Gillon Aitken Associates, Ltd.

CHAPTER 8   **Page 215:** *(Left)* Portrait c. 1919–1920, based on a photograph by B. N. Rehn. © Bettmann/CORBIS. *(Right)* Photo: Ullstein, copyright ullsteinbild. **Document 1, page 234:** *What Is to Be Done? Burning Questions of Our Movement* from *The Lenin Anthology* by Robert C. Tucker. Copyright © 1975 by W. W. Norton & Company, Inc. Used by permission of W. W. Norton & Company, Inc. **Document 2, page 236:** Lenin, *The Emancipation of Women: From the Writings of V.I. Lenin.* Reprinted with permission. **Document 3, page 238:** N. Krupskaya, *Reminiscences of Lenin.* Copyright © 1970 by International Publishers Co. Reprinted with permission. **Document 4, page 240:** From Leon Trotsky, *My Life: An Attempt at Autobiography* (New York: Charles Scribner's Sons, 1930), pp. 201–202, 212–213. **Document 5, page 241:** N. Krupskaya, *Reminiscences of Lenin.* Copyright © 1970 by International Publishers Co. Reprinted with permission. **Document 6, page 242:** The "April Theses" from *The Lenin Anthology* by Robert C. Tucker. Copyright © 1975 by W. W. Norton & Company, Inc. Used by permission of W. W. Norton & Company, Inc. **Document 7, page 245:** Holt, Alix, trans., *Selected Writings of Alexandra Kollontai.* Copyright © 1977 by kind permission of Allison & Busby, London. **Document 8, page 249:** Lenin, *The Emancipation of Women: From the Writings of V.I. Lenin.* Reprinted with permission. **Page 250:** Nadezhda K. Krupskaya, "Woman—Friend, Comrade and Mother," in *Soviet Woman: A Citizen With Equal Right—A Collection of Articles and Speeches* (Moscow: Co-operative Publishing Society, 1937), pp. 58–63. Originally published in *Krestyanka,* no. 17, 1936.

and Done by Simone de Beauvoir, translated by Patrick O'Brian copyright © 1974 by Andre Deutsch & G. P. Putnam. Used by permission of G. P. Putnam's Sons, a division of Penguin Publishing, Inc. Copyright © Editions *Gallimard,* Paris 1972. Appears by permission of the publisher, Marlowe & Company. **Page 356:** DiCaprio, Lisa and Merry Wiesner, *Lives and Voices: Sources of European Women's History.* Copyright © 2000 by Houghton Mifflin Company. Reprinted with permission.

CHAPTER 12   Page 358: *(Left)* Photograph 1983. AP/Wide World Photos. *(Right)* Photograph 1980. © Klaus Drinkwitz/STERN–Magazine. **Document 1, page 380:** "The Basic Law of the Federal Republic of Germany (1949)," in *Source Materials on the Government and Politics of Germany,* ed. James K. Pollack and John C. Lane (Ann Arbor, Mich.: Wahrs Publishing, 1964), pp. 11–12. **Document 2, page 382:** Reprinted from *Thinking Green! Essays on Environmentalism, Feminism, and Nonviolence* (1994) by Petra K. Kelly with permission of Parallax Press, Berkeley, California. **Document 3, page 386:** From *Greenham Common: Women at the Wire* by Barbara Hartford and Sarah Hopkins. (Women's Press, 1984). Reprinted by permission from Sarah Hopkins. **Document 4, page 387:** Copyright © Carl-Christoph Schweitzer et al. Eds. From *Politics and Government in the Federal Republic of Germany* by Carl-Christoph Schweitzer et al Eds. Reprinted with permission of Palgrave. **Document 5, page 389:** Copyright © Carl-Christoph Schweitzer et al. Eds. From *Politics and Government in the Federal Republic of Germany* by Carl-Christoph Schweitzer et al Eds. Reprinted with permission of Palgrave. **Document 6, page 390:** Coates, Ken, Peggy Duff, Dan Smith, Mary Kaldo, E. P. Thompson, and Roy Medvedev, *Eleventh Hour for Europe.* Copyright © 1981 by Spokesman Books. Reprinted with permission. **Document 7, page 392:** Reprinted from *Thinking Green Essays on Environmentalism, Feminism, and Nonviolence* (1994) by Petra K. Kelly with permission of Parallax Press, Berkeley, California. **Document 8, page 395:** Hulsburg, Werner, *The German Greens: A Social and Political Profile.* Copyright © 1988 by Verso. Reprinted with permission. **Document 9, page 395:** Kreisler, Harry *Conversations with History,* Institute of International Studies, University of California, Berkeley, October 23, 1984. <http://globetrotter. berkeley. edu/conversations/KellyBastian/kelly-bastian0.html>. Reprinted with permission.

CHAPTER 13   Page 402: Attending Havel's play, *Largo Desolato,* at the Prague Na Zabradli Theatre, April 8, 1990. CTK Photo – Czech News Agency/Michal Kramphanzl. **Document 1, page 424:** From *Disturbing the Peace* by Vaclav Havel, translated by Paul Wilson, copyright 1990 by Vaclav Havel. Used by permission of Alfred A. Knopf, a division of Random House, Inc. **Document 2, page 426:** Ludvik Vaculik, "2000 Words to Workers, Farmers, Scientists, Artists, and Everyone," in *East Europe,* August 1968, pp. 25–28. Also in Lyman H. Legters, *Eastern Europe: Transformation and Revolution, 1945–1991, Documents and Analyses* (Lexington, Mass.: D.C. Heath and Company, 1992), pp. 211–213. **Document 3, page 428:** Eva Kanturková, *Sesly jsme se v této kniz: Olga Havlová, Marie Rút Krízková, Elzbieta Ledererová,* excerpt trans. Simona Fojtova (Köln: Index, 1980), pp. 10–12. **Document 4, page 429:** From *Living In Truth: Twenty-Two Essays Published on the Occasion of the Award of the Erasmus Prize to Vaclav Havel* by Havel, Vaclav. Copyright © 1989. Reprinted with permission of Faber & Faber Ltd. **Document 5, page 432:** Skilling, H. Gordon, *Charter 77 and Human Rights in Czechoslovakia,* 1981, Routledge. Reprinted with permission. **Document 6, page 435:** From *Letters to Olga* by Vaclav Havel, translated by Paul Wilson, copyright © 1984 by Rowahlt Taschenbuch Verlag. Translation copyright © 1988 by Paul Wilson. Copyright © 1983 by Vaclav Havel. Used by permission of Alfred A. Knopf, a division of Random House, Inc. **Document 7, page 438:** "A Letter from the United States—The Critical Theory Approach" from *How We Survived Communism and Even Laughed* by Slavenka Drakulic. Copyright © 1991 by Slavenka Drakulic. Used by permission of W. W. Norton & Company, Inc. **Document 8, page 441:** From Havlova, Olga, "Letter to the Editor," *The New York Review of Books,* 14 June 1990. **Page 442:** "Cool Consort to the Revolutionary Darling; Olga Havel Interview" by Valerie Grove from *The Sunday Times,* 11 November 1990. © Times Newspapers Limited, London (1990). Reprinted with permission.

INDEX